Deregulatory Takings

and the

Regulatory Contract

Deregulatory Takings and the Regulatory Contract

The Competitive Transformation of Network Industries in the United States

J. Gregory Sidak
Daniel F. Spulber

CAMBRIDGE
UNIVERSITY PRESS

PUBLISHED BY THE PRESS SYNDICATE OF THE UNIVERSITY OF CAMBRIDGE
The Pitt Building, Trumpington Street, Cambridge CB2 1RP, United Kingdom

CAMBRIDGE UNIVERSITY PRESS
The Edinburgh Building, Cambridge CB2 2RU, United Kingdom
40 West 20th Street, New York, NY 10011-4211, USA
10 Stamford Road, Oakleigh, Melbourne 3166, Australia

First published 1997

Printed in the United States of America

Typeset in CG Times

Library of Congress Cataloging-in-Publication Data

Sidak, J. Gregory
    Deregulatory takings and the regulatory contract: the competitive transformation of
network industries in the United States / J. Gregory Sidak, Daniel F. Spulber.
        p.   cm.
    Includes bibliographical references and index.
    ISBN 0-521-59159-7 (alk. paper)
    1. Telecommunication—Deregulation—United States. 2. Telecommunications—Law
and legislation—United States. 3. Electric utilities—Deregulation—United States.
4. Electric utilities—Law and legislation—United States. 5. Public
utilities—Deregulation—United States. 6. Public utilities—Law and legislation—United
States. 7. Right of property—United States. 8. Breach of contract—United States.
I. Spulber, Daniel F. II. Title.
HE7781.S56 1997
384'.041—DC21   97-30786
                                                                                            CIP

*A catalog record for this book is available from
the British Library*

To Our Families

Contents

Preface

Significant deregulation efforts in the telecommunications and electric power industries are following on the heels of reduced regulation of natural gas, airlines, railroads, trucking, banking, and securities brokerage. The transformation of the network industries in the United States promises significant benefits. The removal of government controls over prices, products, and the entry of new firms, and their replacement by markets, should yield substantial productive efficiencies, allocative efficiencies, and innovation in technology and service offerings. Moreover, market allocation of goods and services obviates the costly administrative processes that inevitably accompany public regulation. The question, however, is whether the deregulatory process in network industries will fulfill its great promise.

Traditionally, the utility sector in the United States has been characterized by the combination of private ownership and management of companies with public control over prices, service obligations, and entry. Deregulation generally is interpreted to mean the relaxation of public controls. That type of deregulation is most likely to achieve the benefits of competition. Other types of public policies carried out in the name of deregulation, however, have the effect of encroaching on private ownership of property and increasing public control. Such policies cannot be expected to yield the full benefits of market competition. In this book, we address deregulatory policies that threaten to reduce or destroy the value of private property without any accompanying payment of just compensation, policies that we term "deregulatory takings." We further consider the problem of renegotiation of the regulatory contract, which changes the terms and conditions of operation of utility companies. We argue that constitutional protections of private property from takings, as well as efficient remedies for contractual breach, provide the proper foundation for the competitive transformation of the network industries.

By addressing the problems of deregulatory takings and breach of the regulatory contract, we are not advocating slowing the process of deregulation. Quite the contrary. Transforming the utility sector to allow competitive markets to form means that regulators should exercise forbearance. They should progressively remove regulation without trying to "manage" competition. That objective requires regulators to treat incumbents and entrants symmetrically: Regulators should remove "incumbent burdens" as well as artificial entry barriers. The benefits of competition do not stem from government regulations that redistribute income from utility investors to customers, nor do such benefits stem from regulatory policies for network access that promote entrants' free riding on the incumbent's facilities. Such actions represent a new version of *increased* regulation, not deregulation.

Investors in the network industries made investment in large-scale facilities in the expectation that they would receive from regulators the reasonable opportunity to recover those investments plus a competitive rate of return. Those investments built the U.S. telephone system and electrical systems, whose performance and reliability are self-evident. Such systems were well-suited to a regulated environment but are not likely to be optimal in a competitive market. Moreover, those systems reflect inefficiencies arising from regulatory performance incentives and pricing controls. Yet, such inefficiencies do not imply that we should today disregard the obligations that regulators incurred for past investments made by the firms they regulated. Rather, as in private contracts, the swiftest and surest path to terminating agreements is to compensate the parties for their expectation and allow the parties to pursue the most efficient alternative arrangements.

We present the main issues of the deregulation controversy. We show that there is a fundamental identity between the calculation of just compensation for deregulatory takings and the efficient remedy for breach of the regulatory contract. We further explore the pricing of access to network facilities upon deregulation. We show that "efficient component pricing" is closely related to the estimation of investment-backed expectations that underlie just compensation for takings and damage remedies for breach. Those equivalence principles provide a guide to public policymakers as they seek to open a network industry to competition.

We intend this book to be useful not only to public policymakers in all branches of government, but also to students and researchers in law, economics, and political science. Our analysis is meant to contribute to legal research on property rights and contracts, with particular application to the relationships between the state and private enterprise. Our analysis also addresses issues in regulatory economics, which has tended to focus on mechanisms for implementing regulations rather than on the process of removing those regulations. We attempt to provide guidelines for the redesign and removal of regulatory controls. Finally, our analysis raises public choice questions about the deregulatory process, including income redistribution and jurisdictional issues.

Because no work of this scope can blossom without some prior care and feeding, we thank the editors and staff of several law reviews for their patience in allowing us to shape and refine our ideas through the publication in their respective journals of the articles that formed the building blocks of this book. Specifically, we acknowledge the *New York University Law Review,* the *Columbia Law Review*, and the *Yale Journal on Regulation*.[1] Smaller portions of this book draw upon articles published in the *Harvard Journal of Law and Public Policy* and the *Southern California Law Review*, whose editors and staff we also thank.[2]

In writing this book, we have benefitted from conversations with, and suggestions from, many colleagues. We gratefully acknowledge the feedback from the participants at a conference on takings held at the American Enterprise Institute in March 1996. Most notably in this regard, we appreciate the written comments by Oliver E. Williamson and by Judge Stephen F. Williams in response to our original working paper in this area. For their comments on other earlier papers, we also thank participants at a conference on telecommunications law at Columbia Law School in November 1996 and participants in the March 1997 industrial organization seminar at the Haas School of Business at the University of California, Berkeley. We also thank our students in courses on manage-

---

1. J. Gregory Sidak & Daniel F. Spulber, *Deregulation and Managed Competition in Network Industries*, 15 YALE J. ON REG. (forthcoming 1998); J. Gregory Sidak & Daniel F. Spulber, *Givings, Takings, and the Fallacy of Forward-Looking Costs*, 72 N.Y.U. L. REV. (forthcoming 1997); J. Gregory Sidak & Daniel F. Spulber, *The Tragedy of the Telecommons: Government Pricing of Unbundled Network Elements Under the Telecommunications Act of 1996*, 97 COLUM. L. REV. 1081 (1997); J. Gregory Sidak & Daniel F. Spulber, *Deregulatory Takings and Breach of the Regulatory Contract*, 71 N.Y.U. L. REV. 851 (1996); Daniel F. Spulber, *Deregulating Telecommunications*, 12 YALE J. ON REG. 25 (1995).

2. William J. Baumol & J. Gregory Sidak, *Stranded Costs*, 18 HARV. J.L. & PUB. POL'Y 835 (1995); Robert W. Crandall & J. Gregory Sidak, *Competition and Regulatory Policies for Interactive Broadband Networks*, 68 S. CAL. L. REV. 1203 (1995).

ment strategy and regulation at the Kellogg School of Management and the Yale School of Management for their lively discussions in response to lectures that addressed the topics we present in this book.

We wish to thank a number of our friends and colleagues whose helpful comments, occasional protests, and valuable discussions helped to improve the present work. They include William Barr, William J. Baumol, Keith Bernard, Solveig Bernstein, Ramsen V. Betfarhad, Mark B. Bierbower, Robert T. Blau, JoAnne G. Bloom, Severin Borenstein, Paul Cappuccio, Charles H. Carrathers III, Michael A. Carvin, Katherine K. Combs, Edward Comer, Robert W. Crandall, Michael J. Doane, Kenneth R. Dunmore, James W. Durham, Richard A. Epstein, Christina Forbes, Edward J. Fuhr, Richard D. Gary, Richard Gilbert, Davison W. Grant, Louis Harris, Thomas W. Hazlett, Victor L. Hou, William T. Lake, Alex C. Larson, Lance Liebman, Paul W. MacAvoy, Ferdinand C. Meyers, Jr., Eli M. Noam, Theodore B. Olson, Thomas Parker, Mark A. Perry, Lewis F. Powell III, George L. Priest, John W. Rowe, Alan Schwartz, Michael Senkowski, Howard A. Shelanski, David S. Sibley, Melinda Ledden Sidak, Marshall Smith, Irwin M. Stelzer, Lawrence E. Strickling, Pamela Strobel, John Thorne, Dennis Trimble, Leigh Tripoli, Daniel E. Troy, Hal R. Varian, John Vickers, M. Edward Whelan III, Johannes W. Williams, Michael A. Williams, James Q. Wilson, Glenn A. Woroch, Ward W. Wueste, and anonymous referees selected by the Cambridge University Press. We thank Keitha Macdonald for her able assistance in preparing the manuscript for publication. We also thank Rebecca Armendariz, Mark Obenstine, and Anthony Yoseloff for valuable research assistance.

Some of the insights in this book occurred to us in the course of presenting expert testimony in regulatory proceedings on behalf of Ameritech, Central & South West Corp., the Energy Association of New York State, GTE, Hong Kong Telecommunications Limited, Pacific Bell, PECO Energy Company, and the United States Telephone Association. The opposing testimony of the eminent scholars retained as expert witnesses in those regulatory proceedings, as well as the experience of answering live cross-examination, helped us sharpen the legal and economic reasoning contained in this book. In particular, we wish to recognize the scholars who have expressed their respectful disagreement with portions of our analysis: William J. Baumol, Nicholas Economides, David L. Kaserman, John W. Mayo, Thomas W. Merrill, Janusz A. Ordover, Frederick Warren-Boulton, and Robert D. Willig. We hope that our responses to their criticisms exhibit the same professional respect that we received from them. We are grateful to have had the opportunity to have our theories so immediately applied to real-world problems and so thoroughly vetted by distinguished colleagues. It is our hope that such firsthand exposure to regulatory institutions has helped us to present our theoretical work as more than detached "blackboard economics" and that our analysis and conclusions will therefore be all the more useful and accessible to regulators, legislators, and jurists.

Finally, we are grateful to Dean Donald P. Jacobs of the J. L. Kellogg Graduate School of Management for his encouragement. We give special thanks to Christopher C. DeMuth, president of the American Enterprise Institute, for his steadfast support of our research, particularly in light of its controversial nature, and to Scott Parris of the Cambridge University Press for his supportive editing of the book and his help in bringing the project to fruition. Most of all, we thank our wives and children for their patience and understanding for the time that we denied them while completing this book.

J. GREGORY SIDAK
DANIEL F. SPULBER

About the Authors

J. GREGORY SIDAK is the F. K. Weyerhaeuser Fellow in Law and Economics at the American Enterprise Institute for Public Policy Research and senior lecturer at the Yale School of Management. He directs AEI's Studies in Telecommunications Deregulation and its Studies in Postal Regulation.

Mr. Sidak served as deputy general counsel of the Federal Communications Commission from 1987 to 1989, and as senior counsel and economist to the Council of Economic Advisers in the Executive Office of the President from 1986 to 1987. As an attorney in private practice, he worked on numerous antitrust cases and federal administrative, legislative, and appellate matters concerning regulated industries.

Mr. Sidak is the author of *Foreign Investment in American Telecommunications* (University of Chicago Press 1997). He is the coauthor, with William J. Baumol, of *Toward Competition in Local Telephony* (MIT Press & AEI Press 1994) and *Transmission Pricing and Stranded Costs in the Electric Power Industry* (AEI Press 1995). With Daniel F. Spulber, Mr. Sidak is coauthor of *Protecting Competition from the Postal Monopoly* (AEI Press 1996). He is the editor of *Governing the Postal Service* (AEI Press 1994). Mr. Sidak has published articles on antitrust, telecommunications regulation, corporate governance, and constitutional law in the *Journal of Political Economy*, the *California Law Review*, the *Columbia Law Review*, the *Cornell Law Review*, the *Duke Law Journal*, the *Georgetown Law Journal*, the *Harvard Journal on Law and Public Policy*, the *New York University Law Review*, the *Northwestern University Law Review*, the *Southern California Law Review*, the *Stanford Law Review*, the *Yale Journal on Regulation*, and elsewhere. He has testified before committees of the U.S. Senate and House of Representatives on regulatory and constitutional law matters, and his writings have been cited by the Supreme Court, the lower federal courts, state and federal regulatory commissions, and the Judicial Committee of the Privy Council of the House of Lords.

Mr. Sidak received A.B. and A.M. degrees in economics and a J.D. from Stanford University, where he was a member of the *Stanford Law Review*, and served as law clerk to Judge Richard A. Posner during his first term on the U.S. Court of Appeals for the Seventh Circuit.

DANIEL F. SPULBER is the Thomas G. Ayers Professor of Energy Resource Management and Professor of Management Strategy at the J. L. Kellogg Graduate School of Management, Northwestern University, where he has taught since 1990. He was previously professor of economics and professor of economics and law at the University of Southern California. He has also taught economics at Brown University and the California Institute of Technology.

He has conducted extensive research in the areas of regulation, industrial organization, microeconomic theory, law and economics, energy economics, and management strategy. In a ranking of economists published in the April 1996 issue of *Economic Inquiry*, he was ranked as the sixth most productive economist in the United States on the basis of publications in the top economics journals. He is the founding editor of the *Journal of Economics & Management Strategy*, published by the MIT Press.

Professor Spulber is the author of the textbook *Regulation and Markets* (MIT Press 1989). He is the coauthor with J. Gregory Sidak of *Protecting Competition from the Postal Monopoly* (AEI Press 1996), and coeditor with Leonard Mirman of *Essays in the Economics of Renewable Resource Management* (North Holland 1982).

Professor Spulber has published articles on regulation, pricing, microeconomic theory, competitive strategy, and related topics in numerous academic journals, including the *American Economic Review*, the *Journal of Economic Perspectives*, the *Journal of Economic Theory*, the *Review of Economic Studies*, the *Quarterly Journal of Economics*, the *RAND Journal of Economics*, the *International Economic Review*, the *Columbia Law Review*, the *Journal of Law and Economics*, the *New York University Law Review*, and the *Yale Journal on Regulation*.

Professor Spulber received his B.A. in economics from the University of Michigan in 1974 and his M.A. in 1976 and Ph.D. in 1979 in economics from Northwestern University.

Deregulatory Takings

and the

Regulatory Contract

1

The Nature of the Controversy

THE TAKINGS CLAUSE of the Fifth Amendment commands: "Nor shall private property be taken for public use, without just compensation."[1] The sweeping deregulation of public utilities being proposed and implemented at the state and federal levels promises to bring the benefits of competition to markets for electric power and telecommunications. Those benefits include improvements in operating efficiencies, competitive prices, efficient investment decisions, technological innovation, and product variety. The benefits of competition, however, do not include forced transfers of income from utility shareholders to their customers and competitors as a result of asymmetries in regulation. Asymmetric regulation can serve only to impede competition and impair the financial health of public utilities. As regulators dismantle barriers to entry and other regulatory restrictions, they must honor their past commitments and avoid actions that threaten to confiscate or destroy the property of utility investors on an unprecedented scale.

In this book we examine regulatory commitments and the potential for the deregulation of regulated network industries to cause massive takings to occur. We connect that analysis to what has, until now, been regarded as principally a technical problem in economic theory and regulatory practice: the design of efficient access pricing. We consider the selection of access prices such that, in the new competitive environment, a public utility will have an opportunity to achieve for its investors the expected earnings associated with the former regulatory regime

---

1. U.S. CONST. amend. V.

under which the utility made (and regulators approved as prudent) enormous investments in long-lived facilities and other specialized assets to serve its customers. We weave together here the separate threads of access pricing theory, takings jurisprudence, and the transaction costs analysis of voluntary exchange. The resulting fabric will help to inform an emerging body of analysis in law and economics that one might term the jurisprudence of network industries.

THE TAKINGS LANDSCAPE

The prototypical takings case involves a physical invasion of land. It arises, for example, when the state needs a piece of private land to build a highway and commences a condemnation proceeding that results in the payment of compensation. The dramatic growth of the regulatory state, however, produced another class of takings case—the regulatory taking—in which the owner of private property is not forced to sell it to the government pursuant to a condemnation action, but rather is allowed to keep his property subject to significant constraints concerning its use that are issued in the name of the state's police power.[2] In 1922 Justice Holmes planted the seed for that legal theory when he observed in *Pennsylvania Coal Co.* v. *Mahon* that a state law making it "commercially impracticable to mine certain coal" on one's property had "very nearly the same effect for constitutional purposes as appropriating or destroying it."[3] By 1992 the Supreme Court considered in *Lucas* v. *South Carolina Coastal Council* whether environmental regulations that prevent a landowner from building homes on his beachfront parcel so diminished the value of the property as to constitute an uncompensated confiscation.[4]

The prohibition against uncompensated takings descended from the Magna Charta.[5] Not surprisingly, concern over regulatory takings is

---

2. *See* Yee *v.* Escondido, 503 U.S. 519, 522 (1992); WILLIAM A. FISCHEL, REGULATORY TAKINGS: LAW, ECONOMICS, AND POLITICS (Harvard University Press 1995); SUSAN ROSE-ACKERMAN, RETHINKING THE PROGRESSIVE AGENDA: THE REFORM OF THE AMERICAN REGULATORY STATE 132–43 (Free Press 1992).

3. 260 U.S. 393, 414 (1922).

4. 505 U.S. 1003 (1992).

5. Justice William Strong wrote in Northern Transp. Co. of Ohio *v.* City of Chicago, 99 U.S. 635, 642 (1879), that it was the "view of Magna Charta and the restriction to be found in the Constitution of every State, that private property shall not be taken for public use without just compensation being made." *See* William B. Stoebuck, *A General Theory of Eminent Domain*, 47 WASH. L. REV. 553, 563 (1972). On the philosophical

therefore a legal phenomenon not unique to the United States, but rather one that is manifest in other English-speaking nations that impose limitations on the state's ability to make uncompensated confiscations of property.[6] Moreover, the significance of takings cases involving factual situations other than the physical invasion of property is certain to grow. For the time being, the Supreme Court punctuates its takings cases with the quaint reminder from its 1978 decision in *Penn Central Transportation Co.* v. *New York City*, that "[a] 'taking' may more readily be found when the interference with property can be characterized as a physical invasion by the government . . . than when interference arises from some public program adjusting the benefits and burdens of economic life to promote the common good."[7] The Court will surely let go of that security blanket before long. As William Fischel has observed, "legal 'property' is not a clod of earth but a bundle of legal entitlements."[8] As value in the economy arises to a greater relative extent from intellectual property and information-based assets than from land, legal analogies to physical invasion of real property will cease to shed light on the controversies at hand.

---

foundations of the Takings Clause, see RICHARD A. EPSTEIN, TAKINGS: PRIVATE PROPERTY AND THE POWER OF EMINENT DOMAIN 3–31 (Harvard University Press 1985).

6. Other English-speaking nations have constitutional or common law protections against uncompensated confiscation of property, although those protections do not correspond precisely to the Takings Clause in the U.S. Constitution. For authority in England, see Central Control Bd. *v.* Cannon Brewery Co., Ltd., [1919] A.C. 744. For Australia, see AUSTRALIAN CONST. § 51(xxxi) (granting Parliament the power to make laws concerning "The acquisition of property on just terms from any State or person for any purpose in respect of which the Parliament has power to make laws"); Mutual Pools & Staff Pty. Ltd. *v.* Commonwealth, F.C. 94/005, slip op. (High Ct. of Australia, Mar. 9, 1994). For Canada, see British Colum. Elec. Ry. *v.* Public Utils. Comm'n of Brit. Colum., 25 D.L.R.2d 689 (1961) (determining "fair and reasonable rate of return"); Northwestern Utils. *v.* City of Edmonton, 2 D.L.R. 4 (1929) (same). For Ireland, see *In re* Article 26 of the Constitution and the Housing (Privated Rented Dwellings) Bill, [1983] I.R. 181 (Ir. S.C. 1983). For Northern Ireland, see O.D. Cars Ltd. *v.* Belfast Corp., [1959] N. Ir. 62 (Ct. of Appeals). The principle also exists under European treaties. *See, e.g.*, Article 1 of Protocol No 1, European Convention on Human Rights ("Every natural or legal person is entitled to the peaceful enjoyment of his possessions. No one shall be deprived of his possessions except in the public interest and subject to the conditions provided for by law and by the general principles of international law."); Lithgow *v.* United Kingdom, 8 Eur. H.R. Rep. 329 (Eur. Ct. of Human Rights 1986).

7. 438 U.S. 104, 124 (1978) (citation omitted); *accord, Lucas*, 505 U.S. at 1017; Loretto *v.* Teleprompter Manhattan CATV Corp., 458 U.S. 419, 426 (1982).

8. FISCHEL, *supra* note 2, at 2.

REGULATION AND CONTRACT

Courts will soon face a third genre of takings cases that will make the past analysis of regulatory takings seem simplistic by comparison. Regulatory change is precipitating the competitive transformation of network industries served by public utilities long presumed to be natural monopolies and subjected to extensive price regulation. The takings issue arises because those utilities assumed obligations to serve in return for the regulator's assurance that the utilities would earn a competitive return on invested capital, along with compensation for the full cost of providing service.[9] In that relationship regulators protect the utility's opportunity to earn a competitive return by controlling entry into the firm's market, restrict the maximum earnings of the utility through rate setting, and establish service requirements through universal service, carrier of last resort, and other rules. Such an arrangement, known as the *regulatory contract*, enables the regulators to reconcile their ceilings on the earnings of utilities with the requirement that, in terms of actuarially expected value, prospective investors be offered a competitive rate of return on their investments.[10] The regulator is thus said to have entered into a bargain with the public utility: In return for assuming an obligation to serve and charging not more than "just and reasonable" prices on a nondiscriminatory basis, the utility is guaranteed a franchise protected by entry regulation and income sufficient to recover and to earn a competitive rate of return on its invested capital.[11]

When the state maintains regulatory obligations while simultaneously easing entry restrictions, existing utilities encounter costly competitive disadvantages, known as *incumbent burdens*.[12] Regulators typically

---

9. *See* Paul W. MacAvoy, Daniel F. Spulber & Bruce E. Stangle, *Is Competitive Entry Free?: Bypass and Partial Deregulation in Natural Gas Markets*, 6 YALE J. ON REG. 209, 210 (1989).

10. Another name given that arrangement is the *regulatory compact*. Throughout this book, we treat the regulatory contract and the regulatory compact as synonymous.

11. *See, e.g.,* General Motors Corp. *v.* Tracy, 117 S. Ct. 811, 823 (1997).

12. The term *incumbent burdens* was introduced in MacAvoy, Spulber & Stangle, *supra* note 9, at 210, 224–31, in their analysis of partial deregulation of natural gas transmission. Justice Stephen G. Breyer has made the analogous argument with respect to the asymmetric regulation of AT&T following the breakup of the Bell System. Stephen G. Breyer, *Antitrust, Deregulation, and the Newly Liberated Marketplace*, 75 CAL. L. REV. 1005, 1022–24 (1987); *see also* PAUL W. MACAVOY, THE FAILURE OF ANTITRUST AND REGULATION TO ESTABLISH COMPETITION IN LONG-DISTANCE TELEPHONE SERVICES 35–81 (MIT Press & AEI Press 1996).

require public utilities to provide universal service at a fixed price, regardless of the true cost of service; to act as the carrier of last resort; or to employ production processes mandated by regulators that do not lead to minimization of cost but serve other social objectives, such as use of renewable but more costly fuels. Moreover, even legislation that is popularly viewed as "deregulatory," such as the federal Telecommunications Act of 1996[13] and Pennsylvania's Electricity Generation and Customer Choice and Competition Act of 1996,[14] has *increased* incumbent burdens by expanding the definition of universal service. In addition, regulation denies the public utility the pricing flexibility of the entrant and thus places the utility at a competitive disadvantage. New entrants into regulated markets, of course, first target those customers whom regulators require the regulated firm to charge prices exceeding cost so that other customers may be charged prices below cost. Furthermore, deregulatory legislation may allow new entrants to avoid regulations that thwart the use of the least-cost production technology and thus may enable them to be more efficient producers than the incumbent public utility. As a consequence, when the state removes entry regulation, it will jeopardize the financial solvency of the public utility unless it simultaneously allows the utility to "rebalance" its rate structure to eliminate the implicit subsidies and unless all firms in the market either share the costs of incumbent burdens or some third party explicitly reimburses the public utility for those costs.

In reality, however, federal regulatory agencies and state public utilities commissions (PUCs)—which are subject to the Takings Clause through the Due Process Clause of the Fourteenth Amendment[15]—are allowing entry into regulated network industries before rates are rebalanced and the financing of special-service obligations is accomplished more efficiently and equitably. In the electricity industry, Congress has stimulated entry by passing the Energy Policy Act of 1992,[16]

13. Pub. L. No. 104-104, 110 Stat. 56 (1996).

14. 1996 Pa. Laws 138 (codified at 66 PA. CONS. STAT. § 2801 *et seq.*).

15. U.S. CONST. amend. XIV; Chicago, B. & Q. R. Co. *v.* Chicago, 166 U.S. 226, 239 (1897); *Penn Central*, 438 U.S. at 122; Nollan *v.* California Coastal Comm'n, 483 U.S. 825, 827 (1987). In addition, twenty-six states have constitutional provisions that are stronger than the Takings Clause in that they expressly require compensation for private property "damaged" by state action (as opposed to being confiscated). *See* FISCHEL, *supra* note 2, at 87; William B. Stoebuck, *The Property Right of Access Versus the Power of Eminent Domain*, 47 TEX. L. REV. 733, 734 (1969).

16. Pub. L. No. 102-486, 106 Stat. 2776 (1992).

which amended section 211 of the Federal Power Act[17] to empower the Federal Energy Regulatory Commission to order vertically integrated electric utilities to deliver competitively generated power over their transmission lines to wholesale customers, a process known as wholesale wheeling.[18] Meanwhile, regulators in California and other states have announced plans to allow the same type of transmission to retail customers, known as "retail wheeling" of power.[19]

In local telephony, even before the Telecommunications Act of 1996 a number of states had removed all statutory entry barriers into local exchange service and toll service within a local access and transport area (LATA).[20] Furthermore, several states had ordered local exchange carriers (LECs) to provide interexchange carriers 1+ dialing parity for intraLATA toll calls; customers would then "presubscribe" to such service in the same manner that they presubscribe to AT&T, MCI, or Sprint for long-distance calls that cross LATA boundaries.[21] Presubscription for intraLATA toll services makes entrants more effective providers of such services, but at the same time that policy reduces for the LEC one of its most significant revenue streams making a positive contribution to the firm's overall profitability. Other proceedings in the United States and abroad require interconnection to the

---

17. 16 U.S.C. § 824 *et seq.*

18. *Id.* at § 824j(a); *see also* Inquiry Concerning the Commission's Pricing Policy for Transmission Provided Public Utilities Under the Federal Power Act, Policy Statement, Dkt. No. RM93-19-000, 69 F.E.R.C. ¶ 61,086, 59 FED. REG. 55,031 (1994); WILLIAM J. BAUMOL & J. GREGORY SIDAK, TRANSMISSION PRICING AND STRANDED COSTS IN THE ELECTRIC POWER INDUSTRY (AEI Press 1995) [hereinafter TRANSMISSION PRICING AND STRANDED COSTS].

19. Benjamin A. Holden, *California Regulators Approve Plan to Deregulate Market for Power by 1998*, WALL ST. J., Dec. 21, 1995, at A2; Proposed Policies Governing Restructuring California's Electric Services Industry and Reforming Regulation, R.94-04-031, I.94-01-032 (Cal. Pub. Utils. Comm'n Dec. 20, 1995).

20. *See, e.g.*, INGO VOGELSANG & BRIDGER M. MITCHELL, TELECOMMUNICATIONS COMPETITION: THE LAST TEN MILES (MIT Press & AEI Press 1997).

21. MCI Telecommunications Corp. *v.* Pacific Bell, Case 94-12-032, Case 95-01-009, Decision 95-05-020, slip op. (Cal. Pub. Utils. Comm'n May 10, 1995); Investigation into IntraLATA Presubscription, Dkt. No. 930330-TP PSC-95-0918-FOF-TP, slip op. (Fla. Pub. Serv. Comm'n July 31, 1995); IntraLATA Presubscription, Dkt. No. 930330-TP Order No. PSC-95-0203-FOF-TP, 160 P.U.R.4th 41 (Fla. Pub. Serv. Comm'n 1995); MCI Telecommunications Corp., Case No. U-10138 Remand, 160 P.U.R.4th 19 (Mich. Pub. Serv. Comm'n 1995); City Signal, Inc., Case No. U-10647, 159 P.U.R.4th 532 (Mich. Pub. Serv. Comm'n 1995); Exchanges of Ameritech Wisc., Dkt. No. 6720-TI-111, slip op. (Wisc. Pub. Serv. Comm'n July 25, 1995).

LEC's network or unbundled access to the LEC's basic service elements, such as switches, customer loops, databases, and network software used to produce "enhanced services" such as call waiting and call forwarding.[22] Early experience from New Zealand[23] and from state proceedings in Ohio and Illinois[24] suggested that such proceedings would be contentious, because the access charge that is ultimately set has the potential to subsidize entry and penalize incumbency, or vice versa. In two 1995 decisions, regulators in California and Washington summarily rejected the argument that a "bill and keep" system of reciprocal compensation between interconnected local telephone companies amounted to a taking of the incumbent's property because the volume of calls in its direction grossly outnumbered those originating on its system and terminating on the entrant's.[25]

When the incumbent firm has cast interconnection as a physical

22. Alternative Regulatory Frameworks for Local Exchange Carriers, I.87-11-033, Application 85-01-034, Application 87-01-002, Decision 95-08-022, slip op. (Cal. Pub. Utils. Comm'n Aug. 11, 1995); Competition for Local Exchange Service, R.95-04-043, I.95-04-044, Decision 95-07-054, 163 P.U.R.4th 155 (Cal. Pub. Utils. Comm'n 1995); Establish Permanent Interconnection Arrangements Between Basic Local Exchange Service Providers, Case No. U-10860, slip op. (Mich. Pub. Serv. Comm'n Sept. 21, 1995); City Signal, Inc., Case No. U-10647, 164 P.U.R.4th 166 (Mich. Pub. Serv. Comm'n 1995); Local Competition, Telecom Decision CRTC 97-8 (Canadian Radio-television & Telecommunications Comm'n May 1, 1997); Interconnection Configurations and Basic Underlying Principles, Interconnection and Related Competition Issues Statement No. 6 (Statement by Alexander Arena, Telecommunications Authority of Hong Kong, June 3, 1995); Carrier-to-Carrier Charging Principles, Interconnection and Related Competition Issues Statement No. 7 (Statement by Alexander Arena, Telecommunications Authority of Hong Kong, June 10, 1995); Points of Interconnection, Interconnection and Related Competition Issues Statement No. 8 (Statement by Alexander Arena, Telecommunications Authority of Hong Kong, June 10, 1995).

23. Telecom Corp. of New Zealand Ltd. *v.* Clear Communications Ltd., [1995] 1 N.Z.L.R. 385 (Judgment of the Lords of the Judicial Committee of the Privy Council, Oct. 19, 1994); *see also* William J. Baumol & J. Gregory Sidak, *The Pricing of Inputs Sold to Competitors: Rejoinder and Epilogue*, 12 YALE J. ON REG. 177 (1995) (discussing New Zealand interconnection litigation).

24. Thomas E. Weber, *Time Warner Seeks Mediation in Talks with Ameritech*, WALL ST. J., Dec. 27, 1995, at 17 (cable television company asking Ohio regulators to mediate interconnection pricing); Thomas E. Weber, *AT&T Accuses Ameritech of Charging Unfair Prices to Resell Local Services*, WALL ST. J., Dec. 26, 1995, at B2 (pricing of resale of basic service elements in Illinois).

25. Washington Util. & Transp. Comm'n *v.* U S West Communications, Inc., Fourth Supplemental Order Rejecting Tariff Filings and Ordering Refiling, Dkt. Nos. UT-941464 *et al.*, slip op. (Wash. Util. & Transp. Comm'n Oct. 31, 1995); Competition for Local Exchange Service, Decision 95-09-121, R.95-04-043, I.95-04-044, 165 P.U.R.4th 127 (Cal. Pub. Utils. Comm'n 1995).

invasion of property, the takings argument has received greater attention. In 1994 the U.S. Court of Appeals for the District of Columbia Circuit overturned a Federal Communications Commission rule—as exceeding the agency's authority—that ordered unbundling of the local loop and physical or virtual collocation of competitors' transmission equipment on the premises of the incumbent local exchange carrier.[26] In 1995 the Oregon Supreme Court held that the state public utilities commission violated the Takings Clause of the U.S. Constitution when it ordered collocation on LEC premises of enhanced service providers as part of the commission's policy on open network architecture.[27] Generally, however, state PUCs have dismissed the possibility that their policies of interconnection or unbundling may violate the Takings Clause.[28] The Telecommunications Act of 1996 includes numerous instances of mandatory unbundling, many of which will surely prompt takings challenges if, as seems inescapable, they entail either physical invasion of facilities or demands from entrants for the incumbent regulated firm to offer such access at uncompensatory prices, whether or not such access is deemed to be a physical invasion.

It is easy to cheer the arrival of competition to industries where it previously has been discouraged or forbidden by law. But the predictable appeal that competition holds for legislators and regulators should not obscure the fact that the transition from regulated monopoly to competition, like the transition from dirty air to clean, is not free. The advent of competition in local telephony and the electric power industry will preclude the recovery, through market-determined prices, of the costs that incumbent burdens entail for public utilities. The potential magnitude of that phenomenon is staggering. Electric utilities alone may face $200 billion or more in "stranded costs" as a result of the growth of independent power producers and the advent of wholesale

26. Bell Atlantic Tel. Cos. *v.* FCC, 24 F.3d 1441, 1445 (D.C. Cir. 1994) (noting that the FCC's order of physical collocation "directly implicates the Just Compensation Clause of the Fifth Amendment, under which a 'permanent physical occupation authorized by government is a taking without regard to the public interests it may serve'") (quoting Loretto *v.* Teleprompter Manhattan CATV Corp., 458 U.S. 419, 426 (1982)).

27. GTE Northwest Inc. *v.* Public Util. Comm'n of Ore., 321 Ore. 458, 900 P.2d 495 (1995), *cert. denied*, 116 S. Ct. 1541 (1996).

28. *See, e.g.*, Intermedia Communications of Fla., Inc., Dkt. No. 921074-TP, slip op. (Fla. Pub. Serv. Comm'n, Mar. 10, 1994).

and retail wheeling.[29] That is a public policy challenge at least as large as the savings and loan cleanup.

Not surprisingly, state and federal regulators are already addressing the problem of stranded cost recovery in the electric power industry. Critical questions in that policy debate include how stranded costs are defined, how they are measured, and what percentage of such costs the utility's shareholders should bear. Pennsylvania, for example, enacted legislation that took effect in 1997 to ensure full recovery of stranded costs by electric utilities.[30] Some state PUCs, such as California's, have announced that electric utilities may recover 100 percent of nonmitigable stranded costs through a nonbypassable competition transition charge, although at a reduced rate of return on investment to reflect the reduced degree of risk that utilities supposedly will face in recovering those costs.[31] Other state PUCs have advocated shareholder recovery of a lesser percentage. New Hampshire, for example, has proposed that shareholders of franchised electric utilities bear 50 percent of the burden of stranded costs caused by retail wheeling.[32]

But in local telephony, where substantial competitive entry is likely to occur before 2000, state and federal regulators are only beginning to address the issue of stranded costs. Indeed, at least one state regulator, the California Public Utilities Commission, has refused to consider testimony on the takings question in its proceedings on competition in local telephony until *after* it has ordered mandatory unbundling by that

---

29. AMERICAN BAR ASSOCIATION, ANNUAL REPORT, SECTION OF PUBLIC UTILITY, COMMUNICATIONS AND TRANSPORTATION LAW 188 (1994) ($300 billion estimate); Recovery of Stranded Costs by Public Utilities and Transmitting Utilities, Notice of Proposed Rulemaking, Dkt. No. RM-94-7-000, 67 F.E.R.C. ¶ 61,394, at 20 (1994) (reporting estimates from tens of billions of dollars to $200 billion); *NARUC Eyes Stranded Investment Jurisdictional Issues*, ENERGY REP., vol. 22, no. 9 (Mar. 7, 1994) (reporting $200 billion to $300 billion estimate by an investor-owned utility's vice president of corporate strategic planning). *See also* BAUMOL & SIDAK, TRANSMISSION PRICING AND STRANDED COSTS, *supra* note 18, at 98–114; William J. Baumol & J. Gregory Sidak, *Stranded Costs*, 18 HARV. J.L. & PUB. POL'Y 835 (1995).

30. Electricity Generation and Customer Choice and Competition Act of 1996, 1996 Pa. Laws 138 (codified at 66 PA. CONS. STAT. § 2801 *et seq.*).

31. Proposed Policies Governing Restructuring California's Electric Services Industry and Reforming Regulation, R.94-04-031, I.94-01-032 (Cal. Pub. Utils. Comm'n Dec. 20, 1995). Under the California proposal, the rate of return on generation-related stranded costs would be set at the cost of debt for the debt portion, but the return on the equity portion would be set at 10 percent less than the cost of debt. The overall rate of return is estimated to be approximately 7.4 percent.

32. Preliminary Guidelines, Dkt. No. DE 95-250 (N.H. Pub. Utils. Comm'n 1995).

state's local exchange carriers.[33] The Federal Communications Commission similarly deferred consideration of such cost recovery issues in its May 1997 order on reform of access charges for interstate calls.[34]

THE SCOPE OF ANALYSIS

In chapter 2 we review the basic economic issues associated with deregulation of the network industries served by public utilities, particularly the telecommunications and electric power industries. In particular, we examine the effect of asymmetric regulations borne by the incumbent utility but not entrants, which we call *incumbent burdens*. We consider the effects of deregulation and incumbent burdens on stranded costs, and the consequences of mandatory unbundling and open access regulation.

In chapter 3 we examine at length the regulatory quarantine, one of the most significant of incumbent burdens. Under the quarantine an incumbent utility is forbidden to enter one or more competitive markets. We show that the economic rationale for the quarantine theory is unpersuasive in the important case of local exchange telephony.

In chapter 4 we present the economic, historical, and legal case for the existence of the regulatory contract. We first explain the economic rationale for why a regulatory contract must exist between the utility and the municipality (or its successor, the state). Next, we provide historical evidence that such a contract has long been recognized. We then examine the principal elements of the regulatory contract. In light of what our analysis shows, the state cannot credibly assert that it owes no remedy to the utility when the state breaches the regulatory contract while adopting policies that promote competitive entry.

In chapter 5 we examine the utility's remedy for the regulator's breach of the regulatory contract, which we show to be the standard remedy for breach of any contract: damages for lost expectations. If a regulator permits entry into a network industry served exclusively by a

---

33. Administrative Law Judge's Ruling Clarifying the Scope of Phase II Testimony, Order Instituting Rulemaking on the Commission's Own Motion into Competition for Local Exchange Service, R.95-04-043, I.95-04-044 (Cal. Pub. Utils. Comm'n Oct. 5, 1995).

34. Access Charge Reform; Price Cap Performance Review for Local Exchange Carriers; Transport Rate Structure and Pricing; End User Common Line Charges, First Report and Order, CC Dkt. Nos. 96-262, 94-1, 91-213, 95-72, ¶ 14 (released May 16, 1997).

regulated public utility while leaving the utility's incumbent burdens in place, the regulator will have confiscated the wealth of the utility's shareholders. The regulator will have denied those shareholders the benefit of their bargain with the regulator—that is, their expectation under the regulatory contract. As a matter of economic theory, that remedy will always equal or exceed the amount of the public utility's stranded costs. If the regulator fails to introduce a mechanism by which the public utility can recover its stranded costs, the regulator will have denied the utility the ability to maintain financial solvency.[35] We further consider whether sovereign immunity denies the public utility a remedy for the state's breach of the regulatory contract, and we analyze the public utility's duty to mitigate damages for breach of that contract. We examine whether the regulator would have a plausible defense to breach of contract on a theory of either mistake or impossibility, and we show what the measure of restitution to the regulated utility would be if a court were to set aside the regulatory contract on such a theory. Finally, if the relationship between the state and public utility is deemed *not* to be a contract, but rather at most a gratuitous or donative promise made to the utility by the state, we examine the legal and economic arguments for the utility's recovery of its cost of detrimental reliance—namely, an amount no less than its stranded costs—under the common law doctrine of promissory estoppel.[36]

In chapter 6 we consider property protections for investment in public utilities. Even if one refuses to recognize that the regulatory contract is enforceable as a matter of contract law against the regulator in the event of its breach, the abnegation of that relationship between the regulator and the public utility (whatever legal name one chooses to attach to it) effects a taking of private property for public use—namely, the promotion of competition in a regulated industry—without just compensation. In that case, however, it is not an expanding regulatory state that has worked the taking, but a receding one. For that reason, we call that form of confiscation of private property a *deregulatory*

---

35. *See, e.g.*, Fred Vogelstein, *Electric Utility Bond Holders Face More Risk*, WALL ST. J., Nov. 24, 1995, at C1 (reporting that Niagara Mohawk Power, with $4.2 billion in debt outstanding, is considering declaring bankruptcy); Agis Salpukas, *New York State Utility Seeks Sweeping Changes*, N.Y. TIMES, Oct. 7, 1995, at 35.

36. Just as there is a regulatory contract, so also is it conceivable that the state could commit regulatory *torts*, such as trespass, interference with contractual or prospective economic advantage, and fraud. To keep the scope of this book manageable, however, we confine our analysis to theories of contract and property.

taking.[37] We show that, under three separate lines of Supreme Court cases, the appropriate measure of damages for a deregulatory taking is the public utility's expectation of its forgone net benefit *if the state were to abide by the regulatory contract*.[38] As a matter of economic theory, that amount cannot be less than the opportunity cost of the utility's property under the state's continued adherence to the regulatory contract. That result holds whether one casts a deregulatory taking as a physical invasion of property, as a confiscatory setting of public utility rates, or as a noninvasive regulatory taking. Indeed, we show that the reasoning in the major decisions on regulatory takings applies with greater force to deregulatory takings in regulated industries than it does to the typical case of land use or environmental restrictions imposed on real property. In particular, regulatory takings cases stress the "investment-backed expectation" interest of the private property owner.[39] That consideration is analogous to the reasonable expectation interest of the public utility when it placed in service a long-lived nonsalvageable asset (such as an electrical generation plant or a telecommunications switch or a transmission line) or made similar kinds of nonsalvageable investments giving rise to stranded costs.

In chapter 7 we examine how a court should measure just compensation for a deregulatory taking. We argue that just compensation

---

37. A deregulatory taking is thus an important example of the compensable transformation of economic institutions that William Fischel describes:

> Just compensation is a means of smoothing out transformations in the economy, whether they be for internal improvements or for institutional change. The Takings Clause serves both as a check to excessive public enthusiasm (since money must be paid) and as a facilitator (since property must be surrendered). But it does not prohibit change. Thus if Hawaii wants to reject some of its anachronistic landholding system, there should be no bar to its doing so if compensation is made. It isn't just roads and post offices that qualify as public goods; economic institutions do, too.

FISCHEL, *supra* note 2, at 73 (referring to Hawaii Housing Auth. *v.* Midkiff, 467 U.S. 229 (1984)).

38. We confine our analysis to the Takings Clause of the U.S. Constitution. Analogous provisions in the state constitutions, some of which predate the Fifth Amendment, may offer even stronger protections against uncompensated confiscations of property. *See, e.g.*, Burrow *v.* City of Keene, 122 N.H. 590, 596 (1981) ("the New Hampshire Constitution makes explicit what is implicit in the Fifth Amendment to the Federal Constitution, namely, that no *part* of a man's property shall be taken from him . . . without his consent") (emphasis in original).

39. *Penn Central*, 438 U.S. at 124.

should mirror the outcome of voluntary exchange, which would yield for the seller his full economic cost of willingly parting with the asset. For the regulated utility the measure is the difference between the firm's expected net revenues under regulation and the firm's expected net revenues under competition. That difference corresponds to the change in the value of the utility.

In chapter 8 we review the *efficient component-pricing rule* (ECPR), which specifies that the price of network access must include all opportunity costs incurred by the supplier in providing the product—that is, all potential earnings that the supplying firm forgoes, either by providing inputs of its own rather than purchasing them, or by offering services to competitors that force it to relinquish business to those rivals, and thus to forgo the profits on that lost business. The rule requires that the price of a unit of access to an incumbent's network should equal its average incremental cost, including all pertinent incremental opportunity costs.[40] A number of regulatory bodies have considered or are considering the use of the rule in connection with the deregulation of electricity and local telephony markets.[41] We then summarize the numerous ways in which the ECPR promotes economic efficiency as well as the statutory objectives in unbundling legislation like the Telecommunications Act of 1996. We show in formal economic terms the efficiency of the ECPR under different market structures. The access price derived from the ECPR permits price to fall and output to expand for the final product relative to the price and output that had obtained under regulation. That result holds in contestable markets, under Cournot-Nash competition, and in markets characterized by product differentiation. In each such market structure, the ECPR rewards entry by more efficient rivals and lowers the price of the final product.

In its simplest version the ECPR assumes that there are no substitutes for the bottleneck facility providing network access. In chapter 9 we remove that assumption and examine the *market-determined efficient component-pricing rule* (M-ECPR). The M-ECPR explicitly limits the opportunity cost component of the ECPR to reflect the constraint

---

40. *See* WILLIAM J. BAUMOL & J. GREGORY SIDAK, TOWARD COMPETITION IN LOCAL TELEPHONY 93–116 (MIT Press & AEI Press 1994); William J. Baumol & J. Gregory Sidak, *The Pricing of Inputs Sold to Competitors*, 11 YALE J. ON REG. 171 (1994).

41. *E.g.*, Telecom Corp. of New Zealand Ltd. *v.* Clear Communications Ltd., [1995] 1 N.Z.L.R. 385 (Judgment of the Lords of the Judicial Committee of the Privy Council, Oct. 19, 1994).

that competitive alternatives to the bottleneck facility impose on the incumbent's maximum feasible price for access to that facility.

In chapter 10 we review and answer the numerous criticisms that economists and regulators have lodged against the ECPR or the M-ECPR. We show that those criticisms are misplaced and do not provide a basis for rejecting the use of the M-ECPR for the pricing of mandatory network access. We also emphasize the fact, often not acknowledged by critics of the ECPR or the M-ECPR, that many eminent regulatory economists have endorsed the rule and that many regulatory or judicial bodies have employed the rule. Finally, we dispel the misconception that the creators of the ECPR have rejected use of the M-ECPR for pricing unbundled network elements in local telephony.

In chapter 11 we explain the *equivalence principle*. It posits that an equivalence exists between the following concepts: (1) the expectation damage remedy for breach of the regulatory contract; (2) the calculation of just compensation for a deregulatory taking; (3) the change in the financial value of the regulated public utility as a consequence of regulatory change; and (4) the access price that, in the absence of substitutes for the bottleneck facility, would promote efficient interconnection, resale, and unbundling in network industries opened to competition. The rule that accomplishes those simultaneous goals, in the absence of substitute forms of network access, is the efficient component-pricing rule. In all four cases, the critical insight for courts and regulators to grasp is that the law protects *expectations*, for the essential reason that expectations determine decisions and actions in a market economy. One important implication of the equivalence principle for current regulatory proceedings is that, for any given rate structure, an interconnection price will be confiscatory under the Takings Clause unless that price is computed in a manner that promotes only *efficient* entry into the market at issue. That result is not limited to the Takings Clause of the U.S. Constitution, but rather applies as a matter of fundamental legal and economic logic to any jurisdiction that by constitution, statute, regulation, or common law recognizes an individual's right to just compensation when the state confiscates his property for a public purpose.

In chapter 12 we examine the efficiency characteristics of the principal pricing proposals that critics of the ECPR and the M-ECPR offer—pricing network elements according to total service long-run incremental cost (TSLRIC) or total element long-run incremental cost (TELRIC). We show that TSLRIC pricing and TELRIC pricing create numerous inefficiencies and frustrate important objectives in deregulatory legislation such as the Telecommunications Act of 1996. Moreover, the FCC's mischaracterization of economic cost introduces errors of measurement that increase the inefficiencies associated with using TSLRIC or TELRIC to price mandatory network access and manifest an error of economic reasoning that we call "the fallacy of forward-looking costs."

In chapter 13 we examine several implications of efficient capital markets for the recovery of damages or other remedies by the public utility in response to a deregulatory taking. First, we examine the argument that shareholders of the public utility have already been compensated, in the cost of capital that regulators have allowed the utility to earn, for the risk that the regulator will breach the regulatory contract before the utility has had enough time to recover, through its allowed rates, the cost of nonsalvageable assets that the utility put into service in detrimental reliance on the continued operation of that regulatory contract. We show that such an argument is improbable as a matter of economic theory.

Second, we analyze the Supreme Court's current rule that a statute that diminishes property value is not ripe for challenge on takings grounds until the state has actually enforced the statute against the property owner. That rule, we argue, is naïve because it ignores that an efficient market, such as the equities market in which the common stocks of electric utilities and telephone companies are traded, impounds the value of regulatory change (including breach of the regulatory contract by the regulator) into the relevant stock prices as soon as information becomes publicly available. The taking thus occurs when the state signals its abrogation of the regulatory contract, not when that abrogation subsequently takes official effect. Delaying the litigation of takings claims based on abrogation of the regulatory contract will lead to inefficient resource allocation.

Third, we show why it is myopic for competitive entrants into the market formerly served on an exclusive basis by the public utility to oppose its recovery of stranded costs.

In chapter 14 we consider the principles that limit a person's right to receive compensation for changes in regulation that diminish a firm's value. Would the repeal of agricultural price supports or the elimination of taxicab medallions, for example, give rise to a valid takings claim? The answer, we argue, lies in the unique character of the regulatory contract into which the public utility and the state have entered. It is both feasible and necessary for courts to distinguish between firms that have entered into an explicit or implicit contract with the state and firms that have merely obtained regulation or legislation that has created for them the ability to earn economic rents without any countervailing quid pro quo.

In chapter 15 we recommend three principles for guiding regulators in their quest for "fair competition" in currently regulated network industries: *economic incentive*, *equal opportunity*, and *impartiality*. The economic incentive principle cautions that, if regulators do not allow regulated utilities the reasonable opportunity to recover their stranded investment and the costs of satisfying additional regulatory requirements, then the service and investment incentives of those utilities will be impaired. The equal opportunity principle counsels regulators to restructure or remove regulation to ensure that all competitors enter the market on an equal regulatory footing. The impartiality principle instructs regulators not to attempt to influence the eventual outcomes of competition or to micromanage the market following deregulation and open entry. In advocating those three principles, we challenge the conventional wisdom that in network industries undergoing deregulation the regulator must "promote" and then "protect" competition. Such a policy is not truly deregulation, for it installs the regulator as a permanent referee for competitive disputes. Moreover, such a policy is unnecessary because the returns that firms can expect to earn from serving customers provide sufficient incentive for them to compete in the provision of services in the deregulated market. Attempts to manage competition not only entail administrative costs, but also can prevent the market from achieving the benefits of competition that regulators seek to attain. Similarly, regulators need not "protect" competition once they have allowed it to occur. Market incentives are sufficient to allow competition to flourish. If regulators pick winners or protect less successful firms from their own inefficiency, then the benefits of competition will not result. An important implication of our analysis is that regulators must recognize that the extent of mandatory unbundling affects both transaction costs and production costs and can become the object of the competitive strategies of entrants to create asymmetric burdens for incumbent firms.

We close in chapter 16 by sounding several cautionary notes about how our analysis relates to the choice between public or private ownership of network industries. First, we critique an anarchic argument made for not allowing recovery of stranded costs—an argument ostensibly predicated on the desire to minimize government intervention in network industries. Second, we show how the problem of recovering stranded costs differs under public rather than private ownership. That analysis has special relevance to nations that are contemplating the privatization of a network industry in which stranded costs might accompany the introduction of competition. Third, we argue that the Telecommunications Act of 1996 has fundamentally redefined private property in a network industry. Apart from asking whether such a redefinition is constitutional, we should ask whether it is likely to harm economic welfare by destroying returns to vertical integration and, worse, by precipitating a "tragedy of the commons." The current approach to deregulation of telecommunications rests on an unstated assumption that the network has essentially unlimited capacity to accommodate the additional traffic of competitors that have secured mandatory access to the network. We question whether that assumption is likely to be correct and, if not, what the implications for consumer welfare will be. Fourth, we examine the first major judicial interpretation of the unbundling provisions of the Telecommunications Act of 1996, the Eighth Circuit's 1997 decision in *Iowa Utilities Board* v. *FCC*,[42] which showed that a full evaluation of the relevant takings issues would have to wait until a later day.

---

42. 1997 U.S. App. LEXIS 18183 (8th Cir. July 18, 1997).

2

Deregulation and Network Pricing

THE COMPETITIVE TRANSFORMATION of local exchange tele-communications and the electric power industry raises significant questions about whether regulators should give a public utility the opportunity to recover its stranded costs. As regulators mandate the unbundling of basic network elements in local telephony or wholesale and retail wheeling in the electricity industry, they introduce competitive rules that potentially deny incumbent utilities the opportunity to recover the cost of service. While competition presents incumbents with opportunities to serve customers in new ways, regulators often leave untouched the utility's preexisting incumbent burdens. Such regulatory action threatens to confiscate private property—shareholder value—for the promotion of competition, without just compensation. This chapter addresses the major issues giving rise to the problem of deregulatory takings.

To understand deregulation, it is necessary to identify a number of important economic issues and define essential concepts. Why were the network industries regulated in the first place? What motivated policymakers to undertake deregulation? Although it is not possible to review here all of the social, political, and market forces that motivated the creation and reform of regulation, it is useful to examine some of the key economic arguments for both the creation and the removal of regulation.

Natural Monopoly and
Network Industries

The presence of natural monopoly technology provides a central motivation for establishing regulated industries and accordingly imposing entry barriers, price controls, and obligations to serve. As then Professor, now Justice, Stephen G. Breyer observed, "The most traditional and persistent rationale for governmental regulation of a firm's prices and profits is the existence of a 'natural monopoly.'"[1] The end of natural monopoly technology, moreover, justifies deregulation of the network industries, as we see in the next chapter.

A given production technology is said to exhibit the property of *natural monopoly* if a single firm can supply the market at lower cost than can two or more firms.[2] That textbook definition of natural monopoly is based on a cost function that assigns total costs to outputs. The cost function has the natural monopoly property if a firm with that cost function has lower costs than would an allocation of output among two or more firms *using the same cost function*, a condition also referred to as the *subadditivity of costs*. If the technology of local telephony or of electricity generation and transmission exhibits natural monopoly characteristics, then a single firm can construct and operate that network at a lower cost than can two or more firms.

If the firm's cost function exhibits natural monopoly over a restricted range of outputs, then the existence of natural monopoly depends on the extent of market demand. With demand in the relevant range at some market price, production by one firm is less costly than by two or more firms. With an expansion in demand, efficient production would require an increase in the number of firms.

---

1. *See* STEPHEN G. BREYER, REGULATION AND ITS REFORM 15 (Harvard University Press 1982).

2. *See* DENNIS W. CARLTON & JEFFREY M. PERLOFF, MODERN INDUSTRIAL ORGANIZATION 295–96 (Harper Collins, 2d ed. 1994); KENNETH E. TRAIN, OPTIMAL REGULATION: THE ECONOMIC THEORY OF NATURAL MONOPOLY 6–8 (MIT Press 1991); DANIEL F. SPULBER, REGULATION AND MARKETS 3 (MIT Press 1989); ROGER SHERMAN, THE REGULATION OF MONOPOLY 80–81 (Cambridge University Press 1989); SANFORD V. BERG & JOHN TSCHIRHART, NATURAL MONOPOLY REGULATION: PRINCIPLES AND PRACTICE 22 (Cambridge University Press 1988); JEAN TIROLE, THE THEORY OF INDUSTRIAL ORGANIZATION 19–20 (MIT Press 1988); WILLIAM J. BAUMOL, JOHN C. PANZAR & ROBERT D. WILLIG, CONTESTABLE MARKETS AND THE THEORY OF INDUSTRY STRUCTURE 9 (Harcourt Brace Jovanovich 1982; rev. ed. 1988).

The natural monopoly justification for regulation has a distinguished history. The concept of natural monopoly is generally credited to John Stuart Mill, who emphasized the problem of wasteful duplication of transmission facilities that can occur in utility services.[3] Leon Walras developed the connection between natural monopoly and regulation, with reference to the construction and operation of railroads.[4] The assertion that regulation served to capture the efficiencies of large-scale production while controlling market power characterizes the Progressive "public interest" view of utility regulation in the early part of the twentieth century.[5]

Several aspects of the definition of natural monopoly deserve special attention. That definition begins with a *known technology*, as represented by the natural monopoly cost function. To assert that an industry is characterized by natural monopoly, one implicitly assumes that there is a single "best" technology that is commonly known, that all firms would have access to that technology, and that all firms operating that technology would be at the efficient production-possibility frontier.[6] The natural monopoly cost function is a long-run cost function, so that investment can be adjusted to achieve the efficient level of capital investment required for operating at minimum cost for each output level.

Based on the standard definition, a cost function has the natural monopoly property if the technology exhibits *economies of scale* over the relevant range of output. Economies of scale are present if the marginal costs of production are less than the average costs of production over the relevant range of output.[7] Stated differently, economies of scale are said to exist over the relevant range of output when unit costs decline with the volume of production. Economies of scale are a sufficient condition for natural monopoly for a single-product firm.

---

3. JOHN STUART MILL, PRINCIPLES OF POLITICAL ECONOMY 132–54 (W. J. Ashley ed., Augustus M. Kelly 1961) (1848).

4. LEON WALRAS, ETUDES D'ECONOMIE SOCIALE: THEORIE DE LA REPARTITION DE LA RICHESSE SOCIALE (F. Pichon 1896).

5. *See* ROBERT BRITT HORWITZ, THE IRONY OF REGULATORY REFORM: THE DEREGULATION OF AMERICAN TELECOMMUNICATIONS 25 (Oxford University Press 1989); JOHN BATES CLARK & JOHN MAURICE CLARK, THE CONTROL OF TRUSTS (MacMillan & Co. 1912).

6. SPULBER, *supra* note 2, at 138.

7. *Id.* at 115–18; CARLTON & PERLOFF, *supra* note 2, at 58–63.

Economies of scale need not be present for the firm's technology to have the natural monopoly property. For a single-product firm, average costs may decline as output increases from zero up to a minimum efficient scale, whereupon average costs may stay constant (constant returns to scale) or even increase (decreasing returns to scale). The firm's technology may still have the natural monopoly property even at some output levels above the minimum efficient scale. Even though average costs are increasing, it may still be less costly to produce the output with one firm rather than two or more firms.

Economies of scale can be due to many different technological factors. *Fixed costs* are a source of economies of scale that are particularly significant to industries that require networks, such as telecommunications, electricity, railroads, oil and natural gas pipelines, and water services. Fixed costs are costs that do not vary with fluctuations in output, unlike operating or "variable" costs. The fixed costs of establishing a network system are the costs of facilities such as transmission lines, which are not sensitive to the level of transmission on the lines.

The need to avoid *duplication of facilities*, particularly duplication of the fixed costs of the network system, is an important component of the natural monopoly argument for the regulation of most network industries. For example, that argument was put forward to justify regulation of the local exchange.[8] The reasoning is that, because costs are minimized by not duplicating network infrastructure, regulators should bar the entry of competing carriers. That argument has been advanced in a wide range of regulated industries in which transmission or transportation facilities are a significant portion of total costs.

For a multiproduct firm, the natural monopoly property is sufficient for the existence of economies of scope. The firm's technology is said to exhibit *economies of scope* when it is less costly for one firm to produce a set of goods jointly than for distinct firms to produce individual goods or subsets of goods separately. It is important to notice that although natural monopoly implies economies of scope, the converse is not the case. Most multiproduct firms derive economies of scope from joint production; it is a primary motivation for companies to diversify their product offerings. That achievement of economies of scope does not imply that those companies could serve their entire markets at lower cost than two or more firms.

---

8. United States *v.* Western Elec. Co., 673 F. Supp. 525, 537 (D.D.C. 1987), *aff'd*, 894 F.2d 1387 (D.C. Cir. 1990).

The reason that economies of scope exist is closely related to the avoidance of duplication of facilities. Costs that are not attributable to any particular good or service are called *common costs*. Common costs can be fixed costs, but they need not be. For example, in a simple network system with a single trunk line and multiple distribution lines, the cost of the trunk line is a common cost because it is not attributable to any specific transmission service between any two origination and distribution points. To some extent we can view the trunk line as a fixed cost because it is not sensitive to the usage of the transmission system. In the long run, however, adjusting the system's size to reflect transmission capacity requirements would necessarily entail changing the size of the trunk line. Thus, common costs generally are not fixed costs, because those costs depend on the levels of the outputs of the multiproduct firm.

The cost attributable to an individual product or group of products is referred to as *incremental cost*. The incremental cost of some service *A* is calculated by taking the difference between the total cost of producing a set of services including service *A* and the total cost of producing a set of services excluding service *A*. Common cost is calculated by subtracting from total cost the sum of the incremental costs of each service. Thus, common costs are those costs that are not attributable to any individual service. The greater the proportion of common costs relative to total costs, the greater are the economies of joint production. As we observe in later chapters, the distinction between incremental and common costs is important because regulators seeking to set prices equal to incremental costs may prevent incumbent utilities from recovering their common costs.

Natural monopoly is a traditional economic justification for regulating local telephony or electricity generation, transmission, and distribution. That justification may lose its persuasiveness over time. What was once a naturally monopolistic method for delivering a particular kind of telecommunications service may be supplanted by a lower-cost method that does not necessarily have large sunk costs and low incremental costs.[9] That kind of transformation has already occurred in the generation of electricity with the advent of combined-cycle gas turbine plants, and it appears to be occurring today in local telephony with the development of various wireless technologies. Moreover, the number of alternative technologies available to build and operate the interactive

---

9. *See* Daniel F. Spulber, *Deregulating Telecommunications*, 12 YALE J. ON REG. 25 (1995).

broadband networks of the future leaves unanswered the question of whether such networks will have the cost characteristics of natural monopoly. The wiser course for regulators, therefore, is to encourage competition among technologies and firms.

For there to be a true tournament among all potential providers of a service previously supplied solely by a regulated firm, the market must be free of regulatory barriers to entry—barriers created artificially by statute or regulation rather than by economic cost advantages of incumbents over entrants. Opposition to new entry, of course, is a predictable response among incumbent firms in any industry. Since at least the 1930s, incumbent firms in the United States have repeatedly entreated regulators to prevent, or at least to circumscribe, entry by rival firms exploiting new communications technologies. For example, newspapers resisted the growth of radio broadcasting, radio broadcasters resisted the growth of over-the-air television, over-the-air television broadcasters resisted the growth of cable television, cable television operators resisted the entry of telephone companies into video, and so forth.[10]

With the entry of competing carriers restricted, the incumbent utilities were free from some forms of competition. As a consequence, regulators sought to replace the discipline of the market with administrative controls. State and municipal commissions imposed cost-of-service regulation to limit the prices and earnings of the incumbent utility. The quality of service was mandated and monitored through obligations to serve and other regulatory requirements. Thus, natural monopoly technology provided an impetus for regulation. Regulation would increase consumer welfare if the inefficiencies of costly administrative controls were outweighed by cost savings from a single transmission network. A reevaluation of that critical tradeoff is the catalyst for deregulation. If technological change reduces or eliminates the advantages of natural monopoly technology, or if the efficiency burdens of regulation become too onerous, dismantling the regulatory regime becomes worthwhile.

We are not, of course, suggesting that the presence and later obsolescence of natural monopoly technology fully explains regulation and subsequent deregulation. To do so would imply a "public interest" interpretation of regulation that is often inconsistent with the history of regulatory institutions. A number of other factors—including the high

---

10. *See, e.g.*, BRUCE M. OWEN & STEVEN S. WILDMAN, VIDEO ECONOMICS 14–18 (Harvard University Press 1992).

sunk costs of the network industries and the income redistribution inherent in regulated rate structures—also play a crucial role in regulation and deregulation.

SUNK COSTS, BARRIERS TO
ENTRY, AND STRANDED COSTS

High capital investment costs are another property of the technology of network industries that figures prominently in the creation and reform of regulation. To establish a network, industries such as telecommunications and electric power must make substantial nonrecoverable, market-specific investments, known as *sunk costs*. Networks represent the quintessential sunk costs. The transportation and reticulation facilities in telecommunications, electricity, railroads, oil and natural gas pipelines, and water services are tied to specific geographic locations. The capital from the facilities has little if any scrap value, and the facilities cannot physically be transferred to another market, unless alternative uses for the facilities can be found *in situ*. Other costs, such as investments in specialized capital equipment for nuclear power plants, also are sunk. Such facilities cannot be transferred to other uses.

Sunk costs justify regulation in two distinct ways. The notion that the need to sink costs favors incumbents justifies price regulation to control the monopoly power of incumbents; conversely, technological change that reduces the need to sink costs creates opportunities for deregulation. Alternatively, the presence of sunk costs justifies regulatory entry barriers put in place to allow incumbents to recover their capital investment costs. The recovery of sunk costs is a critical aspect of network industries that complicates deregulation.

Barriers to Entry

George J. Stigler asserted that barriers to entry are costs imposed on entrants but not present for incumbents.[11] Sunk costs are said to be a barrier to entry if entrants must make irreversible investments in capacity—expenses that incumbents have already incurred.[12] If an incumbent,

---

11. GEORGE J. STIGLER, THE ORGANIZATION OF INDUSTRY 67 (Richard D. Irwin, Inc. 1968). The definition is commonly applied. *See, e.g.*, William J. Baumol & Robert D. Willig, *Fixed Costs, Sunk Costs, Entry Barriers and Sustainability of Monopoly*, 96 Q.J. ECON. 405, 408 (1981).

12. *See* SPULBER, *supra* note 2, at 40–42.

but not an entrant, has already incurred the sunk cost of facilities, the incumbent need only price to recover operating and incremental capital expenses, because it can write off the irreversible investment costs of entry. A potential entrant, in contrast, must anticipate earnings exceeding its operating costs, incremental investment, and irreversible costs of establishing its facilities before it will attempt to enter the market.

By itself a natural monopoly technology does not act as a barrier to entry. Firms can enter an industry and compete with incumbents even if production by a single firm is efficient. Natural monopoly technology does not prevent the entrant from investing in new facilities, announcing prices, recruiting customers, and otherwise competing with the incumbent. To deter entry effectively, the incumbent firm must be able to set prices and retain its customers such that entry is no longer profitable. It is important to emphasize that, even if a single firm could serve the market more efficiently than could two or more firms, that state of affairs does not imply that entering firms cannot compete to serve the market. Furthermore, natural monopoly technology does not rule out the possibility of multiple competitors' entering to serve the market simultaneously.

Along with other economic analyses of entry and competition, the economic literature on contestable markets has shown that competition for the market can occur with natural monopoly technology and has stated the conditions under which there may or may not be prices such that an incumbent can sustain a monopoly position. William J. Baumol, John C. Panzar, and Robert D. Willig refer to an industry in which there are negligible barriers to entry as *contestable* and emphasize that companies that are natural monopolies can compete to serve the market.[13] Under certain demand and cost conditions, an incumbent can sustain its position against new entry, but only by choosing prices that yield zero profits. Without the need to sink costs, potential entrants can exert competitive discipline on an incumbent firm's prices and performance. Thus, without sunk costs, "hit-and-run" entry provides competition even in the presence of natural monopoly.

Competition nonetheless remains feasible even with sunk costs. The need to sink costs should not be viewed as an insurmountable barrier to the entry of new competitors. All competitive markets involve some degree of irreversible investment, whether in capital equipment, marketing, or research and development. Entrants commit capital resources in markets where they expect to earn competitive returns on their

---

13. BAUMOL, PANZAR & WILLIG, *supra* note 2, at 7.

investments. The sunk costs involved in establishing a telecommunications system, given currently available technologies, are not qualitatively different from irreversible investments in any other competitive market. Furthermore, in competitive markets there is often duplication of investment, and the entry of excess or insufficient capacity can take place as a consequence of uncertainty regarding costs, technology, or market demand. Therefore, even if sunk costs are present in telecommunications, they need not in themselves confer monopoly rents on incumbents.

In addition, entrants can reduce the risk associated with making investment commitments in a variety of ways, including contracting with customers before making irreversible investments and entering into joint ventures or mergers with incumbents. Moreover, a potential entrant need not be deterred from entry if it has a sufficient cost advantage over the incumbent. Developments in the telecommunications industry since the breakup of the Bell System amply demonstrate that many companies are willing and able to make the irreversible investments required to enter the business of local telecommunications.

The irreversible nature of investment in network industries has provided an additional rationale for the regulation of those industries. Private industries routinely engage in large-scale irreversible investments in capital plant and equipment, research and development, and marketing. The presumed difference is that a large portion of utility investment is in network facilities that also have the natural monopoly property. Thus, entry restrictions avoid duplication of irreversible investment. Moreover, because irreversible investment can create a barrier to entry, some calls for regulation of utilities rest on the need to control monopoly rents.

Just as technological change spells the end of the natural monopoly justification for regulation, so reductions in the required level of irreversible investment eliminate calls for regulation based on sunk-cost entry barriers, as we discuss in chapter 3. With ease of entry, competition *for* the market becomes feasible, even if the technology exhibits economies of scale. *Contestable markets* are markets with low sunk costs or markets subject to competition from substitute products or services provided by industries with low sunk costs. If markets are contestable, there is little call for price regulation to control monopoly rents.[14] Moreover, product innovation that creates substitutes for the

---

14. Harold Demsetz, *Why Regulate Utilities?*, 11 J.L. & ECON. 55 (1968); BAUMOL, PANZAR & WILLIG, *supra* note 2, at 476–79.

incumbent's services allows intermodal competition to develop, which again eliminates the need for regulation to control monopoly rents that are alleged to arise from the operation of "bottleneck" facilities.

Stranded Investment and Stranded Cost

Entry restrictions further provide protection from competition for the earnings of regulated firms and thus enable the incumbent to recover the costs of long-lived specialized capital investment and the returns to investment.[15] That purpose is closely related to avoiding the duplication of facilities, because irreversible investment costs exacerbate that problem. Cost-of-service regulation in the network industries traditionally has based rates on a valuation of the utility's investment and an allowed rate of return on that investment. As we emphasize in the following chapters, the regulatory contract in those industries provides for the recovery of investment costs.

Ordinarily, sunk costs do not affect business decisions, which are only concerned with available benefits and avoidable costs. To base future decisions on those costs is known as *the fallacy of sunk costs*. Nonetheless, the regulatory treatment of stranded costs can have important distributional consequences and can affect incentives for the public utility to make future investments in highly specific and nonsalvageable assets. In that respect, neglect of cost recovery would be ill-advised because it could profoundly affect the outcome of the repeated-play game between the public utility and its regulator.[16] In this book and in our previous writings, we emphasize that the relationship between the regulated firm and its regulator is a bargaining situation. That is, the relationship is not, as it is sometimes characterized, either a setting in which the regulator imposes exogenous rules on passive firms or a setting in which a passive regulator is "captured" by the firms that it ostensibly regulates. Consequently, we do not agree with Oliver E. Williamson's criticism that we have assumed that regulators "exercise informed oversight and administer rates fairly" and that regulated utilities are "candid, compliant, efficient, and nonstrategic."[17] To

15. *See* Victor P. Goldberg, *Regulation and Administered Contracts*, 7 BELL J. ECON. 426 (1976).

16. For a more technical analysis of the relationship of reputation to repeated games, see DAVID M. KREPS, A COURSE IN MICROECONOMIC THEORY 531–36, 764–67 (Princeton University Press 1990).

17. Oliver E. Williamson, *Deregulatory Takings and Breach of the Regulatory Contract: Some Precautions*, 71 N.Y.U. L. REV. 1007, 1009 (1996).

paraphrase James Madison, we do not believe that regulators and regulated firms are angels.[18] To the contrary, we believe that regulators and regulated firms are capable of exhibiting all of the highest and lowest motives of human beings.

By opening regulated markets to competition, regulators can reduce the earnings of the incumbent public utility. The capital equipment and other facilities of that utility may not be suited to the changing requirements of competitive markets. Moreover, competitive rules designed by regulators seeking to "manage" the transition to competition may handicap the incumbent utility relative to entrants. Those changes in regulatory policy can reduce the regulated firm's net revenues and deny its investors an opportunity to earn a fair return on their investments made under the previous regulatory regime. Those changes also can prevent the utility's shareholders from having a return of their invested capital when the utility retires from service the assets that such capital was used to acquire. That inability of utility shareholders to secure the return of, and a competitive rate of return on, their investment gives rise to the condition known as stranded investment or *stranded costs*. More precisely, stranded investment is a subset of stranded costs. The latter includes expenditures (such as the mandatory purchase of energy at the utility's avoided cost but above the market price of such energy) that are not capital investments in physical plant per se, but that nonetheless reflect outlays required by regulators that firms cannot recoup in the presence of competitive entry. Throughout this book, we use the broader concept of stranded costs.[19]

As we demonstrate in chapter 4, one can measure stranded costs as the anticipated shortfall in net revenues under competition as a consequence of changes in regulatory policy. Although private contracts and the regulatory contract are not identical forms of agreements, economic analysis of the common law of contracts illuminates the correct way to

---

18. "But what is government itself but the greatest of all reflections on human nature? If men were angels, no government would be necessary. If angels were to govern men, neither external nor internal controuls on government would be necessary. In framing a government which is to be administered by men over men, the great difficulty lies in this: You must first enable the government to controul the governed; and in the next place, oblige it to controul itself." THE FEDERALIST NO. 51, at 322 (James Madison) (1788) (Jacob E. Cooke ed., Wesleyan University Press 1961).

19. *See generally* WILLIAM J. BAUMOL & J. GREGORY SIDAK, TRANSMISSION PRICING AND STRANDED COSTS IN THE ELECTRIC POWER INDUSTRY (AEI Press 1995); William J. Baumol & J. Gregory Sidak, *Stranded Costs*, 18 HARV. J.L. & PUB. POL'Y 835 (1995).

measure stranded costs and the best approach to recovering stranded costs by applying basic principles from private contracts. We argue in chapter 4 that the regulatory contract protects the utility's reasonable opportunity to earn a competitive return on investments that it made to discharge its obligation to serve.

INCUMBENT BURDENS

Government regulation that takes the form of rules applying unequally to incumbents and entrants can create additional costs for entrants and potentially can restrict market entry entirely. Stigler observed, for example, that licenses are "absolute barriers to entry."[20] Government regulation and sunk costs are the two main types of barriers to entry. Just as regulation can explicitly or implicitly block entry into an industry, so regulation can encourage or promote entry by applying rules asymmetrically on entrants and incumbents. An *incumbent burden* is said to exist if incumbents face costs owing to regulation that are not imposed on entrants.

As a market served exclusively by a public utility is opened to competition, regulators create the possibility of stranded costs if they retain or impose different regulations on the incumbent utility in comparison with those imposed on actual and potential entrants. Such regulatory differences cause greater costs to be placed on the incumbent public utility than on entrants. Incumbent burdens encourage or even subsidize some forms of entry and create the potential for *uneconomic bypass*.[21] Uneconomic bypass is said to occur if entry raises the total industry costs of providing a given level of service; such bypass can result from subsidies to entrants or from asymmetric regulation of incumbent public utilities and entrants.[22]

Thus, an incumbent burden is the opposite of an entry barrier in the sense that the former facilitates entry and bypass of the existing network even if such bypass would be uneconomic in the absence of the regulations. Stated differently, incumbent burdens are analogous to the phenomenon of "raising rivals' costs,"[23] except that in an industry

---

20. STIGLER, *supra* note 11, at 123–25.

21. *See* Paul W. MacAvoy, Daniel F. Spulber & Bruce E. Stangle, *Is Competitive Entry Free?: Bypass and Partial Deregulation in Natural Gas Markets*, 6 YALE J. ON REG. 209, 210 (1989).

22. *Id.*

23. Thomas G. Krattenmaker & Steven C. Salop, *Anticompetitive Exclusion: Raising Rivals' Costs to Achieve Power over Price*, 96 YALE L.J. 209 (1986).

subject to public utility regulation the "rival" whose cost is being raised is the incumbent public utility rather than the entrant. Thus, the raising of a rival's cost is a method not of facilitating inefficient exclusion from a market, but of facilitating inefficient entry into it.

In telecommunications, for example, the regional Bell operating companies (RBOCs) face a variety of regulatory restrictions (including common carrier provisions, quarantines, universal service requirements, and public filing of rates) that are generally not imposed on new entrants. In most major markets in the United States, the local exchange carrier is either one of the seven RBOCs or GTE, a firm comparable in size to any given RBOC but never part of the former Bell System.[24] Other restrictions on the RBOCs create lower limits on certain tariffs that limit the RBOCs' ability to compete with entrants and provide a tariff umbrella for competitors. The regulated rate structure of the RBOCs, with high rates charged to business customers, has created opportunities for selective bypass of the local network, particularly by competitive access providers such as Metropolitan Fiber Systems (MFS) and Teleport Communications Group (TCG), which principally serve large business customers.[25]

The inefficiencies created by incumbent burdens suggest that market entry of competitors should be accompanied by a lifting of uneven restrictions placed on the RBOCs. By removing those restrictions, regulators would eliminate artificial handicaps arising from regulation. That policy would allow an RBOC to respond to competitive challenges through its strategies for pricing, investment, and innovation. Entry would then reflect competitive considerations instead of regulatory restrictions on the incumbent public utility.

Implicit Income Transfers
Embedded in the Rate Structure

Cross-subsidization occurs when a company supplying more than one product or service uses the revenues from product *A* to recover a por-

---

24. *See* MICHAEL K. KELLOGG, JOHN THORNE & PETER W. HUBER, FEDERAL TELECOMMUNICATIONS LAW 199–248, 401–21 (Little, Brown & Co. 1992).

25. MFS COMMUNICATIONS CO., INC., 1995 SEC FORM 10-K, at 1, 11 (1996); TELEPORT COMMUNICATIONS GROUP, INC., PROSPECTUS FOR 23,500,000 SHARES OF CLASS A COMMON STOCK (June 3, 1996); Affidavit of Glenn A. Woroch (June 27, 1994), submitted on behalf of Motion of Bell Atlantic Corporation, BellSouth Corporation, NYNEX Corporation, and Southwestern Bell Corporation to Vacate the Decree, United States *v.* Western Elec. Co., No. 82-0192 (D.D.C. filed July 6, 1994).

tion of the additional costs of producing product *B*. That practice creates economic inefficiencies because the consumers of product *A* would be better off if the products were produced and priced separately, even though such separation would forgo economies from joint production. Moreover, the consumers of product *B* receive incorrect price signals about the incremental costs of producing product *B*. Cross-subsidies can persist only in the presence of regulatory barriers to entry or exit. As Judge Richard A. Posner has observed, regulatory cross-subsidies are "a peculiarly inefficient method of taxation" because regulators could achieve their purpose through excise taxes on one service to support part of the cost of the other service, without the imposition of entry or exit controls.[26] Robert W. Crandall and Leonard Waverman, for example, have estimated the static welfare gains from eliminating cross-subsidies in U.S. telephone rates to be $8 billion annually.[27]

Economists have devised formal tests for cross-subsidization. A regulated firm's rate structure can be said to be free of cross-subsidies if and only if the prices satisfy the stand-alone cost test.[28] That widely applied criterion requires that the revenues generated from either of two services not exceed the stand-alone cost of providing that service. If the revenues from one service exceed its stand-alone cost, then that service is providing a cross-subsidy to the other service. Clearly, the customers of the service that is providing the cross-subsidy would be better off if that service could be obtained independently.

The definition of the stand-alone cost test is given in terms of two services. In the case of more than two services, the test requires that no group of services subsidize any other group of services. The regulated rate structure refers to a break-even rate structure.

A firm's rate structure also is free of cross-subsidies if and only if the prices satisfy the incremental cost test, which is equivalent to the stand-alone cost test for a regulated rate structure.[29] According to the

26. RICHARD A. POSNER, ECONOMIC ANALYSIS OF LAW 360 (Little, Brown & Co., 4th ed. 1992).

27. ROBERT W. CRANDALL & LEONARD WAVERMAN, TALK IS CHEAP: THE PROMISE OF REGULATORY REFORM IN NORTH AMERICAN TELECOMMUNICATIONS 94 (Brookings Institution 1996).

28. *See* WILLIAM J. BAUMOL & J. GREGORY SIDAK, TOWARD COMPETITION IN LOCAL TELEPHONY 81 (MIT Press & AEI Press 1994); BAUMOL, PANZAR & WILLIG, *supra* note 2, at 352–53.

29. For further discussion and a formal definition, see BAUMOL & SIDAK, TOWARD COMPETITION IN LOCAL TELEPHONY, *supra* note 28, at 57, 81–83; WILLIAM J. BAUMOL, SUPERFAIRNESS: APPLICATIONS AND THEORY 113–20 (MIT Press 1986).

incremental cost test, which has been widely applied for more than a century, revenues generated by each service must cover the incremental cost of providing that service. The rationale for the incremental cost test is the requirement that each service must generate revenues that at least cover the additional cost of producing that service. If not, the other service is providing a cross-subsidy, and the customers of the other service would be better off receiving their service independently, at its stand-alone cost. Here, we define the incremental cost test for only two services. In the case of more than two services, the revenues generated by each group of services must cover the incremental cost of providing that group of services.

If the firm's rates are not necessarily break-even rates but instead generate revenues that are greater than or equal to costs, then the incremental cost test should be applied to determine cross-subsidization, regardless of whether regulation exists. If the firm operates in both regulated and unregulated markets, then, for the firm to be free of cross-subsidies, the revenues in the unregulated market should cover the firm's incremental costs of serving the unregulated market. That condition guarantees that serving the unregulated market increases, or at least does not reduce, the firm's profit.

Cross-subsidization has been a typical feature of regulated rate structures in all the network industries. Cross-subsidies come in many forms, including geographic rate averaging, when the costs of service differ substantially based on location; pricing based on customer classes that systematically transfers income from business to residential customers and from urban to rural customers; and pricing based on the types of services, such as long-distance subsidies to local exchange services and subsidies from switched services (call waiting, call forwarding) to basic residential telephone service.

Maintaining cross-subsidies in the rate structure frequently has inclined regulators to suppress entry. Typically, regulators have used the pricing structure for the services of the regulated firm as an off-budget means of subsidizing the delivery of such services to politically favored groups of consumers, such as residential customers or rural customers.[30] But if the incumbent is to remain financially solvent while being obliged to sell services below cost to a particular set of customers, it must charge at least one other set of customers (typically business and industrial customers) prices that exceed the cost of serving them. Open

30. *See, e.g.*, ROBERT W. CRANDALL, AFTER THE BREAKUP: U.S. TELECOMMUNICATIONS IN A MORE COMPETITIVE ERA 16–42 (Brookings Institution 1991).

entry, however, frustrates such pricing: The more that prices for a group of customers exceed the cost of serving them, the greater the incentive for a rival firm to enter the market and "cream skim" by underpricing the incumbent (even if the entrant's costs exceed the incumbent's). To preserve the incumbent's ability to recoup losses on its forced sale of services to the regulator's preferred class of customers at uncompensatory prices, the regulator typically enables the incumbent to earn monopoly rents on the sale of its services to other customers.

But the regulator can keep that fragile edifice of arbitrary prices standing only by restricting entry and by impeding the ability of consumers to substitute rival services (often ones made possible by an advance in technology) for the regulated service. There results a kind of market allocation by regulatory fiat: The regulator defends, though not in so many words, a policy of permitting the incumbent regulated firm to earn supracompetitive returns on sales to certain customers, a portion of which the incumbent will be obliged to sacrifice at the regulator's behest to subsidize service to those classes of customers whom the regulator deems to be deserving. Eventually, large customers demand that the regulator permit competitive entry. The typical result is "partial regulation," under which the incumbent regulated firm faces both continued regulation and, in its more profitable markets, competition.

Thus, rate regulations that involve cross-subsidization and other distortions in the rate structure create incumbent burdens. New entrants generally target the highest-margin customers. Frequently, those are the customers whom regulators require the incumbent utility to charge prices exceeding cost so that other customers may be charged prices below cost. The regulated firm then incurs losses on the services that are overpriced because competitors can target customers of those services. At the same time, the incumbent firm incurs losses on those services that were underpriced under the rate structure with cross-subsidies. Opening markets to competition creates calls for "rebalancing rates" to eliminate cross-subsidies. Finding such a subsidy-free rate structure is particularly difficult, if not impossible, for regulators because the competitive market is a better determinant of relative prices. Moreover, the relative prices that will emerge in a competitive market are free of the political considerations that mark regulated rate structures. In short, opening markets to competition is inconsistent with maintaining regulated cross-subsidies.

The Regulatory Quarantine

The regulatory quarantine is one of the most substantial incumbent burdens the regulated utility bears. Among the most familiar quarantines were the line-of-business restrictions imposed on the RBOCs by the Modification of Final Judgment (MFJ), which broke up the Bell System.[31] The most controversial line-of-business restriction in the MFJ was the prohibition on an RBOC's transporting a call from one local access and transport area (LATA) to another. Telecommunications "deregulation" in 1996 did not end the interLATA ban. To the contrary, Congress continued that quarantine through a complicated "checklist" in section 271 of the Telecommunications Act of 1996 that an RBOC must satisfy before it will be permitted to commence provision of interLATA services.[32] The principal rationale for the quarantine has been the fear (under cost-of-service regulation) that an RBOC would misallocate cost from regulated to unregulated products and a related fear that such misallocation would enable the RBOC to engage in predation against rivals in the unregulated market. A growing number of scholars, however, have questioned the plausibility of that theory, or the need to resort to a quarantine to prevent the perceived competitive risk.[33] The quarantine is so central to current regulatory policy, and regulators have so seriously ignored scholars' warnings of its deleterious effects on consumer welfare, that we devote all of chapter 3 to its examination. Therefore, here we only briefly outline that policy and its capacity to impose incumbent burdens.

An RBOC subject to a quarantine is placed at a competitive disadvantage relative to entrants that can offer a bundle of services and thereby provide customers the convenience of "one-stop shopping." The RBOC is also deterred from entry into markets that could generate revenues for the firm, while competitors are not denied access into those markets. By denying the RBOCs the opportunity to earn revenues

---

31. *See* Kellogg, Thorne & Huber, *supra* note 24, at 291–342.

32. 47 U.S.C. § 271.

33. *See* Paul W. MacAvoy, The Failure of Antitrust and Regulation to Establish Competition in Long-Distance Telephone Services 175–212 (MIT Press & AEI Press 1996); Paul S. Brandon & Richard L. Schmalensee, *The Benefits of Releasing the Bell Companies from the Interexchange Restrictions*, 16 Managerial & Decision Econ. 349 (1995); Spulber, *supra* note 9; J. Gregory Sidak, *Telecommunications in Jericho*, 81 Cal. L. Rev. 1209, 1216–22 (1993).

that their competitors may earn, the interLATA quarantine places the RBOCs at a competitive disadvantage overall. Moreover, the quarantine prevents the RBOCs from earning returns on their technological expertise and market knowledge. That impediment further places them at a competitive disadvantage in comparison with actual and potential competitors in the local exchange. In the absence of the quarantine, the RBOCs would be able to compete in interLATA telecommunications markets as actual or potential entrants.

The incumbent burden created by a regulatory quarantine has three dimensions. First, the public utility subject to the quarantine is denied economies of vertical integration or scope. Second, the utility is denied marketing benefits and transaction-costs savings derived from bundling services, which creates disadvantages relative to entrants who can offer such bundles. Third, with respect to its entry into adjacent markets, the utility in effect is subjected to an antitrust rule of per se illegality rather than a rule of reason having a market power screen and an efficiency defense. Under the rule of reason, of course, the government or private plaintiff must prove that the firm restraining trade possesses market power[34] and that the anticompetitive effects of the firm's restraint outweigh its procompetitive effects.[35] The incumbent burdens thus imposed by the MFJ's line-of-business restrictions, and reimposed by the checklist provisions of section 271 of the Telecommunications Act of 1996, illustrate how regulation can create a competitive disadvantage rather than an advantage for incumbent regulated firms such as the RBOCs.

---

34. Market power is "the power to control prices or exclude competition." United States *v.* E. I. du Pont de Nemours & Co., 351 U.S. 377, 391–92 (1956). It is "the ability to raise prices above those that would be charged in a competitive market." National Collegiate Athletic Ass'n *v.* Board of Regents of the Univ. of Okla., 468 U.S. 85, 109 n.38 (1984) [hereinafter *NCAA*]. *Accord*, Jefferson Parish Hosp. Dist. No. 2 *v.* Hyde, 466 U.S. 2, 27 n.46 (1984); William E. Landes & Richard A. Posner, *Market Power in Antitrust Cases*, 94 HARV. L. REV. 937, 937 (1981). The Supreme Court has imposed the market power screen in a variety of contexts. *See, e.g.,* Brooke Group Ltd. *v.* Brown & Williamson Tobacco Corp., 509 U.S. 209, 233–35 (1993); FTC *v.* Indiana Fed'n of Dentists, 476 U.S. 447, 460–61 (1986) ("the purpose of the inquiries into market definition and market power is to determine whether an arrangement has the potential for genuine adverse effects on competition"); Northwest Wholesale Stationers, Inc. *v.* Pacific Stationery & Printing Co., 472 U.S. 284, 296 (1985).

35. *NCAA*, 468 U.S. at 101–02; Broadcast Music, Inc. *v.* Columbia Broadcasting Sys., Inc., 441 U.S. 1, 18–23 (1979).

Structural Separation and
"Dominant Carrier" Regulations

Structural separation regulations and dominant carrier regulations imposed on incumbent LECs have much the same effect as a quarantine because they create barriers to entry into interexchange telecommunications. Application of the "separate affiliate" safeguards in section 272 of the Telecommunications Act of 1996 is asymmetric relative to the interexchange carriers, and thus it imposes competitive rigidities and cost burdens upon the RBOCs.[36] As a consequence, the playing field is not level for RBOCs in comparison with interexchange carriers. If rules are not applied fairly and evenly, the result is not deregulation but managed competition. Managed competition protects specific competitors, not competition. The resulting market outcome will reflect regulatory choices, not customer preferences and the relative economic efficiency of competing firms.

In 1995 the FCC declared AT&T to be a nondominant carrier in interexchange telecommunications.[37] The agency found that the effects of declaring AT&T to be nondominant would be (1) to free the carrier from price-cap regulation; (2) to allow AT&T to file tariffs on one day's notice and no longer to require AT&T to report or file carrier-to-carrier contracts; (3) automatically to authorize AT&T to extend service to any domestic point, and to construct, acquire, or operate any transmission lines (subject to FCC approval of radio frequencies) and to discontinue or reduce service; (4) to relieve AT&T of the obligation to submit cost-support data for above-cap or out-of-band rate filings; and (5) to release AT&T from other annual reporting requirements, including a financial report, a depreciation report, an annual rate-of-return report, and an access minutes report. Those changes substantially reduced the regulatory constraints and administrative costs of regulation for AT&T. To impose such regulatory constraints and costs on other carriers, as the FCC subsequently proposed in 1996,[38] would create a

---

36. 47 U.S.C. § 272.

37. Motion of AT&T Corp. to Be Reclassified as a Non-Dominant Carrier, Order, 11 F.C.C. Rcd. 3271 (1995).

38. Implementation of the Non-Accounting Safeguards of Sections 271 and 272 of the Communications Act of 1934, as amended; and Regulatory Treatment of LEC Provision of Interexchange Services Originating in the LEC's Local Exchange Area, Notice of Proposed Rulemaking, CC Dkt. No. 96–149, 11 F.C.C. Rcd. 18,877 (1996) [hereinafter *Non-Accounting Safeguards NPRM*].

barrier to entry into interexchange telecommunications, because any costs borne by entrants but not incumbents constitute a barrier to entry. The FCC's asymmetric imposition of those regulatory costs would bias market outcomes in favor of companies that were free of such costs.

Even if such regulatory constraints and administrative costs were to be evenly applied to all interexchange carriers, they would have a greater impact on smaller independent LEC carriers. It is unlikely that the costs of compliance increase proportionately with the size of the firm. The independent LECs thus would experience a greater proportional increase in administrative costs than the large interexchange carriers. As a result, the barriers to entry into interexchange telecommunications could be insurmountable for many firms. That result would only reduce competition in interexchange markets.

Under the FCC's rules, independent LEC provision of interstate, domestic, interexchange services is subject to nondominant treatment if the affiliate (1) maintains separate books of account; (2) does not jointly own transmission or switching facilities with the exchange telephone company; and (3) obtains any exchange telephone company services at tariffed rates and conditions.[39] The first two requirements increase the total costs of a company providing both local exchange service and interexchange service relative to the costs that the company would incur if it could otherwise organize its accounting and facilities ownership. That is so because such regulatory constraints, if they have any force, must result in higher costs in comparison with the choices that an unconstrained firm would make. In addition, the tariff restrictions and reporting associated with the third requirement presumably entail administrative costs for firms.

Interexchange carriers do not face separation and dominant carrier regulations as they enter the local exchange, but local exchange carriers face separations regulations when they enter interexchange telecommunications. The Telecommunications Act of 1996 presupposes that facilities-based competition will occur in the local exchange. Some of that competition will come from facilities created by interexchange carriers. Those carriers will continue to be viewed as interexchange carriers with local exchange facilities. Regulators will treat them differently from local exchange carriers that have local exchange facilities but also provide interexchange services. The net result, therefore, is an accident of history. Why should a firm that wishes to operate in two markets face different regulatory restrictions and administrative costs

39. *Id.* ¶ 59.

depending upon which market it originally served? Put differently, two identical firms, each serving both interexchange and local exchange markets, would be treated disparately by regulators depending on the history of the firm. Because those regulations impose transaction and administrative costs on the LECs, those firms are placed at a competitive disadvantage relative to the interexchange carriers and other entrants into local telephony.

Because those regulations are asymmetrically applied, they place the LECs at a competitive disadvantage if they try to enter interexchange markets; thus, the regulations constitute for the independent LECs a barrier to entry into long-distance service. The cost of maintaining separate books of account will fall heavily on smaller independent LECs and deny them the economies of scope that would result from maintaining combined accounts. The separate ownership of transmission or switching facilities will further reduce economies of scope that firms could achieve by operating local exchange and long-distance facilities jointly. Finally, applying regulatory conditions to the purchase of local exchange services that are not present for interexchange carriers will create costs for local exchange carriers that are not present for interexchange carriers.

Moreover, because interexchange carriers can operate as local exchange carriers through the resale of LEC services, through the use of unbundled LEC network elements, and through the construction (or acquisition) of competing facilities, the interexchange carriers can build companies that take advantage of economies of scope arising from the joint provision of local exchange service and interexchange service. In addition, because the joint provision of local exchange service and interexchange service is attractive to customers, there are potential cost and sales advantages to operating in both types of markets. If the incumbent LEC faces regulatory entry barriers into interexchange telecommunications, regulators will ultimately place the LEC at a competitive disadvantage in the local exchange as well. The net effect will be to impede rather than enhance competition.

Regulators would exacerbate that competitive asymmetry if they were to classify local exchange carriers as "dominant." As explained earlier, the result of classifying incumbent LECs as dominant carriers is to protect interexchange carriers from competition and thus to reduce customer choice and the expected benefits of deregulation. If dominant carrier regulations are imposed on the incumbent LEC and structural separation requirements are continued, then the LEC will have higher administrative costs in comparison with interexchange carriers and entrants. Thus, many LECs would be deterred from entry into interexchange telecommunications. Regulation rather than the competitive market would determine what types of companies will provide customer services in telecommunications. One could not expect such a biased outcome to yield the economic benefits of competition.

Cost Allocation Rules

Cost allocation rules for the incumbent utility are a mainstay of the regulation of network industries. They are also an incumbent burden that impedes the firm's ability to compete in unregulated markets. As soon as the Telecommunications Act of 1996 had become law, the FCC provided yet another example of the regulator's fascination with cost allocation rules. The agency proposed changes in Part 64 of its rules as they affect "cost allocation rules and procedures to accommodate an incumbent local exchange carrier's use of the same network facilities to provide video programming service and other competitive offerings not subject to Title II regulation, as well as telephony and other Title II offerings."[40] As the FCC noted, however, the policy implications and precedential impact of the proceeding would be far broader than would be suggested by that formulation of the immediate question under consideration:

> While much of the focus of this proceeding is on provision of video programming service by incumbent local exchange carriers, we note that this is likely to be only the first major competitive service that will be provided jointly with regulated telephone service . . . . [I]n the short term, video services will account for the majority of non–Title II use of the network facilities of incumbent local exchange carriers. We anticipate that in the long term, however, that a panoply of broadband-based, nonregulated services will share facilities with regulated services.[41]

Mindful of those larger implications, we examine the main issue for LEC provision of "interactive broadband services"—by which we mean not only the video programming services immediately under consider-

---

40. Allocation of Costs Associated with Local Exchange Carrier Provision of Video Programming Services, Notice of Proposed Rulemaking, CC Dkt. No. 96-112, 11 F.C.C. Rcd. 17,211, 17,213 ¶ 2 [hereinafter *LEC Video Cost Allocation NPRM*]. Title II refers to the portion of the Communications Act governing telephony.

41. *Id.*

ation, but also the other current and future broadband services to which the FCC's notice alluded.

The FCC sought to rewrite Part 64 because the agency's "current cost allocation rules were not designed for this task" of ushering local telephony through the metamorphosis from regulation to competition. Yet, Part 64 itself is unnecessary for LECs regulated under price caps that do not include earnings-sharing arrangements. For rate-of-return regulated LECs, and for LECs subject to price caps that do include earnings-sharing arrangements, competition in local telephony will be sufficient on its own to preclude them from cross-subsidizing the provision of broadband services. It is unlikely that cost allocation regulation is now or should be the binding constraint on the behavior of the LECs. Moreover, because demand and supply conditions for LECs' provision of broadband services are highly uncertain and heterogeneous, it would be naïve to suppose that the FCC could improve consumer welfare by mandating today nationwide, standardized cost pools and allocation factors for all LECs to follow when providing diverse broadband services in the years to come.

The FCC's stated goal in its 1996 cost allocation notice of proposed rulemaking (NPRM) was "to establish a system of cost allocation principles that inhibits carriers from imposing on ratepayers the costs and risks of competitive, nonregulated ventures, including nonregulated video service ventures."[42] The FCC presumably intended that any rule that it promulgated for the allocation of common costs associated with LEC provision of video programming services would generate social benefits. In the agency's view, "such a system of cost allocation principles must balance" four subsidiary goals: (1) "administrative simplicity," (2) "adaptability to evolving technologies," (3) "uniform application among incumbent local exchange carriers, in particular those that must file their cost allocation manuals with the Commission," and (4) "consistency with economic principles of cost-causation."[43]

Those four goals are likely to be in conflict. Economic pricing is based on both demand and supply considerations, not cost causation. Moreover, if all costs were attributable to specific outputs, there would be little need for administrative cost allocation rules. The second and third subsidiary goals are in conflict because new technologies will encourage diverse network architectures that will defy the FCC's quest for uniformity. The fourth subsidiary goal merely restates the usual

---

42. *Id.* at 17,222 ¶ 24.
43. *Id.*

purpose, from an accountant's perspective, of *any* cost allocation system.[44] By a process of elimination, it is easy to predict that "administrative simplicity" becomes the agency's predominant goal. Obviously, the optimal cost allocation rule is not the one that minimizes the regulator's administrative costs alone. If a particular cost allocation rule were to stifle efficient, procompetitive entry by LECs into video programming services, it would be no consolation to consumers that the rule required the least amount of the FCC's resources to administer. The claimed savings would be a false economy indeed.

In fact, the FCC's choice in general, and in the specific cost allocation provisions of Part 64, is fully distributed cost (FDC), which is noted for its ease of application without reference to any economically meaningful criterion. In a frequently cited article criticizing FDC pricing, William J. Baumol and others have written:

> The "reasonableness" of the basis of allocation selected makes absolutely no difference except to the success of the advocates of the figures in deluding others (and perhaps themselves) about the defensibility of the numbers. There just can be no excuse for continued use of such an essentially random, or, rather, fully manipulable calculation process as a basis for vital economic decisions by regulators.[45]

There are other problems with FDC pricing as well. As Ronald R. Braeutigam has observed, "FDC pricing will lead to prices which are in general economically inefficient, which is not surprising given the fact that the practice focuses heavily on cost and little on conditions of demand (including demand elasticities) which are important in determining the size of the deadweight losses from any pricing policy."[46]

Any cost allocation rule unavoidably will entail two kinds of costs of nontrivial magnitude. The first is the loss in allocative efficiency if

44. *See, e.g.*, CHARLES T. HORNGREN, GEORGE FOSTER & SRIKANT M. DATAR, COST ACCOUNTING: A MANAGERIAL EMPHASIS 500 (Prentice Hall, 8th ed. 1994).

45. William J. Baumol, Michael F. Koehn & Robert D. Willig, *How Arbitrary Is "Arbitrary"?—or, Toward the Deserved Demise of Full Cost Allocation*, 21 PUB. UTIL. FORTNIGHTLY, Sept. 3, 1987, at 16; *accord,* CRANDALL & WAVERMAN, *supra* note 27, at 258–59. In a reprise of his earlier paper with Koehn and Willig, Baumol has written with one of us: "Fully allocated cost figures . . . have no economic content. They cannot pretend to constitute approximations to *anything*." BAUMOL & SIDAK, TRANSMISSION PRICING AND STRANDED COSTS IN THE ELECTRIC POWER INDUSTRY, *supra* note 19, at 64 (emphasis in original).

46. Ronald R. Braeutigam, *Optimal Policies for Natural Monopolies, in* 2 HANDBOOK OF INDUSTRIAL ORGANIZATION 1289, 1314 (Richard Schmalensee & Robert D. Willig eds., North-Holland 1989).

the rule either (1) fails to deter actual instances of cost misallocation by LECs that reduce the well-being of consumers or the competitive process or (2) deters innocent or procompetitive behavior that is incorrectly identified as having received an improper cross-subsidy from the LEC's regulated activities. Those two situations embody the costs of regulatory error. Distinct from such error costs is the second category, which consists of the administrative costs borne by private firms and the FCC. Those costs include the expense of lawyers, accountants, and the cost reporting systems necessary to comply with the rule.[47]

In its 1996 NPRM the FCC tentatively concluded, without any careful economic analysis or statutory construction, that pricing using demand elasticities to allocate common costs, such as Ramsey pricing, would violate the Telecommunications Act of 1996:

> A fixed factor approach for non-traffic sensitive loop plant presumes that a cost-causative allocation is not possible. When a cost-causative method is not available, the allocation must be based on other considerations such as demand or public policy considerations. Demand for telephone service is at present highly inelastic. Thus, without either regulatory intervention or workable competition, incumbent local exchange carriers have the ability to shift to telephone ratepayers a large portion of the cost of facilities used for both regulated and nonregulated activities. Such a result is contrary to the 1996 Act's requirement that ratepayers of regulated service not bear the costs or risks of competitive ventures and, therefore, would be an unacceptable result. For this reason we tentatively conclude that relative demand cannot form the basis for allocating common loop costs between regulated and nonregulated services.[48]

47. Separation of Costs of Regulated Telephone Service from Cost of Nonregulated Activities, Report and Order, CC Dkt. No. 86-111, 2 F.C.C. Rcd. 1298 (1987) (*Joint Cost Order*), *modified on recons.*, 2 F.C.C. Rcd. 6283 (1987) (*Joint Cost Reconsideration Order*), *modified on further recons.*, 3 F.C.C. Rcd. 6701 (1988) (*Joint Cost Further Reconsideration Order*), *aff'd sub nom.* Southwestern Bell Corp. *v.* FCC, 896 F.2d 1378 (D.C. Cir. 1990).

48. *LEC Video Cost Allocation NPRM*, 11 F.C.C. Rcd. at 17,227 ¶ 41. The FCC was alluding to 47 U.S.C. § 254(k), which provides: "A telecommunications carrier may not use services that are not competitive to subsidize services that are subject to competition. The Commission, with respect to interstate services, and the States, with respect to intrastate services, shall establish any necessary cost allocation rules, accounting safeguards, and guidelines to ensure that services included in the definition of universal service bear no more than a reasonable share of the joint and common costs of facilities used to provide those services."

The FCC's hasty conclusions about Ramsey pricing were misplaced. Competitive multiproduct firms allocate common costs in inverse relationship to the demand elasticities of their respective products, much like Ramsey pricing. Moreover, the FCC seemed to suggest that, without some fix to Part 64, technological change and the uncertainty of consumer demand for broadband services together would make the agency's cost allocation rules for LEC provision of broadband services so complex in the near future as to be unworkable. Given those trends, the FCC's resort to demand-based methods for allocating common costs is inevitable. If the Part 64 process is indeed bound to become intractable, and if the FCC continues to resist the use of Ramsey pricing, then it follows a fortiori that the agency should invoke its forbearance authority to confine the application of Part 64 to the very slim category of cases where the probability of, and magnitude of harm to consumers from, incorrect allocation of common costs are both large.

Administrative cost allocation rules create an incumbent burden for the LECs. A preferable way to reduce the incentive and opportunity for anticompetitive cross-subsidization is to replace cost-of-service regulation with price caps.[49] The FCC is concerned about the possibility of a rate-regulated monopolist's underpricing its rivals by attributing some of the costs of producing the competitive product to its rate-regulated activities and then passing those misallocated costs along to its captive ratepayers. The potential for cost misallocation is attributed to the asymmetry of information between the regulated firm and its regulator: The regulator has imperfect information about the firm's true costs and the appropriate allocation of common fixed costs among regulated and unregulated operations; thus, the regulator is at a disadvantage when seeking to link the firm's profits on regulated operations to its cost of service. The concern over cross-subsidization recurs whenever LECs propose to enter other lines of business. That concern was embodied most dramatically in the line-of-business restrictions imposed on the regional Bell operating companies by the MFJ, which Congress replaced in 1996 with the "checklist" provisions of new section 271 of the Communications Act. The concern over cross-subsidization, however, is not grounds for making a LEC that is sub-

---

49. *See* DAVID E. M. SAPPINGTON & DENNIS WEISMAN, DESIGNING INCENTIVE REGULATION FOR THE TELECOMMUNICATIONS INDUSTRY (MIT Press & AEI Press 1996); David E. M. Sappington, *Revisiting the Line-of-Business Restrictions*, 16 MANAGERIAL & DECISION ECON. 291, 293–96 (1995).

ject to price-cap regulation comply with the burdensome cost allocation provisions of Part 64 when it develops interactive broadband networks, for economists well recognize that pure price-cap regulation removes the incentive and opportunity for the regulated firm to misallocate costs.[50]

The economic implications of technological advances in electronics, fiber optics, digital signal compression, and software will allow some networks to deliver not only narrowband services, but also one-way and switched broadband services. The development of new uses for the network will in turn encourage entry by a number of potential competitors for voice telephony, data transmission, distributive video (what is currently regarded as broadcasting or cable television), interactive video, and other electronic services such as banking, shopping, and advertising.[51] No one, including the FCC's experts, currently knows which system or systems will be technologically and financially viable in the foreseeable future. Although the business press regularly reports that a "convergence" of telecommunications technologies is occurring, it may be more accurate to say that a *divergence* of such technologies is occurring in the sense that a number of alternative architectures simultaneously may evolve for the delivery of various combinations of narrowband and interactive broadband services. A corollary of that analysis is that one may not assume that a system that is viable this year will not be superseded by a superior technology introduced only a few years later. Consequently, the FCC's policy in that arena must proceed cautiously, lest it impose new incumbent burdens that impede the Schumpeterian process by which superior production technologies continuously vie to displace inferior ones.[52]

The FCC is no more able to predict the demand side of the market for broadband services than the supply side. As currently understood, the potential market for interactive broadband services includes pay-

---

50. An analogous situation exists with respect to small local exchange carriers that set their rates on the basis of average schedules determined by the National Exchange Carrier Association. *See* MTS and WATS Market Structure: Average Schedule Companies, Memorandum Opinion and Order, 6 F.C.C. Rcd. 6608 (1991). For any of those carriers, access compensation is determined on the basis of national averages, not the given carrier's own costs. Consequently, that carrier could not benefit from shifting costs from its unregulated activities to its regulated activities.

51. *See* Robert W. Crandall & J. Gregory Sidak, *Competition and Regulatory Policies for Interactive Broadband Networks*, 68 S. CAL. L. REV. 1203 (1995).

52. JOSEPH R. SCHUMPETER, CAPITALISM, SOCIALISM AND DEMOCRACY 81–86 (Harper & Row 1942).

per-view movies and sporting events, home shopping, video games, interactive information services, video conferencing, distance learning, and telemedicine. As in the case of production technologies, the uncertain demand for interactive broadband services should counsel humility, not hubris: Government policy should recognize that current predictions of what consumers will or will not want delivered over the network may prove within a few years to be as dated as Disneyland's 1950s rendition of "Tomorrowland."[53] There will be little hard evidence of the market demand for new interactive services until firms actually build the networks and experiment with new service offerings. In that start-up environment, it is essential that policymakers allow a wide range of new network designs and new service offerings so that consumers may be afforded as wide a range of choices as possible. For the FCC to impose uniform, nationwide standards for the allocation of common costs associated with LEC provision of interactive broadband services would be to erect an incumbent burden that would impede the ability of the LECs to select competitive pricing and service offerings.

The cost allocation procedures of Part 64 also invite strategic abuse of the regulatory process to impede the LECs' competitive entry into other markets. The proponents of any given cost allocation formula will predictably justify their recommendation on the grounds that it will advance "the public interest." Yet elementary price theory will usually reveal the contrary—that the recommendation has the practical effect of suppressing competitive entry into the proponent's market and thus reducing consumer welfare. In the FCC's 1996 cost allocation proceeding, for example, the cable television industry's principal proposal—that 75 percent or more of common costs be allocated to the LEC's video services and 25 percent to its telephony services—had no economic substance. With as much intellectual weight the industry could have proposed that the FCC allocate the LEC's common costs between video and telephony on the basis of the ratio of the total offensive yardage of the Washington Redskins to that of the Dallas Cowboys. Such cost allocation procedures erect regulatory barriers to competitive entry by telephone companies. If the LECs must place a disproportion-

---

53. Within weeks of the passage of the Telecommunications Act of 1996 the Walt Disney Company announced plans to refurbish Tomorrowland because, in the words of one reporter, "the fundamental contradiction of Tomorrowland [is that] the future is unfolding too fast for even the vaunted Imagineers to represent it literally within the confines of a theme park." Marla Dickerson, *Disneyland Steps Back to Get Ahead*, L.A. TIMES, Mar. 22, 1996, at D1.

ate share of the common costs of their broadband networks on video customers, then those carriers will have a dampened incentive to build such networks and to compete in the provision of advanced telecommunications services that consumers may one day consider essential.[54]

Barriers to Use of the Least-
Cost Production Technology

Entrants may be allowed to avoid regulations that thwart the use of the least-cost production technology and in that sense may be more efficient producers than the incumbent public utility. For example, the Public Utility Regulatory Policies Act (PURPA),[55] enacted in 1978, requires an electric utility to buy power from cogenerators and small power producers known as "qualifying facilities" at the utility's avoided cost, even when the utility could purchase cheaper energy for its customers elsewhere.[56] In contrast, independent power producers are free to employ solely the cheapest method of generating electricity.

OPEN ACCESS AND
MANDATORY UNBUNDLING

Deregulation of the network industries often is accompanied by regulatory policies requiring the incumbent utility to provide "open access" to its transmission and reticulation facilities. Deregulation in electricity and telecommunications has been accompanied by regulations aimed at vertical divestiture or separation of vertically integrated activities of incumbent utilities. Regulators specify both what activities should be available for competition and the prices and conditions under which the incumbent shall grant competitors access to its facilities.

---

54. For a related critique of the FCC's 1996 cost allocation proposal, see ALFRED E. KAHN, HOW TO TREAT THE COSTS OF SHARED VOICE AND VIDEO NETWORKS IN A POST-REGULATORY AGE (Cato Institute Nov. 27, 1996).

55. Pub. L. No. 95-617, 92 Stat. 3117 (1978).

56. Under PURPA, a qualifying facility must produce useful thermal energy through the sequential use of the energy used to generate electricity. 16 U.S.C. §§ 796(17), (18); Order No. 70, F.E.R.C. Stats. & Regs. ¶ 30,134 (1980). A qualifying facility must meet certain ownership, operating, and efficiency criteria established by FERC. 18 C.F.R. § 292.205–206. Among the advantages of being designated a qualifying facility are that electric utilities must provide the qualifying facility interconnection, must purchase its output at the purchasing utility's avoided cost, and must provide the qualifying facility back-up power. *Id*. §§ 292.303(c)(2), 292.305(b).

Leverage and the
Essential Facilities Doctrine

Regulatory principles of open access and mandatory unbundling have their counterpart in antitrust law in the form of the essential facilities doctrine.[57] That doctrine is a subtle and expanding body of law. We touch upon the subject here only to the extent necessary to show how antitrust law and the law of regulated network industries substantially overlap with respect to their treatment of a bottleneck facility and their expressions of concern that the owner of the bottleneck facility not "leverage" its market power into other product markets.[58]

Leverage is defined in the antitrust context as the use of monopoly power in one market to extract additional monopoly rents and to secure competitive advantages in a second market.[59] Leverage is designed to exclude competitors from all or part of the second market. Such exclusion is called "foreclosure." Some economists theorize that leverage results from a variety of action, including tying, restricting access to essential facilities, and refusing to deal. The tying and essential facilities examples have often been applied in telecommunications antitrust cases.[60]

Tying refers to a situation in which the seller of a good requires the buyer to purchase a second good, thus selling the two as a product bundle.[61] For example, a tying contract offered by an RBOC would require the buyer of its local service to purchase its long-distance service from the RBOC as well. In such a situation, the RBOC would be said to leverage its market power in the local service (the tying product's market) over to its long-distance service (the tied product's market). Courts have been concerned with the restriction of competi-

---

57. *See* Otter Tail Power Co. *v.* United States, 410 U.S. 366 (1973); United States *v.* Terminal R.R. Ass'n, 224 U.S. 383 (1912).

58. One of us has previously noted that the essential facilities doctrine represents the intersection of antitrust and regulation. BAUMOL & SIDAK, TOWARD COMPETITION IN LOCAL TELEPHONY, *supra* note 28, at 26–27.

59. *See, e.g.,* Berkey Photo, Inc. *v.* Eastman Kodak Co., 603 F.2d 263, 276 (2d Cir. 1979) ("the use of monopoly power attained in one market to gain a competitive advantage in another is a violation of § 2 [of the Sherman Act], even if there has not been an attempt to monopolize the second market"). *But see* Air Passenger Computer Reservation Sys. Antitrust Litig., 694 F. Supp. 1443, 1472 (C.D. Cal. 1988).

60. KELLOGG, THORNE & HUBER, *supra* note 24, at 142.

61. *E.g.,* Eastman Kodak Co. *v.* Image Technical Servs., Inc., 504 U.S. 451 (1992); Hyde *v.* Jefferson Parish Hosp. Dist. No. 2, 466 U.S. 2 (1984); Times-Picayune Publishing Co. *v.* United States, 345 U.S. 594 (1953).

tion in the tied product's market, but the rationale for that concern has been subject to significant academic criticism from the Chicago School of antitrust analysis. Judge Robert H. Bork has called that "transfer of market power" theory "fallacious."[62] Similarly, Judge Richard A. Posner observed in 1976, "One striking deficiency of the traditional, 'leverage' theory of tie-ins, as the courts have applied it, is the failure to require any proof that a monopoly of the tied product is even a remotely plausible consequence of the tie-in."[63] In short, the problem with the tying theory of leverage is that the monopolist has little incentive to tie its products in bundles, because it generally can obtain no additional profits from the tie-in sale and rarely can obtain market power in the market for the tied good.[64]

The firm may obtain benefits from tie-ins if the tied good aids the firm in metering the usage of the tying good for pricing purposes. As Judge Posner has noted, however, that outcome does not imply that there is an incentive to exclude competition.[65] In the telecommunications context, the incumbent LEC certainly is capable of monitoring the usage of its local service without the sale of additional long-distance services or equipment.

Leveraging theory has influenced the development of the essential facilities doctrine. An essential facility is a productive input that others cannot duplicate feasibly or economically. The concept has been applied vaguely in antitrust law and has elements of both natural monopoly and barriers to entry. As in the case of a natural monopoly technology, the essential facility should not be duplicated, because the market is served at minimum cost with one facility. An essential facility is similar to a barrier to entry in that a competitor cannot feasibly or economically duplicate a facility in a market. Thus, the argument goes, an existing facility will not be duplicated because an entrant

---

62. ROBERT H. BORK, THE ANTITRUST PARADOX: A POLICY AT WAR WITH ITSELF 366 (Free Press, rev. ed. 1993) (Basic Books 1978). For earlier contributions to the Chicago School critique of tie-ins, see Ward S. Bowman, *Tying Arrangements and the Leverage Problem*, 67 YALE L.J. 19 (1957); George J. Stigler, United States *v.* Loew's, Inc.: *A Note on Block Booking*, 1963 SUP. CT. REV. 152. For a later Chicago School critique of technological tie-ins, see J. Gregory Sidak, *Debunking Predatory Innovation*, 83 COLUM. L. REV. 1121 (1983).

63. RICHARD A. POSNER, ANTITRUST LAW: AN ECONOMIC PERSPECTIVE 172 (University of Chicago Press 1976). Courts have since required such proof. United Farmers Agents Ass'n *v.* Farmers Ins. Exchange, 89 F.3d 233, 236 n.2 (5th Cir. 1996).

64. POSNER, ANTITRUST LAW, *supra* note 63, at 173.

65. *Id.* at 174–75.

would incur irreversible investment costs. Alternatively, it is suggested that the costs of duplicating the facility are higher for an entrant than for an incumbent.

The essential facilities doctrine, however, transcends the natural monopoly and barriers to entry ideas because it also incorporates vertical elements. The owner of the essential facility not only has monopoly power in one market but also is presumed to deny equitable access to competitors in another market. In *United States* v. *Terminal Railroad Association*, the Supreme Court found a railroad switching junction to be an essential facility.[66] In *Otter Tail Power Co.* v. *United States*, the Court found that the electric power transmission lines of the utility were an essential facility.[67] The standard antitrust remedy for the existence of an essential facility is an injunction (or consent decree) that mandates that competitors receive equal access to that facility.[68] That was the remedy that the MFJ mandated for long-distance carriers even *after* the government and AT&T agreed upon the vertical dismemberment of the former Bell System.

Wheeling Electric Power

In electric power transmission and distribution, federal regulators require an electric utility to transmit power for others—to "wheel" power over its transmission and distribution network that its competitors have generated. Retail wheeling and wholesale wheeling denote the transmission of power to retail and wholesale customers, respectively. A final customer or utility purchases power directly from a generator or from an intermediary. Utilities that supply wheeling services, acting as transporters rather than generators or merchants, transmit the power.

PURPA increased the authority of the Federal Energy Regulatory Commission (FERC) in 1978 to order interconnection of electric utility systems and gave FERC the authority to order wholesale wheeling.[69] Through its enactment of the Energy Policy Act in 1992,[70] Congress amended section 211 of the Federal Power Act to allow any generator

---

66. 224 U.S. 383 (1912).

67. 410 U.S. 366 (1973).

68. KELLOGG, THORNE & HUBER, *supra* note 24, at 140.

69. Pub. L. No. 95-617, 92 Stat. 3117 (1978). PURPA added sections 210, 211, and 212 to the Federal Power Act, ch. 687, 49 Stat. 847 (1935) (codified at 16 U.S.C. § 824 *et seq.*).

70. Pub. L. No. 102-486, 106 Stat. 2776 (1992).

to petition FERC for mandated access to a utility's transmission grid.[71] A substantial portion of wholesale power transactions depends on wheeling,[72] and many states—including California, New York, and Pennsylvania—are in the process of establishing requirements for retail wheeling.

Unbundling Network Elements
in Local Telephony

In telecommunications, open access requires the local exchange carrier to open its network to access and transmission by competing carriers. To understand the deregulation of the local exchange, it is necessary to introduce some terminology. A telecommunications *network* refers to the trunk lines and switches that direct traffic over the trunk lines. The local wireline network traditionally consists of connections between customer premises and central offices, which are themselves connected. If customer premises are connected to the central office by dedicated loops, resembling the spokes connected to the hub of a wheel, the network is said to have a "star" form. If the customers connect by dedicated loops to a trunk line running to the central office, the network has a "bus" form. Finally, if the customers are connected by dedicated loops to a circular trunk that originates and terminates at the central office, the network has a "ring" form.[73]

Access refers to the way in which individual users of the telecommunications system are connected to the network.[74] Access connections include copper-wire loops, coaxial links, fiber-optic lines, and wireless interfaces. *Interconnection* refers to connections between networks, including those operated by different companies, such as interexchange

---

71. 16 U.S.C. § 824j(a). Section 211 now provides: "Any electric utility, Federal power marketing agency, or any other person generating electric energy for sale or resale, may apply to the Commission for an order under the subsection requiring a transmitting utility to provide transmission services (including any enlargement of transmission capacity necessary to provide such services) to the applicant." *Id.*; *see also* Policy Statement Regarding Good Faith Requests for Transmission Services, F.E.R.C. Stats. & Regs. ¶ 30,975 (1993).

72. *See* ENERGY INFORMATION ADMINISTRATION, ELECTRIC TRADE IN THE UNITED STATES, 1992 (DOE/EIA-0531(92) 1994).

73. GEORGE C. CALHOUN, WIRELESS ACCESS AND THE LOCAL TELEPHONE NETWORK 396 (Artech House 1992).

74. *Id.* at 68.

carriers (for example, AT&T or MCI) and local exchange carriers (for example, Bell Atlantic or GTE).

Open-access regulations establish rules for interconnection of networks. Open-access regulations often impose requirements on regulated carriers for the pricing and transmission of traffic originating or terminating on another company's network. For example, the interexchange carriers (IXCs) pay the LECs access charges to originate and terminate traffic of customers using the IXC network.[75] Competition in the local exchange from a variety of companies creates alternative means for companies to gain access to the local exchange and other networks. Technological and regulatory change has caused the emergence of alternative access suppliers, such as wireless providers (including cellular and personal communications systems), fiber-optic systems of competitive access providers, and the fiber-optic and coaxial cable systems of cable television operators.

Unbundling applies to the sale of the incumbent LEC's switching and transmission services. Regulatory definitions of individual services and network "components" are necessarily arbitrary, for any service is a bundle of features. Regulators attempt to distinguish individual services and then require the incumbent LEC to offer them for sale to both customers and competitors. Regulatory unbundling can extend to very specific network components—including interfaces, network functions, switching services, maintenance, customer information, and billing and ordering systems. Such forced unbundling is meant to provide competitive access to local exchange facilities; but, as we explain in chapters 9 and 12, it can easily produce inefficiencies.

Resale refers to the purchase and sale by competitors of the incumbent LEC's network services. Depending on regulatory rules and the incumbent LEC's service offerings, competitors can resell virtually any service already sold by the LEC or new services created by using the LEC's facilities in combination with those of the entrant. Among the services offered for resale are "vertical" components, such as switching services (call waiting, call forwarding), transmission services, and the services of local loops. Resale effectively substitutes the merchant function of the reseller (including marketing, sales, billing, and order-

---

75. Access Charge Reform; Price Cap Performance Review for Local Exchange Carriers; Transport Rate Structure and Pricing; Usage of the Public Switched Network by Information Service and Internet Access Providers, Notice of Proposed Rulemaking, Third Report and Order, and Notice of Inquiry, CC Dkt. Nos. 96-262, 94-1, 91-213, 96-263, 11 F.C.C. Rcd. 21,354 (1996).

ing) for those of the incumbent LEC. Resale permits competitors to enter the market for distribution of services without constructing facilities that would duplicate the incumbent LEC's. Moreover, resale permits entrants to bundle their own services, such as long-distance or cellular service, with the incumbent LEC's services.

CONCLUSION

In the electricity and local telephony industries, regulators have mandated, or will imminently mandate, access to the transmission and reticulation facilities of the incumbent utility at regulated rates. The regulated firm is required to make available the services of the network in "unbundled" form—the incumbent must follow detailed technical or economic specifications that allow competitors, customers, and suppliers to have access to those facilities with a level of ease that is comparable to that of the company's own access. The network often is characterized equivalently as a "bottleneck," a "monopoly component," or an "essential facility." The regulator argues that the utility's competitors cannot profitably duplicate the facilities. That argument is put forward to justify possibly onerous and costly access requirements.

Moreover, by specifying the terms of access, regulators eliminate potential efficiency gains from negotiated access and unbundling. By not relying on market mechanisms to determine the nature and extent of unbundling, regulators run the risk of creating inefficient and inflexible access and interconnection rules that impose costs on all parties and potentially subsidize entrants at the expense of incumbents and, ultimately, consumers. Furthermore, regulators and competitors argue that competition would be served if competing firms had access to those facilities at a regulated and uniform price.

Competitors argue strenuously for open access on the grounds of fairness and on the grounds of the potential benefits from competition. To the extent that competitors receive network services below cost, open-access provisions can result in a transfer of income from the regulated incumbent's investors and captive customers to the entrant's investors and customers. Such an income transfer should not be defended as fair, for its allocation is arbitrary and depends on the ability of customers to switch to the new entrant. Moreover, there is no reason that the claims of entrants to those transfers should take precedence over the expected returns of the incumbents. Such transfers need not achieve the benefits of competition because subsidized entry can result in inefficient duplication and bypass of existing facilities. Moreover, if the regulated incumbent is constrained in its ability to compete with entrants, mandated access should not be portrayed as open competition.

Deregulation through mandatory access has significant implications for the regulated firm. If there is controlled entry into the franchise territory of the regulated utility before open access, then unbundling, interconnection, and other access provisions enable entrants to compete with the incumbent by using the incumbent's facilities. If such entry denies the incumbent utility the reasonable opportunity to earn the allowed rate of return expected under regulation, open access (if not accompanied by an alternative policy for cost recovery) represents a breach of the regulatory contract, as we explain in greater detail in chapter 4. Moreover, if regulated rates do not compensate the incumbent for the cost of providing access and unbundled service, including the opportunity cost of the alternative uses for the facilities used to supply access, then a taking will have occurred, as we explain more thoroughly in chapter 6.

In short, when the state removes statutory barriers to entry, it will jeopardize the financial solvency of the regulated public utility unless it simultaneously allows that utility to "rebalance" its rate structure to eliminate the implicit cross-subsidies and unless the costs of incumbent burdens are either shared by all firms in the market or explicitly reimbursed by some third party—most likely, the state itself. In actuality, however, federal regulatory agencies and state public utility commissions are allowing entry into regulated network industries before rates have been rebalanced and before special-service obligations borne by the incumbent public utility have been financed by some other means. We show in chapters 4 through 7 that, under either the law of contract or the law of property, those circumstances give the regulated utility a remedy against the state.

3

Quarantines and Quagmires

A DOMINANT AND RECURRENT theme in the regulation of network industries has been that the firm possessing a bottleneck facility be restricted in the lines of business in which it may engage. The regulatory quarantine is one incumbent burden of the sort described in the preceding chapter. But it is typically not part of the original regulatory contract. Rather, the quarantine model has developed over time to address a variety of perceived evils of regulated monopoly. Its most visible example has been the line-of-business restrictions imposed on the regional Bell operating companies (RBOCs) by the now-defunct Modification of Final Judgment (MFJ), the consent decree that forbade, among other things, the RBOCs from providing certain forms of long-distance service.[1] Although the quarantine model can be found in the electric utility industry also—most notably in the Public Utility Holding Company Act of 1935—the analysis in this chapter relies principally on examples from telecommunications, where the quarantine model again figured prominently in the Telecommunications Act of 1996.

The 1982 MFJ terminated one of the most significant antitrust suits since the breakup of Standard Oil. The breakup of the Bell System, which took effect on January 1, 1984, constituted a large-scale vertical divestiture. The divestiture assigned the long-distance and equipment manufacturing functions of the Bell System to AT&T. The local exchange services were divided among seven regional operating companies: Ameritech, Bell Atlantic, BellSouth, NYNEX, Pacific

---

1. Modification of Final Judgment § II(D)(1) [hereinafter *MFJ*], *reprinted in* United States v. American Tel. & Tel. Co., 552 F. Supp. 131, 225–34 (D.D.C. 1982), *aff'd sub nom.* Maryland v. United States, 460 U.S. 1001 (1983).

Telesis, Southwestern Bell (now called SBC), and U S WEST.

The terms of the MFJ required the RBOCs to provide "equal access" to the local network to all long-distance carriers and subjected the RBOCs to line-of-business restrictions. Although many regulated monopolies have enjoyed protection from rival entry, the MFJ's line-of-business restrictions quarantined the RBOCs within their markets by barring their entry elsewhere. Initially, the RBOCs were forbidden to "provide any other product or service, except exchange telecommunications and exchange access service, that is not a natural monopoly service actually regulated by tariff."[2] Even the divestiture's disposition of Bell System assets and businesses contravened that principle, however, and soon the RBOCs instead faced three specific line-of-business restrictions.[3] The restrictions forbade the RBOCs from providing interexchange services from one local access and transport area (LATA) to another and from manufacturing telecommunications equipment.[4] A third line-of-business restriction concerning the provision of information services had been effectively removed by the time that the Telecommunications Act of 1996 superseded the divestiture decree.[5]

Paradoxically, the Bell System breakup led to increased regulation and litigation. The MFJ established what became a complex regulatory apparatus that both implemented the terms of the consent decree and reviewed the RBOCs' attempts to enter markets. Although the RBOCs were quarantined, the Department of Justice (DOJ) proposed, and the divestiture court endorsed, a triennial review in which the RBOCs were to be allowed to petition the court for permission to expand into other

2. *MFJ* § II(D)(3).

3. *See* MICHAEL K. KELLOGG, JOHN THORNE & PETER W. HUBER, FEDERAL TELECOMMUNICATIONS LAW 291–342 (Little, Brown & Co. 1992).

4. *MFJ* §§ II(D)(1), (2). The divestiture court partially lifted the interLATA restriction for the RBOCs' wireless services in 1995. An RBOC would have been allowed, subject to various conditions, to provide in-region interLATA service on a resale basis to its wireless subscribers. While the decision was on appeal, the 1996 legislation mooted the MFJ, and the Court of Appeals consequently vacated the district court's order. United States *v.* Western Elec. Co., 890 F. Supp. 1 (D.D.C. 1995), *vacated*, 84 F.3d 1452 (D.C. Cir. 1996).

5. *MFJ* § II(D)(2). For thorough discussions of the economic causes and consequences of the divestiture, see PAUL W. MACAVOY, THE FAILURE OF ANTITRUST AND REGULATION TO ESTABLISH COMPETITION IN LONG-DISTANCE TELEPHONE SERVICES (MIT Press & AEI Press 1996); ROBERT W. CRANDALL, AFTER THE BREAKUP: U.S. TELECOMMUNICATIONS IN A MORE COMPETITIVE ERA (Brookings Institution 1991); PETER TEMIN, THE FALL OF THE BELL SYSTEM: A STUDY IN PRICES AND POLITICS (Cambridge University Press 1987).

markets.[6] The divestiture court, however, managed to have only one such review before the process disintegrated. For more than a decade, the RBOCs, AT&T, and the DOJ engaged in virtually continuous litigation to interpret the MFJ's line-of-business restrictions. That process effectively placed the federal district court of the District of Columbia, and a handful of DOJ lawyers, in the regulation business. In addition, public policy increased the Federal Communications Commission's involvement with the industry in promoting competition, particularly through its administration of open access.[7]

The Telecommunications Act of 1996 supersedes the MFJ and other federal regulation, but section 271 of the newly amended Communications Act continues the interLATA line-of-business restriction in the form of a complex "checklist" process that requires, among other things, that the RBOCs provide unbundled access to their local exchange networks as a quid pro quo for entry into interLATA telecommunications.[8] Such a bargain is unnecessary. Economic efficiency and consumer well-being justify the rapid removal of the remaining line-of-business restrictions imposed on the RBOCs. Moreover, because the 1996 legislation expressly mandates unbundled access to the local network for competitors, it is superfluous to retain the regulatory quarantine as a bargaining chip for regulators.

Indeed, the section 271 checklist procedure imposes more onerous burdens than the MFJ's interLATA restrictions ever did.[9] Before an RBOC undergoes scrutiny under the checklist, it first must enter into an interconnection agreement, approved by the state public utilities commission in the state where the RBOC seeks to originate interLATA calls, with a facilities-based provider of local exchange service.[10] Then the FCC, in consultation with the relevant state public utilities commission (PUC), will determine whether the RBOC's interconnection agreement satisfies the fourteen requirements of the checklist.[11] If the

6. KELLOGG, THORNE & HUBER, *supra* note 3, at 365–66.

7. *See* DANIEL F. SPULBER, REGULATION AND MARKETS 16 (MIT Press 1989).

8. 47 U.S.C. § 271.

9. *See* MACAVOY, *supra* note 5, at 190–98, 200; *see also* PETER W. HUBER, MICHAEL K. KELLOGG & JOHN THORNE, THE TELECOMMUNICATIONS ACT OF 1996: SPECIAL REPORT 32–33 (Little, Brown & Co. 1996).

10. 47 U.S.C. § 271(c)(1)(A). Alternatively, if the state PUC has approved a generic interconnection plan offered by the RBOC but the RBOC has received no request for interconnection within the first seven months after enactment of the Telecommunications Act of 1996, then the RBOC may proceed to be evaluated under the checklist. *Id.* § 271(c)(1)(B).

11. "Competitive checklist.—Access or interconnection provided or generally

interconnection agreement passes the checklist, and if the RBOC has established a structurally separate entity for the provision of in-region interLATA service,[12] then the FCC, after consulting with and giving

offered by a Bell operating company to other telecommunications carriers meets the requirements of this subparagraph if such access and interconnection includes each of the following:

(i) Interconnection in accordance with the requirements of sections 251(c)(2) and 252(d)(1).

(ii) Nondiscriminatory access to network elements in accordance with the requirements of sections 251(c)(3) and 252(d)(1).

(iii) Nondiscriminatory access to the poles, ducts, conduits, and rights-of-way owned or controlled by the Bell operating company at just and reasonable rates in accordance with the requirements of section 224.

(iv) Local loop transmission from the central office to the customer's premises, unbundled from local switching or other services.

(v) Local transport from the trunk side of a wireline local exchange carrier switch unbundled from switching or other services.

(vi) Local switching unbundled from transport, local loop transmission, or other services.

(vii) Nondiscriminatory access to—

(I) 911 and E911 services;

(II) directory assistance services to allow the other carrier's customers to obtain telephone numbers; and

(III) operator call completion services.

(viii) White pages directory listings for customers of the other carrier's telephone exchange service.

(ix) Until the date by which telecommunications numbering administration guidelines, plan, or rules are established, nondiscriminatory access to telephone numbers for assignment to the other carrier's telephone exchange service customers. After that date, compliance with such guidelines, plan, or rules.

(x) Nondiscriminatory access to databases and associated signaling necessary for call routing and completion.

(xi) Until the date by which the Commission issues regulations pursuant to section 251 to require number portability, interim telecommunications number portability through remote call forwarding, direct inward dialing trunks, or other comparable arrangements, with as little impairment of functioning, quality, reliability, and convenience as possible. After that date, full compliance with such regulations.

(xii) Nondiscriminatory access to such services or information as are necessary to allow the requesting carrier to implement local dialing parity in accordance with the requirements of section 251(b)(3).

(xiii) Reciprocal compensation arrangements in accordance with the requirements of section 252(d)(2).

(xiv) Telecommunications services are available for resale in accordance with the requirements of sections 251(c)(4) and 252(d)(3)." *Id.* § 271(c)(2)(B).

12. The structural separations requirements are in section 272 of the act: "Struc-

substantial weight to the views of the Department of Justice,[13] must rule, under the general public interest standard of the Communications Act, on the RBOC's request to provide in-region interLATA service.[14]

Although the FCC must approve or reject the RBOC's application within ninety days, the complexity of the checklist and the related approval process will inevitably produce dispute on matters of fact, law, economics, and engineering. That complexity—along with the provision authorizing the FCC to suspend or revoke its approval of the RBOC's provision of in-region interLATA service and the related provision creating a process for the filing of complaints by private parties upon which the FCC must act within ninety days[15]—creates a rich opportunity for strategic gaming by interexchange carriers seeking to block RBOC entry into long-distance markets. The experience with the MFJ is suggestive. The MFJ allowed for modification of its line-of-business restrictions through a waiver process. That process proved to be a quagmire that was costly in terms of delaying benefits to consumers in the form of greater price competition and new service introductions. By 1993 the average age of pending waiver requests before the Department of Justice was thirty-six months, despite the fact that the DOJ had opposed relief in only 6 of the 266 waiver requests filed by the RBOCs.[16] By the end of 1993 the average age of pending waiver motions before the district court had grown to 54.7 months, despite the fact that the court had approved in full 96 percent of all waiver requests filed.[17]

---

tural and Transactional Requirements.—The separate affiliate required by this section—

(1) shall operate independently from the Bell operating company;

(2) shall maintain books, records, and accounts in the manner prescribed by the Commission which shall be separate from the books, records, and accounts maintained by the Bell operating company of which it is an affiliate;

(3) shall have separate officers, directors, and employees from the Bell operating company of which it is an affiliate;

(4) may not obtain credit under any arrangement that would permit a creditor, upon default, to have recourse to the assets of the Bell operating company; and

(5) shall conduct all transactions with the Bell operating company of which it is an affiliate on an arm's length basis with any such transactions reduced to writing and available for public inspection." *Id.* § 272(b).

13. *Id.* § 271(d)(2)(A).

14. *Id.* § 271(d)(3).

15. *Id.* § 271(d)(6).

16. Paul H. Rubin & Hashem Dezhbakhsh, *Costs of Delay and Rent-Seeking Under the Modification of Final Judgment*, 16 MANAGERIAL & DECISION ECON. 385, 385–86 (1995).

17. *Id.* at 389, 392.

The delay in obtaining waivers of the MFJ's line-of-business restrictions suggests the kinds of costs that consumers could incur under the similar quarantine approach of the checklist. The process of construing and applying the checklist will fuel esoteric litigation. Because the outcome of such litigation will determine when an RBOC will be allowed to compete in lucrative interLATA markets, one can expect incumbent interexchange carriers to contest the litigation fiercely.

Ameritech filed the first section 271 application, to provide interLATA service in Michigan, which it promptly withdrew after interexchange carriers vigorously opposed it as incomplete.[18] The next section 271 application, by SBC to provide interLATA service in Oklahoma, encountered opposition by the Department of Justice, which asserted that SBC had not satisfied the competitive checklist and that its local markets had not "been irreversibly opened to competition."[19] Although such litigation would be costly in its own terms, its greater cost will surely be in terms of delayed or forgone price competition and product innovation in the interLATA market.

THE STRUCTURE OF THE
QUARANTINE ARGUMENT

Telecommunications is a substantial sector of the American economy. Moreover, given the convergence of computers and telecommunications, continued technical progress is a vital part of the information economy. Furthermore, the lessons from the telecommunications industry are applicable to other network industries such as electric power, natural gas, water services, and postal delivery, each of which is experiencing technological change that is breaking down monopolies and destabilizing the established regulatory regimes. Taking into consideration the current and past conditions of the telecommunications industry, we evaluate in this chapter the four principal economic arguments that have been made for imposing or retaining the quarantine on the RBOCs and that have been made to justify the checklist procedures of section 271 of the Communications Act, as amended by the 1996 legislation. We can

18. Jim Kirk, *Ameritech Drops Mich. Bid*, CHI. SUN-TIMES, Feb. 12, 1997, at 65.

19. Evaluation of the United States Department of Justice, Application of SBC Communications Inc. et al. Pursuant to Section 271 of the Telecommunications Act of 1996 to Provide In-Region, InterLATA Service in the State of Oklahoma, CC Dkt. No. 97-121 (filed with FCC, May 16, 1997). After the FCC rejected SBC's application, the company filed suit challenging the constitutionality of the section 271 process on multiple grounds. *SBC Files Challenge to Telecom Law*, WALL ST. J., July 3, 1997, at A3.

summarize those arguments, often directed at local exchange carriers (LECs) generally, as follows:

- The LEC's production technology in the local exchange exhibits the property of natural monopoly.

- The LEC is the beneficiary of significant barriers to entry into the local exchange.

- The LEC can leverage its local-exchange monopoly into other markets.

- The LEC can employ cross-subsidization from local service to gain competitive advantages upon entry into other lines of business.

Those arguments for preserving the regulatory quarantine are irreconcilable with economic and technological developments in the telecommunications industry since the breakup of the Bell System. The first two arguments are related to the characteristics of the local exchange market. The AT&T divestiture and the line-of-business restrictions in the MFJ were predicated on the concern that local exchange telephony was a natural monopoly technology that AT&T had allegedly used to harm competition in other markets. In particular, AT&T was alleged to have provided its rivals in the long-distance market with connections to the local exchange that were inferior to or more costly than AT&T provided to its own Long Lines division—a practice sometimes referred to as "discriminatory access." The MFJ reflected the concern of Judge Harold H. Greene, the presiding district court judge in the divestiture litigation, that the RBOCs would retain a monopoly over the local exchange as a consequence of their natural monopoly technology and barriers to entry. If allowed to enter into interLATA services and equipment manufacturing, the RBOCs allegedly would have the means to deny access to competing suppliers, just as AT&T had been accused of doing before the divestiture of the Bell System.

The final two arguments attempt to predict the behavior of the LECs in the markets for interLATA services and equipment manufacturing. Before the divestiture AT&T allegedly harmed rivals by deceiving its rate-of-return regulators through misallocation of costs from interexchange and other operations to the local operating companies. That cross-subsidization allegedly enabled AT&T to evade rate-of-return regulation and to engage in predatory pricing against efficient competitors in markets adjacent to the local exchange. The divestiture and quarantine provisions of the MFJ reflected Judge Greene's concern that the RBOCs, like predivestiture AT&T, would use their monopoly position in the local exchange markets to obtain a competitive advantage in the long-distance and equipment manufacturing markets.

Judge Greene advanced the four arguments outlined above as justifications for imposing the line-of-business restrictions in the MFJ. But they reflect traditional regulatory arguments that generally do not apply to the existing telecommunications industry. The arguments were presented in testimony in the AT&T case. The Department of Justice contended that the "natural monopoly characteristics" of the local exchange precluded competition "until a point of concentration of interexchange traffic above the end office."[20] The U.S. Court of Appeals for the District of Columbia Circuit explained in 1990 that the motivation for bringing the antitrust case against AT&T and, later, the justification for the consent decree, "was that AT&T had used its natural monopoly over local exchange services to impede competition in related markets."[21] As Judge Greene observed in 1987 with regard to barriers to entry, "The evidence introduced at the trial of this case clearly demonstrated that duplication of the ubiquitous local exchange networks would require an enormous and prohibitive capital investment, and no one seriously questions that this is true."[22] In 1981 he had similarly stated: "The government alleges that defendants have monopoly power in each of these markets and, to prove the existence of such power, evidence has been offered of market share, barriers to entry, size, and the exercise of power."[23]

The ability of the RBOCs to leverage their market power was, in Judge Greene's view in 1982, temporary: "It is probable that, over time, the Operating Companies will lose the ability to leverage their monopoly power into the competitive markets from which they must now be barred."[24] The Justice Department similarly stated in 1982 in its competitive impact statement justifying the consent decree: "The

---

20. Response of the United States to Comments Received on the BOC LATA Proposals at 9–10, United States *v.* Western Elec. Co., No. 82-0192 (D.D.C. Mar. 23, 1982).

21. United States *v.* Western Elec. Co., 894 F.2d 1387, 1389 (D.C. Cir. 1990).

22. United States *v.* Western Elec. Co., 673 F. Supp. 525, 538 (D.D.C. 1987), *aff'd*, 894 F.2d 1387 (D.C. Cir. 1990).

23. United States *v.* American Tel. & Tel. Co., 524 F. Supp. 1336, 1346 (D.D.C. 1981).

24. 552 F. Supp. at 194.

reorganization of AT&T . . . is intended to eliminate the present incentives of the BOCs . . . to discriminate against AT&T's competitors in the markets for interexchange services, information services, customer premises equipment, and the procurement of equipment used to provide local exchange services."[25] The decree's injunctive provisions were seen to "limit the functions of the divested BOCs to preclude the possibility of a recurrence of the type of monopolizing conduct that the United States alleges to have resulted from AT&T's ownership of regulated local exchange carriers and its simultaneous participation in competitive, or potentially competitive, markets."[26] With regard to cross-subsidization, Judge Greene pronounced in 1982 that "the proposed decree would complement the structural changes by various restrictions which are said to be designed (1) to prevent the divested Operating Companies from discriminating against AT&T's competitors, and (2) to avoid a recurrence of the type of discrimination and cross-subsidization that were the basis of the AT&T lawsuit."[27]

In the remainder of this chapter we demonstrate (1) that the RBOCs' technology in the local exchange no longer exhibits cost properties associated with natural monopoly; (2) that the RBOCs are not currently the beneficiaries of any significant entry barriers; (3) that the RBOCs would not be able to leverage unfairly their market positions in the local exchange into other markets; and (4) that the RBOCs would be unable to employ cross-subsidies from local service to achieve competitive advantages in other lines of business. We conclude that the rapid elimination of the line-of-business restrictions that Congress transplanted from the MFJ to the Telecommunications Act of 1996 would enhance the productive, allocative, and dynamic efficiency of the telecommunications sector and thus advance the public interest.

The implications of our argument extend beyond the telecommunications industry. Traditional justifications for regulating industries, such as the presence of natural monopoly technologies, may no longer apply in the presence of technological change and competitive entry. In telecommunications, and in other industries as well, technological change strikes at the heart of the natural monopoly argument. Moreover, technological progress that reduces dependence on irreversible capital

25. Competitive Impact Statement in Connection with Proposed Modification of Final Judgment, 47 FED. REG. 7170, 7175 (1982) (footnote omitted).

26. *Id.*

27. 552 F. Supp. at 142.

investment significantly reduces the need for concern over barriers to entry.

THE NATURAL MONOPOLY ARGUMENT

The first argument used to justify the regulatory quarantine is that the RBOCs have a monopoly over the local exchange because their technology has the property of natural monopoly. That argument is misplaced. We shall now show that the local exchange has lost or is quickly losing the characteristics of a natural monopoly and that natural monopoly is not a barrier to entry.

Natural Monopoly and the Local Exchange

Before the breakup of the Bell System, the local exchange was widely viewed as a natural monopoly. Under Theodore Vail—who as early as 1907 advanced the well-known slogan, "One system, one policy, universal service"—AT&T itself maintained that telephone service was a natural monopoly.[28] The Communications Act of 1934 reflected that view.[29] So did the writings of leading scholars on regulation. In his 1971 treatise *The Economics of Regulation*, Alfred E. Kahn observed: "That the provision of local telephone service is a natural monopoly is generally conceded."[30] Even at that time, however, Kahn presciently observed that substantial technological change had occurred in communications after World War II (including microwave relay systems, satellites, transoceanic cable, and cable television), and that "[i]n the presence of such rapid change, the natural monopoly of yesterday may be transformed into a natural area of competition today; and vice versa."[31] Like Kahn in 1971, the future Justice Stephen G. Breyer similarly wrote in 1982 that "local telephone service seems to be generally accepted as a natural

---

28. MILTON L. MUELLER, JR., UNIVERSAL SERVICE: COMPETITION, INTERCONNECTION, AND MONOPOLY IN THE MAKING OF THE AMERICAN TELEPHONE SYSTEM 4 (MIT Press & AEI Press 1997); ROBERT BRITT HORWITZ, THE IRONY OF REGULATORY REFORM: THE DEREGULATION OF AMERICAN TELECOMMUNICATIONS 99 (Oxford University Press 1989).

29. *See* STEPHEN G. BREYER, REGULATION AND ITS REFORM 291 (Harvard University Press 1982).

30. 2 ALFRED E. KAHN, THE ECONOMICS OF REGULATION: PRINCIPLES AND INSTITUTIONS 127 (MIT Press, rev. ed. 1988) (John Wiley & Sons, Inc. 1971).

31. *Id.* at 127.

monopoly."[32] He observed, like Kahn, that technological change could make competition possible in the future, although at the time Justice Breyer discounted such developments as "speculative."[33]

The belief that the local exchange service constituted a natural monopoly undoubtedly influenced the implementation of the MFJ's line-of-business restrictions. But paradoxically by the time of the Telecommunications Act, when the view that local telecommunications was a natural monopoly had been widely rejected and the preamble to the new telecommunications legislation instead proclaimed Congress's purpose to be "[t]o promote competition and reduce regulation in order to secure lower prices and higher quality services for American telecommunications consumers,"[34] Congress nonetheless embraced the regulatory quarantine in the form of the checklist provisions of section 271. That bit of intellectual inconsistency calls into question whether the relevant parties really took the natural monopoly argument seriously even during the drafting and administration of the MFJ during the 1980s and 1990s. Like some bit of liturgy whose origin and purpose had been forgotten, the regulatory quarantine was reaffirmed as part of the orthodoxy of telecommunications regulation, even as members of Congress were laboring to exalt deregulation and competition.

The natural monopoly argument for the quarantine asserts that the LECs, and hence the RBOCs, have a monopoly over the local exchange because the technology of the exchange exhibits the characteristics of a natural monopoly. In 1987 Judge Greene stated, "The exchange monopoly of the Regional Companies has continued because it is a natural monopoly."[35] "Exchange telecommunications," he wrote, "is characterized by very substantial economies of scale and scope."[36] From the natural monopoly argument for regulation flows the assertion that not only would one LEC serve a given market most efficiently, but also that, if competition were allowed, only one carrier would survive. If that reasoning were sound, regulation of the local exchange might appear to be efficient and justified.

32. *See* BREYER, *supra* note 29, at 291.

33. *Id.* at 292.

34. Telecommunications Act of 1996, preamble, Pub. L. No. 104-104, 110 Stat. 56, 56.

35. 673 F. Supp. at 537.

36. *Id.* at 538 (citing *AT&T Proposed Settlement: Hearing Before the Senate Comm. on Science and Transportation*, pt. 1, 97th Cong., 2d Sess. 59 (1981) (testimony of Assistant Attorney General William F. Baxter)).

The natural monopoly argument for regulation supports restricting entry into the local telecommunications market and awarding a monopoly franchise. In turn, awarding a monopoly franchise provides justification not only for regulating the single firm's prices and other activities, but also for preventing the firm from engaging in other economic activities. If the natural monopoly argument for regulation is no longer valid, however, that fact would suggest that restriction of entry into the local telecommunications loop is not justified. (And, indeed, in section 253 of the Telecommunications Act of 1996, Congress preempted state prohibitions on entry into local telephony.[37]) Moreover, if invalid, the natural monopoly argument cannot be used by extension to prevent an incumbent LEC from undertaking other economic activities outside the local exchange.

The Local Exchange Has Lost or Is Quickly Losing the Characteristics of a Natural Monopoly

Substantial technological change and industry transformation since the AT&T divestiture have rendered the natural monopoly argument invalid. For a number of reasons it is no longer correct to treat the local exchange as a natural monopoly. First, there is no existing single best technology for telecommunications transmission. Second, the best potential technology or mixture of technologies is not yet known, as the industry continues to experience substantial technological change. Third, the "interconnectedness" of networks eliminates the natural monopoly, because multiple carriers can provide access to the interconnecting networks. Fourth, the goal of avoiding duplicative facilities is not applicable as an aspect of natural monopoly in local telecommunications, because substantial duplication of facilities has already occurred.

There Is No Single Best Technology for Local Telecommunications. The natural monopoly argument asserts that cost efficiencies are obtained from a single supplier, given the characteristics of a specific technology for carrying out a specific task. With multiple technologies, each with different characteristics, efficiency may require production by multiple firms, so that monopoly no longer yields cost efficiencies. Perhaps the notion of a best technology once served as an accurate description of the traditional telecommunications system, which consisted of copper wires

---

37. 47 U.S.C. § 253.

for transmission, central switching equipment, and very basic equipment on the customer's premises. That description no longer applies, as a consequence of technological change and industry developments. There is no longer a single best technology for telecommunications transmission.

Instead, now multiple telecommunications technologies in addition to the traditional copper wire provide transmission. The alternative modes of transmission include coaxial cable, fiber-optic cable, satellite, microwave, cellular, and other radio technologies. Each of those technologies has various advantages and disadvantages in terms of cost and performance. It is no longer possible, nor is it desirable, to pick a single mode of transmission to the exclusion of all others. George C. Calhoun has argued that "the abandonment of hierarchical structures is gathering momentum, especially in the core public network and in specialized computer networks."[38] He describes "a series of partly competing, partly complementary, somewhat differentiated, overlapping access fabrics"[39] that he calls the *laminar network:*

> The laminar network, then, will consist of multiple layers of transmission facilities for accessing the core network at an increasing number of gateways. . . . The lowest levels will still be copper-based fabrics, the vast installed base of wireline telephony and coaxial cable TV plant that will continue in use for decades. Growing over these there will be several new layers of fiberoptics plant—and, because of its nature, ever more layers of digital radio. Even within a given "fabric layer" there will almost certainly be a great deal of technical diversity.[40]

The increasing variety of competing transmission technologies implies that it is no longer possible to define a natural monopoly technology for local telephony.

Some may assert that a combination of transmission modes is best, and that a single supplier should efficiently choose that unknown combination. Such an attempt to revive the natural monopoly argument, however, would be plagued with difficulties, because multiple suppliers could provide the correct mix of technologies. Moreover, because the relative cost and performance characteristics of the alternative technologies change continuously, the optimal mix of technologies will frequently change.

38. GEORGE C. CALHOUN, WIRELESS ACCESS AND THE LOCAL TELEPHONE NETWORK 532 (Artech House 1992).
39. *Id.* at 537.
40. *Id.* at 539.

Not only is there no single best technology for traditional telephone service, there is no single best technology for handling the many new types of services that the telecommunications industry now provides. The traditional telecommunications system was designed to handle voice transmission from stationary equipment. Consumers now demand many alternative communications products, including fax, data transmission, interactive services, video transmission, and both mobile and stationary communications. Calhoun forecasts that future telecommunications technology will not be confined to a single form but will include many forms of access, some on a small scale (for example, microcell radio), some of global proportions (very small aperture terminal satellite networks, or VSATs), some optimized for narrowband transmissions, others for broadband, some for vehicular communications, others for fixed or portable, some for data-dominant traffic, others for voice-dominant traffic, and still others for the transmission of image-based traffic—all rather imperfectly stitched together.[41]

The transmission technologies vary in terms of their suitability and performance in completing those diverse transmission tasks. Moreover, telecommunications companies provide a wide array of additional switching services with different sets of switching and computer technologies. Those switching and computer technologies also vary in terms of their cost and performance in the supply of various services. In addition, there are different technological requirements for different portions of the telecommunications system. The technological requirements for transmission and for switching long-distance telecommunications differ considerably from those required for access to the telecommunications network. There are now multiple technological approaches for access to, as well as transmission of, local telephone service. As Calhoun has observed with respect to the large set of choices available simply for providing access:

> So the real question faced by planners is not "Which is cheaper, radio or wire?" but "What is the most cost-effective mix of radio, cable, and fiber in the access network for a given situation?"
>
> The complexity of this question can overwhelm even a fully computerized modeling process. In principle, there are dozens, or hundreds, of solutions (in the mathematical sense of the word) for any given exchange. And when we realize that radio easily transcends the traditional exchange concept . . . , the solution set multiplies further.[42]

41. *Id.* at 527.
42. *Id.* at 470.

The natural monopoly argument becomes even less applicable when one recognizes that a telecommunications company can offer an array of telephone services, in addition to basic voice transmission. The definition of natural monopoly, of course, may be extended to cover multiproduct technology. In the multiproduct case, the technology is said to have the natural monopoly property if a single firm can provide the bundle of products at a lower cost than can two or more firms. Under such conditions, the single firm enjoys economies of scope.[43] If distinct technologies are suitable for providing different products and services, such as voice, data transmission, interactive information services, and mobile communication, the argument that a single provider is optimal ceases to hold. Support for the natural monopoly argument would require satisfying a difficult, if not impossible, burden of proving that a single provider of many diverse technologies would be cost-efficient. The burden of proof becomes even more difficult when the technologies are applied to an ever-widening array of different services.[44]

In addition to the many telecommunications technologies handling many different functions, technology within any particular category can differ substantially across firms as a consequence of technological change. Firms have different production technologies because technological knowledge diffuses unevenly, and because technologies are embodied differently across different types of facilities and different generations of capital equipment. For example, time division multiple access (TDMA) and code division multiple access (CDMA) technology will enable providers of cellular service to offer the customer high-quality transmission and the ability to call anyone, anytime.[45] Different carriers use different technologies, however.[46] With changing technology, therefore, costs can differ substantially across firms, and one cannot conclude a priori that a single firm can produce at lower costs than can two or more firms.

43. *See, e.g.,* SPULBER, *supra* note 7, at 114–17.

44. *See* Sanford V. Berg & John Tschirhart, *A Market Test for Natural Monopoly in Local Exchange*, 8 J. REG. ECON. 103 (1995).

45. *See* Jason Meyers, *Stumping for Digital: PCS Carriers and Equipment Vendors Line up in Rival Camps to Defend Their Technology Platforms,* TELEPHONY (supp.), May 13, 1996, at 8; CELLULAR TELECOMMUNICATIONS INDUSTRY ASSOCIATION, STATE OF THE CELLULAR INDUSTRY 101 (1992).

46. By late 1995 ten of fourteen cellular service providers said they would use CDMA technology. *Qualcomm Inc.*, HOOVER'S COMPANY PROFILE DATABASE (1996); QUALCOMM INC., 1996 SEC FORM 10-K, at 4 (1996) (supplier of CDMA technology).

The natural monopoly argument that all technologies are known and that all firms have access to the best technology no longer describes local exchange telecommunications. There has been substantial technological change in computers, computer-based switching equipment, digital transmission methods, wireless access, fiber optics, and other key technologies. Thus, it is no longer possible to identify a stable best technology that can serve as the basis for the natural monopoly argument. Without such a basis, one cannot use the natural monopoly argument to establish the cost-efficiency of a single protected provider of service. For example, although fiber optics may have a clear advantage over other technologies for some forms of trunkline transmission, numerous alternatives exist for handling connections to the network that continue to be developed.

Many crucial issues remain open, including the configuration of the access network and the standards for digital transmission in access. Calhoun observes:

> [T]he proper architecture for a digital access network is still very much in question. Star, ring or bus? Fiber to the home? Fiber to the curb? Radio tails? "Alternative access?" ISDN, or what?
>
> Moreover, regardless of which *physical* configuration prevails, the efficient digitalization of the access environment will require equipment based on standards that are still under development or, at best, just beginning to be commercialized.[47]

If the best technology is not known, regulators cannot credibly assert that an RBOC will necessarily have access to the best technology or that entry of new suppliers using alternative technologies cannot occur.

The Connectivity of Networks Renders Natural Monopoly Obsolete. The natural monopoly argument is also weakened by the connectivity of networks. Improvements in computers and related switching technology allow different firms to build and operate multiple networks that can then be interconnected. The Telecommunications Act of 1996 requires an incumbent LEC to provide interconnection, at rates that are based on cost and may include no more than a reasonable profit, to competing providers of local telecommunications services.[48] Meanwhile, the costs of interconnection have fallen substantially as the costs of switching

---

47. CALHOUN, *supra* note 38, at 534 (emphasis in original).
48. 47 U.S.C. § 252(d)(1).

technology have decreased. Open network architecture further reduces the benefits of a centrally switched network. In addition, new developments in switching have allowed customer premises equipment, such as the private branch exchange (PBX) and local area networks (LANs), to be substituted for transmission and switching by the telecommunications utility. Those significant developments render the concept of a natural monopoly telecommunications network obsolete.

The Problem of Duplicative Facilities No Longer Applies. At the heart of the natural monopoly argument lies the need to avoid duplication of facilities, particularly costly transmission facilities such as telecommunications lines. The advantage of having only one, as opposed to two or more producers, is that the single producer will create a single network, whereas two or more producers will create two or more networks, duplicating facilities and thus causing higher total costs. That crucial part of the natural monopoly argument has been rendered invalid.

Most important, the avoidance of duplication of networks is no longer an issue because duplication has already occurred. Indeed, the promotion of facilities-based competition has become national policy with the passage of the Telecommunications Act of 1996.[49] Even before 1996, many areas had multiple networks employing fiber-optic, cellular, and microwave techniques, and those networks essentially duplicate some transmission capabilities. As Peter W. Huber, Michael K. Kellogg, and John Thorne have observed: "A technologically vibrant industry does not advance by 'duplication.' New technologies (integrated circuits, lasers), new media (radio instead of copper wire, fiber instead of microwave), new architectures (rings instead of stars), replace old ones."[50] The convergence of applications of alternative technologies suggests that the duplication problem no longer exists.

Numerous alternative means exist to access the network in addition to the LEC's local loop, including fiber, coaxial cable, and wireless. Competitive access providers (CAPs) operate fiber-optic-based networks with local loops and switching capabilities. A high proportion of house-

49. 47 U.S.C. § 271(c)(1)(A); *see also* 142 CONG. REC. S687, S713 (daily ed. Feb. 1, 1996) (statement of Senator John B. Breaux).

50. PETER W. HUBER, MICHAEL K. KELLOGG & JOHN THORNE, THE GEODESIC NETWORK II: 1993 REPORT ON COMPETITION IN THE TELEPHONE INDUSTRY 2.80 (The Geodesic Co. 1992). The authors further observe: "Nor does competition arrive in a single leap. Instead it enters one market segment at a time, switch by switch, trunk by trunk, line by line, beginning where prices are highest and costs lowest." *Id.*

holds has both standard telephone service and cable telecommunications services. The coaxial cable that delivers cable television is capable, with certain modifications,[51] of delivering voice telephony and other telecommunications services, such as high-speed Internet access, although the cable companies have been far slower to introduce such telephony-like services than analysts widely expected in the fall of 1993, when Bell Atlantic proposed to acquire TCI.[52] Business customers have an expanding range of alternatives to voice and data services traditionally provided by the LECs. Competitive local telephony for business customers (and even many residential customers) was already well underway before the passage of the Telecommunications Act of 1996. By 1994 Time Warner was offering local exchange service in Rochester, New York City, and Ohio;[53] and MCI and Sprint (with its cable partners' ownership of Teleport) had each announced plans to offer local exchange service in the suburbs of Chicago.[54] A graphic illustration of the competitive threat that the interexchange carriers pose for the incumbent LECs was AT&T's announcement in May 1996 that it would offer Illinois customers three months of free, unlimited local toll calls.[55] As those examples document, the view that technology confers an inherent advantage on an incumbent LEC, and thus gives it a natural monopoly, is controverted by the fact that multiple wireline local networks are in operation or are being deployed.

The desire to avoid duplication of costly transmission facilities is also inconsistent with the technological changes involving wireless technologies. Even if wire-based transmission technologies exhibit the natural monopoly property, segments of the local loop are being replaced with wireless technologies, many of which may not exhibit natural monopoly

---

51. *See* SCIENTIFIC ATLANTA, COACCESS: CATV TELEPHONE SYSTEM: A DUAL-SERVICE TELEPHONY/VIDEO SYSTEM FOR CATV NETWORKS (1993).

52. *See* ROBERT W. CRANDALL & HAROLD FURCHTGOTT-ROTH, CABLE TV: REGULATION OR COMPETITION? 95–96 (Brookings Institution 1996); Mark Robichaux, *Malone Says TCI Push into Phones, Internet Isn't Working for Now*, WALL ST. J., Jan. 2, 1997, at 1.

53. Edmund L. Andrews, *Ameritech Forcefully Stays Home*, N.Y. TIMES, Nov. 22, 1994, § D, at 1; Edmund L. Andrews, *NYNEX Faces Yet Another Competitor*, N.Y. TIMES, Nov. 10, 1994, § D, at 1.

54. Andrews, *Ameritech Forcefully Stays Home*, *supra* note 53, at 1; Richard Ringer, *MCI Submits Local Phone Service Plan*, N.Y. TIMES, Aug. 18, 1994, § D, at 3.

55. John J. Keller, *AT&T Discounts Signal a National Price War*, WALL ST. J., May 30, 1996, at B1.

characteristics. Competitive entry can and indeed has occurred. Competing firms are serving the telecommunications market with wireless technologies such as cellular, microwave, basic exchange telecommunications radio service (BETRS), wireless wide-area networks (WANs), and VSATs.[56] Additional competitive entry in the form of digital personal communications services (PCS) has taken off with national, regional, and local carriers' building transmission systems after winning FCC licensing.[57]

Finally, the substitution of inexpensive switching technology for transmission capacity further reduces the need for concern over the duplication of wireline transmission facilities. The most obvious example is the substitution by customers of PBX equipment for the LEC's centrex service.[58] Such switching hardware and software are available in a competitive market from the same vendors that supply the incumbent LECs. Similarly, the development of affordable high-speed cable modems may encourage the migration of data traffic from local telephone networks to cable television systems even before firms introduce interactive broadband networks.[59] The prospect of high-speed cable modems is significant as well for household consumption of interactive broadband services because a significant percentage of cable subscribers owns personal computers.[60] In short, technology substantially reduces both the amount

---

56. *See generally* CALHOUN, *supra* note 38.

57. An early entrant was Sprint Spectrum service in the Washington-Baltimore region. SPRINT CORP., 1995 SEC FORM 10-K at 23 (1996).

58. *See* CRANDALL, *supra* note 5, at 92–93; HUBER, KELLOGG & THORNE, THE GEODESIC NETWORK II, *supra* note 50, at 6.2, 6.45.

59. *See* Larry J. Yokell, *Cable TV Moves into Telecom Markets*, BUSINESS COMMUNICATIONS, Nov. 1994, at 43; Russell Shaw, *Business Gets Wired for Cable—Cable Systems Offer Corporate Users High-Speed Data Transmission*, INFORMATION WEEK, Nov. 21, 1994, at 80; Carol Wilson, *Cable Operators Rebound with New Strategies*, TELEPHONY, May 30, 1994, at 10.

60. As early as 1994 a leading equity analyst noted:

Currently, [in the United States] 32 million homes (31%) have PCs. In comparison, the number of homes that are passed by cable is three times that, and the number of cable subscribers is almost twice as high. Perhaps most importantly, in urban markets, two-thirds of cable subscribers have a home-based PC, enabling PC-based communications systems to take advantage of high-bandwidth coaxial cable needed for computer-based interactive applications.

HANCOCK INSTITUTIONAL EQUITY SERVICES, INVESTING IN THE "EMERGING" TELECOMMUNICATIONS INDUSTRY 8 (Dec. 2, 1994) (by Douglas C. Ashton).

of duplication of the LEC's facilities that competing networks require and the cost advantage of a single producer over two or more producers.

Natural Monopoly Technology
Is Not a Barrier to Entry

Even under the very specific demand and cost conditions sufficient for "sustainable" monopoly prices, the possibility of sustainable prices need not prevent entrants from successfully competing *for* the market if the incumbent were to deviate from those prices. Even if those conditions were to hold, therefore, an incumbent firm could not leverage its monopoly position to favor other lines of business, because such action would create opportunities for new entrants to serve customers by not requiring the purchase of additional services. In addition, the monopolist could not generate profits to subsidize entry into other lines of business, because the potential for entry into a contestable market eliminates both profits and cross-subsidies.

For purposes of argument, however, suppose that the production technology of the local exchange were to exhibit the property of natural monopoly, contrary to our hypothesis. That condition would not imply that the LEC could select prices that would deter entry. The existence of multiple technologies, the continuing development of new technologies, and the differences in information that firms have about the technology create opportunities for the entry of competitors. Therefore, an incumbent LEC could not sustain a monopoly position simply through the selection of prices. Given the technological change that has been occurring in the telecommunications industry, the incumbent LEC cannot be expected to sustain a monopoly position. The entry of new carriers providing alternative access and transmission services that are economic substitutes for the services of the incumbent LECs clearly demonstrates that a monopoly over the local loop is not sustainable.

The Natural Monopoly Argument Does Not Apply with Cost Inefficiencies. A firm cannot enjoy the cost advantages of natural monopoly unless the firm uses its production technology at the efficient frontier of the production possibility curve. That requirement means that, given a particular productive technology, the monopoly provider purchases and employs productive inputs efficiently to minimize costs. If that is not the case, then a firm operating in the market is subject to competition from more efficient entrants. Thus, the natural monopoly properties of the technology are not sufficient by any means to guarantee that an incumbent can secure a monopoly position. If the incumbent firm is not operating efficiently, a more efficient entrant can provide equal or better service to customers at a lower price.

A number of reasons, including the presence of regulation, suggest that incumbents in telecommunications are not using their technology in the most economically efficient manner. The survey of incumbent burdens in chapter 2 indicates why one cannot assume that regulators permit an incumbent LEC to operate in a cost-minimizing fashion. Moreover, if investment incentives are distorted, then the firm will not operate the technology at the efficient frontier. A number of factors indicate that we should not presume the investment level of the local telecommunications providers to be at an efficient level. Price regulation, the entry of competing carriers, the quarantine, and regulatory uncertainty will affect the incentives of an incumbent LEC to invest. To the extent that investment departs from efficient levels, the notion that natural monopoly technology prevents entry ceases to apply.

The Existence of Multiple Carriers Calls into Question the Natural Monopoly Argument. Successful competitive entry refutes the argument that the technology of the local exchange exhibits natural monopoly properties and thereby confers a monopoly on the incumbent LEC. The presence of competitors in the local exchange leads to one of two conclusions. First, if natural monopoly technology is sufficient to create a monopoly, then the entry of competitors must imply either that the incumbent LEC's technology is not that of a natural monopoly or that the LEC is not operating the natural monopoly technology efficiently or pricing appropriately. Second, even if we believe that the incumbent LEC's technology were that of a natural monopoly, we would be forced to conclude that the natural monopoly's technology was insufficient to guarantee that an incumbent could achieve a monopoly in the market as a result of its technology. Either way the natural monopoly argument for regulation of the local exchange ceases to hold.

One might argue that the existence of competing local carriers does not refute the view that natural monopoly is not a barrier to entry if regulatory restrictions handicap the incumbent LECs: The restrictions then protect unregulated competitors and effectively subsidize entry. That retort is not convincing, however. If the natural monopoly view were correct, then one would expect the entry of at most *one* other carrier taking advantage of regulatory restrictions and employing the natural monopoly's technology. In fact, and to the contrary, multiple companies are entering the local exchange. As we have already noted, dozens of

CAPs offer fiber-optic transmission service and connection to interexchange carriers, and many other companies provide wireless transmission service, including cellular and PCS telecommunications networks.

Moreover, the interexchange carriers such as AT&T, MCI, Sprint, and WorldCom provide, in addition to interLATA transport, growing levels of intraLATA service in competition with the incumbent LECs. AT&T acquired McCaw Cellular, the largest cellular carrier in the United States, and thus gained wireless access to business and residential customers.[61] MCI became a facilities-based entrant into local telephony through its MCI Metro subsidiary[62] and entered into agreements with suppliers of cellular and PCS service to provide MCI wireless access in the local market.[63] Sprint, itself a large incumbent LEC in certain regions, entered into joint venture agreements with the cable companies that control Teleport Communications Group, a large CAP.[64] In 1996 WorldCom merged with the largest competitive access provider, MFS Communications, and thus became a fully vertically integrated local exchange and long-distance carrier with facilities in most major metropolitan areas.[65]

The entry of competitors into local telephony has shown that no technological properties inherent to the local exchange are sufficient to guarantee a monopoly to the incumbent LEC. Such competitive entry implies that policymakers should not use the natural monopoly argument to justify forbidding entry by the RBOCs into other lines of business.

Summary

Even if the technology of transmission were to exhibit natural monopoly properties, that technology would not necessarily constitute a barrier to

---

61. AT&T CORP., 1995 SEC FORM 10-K at 3 (1996).

62. MCI CORP., 1995 SEC FORM 10-K at 6 (1996).

63. Lawrence M. Fisher, *MCI Joins Nextwave in Wireless Communications Venture*, N.Y. TIMES, Aug. 27, 1996, at C3; John J. Keller, *MCI Proposes a $20 Billion Capital Project*, WALL ST. J., Jan. 5, 1994, at A3.

64. SPRINT CORP., 1995 SEC FORM 10-K at 65 (1996). When Congress enacted the Telecommunications Act of 1996, Sprint trailed only the RBOCs and GTE in size as a LEC, with 6,425,330 access lines and operating revenues from local services exceeding $3.8 billion. UNITED STATES TELEPHONE ASSOCIATION, PHONE FACTS 1995, at 10 (1996).

65. WORLDCOM, INC., 1996 SEC FORM 10-Q, at 9–10 (Sept. 30, 1996); Mark Landler, *Worldcom to Buy MFS for $12 Billion, Creating a Phone Giant*, N.Y. TIMES, Aug. 27, 1996, at C1; E. S. Browning, *Worldcom Deal Gives "Local Access" a Buzz*, WALL ST. J., Aug. 27, 1996, at C1.

entry into local telephony. Not only can new entrants compete with the incumbent LEC to serve the market, but they have done so. Moreover, even if the technology had natural monopoly properties, it does not necessarily follow that the incumbent LEC uses the technology so efficiently as to render the market invulnerable to more efficient entrants. If the technology of the local exchange is no longer a natural monopoly, then entry into the local loop will continue, and sound public policy counsels that the regulator's reliance on the quarantine should be minimized, if it cannot be eliminated altogether.

THE BARRIERS TO ENTRY ARGUMENT

The second argument used to justify the regulatory quarantine is that barriers to entry in the local exchange will maintain the monopoly position of the RBOCs. We examine now whether barriers to entry are present in local exchange markets. We demonstrate that the sunk cost argument for regulation of local telephony (and hence for the regulatory quarantine of the RBOCs) no longer applies and that entrants have incurred sunk costs for multiple networks.

Barriers to Entry
and the Local Exchange

There is no question that the RBOCs have a predominant market share for the provision of certain local telecommunications services and that those companies are large in terms of various measures of size, including number of customers and miles of transmission lines. Those facts, however, need not indicate that the RBOCs have market power in the local exchange. An incumbent firm is subject to the competitive discipline of potential entry when its market power is not substantial. As Judge Greene conceded in 1982 regarding AT&T, "Although monopoly power may be inferred from a firm's predominant market share, size alone is not synonymous with market power, particularly where entry barriers are not substantial."[66]

Although we noted above that both sunk costs and government regulation are sources of barriers to entry, sunk costs are the barrier to entry primarily associated with the local exchange. According to Judge Greene in 1987, "Local exchange competition has failed to develop, not so much because state and local regulators prohibit entry into the market

---

66. 552 F. Supp. at 171.

by would-be competitors of the Regional Companies, but because of the economic and technological infeasibility of alternative local distribution technologies."[67] Even if one assumes for the sake of argument the economic validity of that proposition in 1987, technological change has made it implausible that barriers to entry owing to sunk costs could still significantly deter entry into local telephony. Moreover, the substantial competitive entry into local telephony that has already occurred has mooted the question of whether sunk costs are a barrier to entry.

In addition, an examination of federal and state regulation of the telecommunications industry suggests that such regulation does not represent barriers to entry into the local exchange. In many markets, the LECs in fact face incumbent burdens, in which regulation imposes greater costs on incumbents than on entrants; in those cases, regulation encourages, or even subsidizes, some forms of entry and creates the potential for uneconomic bypass.[68] Uneconomic bypass occurs when competitive entry raises the total industry costs of providing a given level of service. As we explain in chapter 2, such bypass can result from subsidies or differences in regulation between incumbents and entrants.

The Sunk Cost Argument for Regulation of the Local Loop No Longer Applies

The evolution of telecommunications technology invalidates the argument that there are barriers to entry into local telecommunications markets stemming from the high sunk costs of establishing a telecommunications network. The notion that capital requirements to duplicate the local exchange network are prohibitive rests on several economic and technological misconceptions.

First, a new entrant need not duplicate the incumbent LEC's entire transmission and switching systems to enter the market profitably. The entrant need only enter portions of the market where the expected revenues exceed the expected costs of providing new service. Thus, an entrant must sink the costs required to serve only its specific customers. The size of the *incumbent's* sunk costs is irrelevant to the entrant. By

---

67. 673 F. Supp. at 537–38.

68. *See, e.g.*, Access Charge Reform; Price Cap Performance Review for Local Exchange Carriers; Transport Rate Structure and Pricing; Usage of the Public Switched Network by Information Service and Internet Access Providers, Notice of Proposed Rulemaking, Third Report and Order, and Notice of Inquiry, CC Dkt. Nos. 96-262, 94-1, 91-213, 96-263, 11 F.C.C. Rcd. 21,354, 21,376–77 ¶ 42 (1996).

choosing to serve only part of the local exchange market, the entrant substantially reduces its irreversible investment.

Second, the entrant need not duplicate the technology of the incumbent LEC's transmission and switching systems. The technology of telecommunications transmission has changed substantially in a manner that alters the types of investments required to establish a network. Although transmission wires represent the primary irreversible investment incurred by the LECs, many new technologies (such as cellular, mobile radio technology, and satellite transmission) substantially reduce the wired portion of the transmission system. By serving areas using wireless transmission, particularly for the "last mile" to the customer's location, the new technologies are not tied to specific customers through irreversible investment in transmission. For example, a transmission tower and receiver are not customer-specific, for they can serve any customer in a given geographic area. Moreover, radio transmission facilities themselves do not necessarily represent sunk costs, because they can be physically moved to serve other markets. Those features of some new transmission technologies obviate significant transaction-specific or customer-specific investments.

Third, technological change has altered the design of telecommunications systems. Telecommunications systems provide transmission services by using a combination of switches and transmission. The increased power and reduced cost of computer chips have correspondingly increased the power and reduced the cost of switches. And, as noted earlier, multiple vendors supply switches in a competitive market that is open to entrants and incumbent LECs alike. To the extent that firms can substitute switches for transmission lines, the cost-minimizing input mix will involve a greater reliance on switches and a correspondingly lesser reliance on lines. Also, as the power of switches has increased, so has their productivity. Increased productivity of switches reduces the number of switches required to produce a given level of transmission capacity. For example, the private branch exchange switching technology reduces the number of lines required to provide a given level of capacity to a customer's premises.

A reduction in the number of lines required to provide a given level of capacity implies that such a potential source of sunk costs is reduced for a new entrant into the local telecommunications market. Moreover, the switches operated by a telecommunications company, unlike lines, are not tied to a particular customer location. The switches may be shifted to other applications and thus do not represent sunk costs. Also, the switches owned and operated by customers certainly do not represent sunk costs for a telecommunications supplier. Thus, as technological change has significantly reduced sunk costs, the argument that sunk costs create a barrier to entry into the local exchange ceases to apply.

In another important way technological change in telecommunications has eliminated the argument that sunk costs are a barrier to entry. Given the extent of technological change since the incumbent LEC installed its infrastructure for the local loop, the incumbent's technology and the entrant's technology differ substantially. The incumbent LEC operates an old technology, such as a network that uses copper wires for transmission, whereas the entrant operates a new technology, such as one using more efficient radio or fiber-optic transmission.

The barrier to entry argument is then invalid with respect to local telecommunications in two ways. First, the operating cost differences between existing and new technologies can be substantial. The fact that the incumbent has sunk costs does not deter entry, because the entrant offering a more efficient technology, such as radio or fiber-optic transmission, can expect to compete successfully with the incumbent and to recover sunk costs.

Second, the need to sink costs is not a barrier to entry if the entrant can invest in a new technology with a performance advantage over an obsolescent telecommunications technology. The performance characteristics of incumbent and entrant technologies differ substantially. New access technologies offer various benefits that are not available through copper-wire access technology in the local loop. Those benefits include the mobility of radio services and the increased bandwidth of fiber-optic cable and coaxial cable. If the incremental revenues that a firm can obtain from providing value-added services, such as mobility or data transmission, will be sufficient to cover the costs of establishing and operating a new system, then it is irrelevant to the prospective entrant that the incumbent LEC has an advantage because of its existing copper wire and other investments in the local loop.

Competitive access providers, for example, attempt to distinguish their services from those provided by incumbent LECs on the basis of superior network reliability. In 1996 MFS described its corporate strategy as follows:

> The Company's strategy is to become the primary provider of telecommunications services to business and government end users. The Company believes business and government users have distinct telecommunications service requirements, including maximum reliability, consistent high quality, capacity for high-speed data transmission, responsive customer service and continuous attention to service enhancement

and new service development. The Company believes it has significant advantages over its competitors as a result of the Company's . . . expertise in developing highly reliable, advanced digital fiber optic networks which offer substantial transmission capacity.[69]

To achieve the higher reliability that its customers demand, MFS provides intentional redundancy throughout its fiber-optic network.[70] Another CAP, Teleport Communications Group (TCG), similarly stated in a 1996 prospectus:

> The Company uses the latest technologies and network architectures to develop a highly reliable infrastructure for delivering high-speed, quality digital transmissions of voice, data and video telecommunications. The basic transmission platform consists primarily of optical fiber equipped with high capacity SONET equipment deployed in self-healing rings. These SONET rings give TCG the capability of routing customer traffic simultaneously in both directions around the ring thereby eliminating loss of service in the even of a cable cut.
>   . . . Redundant electronics, with automatic switching to the backup equipment in the event of failure, protects against signal deterioration or outages. Continuous monitoring of system components focuses on proactively avoiding problems rather than just reacting upon failure.[71]

TCG further stated that one factor that promoted competition in local telecommunications markets after the AT&T divestiture was "technological advances in the transmission of data and video requiring greater capacity and reliability levels than copper-based ILEC [incumbent local exchange carrier] networks were able to accommodate."[72] TCG (which is controlled by a consortium of cable companies including TCI, Cox, Comcast, and Continental) noted that "CAPS generally offered . . . improved reliability in comparison to [sic] the ILECs," but that "[i]n recent years, the ILECs steadily have been increasing the amount of fiber

---

69. MFS Communications Co., 1995 SEC Form 10-K at 1 (1996). "Because MFS believes it has certain advantages relative to quality control . . . resulting from its use of the Company's existing fiber optic networks, MFS Intelenet believes that it may enjoy certain advantages with respect to certain of its competitors." *Id.* at 6.

70. "The end user's transmission signals are generally transmitted through the network simultaneously on both primary and alternate protection paths." *Id.* at 2.

71. Teleport Communications Group, Inc., Prospectus for 23,500,000 Shares of Class A Common Stock 50 (June 3, 1996).

72. *Id.* at 42.

used in their networks, thereby decreasing the competitive advantage held by the CAPs in the special access and private line markets."[73]

In short, the existing and planned competitive entry into local telecommunications shows that the new technologies offer cost and performance advantages over existing technologies. It follows that those advantages are sufficient to eliminate the barriers to entry that arise from the facilities of the incumbent LECs and the need for new entrants to sink costs. Of course, the LECs can invest in the new technologies—such as fiber-optic transmission capacity—as readily as can any entrant, absent any regulatory hurdles. Our discussion in chapter 2, however, shows that such regulatory hurdles are *not* absent, but rather lie at the heart of the controversy over how an incumbent LEC may allocate among its telephony and video customers the common costs of its investments in broadband capacity. *If* such regulatory hurdles did not exist for the incumbent LEC, then the incumbent LEC and the entrants would be on an equal footing with regard to their choices of network technology on a forward-looking basis: The need to sink costs in a *new* technology falls evenly on the incumbent and entrant and thus cannot constitute a barrier to entry.

Entry Barriers Are Not
an Issue Because Costs Have
Already Been Sunk for Multiple Networks

The substantial entry into local telecommunications that has already occurred also invalidates the argument that sunk costs constitute a substantial barrier to entry into the local exchange: As we already noted, interexchange carriers, competitive access providers, cable companies, cellular companies, and other wireless transmission suppliers have made significant investments in local telecommunications capacity. In 1994 AT&T paid more than $11 billion in stock for McCaw Cellular.[74] In 1994 MCI Metro embarked on a program to invest $2 billion in fiber rings and local switching infrastructure in major U.S. metropolitan markets.[75] In 1993 Sprint acquired Centel, a local exchange carrier and cellular operator, for $2.5 billion.[76] Through June 1996 the cellular

73. *Id.*
74. AT&T, 1995 SEC FORM 10-K at 8 (1996).
75. MCI CORP., 1995 SEC FORM 10-K at 10 (1996).
76. SPRINT CORP., 1995 SEC FORM 10-K at 20 (1996); *Gambling on Thin Air*,

industry had made a cumulative capital investment of $26.7 billion[77] and, by the end of 1996, had more than forty-two million subscribers.[78] Twelve competitive access providers (excluding MCI Metro) reporting cumulative investment to the FCC had sunk $227.3 million by the end of 1995.[79] One should add to those levels of network investment the combined investment of the cable television companies in developing their networks, although reliable estimates of cumulative industry investment are not readily available. The substantial levels of investment by rival telecommunications companies in the local market conclusively confirm that sunk costs do not create a barrier to entry into that market that would suffice to confer a monopoly on incumbent LECs.

In addition, the significant entry into the local exchange implies that entrants do not necessarily have a cost disadvantage relative to incumbent LECs, for those entrants have made irreversible investments. After making irreversible investments, entrants become incumbents. From that point forward, one cannot use the costs of entry to distinguish incumbent LECs from new communications providers.

Regulation of the RBOCs Creates Incumbent Burdens Rather Than Entry Barriers

Another form of entry barrier arises when a regulator awards an exclusive franchise to a LEC, thus precluding the entry of new carriers. The view that such a grant of statutory monopoly over local telecommunications exists today, however, is incorrect. Although state PUCs once tightly regulated entry into the local exchange, they no longer do

ECONOMIST, Aug. 21, 1993, at 49.

77. CELLULAR TELECOMMUNICATIONS INDUSTRY ASSOCIATION, 1996 MID-YEAR DATA SURVEY (Sept. 1996) ("Cumulative Capital Investment") (available on the Internet at http://www.wow-com.com/graphs/cap.htm).

78. CELLULAR TELECOMMUNICATIONS INDUSTRY ASSOCIATION, 1996 MID-YEAR WIRELESS SURVEY TABLE (Jan. 8, 1997) (available on the Internet at http://www.wow-com.com/data.htm).

79. FEDERAL COMMUNICATIONS COMMISSION, FIBER DEPLOYMENT UPDATE: END OF YEAR 1995, table 15 (1996) [hereinafter 1995 FIBER DEPLOYMENT UPDATE] (available on the Internet at http://www.fcc.gov/Bureaus/Common_Carrier/Reports/FCC-State_Link/infra.html/Fiber95.zip). The twelve CAPs were Brooks Fiber Properties, Eastern Telelogic, Electric Lightwave, IntelCom Group, Intermedia Communications (ICI), Kansas City Fiber Net, MFS, MWR Telecom (Iowa Resources), Phoenix Fiberlink, Inc., Teleport Communications Group, Time Warner Communications, and US Signal.

so. As we mentioned earlier, the Telecommunications Act of 1996 preempted state prohibitions on entry into local telecommunications markets.[80] Even before the passage of the 1996 federal legislation, the entry of many new carriers into the local exchange markets indicated that such regulatory barriers to entry were not effective. Indeed, in 1994 the majority of state regulatory authorities allowed competitive entry into their intraLATA toll markets and permitted CAPs to interconnect with the local exchange network.[81]

If anything, federal and state regulations create incumbent burdens, imposing costs and restrictions on incumbent LECs (and particularly the RBOCs) that are not placed on entrants, as we note in chapter 2. An incumbent burden facilitates entry and bypass of the existing telecommunications network even if such bypass would be uneconomic in the absence of the regulations. It is therefore the opposite of a barrier to entry.

The incumbent LECs are subject to numerous regulatory restrictions, including common carrier provisions, universal service requirements, and public filing of rates, none of which is generally imposed on new entrants. Other restrictions on incumbent LECs create lower limits on certain tariffs, which restrict the ability of the LECs to compete with entrants and create a tariff umbrella for competitors. Because the incumbent LECs have regulated rate structures that require charging high rates to business customers, entrants have incentives to provide selective bypass of the local network. One incumbent burden created by federal regulation is the differential treatment of access charges that AT&T pays to traditional LECs versus those it pays to new access providers. AT&T is required to pass along to its customers savings in access charges paid to traditional LECs, but it need not pass along the savings on access charges paid to new access providers.[82] Therefore, the argument that regulations create entry barriers that confer a statutory monopoly on incumbent LECs belies the current state of industry regulation.

Because incumbent burdens cause economic inefficiency, regulators, when allowing competitive entry, should lift uneven restrictions placed on the incumbent LECs, including the quarantine imposed on the RBOCs. Removing such restrictions would level the playing field and

---

80. 47 U.S.C. § 253.

81. NATIONAL ASSOCIATION OF REGULATORY UTILITY COMMISSIONERS, THE STATUS OF COMPETITION IN INTRASTATE TELECOMMUNICATIONS 198–200 (1994).

82. Policy and Rules Concerning Rates for Dominant Carriers, Report and Order and Second Further Notice of Proposed Rulemaking, CC Dkt. No. 87-313, 4 F.C.C. Rcd. 2873, 3005–06 ¶¶ 259–61, 3026–30 ¶¶ 315–21 (1989).

would allow the RBOCs to respond to competitive challenges through pricing, investment, and innovation. If regulators lifted the in-region interLATA restrictions on the RBOCs, any further entry would reflect a truly competitive market, rather than a market that asymmetric regulation had artificially made to appear competitive.

Like the former MFJ, the newly enacted section 271 prevents the RBOCs from entering in-region interLATA markets that could generate revenues, while competitors in the local exchange are not similarly denied access to those markets. Because the quarantine denies an RBOC the opportunity to earn revenues that its competitors may earn, regulators place the RBOC at a disadvantage and deny it returns to its technological expertise and market knowledge. That constraint does more than handicap the RBOCs against actual and potential competitors in the local exchange. It denies or delays the benefits that consumers would derive from RBOC entry into the in-region interLATA market. In the absence of the quarantine, an RBOC could compete in the same markets as its competitors. In short, the incumbent burdens that the quarantine creates further demonstrate that regulation is not a barrier to entry to the local exchange; rather the quarantine creates a competitive disadvantage for the RBOC in its home market.

THE LEVERAGE ARGUMENT

The third argument used to justify the quarantine on the RBOCs is that, if permitted entry into the manufacturing and interLATA markets, an RBOC could leverage its monopoly position in the local exchange to obtain an unfair competitive advantage over potential competitors in those markets. The leverage argument rests on the antitrust law concept of vertical restraints. A vertical restraint restricts a company's buyer or seller relationships with other companies. Antitrust plaintiffs may challenge a vertical restraint as an "exclusionary practice," which Judge Richard A. Posner has defined as occurring when a firm "trades a part of its monopoly profits, at least temporarily, for a large market share, by making it unprofitable for other sellers to compete with it."[83]

We examine now the application of the leverage argument to the local exchange carriers. As we demonstrate below, the leverage argument is generally flawed in any market. Because a monopolist can always extract

---

83. RICHARD A. POSNER, ANTITRUST LAW: AN ECONOMIC PERSPECTIVE 28 (University of Chicago Press 1976).

monopoly rents in the market that it controls, it cannot increase its rents by expanding into a second market. Furthermore, competition in the local exchange market eliminates the possibility that the LEC can exercise such leverage.

Leverage and the Local Exchange

In 1982 Judge Greene stated with regard to interLATA services, "The complexity of the telecommunications network would make it possible for [the RBOCs] to establish and maintain an access plan that would provide to their own interexchange service more favorable treatment than that granted to other carriers."[84] Similarly, with respect to the manufacture of telecommunications equipment, Judge Greene stated that "non-affiliated manufacturers would be disadvantaged in the sale of such equipment and the development of a competitive market would be frustrated."[85] Finally, with regard to information services, he stated, "The Operating Companies would . . . have the same incentives and the same ability to discriminate against competing information service providers that they would have with respect to competing interexchange carriers."[86]

The leverage argument has thus been applied to the RBOCs in two ways. First, it has been argued that the RBOC could use its monopoly to sell its own interLATA services or telecommunications equipment to itself or to its existing customers. Second, the argument asserts, the RBOC could use its control over its essential facilities, or local bottleneck, to extract monopoly rents by rationing its customers' access to equipment or interLATA services. Judge Greene stated in 1981 that "the local facilities controlled by Bell are 'essential facilities'" for long-distance carriers.[87] As we explain below, those two arguments are inconsistent with technological changes and industry developments.

Erosion of the Local Exchange Monopoly Eliminates
the Possibility of Leverage and Self-Dealing

The argument that an RBOC will use its monopoly in the local exchange to sell interLATA services and telecommunications equipment to its own

---

84. 552 F. Supp. at 188.
85. *Id.* at 190.
86. *Id.* at 189.
87. 524 F. Supp. at 1346.

customers in a manner that denies access to other firms is inconsistent with current industry conditions. As we have explained, the view that an incumbent LEC has a monopoly over the local exchange by virtue of natural monopoly technology is no longer valid. Moreover, the assertion that the LEC has a monopoly resulting from barriers to entry due to sunk costs or regulation is invalid. In addition, the presence of competition and the potential for substantial additional entry into the local exchange invalidate the notion of the existence of a monopoly in the local loop.

As Judge Greene noted in 1982 with regard to concerns over AT&T's market share in the market for interexchange services, low entry barriers and the "trend of increasing competition" imply a lack of market power.[88] One can now apply the same argument to the incumbent LECs, for the technology of the local exchange exhibits substantially reduced entry barriers, and there is a clear trend toward increased competition. The absence of either monopoly or the potential for monopoly in the local exchange implies that the "pivot" required to support leverage does not exist. The monopoly-leverage argument consequently fails.

In the case of interLATA services, customers have a choice of interexchange carriers, including AT&T, MCI, Sprint, and WorldCom. Moreover, customers have alternative means of accessing interexchange carriers through wireless or fiber-optic networks. Therefore, many customers can access long-distance providers without going through the local exchange. Those alternatives will continue to expand as the interexchange carriers themselves vertically integrate into the provision of local access. Furthermore, under equal-access regulations, the RBOC's interLATA services would have to compete on an equal footing with those of interexchange carriers that currently reach customers through the local exchange. The Telecommunications Act of 1996 requires an RBOC that has been permitted to originate in-region interLATA service through a separate affiliate to "charge the affiliate . . . , or impute to itself (if using the access for its provision of its own services), an amount for access to its telephone exchange service and exchange access that is no less than the amount charged to any unaffiliated interexchange carriers for such service."[89] Thus, the quarantine on the provision of interLATA services by RBOCs ignores the alternative forms of access that are available to consumers and the competitive parity that

88. 552 F. Supp. at 171.
89. 47 U.S.C. § 272(e)(3).

section 272's imputation requirement would impose on the RBOC's sale of access to interexchange carriers.

We have seen that, if it were allowed to enter the in-region interLATA market, an RBOC could not prevent its local exchange customers from gaining access to other interexchange carriers. As we later show, the argument that an RBOC could leverage its monopoly position to control its customers' access to telecommunications equipment is also inconsistent with current industry conditions. For our present purposes, we can classify equipment into customer premises equipment and telephone company switching and transmission equipment. With respect to either broad category, the monopoly-leverage argument has little or no basis. Although AT&T exercised control over customer premises equipment and telephone company purchases of switching and transmission equipment before the breakup, no one retains that type of control.

For equipment purchased by customers for use on their own premises—such as handsets, answering machines, fax machines, computers, inside wiring, and PBX—there is absolutely no basis for concluding that an RBOC can exercise any control at all on the choices of supplier. Customers buy such equipment in the marketplace. An RBOC has no more control over those purchases than does a broadcast television network over the brand of television set purchased by its viewers.[90]

The RBOCs' Networks Are
No Longer Essential Facilities

The essential facility argument outlined above was used to justify the quarantine on the RBOCs by implying that they would use their control of the local exchange to deny their customers access to other long-distance services, to require customers to purchase the RBOCs' own equipment, or to require customers to purchase the RBOCs' own information services. In 1987 Judge Greene called the local switches and circuits an "essential facility" and concluded that "the Regional

---

90. *See generally* Jerry A. Hausman, *Competition in Long-Distance and Telecommunications Markets: Effects of the MFJ*, 16 MANAGERIAL & DECISION ECON. 365 (1995); Franklin M. Fisher, Robert J. Larner, Michael Hunter & Amy Salsbury Serrano, *BOC Manufacture of Telecommunications Equipment: An Assessment of Benefits and Competitive Risks*, 16 MANAGERIAL & DECISION ECON. 439 (1995).

Companies have retained control of the local bottlenecks."[91] In 1995 he wrote that termination of the interLATA restrictions in the MFJ

> can only be accomplished when the conditions which gave rise to those restrictions no longer exist. Put most simply and bluntly, restrictions on long distance service by the Regional Companies can be completely eliminated only when these companies no longer have the capacity to exploit what has throughout this litigation been termed the "bottleneck."[92]

Judge Greene stated that his 1987 conclusions concerning essential facilities "still apply today, and the Court continues to be informed by their logic. The continued existence of bottlenecks remains the factual predicate for the interexchange restriction."[93] That factual predicate, however, was questionable even when made in the 1980s and surely was insupportable by the time Congress enacted the Telecommunications Act of 1996. The premise that an incumbent LEC could control the local exchange is inconsistent with regulatory and industry developments since the AT&T divestiture. Those developments imply that the local loop is no longer an essential facility, just as they imply that the incumbent LECs no longer qualify as natural monopolists or benefit from barriers to entry. The essential facilities argument for the quarantine is no longer valid for three reasons.

First, the local loop is not an essential facility because there are many alternatives to the existing local exchange network provided by the regulated incumbent LEC. The multiple technologies currently available for telecommunications transmission (including coaxial cable, fiber-optic cable, and wireless technologies such as cellular and microwave) are sufficient to establish the feasibility of constructing alternative transmission facilities to supplement, compete with, or even replace portions of the local exchange network provided by the incumbent LEC. The essential facilities argument implies that the incumbent LEC metaphorically owns and controls a bridge that crosses a river at the only feasible crossing point within some geographic area. To extend that analogy, the availability of multiple transmission technologies is sufficient to establish that there are many other ways to cross the river.

Second, the essential facilities argument is no longer valid because entry into the local loop has already occurred. The economic viability of

91. 673 F. Supp. at 540.
92. 890 F. Supp. at 4.
93. *Id.* at 5.

competitors that supply transmission services using coaxial cable, fiber optics, and wireless systems establishes that firms can economically construct alternative facilities. Thus, it is not only technically feasible to construct alternative facilities, but also economically feasible. For example, CAPs offer access to long-distance carriers on facilities that bypass the incumbent LEC's transport and switching facilities. By definition, facilities that have already been bypassed cannot still be considered "essential." Although the CAPs' fiber-optic systems are small in size compared with those of the incumbent LECs, the entry of CAPs has demonstrated the economic feasibility of bypassing portions of the local exchange. Similarly, the rapid growth of the cellular industry demonstrates the economic feasibility of other means of access. It would be myopic to point to the absolute size of an incumbent LEC's local loop plant as evidence that it is an essential facility.

Although the local loop is no longer an essential facility, regulations still exist guaranteeing access to the local exchange for long-distance carriers. The existence of those provisions also serves to invalidate the essential facilities argument with respect to in-region interLATA services: Even if the local exchange were to involve facilities that could not be duplicated, the equal-access provisions eliminate any advantage that an RBOC could otherwise gain by offering long-distance services.

In short, the essential facilities argument fails to apply because the local exchange is no longer an essential facility for access to the telecommunications network. An RBOC cannot leverage an essential facility that it does not possess.

THE CROSS-SUBSIDIZATION ARGUMENT

The fourth argument for the regulatory quarantine advances the proposition that an RBOC, if allowed to offer in-region interLATA service, would use profits from its local exchange services to cross-subsidize its provision of interLATA services. The argument suggests that the RBOC would thereby gain an unfair competitive advantage. We consider now the application of the cross-subsidization argument to the incumbent LECs. We show that the RBOCs do not have an incentive to cross-subsidize long-distance service or equipment manufacturing and that growing competition reduces the profits (if any) from the local exchange that could be used for cross-subsidies.

Cross-Subsidization
and the Local Exchange

In 1982 Judge Greene ruled that the RBOCs would employ cross-subsidization to foreclose competition in interexchange services, information services, and the manufacture of telecommunications equipment. The RBOCs, he wrote, would be able "to subsidize their interexchange prices with profits earned from their monopoly services" and "to subsidize the prices of their [information] services with revenues from the local exchange monopoly."[94] Moreover, they "would have an incentive to subsidize the prices of their equipment with the revenues from their monopoly services."[95] To justify the regulatory quarantine, Judge Greene thought it was necessary to determine whether the RBOCs have both "the incentive and opportunity to act anticompetitively."[96]

The RBOCs have lost any opportunity to cross-subsidize. Existing and potential competition in local telephony has significantly reduced the profits from the local exchange service that could be used to provide cross-subsidies to in-region interLATA services or equipment manufacturing. Judge Greene observed that "AT&T's opportunity for cross-subsidization will become increasingly curtailed as interexchange competition increases."[97] That same observation now applies to the situation of the RBOCs in the local exchange: Competition in the local loop has curtailed their opportunity for cross-subsidization. Moreover, the belief that an RBOC has the incentive to cross-subsidize predatorily is based on specious economic reasoning.

An RBOC Does Not
Have an Incentive to Subsidize
Activities outside the Local Exchange

The cross-subsidy argument relies on the notion that an RBOC has an incentive to subsidize its entry into other lines of business, particularly those from which the regulatory quarantine now bars it. In other words, for the cross-subsidy argument to apply, the RBOC would have to earn incremental revenues that are less than the incremental cost of providing other services; thus, the RBOC would have to incur an economic loss on

---

94. 552 F. Supp. at 188, 172.
95. *Id.* at 188–90.
96. *Id.* at 187.
97. *Id.* at 173.

those additional lines of business. Such an action would be inconsistent with profit maximization; an RBOC would not act that way because to do so would be inconsistent with the interests of its shareholders. That is not to say that other lines of business would not incur the normal initial losses that occur as firms establish new businesses. It is normal for investors to accept losses in the initial phases of establishing a new line of business. Moreover, a line of business may incur losses as a consequence of the normal market risks any business faces. It is, however, inconsistent with business objectives and economic analysis to expect that an RBOC would enter a market with the intention of incurring a loss, even if earnings in another part of its business subsidized that loss. The interests of the RBOC's owners would be to invest those earnings in a venture expected to be profitable. Therefore, the notion that an RBOC would obtain a competitive advantage through cross-subsidies is incorrect and at odds with the profit-making objectives of shareholder-owned companies. A business will not cross-subsidize a new business venture that it expects to be unprofitable.

Another assumption of the cross-subsidy argument is that an RBOC would use cross-subsidies to obtain a temporary competitive advantage over its rivals in other lines of business, with the objective of eliminating competitors. That view implies that the RBOC would engage in behavior resembling predatory pricing, which is said to occur when firms incur a loss with the intention of eliminating rivals and later raising prices to recoup earnings after the rivals have exited the market.[98] That argument has been discredited. Both scholars in law and economics and the Supreme Court generally agree that predatory pricing is unlikely to succeed because (1) there is little guarantee of successful recoupment, (2) rivals can also incur losses in anticipation of future profits, and (3) new entrants will appear if prices are raised after the existing competitors have exited the industry.[99] Moreover, it is difficult in practice to

---

98. *See, e.g.*, WILLIAM J. BAUMOL & J. GREGORY SIDAK, TOWARD COMPETITION IN LOCAL TELEPHONY 63 (MIT Press & AEI Press 1994); SPULBER, *supra* note 7, at 475–76.

99. Brooke Group Ltd. *v.* Brown & Williamson Tobacco Corp., 509 U.S. 209, 224–26 (1993); Matsushita Elec. Indus. Co. *v.* Zenith Radio Corp., 475 U.S. 574, 589 (1986); ROBERT H. BORK, THE ANTITRUST PARADOX: A POLICY AT WAR WITH ITSELF 144–59 (Free Press, rev. ed. 1993) (Basic Books 1978); YALE BROZEN, CONCENTRATION, MERGERS, AND PUBLIC POLICY 163, 392 (Macmillan Publishing Co. 1982); POSNER, ANTITRUST LAW, *supra* note 83, at 184–96; Phillip Areeda & Donald F. Turner, *Predatory Pricing and Related Practices Under Section 2 of the Sherman Act*, 88 HARV. L. REV. 699, 718 (1975); J. Gregory Sidak, *Debunking Predatory*

distinguish low competitive prices from predatory prices and to distinguish low earnings from predatory losses.[100]

The scenario of cross-subsidization and predatory pricing grows increasingly implausible when one considers that the interLATA and equipment markets that the RBOC would enter have multiple incumbent suppliers with substantial capacity. In the interLATA market, particularly, any attempt by an RBOC at predatory pricing would be futile because AT&T, MCI, Sprint, and WorldCom all have substantial capacity. Furthermore, the durability and expanding transmission capacity of fiber-optic cable would make it impossible for an RBOC to restrict industry output and raise prices above incremental costs during the recoupment phase of the predation scenario. Even in the unlikely event that an RBOC could drive one of the four large interexchange carriers into bankruptcy, the fiber-optic transmission capacity of that carrier would remain intact, ready for another firm to buy the capacity at a distress sale and immediately undercut the RBOC's noncompetitive prices. In 1996 the FCC, citing a passage from an earlier article from which this chapter is adapted, embraced that reasoning with respect to newly enacted section 272:

> [E]ven if a BOC is able to allocate improperly the costs of its affiliate's interLATA services, it is questionable whether a BOC affiliate could successfully engage in predation. At least three interexchange carriers—AT&T, MCI, and Sprint—have nationwide or near-nationwide network facilities. These are large well-established companies with customers throughout the nation. It may be unlikely, therefore, that a BOC affiliate, whose customers presumably would be concentrated in one geographic region, could drive one or more of these companies from the market. Even if it could do so, there is a question whether the BOC affiliate would later be able to raise prices in order to recoup lost revenues.[101]

That assessment is in accord with the conclusion of many other regulatory economists.[102] In short, an RBOC engaging in predatory

Innovation, 83 COLUM. L. REV. 1121 (1983); Frank H. Easterbrook, *Predatory Strategies and Counterstrategies*, 48 U. CHI. L. REV. 263 (1981).

100. BORK, *supra* note 99, at 144–55.

101. Implementation of the Non-Accounting Safeguards of Sections 271 and 272 of the Communications Act of 1934, as Amended; and Regulatory Treatment of LEC Provision of Interexchange Services Originating in the LEC's Local Exchange Area, Notice of Proposed Rulemaking, CC Dkt. No. 96-149, 11 F.C.C. Rcd. 18,877, 18,943 ¶ 137 (1996) (citing Daniel F. Spulber, *Deregulating Telecommunications*, 12 YALE J. ON REG. 25, 60 (1995); other citations omitted).

102. *E.g.*, MACAVOY, *supra* note 5, at 186–90; Susan Gates, Paul Milgrom &

pricing in the interLATA market could not expect to recoup its investment in sales made below incremental cost.

Even if one were to accept the predatory pricing argument, the connection made to the possibility of cross-subsidization is fundamentally flawed. If, indeed, an RBOC believed that it could enter a line of business profitably by initially incurring losses and then eliminating rivals and recouping profits, it could certainly do so by raising the requisite funds from investors. Through the normal functioning of the capital markets, investors will fund a business that is anticipated to be profitable, and cross-subsidies from one line of business to another are not needed. The view that an RBOC would cross-subsidize what would otherwise be a profitable business venture is therefore incorrect, because it ignores the willingness of investors to fund the venture and thereby share in its returns.

Competition in the Local Exchange
Has Reduced the Profits with Which the
RBOC Could Cross-Subsidize Other Businesses

We have shown that there is no economic incentive for an RBOC to cross-subsidize entry into other lines of business, whether or not the other businesses are expected to be profitable. Even if one were to believe that such incentives existed, any concerns should be allayed by the growing competition in the local loop. Leland L. Johnson, who has argued that the LECs might cross-subsidize their provision of video services, has nonetheless observed that "evolving market pressures are reducing the ability of LECs to cross-subsidize."[103] "The threat of cross-subsidization," he argued, "is constrained because the pool of potential LEC monopoly revenues available to absorb cost shifting is shrinking."[104] That reasoning will apply even more conclusively by the time that interactive broadband networks become operational. "The threat of

---

John Roberts, *Deterring Predation in Telecommunications: Are Line-of-Business Restraints Needed?*, 16 MANAGERIAL & DECISION ECON. 427 (1995); Paul S. Brandon & Richard L. Schmalensee, *The Benefits of Releasing the Bell Companies from the Interexchange Restrictions*, 16 MANAGERIAL & DECISION ECON. 349 (1995); Hausman, *supra* note 90; Kenneth J. Arrow, Dennis W. Carlton & Hal S. Sider, *The Competitive Effects of Line-of-Business Restrictions in Telecommunications*, 16 MANAGERIAL & DECISION ECON. 301 (1995).

103. LELAND L. JOHNSON, TOWARD COMPETITION IN CABLE TELEVISION 80 (MIT Press & AEI Press 1994).

104. *Id.*

cross-subsidy is less today than previously," Johnson concluded in 1994, "and it will continue to diminish."[105]

The significant level of competition in the local loop reduces or eliminates the RBOC's economic profits that could be diverted to other activities. That does not mean that the RBOCs are not currently profitable. The accounting profits earned by the RBOCs may include a return to their shareholders for the cost of capital. Rather, the RBOCs' economic profits, which represent earnings above the cost of capital and other costs, are controlled by the actions of actual and potential competitors. Furthermore, the RBOCs face regulatory controls on prices or rates of return that further limit their profits.

The presence of competition in local telecommunications markets, moreover, eventually will eliminate any cross-subsidies that governmental authorities have built into the existing regulated rate structure, such as the subsidization of residential customers by business customers.[106] If competitors are as efficient as the RBOC, then the RBOC cannot set the price for any service at a level above the stand-alone cost of providing that service. If an RBOC attempted to do so, a competitor could profitably enter that market and provide the service on a stand-alone basis or in conjunction with other services. If the competitor is more efficient than the RBOC, which is certainly possible given the rapid pace of technological advances in telecommunications, the RBOC cannot price its services at or above the efficient stand-alone cost.

The RBOCs Are Unlikely to Use
Other Lines of Business to Shelter Income

Another variant of the cross-subsidy argument asserts that if the quarantine were lifted, an RBOC would use cross-subsidies to shelter income from the regulated local loop by transferring it to its unregulated equipment business by setting above-market transfer prices for its self-manufactured equipment. In states in which the RBOC is regulated by price caps or other incentive-based regulations, there is no incentive for such income transfers to take place, as the RBOC's earnings are not controlled. In states that still use rate-of-return regulation, various controls

---

105. *Id.* at 81.

106. On the elimination of cross-subsidies by competition in contestable markets, see WILLIAM J. BAUMOL, JOHN C. PANZAR & ROBERT D. WILLIG, CONTESTABLE MARKETS AND THE THEORY OF INDUSTRY STRUCTURE 202 (Harcourt Brace Jovanovich, rev. ed. 1988).

can prevent such income transfers. States that have not yet done so could adopt incentive-based regulations. In addition, the states could apply equal-access and competitive-bidding regulations—for example, mandating that the RBOC obtain competitive bids for equipment, thereby forcing it to bid against other equipment suppliers.

Owing to the minimum efficient scale of manufacturing such sophisticated telecommunications equipment as central office switches, an RBOC is unlikely to find it profitable to produce only enough equipment to satisfy its own needs. The RBOC's need to sell equipment to unaffiliated third parties would therefore provide regulators an objective measure of the competitive price for such equipment. In states with rate-of-return regulation, regulators could readily observe whether the RBOC's internal transfer price for the same equipment exceeded the market price. Regulators could also observe the competing prices of other manufacturers as further evidence of the market value of such equipment.

Finally, an RBOC cannot use income transfers to shelter income, because such transfers would raise the costs of providing local exchange services above competitive levels. The RBOC would then lose customers to existing and potential competitors in the local loop. Active competition in the local loop requires an RBOC to control its costs, which would be inconsistent with above-market transfer prices for equipment and other services.

CONCLUSION

Entry of the RBOCs into the provision of interLATA services would enhance competition in those markets. The quarantine is a regulatory barrier to entry that protects existing firms in the interLATA and equipment markets. Thus, for the RBOCs the quarantine is an incumbent burden that not only restricts the competitiveness of the RBOCs in the local loop, but also affords new entrants in that market the opportunity to exploit a broader range of technologies in their service offerings and design of local networks.

Allowing the RBOCs to enter the in-region interLATA market would enhance economic efficiency in at least four ways. First, there are likely to be efficiency gains from the joint provision of access and interexchange services that arise from the use of common inputs, such as switching facilities. AT&T's acquisition of McCaw Cellular, as well as MCI's intention to integrate into the local telecommunications market, imply that the companies expect such efficiency gains to be substantial.

Such gains from vertical integration are called *economies of sequence.*[107] The RBOCs' entry into the in-region interLATA market would allow them to exploit any potential economies of sequence between either local exchange and interLATA services or between intraLATA toll and interLATA services. To deny the RBOCs entry into the in-region interLATA market would be to deny consumers the savings from the cost efficiencies that such a combination would entail.

Second, to the extent that joint production yields economies of sequence, effective competition against vertically integrated firms in interexchange services, primarily AT&T-McCaw and MCI, may require a rival to be similarly vertically integrated.[108] If the quarantine were eliminated, an RBOC not only could pursue alliances and resale arrangements with other carriers in the interLATA market, but also could extend its existing network for intraLATA toll services to provide interLATA service within its region. Such an extension would enhance competition in interexchange services.

Third, the RBOCs bring considerable technical and business expertise to the provision of interexchange services, which should serve to enhance efficiency in the interLATA segment of the market. The RBOCs possess technical and managerial experience in operating large telecommunications networks. In particular, with more than three times the fiber miles of the interexchange carriers, the RBOCs have technological expertise in fiber-optic transmission, which is the backbone of the interexchange system.[109]

Fourth, if the RBOCs were allowed to offer interLATA services, those that chose to do so would be able to apply their technological experience to research and development. The RBOCs bring experience in switching, providing access to long-distance services, and operating telecommunications networks. Each of those skills can be applied to innovation in interexchange services. Because access, switching, and transmission technologies continue to evolve, multiple research approaches are desirable. Continuing to forbid the RBOCs to provide interLATA services would therefore deny consumers the full dynamic efficiencies that result from rivalry in technological innovation.

107. SPULBER, *supra* note 7, at 118–20.

108. *See* Armen A. Alchian, *Vertical Integration and Regulation in the Telephone Industry*, 16 MANAGERIAL & DECISION ECON. 323 (1995).

109. In 1995 the RBOCs had 9,414,413 fiber miles, as compared with 2,773,300 fiber miles for all interexchange carriers. 1995 FIBER DEPLOYMENT UPDATE, *supra* note 79, tables 2, 6.

In short, continuing to bar the RBOCs' entry into in-region interLATA services would impede the achievement of cost efficiencies, reduce the dynamic efficiencies from innovation, and deprive consumers of the benefits of increased competition. Clearly, it is in the public interest for the FCC, acting in conjunction with the state PUCs and the Department of Justice, to administer section 271 in a way that lifts that regulatory quarantine as quickly as possible. The interexchange market is substantial—approximately the size of the local exchange market. The market's size alone is sufficient to emphasize the public interest in opening the market to formidable competitors possessing highly specialized technological expertise. Increased domestic competition will create efficient and innovative companies. We can expect that development to enhance the competitive position of American companies in the large international telecommunications market.

Long-distance telecommunications services are also closely related to the development of technology for the access, transmission, and switching facilities required for the so-called information superhighway. We expect those interconnecting telecommunications networks to improve the productivity and competitiveness of American industry and to provide a variety of consumer benefits. Continuing to bar the RBOCs from entering the interLATA market, however, could reduce the industry's speed and effectiveness in creating those superhighways.

There is no economic basis for continuing to forbid the RBOCs from providing interLATA services. The main arguments in support of the quarantine no longer apply to local exchange telecommunications. First, as a consequence of technological change and the transformation of the telecommunications industry, an RBOC's technology in the local exchange no longer exhibits the natural monopoly property. Second, as a result of technological change and industry transformation, the RBOCs no longer benefit from any significant entry barriers. Third, an RBOC could not unfairly leverage its market position in the local exchange into other markets. Fourth, an RBOC could not employ cross-subsidies from local service to achieve competitive advantages when entering other lines of business.

At the same time, the quarantine reduces competition and deters innovation. As entrants in the in-region interLATA market, the RBOCs would likely be able to exploit economies of scope and sequence. The result would be an improvement in consumer welfare through lower costs and more vigorous competition in those markets. In a dynamic sense, such entry by the RBOCs would further benefit consumers by enabling the RBOCs to apply their specialized knowledge to the research and development of a broader spectrum of telecommunications products and services.

It is open to question whether the MFJ's line-of-business restrictions benefited consumer welfare when they took effect on January 1, 1984. Today those restrictions, reincarnated in the checklist, most assuredly do not. The quarantine sacrifices competition, efficiency, and innovation while attempting to prohibit conduct that is already prevented by economic forces and punishable by existing antitrust law. The regulatory quarantine, as embodied in the checklist, has more potential to harm consumers than to benefit them. Regulators and the courts should apply and construe those unfortunate provisions accordingly.

4

The Regulatory Contract

STATE PUBLIC UTILITY regulation of electric power generation, transmission, and distribution and of local telephony represents a contract between the state and the regulated company. The economic functions of the regulatory contract, as well as the legal duties and remedies associated with it, are identical to those of a contract between private parties.

ECONOMIC FOUNDATIONS OF
THE REGULATORY CONTRACT

Consumers and businesses voluntarily participate in a market transaction only if they receive *gains from trade*—that is, only if the transaction yields positive net benefits for them. A supplier will not invest in a transaction unless he expects the returns from the transaction to cover all economic costs, including a competitive return to invested capital. That principle is summarized in Armen A. Alchian's classic definition of cost: "In economics, the cost of an event is the highest-valued opportunity *necessarily* forsaken."[1] The supplier's costs of investing in the transaction include the highest net benefit of all opportunities forgone, known as *opportunity cost*.

---

1. Armen A. Alchian, *Cost, in* 3 INTERNATIONAL ENCYCLOPEDIA OF THE SOCIAL SCIENCES 404, 404 (David L. Sills ed., MacMillan Co. & Free Press 1968). We have added emphasis to the word *necessarily* at the request of Professor Alchian, who informed us in private correspondence that he intended the word to be italicized in the original.

Cost Recovery for
Transaction-Specific Investment

Cost recovery is an essential element of contract law. A contract must provide *consideration* to each of the parties, which implies that those incurring costs must expect to recover those costs, including a return to invested capital. Victor P. Goldberg, for example, has noted of contracts generally:

> Suppose that one party has to make a considerable initial investment and that the value of the investment depends on the continuation of the relationship. An employee investing in firm-specific capital is one example; a second would be an electric utility building a plant to serve a particular area. Both will be reluctant to incur the high initial costs without some assurance of subsequent rewards. Other things equal, the firmer that assurance, the more attractive the investment. So, for example, if the utility customers agree to give it the exclusive right to serve them for twenty years, then the utility would find construction of a long-lived plant more attractive than if it did not have such assurance. Of course, if a new, superior technology were likely to appear within three years, the customers would not want the long-lived plant built. Nevertheless, there will be lots of instances in which the parties will find it efficacious to protect one party's reliance on the continuation of the relationship.[2]

Cost recovery is an essential aspect of utility regulation as well.[3] Utilities would not have undertaken the extensive investments required to provide regulated service within their franchise region without the opportunity to recover their costs. In a manner similar to Goldberg's, one of us has specifically written about the public utility's recovery of transaction-specific investments under the regulatory contract:

> The regulatory contract is often justified as a means of mitigating the risks of making large irreversible investments that are faced by regulated utilities. Customers of utilities gain from such commitments, since efficient levels of investment yield lower costs of service. There is an

---

2. Victor P. Goldberg, *Relational Exchange: Economics and Complex Contracts*, 23 AM. BEHAVIORAL SCIENTIST 337, 340 (1980), *reprinted in* READINGS IN CONTRACT LAW 16, 18 (Victor P. Goldberg ed., Cambridge University Press 1989); *see also* Victor P. Goldberg, *Regulation and Administered Contracts*, 7 BELL J. ECON. 426 (1976).

3. *See* JEAN-JACQUES LAFFONT & JEAN TIROLE, A THEORY OF INCENTIVES IN PROCUREMENT AND REGULATION 53–127 (MIT Press 1993).

incentive to honor commitments regarding compensatory rates of return to assure that regulated firms will undertake future investment and that they will maintain their existing capital equipment. In practice, honoring commitments to investors in regulated utilities keeps down future borrowing costs by reducing investor risk.[4]

The President's Council of Economic Advisers endorsed that economic reasoning in its 1996 report:

[T]here is an important difference between regulated and unregulated markets. Unregulated firms bear the risk of stranded costs but are entitled to high profits if things go unexpectedly well. In contrast, utilities have been limited to regulated rates, intended to yield no more than a fair return on their investments. If competition were unexpectedly allowed, utilities would be exposed to low returns without having had the chance to reap the full expected returns in good times, *thus denying them the return promised to induce the initial investment.* A strong case therefore can be made for allowing utilities to recover stranded costs where those costs arise from after-the-fact mistakes or changes in regulatory philosophy toward competition, as long as the investments were initially authorized by regulators.[5]

The same logic underlies the observation by the Supreme Court of Texas in 1994 that the state's public utility act

balances the important objective of protecting consumers from monopoly power with the need for financial stability which is required to attract the large amounts of investment capital essential to dependable utility service. When balancing the interests of consumers and utilities, the financial integrity of the utility weighs in favor of both sides. If the

---

4. DANIEL F. SPULBER, REGULATION AND MARKETS 610 (MIT Press 1989). For similar analyses in the tradition of Goldberg, see Paul L. Joskow & Richard Schmalensee, *Incentive Regulation for Electric Utilities*, 4 YALE J. ON REG. 1, 8–12 (1986); Dennis L. Weisman, *Default Capacity Tariffs: Smoothing the Transitional Regulatory Asymmetries in the Telecommunications Market*, 5 YALE J. ON REG. 149, 157–61 (1988); Glenn Blackmon & Richard Zeckhauser, *Fragile Commitments and the Regulatory Process*, 9 YALE J. ON REG. 73, 76–78 (1992).

5. 1996 ECONOMIC REPORT OF THE PRESIDENT 187 (Government Printing Office 1996) (emphasis added); *see also* 1997 ECONOMIC REPORT OF THE PRESIDENT 204–05, 207 (Government Printing Office 1997). In 1997 the Antitrust Division of the Department of Justice endorsed the proposition that "stranded costs . . . be assessed on a competitively neutral basis." Hearings before the House Comm. on the Judiciary, 105th Cong., 1st Sess. (June 4, 1997) (testimony of A. Douglas Melamed, Principal Deputy Assistant Attorney General, Antitrust Division, U.S. Department of Justice).

utility is forced to pay higher costs of capitalization, the increased costs will eventually be borne by the consumer.[6]

Cost-of-service regulation of public utilities is based on allowing a utility the opportunity to recover its investment, including a competitive rate of return.[7] Utilities have had to undertake substantial investments to discharge their obligation to serve. The purpose of a regulatory contract is to provide for recovery of "economic costs," by which we mean the full cost of an activity, including direct expenditures, the time cost of money expended for capital investment, and any other opportunity costs. As mentioned earlier, an opportunity cost of an activity is the net benefit forgone from the best alternative activity. The time cost of money is an opportunity cost of an investment because it represents the highest return that the investor could have earned by investing the money elsewhere.

The expectation that a utility will be able to recover its costs applies as well to new expenditures that the utility makes to satisfy regulatory obligations, even if the industry is partially or fully deregulated. The utility cannot be asked to provide services in the competitive market at regulated prices that are noncompensatory—that is, at prices that do not allow for full cost recovery, particularly when the firm is mandated to offer unbundled services. Moreover, deregulation of the local telephone exchange, or mandatory unbundling of electricity generation and transmission, does not eliminate the responsibilities of regulatory authorities to allow the incumbent utility the reasonable opportunity to recover costs *already incurred* to satisfy the utility's obligation to serve. Regulators have a continuing responsibility to allow the utility the opportunity to recover those costs.

Opportunism and Asset Specificity

Oliver E. Williamson defines *opportunism* as "self-interest seeking with guile"[8] and describes utility regulation as a "highly incomplete

---

6. Texas *v.* Public Utility Comm'n of Tex., 883 S.W.2d 190, 202 (1994) (citations omitted).

7. Jean-Jacques Laffont and Jean Tirole observe, "In the absence of a detailed long-term contract, the regulated firm may refrain from investing in the fear that once the investment is in place, the regulator would pay only for variable cost and would not allow the firm to recoup its sunk cost." LAFFONT & TIROLE, *supra* note 3, at 54.

8. OLIVER E. WILLIAMSON, MARKETS AND HIERARCHIES: ANALYSIS AND ANTITRUST IMPLICATIONS 26 (Free Press 1975); OLIVER E. WILLIAMSON, THE ECONOMIC INSTITUTIONS OF CAPITALISM: FIRMS, MARKETS, RELATIONAL CONTRACTING 47 (Free

form of long-term contracting" in which the terms are adapted to "changing circumstances" to ensure the supplier of a fair rate of return.[9] Simply auctioning franchises in the manner that Harold Demsetz proposed[10] creates difficulties, Williamson argues, because parties to the franchise agreement could behave opportunistically and renege on their contractual promises. He emphasizes the possibility that cable television operators would bid low on the franchise and later raise prices to take advantage of the regulator's sunk costs of searching for a franchise operator.[11] Conversely, empirical evidence indicates that cities awarding cable franchises may take advantage of the cable operator's irreversible investment in transmission facilities.[12]

The problem of regulatory opportunism stems from the fact that regulatory assets, including expenditures for plant and equipment and capitalized outlays to perform duties mandated by regulators, are likely to be transaction-specific. That is, the assets have little value outside the regulatory transaction. Although they used different terminology, scholars on regulation have recognized the problem of asset specificity since the early part of the twentieth century. In 1934 John Bauer wrote of investment by public utilities: "Capital is largely embodied in fixed structures which are useless except for their special purposes."[13] Many years later, Paul Milgrom and John Roberts defined an asset's degree of specificity to be "the fraction of [the asset's] value that would be lost if it were excluded from its major use."[14] Applying the Milgrom-Roberts measure to Bauer's assessment of public utility investment would imply 100 percent asset specificity. Even if public utility investment were not quite so specific, it is easy to understand why Williamson has observed that "asset specificity is the big locomotive to which transaction cost economics owes much of its predictive content."[15] He

Press 1985).

9. Oliver E. Williamson, *Franchise Bidding for Natural Monopolies—in General and with Respect to CATV*, 7 BELL J. ECON. 73, 91 (1976) [hereinafter *Franchise Bidding*].

10. Harold Demsetz, *Why Regulate Utilities?*, 11 J.L. & ECON. 55 (1968).

11. Williamson, *Franchise Bidding, supra* note 9, at 92.

12. *See* Mark A. Zupan, *Cable Franchise Renewals: Do Incumbent Firms Behave Opportunistically?*, 20 RAND J. ECON. 473 (1989).

13. John Bauer, *Public Utilities: United States and Canada, in* 12 ENCYCLOPAEDIA OF THE SOCIAL SCIENCES 677, 680 (Edwin R. A. Seligman & Alvin Johnson eds., Macmillan Co. 1934).

14. PAUL MILGROM & JOHN ROBERTS, ECONOMICS, ORGANIZATION AND MANAGEMENT 307 (Prentice Hall 1992).

15. WILLIAMSON, THE ECONOMIC INSTITUTIONS OF CAPITALISM, *supra* note 8, at 56.

notes that markets that are contestable are those without asset specificity, so that "contestability theory and transaction cost economics are looking at the same phenomenon—the condition of asset specificity—through the opposite ends of the telescope."[16]

Technological changes that affect the degree of asset specificity are facilitating the transition from regulation to competition being observed in markets traditionally served by public utilities. The regulatory contract that was suited to an industry with significant asset specificity is not suited to an industry in which asset specificity has declined considerably. The problem of incompatibility between the degree of asset specificity and the regulatory regime arises in the transition to competition: Incumbent utilities have not yet recovered the costs of their assets that are specific to a regulated market, and entrants meanwhile can invest in facilities that have considerably less asset specificity (wireless telecommunications, for example) or can provide service with minimal investment (resale of incumbent telecommunications services, for example).

It would breach the regulatory contract for the regulator to make unilateral changes in regulation that might prevent a utility from recovering the economic costs of investments that it made to discharge its regulatory obligations to serve. Contractual protections of the interests of the utility and its investors exist so that the state and private companies can continue to make agreements requiring investments in highly specialized capital. Analogously, Paul Joskow has studied the nature of the long-term contracts by which coal mines supply electric utilities with coal.[17] He found that, because that contractual relationship entails durable transaction-specific investments by both parties, the supply contracts have detailed price-escalation clauses to reflect changes in the cost of supplying coal. Rather than set specific prices, the contracts establish the framework for determining how price adjustments should be made in the event that circumstances change in a way that the parties could not have foreseen when entering into the contract. Just as the institution of contract law reduces the cost of forming private agreements that entail transaction-specific investments, so agreements be-

---

16. *Id.* at 56 n.14.

17. Paul L. Joskow, *Vertical Integration and Long-Term Contracts: The Case of Coal-Burning Electric Generating Plants*, 1 J.L. ECON. & ORG. 33 (1980); Paul L. Joskow, *Contract Duration and Durable Transaction-Specific Investments: The Case of Coal*, 77 AM. ECON. REV. 168 (1987); Paul L. Joskow, *Asset Specificity and the Structure of Vertical Relationships: Empirical Evidence*, 4 J.L. ECON. & ORG. 95 (1988).

tween the state and private companies depend on analogous contractual protections to reduce and allocate the risk of cost recovery for specialized assets that cannot be salvaged if the contract is not performed.

As with private contracts, the regulatory contract is designed to address "holdup" problems. By incurring substantial capital expenditures to perform its obligation to serve, the utility is vulnerable to confiscation.[18] In the absence of contract enforcement, the utility is at the mercy of the regulatory authority: By lowering rates to levels that do not allow a full recovery of costs, after the facilities have been created, a regulator could take advantage of the utility and its investors. A company supplying telecommunications or electricity services can raise or lower its posted prices without incurring more than the costs of communicating the new tariffs to customers. The regulated rates are thus much more flexible than are the utility's capital facilities in contrast since those are irreversible, market-specific investments. To the extent that they were tailored to meet regulatory obligations to serve, the utility's investments need not be fully recovered in a competitive market setting. That means that the regulatory contract is necessary to protect the regulated utility from regulatory "holdup."

The opening of the telecommunications or electricity markets to competition provides a temptation for regulators to behave in an opportunistic manner. The utilities have already constructed their network facilities. They will keep those facilities in operation as long as revenues cover their operating costs, even if revenues are not sufficient to allow even partial recovery of capital costs.

"Core" customers are those customers of the regulated utility who have limited opportunities to switch to competitive suppliers, while "noncore" customers are better able to seek alternatives. Noncore customers can take advantage of common carrier regulations by relying on the incumbent utility as a backup service or carrier of last resort. Typically, core customers are residential and small business customers, while noncore customers are large commercial and industrial customers. Core customers thus often bear a greater share of overhead costs when deregulation leads to selective entry and bypass of the incumbent utility. With continued regulation of the utility's core markets, some of

18. For a similar argument, see Timothy J. Brennan & James Boyd, Political Economy and the Efficiency of Compensation for Takings, Resources for the Future Discussion Paper 95-28, at 25 (June 1995) ("there is the possibility of regulatory moral hazard . . . when the government can act opportunistically to capture the benefits of private investment through changes in regulatory policy").

those costs would be shifted to remaining core customers while others would represent losses for utility investors. Thus, some putative benefits of competition are merely an income transfer from the utility's investors and core customers to noncore customers, rather than a gain due entirely to enhanced productivity. Some rate rebalancing is desirable to eliminate cross-subsidization from regulated rate structures. Deregulation should not, however, be used as a means to achieve gains for some customers by imposing losses on utility investors or core customers.

Credible Commitments

Economic theory widely recognizes that commitments made in bargaining situations influence the behavior of other actors only to the extent that the person making such commitments is credibly bound (by himself or others) to honoring them.[19] The notion of enforceable agreements plays a similar role in regulated industries as it does in competitive markets. As Pablo T. Spiller and others have shown both theoretically and empirically, the level of investment in long-lived infrastructure undertaken by a regulated (or recently privatized) public utility depends critically on regulatory institutions' having been designed to ensure the credibility of the regulator's commitments that it will not act opportunistically once the utility has placed those nonsalvageable assets into service.[20] The President's Council of Economic Advisers has made the same argument concerning recovery of stranded costs:

> [R]ecovery should be allowed for legitimate stranded costs. The equity reason for doing so is clear, but there is also a strong efficiency reason for honoring regulators' promises. Credible government is key to a successful market economy, because it is so important for encouraging long-term investments. Although policy reforms inevitably impose

---

19. *See, e.g.*, MILGROM & ROBERTS, *supra* note 14, at 131; OLIVER E. WILLIAMSON, THE MECHANISMS OF GOVERNANCE 120–44 (Oxford University Press 1996); WILLIAMSON, THE ECONOMIC INSTITUTIONS OF CAPITALISM, *supra* note 8, at 167; THOMAS C. SCHELLING, THE STRATEGY OF CONFLICT (Oxford University Press 1960).

20. Pablo T. Spiller, *Institutions and Regulatory Commitment in Utilities' Privatizations*, 2 INDUS. & CORP. CHANGE 387 (1993); Brian Levy & Pablo T. Spiller, *The Institutional Foundations of Regulatory Commitment: A Comparative Analysis of Five Country Studies of Telecommunications Regulation*, 10 J.L. ECON. & ORG. 201 (1994); Shane Greenstein, Susan McMaster & Pablo T. Spiller, *The Effect of Incentive Regulation on Infrastructure Modernization: Local Exchange Companies' Deployment of Digital Technology*, 4 J. ECON. & MGMT. STRATEGY 187 (1995).

losses on some holders of existing assets, good policy tries to mitigate
such losses for investments made based on earlier rules.[21]

The utility's investors would not be willing to commit vast amounts of
capital to carry out an obligation to serve unless the regulator's offer of
an opportunity to earn a fair rate of return were credible. Regulated
utilities relied upon those contractual assurances in planning and carrying out their investment and service plans. Conversely, the regulator
would not be willing to provide a franchise protected by entry regulation and to authorize the utility's pricing and investment plans unless
the utility's promises to provide services were credible. The legal and
public policy context in which the regulatory process operates provides
guarantees to the parties to the regulatory contract.

As with private contracts, the regulatory contract must involve
consideration, for the agreement is voluntary. The first utilities did not
spring into existence as a result of some government conscription of
private capital. The regulated utility submits to various regulatory restrictions including price regulations, quality-of-service requirements,
and common carrier regulations. In return, the regulated firm receives
a protected franchise in its service territory, and its investors are allowed an opportunity to earn revenues subject to a rate-of-return constraint. Without the expectation of earning a competitive rate of return,
investors would not be willing to commit funds for establishing and
operating the utility. The funds are committed to provide services to
the customers of the regulated utility. Once the utility invests those
funds, the long depreciation schedules typical in electricity and telecommunications regulation credibly commit the utility to performing its
obligations under the regulatory contract by denying it the opportunity
to recover its capital before the end of its useful life.

Relational Contracting

A question sometimes asked of expert witnesses in regulatory proceedings is, "Where, Professor *X*, is this regulatory contract to which your
testimony refers?" That question is akin to asking an Englishman to
produce a copy of his constitution. The regulatory contract is a bundle
of public utility statutes, utility commission precedents, adjudicatory
decisions, rulemakings, hearings on the record, formal notices of pro-

---

21. 1996 ECONOMIC REPORT OF THE PRESIDENT 187 (Government Printing Office 1996).

posed rulemaking, and public commentary. Such reasoning is neither novel nor inherently economic, for it is the same logic that propels the Supreme Court's analysis of state legislation that has given rise to a contractual obligation:

> In general, a statute is itself treated as a contract when the language and circumstances evince a legislative intent to create private rights of a contractual nature enforceable against the State. In addition, statutes governing the interpretation and enforcement of contracts may be regarded as forming part of the obligation of contracts made under their aegis.[22]

Although the original franchise agreement between the public utility and a municipality is usually the critical first document in the bundle of agreements concerning the relationship between the state and the utility, no single document is likely to encapsulate the entire regulatory contract. The relational contract between the utility and the regulated firm is analogous to a corporation, which is an easily identified entity but consists of multiple contracts that define the firm. The corporation is often said to be a "nexus of contracts" between the firm and its investors, employees, suppliers, and customers.[23] Although there may be articles of incorporation, a single document cannot unify the contracts that compose the firm.

Victor P. Goldberg provides an important early characterization of the regulatory contract. He observes that private contracts involve both a *continuing relationship* that uses "rough formulae or mutual agreement to adjust the contract to current situations" and *agency*, which occurs when a firm deals with many customers who "find it desirable to act collectively through an agent both to negotiate the terms and to administer the contract over time."[24] Goldberg asserts that "[r]egulation can be viewed as an implicit administered contract in which both elements are significant."[25]

---

22. United States Trust Co. *v.* New Jersey, 431 U.S. 1, 17 n.14 (1977).

23. *E.g.*, FRANK H. EASTERBROOK & DANIEL R. FISCHEL, THE ECONOMIC STRUCTURE OF CORPORATE LAW 8–12 (Harvard University Press 1991); ROBERTA ROMANO, THE GENIUS OF AMERICAN CORPORATE LAW (AEI Press 1993).

24. Goldberg, *Regulation and Administered Contracts*, *supra* note 2, at 428, 429.

25. *Id.* at 427. For a survey of the subsequent literature building on Goldberg's analysis, see Keith J. Crocker & Scott E. Masten, *Regulation and Administered Contracts Revisited: Lessons from Transaction-Cost Economics for Public Utility Regulation*, 9 J. REG. ECON. 5 (1996). One indicator of the degree to which Goldberg and Williamson revolutionized scholarship on public utility regulation is that, of the various rationales

Even if there were no explicit documentation of the relationship between the regulator and the firm, the regulatory contract would still represent an unambiguous meeting of the minds. All the arguments concerning the economic function of the legal requirements of a contract between private parties apply with equal, if not greater, force to the regulatory contract between the state (or federal regulator) and the regulated firm. Thus, the state (or federal regulator) cannot credibly assert that it owes no remedy to the incumbent when it breaches the regulatory contract while adopting policies that promote competitive entry.

As with private contracts, the regulatory contract has both express and implied provisions. The franchise award, orders approving rates, and orders approving capital expenditures are clearly formal written agreements. Including capital expenditures in the regulated rate base is certainly a formal contractual agreement. The regulatory contract also has implied features. The utility undertakes capital expenditures of some extended economic lifetime in anticipation of cost recovery. Regulatory approval of such capital expenditures implies that there will not be fundamental changes in the regulator's approach to the company's market environment during the economic lifetime of those investments without addressing the issue of compensating investors.

Transactions usually do not involve simultaneous performance, as with a simple exchange. Contracts are necessary to address the problems that may arise with the passage of time. Generally, there is a delay between the time the contract is entered into and the time that performance is completed. In the interim, foreseen and unforeseen changes in the circumstances of the parties may arise. The contract is designed to adjust the terms of the transaction to handle contingencies.

Just as vertical integration is a transaction-cost-reducing substitute for complete contingent-claim contracting, so also is the administrative process surrounding the regulatory contract. The implicit terms, fleshed out by the administrative process, are as important as the explicit ones, especially given the contract's duration. The regulatory contract can therefore be left as improvisational and relational, like the loose weave of the Delaware Corporate Code or Article II of the Con-

that Richard A. Posner considered and rejected for distinguishing public utilities from unregulated companies in his classic 1969 disquisition on the regulation of natural monopoly, none concerned the problem of inducing private investment in nonsalvageable assets subject to regulatory opportunism. Richard A. Posner, *Natural Monopoly and Its Regulation*, 21 STAN. L. REV. 548, 615 n.132 (1969).

stitution.[26] It is more efficient for the parties to eschew specificity in their enumeration of rights and duties under the regulatory contract in innumerable contingent situations over the long life of the useful assets employed and to rely instead on an alternative mechanism for ensuring that neither party will act opportunistically with respect to the other; such mechanisms include vertical integration and credible commitments, including administrative procedures enforced by an independent judiciary.[27] An absence of contract specificity, however, is not the same as the public utility's ceding unconditional discretionary powers to the regulator.

The regulatory process itself is a formal proceeding, whether it transpires at the federal or state level. Parties present testimony and evidence in formal public proceedings for the record. The agency gives formal notice of proposed rulemakings and considers the comments of interested parties. That process establishes the regulatory bargain and serves not only to make the process transparent, but also to assure the participants that their interests are protected, just as contract rights and remedies protect the parties to private contracts. The formal proceedings make a public record that helps to protect the legal and economic interests of consumers and the firm's investors.

Regulatory hearings, particularly for rate setting, provide a forum in which market participants can interact directly with each other and the regulatory commission. The hearings serve an important economic purpose. Just as the terms of private contracts result from negotiations between the parties, so the regulatory process involves *bargaining* among the regulatory authority, the regulated firm, its customers, and other interested market participants.[28] The bargaining process encompasses cost measurement, cost allocation, quality of service, and allowed rate of return. Negotiation results in rates and investment plans for the utility to provide service within its service area.

Bargaining between consumers and firms under the auspices of the regulatory agency does not necessarily indicate that the regulatory commission acts in the public interest, by maximizing social welfare, simply to carry out its public duties. Regulatory commissioners may

---

26. *See* J. Gregory Sidak, *The President's Power of the Purse*, 1989 DUKE L.J. 1162, 1235–38.

27. WILLIAMSON, THE ECONOMIC INSTITUTIONS OF CAPITALISM, *supra* note 8, at 69; Oliver E. Williamson, *Transaction-Cost Economics: The Governance of Contractual Relations*, 22 J.L. & ECON. 233, 236 (1985).

28. SPULBER, *supra* note 4, at 85–86, 269–71.

pursue entirely private objectives, including personal notions of fairness, the quest for power and self-aggrandizement, or merely avoidance of criticism. Furthermore, regulatory commissions are subject to capture by one industry interest or another or by one consumer interest or another, depending on whether the bargaining power of any particular interest group dominates that of other groups. The regulated outcome often is a compromise when interest groups have countervailing bargaining power. Bargaining power in the regulated setting results from direct influence of the parties over the bureaucrats serving on the regulatory commissions as well as indirect influence. Generally, interested parties obtain bargaining power through the exercise of indirect influence over regulatory commissions. Indirect influence stems from legislative, executive, and judicial oversight of commission activities. Interest groups may apply to the legislature for special hearings or legislation that limits commissioner discretion. They may appeal to the executive branch for political pressure or appointment of new commissioners. Finally, interested parties may appeal commission actions to the courts, seeking to remand or reverse unfavorable decisions.

THE PRINCIPAL COMPONENTS OF
THE REGULATORY CONTRACT

The three components of the regulatory contract are entry controls, rate regulation, and utility service obligations. The state commission controls the entry of the utility's competitors and authorizes rates that give the utility's investors the opportunity to earn a "fair" rate of return on their investment. In return, the regulated utility must comply with regulatory accounting procedures for the disclosure of its costs, abide by price regulations, limit its business activities in other markets, invest in sufficient transmission and access services to all customers within its service territory who request service, operate efficiently as determined by the regulatory commission, make only investments that are "prudent," meet regulatory standards for quality of service, and comply with a host of other provisions.

The broad terms of the regulatory contract are governed by the regulatory authority's preceding decisions, legislation, and judicial oversight. Regulated rates are set through public rate hearings that generally follow rules of administrative procedure. Interested parties must be informed of the time, place, and nature of the hearings, the legal authority and jurisdiction upon which the hearing is to be held, and the matters of fact and law that are asserted.[29]

The regulatory authority approves the utility's investment projects through prudency reviews and used-and-useful hearings.[30] The regulators approve the prices charged by the regulated utility and review its financial performance. Thus, the regulatory contract is between the utility and the regulatory commission, as the agent of the legislature, which in turn represents the general public. It is not necessary to believe that the commission acts in the public interest to conclude that the commission undertakes obligations as the public's representative. The actions of regulatory commission are government commitments that potentially obligate public funds.

Entry Regulation

Regulations limiting the entry of competitors into the service territory of the incumbent utility are a standard feature of the regulatory contract. Regulatory commissions control entry through the awarding of franchises and the requirement of a certificate of public convenience and necessity. Regulators have restricted entry into telecommunications, the electric power industry, natural gas, water services, hospitals, broadcasting, and many other industries.

The Rationale for Entry Controls. Entry controls have traditionally limited competition for the utilities and allowed them the opportunity to earn a fair rate of return on their investments while conforming to rate regulation and regulatory service obligations. The elimination of regulatory entry barriers to achieve the benefits of competition represents a fundamental change in the terms of the regulatory contract. To avoid confiscatory outcomes, those changes need to be counterbalanced by altering both the responsibilities and compensation for the incumbent utilities.

The traditional justification for entry restrictions in telecommunications has been to achieve the cost gains from *natural monopoly*. For example, in 1982 then-Judge Stephen Breyer wrote that "local telephone service seems to be generally accepted as a natural monopoly."[31]

---

29. *See, e.g.*, CAL. PUB. UTIL. CODE § 311 (hearings, evidence, and decisions).

30. *See* SPULBER, *supra* note 4, at 269–71.

31. *See* STEPHEN G. BREYER, REGULATION AND ITS REFORM 291 (Harvard University Press 1982).

A technology is said to exhibit the property of natural monopoly if one firm can produce the product or service at lower cost than can two or more firms.[32] A sufficient condition for the cost function to have the natural monopoly property is for the technology to exhibit economies of scale over the relevant range of output. Economies of scale are said to be present if the marginal costs of production are less than the average costs of production over the relevant range of output.[33]

Technological change and industry transformations in telecommunications and other markets have cast doubt on the natural monopoly argument for regulation.[34] Furthermore, competition brings cost efficiencies and incentives for innovation that cannot be achieved through entry and rate regulation. Those benefits are manifest in the markets that experienced the first deregulation wave—airlines, trucking, and rail freight transportation. Moreover, the high transaction costs associated with cost-of-service regulation lead many to question whether any potential cost gains can possibly justify continuing to regulate entry.

Accordingly, state PUCs have begun to dismantle regulatory barriers to entry into the local exchange and into the retail distribution of electricity. The elimination of franchise protection by the state PUCs is a unilateral change of a fundamental term in the regulatory contract. Although cost efficiencies may no longer justify continuing entry regulations, that changed circumstance does not eliminate the regulator's responsibility to allow utilities to recover their costs incurred before the change in the regulatory contract.

Exclusive versus Nonexclusive Franchises. A common misunderstanding of the regulatory contract is that an essential component of that agreement is the government's grant of a monopoly to the investor-owned utility. The grant may take the form of an exclusive franchise

---

32. *See, e.g.*, WILLIAM J. BAUMOL, JOHN C. PANZAR & ROBERT D. WILLIG, CONTESTABLE MARKETS AND THE THEORY OF INDUSTRY STRUCTURE 17 (Harcourt Brace Jovanovich, rev. ed. 1988) (defining natural monopoly in terms of an industry in which all firms have the same cost function).

33. The firm's average cost function refers to the cost per unit of output evaluated at each output level. The firm's marginal cost function refers to the additional cost of producing one more unit of output, evaluated at each level of output. Economies of scale are not necessary for natural monopoly. The natural monopoly property can be present at an output level at which the cost function exhibits decreasing returns to scale. *See* SPULBER, *supra* note 4, at 117.

34. *See* Daniel F. Spulber, *Deregulating Telecommunications*, 12 YALE J. ON REG. 25 (1995).

or a statutory prohibition on competitive entry. To the contrary, the regulatory contract does *not* require monopoly, and the misapprehension that it does, in turn, supplies the erroneous premise for two misplaced arguments. The first is the assertion that those who defend the regulatory contract are necessarily opposed to competition and unconditionally maintain that, by itself, the government's introduction of competition into the market in question would constitute breach of the regulatory contract. The second misplaced argument is the assertion that one can disprove the existence of the regulatory contract in a given state by pointing to the existence there of a statute or state constitutional provision that forbids the state or any of its municipalities from granting an exclusive franchise. Neither of those two arguments is correct.

Suppose that a state not only forbade exclusive franchises but also failed to create—by statute, common law, or regulatory practice of long standing—any alternative cost recovery mechanism that credibly assured the utility that the regulator would provide the utility the opportunity to recover its irreversible, nonsalvageable investments. In that institutional setting, a private company would be reluctant to contract with municipalities for the long-term supply of any amount of service that would necessitate any incremental investment in nonsalvageable assets; and even if the company *were* willing enter into such a contract, investors would be unwilling to supply the company with the requisite capital unless they were paid a risk premium substantial enough to compensate for the risk that the firm might never recover the capital used to make those investments in nonsalvageable assets and that the firm might never receive a competitive return on that capital. Investors routinely demand that sort of risk premium from irreversible investments in third-world countries that suffer from political instability and correspondingly unreliable judicial and regulatory institutions for the protection of private property. Most important, consumers suffer under such circumstances because they ultimately pay the risk premium that is necessary to attract the investment required for the utility to render service and because they will bear the disruption in service if regulatory instability induces the public utility to disinvest.

Clearly, therefore, the existence of a statute or state constitutional provision that forbids the state or any of its municipalities from granting an exclusive franchise does not disprove the existence of the regulatory contract in that state. It is a factual matter beyond any dispute that some states, such as Texas, forbid the grant of an exclusive franchise.[35] The existence of such a prohibition, however, is hardly evidence that the state does not have a regulatory contract. All that such a fact proves is that the state has selected a different means by which to achieve the ends for which franchise exclusivity is the chosen means in other states. The common objective in the two cases is to create the opportunity for the utility to recover the prudently incurred costs of irreversible, nonsalvageable investments that it made to discharge its obligation to serve customers within its service area. For example, a municipality or state, while not granting exclusivity to the incumbent utility, may nonetheless refrain from taking actions that would threaten the firm's recovery of nonsalvageable investments. In the absence of rate rebalancing, the most obvious way for the municipality or state to preserve a reasonable opportunity for the incumbent utility to recover its costs would be to permit entry only by firms that will either assume public service obligations comparable to the incumbent's or contribute their appropriate share to the funding of such obligations. That limitation on the discretion of the licensing authority may include the statutory directive to the public utilities commission not to grant an overlapping certificate of public necessity without good cause. In Texas, for example, the Public Utility Regulatory Act of 1995 provides that the Public Utilities Commission of Texas shall grant a certificate of convenience and necessity after considering not only "the adequacy of existing service" and "the need for additional service," but also the effect of the grant on a number of factors, including its effect "on any public utility of the same kind already serving the proximate area."[36]

Further, the government's introduction of competition into the regulated market in itself would not breach the regulatory contract. Entry regulation is simply a means to an end; it is not the end in itself. The appropriate objective—the objective that advances economic efficiency and consumer welfare—is for the regulator to provide a credible mechanism by which the utility will have the opportunity to recover the costs of (and a competitive return *on*) its irreversible, nonsalvageable investments over the course of their useful lives. If a state in the past has chosen franchise exclusivity as the mechanism to achieve that objective but now wants to reverse course and allow open entry, then it must simultaneously introduce an alternative policy that is equally

---

35. TEX. CONST. art. I, § 26. For a 1913 survey of the limitations on the grant of exclusive franchises, see OSCAR L. POND, A TREATISE ON THE LAW OF PUBLIC UTILITIES OPERATING IN CITIES AND TOWNS §§ 117–31, 156–71 (Bobbs-Merrill Co. 1913).

36. TEX. REV. CIV. STAT. ANN., art. 1446c-0, § 2.255(c).

efficacious in creating the opportunity for achieving that cost-recovery objective. In short, a breach of the regulatory contract does *not* necessarily occur when the state abolishes entry regulation; but a breach *does* necessarily occur when the state abolishes entry regulation without simultaneously imposing an alternative policy that will achieve the same cost-recovery objective for which entry regulation was originally intended.

Regulation of Rates

The regulation of rates by federal agencies and state PUCs is another standard feature of the regulatory contract. Rate regulation to control monopoly power generally accompanies entry restrictions that were put in place to protect natural monopoly. Control over rates also places responsibilities on regulators. The need to raise capital repeatedly, and constitutional protections against takings under the Fifth and Fourteenth Amendments, require regulators to take into account the interests of investors.

Economists have advanced many justifications for rate regulation.[37] In addition to controlling monopoly power, rate regulation often is perceived as a means of achieving universal service and maintaining reasonable rates for consumers and industry. Federal agencies and state PUCs have followed a standard procedure in cost-of-service ratemaking. The utility estimates its operating costs including depreciation for a selected year, known as a "test year." The estimate reflects expectations about demand and operating costs. In addition, the utility calculates its capital costs, which generally are estimated by using the book value of capital expenditures net of depreciation. The regulatory commission sets an "allowed rate of return" for the company's financial costs. Methods of determining the rate of return vary, but in many cases the PUC averages the costs of the utility's debt with an estimate of the costs of capital for equity owners. Following regulatory accounting rules, the regulatory commission calculates the total costs of the utility as its operating cost, plus the rate base times the allowed rate of return. That estimate of costs is the utility's "revenue requirement." On the

---

37. For further discussion, see ALFRED E. KAHN, THE ECONOMICS OF REGULATION: PRINCIPLES AND INSTITUTIONS (MIT Press, rev. ed. 1988) (John Wiley & Sons, Inc. 1970); BREYER, *supra* note 31; RICHARD SCHMALENSEE, THE CONTROL OF NATURAL MONOPOLIES (Lexington Books 1979); SPULBER, *supra* note 4.

basis of the revenue requirement, the utility proposes rates to the regulator that are designed to recover estimated costs.

It should be evident that the regulatory commission cannot unilaterally terminate its obligation to the utility. Deregulation does not absolve the regulators of their responsibility to permit regulated companies to earn competitive rates of return on their investments. Rates can be expected to fall under competition, while regulators continue to impose performance requirements on the utilities. The "end-result" test, which we examine in chapter 6, should be applied to the effects of competitive rules so that investors are permitted to earn a competitive return on capital investment under regulation.

The Obligation to Serve

As a general rule in antitrust law, a firm may unilaterally refuse to deal with any prospective customer.[38] That rule even extends to a monopolist's unilateral refusal to deal, so long as the firm by doing so does not intend to create or maintain a monopoly.[39] That rule does not apply to utilities, however. As Justice Benjamin N. Cardozo observed in 1920, "the duty to serve . . . results from the acceptance of the franchise of a public service corporation."[40]

A utility carries an obligation to serve customers in its franchise region at posted prices. That duty to serve requires the company to expand its transmission and switching capacity to meet the growth and location of customer demand. Utilities have constructed facilities to provide reliable telephone, electricity, or natural gas service. Regulators monitor the performance of regulated utilities in a variety of other areas, including responsive customer relations, speed of repairs, or other services. The cost of capacity investments is recovered through their inclusion in the rate base. The utility earns the allowed rate of return on its capital expenditures net of depreciation. The utility recovers the cost of assets through depreciation allowances that are treated as operating costs.

38. United States *v.* Colgate & Co., 250 U.S. 300, 307 (1919).

39. *Id.* at 307.

40. Tismer *v.* New York Edison Co., 228 N.Y. 156, 161, 126 N.E. 729, 731 (1920) (citing People *ex rel.* Cayuga Power Corp. *v.* Public Serv. Comm'n, 226 N.Y. 527, 532, 124 N.E. 105, 106 (1919) (Cardozo, J.)); *see also* IRSTON R. BARNES, THE ECONOMICS OF PUBLIC UTILITY REGULATION 42, 740–42 (F. S. Crofts & Co. 1942).

The regulatory contract requires performance from utilities that has necessitated substantial capital expenditures, which were made subject to regulatory approval and oversight. If the regulator unilaterally changes the regulatory contract, a complete review of the utility's performance obligations becomes necessary.

The Obligation to Extend the Network to Provide Service to All Consumers. The public utility's obligation to serve entails the obligation to extend its network to serve new customers. Why must a utility be *forced* to make additional sales? The answer, in general terms, is that the private marginal benefit of extending service is less than the private marginal cost. Left to its own devices, the utility would build a network reaching a lower percentage of the populace than regulators would desire. For a fixed, geographically averaged price, the utility would stop expanding its network when the private marginal cost of doing so began to exceed the private marginal benefit. Regulators would prefer to have the network expanded to the point where *social* marginal cost equals *social* marginal benefit.[41] Alternatively, the utility would depart from pricing its services at a fixed price and, instead, charge higher prices to customers in high-cost areas. Thus, the need to impose on the utility an obligation to extend its network is the direct implication of policies of universal service and rate averaging.

Early in the experience of public utility regulation, the Supreme Court recognized that interrelationship. When confronted with a utility's constitutional challenge to the obligation to extend its network, the Court announced a rule that coincides precisely with the test that economists decades later would articulate for defining the existence of subsidized prices.

In 1917 the Court decided *New York* ex rel. *New York & Queens Gas Co.* v. *McCall*, a case in which the New York Public Service Commission ordered a gas utility having an exclusive franchise to extend its gas mains and service pipes to the community of Douglaston, "located about a mile and a half beyond the then terminus of the company's gas mains, but within the Third Ward of the Borough

---

41. For a theoretical exposition of that proposition by a former state regulatory commissioner, see ELI NOAM, *Network Tipping: The Rise and Fall of the Public Network Monopoly, in* TELECOMMUNICATIONS IN EUROPE 26 (Oxford University Press 1992). We return to the issue of network externality in chapter 16. For early skepticism of that phenomenon that predates the recent literature by economic theorists, see JAMES C. BONBRIGHT, PRINCIPLES OF PUBLIC UTILITY RATES 17 n.16 (Columbia University Press 1961).

of Queens."[42] From the Court's description, Douglaston would have been a desirable market to serve—affluent and rapidly growing.[43] The utility's reluctance to extend service stemmed from the fact that "the mains of the company, which extended to the point nearest to Douglaston, were being used to almost their full capacity, and for this reason the estimated cost of making the improvement included new mains of some eight miles in length."[44] The utility estimated that its return on investment for the extension would be only 2¼ percent, which (although not expressly stated in the opinion) was presumably below the cost of capital. Although the utility attacked the order as a deprivation of due process, it did not claim "that the comparatively small loss . . . would render its business as a whole unprofitable," and it did not explicitly allege a taking of property.[45] The Court, in a unanimous opinion by Justice John H. Clarke, rejected the utility's due process argument and affirmed the order to extend the line:

> Corporations which devote their property to a public use may not pick and choose, serving only the portions of the territory covered by their franchises which it is presently profitable for them to serve and restricting the development of the remaining portions by leaving their inhabitants in discomfort without the service which they alone can render. To correct this disposition to serve where it is profitable and to neglect where it is not, is one of the important purposes for which these administrative commissions, with large powers, were called into existence. . . .[46]

McCall thus establishes the following rule: If a public utility with entry regulation and uniform rate structure is meeting or exceeding its reve-

---

42. 245 U.S. 345, 346 (1917).

43. "The community of Douglaston . . . was a rapidly growing settlement of three hundred and thirty houses, of an average cost of $7,500, thus giving assurance that the occupiers of them would be probable users of gas, and which, with very few exceptions, were occupied by families the entire year. While the community is described in the assignment of error as 'independent and remote,' the record shows that it was served at the time by franchise-holding companies, which supplied water, electric light, and telephone to its inhabitants, and that the number of houses had doubled within a few years." *Id.* at 349.

44. *Id.* at 349–50.

45. *Id.* at 351.

46. *Id. See also* RICHARD J. PIERCE, JR., ECONOMIC REGULATION: CASES AND MATERIALS 169–70 (Anderson Publishing Co. 1994).

nue requirement, then it cannot refuse a request to extend its network to serve a new customer below incremental cost.

That proposition can be restated in a manner more familiar to contemporary economic analysis of network industries. A utility would not voluntarily extend its network to a given customer i if doing so would generate an incremental loss for the utility—that is, if

$$R_i < IC_i,$$

where R_i is the utility's revenue from customer i and IC_i is the utility's incremental cost of serving customer i. Under the regulatory contract, however, the utility can be excused from its duty to extend service even at a loss if and only if the utility as a whole is unprofitable—that is, if its total revenues TR are less than its total costs TC:

$$TR \equiv \sum_{j=1}^{n} R_j < TC.$$

It follows that, if the utility is precisely meeting a break-even constraint on its overall operations,

$$TR \equiv \sum_{j=1}^{n} R_j = TC,$$

as is the stylized objective of rate-of-return regulation. If the utility is required by the *McCall* rule to extend service unprofitably to customer i, then there must be at least one other customer k from whom the utility earns revenues exceeding incremental costs:

$$R_k > IC_k.$$

Economies of scope imply that the sum of incremental cost across the services that the company provides is less than total costs. The sum of incremental costs can equal total cost if the services are independent. Note that in the absence of economies of scope, it is inefficient to operate the services jointly. Even if each service covers its incremental cost, therefore, one or more services must cover joint and common costs as well. If, in addition, a service does not cover all of its incremental costs, then other services must also carry them.

The *McCall* rule thus guarantees the existence of a cross-subsidy in the utility's rate structure. A regulated firm's rate structure is said to be free of cross-subsidies if and only if the prices satisfy the *incremen-*

tal cost test.[47] Applying the incremental cost test, revenues generated by each service cover the incremental cost of providing that service.[48] The rationale for the incremental cost test is the requirement that each service must generate revenues that at least cover the additional cost of producing that service. If not, the other service is providing a cross-subsidy, and the customers of the other service would be better off receiving their service independently, at its stand-alone cost.

If a firm is regulated, it is desirable to design a rate structure that is free of cross-subsidies. Otherwise, the economic incentives can lead to allocative inefficiency. Customers receiving the subsidy do not observe the full economic costs of their service and consequently demand an inefficiently high amount; customers providing the subsidy demand an inefficiently low amount or seek bypass alternatives that may be uneconomic under some conditions. As explained earlier, however, regulators almost invariably require the public utility to conform to a rate structure that is rife with cross-subsidies.

As we shall see shortly, the prohibition against a public utility's exiting its franchise area is another instance in which the regulatory contract compels the utility to deviate from subsidy-free prices so that the state can continue to effect income transfers through the utility's rate structure.

Service Quality. Regulators require a public utility to maintain specified levels of service quality. Quality of service is a fundamental part

---

47. *See* WILLIAM J. BAUMOL & J. GREGORY SIDAK, TOWARD COMPETITION IN LOCAL TELEPHONY 57, 81–83 (MIT Press & AEI Press 1994); WILLIAM J. BAUMOL, SUPERFAIRNESS: APPLICATIONS AND THEORY 113–20 (MIT Press 1986). Alternatively, a break-even regulated rate structure is said to be free of cross-subsidies if and only if the prices satisfy the *stand-alone cost test. See, e.g.,* BAUMOL & SIDAK, TOWARD COMPETITION IN LOCAL TELEPHONY, *supra*, at 84; BAUMOL, PANZAR & WILLIG, *supra* note 32, at 352–53. Stand-alone cost refers to the firm's long-run total cost of each service operated separately. The stand-alone cost test requires that the revenues generated from either of two services not exceed the stand-alone cost of providing that service. If the revenues from one service do exceed its stand-alone cost, then that service is providing a cross-subsidy to the other service. (The definition of the stand-alone cost test is given in terms of two services. In the case of more than two services, the test requires that no group of services subsidize any other group of services.) The test for cross-subsidization demonstrates that the customers of the service providing the cross-subsidy would be better off if that service could be obtained independently of the other service.

48. Here, we define the incremental cost test for only two services. In the case of more than two services, the revenues generated by each group of services must cover the incremental cost of providing that group of services.

of the universal service requirement. Regulated utilities must maintain sufficient capacity not only to provide service to all customers who request it, but also to meet the peak demands of its customers. With variability of demand, the firm needs to carry the cost of substantial capital investment that can remain idle off-peak. The effect of service quality regulation is that the type of capital equipment that the utility employs to meet its service obligations is tailored to satisfying regulatory specifications, which are often articulated in terms of engineering standards for reliability, capacity, and so on. Moreover, capacity investments are designed to meet service requirements while passing the test of prudency reviews and used-and-useful tests for cost recovery.

Service quality regulations have several significant implications for the recovery of stranded investment. First, the types of facilities that are needed to meet regulatory requirements are often ill-suited to competitive markets. That fact does not in itself indicate that the regulated firm failed to invest wisely or that it embraced obsolete technology. Rather, the capacity that is best adapted for one type of market structure should not be expected to fit another type of market structure. For example, after airline deregulation, as airlines switched from direct routes to a hub-and-spoke system, they needed different airport accommodations and different types of planes. The capital equipment that a regulated monopoly needs to provide service is unlikely to match the needs of a competitive firm.

Second, the capital equipment that competitive firms need is meant to satisfy customer needs rather than one-size-fits-all technological standards. Thus, compared with a firm whose capital investment is designed to serve all in a uniform manner, entrants can target service offerings to specific customer needs and provide better service to some classes of customers.

Third, because the incumbent regulated firm built a system with substantial excess capacity, its cost of maintenance and operation can be expected to differ from those of entrants, who have the prerogative to ration customers. Moreover, the capital facilities of incumbents are long-lived, so that entrants can take advantage of technological change in the design of their facilities. Technological obsolescence of incumbent facilities thus need not indicate errors in the incumbent's investment strategy.

In the case of electric power, the utility must maintain sufficient generation, transmission, and distribution capacity to meet the pattern of demand with baseload, shoulder, and peaking capacity. Because the cost of storing power is prohibitive, and because regulators do not permit rationing of residential and commercial customers, the utility must recover the costs of capacity through demand charges based on maximum use, and through energy charges. Moreover, the utility provides standby capacity because it must remain prepared to serve customers that self-generate or purchase power elsewhere, whenever they have additional needs for power.

Regulatory standards for generation, transmission, and distribution capacity generally specify high levels of reliability—typically one day of major power outages in ten years.[49] Utilities attempt to meet their power demand at lowest reasonable cost by operating an assortment of power plants (including nuclear, gas, fuel oil, and coal) and by purchasing power. Their supply problem differs from that of specialized entrants who can simply contribute power for resale within a pool arrangement. Utilities attempt to smooth the patterns of electricity usage through peak-load pricing or time-of-day pricing and through other programs to shift the costs of usage toward peak users. Rate regulation constrains such efforts, however. In addition, utilities address the variability of demand through the design of interruptible or curtailable rates that permit industrial users to obtain discounts in return for allowing their load to be dropped if capacity shortages occur during peak periods.

In telecommunications, utilities also must have sufficient transmission and switching capacity available to meet peak demand. Systems are designed in terms of reserve capacity, instead of limiting customer usage with system limits. Telecommunications facilities are designed to meet technical specifications for reliability and accuracy of transmission. Those standards can quickly become obsolete in a market with multiple providers and new transmission technologies such as digital signals and wireless personal communications services. In addition to such service-quality rules that affect capital investment, other rules set standards for time to answer (for operator pick-up), repair time, billing requirements (accuracy and specificity), and reliability in terms of reserve capacity. Those rules can create competitive disadvantages if they are imposed on incumbent utilities but not on entrants.

The Implicit Obligation to Maintain Capacity for the Return of the "Prodigal Son." The utility's obligation to maintain capacity for the return of departed customers is analogized to the parable of the prodi-

---

49. *See* LEONARD S. HYMAN, AMERICA'S ELECTRIC UTILITIES: PAST, PRESENT AND FUTURE 30 (Public Utilities Reports, Inc., 5th ed. 1994).

gal son.[50] In the parable, one son asks for his inheritance, leaves his father, and squanders his legacy; the other son stays and manages his father's farm. When the prodigal son returns, impoverished, and begs to be given a job as a mere laborer, the father instead lovingly welcomes the son back into the family and holds a feast to celebrate his return, which angers the loyal son.

Often a large customer will terminate service from the utility and turn either to a competing provider of service or to self-provision of the service. For example, a factory may install its own electrical generators. Nonetheless, the departing customer continues to enjoy the benefits of a service that the utility provides to it: insurance that the customer will be able to rely on the utility to supply service if the customer's alternative source of supply is inadequate. The utility must maintain sufficient capacity to serve the departed customer *if he returns*.

Until he actually returns to the utility, however, the departed customer makes no contribution to recovery of the utility's cost of maintaining standby capacity. Needless to say, the departed customer makes no contribution to margin with which the utility can recoup losses on services provided below cost to politically preferred constituencies. The departed customer is a free rider, and the remaining customers pay the premium on the insurance that he consumes. That insurance subsidy artificially raises the price of service to remaining customers and makes alternative provision of the utility's service increasingly attractive to the utility's remaining customers, particularly large users.

The Current Use and Usefulness of "Excess" Capacity. Given the utility's obligation to serve future demand, it should be clear that available generation capacity is used and useful in conferring a current benefit on consumers apart from their current consumption of power. Current consumers derive a current benefit from the ability of the utility's existing infrastructure to accommodate unexpected peaks in usage or growth in demand. Whether an investment is economically beneficial depends upon a wide variety of factors. Obviously, if current capacity is insufficient to meet demand at prevailing prices and an investment in plant yields added capacity, then the output generated by

---

50. *Luke* 15:11–32. *See, e.g.*, Establishment of Backup and Maintenance Rates, Dkt. No. 94-176, slip op. (Me. Pub. Utils. Comm'n May 25, 1994); Backup and Maintenance Rates and the Treatment of Stranded Costs, Dkt. No. 94-176, 152 P.U.R.4th 349 (Me. Pub. Utils. Comm'n 1994).

that added capacity unquestionably constitutes an economic benefit. Where capacity is not in short supply, further analysis may nonetheless reveal that some other form of current economic benefit accrues to utility customers and to the general public from capacity expansion. Those benefits may include greater network reliability and insurance against longer-period capacity shortages resulting from unforeseeable increases in demand. In addition, the availability of capacity at any given moment reflects that technology and other factors make investment inherently "lumpy."

Consumers of electric power currently benefit from all of those possible consequences. Although at first glance it may appear otherwise, a benefit such as the avoidance of capacity shortages is not different in principle from direct financial benefits, such as lower operating costs. Each benefit has a savings in costs that corresponds to and appropriately measures its economic value, even if that value cannot be definitively quantified in monetary terms. For example, consumers clearly benefit if the utility has enough additional generation capacity to reduce the risk of outages and network failure. Provision against risk is a tangible product that is bought and sold in a market at observable prices, as the existence of the insurance industry attests.

The existence of available capacity that reduces risk frees the utility, and ultimately its customers, from the need to bear the costs that would be entailed in incurring those risks. It also frees the utility's business customers from incurring the cost of business-interruption insurance against any financial damages to them arising from a power outage. Each of those burdens has an obvious financial cost whose magnitude can, at least in principle, generally be estimated.

Exit Regulation. One significant but neglected implication of the utility's obligation to serve is that the utility cannot exit a market at will. A utility must secure the regulator's authorization through an abandonment proceeding to withdraw service.[51] Unlike the utility, competitive entrants can abandon any of their facilities at will. The pro-

---

51. CHARLES F. PHILLIPS, JR., THE REGULATION OF PUBLIC UTILITIES 570 (Public Utilities Reports, Inc., 3d ed. 1993) ("Voluntary abandonment, either partial or complete, must be approved by the regulatory commissions."); WILLIAM K. JONES, REGULATED INDUSTRIES: CASES AND MATERIALS 333–39 (Foundation Press 1976); Oliver P. Field, *The Withdrawal from Service of Public Utility Companies*, 35 YALE L.J. 169 (1925); Ford P. Hall, *Discontinuance of Service by Public Utilities*, 13 MINN. L. REV. 181, 325 (1929); Note, *The Duty of a Public Utility to Render Adequate Service: Its Scope and Enforcement*, 62 COLUM. L. REV. 312, 319–22 (1962).

hibition on abandonment is therefore clearly an incumbent burden, one closely related to the utility's universal service obligation. Regulators should lift the prohibition on abandonment as soon as they permit competitive entry into the utility's service area. Until that time, the utility, compared with the unregulated firm, faces a barrier to exit. That barrier is substantial because, given rate averaging, the utility is inevitably required to offer some customers service at uncompensatory prices.

In fact, the prohibition against a public utility's exiting its franchise area is symmetrical to the *McCall* rule compelling the utility to extend service: If the utility is at least breaking even, then it can be denied the freedom to terminate service on a line that produces an incremental loss, just as it can be compelled to extend service to new customers who would produce an incremental loss.[52] A representative statement of the rule appears in a 1918 decision involving a municipal railway:

> If a railway company is under a statutory or a contract duty to maintain and operate a line, it will be compelled by injunction or mandamus so to do, even though the further operation should be at a loss. It is only when there is no valid or binding obligation to continue operations that the company may, at its discretion, abandon an unprofitable line or branch. If there is a binding obligation to maintain and operate a part of a system, it is questionable whether that part or branch can ever be abandoned, unless the losses inflicted by its continued operation are such as will wreck the entire system.[53]

The prohibition on exit is thus another aspect of the regulatory contract that compels the utility to deviate from subsidy-free prices.

The question of abandonment and the utility's right to withdraw service provides a valuable perspective on the regulatory contract con-

---

52. Fort Smith Light & Traction Co. *v.* Bourland, 267 U.S. 330 (1925); Iowa *v.* Old Colony Trust Co., 215 F. 307 (8th Cir. 1914); Crawford *v.* Duluth Street Ry., 60 F.2d 212 (7th Cir. 1932); Columbus Ry. Power & Light Co. *v.* Columbus, 253 F. 499 (S.D. Ohio 1918), *aff'd*, 249 U.S. 399 (1919); Salina *v.* Salina Street Ry., 114 Kan. 734, 220 P. 203 (1923); Northern Ill. Light & Traction Co. *v.* Commerce Comm'n *ex. rel.* City of Ottawa, 302 Ill. 11, 134 N.E. 142 (1922). The Supreme Court stated in Texas R.R. Comm'n *v.* Eastern Texas R.R., 264 U.S. 79, 85 (1924), that "if at any time it develops with reasonable certainty that future operations must be at a loss, the company may discontinue operation and get what it can out of the property by dismantling the road." To require otherwise would effect a confiscation of property: "To compel it to go on at a loss, or to give up the salvage value, would be to take its property without just compensation which is a part of due process of law." *Id.*

53. Columbus Ry. Power & Light Co. *v.* Columbus, 253 F. 499, 505 (D. Ohio 1918), *aff'd*, 249 U.S. 399 (1919).

cerning the question of whether that contract is enforceable against the utility. The contractual or statutory limits on abandonment resemble a specific performance requirement for the utility. When a party to private contract commits a breach, an Anglo-American court disfavors specific performance and will order it only when the service or good is unique or when the buyer could not obtain a similar contract in the market.[54] The idea that the municipality or regulatory commission cannot obtain a similar contract in the market motivates the prerogative that the commission enjoys at common law, a prerogative resembling the remedy of specific performance, to demand that the utility discharge its obligation to serve by not abandoning routes or lines serving an incrementally unprofitable group of customers. With the arrival of competition, however, the motivation for restrictions on abandonment would seem to vanish, for the regulator then can rely on the market to obtain services for those customers whom the utility would abandon. That rationale can be found in the existing cases. Courts have considered the availability of adequate substitute service relevant to whether the regulated firm may be allowed to abandon service on a line or to a group of customers that is incrementally unprofitable.[55] When such substitutes are available, courts have even allowed the regulated firm that is profitable as a whole to exit an incrementally unprofitable segment of the market.[56]

THE DURATION OF
THE REGULATORY CONTRACT

How long does the regulatory contract last? Contracts in general exist because performance takes time. Thus, the duration of the contract reflects the time required for performance to be completed. The duration of the regulatory contract corresponds to the economic lifetime of the assets

---

54. *See* Anthony T. Kronman, *Specific Performance*, 45 U. CHI. L. REV. 351 (1978); Alan Schwartz, *The Case for Specific Performance*, 89 YALE L.J. 271 (1979); Thomas S. Ulen, *The Efficiency of Specific Performance: Toward a Unified Theory of Contract Remedies*, 83 MICH. L. REV. 341 (1983); Steven Shavell, *The Design of Contracts and Remedies for Breach*, 99 Q.J. ECON. 121 (1984); William Bishop, *The Choice of Remedy for Breach of Contract*, 14 J. LEGAL STUD. 299 (1985).

55. Mississippi R.R. Comm'n v. Mobile & O.R.R. Co., 244 U.S. 388 (1917); State *ex rel.* Kirkwood v. Public Serv. Comm'n, 330 Mo. 507, 50 S.W.2d 114 (1932).

56. Cincinnati N. R.R. v. Public Utils. Comm'n, 119 Ohio St. 568, 165 N.E. 38 (1929) (railroad passengers adequately served by bus); Union Pac. R.R. v. Public Serv. Comm'n, 102 Utah 465, 132 P.2d 128 (1942) (same).

employed by the utility to perform its service obligations. The regulatory contract typically lasts a long time because the assets employed in network industries are irreversible and market-specific with a long lifetime. The utility performs its contractual obligations during the period of time that its facilities are used and useful. Consumers continue to receive the services of those assets even after the costs have been fully recovered through amortization.

The high costs of investment in network facilities and the extended economic lifetime of those facilities make it desirable for consumers to pay for services as they are received. Thus, investors in regulated utilities not only finance the firm's investment, but also implicitly finance the payments of consumers. Consumers receive the services of long-lived assets in a manner similar to leasing capital equipment.

Because of the irreversible nature of investment, the duration of the regulatory contract also depends on the buyer's performance. Thus, the regulatory contract lasts until the firm has had a reasonable opportunity to recover the nonsalvageable investments that it made to provide service to the public. In contracts with explicit durations, that concern for cost recovery manifests itself in a lengthy term of the utility's franchise. The legal answer to the question of the regulatory contract's duration mirrors that economic reasoning. Oscar L. Pond wrote in his 1913 treatise that "the erection and maintenance of [public utility] systems require so large an investment that private capital will not undertake such enterprises under franchises running for unreasonably short periods of time."[57] Moreover, Pond noted, "the property so used can not be easily turned or converted into cash," a clear recognition of the risk to the utility of the asset specificity inherent in its investment in infrastructure.[58]

It bears emphasis, particularly in the absence of an explicitly defined duration for the contract, that the regulator, by imposing depreciation policies (or other regulatory policies) that cause cost recovery to lag behind actual economic depreciation, in effect extends the duration of the contract until such time as the utility has received the reasonable opportunity to recoup its true economic costs—both operating costs and capital costs. Irston R. Barnes described two possible legal forms consistent with that economic proposition. The first was a *perpetual franchise*. Though a franchise was "seldom made perpetual by its terms," Barnes noted, "if the franchise is silent with respect to its duration and if there are not general

---

57. POND, *supra* note 35, at § 120 at 158 .
58. *Id*. § 121 at 158.

laws of the state imposing a limitation with respect to their duration, the courts may hold the franchise to be perpetual."[59]

The second form was the *indeterminate permit* or *terminable franchise*. Under such a franchise, which eighteen states permitted at the time that Barnes wrote in 1942, "[t]he utility continues to enjoy the privileges of the franchise until the municipality acts to take over the property," which as a practical matter "means that the franchise endures as long as the service continues to be satisfactory."[60] A public utility that satisfactorily performed its public service obligations would have "what is in effect a perpetual franchise," subject to the municipality's option to terminate the franchise and "pay the purchase price of the property."[61] The terminable franchise closely resembles the long-term relational contracting that Goldberg, Williamson, and other economists would describe several decades later. Barnes seemed to consider the terminable franchise to be the most efficient contracting form of his day for balancing the competing interests of the utility, the municipality, and consumers. The benefits to the utility were lessened risk for its asset-specific investment and, hence, a lower cost of capital:

> The company is secure in the possession and operation of its property. . . . [T]he investment of capital is readily induced on favorable terms. Expenditures for improvements and extensions are willingly undertaken, since all of the legitimate investment must be fully compensated if the municipality decides to take possession of the property.[62]

The terminable franchise gave the municipality "full control with respect to the future conduct of the utility."[63] At the same time, however, the municipality forbore from holding periodic proceedings to renew the franchise. The municipality thus avoided the "bickering and controversy" over

---

59. BARNES, *supra* note 40, at 219 (citing Owensboro *v.* Cumberland Tel. & Tel. Co., 230 U.S. 58 (1913); Ohio Pub. Serv. Co. *v.* Ohio, 274 U.S. 12 (1927)).

60. *Id.* at 221. The states were Arkansas, California, Colorado, Connecticut, Idaho, Illinois, Indiana, Kansas, Louisiana, Maryland, Missouri, Montana, New Hampshire, North Dakota, Ohio, South Carolina, Vermont, and Wisconsin. *Id.* at 212 n.3. The two other types of franchises that Barnes described were the *long-term franchise*, lasting twenty to fifty years, and the *short-term franchise*, lasting ten years or fewer but frequently having a virtually automatic privilege of renewal for an equal number of years. *Id.* at 219–20.

61. *Id.* at 221. "It is therefore of crucial importance," Barnes added, "that the franchise define precisely the procedure by which the property shall be valued." *Id.*

62. *Id.*

63. *Id.*

franchise renewal that one can imagine could have signaled opportunism by the municipality.[64]

THE CONTRACTUAL FOUNDATIONS OF *CHARLES RIVER BRIDGE* AND *MUNN* V. *ILLINOIS*

Some who oppose the recovery of stranded investment by the regulated firm assert that the regulatory contract is a recent fabrication. Economist Robert J. Michaels, for example, wrote in 1995:

> Voltaire said that history was nothing but a fable that had been general-ly agreed upon. The fictitious regulatory compact that justifies stranding compensation makes for poor history and misleading fable. Despite fre-quent claims that its roots go back to *Hope* and *Bluefield*, the compact is a recent intellectual invention. According to a LEXIS® search, the first regu-latory and court decisions to mention it only appear in 1983 and 1984. The legislative history of regulation is strikingly devoid of references to a com-pact, and no known regulation arose from a collaborative effort at which anything resembling a compact was on the agenda. "Stranded investment" carries a similarly short pedigree, and is to this day absent from textbooks on regulation and industrial organization.[65]

Other economists—including William A. Niskanen, Michael T. Maloney, and Robert E. McCormick—have repeated that claim.[66] No amount of

---

64. *Id.*

65. Robert J. Michaels, *Stranded Investment Surcharges: Inequitable and Inefficient*, PUB. UTIL. FORTNIGHTLY, May 15, 1995, at 21, 21. Presumably, Michaels is referring to New England Coalition on Nuclear Pollution *v.* Nuclear Reg. Comm'n, 727 F.2d 1127, 1130 (D.C. Cir. 1984) ("It may be possible to believe (though we do not pass upon the point), as the Commission evidently believed when it issued its proposed rule, that the very nature of government rate regulation—a compact whereby the utility surrenders its freedom to charge what the market will bear in exchange for the state's assurance of adequate profits—assures financial stability for public utilities.") (Scalia, J.); Washington Utils. & Transp. Comm'n *v.* Puget Sound Power & Light Co., 62 P.U.R.4th 557, 589 (Wash. 1984) ("Understanding the dichotomy between the treatment of expenses prudently undertaken to provide service and providing a return on investment and that they are two separate matters is critical to the understanding of the regulatory compact and the operation of utilities.").

66. William A. Niskanen, *A Case Against Both Stranded Cost Recovery and Mandatory Access*, REGULATION, 1996 no. 1, at 16 (1996); 1 MICHAEL T. MALONEY & ROBERT E. MCCORMICK WITH RAYMOND D. SAUER, CUSTOMER CHOICE, CUSTOMER VALUE: AN ANALYSIS OF RETAIL COMPETITION IN AMERICA'S ELECTRIC INDUSTRY 6 (Citizens for a Sound Economy Foundation 1996). Niskanen asserts that "[t]here never was a 'regulatory compact'" but then supports that claim with the statement that "consumers would never have agreed to guarantee the value of investments against major changes in technology or the

repetition, however, alters the fact that Michaels's claim is false. It does not comport with American legal and economic history.

In his 1942 treatise, *The Economics of Public Utility Regulation*, Irston R. Barnes of Yale University chronicled the various "theories as to the basis of the public interest," one of which he called the "implied-contract theory."[67] Barnes described that theory, which he distinguished from four other legal theories of the basis for public utility regulation, in the following terms:

> It has been said that the basis for the distinction between those businesses whose prices are subject to governmental control and those that are free from such control is to be found in the implied contract that may be assumed to exist when the business enjoys peculiar rights or privileges from the government. If the business operates under special franchises which give it the right to occupy the public streets with its structures and equipment, the contention may be advanced that it is under an implied contract to accept regulation in the interest of the general public. Or again, if the corporation has been given the right to use the power of eminent domain in the acquisition of property, it is said that it has thereby acquiesced in the supervision of its business by the public.[68]

Barnes argued that, during the half-century between 1877 and 1927, the implied-contract theory had had such "supporters on the Supreme Court" as Chief Justice William Howard Taft and Justices Stephen J. Field, Joseph R. Lamar, and George Sutherland.[69] Barnes was correct in his observation that a contract existed, but he did not understand all the terms of the contract as we described them in the preceding section.

---

market." Niskanen, *supra*, at 16. As chapter 6 explains, however, it is major change in *regulation*, not technology or the market, that gives rise to compensable stranded costs. Maloney and McCormick dismiss the existence of the regulatory contract solely on the basis of one irrelevant decision in which the Temporary Court of Emergency Appeals rejected a party's poorly briefed argument that the Ninth Amendment created a constitutional right "to trust the federal government and to rely on the integrity of its pronouncements." Mapco Inc. v. Carter, 573 F.2d 1268, 1277–78 (Temp. Ct. Emergency App. 1978), *quoted in* Maloney & McCormick, *supra*, at 6. Maloney and McCormick do not discuss the law of contract or takings jurisprudence.

67. BARNES, *supra* note 40, at 13, 14.

68. *Id.* at 14.

69. *Id.* at 14 & nn.43–46 (citing Munn v. Illinois, 94 U.S. (4 Otto) 113, 146–47 (1877) (Field, J., dissenting); German Alliance Ins. Co. v. Kansas, 233 U.S. 389, 426 (1914) (Lamar, J.); Wolff Packing Co. v. Industrial Ct., 262 U.S. 522, 535 (1923) (Taft, C.J.); Tyson & Brother v. Banton, 273 U.S. 418, 439 (1927) (Sutherland, J.)).

The Supreme Court showed greater sophistication of its understanding of the causes and consequences of the regulatory contract. Other prominent jurists—including Justices John Marshall Harlan, Oliver Wendell Holmes, Charles Evans Hughes, and Rufus W. Peckham—wrote opinions for the Court during the late nineteenth and early twentieth centuries that emphasized the contractual nature of public utility regulation. As numerous decisions document, the Court repeatedly expressed its understanding that asset-specific investment by public utilities would take place only if the government credibly committed itself not to expropriate the value of that private investment.

One can find even earlier origins of the regulatory contract in two of the Supreme Court's most notable decisions concerning regulation and public contracting: *Charles River Bridge* v. *Warren Bridge*[70] and *Munn* v. *Illinois*.[71] The two cases show that the concept of a public utility, as well as the subsequent premise for public utility regulation, rested explicitly on contract law.

Charles River Bridge

In 1837 the Court emphasized the power of the state to safeguard the interests of the community when it ruled against the interests of an operator of a private toll bridge in *Charles River Bridge*. For present purposes the decision is notable because of the common understanding throughout it that the relationship between the state and the private firm was contractual in nature. By an act of 1785, the Massachusetts legislature incorporated the Proprietors of the Charles River Bridge, authorizing the corporation to construct a bridge over the Charles River between Boston and Charlestown. The legislature granted the Proprietors of the Charles River Bridge the right to own the bridge and to collect tolls for passage over it for a period of forty years. The bridge opened to traffic in 1786. In 1792 the state legislature extended the life of the charter until 1856. In 1828 the Massachusetts legislature incorporated the Proprietors of the Warren Bridge, authorizing the corporation to construct another bridge over the Charles River near the Charles River Bridge. After the Proprietors of the Warren Bridge had earned the agreed-upon return on their investment by operating the bridge as a rival toll bridge, ownership of the bridge was to revert to the state. The Proprietors of the Charles River Bridge sought to enjoin the construction of the Warren Bridge. During the pendency of the

70. 36 U.S. (11 Pet.) 420 (1837).
71. 94 U.S. (4 Otto) 113, 124 (1877).

case, the Warren Bridge was built and the Proprietors of the Warren Bridge reaped sufficient return from tolls so that the ownership of the bridge reverted to the state, at which point the state made the Warren a free bridge, and "the value of the franchise granted to the proprietors of the Charles River Bridge [was] entirely destroyed."[72]

Writing for the Court, Chief Justice Roger B. Taney ruled that the case should turn simply on whether the authorization and subsequent construction of the Warren Bridge was an act of the Massachusetts legislature that impaired obligations of the contract between the Proprietors of the Charles River Bridge and the state of Massachusetts. Citing precedent, he affirmed that an abandonment of a state's power to enact subsequent legislation "ought not to be presumed, in a case, in which the deliberate purpose of the State to abandon it does not appear."[73] Chief Justice Taney, therefore, gave strict construction to the Charles River Bridge charter and found that, in the absence of an explicit grant, the Massachusetts legislature did not convey any implied right of exclusivity to the Proprietors of the Charles River Bridge; although the creation of the Warren Bridge completely destroyed the value of the Charles River Bridge franchise, it did not impair any obligations under the contract in question.[74]

Chief Justice Taney assumed a particularly narrow perspective in considering the existence of a contract between the state and the Proprietors of the Charles River Bridge. He declined to examine the totality of the relationship as it arose under the charter. Instead, he simply inquired whether there was a contract that specifically forbade the state from chartering a second bridge. Chief Justice Taney concluded that no implied contract existed that prohibited the state's actions with regard to the Warren Bridge.[75] In essence, Chief Justice Taney failed to look at the legal relationship established under the act of the Massachusetts in 1785 and to analyze whether the creation of the second bridge detrimentally affected any legal rights arising under that relationship. With his strict construction of the charter, he sought to answer only whether there existed an implied contract to maintain the exclusivity of the charter.

Chief Justice Taney wrongly addressed the amendment of the charter in 1792. In that year, the state legislature chartered the West Boston Bridge to be located at a different point along the river, "which they knew would

---

72. 36 U.S. (11 Pet.) at 538.
73. *Id.* at 548 (citing Providence Bank *v.* Billings & Pittmann, 29 U.S. (4 Pet.) 514 (1830)).
74. *Charles River Bridge*, 36 U.S. at 548.
75. *Id.* at 551.

lessen [the Charles River Bridge's] profits."[76] As compensation for the lost profits, the legislature granted to the Proprietors of the Charles River Bridge an extension to their charter. Rather than recognize the quid pro quo inherent in the charter's amendment, Taney mischaracterized the legislative intent to maintain the investment expectations of the Proprietors of the Charles River Bridge:

> On the contrary, words are cautiously employed to exclude that conclusion; and the extension is declared to be granted as a reward for the hazard they had run, and "for the encouragement of enterprise." The extension was given because the company had undertaken and executed a work of doubtful success; and the improvements which the Legislature then contemplated, might diminish the emoluments they had expected to receive from it.[77]

The other justices writing opinions did not share Chief Justice Taney's narrow perspective.

In his concurrence, Justice John McLean recognized the relationship between the state of Massachusetts and the Proprietors of the Charles River Bridge as a contract:

> Where the Legislature, with a view of advancing the public interest by the construction of a bridge, a turnpike road, or any other work of public utility, grants a charter, no reason is perceived why such a charter should not be construed by the same rule that governs contracts between individuals.
>
> The public, through their agent, enter into the contract with the company; and a valuable consideration is received in the construction of the contemplated improvement. This consideration is paid by the company, and sound policy requires, that its rights should be ascertained and protected, by the same rules as are applied to private contracts.[78]

Justice McLean considered his construction of charters or franchises to be necessary to stimulate private undertaking for the public good:

> The unrestricted profits contemplated, were necessary to induce or justify the undertaking. Suppose within two or three years after the Charles River Bridge had been erected, the Legislature had authorized another bridge to be built alongside of it, which could only accommodate the same line of travel. Whether the profits of such a bridge were realised by a company or by the State, would not the act of the Legislature have been deemed so

76. *Id.* at 550.
77. *Id.* at 551.
78. *Id.* at 557 (McLean, J., concurring).

gross a violation of the rights of the complainants, as to be condemned by the common sense and common justice of mankind?"[79]

In an early recognition of the concept of opportunity costs, Justice McLean noted that "[t]he value of the bridge is not estimated by the quantity of timber and stone it may contain, but by the travel over it."[80] In his view, the state eliminated the value of the Charles River Bridge by authorizing the construction of the Warren Bridge and establishing it as a free bridge: "The sovereign power of the State has taken the tolls of the complainants, but it has left them in possession of their bridge. Its stones and timbers are untouched, and the roads that lead to it remain unobstructed."[81] Nonetheless, by the end of his meandering concurrence, Justice McLean declined to view the Massachusetts legislature as having impaired any obligations under the Charles River Bridge contract, the existence of which he had belabored to demonstrate. Justice McLean's conclusion appears to have turned on his tacit assumption that, from 1785 to roughly 1828, the Proprietors of the Charles River Bridge had reaped enough profit from their undertaking to more than recover their invested capital, which thereby relieved the state from its contractual obligations and freed it to charter a second bridge.

Even Justice Joseph Story in dissent found the charter to be a contract. After surveying much common law and explaining the king's prerogative to repeal or amend his conveyance, Justice Story countered with a statement of his view of the law:

[A]ll this doctrine in relation to the king's prerogative of having a construction in his own favor, is exclusively confined to cases of mere donation, flowing from the bounty of the crown. Whenever the grant is upon a valuable consideration, the rule of construction ceases; and the grant is expounded exactly as it would be in the case of a private grant, favorably to the grantee. Why is this rule adopted? Plainly, because the grant is a contract, and is to be interpreted according to its fair meaning. It would be to the dishonor of the government, that it should pocket a fair consideration, and then quibble as to the obscurities and implications of its own contract.[82]

Applying his rule to the facts of the case at hand, Justice Story concluded that, "upon the principles of common reason and legal interpretation, the

---

79. *Id.* at 562.
80. *Id.*
81. *Id.* at 565.
82. *Id.* at 597 (Story, J., dissenting).

present grant carries with it a necessary implication that the Legislature shall do no act to destroy or essentially to impair the franchise."[83]

Munn v. Illinois

The Court's historic 1877 decision in *Munn* v. *Illinois* begins its defense of the constitutionality of rate regulation of grain elevators with a long-winded recitation of how membership in a civil society entails the consent of each citizen to what the preamble of the Constitution of Massachusetts called a "social compact."[84] That compact, while it "does not confer power upon the whole people to control rights which are purely and exclusively private," wrote Chief Justice Morrison Waite for the majority, "does authorize the establishment of laws requiring each citizen to so conduct himself, and so use his own property, as not unnecessarily to injure another."[85] In only four more sentences Chief Justice Waite purported to establish the direct lineage of such weighty political theory to the more prosaic practice "customary in England from time immemorial, and in this country from its first colonization, to regulate ferries, common carriers, hackmen, bakers, millers, wharfingers, innkeepers, &c."[86]

Munn discusses the unique character of the property of a regulated firm, and for that reason we return to the decision in our discussion in chapter 6 of property-based protections for abrogation of the regulatory contract. For present purposes, however, *Munn* is illuminating because it described a kind of metamorphosis that property was thought to undergo when it became so productive as to command a substantial market:

> Looking . . . to the common law, from whence came the right which the Constitution protects, we find that when private property is "affected with a public interest, it ceases to be *juris privati* only." This was said by Lord Chief Justice Hale more than two hundred years ago . . . and has been accepted without objection as an essential element in the law of property ever since.[87]

To Chief Justice Waite and the majority, property becomes "clothed with a public interest when used in a manner to make it of public consequence,

---

83. *Id.* at 646.
84. 94 U.S. (4 Otto) 113, 124 (1877).
85. *Id.*
86. *Id.*
87. *Id.* at 125–26.

and affect the community at large."[88] That process, the Court reasoned, effected an implicit transfer of a property rights from the owner to the public: "When . . . one devotes his property to a use in which the public has an interest, he, in effect, grants to the public an interest in that use, and must submit to be controlled by the public for the common good, to the extent of the interest he has thus created."[89] From his analogies to common carriers under English law, it was clear that Chief Justice Waite envisioned a bargain between the state and the owner of the property that had become clothed with a public interest.[90]

In a better-reasoned dissent, Justice Stephen Field thought that Chief Justice Waite's statement of the rule was excessively broad:

> When Sir Matthew Hale, and the sages of the law in his day, spoke of property as affected by a public interest, and ceasing from that cause to be *juris privati* solely, that is, ceasing to be held merely in private right, they referred to property dedicated by the owner to public uses, or to property the use of which was granted by the government, or in connection with which special privileges were conferred. Unless the property was thus dedicated, or some right bestowed by the government was held with the property, either by specific grant or by prescription of so long a time as to imply a grant originally, the property was not affected by any public interest so as to be taken out of the category of property held in private right.[91]

Despite the fact that he was dissenting, from that passage it should be clear that even Justice Field could have agreed that the typical bargain between a public utility and its regulator entailed a quid pro quo in the form of a private franchise. Later in his dissent, Justice Field expressly spoke of the government's right to regulate rates as an implicit condition

88. *Id.* at 126.

89. *Id.* The Court explained that the owner could rescind his grant of property rights to the public: "He may withdraw his grant by discontinuing the use; but, so long as he maintains the use, he must submit to the control." *Id.* As our previous discussion of abandonment indicates, however, a public utility would subsequently be found to face barriers to withdrawing its property from public use, notwithstanding that language in *Munn.*

90. Richard A. Epstein's reading of *Munn* comports with our contractual interpretation of that decision. He observes that Chief Justice Waite "noted that traditional common carrier obligations imposed upon a party receiving a legal monopoly the obligation to charge only reasonable fees for the services rendered, where the restriction on the power to charge what one sees fit is the quid pro quo for the monopoly in question." RICHARD A. EPSTEIN, TAKINGS: PRIVATE PROPERTY AND THE POWER OF EMINENT DOMAIN 168 n.15 (Harvard University Press 1985).

91. *Id.* at 139–40 (Field, J., dissenting).

of the bargain under which it conferred special benefits on the regulated firm.[92] He argued that in the frequently cited cases of

> public ferries, bridges, and turnpikes, of wharfingers, hackmen, and draymen, ... there was some special privilege granted by the State or municipality; and no one, I suppose, has ever contended that the State had not a right to prescribe the conditions upon which such privilege should be enjoyed. The State in such cases exercises no greater right than an individual may exercise over the use of his own property when leased or loaned to others.[93]

To Justice Field, therefore, the state's power to impose rate regulation was the result of a bargain in which the state conferred special benefits on the regulated firm in return for its acceptance of rate regulation and public service obligations.

EXPLICIT CONTRACTING BETWEEN MUNICIPALITIES AND PUBLIC UTILITIES

The notions of bargaining between the regulator and the regulated firm, which pervade *Munn* in both Chief Justice Waite's majority opinion and Justice Field's dissent, are repeated many times over in practice. Numerous court decisions and scholarly writings from the late nineteenth and early twentieth centuries flatly contradict Robert J. Michaels's assertion that the regulatory contract is a recent concoction, as does recent research showing the contractual origins of public utility regulation.[94] That Michaels's LEXIS research did not produce more or earlier reported cases may reflect nothing more profound than his evident failure to recognize that, as Justice Story noted in *Green* v. *Biddle* in 1823, "the terms com-

---

92. "It is only where some right or privilege is conferred by the government or municipality upon the owner, which he can use in connection with his property, or by means of which the use of his property is rendered more valuable to him, or he thereby enjoys an advantage over others, that the compensation to be received by him becomes a legitimate matter of regulation. Submission to the regulation of compensation in such cases is an implied condition of the grant, and the State, in exercising its power of prescribing the compensation, only determines the conditions upon which its concession shall be enjoyed. When the privilege ends, the power of regulation ceases." *Id.* at 146–47 (Field, J., dissenting).

93. *Id.* at 148–49.

94. George L. Priest, *The Origins of Utility Regulation and the "Theories of Regulation" Debate*, 36 J.L. & ECON. 289 (1992). For a critique of Priest's article, see Geoffrey P. Miller, *Comment on Priest, "The Origins of Utility Regulation and the 'Theories of Regulation' Debate,"* 36 J.L. & ECON. 325 (1993).

pact and contract are synonymous."[95] Even if Michaels could prove that the phrase "regulatory compact" was recently coined to refer to the contractual relationship under discussion, that fact would not begin to rebut the evidence that municipalities and public utilities routinely entered into explicit contracts in the nineteenth and early twentieth centuries, before the advent in most states of public utilities commissions.

Voluntary Exchange

The regulatory contract in the United States was born roughly 180 years ago, the offspring of public necessity and private undertaking. During the first half of the nineteenth century, city governments lacked the necessary financial resources and expertise to provide their citizens all the benefits that might flow from the momentous scientific and industrial developments of that era. So the cities solicited the help of private entrepreneurs.[96] State legislatures or local municipalities offered charters or franchises to railroads and utilities. Those contracts gave the private firms critical access to public rights-of-way and often delegated to them the power of eminent domain. In return, the companies committed to building the costly infrastructures, and they accepted the obligation to serve the public on a nondiscriminatory basis at reasonable rates. Each franchise was the product of a bargained-for exchange, satisfying the public need for services such as water and electricity, while allowing the private enterprise the opportunity to earn a competitive return and the recovery of its invested capital. It is therefore inaccurate to deny either the contractual origins of the present regulatory relationship, the contractual motivations for the subsequent transition from municipal franchising to state regulatory commissions, or the contractual essence of the regulatory relationship that resulted from that transition. "The franchise is a contract between the utility and the municipality," wrote Irston R. Barnes in 1942, "and since both parties are

---

95. 21 U.S. (8 Wheat.) 1, 92 (1823).

96. WILLIAM M. IVINS & HERBERT DELAVAN MASON, THE CONTROL OF PUBLIC UTILITIES 4–15 (Baker, Voorhis & Co. 1908); 1 DELOS F. WILCOX, MUNICIPAL FRANCHISES 1–3 (Gervaise Press 1910); JOSEPH A. JOYCE, A TREATISE ON FRANCHISES 542–54 (Banks Law Publishing Co. 1914); HERBERT B. DORAU, MATERIALS FOR THE STUDY OF PUBLIC UTILITY ECONOMICS 2–9, 12–22, 33–61 (Macmillan Co. 1930); Felix Frankfurter & Henry M. Hart, Jr., *Rate Regulation*, *in* 13 ENCYCLOPAEDIA OF THE SOCIAL SCIENCES 104, 105 (Edwin R. A. Seligman & Alvin Johnson, eds., Macmillan Co. 1934); ELI WINSTON CLEMENS, ECONOMICS AND PUBLIC UTILITIES 72–73 (Appleton-Century-Crofts, Inc. 1950). For a thorough discussion of the various types of franchises that municipalities and utilities devised, see BARNES, *supra* note 40, at 218–41.

bound thereby it is important that its terms be carefully drawn with due regard to the legitimate interests of each."[97]

Half a century later, another Yale professor, George L. Priest proposed an explanation for the use of municipal franchising that is grounded in voluntary exchange and contractual adaptation:

> Public utility companies voluntarily entered contracts subjecting themselves to regulation in order to gain authority to use public rights-of-way for laying gas and water pipes, stringing telephone and electric poles, burying electrical wires, and laying street railway tracks. Regulation of the utility's activities and terms of business resulted from a negotiation between the municipal government and the utility in a context that both parties recognized saved the utility the costs of negotiating with and securing rights from the individual property owners they intended to serve.[98]

New York City, for example, introduced franchise contracts as early as the 1820s for gas and the 1830s for street railway transportation.[99] Other franchises for services such as electricity, water, street railways, toll bridges, and telephone service soon followed.

The franchise was a legal instrument—a contract having all the constitutional protection that a contract between private parties would enjoy. Joseph Joyce, writing at the turn of the twentieth century in his treatise on municipal franchises, observed:

> [F]ranchises are based in this country upon contracts between the sovereign power and a private citizen, made upon a valuable consideration for purposes of public benefit as well as for individual advantage; and it is said by Chancellor Kent that franchises "contain an implied covenant on the part of the government not to invade the right vested, and on the part of the grantees to execute the conditions and duties prescribed in the grant. Some of these franchises are presumed to be founded on a valuable consideration, and to involve public duties, and to be made for public accommodation, and to be affected with *jus publicum*, and they are necessarily exclusive in

---

97. *Id.* at 219.

98. Priest, *supra* note 94, at 303. Economist Kenneth Rose makes the contradictory—and, in our view, historically indefensible—argument that "[t]he regulatory contract is not necessarily a voluntary agreement accepted by utilities." KENNETH ROSE, AN ECONOMIC AND LEGAL PERSPECTIVE ON ELECTRIC UTILITY TRANSITION COSTS 42–43 (National Regulatory Research Institute, July 1996).

99. Priest, *supra* note 94, at 301.

their nature. The government cannot resume them at pleasure, or do any act to impair the grant, without a breach of contract."[100]

From that absolutist view of the municipal franchise as contract, which the government could not unilaterally amend, the modern regulatory contract emerged. In a 1912 decision concerning municipal regulation of gas prices, *Cedar Rapids Gas Light Co.* v. *City of Cedar Rapids*, Justice Oliver Wendell Holmes wrote for a unanimous Supreme Court that such regulation "has to steer between Scylla and Charybdis,"[101] for it resulted from bilateral bargaining in the shadow of takings jurisprudence:

> On the one side if the franchise is taken to mean that the most profitable return that could be got, free from competition, is protected by the Fourteenth Amendment, then the power to regulate is null. On the other hand if the power to regulate withdraws the protection of the Amendment altogether, then the property is nought. This is not a matter of economic theory, *but of fair interpretation of a bargain.* Neither extreme can have been meant. A midway between them must be hit.[102]

The municipality did not unilaterally thrust regulation on the utility. Rather, municipal regulation resulted from voluntary exchange: "It is true that the contract was in the form of an ordinance, but the ordinance was drawn as a contract to be accepted and it was accepted" by the utility.[103]

The Ascent of Contract

The courts have defined the degree to which government may regulate utilities during any given period. The extent of regulation allowed by the courts, in turn, reflected the degree to which the government depended upon and strove to nurture the utility, given the current economic and social climate. Thus, as the railroads became a powerful economic force sooner than the electric, water, or telephone companies, the courts were more willing to allow greater regulation of the railroads a few decades before the latter companies. Yet, despite the differences in relative economic might, the regulatory contract in each of those industries was formed in the late nineteenth and early twentieth centuries while the Su-

---

100. JOYCE, *supra* note 96, at 12 (quoting JAMES KENT, COMMENTARIES ON AMERICAN LAW *458 (Little, Brown & Co., 14th ed. 1896)).
101. 223 U.S. 655, 669 (1912).
102. *Id.* at 669–70 (emphasis added).
103. *Id.* at 667–68.

preme Court vacillated on the definitions of three constitutional doctrines: the prohibition of a state to impair the obligation of contracts, the prohibition of government to take private property without just compensation, and the rise and fall of substantive due process. In the context of each of those doctrines the Court examined the extent to which the state could exercise its police power over a regulated utility.

By 1848 the Court recognized, in *West River Bridge* v. *Dix*, a state's power to commandeer—for just compensation—a toll bridge built by a private party subject to an exclusive franchise.[104] In 1795 Vermont granted an exclusive 100-year franchise to build and operate a toll bridge. In 1843 the local government took the bridge for public use and paid the bridge company $4,000. Justice Peter V. Daniel wrote for the Court that the taking did not constitute an impermissible impairment of the bridge company's contract.[105]

Fewer than twenty years later, the Court proclaimed the importance of franchise rights and the inviolability of contract, again in the context of a challenge to the holder of a bridge franchise. In 1865, in defending an exclusive bridge franchise from impairment, Justice David Davis delivered the Court's opinion in *The Binghamton Bridge.*[106] The opinion embodied the general economic ideology that pervaded judicial opinions on franchise regulation of that era and characterized the inviolability of contract as the keystone to the relationship between government and private enterprise:

> The purposes to be attained are generally beyond the ability of individual enterprise, and can only be accomplished through the aid of associated wealth. This will not be risked unless privileges are given and securities furnished in an act of incorporation. The wants of the public are often so imperative that a duty is imposed on the Government to provide for them; and, as experience has proved that a State should not directly attempt to do this, it is necessary to confer on others the faculty of doing what the sovereign power is unwilling to undertake. The legislature, therefore, says to public-spirited citizens: "If you will embark, with your time, money, and skill, in an enterprise which will accommodate the public necessities, we will grant to you, for a limited period, or in perpetuity, privileges that will justify the expenditure of your money, and the employment of your time and skill." Such a grant is a contract, with mutual considerations, and jus-

---

104. 47 U.S. (6 How.) 507 (1848).
105. *Id.* at 533.
106. 70 U.S. (3 Wall.) 51 (1865).

tice and good policy alike require that the protection of the law should be assured to it.[107]

That economic philosophy and respect for voluntary exchange typified many utility regulation cases of the period.

The protection against governmental takings of private property functioned as a complement to the prohibition of impairment of contractual obligations. During the nineteenth century, the protection of the Contracts Clause was the principle more often applied to cases of utility regulation.[108] The Takings Clause, however, would emerge as the primary protection against regulatory incursions by government. During the years spanned by *West River Bridge* and *The Binghamton Bridge*, the Court devised the doctrine of substantive due process. Although in 1887 the Court in *Munn* v. *Illinois* upheld a regulation of rates of grain elevators "affected with a public interest,"[109] by 1905 in *Lochner* v. *New York* the Court found "no reasonable foundation for holding" a statute limiting the number of hours that bakers may work in a week "to be necessary or appropriate as a health law."[110] The Court began to rule upon the reasonableness of statutes, particularly those effecting economic regulation; that orientation probably affected the Court's view of utility regulation cases as well, including those decided under the Contracts Clause.

THE REGULATORY CONTRACT
IN THE SUPREME COURT

The understanding of utility regulation as contract permeates a number of Supreme Court decisions from the late nineteenth and early twentieth centuries. Those decisions were usually unanimous and are striking for the sophistication with which they described in nontechnical terms the economic rationale for the regulatory contract and based their legal conclusions on such reasoning. Our purpose in discussing the following decisions by the Court is not to endorse the logic of particular legal doctrines, some of which the Court has abandoned since the *Lochner* era, but rather to show as a *factual* matter that in various kinds of cases predating the rise

---

107. *Id*. at 73.
108. U.S. CONST. art. I, § 10, cl. 2 ("No State shall . . . pass any . . . Law impairing the Obligation of Contracts").
109. 94 U.S. 113 (1877).
110. 198 U.S. 45, 58 (1905).

of the state regulatory commission the Court regarded the municipal franchise as an enforceable contract.

New Orleans Water Works

In 1885 the Court held unconstitutional, in *New Orleans Water Works Co. v. Rivers*, a local government's ordinance that infringed upon the exclusive rights that the state legislature granted a water company.[111] The Louisiana legislature in 1877 granted the New Orleans Water-Works Company the exclusive right to provide water to the city of New Orleans for fifty years. In 1882 the city council of New Orleans passed an ordinance to allow an individual to lay pipes to provide his New Orleans hotel with water. The Court upheld the exclusivity of the New Orleans Water-Works' franchise and, in a unanimous opinion by Justice John Marshall Harlan, reasoned:

> The right to dig up and use the streets and alleys of New Orleans for the purpose of placing pipes and mains to supply the city and its inhabitants with water is a franchise belonging to the State, which she could grant to such persons or corporations, and upon such terms, as she deemed best for the public interests. And as the object to be attained was a public one, for which the State could make provision by legislative enactment, the grant of the franchise could be accompanied with such exclusive privileges to the grantee, in respect of the subject of the grant, as in the judgment of the legislative department would best promote the public health and the public comfort, or the protection of public and private property. Such was the nature of the plaintiff's grant, which, not being at the time prohibited by the constitution of the State, was a contract, the obligation of which cannot be impaired by subsequent legislation, or by a change in her organic law. It is as much a contract, within the meaning of the Constitution of the United States, as a grant to a private corporation for a valuable consideration, or in consideration of public services to be rendered by it, of the exclusive right to construct and maintain a railroad within certain lines and between given points, or a bridge over a navigable stream within a prescribed distance above and below a designated point.[112]

In the companion case, *New Orleans Gas Co.* v. *Louisiana Light Co.*, a unanimous Court, again speaking through Justice Harlan, recognized that a state may exercise its police power to protect the health, morals, and safety of its citizens, but the power to regulate is tempered by an inability

---

111. 115 U.S. 674 (1885).
112. *Id.* at 681.

to impair contractual obligations.[113] On facts similar to those in *New Orleans Water Works*, the Court observed: "That the police power . . . is restricted . . . is further shown by those cases in which grants of exclusive privileges respecting public highways and bridges over navigable streams have been sustained as contracts, the obligations of which are fully protected against impairment by State enactments."[114]

Walla Walla Water

In *Walla Walla City* v. *Walla Walla Water Co.* the Court extended its defense of contract to a municipal franchise.[115] In 1883 the legislature of Washington Territory incorporated the city of Walla Walla. One of its enumerated powers under the charter was the power to provide water for the city, as well as the right to permit the use of city streets for the purpose of laying pipes for furnishing such supply. Pursuant to its power, the city of Walla Walla by contract granted to the Walla Walla Water Company in 1887 the right to lay and maintain water mains and related infrastructure for twenty-five years. The water company accepted and complied with all conditions in the contract. In 1893, however, the city passed an ordinance to provide for the construction of a system of water works to supply the city with water. The question thus arose whether the federal court had jurisdiction to decide whether the city had unconstitutionally impaired the obligation of its franchise contract. On his way to concluding that the federal courts did indeed have jurisdiction, Justice Henry B. Brown wrote for a unanimous panel that "this court has too often decided for the rule to be now questioned, that the grant of a right to supply gas or water to a municipality and its inhabitants through pipes and mains laid in the streets, upon condition of the performance of its service by the grantee, is the grant of a franchise vested in the State, in consideration of the performance of a public service, and after performance by the grantee, is a contract protected by the Constitution of the United States against state legislation to impair it."[116]

---

113. 115 U.S. 650 (1885).

114. *Id.* at 661.

115. 172 U.S. 1 (1898).

116. *Id.* at 8–9. "It is true that in these cases the franchise was granted directly by the state legislature, but it is equally clear that such franchises may be bestowed upon corporations by the municipal authorities, provided the right to do so is given by their charters. State legislatures may not only exercise their sovereignty directly, but may delegate such portions of it to inferior legislative bodies as, in their judgment, is desirable for local purposes." *Id.*

Although the city's franchise did not confer a monopoly, Walla Walla Water's contract specifically stipulated that the city would not compete with the company. The city argued that the noncompete provision made the contract void as against public policy. But the Court rejected the argument and interpreted that provision, along with an eminent domain provision, as ancillary restraints that protected the franchisee's opportunity to recover the cost of its investment in infrastructure:

> There was no attempt made to create a monopoly by granting an exclusive right to this company, and the agreement that the city would not erect water works of its own was accompanied, in section 8 of the contract, with a reservation of a right to take, condemn and pay for the water works of the company at any time during the existence of the contract. Taking sections 7 and 8 together, they amount simply to this: That if the city should desire to establish water works of its own it would do so by condemning the property of the company and making such changes in its plant or such additions thereto as it might deem desirable for the better supply of its inhabitants; but that it would not enter into a direct competition with the company during the life of the contract. As such competition would be almost necessarily ruinous to the company, it was little more than an agreement that the city would carry out the contract in good faith.[117]

The Court regarded the noncompete provision as "a natural incident to the main purpose of the contract,"[118] without which a private company would not voluntarily make the substantial asset-specific investments required to provide water service:

> In establishing a system of water works the company would necessarily incur a large expense in the construction of the power house and the laying of its pipes through the streets, and, as the life of the contract was limited to twenty-five years, it would naturally desire to protect itself from competition as far as possible, and would have a right to expect that at least the city would not itself enter into such competition. It is not to be supposed that the company would have entered upon this large undertaking in view of the possibility that, in one of the sudden changes of public opinion to which all municipalities are more or less subject, the city might resolve to enter the field itself—a field in which it undoubtedly would have become the master—and practically extinguish the rights it had already granted to the company.[119]

117. *Id.* at 17.
118. *Id.*
119. *Id.* at 17–18.

In short, the Court articulated in *Walla Walla Water* the same concern over contractual opportunism that emerged three-quarters of a century later as a guiding principle in the economic analysis of utility regulation.

Russell v. Sebastian

In *Russell* v. *Sebastian*, the Court, in 1914, reiterated that concern over contractual opportunism and specifically endorsed a public service corporation's expectation of a profitable rate of return on its investment.[120] Writing for a unanimous Court, Justice Charles Evans Hughes reasoned that a private enterprise accepted a franchise offer with the expectation to earn a profitable rate of return on the investments required to fulfill its obligations under the franchise contract.[121] The Court viewed such an expectation to be inherent in the parties' bargained-for exchange. *Russell* held that a state constitutional amendment and subsequent municipal ordinances impaired contract rights vested in the Economic Gas Co. by a franchise grant entailed in section 19 of article XI of California's 1879 constitution, which provided:

> In any city where there are no public works owned and controlled by the municipality for supplying the same with water or artificial light, any individual, or any company duly incorporated for such purpose, under and by authority of the laws of this state, shall, under the direction of the superintendent of streets, or other officer in control thereof, and under such general regulations as the municipality may prescribe, for damages and indemnity for damages, have the privilege of using the public streets and thoroughfares thereof, and of laying down pipes and conduits therein, and connections therewith, so far as may be necessary for introducing into and supplying such city and its inhabitants, either with gaslight, or other illuminating light, or with fresh water for domestic and all other purposes, upon the condition that the municipal government shall have the right to regulate the charges thereof.[122]

Justice Hughes remarked upon the informal and spontaneous manner in which offer and acceptance of the regulatory contract would occur under such an ordinance:

---

120. 233 U.S. 195, 210 (1914).
121. *Id*. Justice Horace H. Lurton took no part in the decision.
122. *Id*. at 198–99. Economic Gas also claimed that the constitutional amendment and ordinance deprived the company of property without due process in violation of equal protection of the laws under the Fourteenth Amendment. *Id*. at 199–200. The Court did not reach that issue.

It is pointed out that the language of the provision was general both with respect to persons and to places; that it embraced all the cities in the State; and that *it did not provide for any formal or written acceptance of the offer*. But the lack of a requirement of an acceptance of a formal character did not preclude acceptance in fact. . . . [W]hen as to such a city the offer was accepted, the grant became as effective as if it had been made specially to the accepting individual or corporation.[123]

Justice Hughes's reasoning sheds light on the current debate over the regulatory contract. In that debate, some who oppose compensating utilities for their stranded costs dispute the very existence of the regulatory contract because, they argue, no formal writing documents its formation.[124]

In 1909 Economic Gas began its manufacture and distribution of gas to supply the city of Los Angeles with lighting under a claim of right based upon section 19.[125] In 1911 California amended that section of its constitution to allow municipalities to prescribe conditions and regulations upon such corporations.[126] In pursuance of the amendment, the city of Los Angeles adopted two ordinances. The first barred anyone from exercising any franchise or privilege to lay or maintain utility pipes without first obtaining a grant from the city,[127] and the second outlawed street excavation without written permission from the public works board.[128]

The determinative issue in *Russell* was the nature and extent of the rights that Economic Gas acquired under section 19 of California's 1879 constitution upon accepting the franchise offer. The state contended that the scope of Economic Gas's acceptance, and hence the scope of its operations, were limited to the range of streets in use at the time of the 1911 constitutional amendment.[129] Economic Gas claimed that it would lose $2,000 per month if the state were to confine the company's operations solely to the streets in use as of 1911.[130]

For three reasons the Court concluded that Economic Gas had a contractual right to the larger service area that it believed its franchise entailed. First, the Court held that accepting the state's offer would oblige

---

123. *Id.* at 203 (emphasis added).

124. We discuss the related question of the voidability of the regulatory contract in our discussion of the Statute of Frauds in chapter 5.

125. 233 U.S. at 200.

126. *Id.* at 198–99.

127. *Id.* at 199.

128. *Id.*

129. *Id.* at 202.

130. *Id.* at 201.

the company to supply the city with light.[131] That obligation, in turn, would require the company to make considerable investments to construct permanent reservoirs with suitable storage capacity, to build plants large enough to meet reasonably anticipated demands, and to lay conduits necessary for distribution.[132] Second and more notably, the Court found that when an offer of a franchise entailed extensive investment by the franchisee, either explicitly or implicitly, the right of the franchisee to a chance of profit was inherent in the offer, and the chance of profit was essential to the efficacy of an enterprise.[133] Finally, the Court reasoned that because firms evaluated business ventures on the basis of calculations of future growth and expansion, a utility would necessarily expect that the city would open new streets and extend old ones over time—especially where the utility was obligated to extend service throughout the city as reasonable demands required.[134] Economic Gas's construction of facilities capable of supplying gas to a territory much larger than that supplied before the 1911 ordinance evidenced the company's future intentions; indeed, the company had invested $100,000 more than would have been necessary to supply only the inhabitants reached by the pipes in 1911.[135] Hence, the Court concluded that the right to lay the pipes carrying the gas necessary to provide light to Los Angeles inhabitants was "absolutely essential to the undertaking"[136] and that the grant was therefore binding as an entirety and "not foot by foot, as pipes were laid."[137]

Justice Hughes relied heavily on notions of detrimental reliance and investment-backed expectations. Such considerations underlay his emphatic rhetoric concerning contract formation:

> When the voice of the State declares that it is bound if its offer is accepted, and the question simply is with respect to the scope of the obligation, we should be slow to conclude that only a revocable license was intended. Moreover the provision plainly contemplated the establishment of a plant devoted to the described public service and an assumption of the duty to perform that service. That the grant, resulting from an acceptance of the State's offer, constituted a contract, and vested in the accepting individual

131. *Id.* at 209.
132. *Id.* at 206.
133. *Id.* at 208.
134. *Id.* at 209.
135. *Id.* at 200.
136. *Id.*
137. *Id.* at 207–08.

or corporation a property right, protected by the Federal Constitution, is not open to dispute in view of the repeated decisions of this court.[138]

Having shown that formation of the regulatory contract had occurred, Justice Hughes turned to interpreting the contract and emphasized that the Court would not permit rules of construction thereupon to suck the content from the agreement. After conceding the black-letter rule that "public grants are to be construed strictly in favor of the public" and that "ambiguities are to be resolved against the grantee," Justice Hughes emphasized that "this principle of construction does not deny to public offers a fair and reasonable interpretation, or justify the withholding of that which it satisfactorily appears the grant was intended to convey."[139] Instead, he insisted on giving "a practical, common-sense construction" to the regulatory contract.[140] That common-sense construction led Justice Hughes to emphasize the potential for stranded costs to arise if the state were to act opportunistically with respect to the investments that Economic Gas had made to perform the contract:

> The breadth of the offer was commensurate with the requirements of the undertaking which was invited. The service to which the provision referred was a community service. It was the supply of a municipality—which had no municipal works—with water or light. This would involve, in the case of water-works, the securing of sources of supply, the provision of conduits for conveying the water to the municipality, and the permanent investment in the construction of reservoirs with suitable storage capacity; and, in the case of gas-works, the establishment of a manufacturing plant on a scale large enough to meet the demands that could reasonably be anticipated. *But water-works and gas-works constructed to furnish a municipality with water or light would, of course, be useless without distributing systems;* and the right of laying in the streets the mains needed to carry the water or gas to the inhabitants of the community was absolutely essential to the undertaking as a practical enterprise. This, the constitutional provision recognized. It was clearly designed to stop favoritism in granting such rights, not to withhold them. It is not to be supposed that it was expected that water-works and gas-works of the character required to supply cities would be erected without grants of franchises to use the streets for laying the necessary distributing pipes. . . . The scheme of the constitutional provision was not to make it impossible to secure such grants, or to restrict the street rights to be acquired, but, as already stated, to end the existing abuses by making these grants directly through the

138. *Id.* at 204.
139. *Id.* at 205.
140. *Id.*

constitution itself instead of permitting them to be made by the legislature or by municipalities acting under legislative authority.[141]

Justice Hughes rejected the proposition that "the investment in extensive plants—in the construction of reservoirs, and in the building of manufacturing works—was invited without any assurance that the laying of the distributing system could be completed or that it could even be extended far enough to afford any chance of profit."[142] Echoing the reasoning of economists more than half a century later, Justice Hughes concluded his opinion for the Court by once more underscoring the significance of investment as an act of contract formation: "The company, by its investment, had irrevocably committed itself to the undertaking and its acceptance of the offer of the right to lay its pipes, so far as necessary to serve the municipality, was complete."[143]

Detroit Citizens' Street Railway
and Other Contract Impairment Cases

Other early decisions concerning the regulatory contract addressed the municipality's power to reduce prices to uncompensatory levels. With

141. *Id.* at 206–07.
142. *Id.* at 208.
143. *Id.* at 210. Later the same year, Justice Hughes wrote the opinion for a unanimous Court in New York Elec. Lines *v.* Empire City Subway Co., 235 U.S. 179 (1914), which posed the question of whether a franchise to use the streets of New York City to bury electrical lines constituted a contract and, if so, whether the contract had been unconstitutionally impaired. On the existence of the contract, Justice Hughes wrote:

> These municipal consents are intended to afford the basis of enterprise with reciprocal advantages, and it would be virtually impossible to fulfil the manifest intent of the legislature and to secure the benefits expected to flow from the privileges conferred, if, in the initial stages of the enterprise when the necessary proceedings preliminary to the execution of the proposed work are being taken with due promptness, or when the work is under way, the municipal consent should be subject to revocation at any time by the authorities—not upon the ground that the contract had not been performed, or that any condition thereof, express or implied, had been broken, but because as yet no contract whatever had been made and there was nothing but a license which might be withdrawn at pleasure. Grants like the one under consideration are not nude pacts, but rest upon obligations expressly or impliedly assumed to carry on the undertaking to which they relate. They are made and received with the understanding that the recipient is protected by a contractual right from the moment the grant is accepted and during the course of performance as contemplated, as well as after that performance.

Id. at 193 (citations omitted).

apparent disregard for its holding in *Munn*, the Court in 1902 held unconstitutional, in *Detroit v. Detroit Citizens' Street Railway Co.*, a city ordinance attempting to reduce the rates of a street railway that had been fixed in the company's franchise.[144] The Detroit Citizens' Railway had operated pursuant to its franchise for several years when, in 1899, the Detroit city council enacted an ordinance to reduce the company's rates. Writing for a unanimous Court, Justice Rufus W. Peckham reasoned that a municipality, duly authorized by the state legislature, once having entered into a franchise contract with a public service corporation had its powers, "so far as altering the rates of fare or other matters properly involved in and being a part of the contract," suspended for the duration of the contract period.[145]

The Court recognized that, as in the case of a contract between private parties, the rate of fare or price was a crucial element of the regulatory contract that could not be unilaterally altered:

> The rate of fare is among the most material and important of the terms and conditions which might be imposed by the city in exchange for its consent to the laying of railroad tracks and the running of cars thereon through its streets. It would be a subject for grave consideration and conference between the parties, and when determined by mutual agreement, the rate would naturally be regarded as fixed until another rate was adopted by a like agreement.[146]

Again, as in *Walla Walla Water* and *Russell* v. *Sebastian*, the Court's rationale for denying the city of Detroit the unilateral power to reduce price under the contract emphasized cost recovery, asset specificity, opportunism, and credible commitments:

> It would hardly be credible that capitalists about to invest money in what was then a somewhat uncertain venture, while procuring the consent of the

---

144. 184 U.S. 368 (1902).

145. *Id.* at 383.

146. *Id.* at 384. The Court also elaborated on the need for bilateral agreement to modify the contract price: "The rate of fare having been fixed by positive agreement under the expressed legislative authority, the subject is not open to alteration thereafter by the common council alone, under the right to prescribe from time to time the rules and regulations for the running and operation of the road. Nor does the language of the ordinance, which provides that the rate of fare for one passenger shall not be more than five cents, give any right to the city to reduce it below the rate of five cents established by the company. It is a contract which gives the company the right to charge a rate of fare up to the sum of five cents for a single passenger, and leaves no power with the city to reduce it without the consent of the company." *Id.* at 389.

city to lay its rails and operate its road through the streets in language which as to the rate of fare amounted to a contract, and gave the company a right to charge a rate then deemed essential for the financial success of the enterprise, would at the same time consent that such rate then agreed upon should be subject to change from time to time by the sole decision of the common council. It would rather seem that the language above used did not and was not intended to give the right to the common council to change at its pleasure from time to time those important and fundamental rights affecting the very existence and financial success of the company in the operation of its road, but that by the use of such language there was simply reserved to the city council the right from time to time to add to or alter those general regulations or rules for the proper, safe and efficient running of the cars, the character of service, the speed and number of cars and their hours of operation and matters of a like nature.[147]

Thus, the Court well recognized by the turn of the twentieth century that key provisions in the regulatory contract existed to ensure cost recovery for specialized investments and to deter opportunism.

Moreover, in *Detroit Citizens' Street Railway* the Court clearly recognized that the franchise was a contract and that under the Constitution a state (and certainly a municipality) could not infringe upon the rights vested under the contract, especially with regard to allowable rates. The binding character of regulatory agreements respecting rates embodied in municipal ordinances was a rule that subsequent Supreme Court cases recognized as first being promulgated in *Detroit Citizens' Street Railway*.[148] By 1908, a more comprehensive restatement of that rule had become settled law: "The State may authorize one of its municipal corporations to establish by an inviolable contract the rates to be charged by a public service corporation (or natural person) for a definite term, not grossly unreasonable in point of time, and that the effect of such a contract is to suspend, during the life of the contract, the governmental power of fixing and regulating the rates."[149] One can trace the evolution of that articulation of the rule to a number of decisions following *Detroit Citizens' Street Railway*. In those decisions the Court also struck down city ordinances attempting to reduce the rates of fare charged by street railway

---

147. *Id.* at 385.

148. *See* City of Cleveland *v.* Cleveland City Ry., 194 U.S. 517, 536 (1903).

149. Home Tel. & Tel. Co. *v.* City of Los Angeles, 211 U.S. 265, 273 (1908) (citing Detroit *v.* Detroit Citizens' Street Ry., 184 U.S. 368, 382 (1902); Vicksburg *v.* Vicksburg Waterworks Co., 206 U.S. 496, 508 (1907)). For a later case affirming the rule, see St. Cloud Pub. Serv. Co. *v.* City of St. Cloud, 265 U.S. 352, 355 (1924).

companies that were predetermined under the companies' original franchise contracts.[150]

In *City of Cleveland* v. *Cleveland City Railway*, the Court unanimously
held in 1904 that an 1898 Cleveland city ordinance seeking to decrease
street railroad fares charged by Cleveland City Railway impaired the city's
obligations under its franchise contract.[151] In an opinion by Justice Edward
D. White, the Court found that the contract obligations were embodied in
two prior city ordinances enacted in 1885 and 1887. Accordingly, the
Court stated that the contractual right to the higher rates of fare had vested
in Cleveland City Railway because its predecessors in interest, with whom
it was in privity of contract, had accepted the city's offer of building,
maintaining, and operating street railways at rates specified in the 1885
and 1887 ordinances.[152]

In 1910 the Court in *City of Minneapolis* v. *Minneapolis Street Railway
Co.* unanimously held a 1907 Minneapolis ordinance to be unconstitutional
on the grounds that it impaired contract rights secured by the Minneapolis
Street Railway Co. through a 1875 city ordinance that the state legislature
later ratified in 1879.[153] The 1875 ordinance, as ratified, secured to the
company for a fifty-year period beginning in 1873 the contract right to
charge five cents per passenger for one continuous trip. The 1907 ordinance, alternatively, required that the company sell six tickets for a quar-
ter. Writing for the Court, Justice William R. Day found the 1907 ordinance to have violated the terms of "a previous and subsisting contract,
prescribing the rates of fare to be charged by the company in the city of
Minneapolis."[154] Justice Day held that "grants of the character of the one
under consideration[], when embodying the terms of a contract," were
"protected by the Federal Constitution from impairment by subsequent
state legislation, and notwithstanding the principle of strict construction,
whatever [was] plainly granted c[ould] not be taken from the parties entitled thereto by such legislative enactments."[155]

---

150. *See* Detroit *v.* Detroit Citizens' Street Ry., 184 U.S. 368 (1902); Home Tel. & Tel.
Co. *v.* City of Los Angeles, 211 U.S. 265 (1908); Vicksburg *v.* Vicksburg Waterworks Co.,
206 U.S. 496 (1907); City of Cleveland *v.* Cleveland City Ry., 194 U.S. 517 (1904); City of
Minneapolis *v.* Minneapolis Ry., 215 U.S. 417 (1909); Milwaukee Elec. Ry. & Light Co. *v.*
Railroad Comm'n of Wis., 238 U.S. 174 (1915).

151. City of Cleveland *v.* Cleveland City Ry., 194 U.S. 517, 537 (1904). Justice Harlan
took no part in the decision.

152. *Id.* at 534.

153. 215 U.S. 417, 436 (1910).

154. *Id.*

155. *Id.* at 427.

As it did in *Detroit Citizens' Street Railway*, the Court began its inquiry in other contract impairment cases by identifying the state statute empowering the municipal authority to contract with utilities such as street railway companies. In *Detroit Citizens' Street Railway* the contract was made pursuant to a state statute specifically requiring that rates of fare be established by agreement between the railway company and the municipality.[156] Although the Court did not question the competency of a state legislature to authorize a municipality to contract with a street railway company as to rates of fare, it nonetheless "conceded that clear authority from the legislature [was] needed to enable the city to make a contract or agreement like the ordinances in question, including rates of fare."[157] In *Cleveland City Railway* the Court found the statutory grant adequate because it conferred "comprehensive powers to contract with street railway companies with respect to terms and conditions upon which such roads might be constructed, operated, extended and consolidated."[158] In *Vicksburg* v. *Vicksburg Waterworks Co.*,[159] the Court, speaking unanimously through Justice Day, recognized as adequate a grant of legislative powers to the municipality that on its face was unrestrictive.[160] The Court stated that "under a broad grant of power, conferring, without restriction or limitation, upon the city of Vicksburg the right to make a contract for a supply of water, it was within the right of the city council, in the exercise of this power, to make a binding contract, fixing a maximum rate at which water should be supplied to the inhabitants of the city for a limited term of years."[161]

In later cases, however, the Court looked for clear and unmistakable legislative authority empowering a municipality to enter into contracts delineating rates of fare.[162] In *Home Telephone & Telegraph Co.* v. *City of Los Angeles*,[163] Justice William H. Moody wrote for a unanimous Court in 1908 that such contracts were tantamount to the surrender of the governmental power to regulate rates of fare and as such were very grave acts requiring the close scrutiny of both the surrender itself and the authority to

156. *Detroit Citizens' Street Ry.*, 184 U.S. at 385.

157. *Id.* at 382.

158. *Cleveland City Ry.*, 194 U.S. at 534.

159. 206 U.S. 496 (1907).

160. *Id.* at 515.

161. *Id.*

162. Home Tel. & Tel. Co. *v.* City of Los Angeles, 211 U.S. 265, 273 (1908); Milwaukee Elec. Ry. *v.* Railroad Comm'n of Wis., 238 U.S. 174, 180 (1915); City of Paducah *v.* Paducah Ry. Co., 261 U.S. 267, 272 (1923).

163. 211 U.S. 265 (1908).

make it.[164] Justice Moody emphasized that "[n]o other body than the supreme legislature ha[d] the authority to make such a surrender, unless the
authority [was] clearly delegated to it by the supreme legislature."[165] He
reasoned that because contracts stipulating rates of fare to be charged had
"the effect of extinguishing pro tanto an undoubted power of government"
to regulate such rates, their existence and the authority to make them must
be clear and unmistakable.[166] Otherwise, the Court cautioned that "all
doubts must be resolved in favor of the continuance of the power" to regulate.[167] That ruling may have contributed to the rapid shift from municipal
regulation to state public utility commissions, a development supported by
the utilities themselves, that occurred over the next fourteen years.

In *Home Telephone*, the Court explained that the pertinent California
state legislation gave the Los Angeles city council the power only "to
regulate telephone service and the use of telephones within the city, . . .
and to fix and determine the charges for telephones and telephone service
and connections" through ordinances.[168] That provision, the Court said,
gave the municipality "ample authority" to exercise the governmental
power of regulating charges, but was not adequate to vest in the municipality the authority to enter into a contract to abandon the governmental
power itself.[169] The Court stated that the legislation "sp[oke] in words
appropriate to describe the authority to exercise the governmental power,
but entirely unfitted to describe the authority to contract. It authorized
command, but not agreement."[170] Nonetheless, *Home Telephone* recognized that a legislature could authorize agreement as to rates to be made
by ordinance. But such an ordinance, it noted, could not be an ordinance
"to fix and determine the charges."[171] Rather, it had to be an ordinance to
agree upon the charges.

In contract impairment cases, the Court, after identifying the relevant
empowering state statutes, would then reason that an empowered municipal council, when entering into contracts, "was exercising a portion of the
authority of the State, as an agency of the State."[172] For example, in
Cleveland City Railway, the Court reasoned that in passing the 1885 and

164. *Id.* at 273.
165. *Id.*
166. *Id.*
167. *Id.*
168. *Id.* at 275.
169. *Id.*
170. *Id.*
171. *Id.*
172. *Cleveland City Railway*, 194 U.S. at 534.

1887 ordinances the municipal council of Cleveland was exercising the power to contract as an agent of the state of Ohio.[173] Thus, it held that those ordinances embodied contractual obligations binding the council and the Cleveland City Railroad with respect to the rates of fare to be charged on street railway lines affected by the ordinances.[174] In *Detroit Citizens' Street Railway*, the Court implicitly recognized the agency relationship with regard to the power to contract and stated that, when a state statute authorized a municipality to contract with a street railway company, the municipality's power to alter "the rates of fare or other matters properly involved in and being a part of the contract, was suspended for the period of the running of the contract."[175]

A municipality, as an agent of the state, when duly empowered by clear and unmistakable legislative authority, could enter into an agreement with a public service corporation affixing rates for a specified period of time. Generally, a franchise offer extended through a municipal ordinance became a binding contract when a utility accepted the offer. The Court in *Detroit Citizens' Street Railway* approvingly cited *City Railway Co.* v. *Citizens' Street Railroad Co.*[176] for the proposition that once a railway company accepted an offer for the use of city streets, entailed in a municipal ordinance, in consideration for its building and operating a street railway and built and operated the railway, then a contract was formed "which the State was not at liberty to impair during its continuance."[177]

The manner of acceptance does not appear to have played a dispositive role in those cases. In at least one case, the Court, in ascertaining whether an agreement binding both the municipality and the public service corporation was intended, found the fact that the ordinance had required a written acceptance especially significant.[178] On the other hand, in *Russell* v. *Sebastian* the Court said that "the lack of a requirement of an acceptance of a formal character did not preclude acceptance in fact."[179] The Court added that when a utility began preparations for distributing service and changed its position "beyond recall," acceptance was valid.[180] Moreover, as noted

---

173. *Id.*

174. *Id.* In actuality, the ordinances were accepted by the railroad's predecessors in interest.

175. *Detroit Citizens' Street Ry.*, 184 U.S. at 382.

176. 166 U.S. 557 (1897).

177. *Detroit Citizens' Street Ry.*, 184 U.S. at 387 (citing *City Ry. Co.*, 166 U.S. at 417–18).

178. *Cleveland City Railway*, 194 U.S. at 536.

179. Russell *v.* Sebastian, 233 U.S. at 203.

180. *Id.* at 208.

earlier, the Court found that the grant resulting from the company's acceptance of the state's offer of a franchise constituted a contract, thereupon vesting the company with a property right protected by the Constitution.[181]

Beginning with *Detroit Citizens' Street Railway*, the Supreme Court held that municipal ordinances engendered contractual obligations regarding rates when "the provisions as to rates of fare were fixed in ordinances for a stated time and no reservation was made of a right to alter [them]."[182] The Court deemed the specific limitation of the time in which rates were to be fixed to be of particular significance.[183] The Court reasoned that through such "ordinances existing rights of the corporations were surrendered, benefits were conferred upon the public, and obligations were imposed upon the corporations to continue those benefits during the stipulated time."[184] The Court therefore saw "no escape from the conclusion, that [such] ordinances were intended to be agreements binding upon both parties definitely fixing the rates of fare which might be thereafter charged."[185]

THE EVOLUTION FROM MUNICIPAL FRANCHISES
TO STATE PUBLIC UTILITIES COMMISSIONS

As the contract infringement cases indicate, by the late nineteenth century state legislatures had delegated to municipalities the power to award franchises. But, as one would expect of relational contracting, the utility franchises themselves evolved over time, ultimately creating administrative boards that were the precursors to the state public utilities commissions. Early franchises often were vague and left discretion to the utility company. City governments tried to stipulate more precise conditions in the franchise agreement, but changing economic and technological circumstances demanded greater flexibility, and the precise franchises grew to be unworkable. According to George L. Priest, the solution was to eliminate the restrictive details and introduce an administrative board, often having representatives from both the utility and the local government.[186] From those administrative boards grew the state regulatory commissions, most of which came into existence between 1907 and 1922.[187] Those state com-

---

181. *Id*. at 204.
182. *Cleveland City Railway*, 194 U.S. at 536.
183. *Id*.
184. *Id*.
185. *Id*.
186. Priest, *supra* note 94, at 321.
187. "State regulatory commissions were first created in the late 1880s (in Massachu-

missions gradually assumed the powers of the individual municipal franchise authorities in most states. That transition raised the question of whether state public utilities commissions had the right to supersede the regulatory contract between municipal franchise authorities and public service corporations and to regulate the rates and services of individual utilities directly.

Presumably utilities would not have agreed to switch from municipal franchising to state public utility regulation unless they expected that change to produce net benefits for them. From Priest's analysis, it would appear that the utilities did not incur greater costs under state regulation in terms of diminished property protections. The prevailing understanding of the Contract and Takings Clauses and of substantive due process from 1907 through 1922 would have afforded the public utility security against state interference with the terms of its preexisting municipal franchise. At the same time, state regulation likely offered a utility three kinds of benefits over municipal franchising.

First, the horizontal expansion of electrical and telephony networks implied that those networks likely crossed municipal boundaries. Such horizontal expansion presumably reflected the exploitation of economies of scale or of network externalities related to increased subscribership.[188] But that horizontal expansion also implied that electrical and telephony networks would face the new problem of allocating common costs to different municipal jurisdictions for purposes of setting reasonable rates. The complexity of that task could be avoided if state regulators instead set rates over a larger geographic area. For example, Felix Frankfurter and Henry M. Hart, Jr., wrote in 1934 that because the utilities' "activities were confined in the beginning to individual communities, regulation by localities sufficed," but that "the extension of the area of service by the utilities" and "new forms of analogous public services, like pipe lines and electric power, patently beyond the reach of any but state authority" contributed to the creation of state public utilities commissions.[189]

---

setts) but then were inaugurated with sudden uniformity in the decade and a half following 1907. By 1922, electric regulatory commissions had been introduced in thirty-seven of the forty-eight states and gas commissions in eighteen of the twenty large states." *Id.* at 296. For the date of formation for each commission, see BARNES, *supra* note 40, at 206 chart 5.

188. For a discussion of the horizontal integration of local exchange companies during that period, see MILTON L. MUELLER, JR., UNIVERSAL SERVICE: COMPETITION, INTERCONNECTION, AND MONOPOLY IN THE MAKING OF THE AMERICAN Telephone System (MIT Press & AEI Press 1997).

189. Frankfurter & Hart, *supra* note 96, at 105.

Second, as electric utilities and local exchange carriers entered into horizontal mergers, they would be subject to regulation by multiple cities. Alternatively, a state public utility commission offered the public utility "one-stop shopping" on matters of regulation. Thus, the advent of state public utilities commissions may have been a way to minimize the transaction costs of utility regulation once efficient production mandated that the regulated firms merge across geographic markets within a state.

Third, as Geoffrey P. Miller has speculated, utilities may have favored the creation of state commissions as a way to escape city politicians who demanded bribes or less felonious side payments.[190] Certainly, some scholars have argued that the process by which public utilities received their franchises was politically corrupt.[191] The city was in a superior bargaining position in the sense that it controlled access to public rights-of-way, which offered the cost-minimizing route for the utility to lay down its fixed infrastructure. City officials could hold up utility investors by denying them access to those rights-of-way. Moreover, once the utility had sunk costs to build its infrastructure, it would be vulnerable to attempts by the city to set prices at uncompensatory levels or to deny renewal of the franchise in a manner that might strand the cost of undepreciated facilities.[192] The *Home Telephone* decision in 1908 may have eroded the credi-

190. Miller, *supra* note 94, at 327.

191. *E.g.*, FORREST MCDONALD, INSULL 86 (University of Chicago Press 1962). The concern over municipal corruption also gives rise to the argument that the regulatory contract was void *ab initio*, such that there would be no basis to complain if regulators were to repudiate the contract today. That argument is problematic. It would be self-serving and circular for a state regulatory commission to argue decades later that the regulatory contract is void because corrupt city officials who originally granted the franchise demanded and received side payments as a condition of the grant. If such an argument withstood scrutiny, one party's opportunism in the formation of the contract would subsequently provide that party (or its successor in interest) the avenue of escape from its obligations under the contract.

Alternatively, the argument might be that, in return for its payment of bribes demanded by city officials, the utility enjoyed lax rate regulation that enabled the utility to earn monopoly rents. *Cf.* David Gabel, *Competition in a Network Industry: The Telephone Industry, 1894–1910*, 54 J. ECON. HIST. 543, 562 (1994) (telephone company executive convicted in 1907 of bribing city supervisors to refuse to franchise a competitor). If such corrupt practices were efficacious for the utility, however, it would have no incentive to support replacing municipal regulation with regulation by a state public utilities commission. We return to such issues of defective regulation and regulatory capture in chapter 13, when discussing the libertarian argument against permitting the recovery of stranded costs under the regulatory contract, and in chapter 14, when discussing the limiting principles for such recovery.

192. David Gabel notes:

bility of municipal commitments to forbear from opportunistic rate reductions. At a minimum, state commissions offered the utility a new set of regulators.

CONTRACTING WITH THE SOVEREIGN

Despite the ample evidence in Supreme Court decisions of the contractual nature of municipal regulation of public utilities, at least some legal scholars in the early twentieth century adhered to a more statist view that a franchise awarded to a public utility was "a particular privilege which d[id] not belong to an individual or a corporation as of right, but [was] conferred by a sovereign or government upon, and vested in, individuals or a corporation."[193] Thus, in their view, "[i]t [was] essential that the franchise be a grant from a sovereign authority, and . . . none [was] valid unless derived from a law of the state."[194] That reasoning conflates agency and contract formation. It is one thing to require that the municipality have a clear agency relationship with the state when committing itself to forbear from its exercise of regulatory prerogatives under its delegated police powers. But that requirement in no way implies that a municipal franchise lawfully awarded to a public utility is a gratuity—a mere revocable license—rather than an enforceable contract. It is completely under-

---

[A] telephone franchise was highly valued, intangible property. City officials in the early twentieth century, unlike those in the 1870s, were not going to give this right away without imposing conditions. When franchises were issued to the Independents [non-AT&T companies], therefore, they typically included stipulations that set maximum rates, required free telephone service to the city government, free use of the telephone poles and underground conduits for fire and police lines, and royalty fees.

Id. at 561–62. Gabel argues that such conditions were barriers to entry because municipalities did not demand them of the Bell System when its "franchises had been granted when telephony was new and its commercial value uncertain." *Id.* But Gabel's own assessment is also consistent with the hypothesis that, in terms of concessions given to municipalities, the incumbent LEC and its subsequent competitors paid the same *risk-adjusted* price for their respective franchises. David F. Weiman & Richard C. Levin, *Preying for Monopoly? The Case of Southern Bell Telephone Company, 1894–1912*, 102 J. POL. ECON. 103, 121 (1994), agree with Gabel, yet they note, evidently without recognition of the contradiction, that by 1907 the Southern Bell Telephone Company, a successful predator in their assessment, was itself offering similar "concessions to municipal officials and agencies."

193. Harold F. Kumm, *The Legal Relations of City and State with Reference to Public Utility Regulation*, 6 MINN. L. REV. 32, 140 (1922) (citing 3 JOHN F. DILLON, COMMENTARIES ON THE LAW OF MUNICIPAL CORPORATIONS 1905 (Little, Brown & Co., 5th ed. 1906)).

194. *See id.* at 141.

standable that the Court would rule that no grant of a municipal franchise was valid unless sanctioned by "clear and unmistakable" state legislation empowering the municipality to enter into such a contract with the public service corporation.[195] Hence, the franchise contract between a utility and a municipality was in effect a contract between the utility and the state with the municipality acting as the agent of the state. Any municipal authority in that matter "[was] purely derivative and must [have] flow[ed] from the legislative fountain."[196] It was the authority of the municipality to bind the state to a contract—not whether valid municipal franchises were enforceable contracts—that was subject to dispute in particular cases.

Ultimately, a municipal franchise grant, when accepted and acted upon by the utility, became a contract within the meaning of the Constitution. The state public utilities commission's power to alter a franchise contract between a municipality and utility, and the duties and obligations contained in the contract, were limited only by the extent of the state's police powers. When state public utilities commissions began to take over for municipal franchise authorities, the law was well settled that:

> [T]he interdiction of statutes impairing the obligation of contracts does not prevent the State from exercising such powers as are vested in it for the promotion of the common weal, or are necessary for the general good of the public, ... This power, which in its various ramifications is known as the police power, is an exercise of the sovereign right of the Government to protect the lives, health, morals, comfort and general welfare of the people, and is paramount to any rights under contracts between individuals.[197]

The right to regulate the rates that utilities charged fell under the state's police powers and therefore was not dependent upon its being reserved in the regulatory contract. Nonetheless, the Court carved out an important exception to the general rule that the state's police power may not be alienated or suspended through contract. The exception applied "where the public utility and the state, or a municipality acting as an agent of the state, ha[d] entered into a contract for a term of years, wherein it [was] expressly provided that the rates there established shall not be lowered during the period of agreement."[198] The Court had consistently held that the effect of such a contract was to suspend the power of the state to regu-

---

195. *Home Telephone*, 211 U.S. at 273; *Milwaukee Electric Railway*, 238 U.S. at 180.
196. Kumm, *supra* note 193, at 141.
197. Manigault *v.* Springs, 199 U.S. 473, 480 (1905).
198. Kumm, *supra* note 193, at 145.

late rates for the term of the contract so as not to affect adversely the public service corporation.[199]

If the contract complied with those conditions, a court would uphold it. During the term of the agreement, the public utilities commission was held powerless to alter the rates to the detriment of the utility. In *Milwaukee Electric Railway & Light Company* v. *Railroad Commission of Wisconsin*,[200] for example, Justice William R. Day wrote for a unanimous Court in 1915:

> The fixing of rates which may be charged by public service corporations, of the character here involved, is a legislative function of the State, and while the right to make contracts which shall prevent the State during a given period from exercising this important power has been recognized and approved by judicial decisions, it has been uniformly held in this court that the renunciation of a sovereign right of this character must be evidenced by terms so clear and unequivocal as to permit of no doubt as to their proper construction. This proposition has been so frequently declared by decisions of this court as to render unnecessary any reference to the many cases in which the doctrine has been affirmed.[201]

The Milwaukee Electric Railway sought to enjoin the Wisconsin Railroad Commission from enforcing its order reducing the rate of fares that the railway could charge. The rates were below levels previously fixed by a Milwaukee ordinance enacted in 1900. The company contended that under the provisions of the ordinance, it had obtained the right to charge five cents per ticket or to sell tickets in packages of twenty-five for one dollar and packages of six for twenty-five cents until December 31, 1934. In complaints filed by the city of Milwaukee with the state railroad commission in 1906 and 1908, the city had sought to reduce those rates. The complaints resulted in the railroad commission's ordering the company to discontinue its rate of one dollar for twenty-five tickets and to replace it with a package of thirteen tickets for fifty cents.

The Court did not enjoin the state railroad commission's order holding that no irrevocable contract was created by the 1900 ordinance.[202] Thus, it found that the rate reduction, as mandated by the state railroad commission's order, had not impaired the obligation of contract between the city

---

199. *Detroit Citizens' Street Ry.*, 184 U.S. at 383; *Home Telephone*, 211 U.S. at 273; *Cleveland City Ry.*, 194 U.S. at 536; *Vicksburg Waterworks*, 206 U.S. at 508.
200. 238 U.S. 174 (1915).
201. *Id*. at 180.
202. *Id*. at 184.

and the railway. The Court reasoned that the state statute empowering Milwaukee to grant the franchise to the Milwaukee Electric Railway did not "unequivocally grant[] to municipalities the power to deprive the legislature of the right to exercise the rate-making function in the future," which Justice Day called "an acknowledged function of great public importance."[203] *Milwaukee Electric Railway* approvingly cited Justice Moody's opinion in *Home Telephone* stating that the general powers of a municipality were not sufficient to surrender a power of the government by contract unless such a surrender was clearly and unmistakably contemplated by the state legislature.[204]

In 1929 the Court, citing Justice Moody's opinion in *Home Telephone*, reaffirmed in *Railroad Commission of California* v. *Los Angeles Railway Corp.* the rule that a state's grant of authority to a municipality wherein it surrenders its power to regulate rates cannot be "inferred in the absence of a plain expression of purpose to that end."[205] It added that "[t]he delegation of authority to give up or suspend the power of rate regulation will not be found more readily than would an intention on the part of the State to authorize the bargaining away of its power to tax."[206] Hence, the Court cautioned that all doubt should be resolved in favor of the state's authority to prescribe rates.[207]

The facts of the case are as follows. The Los Angeles Railway Corp. operated a street railway system and buses in the city of Los Angeles and in parts of the Los Angeles county. The company was operating under the authority of 102 franchises granted by the city and the county from 1886 to 1928. Those franchises permitted the company to use various city streets for its cars. Seventy-three of the franchises granted between 1890 and 1918 and covering some 113 miles provided that "the rate of fare . . . shall not exceed five cents."[208] Another eighteen covering twelve miles that were granted between 1920 and 1928 provided that "the rate of fare . . . shall not be more than five cents . . . except upon a showing before a competent authority having jurisdiction over rates of fare that such greater charge is justified."[209] The other franchise grants were silent as to the rate of fare. In 1926 the company petitioned the state railroad commission for a basic fare rate increase from five to seven cents. The commission denied

203. *Id.*
204. *Id.* at 180.
205. 280 U.S. 145, 152 (1929) (Butler, J.).
206. *Id.*
207. *Id.*
208. *Id.* at 150.
209. *Id.*

the company's petition in 1928. The company sued in federal court seeking an injunction restraining the commission from enforcing the five-cent rate and also an order adjudicating the rates as being confiscatory.

The Supreme Court affirmed the lower court's decree and permanently enjoined the commission from enforcing those rates on the grounds that they would not permit the company to earn a reasonable return on its investments.[210] Although *Los Angeles Railway* upheld the district court's injunction, it did not address the issue of whether the rates were confiscatory because the appellants had not preserved the issue for appeal.[211] The Court identified the "sole controversy" in the case as being whether the railway company was contractually bound to charge rates denoted in its franchise agreement with the city.[212] In following the precedent of *Detroit Citizens' Street Railway* and its progeny, the Court held that "[i]t [was] possible for a State to authorize a municipal corporation by agreement to establish public service rates and thereby to suspend for a term of years not grossly excessive the exertion of governmental power by legislative action to fix just compensation to be paid for service furnished by public utilities."[213] The Court added that "where a city, empowered by the State so to do, makes a contract with a public utility fixing the amounts to be paid for its service, the latter may not be required to serve for less even if the specified rates are unreasonably high. And, in such case, the courts may not relieve the utility from its obligation to serve at the agreed rates however inadequate they may prove to be."[214]

The Court, upon reviewing all pertinent California state court decisions and construing all relevant state statutes, concluded that the city of Los Angeles was not empowered by the state to enter into rate contracts with the railway company.[215] Nonetheless, the Court in *Los Angeles Railway* assumed that the municipal franchise contracts had established the existing fares and held that the state commission's exercise of its jurisdiction in the case had abrogated those contracts.[216] The Court found such an abrogation when the commission, upon successive applications of the Los Angeles

---

210. *Id.* at 158.

211. *Id.*

212. *Id.* at 151.

213. *Id.* at 151–52 (citing *Detroit Citizens' Street Ry.*, 184 U.S. at 382; *Vicksburg Waterworks*, 206 U.S. at 508, 515; Public Serv. Co. *v.* St. Cloud, 265 U.S. 352, 355 (1924)).

214. *Id.* at 152 (citing *Detroit Citizens' Street Ry.*, 184 U.S. at 389; *Public Service Co.*, 265 U.S. at 355).

215. *Id.* at 156.

216. *Id.*

Street Railway Co., reviewed the rate structure as imposed by the municipal franchises. In 1921, after the required hearings, the commission found the existing fares insufficient and ordered a small rate increase. The rate increase never materialized because the railway opted not to put it into effect. Upon a later petition by the railway in 1926, a commission report and order in 1928 found the existing rates sufficient and therefore reasonable and just. Hence, the company was legally required to continue observing the five-cent rate.

The Court explained that a state had the power, upon the application of a street railway company, to terminate rates of fare fixed by contract between the company and a municipal corporation of the state. It reasoned that under article XII, section 23, of the California Constitution, as amended in 1914, and the Public Utilities Act of 1915, the state railroad commission had exclusive power to regulate rates.[217] And section 27 of the act gave to street railway companies the right to charge more than five cents upon showing the commission that the higher charge was justified. The Court noted that the legislation had made no distinction between rates established by franchise contracts and those otherwise fixed.[218] Hence, the Court concluded that the five-cent street railway fare, even if it had been established by franchise contract, could be increased by the commission upon its finding that the rate was unjust or insufficient.[219] The commission had the statutory authority to establish the just and reasonable rate thereafter to be observed.[220]

THE REGULATORY CONTRACT IN TEXAS

We have seen that the many Supreme Court decisions rest on the understanding that an enforceable contract defined the relationship between a public utility and a franchising municipality. Similar decisions exist in the state supreme courts and are too numerous to survey. Nonetheless, one state, Texas, is particularly instructive because it was among the last to transfer the regulation of public utilities from municipalities to a state commission.[221] Six decades after the widespread move to state public utilities commissions began, the Texas Supreme Court was still interpret-

---

217. *Id.* at 157.
218. *Id.*
219. *Id.* at 157–58.
220. *Id.*
221. *See* Jack Hopper, *A Legislative History of the Texas Public Utility Regulatory Act of 1975*, 28 BAYLOR L. REV. 777 (1976); Dan Pleitz & Robert Randolph Little, *Municipalities and the Public Utility Regulatory Act*, 28 BAYLOR L. REV. 978 (1976).

ing the contractual rights of public utilities under the municipal franchise agreements that regulated their conduct.

In *Texas Power & Light Co.* v. *City of Garland*, the Supreme Court of Texas in 1968 permanently enjoined Garland, Texas, from requiring a franchised electric utility to obtain a permit as a condition precedent to the extension of its line to a new customer.[222] In 1915 the city entered into a fifty-year nonexclusive franchise with the Texas Power & Light Co. that gave the utility the right to serve all inhabitants of the city. In 1949 the city, which itself had entered the electricity business, passed an ordinance that authorized it to deny the utility a permit to extend service to new customers. The Supreme Court of Texas found that and other provisions to violate the franchise contract:

> [The ordinances] authorizing the denial of a permit by reason of competitive interference with the City's electrical service, are aimed directly at the advancement of the City's economic and proprietary interests. Under these provisions the City urges that it possesses the power to amend the franchise and that its power is broad enough to require City Council approval as a prerequisite to expansion by the Company. In other words, the City contends that it may wholly curb any expansion under the non-exclusive franchise held by the Company. Obviously these provisions have for their purpose the elimination of the Company as a competitor beyond its existing lines. They accord preferments ousting the Company from exercising rights in an area granted by its franchise. These things the City cannot do. Essential franchise rights cannot be taken under a pretense of regulation designed to gain a competitive advantage to the City acting in its proprietary capacity.[223]

Such reasoning would hold even more forcefully if the city had violated the incumbent utility's franchise agreement in the name of assisting the competitive expansion of a *private* company, which would more closely resemble the facts of mandatory retail wheeling.

A close reading of the case strongly suggests that the opportunistic behavior by the city had the effect of impairing the incumbent utility's ability to recover its costs. The city wished to exclude the company from serving a set of apartments in an undeveloped area. Given geographically averaged rates, the economies of density that presumably would characterize service to the apartment buildings would have made those new customers incrementally more profitable than the average customer already

---

222. 431 S.W.2d 511 (1968).
223. *Id.* at 518.

served by the utility, and thus the new customers would have made a positive contribution to utility's revenue requirement. The city, in other words, was attempting to cream skim to the detriment of the franchised utility. The Supreme Court of Texas could "see no reason to allow the municipally owned corporation a competitive advantage over the privately owned corporation in this situation."[224]

Finally, the Court ruled that a "1964 ordinance which extended the 1915 franchise [until 1990] did not impliedly incorporate the 1949 ordinance as additional contractual limitations upon the Company's franchise."[225] The city could not impair the utility's contractual rights in that manner: "The 1949 ordinance could not have been enacted as a valid contractual limitation upon the 1915 franchise. The 1949 ordinance, aimed at controlling activities outside the City's police power, was an invalid impairment of the original franchise ordinance when it was enacted; therefore, it cannot now be impliedly incorporated into the valid franchise ordinance passed in 1964."[226] The Court analyzed the case in explicitly contractual terms, noting that "there is a difference between an extension of an existing contract and the making of a new one."[227] In short, the Supreme Court of Texas approached the case with as much skepticism as it would any instance of overt opportunism by one party to a long-term commercial contract:

> The franchise was a broad grant to operate on the present and future streets of Garland. The City's contention is that the franchise by implication was limited to areas in Garland where the Company was then located, and without the right to expand. The conflict between the express terms of the grant and the claimed implications by the City, taken with the history and invalidity of the ordinance at the time it was passed, is so sharp that we must reject the contention the ordinance was impliedly incorporated as a part of the contract.[228]

In that respect the decision in *Texas Power & Light* continued the view of the Supreme Court of Texas in earlier cases involving utility franchisees that the franchise agreement was a contract. In *Texas* v. *Central Power & Light Co.*, the same court considered an antitrust case brought by the state attorney general: "The question to be decided is whether or not the provisions of the contract whereby the city bound itself not to erect a municipal

---

224. *Id*. at 519.
225. *Id*.
226. *Id*.
227. *Id*. at 520.
228. *Id*.

power plant for a period of ten years created a 'trust' in violation of" the state antitrust statute.[229] The court concluded that it was not necessary to decide the question, and it did so on a rationale that implied that the court did not want to upset the original bargain voluntarily struck between the municipality and the utility: "The State would not be entitled to cancellation of the agreement because it was made by the City in part for its benefit, and the City is not a party to this suit. The City would be a necessary party to a suit to cancel an agreement made by it for its own benefit."[230] Thus, a municipality could not rely upon state intervention to release the municipality from a franchise contract into which it voluntarily entered with an investor-owned utility.

WINSTAR AND THE UNMISTAKABILITY
OF THE REGULATORY CONTRACT

The Supreme Court's 1996 decision in *United States* v. *Winstar Corporation*, while not addressing a regulated network industry, does indicate how the Court would likely view a case involving recovery of stranded costs arising from breach of the regulatory contract in such an industry.[231] Perhaps for that reason, public utilities commissions have been quick to assert that *Winstar* is irrelevant to the restructuring of the regulated network industries.[232] It is not. To appreciate *Winstar*'s relevance to the regulatory contract, it is necessary first to review the essential facts of the case.

---

229. 139 Tex. 51, 52, 161 S.W.2d 766, 766 (1942).

230. 139 Tex. at 56, 161 S.W.2d at 768.

231. 116 S. Ct. 2432 (1996). For a critique of our analysis of the relevance of *Winstar* to the regulatory contract, see William J. Baumol & Thomas W. Merrill, *Deregulatory Takings, Breach of the Regulatory Contract, and the Telecommunications Act of 1996*, 72 N.Y.U. L. REV. (forthcoming 1997).

232. For example, New Hampshire's commission stated in 1997:

> Although *Winstar* has become a new rhetorical arrow in our utilities' empty quiver, *Winstar* need not give us pause. In *Winstar*, the threshold question, "whether there were contracts at all between the government and respondents[,]" was not before the Court. Therefore the case is of no assistance in determining whether a contract exists.

Restructuring New Hampshire's Electric Utility Industry, DR 96-150 Order No. 22,514, 175 P.U.R.4th 193 (N.H. Pub. Utils. Comm'n Feb. 28, 1997) (quoting *Winstar*, 116 S. Ct. at 2448). *But see* Electric Utility Industry Restructuring, Dkt. No. 95-462 (Maine Pub. Utils. Comm'n July 19, 1996) ("While not directly applicable, . . . *United States* v. *Winstar Corp.*, suggests, at least, that government should act responsibly in changing the 'rules of the game.'" (citation omitted)).

Three thrifts sued the United States for breach of contract after they had been declared in violation of the capital requirements of the new Financial Institutions Reform, Recovery and Enforcement Act of 1989 (FIRREA).[233] The thrifts argued that savings and loan regulators had promised to indemnify them from the type of regulatory change that FIRREA produced. During the savings and loan crisis of the 1980s, the Federal Home Loan Bank Board sought to induce healthy thrifts to merge with failing ones. The board signed agreements with the healthy thrifts that allowed them to count the excess of the purchase price over the fair market value of the acquired assets as an intangible asset—"supervisory goodwill"—that counted toward fulfilling capital reserve requirements. The board agreed to allow the healthy thrifts to amortize supervisory goodwill over twenty-five to forty years—an extended period that would give the healthy thrifts a reasonable opportunity to recover their costs of rehabilitating the sick thrifts. Without those regulatory agreements, the thrifts created by the mergers would have violated the capital reserve requirements. Thus, the healthy thrifts' investment in the sick thrifts never would have happened. Overall, however, the board's practice of encouraging such merged thrifts turned out to be a failure and promised to lead to the insolvency of federal deposit insurance funds for the thrifts. Eventually, Congress enacted FIRREA, which forbade thrifts from counting supervisory goodwill toward capital requirements. Regulators promptly seized and liquidated two of the three plaintiff thrifts in *Winstar* for failing to comply with the new capital reserve requirements; the third avoided seizure only by aggressively recapitalizing.

A plurality of the Supreme Court upheld the determination by the U.S. Court of Appeals for the Federal Circuit that the government had breached contractual obligations to the thrifts and was liable for breach of contract. One of the government's defenses was the "unmistakability" doctrine, under which surrenders of sovereign authority, to be enforceable, must appear in unmistakable terms in a contract. Justices David H. Souter, John Paul Stevens, Sandra Day O'Connor, and Stephen G. Breyer found that the defense did not apply to the contracts at issue, because the plaintiffs were suing not to stop the government from changing capital reserve requirements applicable to thrifts, but only to compel the government to indemnify them for the effects of such changes.[234] Justices Antonin Scalia, Anthony M. Kennedy, and Clarence Thomas did not accept that distinction between injunctive relief and damages but nonetheless found that the

---

233. Pub. L. No. 101-73, 103 Stat. 183.
234. 116 S. Ct. at 2458 (Souter, Stevens, O'Connor, Breyer, J.J., plurality).

particular contracts at issue established that the government had unmistakably agreed to indemnify the thrifts.[235] Chief Justice William H. Rehnquist dissented in an opinion joined by Justice Ruth Bader Ginsburg.[236]

Writing for the majority, Justice Souter reasoned that application of the unmistakability defense "would place the doctrine at odds with the Government's own long-run interest as a reliable contracting partner in the myriad workaday transaction of its agencies."[237] The government would lose its ability to make credible commitments. "Injecting the opportunity for unmistakability litigation into every common contract action," Justice Souter wrote, "would . . . produce the untoward result of compromising the Government's practical ability to make contracts, which we have held to be 'the essence of sovereignty itself.'"[238] He further explained:

> The Court has often said, as a general matter, that the "rights and duties" contained in a government contract "are governed generally by the law applicable to contracts for private individuals." . . . This approach is unsurprising, for in practical terms it ensures that the government is able to obtain needed goods and services from parties who might otherwise, quite rightly, be unwilling to undertake the risk of government contracting.[239]

The plurality's reasoning in *Winstar* is directly analogous to the contractual issues that result from the mandatory unbundling of regulated network industries. Justice Souter noted that it is particularly important to treat the government's contracts with regulated firms as binding:

> It is important to be clear about what these contracts did and did not require of the Government. Nothing in the documentation or the circumstances of these transactions purported to bar the Government from changing the way in which it regulated the thrift industry. Rather . . . "the Bank Board and the FSLIC [the federal savings and loan insurance fund] were contractually bound to recognize the supervisory goodwill and the amortization periods reflected" in the agreements between the parties. We read this promise as the law of contracts has always treated promises to provide something beyond the promisor's absolute control, that is, as a promise to insure the promisee against loss arising from the promised condition's nonoccurrence. . . . *Contracts like this are especially appropriate in the*

235. *Id.* at 2476 (Scalia, Kennedy, Thomas, J.J., concurring).
236. *Id.* at 2479 (Rehnquist, C.J., Ginsburg, J., dissenting).
237. *Id.* at 2459.
238. *Id.* (quoting United States v. Bekins, 304 U.S. 27, 51–52 (1938)).
239. *Id.* at 2473 (quoting Lynch v. United States, 292 U.S. 571, 579 (1934)).

world of regulated industries, where the risk that legal change will prevent the bargained-for performance is always lurking in the shadows.[240]

That admonition is compelling where the government wishes to use contract as an instrument of regulation: "Since the facts of the present case demonstrate that the Government may wish to further its regulatory goals through contract, we are unwilling to adopt any rule of construction that would weaken the Government's capacity to do business by converting every contract it makes into an arena for unmistakability."[241] Thus, Justice Souter's reasoning in *Winstar* would apply even more forcefully to a regulated electric utility—which has made enormous, nonsalvageable investments in long-lived assets such as generation plants, transmission grids, and distribution networks—or to a local exchange carrier, which has made analogous investments in switching and transport facilities. Clearly, the logic of Justice Souter's plurality opinion extends to agreements that state or municipal regulators have made with private parties. It is permissible to bind those regulators even to commitments that are not "unmistakable" if the regulated firm seeks not to enjoin a change in regulatory policy, but only to receive financial compensation for the harm resulting from that change. Such a rule describes the situation in which an electric utility or local exchange carrier seeks not to enjoin statutes or regulations mandating network unbundling, but only to receive compensation for the stranded costs that result from such new laws.

More important than that distinction between remedies were Justice Souter's concluding remarks underscoring the Court's need to consider the contracts in the broader context of the parties' intent: "It would . . . have been madness for [the healthy thrifts] to have engaged in these transactions with no more protection than the Government's reading [of the contracts] would have given them, for the very existence of their institutions would then have been in jeopardy from the moment their agreements were signed."[242] As we saw earlier in this chapter, the same reasoning about contractual intent permeates the Court's interpretations of the regulatory contract in the late nineteenth and early twentieth centuries. Not surprisingly, in *Winstar* Justice Souter[243]—and Justice Breyer in his concurrence[244]—relied upon those decisions construing the regulatory contract.

---

240. *Id.* at 2451–52 (quoting Winstar Corp. *v.* United States, 64 F.3d 1531, 1541–42 (Fed. Cir. 1995) (en banc) (emphasis added)).

241. *Id.* at 2460.

242. *Id.* at 2472.

243. *Id.* at 2449 (quoting The Binghamton Bridge, 70 U.S. (3 Wall.) 51, 78 (1866), for the proposition that the Court "refus[ed] to construe charter in such a way that it would have been 'madness' for private party to enter into it").

244. *Id.* at 2472–73 (Breyer, J., concurring) (citing *The Binghamton Bridge*, 70 U.S. (3

Although Justice Souter could "imagine cases in which the potential gain might induce a party to assume a substantial risk that the gain might be wiped out by a change in the law, it would have been irrational in this case for [one of the healthy thrifts] to stake its very existence upon continuation of current policies without seeking to embody those policies in some sort of contractual commitment."[245]

In his concurrence, Justice Scalia believed that an enforceable duty imposed on the government to pay damages in the event of breach would "constrain the exercise of sovereign power" as much as compelling the government to perform the contract.[246] He thought that the unmistakability doctrine "has little if any independent legal force beyond what would be dictated by normal principles of contract interpretation."[247] In Justice Scalia's view the doctrine "is simply a rule of presumed (or implied-in-fact) intent."[248] He then offered a stark presumption of contract interpretation. Whereas Justice Souter feared that the government might lose its ability to make credible commitments, Justice Scalia implicitly assumed that the government had already lost it:

> Generally, contract law imposes upon a party to a contract liability for any impossibility of performance that is attributable to that party's own actions. That is a reasonable estimation of what the parties intend. When I promise to do *x* in exchange for your doing *y*, I impliedly promise not to do anything that will disable me from doing *x*, or disable you from doing *y*—so that if either of our performances is rendered impossible by such an act on my part, I am not excused from my obligation. When the contracting party is the government, however, it is simply *not* reasonable to presume an intent of that sort. To the contrary, it is reasonable to presume *(unless the opposite clearly appears)* that the sovereign does *not* promise that none of its multifarious sovereign acts, needful for the public good, will incidentally disable it or the other party from performing one of the promised acts. The requirement of unmistakability embodies this reversal of the normal reasonable presumption. Governments do not ordinarily agree to curtail their sovereign or legislative powers, and contracts must be interpreted in a common-sense way against that background understanding.[249]

Wall.) at 74; Russell *v.* Sebastian, 233 U.S. 195, 205 (1914); Detroit *v.* Detroit Citizens' Street Ry., 184 U.S. 368, 384 (1902)).

245. *Id.* at 2449 (Souter, J., plurality).
246. *Id.* at 2476 (Scalia, J., concurring).
247. *Id.*
248. *Id.*
249. *Id.* (emphasis in original).

If it were unreasonable *as a matter of law* for a private party to trust the government's contractual promise, contract negotiations with the government would entail higher transaction costs, and private parties to such contracts would demand a substantial risk premium, as such parties do when contracting with the governments of politically unstable nations.

Justice Scalia's skepticism about the appropriate legal presumption concerning contractual intent did not prevent him from concluding that the three thrifts had "overcome this reverse-presumption that the Government remains free to make its own performance impossible through its manner of regulation."[250] In reasoning reminiscent of the Court's early interpretations of regulatory contracts in cases such as *The Binghamton Bridge*,[251] *Walla Walla Water*,[252] *Russell* v. *Sebastian*,[253] and *Detroit Citizens' Street Railway*,[254] Justice Scalia agreed with the thrifts that "the very *subject matter* of these agreements, an essential part of the *quid pro quo*, was government regulation" and that "unless the Government is bound as to that regulation, an aspect of the transactions that reasonably must be viewed as a *sine qua non* of their assent becomes illusory."[255] He rejected the notion that "unmistakability demands that there be a *further* promise not to go back on the promise to accord favorable regulatory treatment."[256] The unmistakability doctrine does not require a private party to demand "the Government's promise to keep its promise."[257] Echoing as Justice Souter did the reasoning in the Court's early decisions on regulatory contracts, Justice Scalia stressed the relationship between cost recovery, contract duration, and consideration: "[I]t is quite impossible to construe these contracts as providing for only 'short term' favorable treatment, with the long term up for grabs: either there was an undertaking to regulate [the healthy thrifts] as agreed for the specified amortization periods, or there was no promise regarding the future at all—not even so much as a peppercorn's worth."[258]

What conclusions does one therefore draw from reconciling Justice Souter's plurality opinion with Justice Scalia's concurrence? Only four Justices in *Winstar* would interpret the unmistakability doctrine to permit

---

250. *Id.*
251. 70 U.S. (3 Wall.) 51, 73 (1866).
252. Walla Walla City *v.* Walla Walla Water Co., 172 U.S. 1, 17–18 (1898).
253. 233 U.S. 195, 206–07 (1914).
254. Detroit *v.* Detroit Citizens' Street Ry., 184 U.S. 368, 385 (1902).
255. *Winstar*, 116 S. Ct. at 2477 (emphasis in original).
256. *Id.* (emphasis in original).
257. *Id.* at 2478.
258. *Id.* at 2477–78.

damage remedies in cases where it was not unmistakable that the government had contracted to retain an existing regulatory regime for the benefit of the regulated firm. Of far greater consequence for the restructuring of the regulated network industries, however, is the fact that *seven* Justices—Breyer, Kennedy, O'Connor, Scalia, Souter, Stevens, and Thomas—supported their divergent legal conclusions with the same economic reasoning that stressed cost recovery, incentive for investment, opportunism, and the government's need to make credible commitments. In that important respect, *Winstar* builds on the intellectual foundation that such justices as Holmes, Hughes, Harlan, and Taft laid more than a century earlier to construe the rights and remedies of public utilities under their regulatory contracts with municipalities. *Winstar* confirms the continued vitality of the reasoning in those early decisions.

CONCLUSION

Powerful efficiency arguments demonstrate why one would expect the regulatory contract to have evolved. The regulatory contract contains three essential terms—price regulation, entry regulation, and the obligation to serve—that simultaneously constrained the private exercise of market power and ensured that the utility would have a reasonable opportunity to recover the economic costs of the long-lived, nonsalvageable investments that it made to serve its customers. The theoretical economic arguments for the existence of the regulatory contract comport with observed fact, for many court decisions from the late nineteenth and early twentieth centuries described and interpreted the utility's franchise in explicitly contractual terms.

5

Remedies for Breach of
the Regulatory Contract

CONTRACT REMEDIES provide guidance on the measurement of stranded costs and the proper economic approach to determining compensation for those costs. Given that the utility incurred its costs under the regulatory contract, the opening of the utility's market to competition—that is, the termination of the exclusivity of the utility's franchise—is a breach of a material term of that contract if not accompanied by an offsetting removal of incumbent burdens. It is opportunistic behavior by the promisor—namely, the regulator.

In private contracts, damage remedies for breach guard against opportunistic behavior. The standard remedy for breach of contract is to award the promisee its *expectation interest*.[1] The proper remedy for breach of the regulatory contract is therefore to give the utility the expected level of profit that it would have received had there not been a breach of the regulatory contract. The contract price under the regulatory contract equals the sum of the utility's revenue requirements over the years that the regulatory contract was expected to remain in force. As noted previously, the revenue requirement equals the utility's operating cost (plus depreciation), plus its allowed rate of return

1. E. Allan Farnsworth, *Legal Remedies for Breach of Contract*, 70 COLUM. L. REV. 1145 (1970); Lon Fuller & William Perdue, *The Reliance Interest in Contract Damages*, 46 YALE L.J. 52 (1936); *see also* Douglas G. Baird, *The Law and Economics of Contract Damages*, U. CHI. L. & ECON. WORKING PAPER NO. 30 (2d series) (1994); DAN B. DOBBS, REMEDIES: DAMAGES, EQUITY, RESTITUTION 786–88 (West Publishing Co. 1973).

multiplied by its rate base. The utility's variable cost equals its operating cost plus depreciation.

THE PUBLIC UTILITY'S RIGHT TO EXPECTATION DAMAGES FOR THE REGULATOR'S BREACH OF THE REGULATORY CONTRACT

One can calculate the expectation-damage remedy for breach of the regulatory contract on the basis of principles of contract law. It is useful to specify the method of determining those damages in the context of regulation.

Consider the simplest case of a two-period investment problem. In the initial period, the regulated firm makes an irreversible investment of I dollars in plant and equipment. The regulated utility expects to earn revenues R^e and to incur operating costs C^e in the second period. The regulated firm discounts its earnings at rate i, which represents the opportunity cost of capital in an investment of comparable risk. The expected profit of the regulated firm is therefore equal to discounted expected revenues net of operating costs minus capital investment:

$$expected\ profit = [(R^e - C^e)/(1 + i)] - I.$$

Economists refer to the profit as *economic rent* and to the net revenues $R - C$ as *quasi rent*.

Economic rent provides an incentive for a firm to enter the market. That means that the contract must be such that expected profit is greater than or equal to zero. The regulated firm would not make an investment unless the present discounted value of net revenues exceeds investment cost.

Economic quasi rent provides an incentive for a firm not to exit the market. Once the firm has sunk its irreversible investment I, the firm in this simple two-period model no longer considers the investment in its decision making. It decides whether or not to produce depending on whether expected revenues cover expected costs, $R^e \geq C^e$. That is precisely the temptation for the other party to the contract to behave opportunistically. The regulator has an incentive at that point, after the investment has been made, to seek to lower revenue payments to the level of expected operating costs. The regulated firm would continue to operate even if revenues were lowered all the way to the level of expected operating costs. Thus, regulatory opportunism is an attempt to capture the regulated firm's quasi rent.

Suppose that the regulator breaches the contract after the regulated firm has made the irreversible investment in plant and equipment. If the regulated firm does not operate, it does not receive revenues R, but it also does not incur operating cost C. Thus, expectation damages for breach of contract equal the net revenues forgone:

$$expectation\ damage\ payment = R^e - C^e.$$

Thus, expectation damages equal the firm's expected net earnings and correspond exactly to the firm's quasi rent. If the expectation-damage payment is made, then the regulated firm earns the profit that it would have made had the contract been honored. Moreover, the regulator is not tempted to breach the contract simply to capture the quasi rent, because that would be the precise amount of the damage payment.

If the damages are to be paid in the preceding period, it is necessary to discount damages. The appropriate discount rate should reflect the regulated firm's cost of capital, which depends on the riskiness of regulated returns. Then, the present value of the expectation-damage payment is $(R^e - C^e)/(1 + i)$. Typically, the assets of regulated utilities have long lifetimes. Thus, expectation damages in the initial period should equal the expected present discounted value (PDV) of cash flow over the time horizon T that the firm expected to earn revenues from the regulated assets:

$$PDV = \sum_{t=0}^{T} \frac{R_t^e - C_t^e}{(1 + i)^t}.$$

In the PDV calculation, the terms R_t^e and C_t^e denote expected revenues and operating costs in period t, and i is the discount rate.

COMPETITION AND MITIGATION
OF DAMAGES

If the regulated utility's productive assets are removed from service as a result of competitive rules and continuing regulation, then its stranded cost is a loss to society. As in the case of any loss of resources, steps to mitigate the loss should be taken by parties in a position to do so.[2] The common law is replete with instances in which a party legally entitled to compensation for a harm it has suffered nonetheless is obliged to mitigate that harm if possible.[3] Not surprisingly, state PUCs have addressed the recovery of "nonmitigable" stranded costs, a concept whose meaning we now explore.

The Utility's Duty to Mitigate and the Regulator's Duty Not to Impede Mitigation

Although it is clear that the utility's duty to mitigate stranded costs serves the interest of consumers, on closer inspection we see that mitigation serves the utility's best interest as well. That is so because the utility's large business customers do not have service contracts that terminate simultaneously. As customers with early expiration dates depart, they leave the as-yet-unrecovered portion of stranded costs to be borne by a dwindling number of remaining customers. But the overwhelming number of those remaining (commercial and industrial) customers can be presumed to operate in competitive markets for their own goods and services. A firm in a competitive market that is made to pay a higher price than its rivals for an essential input such as electricity or telecommunications will suffer losses and, in the extreme case, eventually cease operations. Companies that cease operations do not buy any services from the utility, even if they remain contractually obligated to do so. Knowing that it cannot bankrupt or financially jeopardize its remaining customers, the utility has a strong incentive to find new customers for its excess capacity. The duty to mitigate illustrates that the economic interests of the utility and consumers are indeed often entirely compatible, despite appearances to the contrary.

Revenues that the utility will earn in the marketplace by using the same facilities that it employed to produce regulated services offset its losses from the regulator's breach of the regulatory contract. As in the preceding example, the expectation damages that would restore the utility

---

2. Our discussion of the duty to mitigate extends the discussion found in WILLIAM J. BAUMOL & J. GREGORY SIDAK, TRANSMISSION PRICING AND STRANDED COSTS IN THE ELECTRIC POWER INDUSTRY 111–13 (AEI Press 1995).

3. For discussion of the common law duty to mitigate contract damages, see Sauer *v.* McClintic-Marshall Construction Co., 179 Mich. 618, 146 N.W. 422 (1914); Rich *v.* Daily Creamery Co., 296 Mich. 270, 296 N.W. 253 (1941); RESTATEMENT (SECOND) OF CONTRACTS § 350 comment b.

to the position that it would have occupied had the regulatory contract not been breached equal the utility's revenue requirement net of competitive market revenues. *Therefore, the proper economic measure of stranded costs equals the difference between the public utility's net revenue requirement under regulation and entry controls and the net revenues the utility earns from those stranded facilities in the competitive market.*

It is important not to deduct all the utility's potential earnings in the competitive market, for they may include earnings from newly expanded facilities that would have been obtained even if the regulatory contract had continued in force. Only those revenues earned from facilities that were released by the termination of the regulatory contract should be used to offset the losses.

Some harm is nonmitigable. Regulatory assets generally have no market value because they are no more than accounting conventions. They represent additions to the rate base used to recover operating expenses for such regulatory programs as demand-side management. Common sense and economic efficiency dictate that the regulator not perpetuate policies that continue to increase the magnitude of such regulatory assets at the same time that the regulator is contemplating remedies for breach of the regulatory contract. Even if the regulator takes steps on its own to mitigate the stranding of regulatory assets by ending programs such as demand-side management, the utility will still have difficulty mitigating damages resulting from its inability to recover the cost of facilities that deregulation has made obsolete. It may be the case that *no* form of mitigation is available to the utility other than to do what competition would require—to retire facilities whose revenues fail to cover operating costs.

Furthermore, the regulator has a duty not to interfere with the utility's efforts to mitigate stranded costs. Mitigation requires the utility to make the best use of capital facilities created under regulation. It is therefore essential that the regulator not restrict the incumbent utility's pricing and product offerings in the new competitive environment. The regulator's imposition or continuation of pricing restrictions and quarantines can only increase the magnitude of the utility's nonmitigable stranded costs, which ultimately will harm consumers.

The Measurement of the Utility's Expectation Damages Net of Mitigation

Expectation damages emphasize the public utility's forgone earnings as a consequence of the regulator's breach of the regulatory contract. One should therefore compute the value of stranded assets by calculating the utility's expected net revenue stream under regulation and subtracting the utility's expected net revenue stream under competition.

The regulator breaches the regulatory contract by opening the market to competition. The utility is likely to continue operating. It may experience lower revenues, but its costs may change as well. Let R_1^e and C_1^e denote expected revenues and costs under regulation, and let R_2^e and C_2^e denote expected revenues and costs under competition. Then, the fundamental measure of the change in the firm's net expected earnings is defined as:

$$\Delta \equiv (R_1^e - C_1^e) - (R_2^e - C_2^e).$$

The expectation damages for a given period equal the difference between the contract price net of regulated costs and the market price net of competitive market costs:

$$expectation\ damages\ =\ \Delta.$$

The net revenues in the competitive market, $R_2^e - C_2^e$, represent the *mitigation* of contract damages. If the regulated firm earns that amount and receives the damage payment, that is sufficient to restore the seller's expected profit. The expectation-damage payment assumes that the payment is made at the time that the firm would have earned the net revenues.

Measurement of expectation damages is further complicated because the assets of the deregulated utility have long lives. Let PDV_1 denote the present discounted value of expected net revenues under regulation as previously defined. Similarly, define PDV_2 as the present discounted value of expected net revenues that the firm earns under competition. The economically correct measure of damages net of mitigation is to take the difference, Δ^*, between the present discounted values of the two cash flows:

$$expectation\ damages\ =\ \Delta^*\ \equiv\ PDV_1 - PDV_2.$$

When there is only a single period, that expression coincides with the single-period expectation-damage measure. When there is more than one period, the calculation of damages encounters at least two difficulties. First, the time horizons for the two *PDV* calculations can easily differ. For example, a firm may retire the assets from service much sooner in the competitive case than under regulation. So there are two distinct time horizons, T_1 under regulation and T_2 under competition. Second, the discount rates will most likely differ in the two *PDV* calculations. For example, increased risk in the competitive market will require a higher rate of discount in the competitive *PDV*. Therefore, there are two discount rates, i_1 under regulation and i_2 under competition. Because the competitive firm expects to earn PDV_2 under competition, it follows that the expectation damage payment (possibly with different time horizons and discount rates for the two *PDV* calculations) restores the expectation of the firm to its initial expectation, which is PDV_1.

The Superiority of the Net-Revenue Approach to the Asset-by-Asset Approach to Measuring Damages for Breach

The expectation-damage approach emphasizes the net revenues of the regulated utility. That approach contrasts with the *reliance interest* of the public utility, which equals the irreversible, transaction-specific investment that the utility made in reliance on the continuation of the regulatory contract. That amount is equal to the rate base, which is the book value of the investment in facilities, net of depreciation. Because of the regulated revenue requirement, expectation damages and reliance damages coincide if reliance damages include the utility's rate base net of depreciation plus additional liabilities that the utility expected would be included in the rate base. The two damage measures do not coincide with a narrow interpretation of stranded investment that does not take into account the full set of costs.

The expectation-damage approach has a distinct advantage over remedies that are based on an assessment of the regulated firm's capital expenditures. Most significantly, expectation damages provide the correct incentives for regulators to honor the regulatory contract when it is efficient to do so, thus deterring regulatory opportunism. Moreover, expectation damages provide incentives for efficient breach. If the benefits of competition exceed the benefits of regulation, the expectation-damage remedy will send the correct signal.

If competition lowers operating costs, then it is worthwhile to shift from regulation to competition. That is, competition is desirable if $C_1 > C_2$. Note that the damage payment is positive only if revenue payments fall under competition as well. Breach of the regulatory contract is called for if and only if the payment to the firm under regulation exceeds the payment to the firm under competition plus the payment for breach of contract:

$$R_1 > R_2 + [(R_1 - C_1) - (R_2 - C_2)].$$

By canceling the revenue terms on both sides of the inequality, we obtain again the cost inequality $C_1 > C_2$. That inequality establishes that with the expectation-damage remedy, the regulator will breach the regulatory contract if and only if competition lowers operating costs.

That insight addresses the common complaint that the benefits of competition will not be achieved if a damage remedy must be paid to incumbent utilities before moving to competition. On the contrary, the benefits of competition stem from operating efficiencies and the corresponding lowering of revenue payments. Paying damages to compensate the regulated firm still leaves benefits for consumers. The benefits derive from lower costs, not income transfers from investors to consumers.

A revenue-based approach produces other benefits, not the least of which is avoidance of reopening past regulatory hearings. Under the established regulatory process, regulators and intervenors carefully scrutinized the utility's investments before they were made. Those investments included in the rate base were judged to have been prudently incurred. The only investments stranded by competition are those in the rate base. In the electric power industry, some persons opposed to allowing a public utility the opportunity to recover stranded costs characterize those costs as imprudent investments in inefficient and uncompetitive generation facilities. That characterization ignores that the public utilities commission considered those generation facilities to be efficient when it approved them as part of the overall set of utility generating facilities. Moreover, those facilities were designed on the basis of expectations of technology, capacity utilization, and customer requirements *at the time that those assets were installed.* For regulators to reevaluate those decisions on the basis of current market conditions is entirely appropriate for current planning purposes, but it is entirely inappropriate as a review of past choices using 20–20 hindsight.

The utility's loss from the regulator's breach of the regulatory contract equals the contract payments net of operating costs for the time period that the firm expected the regulatory contract to remain in force. In any single year, the utility's stranded investment equals the utility's rate base times its allowed rate of return. The loss therefore includes the book value of capital facilities and the capitalized value of "regulatory assets" that the regulator has permitted or directed the utility to include in its rate base.

The earnings-based approach is preferable to revisiting each of the utility's specific capital investments and expenditures and then summing those that have become "stranded." First, it is not necessary to value the utility's costs and investments in an asset-by-asset manner, for that analysis already took place in regulatory rate hearings and prudency reviews.[4] Listing specific costs and evaluating whether or not they were stranded reopens all the past rate hearings and prudency reviews. Second, an asset-by-asset review could introduce errors in estimating stranded investment if the calculation excluded some reliance expenditures. Third, the asset-by-asset approach ignores that the relevant inquiry posed by the problem of stranded costs is how to compensate the utility for its forgone *expectations* under the regulatory bargain. A retrospective, asset-by-asset approach is likely to underestimate the utility's damages and thus to create incentives for the regulator to resort to inefficient breach of the regulatory contract.

The expectation-damage approach emphasizes that contracts do not protect investment per se; rather they serve to protect *expected gains from trade*. As Justice John McLean observed, the value of the Charles River Bridge lay in the tolls that it could be expected to earn, not in the quantity of timber and stone that the structure contained.[5] It is therefore not necessary to itemize and reevaluate every component of stranded investment and other costs to assess the value of stranded investment unless such a procedure is performed in the context of estimating the regulated revenue requirement.

By emphasizing the revenue requirement, the expectation-damage approach also makes it clear how to compare regulated earnings with the relevant portion of the utility's earning after deregulation, without the need to designate specific assets as competitive or stranded.

The net-revenue approach clearly shows that there are benefits from removing some of the utility's obligations to serve and other incumbent burdens. Doing so will raise net revenues for the incumbent public utility and hence lower required compensation. The award of expectation damages for stranded costs implies that the removal of incumbent burdens by the public utilities commission or state legislature will lower the incumbent utility's stranded costs.

---

4. Nonetheless, some thoughtful scholars have advocated ex post prudency reviews as part of a policy of stranded cost recovery. *See* Oliver E. Williamson, *Deregulatory Takings and Breach of the Regulatory Contract: Some Precautions*, 71 N.Y.U. L. REV. 1007, 1016–18 (1996); Stephen F. Williams, *Deregulatory Takings and Breach of the Regulatory Contract: A Comment*, 71 N.Y.U. L. REV. 1000, 1003, 1005 (1996).

5. Charles River Bridge *v.* Warren Bridge, 36 U.S. (11 Pet.) 420, 562 (1837) (McLean, J., concurring).

CONTRACT MODIFICATION: REPLACING
RATE-OF-RETURN REGULATION
WITH INCENTIVE REGULATION

Parties to a contract sometimes modify their agreement and thus supersede the old contract with a new one. With respect to the regulatory contract, modification has occurred when the regulator and the public utility have agreed, through the formality of public rulemakings, to alter a key provision of the contract, such as the manner in which the commission determines the price of the utility's output and whether the commission will regulate the utility's profit level along with its price. That modification has taken the form of the transition from cost-of-service, rate-of-return regulation to incentive regulation such as price caps.[6] Even before 1996 some state legislatures modified the regulatory contract by repealing statutes that prohibited competitive entry into regulated services such as local exchange telephony.[7] Some of the new regulatory structures even carry the name "social contract."[8]

A change in regulatory procedures, such as a switch from rate-of-return regulation to a system of price caps, does not necessarily represent a termination of the regulatory contract. Generally, such changes in telecommunications and electricity regulation have preserved the regulator's obligation to provide the utility with an opportunity to earn a competitive rate of return on its investment.

The basic system of price caps often keeps in place other aspects of rate regulation. The regulator continues to control rates through the caps; the utility has price flexibility below the price limit. Price-cap formulas frequently feature sharing rules that require the utility to divide earnings above some threshold amount with its customers. Regulators typically continue to assume responsibility for the financial health of the regulated

---

6. *See* DAVID E. M. SAPPINGTON & DENNIS L. WEISMAN, DESIGNING INCENTIVE REGULATION FOR THE TELECOMMUNICATIONS INDUSTRY (MIT Press & AEI Press 1996).

7. *E.g.*, CAL. PUB. UTIL. CODE § 2882.3; VA. CODE § 56-235.5.

8. Alternative Regulatory Frameworks for Local Exchange Carriers, 33 C.P.U.C.2d 43, 107 P.U.R.4th 1, I.87-11-033 *et al.* (Cal. Pub. Utils. Comm'n 1989); Proposed Policies Governing Restructuring California's Electric Services Industry and Reforming Regulation, R.94-04-031, I.94-04-032, Decision 94-12-027, 151 P.U.R.4th 73 (Cal. Pub. Utils. Comm'n 1994); New England Tel. & Tel. Co., D.P.U. 94-50, 153 P.U.R.4th 355 (Mass. Dep't Pub. Utils. 1994); New England Tel. & Tel. Co., DR 89-010, Order No. 20,149, 123 P.U.R.4th 289 (N.H. Pub. Utils. Comm'n 1991); Comprehensive Review of Telecommunications, Dkt. No. 1997, Order No. 14038, 138 P.U.R.4th 620 (R.I. Pub. Utils. Comm'n 1992).

utility. The basic dimensions of the regulatory contract remain in place if regulators retain the system of entry controls as revenue protection devices and maintain the utility's service obligations.

For example, the California Public Utilities Commission (CPUC) included *financial and rate stability* among its goals in establishing its system of incentive regulation for local exchange carriers called the "New Regulatory Framework."[9] The financial stability goal meant that the financial condition of the local telephone exchange carriers should not change markedly under the New Regulatory Framework. According to the CPUC:

> Stability is an important aspect for any plan. As financial stability promotes rate stability, customers, utilities and other market participants will each benefit from predictable prices for utility services.[10]

Despite the use of a price-cap formula for adjusting rates, the CPUC continued extensive monitoring of the regulated companies' financial and operational information, indicating the regulator's continued responsibility for the financial return of the LECs. The CPUC indicated its intent to maintain the utilities' financial returns through *increased* regulation:

> A regulatory structure which combines the price cap indexing approach with a sharing mechanism can provide protection to both shareholders and ratepayers from the risks that the indexing method may over- or underestimate the revenue changes which are needed to keep the utility financially healthy, but not too healthy. The increased regulatory involvement required to implement and maintain a sharing mechanism is a price we are willing to pay at this time for this added protection.[11]

Thus, the switch to incentive regulation, while maintaining other components of the regulatory contract, represents at most modification, not abandonment, of the contract.

Changes in the mechanism of rate adjustment are an administrative procedure instead of a fundamental change in contract terms. Price-cap mechanisms provide incentives for efficiency by allowing utilities to keep

---

9. As the commission defines it, the New Regulatory Framework is an incentive-based regulatory arrangement "centered around a price cap indexing mechanism with sharing of excess earnings above a benchmark rate of return level." Alternative Regulatory Frameworks for Local Exchange Carriers, 33 C.P.U.C.2d 43, 107 P.U.R.4th 1, I.87-11-033 *et al.*, Decision 89-10-031 (Cal. Pub. Utils. Comm'n 1989).

10. 33 C.P.U.C.2d at 198.

11. *Id.* at 134.

some of the gains from cost reductions. Such benefits existed under rate-of-return regulation as a consequence of lags between rate hearings. Price caps confer pricing flexibility that allows the regulated utility to carry out some limited changes in its rate structure, while keeping regulatory control over total revenues. Incentive regulation begins to constitute a fundamental renegotiation of the regulatory contract only when it is coupled with relaxation of entry controls and changes in the utility's obligations to serve.

The use of price caps and other forms of incentive regulation does not alter the manner in which damages for breach of the regulatory contract are calculated. The damages should still equal the present value of net revenues forgone. The amount of damages should be adjusted to the extent that the pricing method alters the net revenue expectations of the utility. The relaxation of entry barriers reduces earnings, and competitive opportunities allow for mitigation as before. The formula for calculating damages thus remains the same.

THE RULE AGAINST RETROACTIVE RATEMAKING

One might question whether the rule against retroactive ratemaking precludes the recovery of stranded costs. It does not. "The rule prohibits a public utility commission from setting future rates to allow a utility to recoup past losses or to refund to consumers excess utility profits."[12] It "prohibits a utility commission from making a retrospective inquiry to determine whether a prior rate was reasonable and imposing a surcharge when rates were too low or a refund when rates were too high."[13] The recovery of stranded costs does not violate the rule because such recovery is not a retrospective attempt to rectify losses incurred while the regulatory contract was in effect.

Although it was in the past that the utility incurred the investments and regulatory obligations that later give rise to stranded costs, those costs are forward-looking in the sense that they remain inchoate, "strandable" costs—and are not actually stranded—until the regulator subsequently adopts policies that unilaterally breach the regulatory contract. By definition, the regulatory commission, by the timing of its announcement of policy changes, endogenously determines the exact moment in the future when the actual stranding of costs will occur. The

---

12. State *v.* Public Util. Comm'n of Tex., 883 S.W.2d 190, 199 (Tex. 1994).
13. *Id.*

utility's expected reductions in net revenues under open-access policies therefore reflect its *future* inability, owing to endogenous regulatory change, to recover its total costs. End-user charges or other mechanisms for recovering stranded costs do not enable the utility to recoup any losses that it incurred in the past while charging regulated rates under a regulatory contract that the regulator, at that time, had not yet chosen to abrogate.

SOVEREIGN IMMUNITY

One could expect a state public utilities commission sued for breach of the regulatory contract to claim sovereign immunity as a defense. Sovereign immunity in that context does not refer to the limitation that the Eleventh Amendment imposes on the jurisdiction of the federal courts to hear suits against the states.[14] Rather, it refers to the state's claim of immunity from suit, even in state court, unless the state has consented to be sued. Although some of the relevant considerations discussed below come from cases construing the Eleventh Amendment, the boundaries of federal jurisdiction are not pertinent to our examination of enforcement of the regulatory contract.[15]

One can safely assume that, before they would have made massive irreversible investments in facilities, the managers of an investor-owned public utility around the turn of the twentieth century would have demanded representations and warranties from the municipality or state that its potential breach of the regulatory contract would not leave the utility without an effective remedy. Such assurance could have taken one or more legal forms: (1) explicit statutory waiver of sovereign immunity;[16] (2) explicit contractual waiver of sovereign immunity; (3) implicit

14. "The judicial power of the United States shall not be construed to extend to any suit in law or equity, commenced or prosecuted against one of the United States by citizens of another state, or by citizens or subjects of any foreign state." U.S. CONST. amend. XI. The Supreme Court later ruled that the principle of state sovereign immunity also prevented a citizen from suing his *own* state in federal court unless the state had consented to be sued. Hans *v.* Louisiana, 134 U.S. 1 (1890); *see* DAVID P. CURRIE, THE CONSTITUTION IN THE SUPREME COURT: THE SECOND CENTURY, 1888–1986, at 7–9, 568–69 (University of Chicago Press 1990).

15. Furthermore, "neither sovereign immunity nor the eleventh amendment bars Supreme Court review of state court judgments in suits in which a state is a party, since supremacy of federal law requires review of federal questions presented by such judgments." LAURENCE H. TRIBE, AMERICAN CONSTITUTIONAL LAW 175 (Foundation Press, 2d ed. 1988) (citing Cohens *v.* Virginia, 19 U.S. (6 Wheat.) 264, 379–83, 407 (1821); Smith *v.* Reeves, 178 U.S. 436, 445 (1900)).

16. *See* Gillespie *v.* City of Los Angeles, 114 Cal. App. 2d 513, 515, 250 P.2d 717,

waiver of sovereign immunity; (4) reliance upon the Contract Clause that the state could not subsequently enact any law impairing the original regulatory contract;[17] and (5) the mutual understanding that the state's breach of the regulatory contract would give rise to a takings case, for which waiver of sovereign immunity would be self-executing. Little case law exists on those issues. The absence of reported cases, coupled with the substantial investment actually made in infrastructure for local telephony and electric power, strongly implies that in some manner the public utility was able to secure reasonable assurances that its long-lived investments would be protected from opportunism. That absence of reported decisions may reflect Henry M. Hart's observation that reputational considerations rather than binding legal constraints may compel a government to waive sovereign immunity:

> [T]he government may be under other kinds of practical pressure not to insist on its immunity. Take government contracts, for example. The law gives no immunity against being branded as a defaulter. The business of government requires that people be willing to contract with it.[18]

The scant case law that does exist suggests that the answer to whether a state today could invoke sovereign immunity as a defense to deny the utility a remedy for breach of the regulatory contract would vary from

---

718 (Cal. App. 1952) ("Prior . . . to 1893 persons having causes of action against the state for injuries arising by reason of the negligence of its officials or employees were not permitted a recovery against the state in the courts, but were relegated to the uncertain mercies of the legislature for relief. It was doubtless for the purpose of a definite departure from the long-held rule that the sovereign could not be made a party to actions of any sort against it without its consent, that the legislature of California, in its wisdom, saw fit to adopt the act of 1893. . . [which] provides that 'All persons who have, or shall hereafter have, claims on contract or for negligence against the state . . . are hereby authorized . . . to bring suit thereon against the state.'") (quotations omitted).

17. Sovereign immunity could still, however, prevent a plaintiff's recovery from the state in a suit based on the Contract Clause. Quayle *v.* New York, 192 N.Y. 47, 50, 84 N.E. 583, 584 (N.Y. App. 1908) ("The Federal Constitution inhibits the state from passing any law impairing the obligation of contracts, and this provision applies to contracts with the state itself as well as to those of third parties. Therefore, a breach of its contract by the state creates a valid cause of action. Immunity of the state from suit merely prevents its enforcement.").

18. Henry M. Hart, *The Power of Congress to Limit the Jurisdiction of Federal Courts: An Exercise in Dialectic*, 66 HARV. L. REV. 1362, 1371 (1953), *reprinted in* PAUL M. BATOR, PAUL J. MISHKIN, DAVID L. SHAPIRO & HERBERT WECHSLER, HART AND WECHSLER'S THE FEDERAL COURTS AND THE FEDERAL SYSTEM 335–36 (Foundation Press, 2d ed. 1973).

jurisdiction to jurisdiction and would depend on the following: whether the state had explicitly or implicitly waived sovereign immunity, whether it would be constitutional for the state to invoke the defense, and whether breach of the regulatory contract would be cast simply as an action exceeding the lawful authority of the public utilities commission.

Sovereign immunity determines whether a plaintiff has a remedy against the state—not whether the plaintiff has a right of action in the first place.[19] In a federal takings case, the plaintiff may proceed even if sovereign immunity would have barred a common law action against the state defendant.[20] There appear to be few state cases in which the state argued that a takings claim could not proceed when sovereign immunity barred the underlying common law claim. The few that do exist, however, agree with the rule in the federal cases. In *State Road Department of Florida* v. *Tharp*, the Florida Supreme Court considered whether the state's immunity from suit barred a suit to enjoin the state road department from interfering with the operation of a water wheel, when the state had refused to offer compensation for its activities.[21] The court dismissed the sovereign-immunity argument:

> If a State agency can deliberately trespass on and destroy the property of the citizen in the manner shown to have been done here and then be relieved from making restitution on the plea on non-liability of the State for suit, the constitutional guaranty of the right to own and dispose of property becomes nothing more than the tinkling of empty words. Such a holding would raise administrative boards above the law and clothe them with an air of megalomania that would eternally jeopardize the property rights of the citizens.[22]

The federal courts have gone even further in protecting the interests of private plaintiffs against claims of sovereign immunity. In one category of cases, courts have under limited circumstances treated the govern-

19. Trippe *v.* Port of New York Authority, 14 N.Y.2d 119, 198 N.E.2d 585, 249 N.Y.S.2d 409 (N.Y. App. 1964) (quoting Buckles *v.* N.Y., 221 N.Y. 418, 423–24 (N.Y. App. 1917)).

20. Causby *v.* United States, 328 U.S. 256 (1946); Richards *v.* Washington Terminal Co., 233 U.S. 546, 550 (1914); Pumpelly *v.* Green Bay Co., 80 U.S. (13 Wall.) 166 (1871).

21. 146 Fla. 745, 1 So. 2d 868 (1941).

22. 146 Fla. at 749, 1 So. 2d at 869–70. For similar holdings in other states, see Engelhart *v.* Jenkins, 273 Ala. 352, 141 So. 2d 193 (1962); Department of Highways *v.* Corey, 247 S.W.2d 389, 390 (Ky. Ct. App. 1952).

ment's retroactive assertion of sovereign immunity as a taking.[23] In a second category of cases, courts have treated the government's breach of contract as a taking.[24] The plaintiff's chief difficulty in those two categories of cases has been in establishing the existence of a property or contract right, not in defeating the assertion of sovereign immunity.[25]

The logical extension of viewing sovereign immunity as concerning only the plaintiff's remedy, not the plaintiff's underlying right, would be to treat every assertion of sovereign immunity as a taking. Some state courts have reasoned in dicta that the state's refusal to waive sovereign immunity for takings might violate the U.S. Constitution.[26] Although no court appears to have based its holding on that rationale, the Wisconsin Supreme Court has held that the takings clause of the state constitution is self-executing and requires no statutory waiver of immunity.[27]

A second reason why sovereign immunity would be unlikely to block a suit against a state PUC for breach of the regulatory contract is that most states have statutes waiving sovereign immunity to some degree. New York,[28] Illinois,[29] and Ohio[30] have broad waivers subject to specific statutory exceptions. Pennsylvania[31] and Wisconsin[32] have narrower statutory waivers, particularly with respect to tort suits. All five states and California have waived sovereign immunity in contract suits.[33]

---

23. Armstrong v. United States, 364 U.S. 40 (1960).

24. Lynch v. United States, 292 U.S. 571 (1934).

25. Bowen v. Public Agencies Opposed to Soc. Security Entrapment, 477 U.S. 41, 55 (1986); Peterson v. United States Dep't of Interior, 899 F.2d 799 (9th Cir. 1990).

26. P.T. & L. Contr. Co. v. Commissioner, Dep't of Transp., 60 N.J. 308, 288 A.2d 574 (1972); Grant Constr. Co. v. Burns, 92 Idaho 408, 443 P.2d 1005 (1968).

27. Zinn v. State, 112 Wis. 2d 417, 436, 334 N.W.2d 67, 76 (1983). New York's highest court disagrees. *Trippe*, 14 N.Y.2d at 124–26, 198 N.E.2d at 586–88, 249 N.Y.S.2d at 412–14.

28. N.Y. Ct. Cl. Act art. II, § 8 (McKinney 1994).

29. The Illinois Constitution of 1970 abolished sovereign immunity, subject to exceptions made by the general assembly. Ill. Const. 1970, art. XIII, § 4. The General Assembly enacted the Court of Claims Act, giving the Court of Claims exclusive jurisdiction over claims against the state. Ill. Rev. Stat., ch. 37, ¶ 439.

30. Ohio Rev. Code § 2743.02(A)(1).

31. 1 Pa. Con. Stat. § 2310 (reaffirming principle of sovereign immunity generally); 42 Pa. Con. Stat. § 8501, 8521, 8522 (exceptions to sovereign immunity).

32. Lister v. Board of Regents, 72 Wis. 2d 282, 291, 240 N.W.2d 610, 617 (1976).

33. Ill. Ann. Stat. ch. 37, ¶ 439.8 (Smith-Hurd Supp. 1972); N.Y. Ct. Cl. Act art. II, § 8 (McKinney 1989); Ohio Rev. Code Ann. § 2743.02 (Anderson Supp. 1989); 72 Pa. Cons. Stat. Ann. § 4651-1 (Purdon Supp. 1989); Wisconsin Retired Teachers Ass'n, Inc. v. Employee Trust Funds Bd., 195 Wis. 2d 1001, 537 N.W.2d 400 (1995) (takings suit against state agency for breach of fiduciary duties may proceed, since takings

Because mandatory unbundling in electric power and local telecommunications markets began to occur only in the 1990s, it is no surprise that, before 1996, there appear to have been no reported cases in which a public utility sued a state public utilities commission on a common law theory of breach of contract.[34] It is not clear whether the state statutes waiving sovereign immunity would be broad enough to permit claims based on breach of the regulatory contract. One might infer that the waiver statutes would allow such claims to proceed, simply because there appears to be no such contract case brought against a PUC in which the commission raised the issue of sovereign immunity.[35] A Texas case involving a takings claim against a public utilities commission, *Public Utility Commission of Texas* v. *City of Austin*, did raise the issue of sovereign immunity.[36] The court followed Texas cases holding that a challenge to an agency's actions as being outside the scope of its authority may proceed without a statutory waiver of sovereign immunity.[37] In essence the utility's complaint was that the PUC was "attempting to act outside the delegated scope of its authority" such that "the type of declaratory relief which the City requests, determining the lawfulness of the Commission's actions and proposed actions . . . may not be shielded by jurisdictional claims of sovereign immunity."[38] The absence of similar precedent in other jurisdictions presents a puzzle. It may be that Texas

---

clause of Wisconsin constitution requires remedy); *see also* Souza & McCue Constr. Co. *v.* Superior Ct. of San Benito, 57 Cal. 2d 508, 510, 370 P.2d 338, 339, 20 Cal. Rptr. 634, 635 (1962); CAL. GOV. CODE § 814.

34. In Central Ill. Light Co. *v.* Illinois Comm. Comm'n, 255 Ill. App. 3d 876, 626 N.E.2d 728 (1993), an Illinois court considered a challenge to the state commission's order that the costs of cleaning up coal-tar dumps were to be shared between utility customers and shareholders. At first, the commission concluded that the customers would bear the costs, but it changed its mind upon the appointment of new commissioners. The utilities argued that "under the regulatory bargain between themselves and their customers," the utilities were entitled to recover their costs. 255 Ill. App. 3d at 887, 626 N.E.2d at 737. That "regulatory bargain" theory did not appear to have been pleaded in any detail, however. The court upheld the commission's ruling, with little or no discussion of the takings issue based on the contract theory.

35. PUCs have raised sovereign immunity defense to tort suits, however. Harris *v.* Public Utils. Comm'n of Ohio, Slip Opinion No. 77AP–256 (unpublished opinion) (statute waiving sovereign immunity does not create a right of action against the state for negligent nonperformance of duties, but merely permits actions to be brought against the state that were previously barred by the doctrine of sovereign immunity); Elson *v.* Public Utils. Comm'n, 51 Cal. App. 3d 577, 124 Cal. Rptr. 305 (Cal. App. 1975).

36. 728 S.W.2d 907 (Tex. App. 1987).

37. *Id.* at 911.

38. *Id.*

law is also the unspoken law elsewhere, and thus that public utilities commissions do not raise sovereign-immunity defenses because most takings suits against them are brought on the theory that the commissions are acting outside their statutory authority. On the other hand, it may be that PUCs do not raise sovereign-immunity defenses in takings cases because of the breadth of the waiver statutes. Both factors may be at work.[39]

At common law, courts have limited the extent to which municipalities may avail themselves of sovereign immunity. Generally, the issue arises in tort suits, where sovereign immunity insulates the municipality's "governmental" activities, but not its "proprietary" activities.[40] Commentators and courts treat the inquiry into the "proprietary" nature of the municipality's activity as a tort doctrine[41] and reason that sovereign immunity would not bar recovery on a contract theory.[42] As chapter 4 shows, courts have treated contracts between a municipality and public utility as binding on both.[43]

A growing number of cities are "municipalizing" the local investor-owned electric utility.[44] The city condemns the utility's franchise and

39. *See, e.g.*, Texas Dep't of Health *v.* Texas Health Enter., 871 S.W.2d 498, 506 (Tex. App. 1993) ("If the State commits an act which by statute it may not do, sovereign immunity is not available. . . . Furthermore, the sovereign immunity doctrine does not apply to contracts made by the State or its agencies.").

40. *E.g.*, Parker *v.* City of Highland Park, 404 Mich. 183, 193–95, 273 N.W.2d 413, 416–17 (Mich. 1973), *modified*, 434 N.W.2d 413 (Mich. 1989); Schwartz *v.* Borough of Stockton, 32 N.J. 141, 149–51, 160 A.2d 1, 5–7 (N.J. 1960); Bucher *v.* Northumberland County, 209 Pa. 618, 59 A. 69 (Pa. 1904); Board of Commissioners of Hamilton County *v.* Mighels, 7 Ohio St. 109 (Ohio 1857).

41. *See* Janice C. Griffith, *Local Government Contracts: Escaping from the Governmental/Proprietary Maze*, 75 IOWA L. REV. 277, 325–26 (1990).

42. Woodfield Lanes, Inc. *v.* Village of Schaumburg, 168 Ill. App. 3d 763, 768, 523 N.E.2d 36, 39 (Ill. App. 1988); Riverside Corp. Trustee *v.* City of Cincinnati, slip op. C-780794 (Ohio App. Feb. 27, 1980) (unpublished) ("We do not accept the postulation that the defense of governmental immunity may be interposed here. Governmental immunity does not apply to contracts freely entered into by a municipality and moreover seems a concept generally, if not exclusively, related to torts rather than contracts. . . . It would seem a travesty of justice to allow municipalities to walk away from contracts into which they have freely entered.").

43. *E.g.*, City of Columbus *v.* Public Utils. Comm'n, 103 Ohio St. 79, 133 N.E. 800 (Ohio 1921) (PUC lacked statutory authority to overturn the terms of contract between municipality and telephone company setting rates).

44. *Va. SCC Clarifies Its Jurisdiction in Falls Church 'Muni Lite' Effort*, ELEC. UTIL. WK., Dec. 18, 1995, at 19; *City of San Francisco Hires Consultant to Study Forming Muni to Replace PG&E*, ELEC. UTIL. WK., Dec. 4, 1995, at 16; Peter Nulty, *Utilities Go to War*, FORTUNE, Nov. 13, 1995, at 200; *Five N.Y. Towns Look to Municipalize; LILCO*

local distribution assets and takes over operation of those facilities. The city's motivation for municipalization is to engage in "jurisdiction shopping" between state and federal regulators. As a wholesale purchaser of power, the city may invoke federal law to effect wholesale wheeling transactions for low-cost bulk power at a time when state law may not yet permit even large industrial customers to buy bulk power through retail wheeling. Municipalization can be a form of opportunistic behavior in which a city reneges on its franchise agreement with an investor-owned utility. In a lawsuit by an electric utility against a municipality for breach of the regulatory contract, or tortious interference with it, it is unlikely that the municipality could invoke sovereign immunity.

In short, if a state has waived sovereign immunity, or if that defense is inapplicable as a matter of law to the state's breach of the regulatory contract, then a public utility would face no impediments to recovery of its remedies for breach beyond those defenses that would exist as a matter of common law in contract litigation between two private parties. Alternatively, sovereign immunity might deny the utility a remedy for the state's breach of the regulatory contract, even though that defense would not necessarily support the state's motion to dismiss for the utility's failure to state a claim. Stated differently, the utility's remedy in that situation might be limited to a declaratory judgment stating that the public utilities commission is in breach of the regulatory contract, without any order for damages or injunctive relief. In that case, or if sovereign immunity were interpreted to deny the utility even a cause of action (without remedy) for breach of the regulatory contract, then it would be clear that the credible commitment of the state to permit the public utility to recover the substantial cost of its specialized investment could only come from the prohibition against uncompensated takings contained in that state's constitution or in the Takings Clause of the U.S. Constitution.

The Supreme Court's 1996 decision in *United States* v. *Winstar Corporation* reduced the likelihood that a regulator could successfully invoke sovereign immunity to defeat a claim for breach of the regulatory contract.[45] In *Winstar*, already discussed at length in chapter 4, the government raised the "sovereign act" defense, under which a "public and general" sovereign act could not trigger contractual liability. Justices

---

Says Consultant Has Interest, ELEC. UTIL. WK., Apr. 24, 1995, at 7; *Four Maine Towns to Vote in November on Setting up Munis to Replace CMO*, ELEC. UTIL. WK., Oct. 3, 1994, at 9.

    45. 116 S. Ct. 2432 (1996).

David H. Souter, John Paul Stevens, and Stephen G. Breyer agreed that
the Financial Institutions Reform, Recovery and Enforcement Act of
1989[46] was not public and general, for the legislative history clearly
showed that the act's purpose was to relieve the government of certain
obligations. In their concurrence, Justices Antonin Scalia, Anthony M.
Kennedy, and Clarence Thomas found that the sovereign acts defense
could not be used when the government tries to abrogate the essential
bargain of the contract.[47]

Sovereign immunity was not at issue in *Winstar*, because the Tucker
Act[48] waives governmental immunity for breaches of contract.[49] Nonetheless, the sovereign act defense is closely analogous to the defense of
sovereign immunity. Both defenses help to ensure that the government
will not bargain away its police power or other powers to legislate for
the public welfare and to limit the taxpayers' obligation to pay for
bureaucratic mistakes. The defenses are not, however, construed so
broadly as to allow the government to elude particular contractual
obligations, for that ability would discourage any private party from
contracting with the government. In *Winstar* Justice Souter explained that
the purpose of the sovereign acts defense is to place the government on
a par with private contracting parties.[50] For that reason Congress waived,
in the Tucker Act, its sovereign immunity defense in contract actions.[51]
Thus, *Winstar*'s outcome and language strongly suggest that the Court
would reject a defense of sovereign immunity to a claim for breach of
the regulatory contract. To rule otherwise would discourage private
parties from contracting with the government for the provision of
services satisfying consumer needs every bit as essential as the mortgage
services supplied by the thrifts in *Winstar*.

MISTAKE AND IMPOSSIBILITY

When, in private contracts, an unforeseen event makes the performance
of a contract substantially more costly for one of the parties than at the
time the parties entered into their agreement, the party facing that higher
cost of performance understandably can be expected to argue that he

46. Pub. L. No. 101-73, 103 Stat. 183.
47. 116 S. Ct. at 2478–79.
48. 24 Stat. 505 (1887) (codified in various sections of 28 U.S.C.).
49. 28 U.S.C. § 1491(a)(1).
50. 116 S. Ct. at 2469.
51. *Id.* at 2473–74.

should be excused from performing the contract because it is impossible to do so.[52] Similarly, one party in those circumstances may seek to be excused from performance on the grounds that no contract in fact exists because of the (presumably mutual) mistake of the promisor and promisee. Regulators may similarly claim mistake or impossibility as a defense to efforts by the regulated firm to enforce the regulatory contract.[53] It was a mutual mistake of fact, the state would assert, not to foresee that a competitive market structure could arise in the relevant network industry. Similarly, the advent of a competitive market, the state would argue, makes it impossible for it to ensure that the regulated firm will receive the reasonable opportunity to recover its invested capital and earn a competitive rate of return on it.

Before we examine the plausibility of such arguments, its bears emphasis that by their very nature such defenses raised by the regulator reinforce the conclusion that the regulated firm and the state entered into a contract. The thrust of those defenses is that the formation of the regulatory contract was faulty because of mutual mistake, or that forces beyond its control prevent the regulator's performance of that contract at a cost that the parties ex ante would have considered reasonable. In either case, the regulator's defense forecloses the argument that it never had a contractual relationship with the regulated firm. Furthermore, whenever a party invokes the defense of impossibility or mistake, the natural question to ask is whether the parties already contracted, implicitly if not explicitly, for the risk in question to be borne by the party now seeking to have the contract declared void. In the case of a regulated utility, that question is especially compelling, for a critical objective of the regulatory contract is to reduce the volatility surrounding the allowed rate of return so that the utility can efficiently use debt to fund its investments in trans-action-specific, long-lived investments in infrastructure.

Consider now the remedy if the regulatory contract were declared void and service were terminated. When, because of mistake or impossibility, a contract is rescinded or deemed never to have been formed in the first place, the court orders the parties to make restitution of the benefits conferred upon one another.[54] That remedy is intended to

<hr />

52. *See* Richard A. Posner & Andrew M. Rosenfield, *Impossibility and Related Doctrines in Contract Law: An Economic Analysis*, 6 J. LEGAL STUD. 83 (1977).

53. For a discussion of that problem in the guise of disallowances of prudently incurred capital investments, see Richard J. Pierce, Jr., *The Regulatory Treatment of Mistakes in Retrospect*, 132 U. PA. L. REV. 497 (1984).

54. RESTATEMENT OF CONTRACTS § 468 (1932); RESTATEMENT OF RESTITUTION § 150 (1939); DOBBS, *supra* note 1, at 266, 722, 741, 974.

prevent one of the parties from being unjustly enriched at the expense of the other or unjustly penalized. The court attempts to restore the parties to the position that they would have occupied had they not formed the contract. That exercise presents difficulties, for there are costs incurred as a result of the transaction—namely, the investment of the regulated firm—that cannot be reversed.

For the regulated utility, restitution damages should reflect the benefits that it conferred upon the state (for consumers, as third-party beneficiaries). Up until the moment of rescission, what benefits have consumers received from the regulated firm? During each preceding year that a regulatory contract was thought to be in effect, consumers compensated the utility under cost-of-service regulation for the value of service delivered. The services consumed cannot be returned, and some payments have already been made. A number of factors complicate the calculation of restitution damages, however. Restitution in the context of a regulated utility differs from restitution with respect to arms-length contracts that operate over short periods of time. Because of the extended duration of regulatory contracts, the payments from consumers may not fully reflect the value of benefits that they received as of the moment of recission. There may be intertemporal subsidies in the form of regulatory assets and extended depreciation schedules such that the payments by consumers have been substantially less than the benefits they have received. The depreciation schedule required by the regulator meant that consumers received service at a price that paid for the retirement of a lesser amount of the utility's invested capital than was realistic in light of the economic obsolescence of assets precipitated by newer, more efficient technologies or changes in regulation. Similarly, consumers received the benefits of all the incumbent burdens, discussed at length earlier, that were borne by the regulated firm between the outset of the contract and the time of its being set aside. Moreover, owing to cross-subsidies in the utility's rate schedule, some customers may have paid substantially more for the benefits received than did other customers. For both the utility and its customers, therefore, the estimation of the net benefits received is an empirical matter that depends on the regulatory policy of the particular jurisdiction and on facts unique to the particular utility. Outcomes may therefore vary from case to case.[55]

---

55. Our thinking on the question of restitution damages has evolved somewhat since our earlier discussion in J. Gregory Sidak & Daniel F. Spulber, *Deregulatory Takings and Breach of the Regulatory Contract*, 71 N.Y.U. L. REV. 851, 929–31 (1996).

Because the utility is subject to cost-of-service regulation, the utility's expected revenues were meant to recover the economic costs of providing service. Thus, the utility was expected to receive the reasonable opportunity to recover the cost of its investment and a competitive rate of return. To the extent that the utility did not recover some portion of its costs under the agreement, it should be allowed to recover the remaining amount from consumers. A court should offset such recovery by deducting any benefits that the regulated firm received up until the moment of rescission. That offset would include the maximum of the scrap value of the capital investment or the returns that could be obtained from continued operation of the facilities to provide service in the competitive market. By deducting the returns from continued use of the facilities, the regulated firm would not benefit from the continued services of facilities, from continued use of public rights of way (presumably at incremental cost), or from facilities constructed using eminent domain. The past benefits of entry regulation need not be reimbursed because rate (or price) regulation already constrained the utility's revenues. In retail wheeling of electric power and in the unbundling of the local telephone network, the regulator has already taken the benefit of entry regulation away from the incumbent regulated firm.

The question is, Who is responsible for preventing mistakes in contract formation? The efficient solution to that question is to place the responsibility for preventing mistakes on the party who can do so at the least cost. The regulated firm has a responsibility to present accurate data of cost and performance of its service obligations to the regulatory authority. Those responsibilities already are reflected in disclosure requirements. The regulator has a responsibility to make clear its own regulatory policy, in terms of what types of investments it approves for inclusion in the rate base, what prices the utility may charge, and what the utility's service obligations are. The regulatory authority surely is the party best informed about impending changes in its own policies, particularly with regard to substantial deregulation. The regulator has a professional staff and operates a system of public hearings on the record. It should not be able to sustain a defense that it did not understand the terms of the regulatory contract.

THE REGULATORY CONTRACT
AND THE STATUTE OF FRAUDS

The Statute of Frauds, enacted in England in 1677, required, among other things, that any contract that could not be performed in one year would have to be in writing: "no action shall be brought . . . upon any agreement that is not to be performed within the space of one year from the making thereof . . . unless the agreement upon which such action shall be brought, or some memorandum or note thereof, shall be in writing, and signed by the party to be charged therewith, or some other person thereunto by him lawfully authorized."[56] American states enacted their own legislation codifying that rule,[57] even though England in 1954 repealed all but two other clauses not germane to the passage just quoted.[58] Some who question the existence of the regulatory contract, including some regulatory commissions, assert that, even if an unwritten contract existed between the utility and the state or municipality, it would be a long-term contract that by its nature could not be performed in a year's time. Consequently, the argument concludes, the unwritten regulatory contract violates the Statute of Frauds and is unenforceable.[59]

The argument, however, is not likely to compel the conclusion that the regulatory contract is void. And, even if the defense were valid in a particular case, it would not enable the state to avoid paying compensation, under equitable principles, for the stranded costs that the state's abrogation of existing regulatory principles would impose on the utility.

The Subsequent Memorandum of the Regulatory Contract

As we noted earlier in this chapter, opponents of cost recovery sometimes ask in regulatory proceedings in what manner the utility and the PUC have recorded their mutual assent to the regulatory contract by having signed a document. The question whether the regulatory contract has been signed, however, differs from whether that contract is voidable under the Statute of Frauds on the grounds that it is an agreement not performable within one year that has not been memorialized in writing. To satisfy the Statute of Frauds, the memorandum need not be integrated into a single document executed by both parties, as the parol evidence

---

56. An Act for the Preservation of Frauds and Perjuries, St. 29 Car. 2, ch. 3, § 4 (1677).

57. *E.g.*, TEX. BUS. CODE §§ 2.201, 26.01.

58. 2 & 3 Eliz. 2, ch. 34 (1954).

59. *E.g.*, Application of Central Power and Light Co. for Authority to Change Rates, Proposal for Decision, SOAH Dkt. No. 473-95-1563, PUC Dkt. No. 14965, at 508, 643 ¶ 68 (Tex. Pub. Util. Comm'n & State Office of Admin. Hearings Jan. 21, 1997) (ALJ proposed decision), *aff'd*, Order, Dkt. No. 14965 (Pub. Util. Comm'n Tex. Mar. 31, 1997).

rule requires.[60] The subsequent memorandum of the regulatory contract may therefore consist of an aggregation of documents—including, for example, proposals for rate increases, authorization for construction, and the resulting orders issued by the regulatory commission. For purposes of the Statute of Frauds, those documents need not evidence the knowledge or consent *of the utility* if the utility is the party attempting to enforce the regulatory contract against the state.[61] Nonetheless, as a practical matter the utility's assent would already be obvious from its actual performance.

Although the particular legislation may vary from state to state, the Statute of Frauds as traditionally conceived would not require an authorized signature of the PUC on a writing that served as a memorandum of the commission's regulatory contract with the utility. Note, however, that, apart from question of the voidability of the regulatory contract, the execution of a document setting forth the regulatory contract is an issue that may be considered by those challenging the regulatory contract as being probative of whether a contract was ever formed in the first place.[62] But again, as a practical matter, there is not likely to be any shortage of evidence of executed documents constituting the regulatory contract. Every time that the utility asks the PUC to authorize a rate increase, approve an investment, certify the extension or discontinuation of service, and the like, the utility submits a written application signed by someone authorized to bind the company. Every time that the PUC rules on any such application, it records the votes of the individual commissioners (who in turn typically must sign some document to verify their votes[63]) and issues an order approving or disapproving the utility's application. The PUC's order is typically signed by the commissioners themselves or by the secretary of the commission and contains an explanation for the decision. As a matter of contract formation, there is a signed written offer from the utility and, in cases of approved applications, a signed written acceptance by the

---

60. John P. Dawson, William Burnett Harvey & Stanley D. Henderson, Cases and Comment on Contracts 969 (Foundation Press, 6th ed. 1993). "The 'note or memorandum' that satisfies most of the [state] statutes can . . . take almost any form." *Id*.

61. *Id*.

62. *Cf*. Restructuring New Hampshire's Electric Utility Industry, DR 96-150 Order No. 22,514, 175 P.U.R.4th 193 (N.H. Pub. Utils. Comm'n Feb. 28, 1997) ("In the context of utility regulation in New Hampshire, there is no offer, no acceptance and no consideration.").

63. *E.g.*, Tex. Gov't Code § 2001.090(a)(2).

commission. So, for example, the California PUC, referring to one of its previous orders by its decision number, wrote in 1991 of utilities' need to "satisfy their obligations under the regulatory compact struck in D.88-01-063."[64] Just as there is no mystery here regarding contract formation, so also there is no mystery concerning compliance with the Statute of Frauds. In other words, if confusion over the Statute of Frauds arises, it is likely because the regulator or an interested party other than the incumbent utility disputes that a regulatory contract was ever formed.

The Party to Be Charged

Under the Statute of Frauds only "the party to be charged" must have reduced the agreement to writing. In the case of breach of the regulatory contract, "the party to be charged" is the state, acting through its agent, the public utilities commission. Breach of the regulatory contract is opportunistic behavior by the regulator for the state's benefit. Consequently, all that the utility would need to show to defeat the PUC's claim that the Statute of Frauds voids the regulatory contract would be a memorandum *by the regulator* that recorded the contract's undertaking. The essential terms of that memorandum are the parties, the assets forming the subject of the contract, and the price.[65] Again, the PUC's orders on rates, prudency of investment, and the like provide ample documentation for such a memorandum.

Moreover, the PUC's memorandum may be supplied at any time before the action is filed (or, in some states, tried) for breach of contract.[66] Consequently, subsequent statements by PUCs or legislatures acknowledging the existence of the "regulatory contract" or the "regulatory compact" between the utility and the state (or its agent, the PUC) have more than symbolic significance. Examples of such statements are numerous. They vary, of course, from state to state in terms of how clearly they describe the essential terms of the regulatory contract. In a discussion captioned, "Legal Framework—The Social and Economic Compact of Utility Regulation," the Washington Utilities and

---

64. Application of SCEcorp and Its Public Utility Subsidiary Southern California Edison Co. (U 338 E) and San Diego Gas & Elec. Co. (U 902-M) for Authority to Merge San Diego Gas & Elec. Co. Into Southern California Edison Co., Decision No. 91-05-028, Application No. 88-12-035, 1991 Cal. PUC LEXIS 253 at *202–03; 122 P.U.R.4th 225; 40 C.P.U.C.2d 159 (Cal. Pub. Utils. Comm'n 1991).

65. DAWSON, HARVEY & HENDERSON, *supra* note 60, at 970.

66. *Id.* at 969.

Transportation Commission in 1984 set forth an early, though general, statement of the regulatory compact:

> A note on the concept and existence of the social and economic compact of utility regulation is necessary to in part help communicate the reasons for the decisions made by the Commission in this order. The social and economic compact of utility regulation begins with the premise that a regulated utility has an obligation to serve the public. In a decision by an earlier Commission an effort was made to put a limit on that obligation. . . . That effort was rejected. . . . This leaves the state of the law as a utility possesses an unending obligation to provide service to anyone within the service territory of that utility who demands service in accordance with approved tariffs.
>
> However, in order for the social duty to serve to be viable, the compact must also provide for a utility to recover expenses it prudently undertakes to meet that obligation. This does not mean a guaranteed rate of return. The elements which determine a rate of return are another part of the compact. Understanding the dichotomy between the treatment of expenses prudently undertaken to provide service and providing a return on investment and that they are two separate matters is critical to the understanding of the regulatory compact and the operation of utilities. . . .
>
> This then is the basic precept and an outline of the application of the regulatory compact. The Commission believes this compact must be upheld.[67]

Later written statements by regulatory commissions have had greater specificity in describing the regulatory contract. In the following words, the Illinois Commerce Commission in 1991 summarized the testimony of Nobel laureate George J. Stigler, which the commission accepted as consistent with its determination that certain investments were "used and useful," on the question of the regulatory compact:

> The long run goal is to provide the amount of electricity needed as cheaply as possible. The traditional regulatory compact does this. The regulatory compact or bargain is a sensible arrangement by which shareholders are told how they are going to be treated, and lend money on that basis, and the utility is told by its commission on behalf of ratepayers how it should conduct itself within specified rules of efficiency or prudency in order to be paid a compensatory rate of return.[68]

---

67. Washington Util. & Transp. Comm'n v. Puget Sound Power & Light Co., Cause No. U-83-54, 1984 Wash. UTC LEXIS 12, at *57–*58, *65, 62 P.U.R.4th 557 (Washington Util. & Transp. Comm'n 1984).

68. Commonwealth Edison Company: Proposed General Increase in Electric Rates;

Also in 1991 the Michigan PSC wrote:

> The regulatory compact . . . is a well established policy under which a
> utility is granted a monopoly franchise that requires it to meet the needs
> of ratepayers, to provide adequate service, and to plan for the future
> needs of ratepayers. In return, the utility is assured recovery of reason-
> able operating expenses, recovery of capital prudently invested, and an
> opportunity to earn a reasonable return on its prudently invested capital.[69]

Although such discussions of the regulatory contract may be more
favorable to the utility than our own definition (which reflects an
evaluation of the law of other states), those examples of written
acknowledgment of the existence of the regulatory contract would surely
satisfy the Statute of Frauds.

More recent discussions of the regulatory contract provide other
instances of regulatory commissions' conceding the existence of the
contract. The Pennsylvania PUC wrote in 1994:

> The universal service precept is rooted in the regulatory compact struck
> between the industry and government in the early part of the 20th century.
> In exchange for a monopoly franchise, a telephone company was obligated
> to serve all customers within its geographic, exclusive territory.[70]

"At the heart of the regulatory framework," wrote the Indiana Utility
Regulatory Commission in 1995, "is the so-called 'regulatory compact,'"
which the commission described by using the words of a state appellate
court decision:

Commonwealth Edison Company: Petition for Authority to Record Carrying Charges and
Deferred Depreciation for Byron Units 1 and 2 and Braidwood Unit 1; Commonwealth
Edison Company: Proposed General Increase in Electric Rates; Staff of the Illinois
Commerce Commission: Petition for an Investigation of the Rates of Commonwealth
Edison Company and of an Offer of Settlement of Docket Nos. 87-0169, 87-0427, and
88-0189; Commonwealth Edison Company: Petition for Authority to Record Carrying
Charges and Deferred Depreciation for Braidwood Unit 2, 87-0427; 87-0169, Consol.;
88-0189; 88-0219; 88-0253, On Remand, 1991 Ill. PUC LEXIS 145, at *324 (Ill.
Commerce Comm'n 1991).

69. Application of Consumers Power Co. for Authority to Increase Its Rates for the
Sale of Electricity, Case No. U-7830, Step 3B, 1991 Mich. PSC LEXIS 119, at *316 n.34
(Mich. Pub. Serv. Comm'n 1991).

70. Formal Investigation to Examine and Establish Updated Universal Service
Principles and Policies for Telecommunications Service in the Commonwealth, Dkt. No.
I-940035, 1994 Pa. PUC LEXIS 15, at *1 (Pa. Pub. Util. Comm'n 1994).

[t]he regulation of utilities arises out of a "bargain" struck between the utilities and the state. As a quid pro quo for being granted a monopoly in a geographical area for the provision of a particular good or service, the utility is subject to regulation by the state to ensure that it is prudently investing its revenues in order to provide the best and most efficient service possible to the consumer.[71]

Similarly, the California PUC wrote in 1996: "For several reasons, we choose not to grant PG&E the waiver it seeks. First, to do so would enable PG&E to escape its part of the regulatory contract."[72] The same year, the California PUC wrote that "'[t]he fundamental tenets of California's contemporary regulatory compact emerged when the monopoly character of the electric utility industry was strong and secure.'"[73] Similarly, the PUC of Ohio wrote in 1996:

The near monopoly provision of local exchange telephone service, characterized by one provider per market, has served well the purpose for which it was intended. The downside of monopoly authority is that regulation and regulators must replace the competitive marketplace in order to ensure that monopoly providers use their authority in a manner which benefits the public interest. The technological advances of the second half of the twentieth century along with legislative changes embodied in Section 4905.02, Revised Code, recently passed Senate Bill 306 and the 1996 Act have made it possible to reconsider the regulatory

71. Petition of Northern Indiana Public Service Company for Approval of Changes in Its Gas Cost Adjustment Mechanism, Cause No. 40180, 1995 Ind. PUC LEXIS 392, at *37-*38, 166 P.U.R.4th 213 (Ind. Util. Reg. Comm'n 1995) (quoting Indiana Gas Co. *v.* Office of the Consumer Counselor, 575 N.E.2d 1044, 1046 (Ind. App. 3d Dist. 1991)).

72. Application of Pacific Gas and Elec. Co. for Authority, Among Other Things, to Increase Its Electric Base Revenue Requirement Effective January 1, 1997 for Electric System Maintenance and Reliability and Customer Service Activities (U 39 E), Decision No. 96-12-066, Application 96-04-002, 1996 Cal. PUC LEXIS 1111, at *9 (Cal. Pub. Utils. Comm'n 1996).

73. Order Instituting Rulemaking on the Commission's Proposed Policies Governing Restructuring California's Electric Services Industry and Reforming Regulation; Order Instituting Investigation on the Commission's Proposed Policies Governing Restructuring California's Electric Services Industry and Reforming Regulation, Decision No. 95-12-063 as modified by Decision No. 96-01-009, Rulemaking No. 94-04-031, Investigation No. 94-04-032, 1996 Cal. PUC LEXIS 28, at *3, 166 P.U.R.4th 1 (Cal. Pub. Utils. Comm'n 1996) (quoting CALIFORNIA PUBLIC UTILITIES COMMISSION, DIVISION OF STRATEGIC PLANNING, CALIFORNIA'S ELECTRIC SERVICES INDUSTRY: PERSPECTIVES ON THE PAST, STRATEGIES FOR THE FUTURE 140 (Feb. 3, 1993)).

compact and to determine to what extent, if any, this Commission can substitute competitive market forces in place of regulatory forces.[74]

In 1997 the Louisiana PSC wrote:

> The "regulatory compact" provides an investor a reasonable opportunity to recover all its prudent costs incurred to serve consumers. At the same time, cost-based regulation does not permit the utility to recover amounts in excess of prudent costs because that would also violate the regulatory compact.[75]

---

74. Commission Investigation Relative to the Establishment of Local Exchange Competition and Other Competitive Issues, Case No. 95-845-TP-COI, 1996 Ohio PUC LEXIS 361, at *3–*4 (Pub. Utils. Comm'n Ohio 1996).

75. Ratemaking and Financial Investigation of Cajun Electric Power Cooperative Evaluation of Bids Submitted to the United States Bankruptcy Court in the Cajun Bankruptcy Proceeding, Docket No. U-17735, Order No. U-17735-I, 1997 La. PUC LEXIS 1, at *51 (La. Pub. Serv. Comm'n 1997). For other examples of state PUCs' making written acknowledgement of the regulatory contract, see South Central Bell Telephone, Order No. U-17949-G, 1991 La. PUC LEXIS 18, at *79–*80; 121 P.U.R.4th 338 (La. Pub. Serv. Comm'n 1991); United Cities Gas Company's Proposed Tariffs to Increase Rates for Gas Service Provided to Customers in the Missouri Service Area of the Company, Case No. GR-93-47, 1993 Mo. PSC LEXIS 37, at *15, (Mo. Pub. Serv. Comm'n 1993); Investigation into Electric Power Competition, Docket No. I-940032, 1994 Pa. PUC LEXIS 24, at *33 (Pa. Pub. Util. Comm'n 1994) ("The regulatory compact has deftly minimized financial risk over the last several decades."); Order Instituting Rulemaking on the Commission's Proposed Policies Governing Restructuring California's Electronic Service Industry and Reforming Regulation; Order Instituting Investigation on the Commission's Proposed Policies Governing Restructuring California's Electric Services Industry and Reforming Regulation, Decision No. 95-05-045, Rulemaking No. 94-04-031, Investigation No. 94-04-032, 1995 Cal. PUC LEXIS 429 at *11 n.34, 161 P.U.R.4th 217 (Cal. Pub. Utils. Comm'n 1995); Pennsylvania Pub. Util. Comm'n *v.* PECO Energy Co., R-00943281; R-00943281C0001; R-00943281C0002; R-00943281C0003, 1996 Pa. PUC LEXIS 34, at *32 (Pa. Pub. Util. Comm'n 1996) ("Under the existing regulatory compact, electric utilities do long-term planning and build generation capacity to meet the power needs of all of its customers—industrial, commercial and residential."); Application of Pacific Gas and Electric Co. for Authority, Among Other Things, to Decrease Its Rates and Charges for Electric and Gas Service, and Increase Rates and Charges for Pipeline Expansion Service; Commission Order Instituting Investigation into the Rates, Charges, Service and Practices of Pacific Gas and Electric Co., Decision No. 96-09-045, Application No. 94-12-005, Investigation No. 95-02-015, 1996 Cal. PUC LEXIS 912, at *6 (Ca. Pub. Utils. Comm'n 1996) ("The notion that customers are entitled to reliable service is an essential aspect of the regulatory compact."). *But see* Order Instituting Rulemaking on the Commission's Own Motion into Competition for Local Exchange Service; Order Instituting Investigation on the Commission's Own Motion into Competition for Local Exchange, Decision No. 96-09-089, Rulemaking No. 95-04-043, Investigation No. 95-04-044, 1996 Cal. PUC LEXIS 962, at *57–*61 (Cal. Pub. Utils. Comm'n 1996) (avoiding ruling on the

Those numerous written statements by state PUCs exemplify a subsequent memorandum by the party to be charged in any case that the utility might bring alleging breach of the regulatory contract. Depending on their specificity, those statements are capable of satisfying the Statute of Frauds and curing the alleged absence of a written agreement at the time the contract was formed, perhaps decades earlier.

Remedies for a Voidable Regulatory Contract

Even if the regulatory contract were deemed to be unenforceable owing to the Statute of Frauds, it does not follow that the state, after repudiating the contract on those grounds, could escape the obligation to provide a remedy to the utility after it had performed, up to that moment, its duties under the voidable contract. The Restatement (Second) of Contracts provides: "A promise which the promisor should reasonably expect to induce action or forbearance on the part of the promisee or a third person and which does induce the action or forbearance is enforceable notwithstanding the Statute of Frauds if injustice can be avoided only by enforcement of the promise."[76] Moreover, although the Statute of Frauds would deny parties to a voidable contract their expectation interests, "the statute does not preclude restitution of a part performance rendered by a party not in default, after substantial breach by the other party who has received the performance."[77] In addition, the Statute of Frauds does not prevent the party not in default from suing the party who received the performance for the tort of deceit.[78] The utility, in other words, could sue

question of whether a regulatory compact exists with respect to local exchange carriers).

76. RESTATEMENT (SECOND) OF CONTRACTS § 139(1); *see also* Merex A.G. *v.* Fairchild Weston Systems, Inc., 29 F.3d 821, 824 (2d Cir. 1994) ("Promissory estoppel has . . . become increasingly available to provide relief to a party where the contract is rendered unenforceable by operation of the Statute of Frauds."); Brody *v.* Bock, 897 P.2d 769 (Colo. 1995); Eavenson *v.* Lewis Means, Inc., 105 N.M. 161, 730 P.2d 464 (1986); Jeffrey G. Steinberg, Note, *Promissory Estoppel as a Means of Defeating the Statute of Frauds*, 44 FORDHAM L. REV. 114 (1975).

77. DAWSON, HARVEY & HENDERSON, *supra* note 60, at 973; *accord*, DOBBS, *supra* note 1, at 857–58.

78. "Since a promise necessarily carries with it the implied assertion of an intention to perform it follows that a promise made without such an intention is fraudulent and actionable in deceit. . . . This is true whether or not the promise is enforceable as a contract. If it is enforceable, the person misled by the representation has a cause of action in tort as an alternative at least, and perhaps in some instances in addition to his cause of action on the contract. If the agreement is not enforceable as a contract, as when it is

the PUC for what one might term "deregulatory fraud."

In short, as a matter of contract law the defense of the Statute of Frauds does little to blunt the theory of the regulatory contract. Depending on the facts of the particular case, the effect of the statute would be to shift a court's attention from the remedies available at law to those available in equity.

PROMISSORY ESTOPPEL

The relationship between the public utility and the regulator is a contract. For sake of argument, however, assume the counterfactual: that no contract can be found to exist between the utility and its regulator. Still, the regulated firm would be entitled to recover damages from the state at least in the amount of the utility's costs incurred in detrimental reliance on representations that the regulator made to it.[79]

The doctrine of promissory estoppel entitles a promisee to recover damages even though no contract existed between him and the promisor, usually for lack of consideration flowing from the promisee to the promisor. The Restatement (Second) of Contract provides: "A promise which the promisor should reasonably expect to induce action or forbearance on the part of the promisee or a third person and which does induce such action or forbearance is binding if injustice can be avoided only by enforcement of the promise."[80] At a minimum, the damages that the promisee may recover under promissory estoppel are reliance

---

without consideration, the recipient still has, as his only remedy, the action in deceit. . . . The same is true when the agreement is oral and made unenforceable by the statute of frauds, or when it is unprovable and so unenforceable under the parol evidence rule." RESTATEMENT (SECOND) OF TORTS § 530 cmt. c (1977), *quoted in* Winger v. Winger, 82 F.3d 140, 145–46 (7th Cir. 1996). *Accord,* Hiller v. Manufacturers Prod. Research Group, 59 F.3d 1514, 1537 (5th Cir. 1995); Tenzer v. Superscope, Inc., 39 Cal. 3d 18, 28–31, 702 P.2d 212, 218–19, 216 Cal. Rptr. 130 (1985).

79. *See, e.g.*, Restructuring of the Electric Utility Industry in Vermont, Dkt. No. 5854 (Vt. Pub. Serv. Bd. Dec. 30, 1996) ("Notwithstanding the lack of a contractual claim that is enforceable at law, the utilities' arguments with respect to a regulatory compact or bargain do carry some equitable force, which [is relevant to] an appropriate standard for recovery of stranded costs.").

80. RESTATEMENT (SECOND) OF CONTRACTS § 90(a) (1979). An earlier version appeared in RESTATEMENT OF CONTRACTS § 90 (1932). *See generally* Robert Birmingham, *Notes on the Reliance Interest*, 60 WASH. L. REV. 217 (1985); Jay M. Feinman, *Promissory Estoppel and Judicial Method*, 97 HARV. L. REV. 678 (1984); Melvin Eisenberg, *Donative Promises*, 47 U. CHI. L. REV. 1 (1979); Richard A. Posner, *Gratuitous Promises in Economics and Law*, 6 J. LEGAL STUD. 411 (1977).

damages. Moreover, legal scholars note that, as such cases have increasingly involved business relationships rather than the traditional classroom hypothetical of the rich uncle who promises to pay his nephew's college tuition, courts have become more inclined to protect the promisee's expectation interest, presumably on the reasoning that "in business cases, expectation recovery may better reflect opportunity losses than would reliance recovery."[81] Thus, a number of courts have awarded the promisee lost profits under a promissory-estoppel theory.[82]

The natural question that arises when promissory estoppel is applied to the relationship between the regulator and the regulated firm is whether the regulator has indeed made a promise. Under traditional contract principles, the answer is yes. The Restatement (Second) of Contracts defines a promise as "a manifestation of intention to act or refrain from acting in a specified way, so made as to justify a promisee in understanding that a commitment has been made."[83] Compare that definition with the notice of proposed rulemaking, and its subsequent report and order, that typify the actions of a regulatory body with jurisdiction over telephone companies, electric utilities, and other regulated network industries. Those documents routinely are dozens of pages long and reflect hundreds or even thousands of pages of comments of interested parties to whom the regulator is required, by state or federal administrative procedure statutes, to give notice of proposed changes in regulation.[84] And, although a regulatory agency is free to repudiate an earlier policy upon which private parties may have relied, it must give a reasoned explanation when doing so.[85] In the specific case of long-lived investments made by local exchange carriers or electric power companies, the regulator's "manifestation of intention to act or refrain from acting in a specified way" is even more inescapable, for the regulator convened proceedings to review specific proposed capacity additions and rate-base inclusions of investment in facilities, which

---

81. Feinman, *supra* note 80, at 688; *id.* at 691 n.59 ("promissory estoppel cases now arise chiefly in commercial contexts").

82. Walters *v.* Marathon Oil Co., 642 F.2d 1098 (7th Cir. 1981); Universal Computer Sys. *v.* Medical Servs. Ass'n, 628 F.2d 820 (3d Cir. 1980); Arnold's Hofbrau, Inc. *v.* George Hyman Constr. Co., 480 F.2d 1145 (D.C. Cir. 1973); Walker *v.* KFC Corp., 515 F. Supp. 612 (S.D. Cal. 1981); *cf.* MICHAEL J. TREBILCOCK, THE LIMITS OF FREEDOM OF CONTRACT 164–87 (Harvard University Press 1996).

83. RESTATEMENT (SECOND) OF CONTRACTS § 2 (1979).

84. *E.g.*, 5 U.S.C. § 553.

85. Motor Vehicle Mfrs. Ass'n of the U.S., Inc. *v.* State Farm Mutual Automobile Ins. Co., 463 U.S. 29 (1983).

interested parties often hotly contested. What else could such proceedings purport to do if not "justify a promisee in understanding that a commitment has been made"?[86]

In short, "contract" or not, the commitments the regulator made to the regulated firm constitute a promise upon which that firm could be expected to rely. Thus, the promise gives rise to a remedy of at least reliance damages, if not expectation damages.[87]

CONCLUSION

The remedies for breach of the regulatory contract are the same as those for more familiar long-term commercial contracts. The appropriate damage measure is the utility's lost expectation, net of mitigation. That amount corresponds to the difference between the firm's net revenues under regulation and under competition. Such a damage measure produces efficient incentives for the regulator to breach the regulatory contract: The regulator will repudiate the regulatory contract only if there are net gains remaining after compensating the utility for its lost expectation of a reasonable opportunity to recover its nonsalvageable investment in long-lived infrastructure. Faced with that damage rule, the regulator will not be tempted to act opportunistically in an effort to appropriate the utility's quasi rents. One would expect that the traditional defenses raised in more familiar commercial contract litigation would be raised in a dispute over breach of the regulatory contract. But those defenses—as well as the defense of sovereign immunity—would not be likely to defeat a claim for breach of the regulatory contract.

---

86. "The standard, consistent with the definition in section 90, is not whether the promisor clearly made a promise, but whether, given the context in which the statement at issue was made, the promisor should reasonably have expected that the promisee would infer a promise. This standard may be met not only by a particular promise or representation, but also by general statements of policy or practice." Feinman, *supra* note 80, at 691.

87. Some of the jurisprudence on regulatory takings cases has a flavor of promissory estoppel, even though the courts eschew such terminology. *E.g.*, Kaiser Aetna *v.* United States, 444 U.S. 177, 179 (1979) ("While the consent of individual officials representing the United States cannot 'estop' the United States . . . , it can lead to the fruition of a number of expectancies embodied in the concept of 'property'—expectancies that, if sufficiently important, the Government must condemn and pay for before it takes over management of the landowner's property."); Ruckelshaus *v.* Monanto Co., 467 U.S. 986, 1011 (1984); Tri-Bio Laboratories, Inc. *v.* United States, 836 F.2d 135, 140–41 (3d Cir. 1987).

6

Takings and the Property of the Regulated Utility

THE SUPREME COURT has placed takings cases into three categories. In declining order of judicial solicitude given the property owner, the categories are physical invasions of property, confiscatory public utility rates, and regulatory takings.[1] Breach of the regulatory contract does not fit automatically into any one of those categories because, being unprecedented, it necessarily is a case of first impression under the Takings Clause. That is true even with respect to the precedents addressing public utility regulation. Although arguments can be made for and against recovery of stranded costs, ultimately the Supreme Court (and its counterpart in other nations) will have to rely on first principles of legal and economic theory to decide whether to recognize a deregulatory taking as an event necessitating the state's payment of just compensation. Those principles, we argue here, support such payment. We then examine the Court's reasoning under each of its three doctrinal branches of takings jurisprudence to determine the extent to which a deregulatory taking can be analogized to cases decided under those doctrines. We conclude that under all three branches of existing takings jurisprudence the regulator's abrogation of the regulatory contract is a compensable confiscation of the property of the regulated firm.

---

1. *See* Richard A. Epstein, *Takings: Of Property Common and Private*, 64 U. CHI. L. REV. 21 (1997).

ECONOMIC RATIONALES
FOR PROPERTY PROTECTIONS

It is difficult to imagine a market economy without legal protections for private property. The definition and enforcement of property rights are the legal foundation of a market economy. The economic functions of property rights are several.

Completeness, Exclusivity, and Transferability As Prerequisites of Allocative Efficiency

Clearly defined property rights are necessary for the exchange of goods and services between individuals. Market exchange cannot take place in the absence of complete, exclusive, and transferable property rights. Before one can transfer ownership of a resource in a market transaction, there must be a meeting of the minds over what bundle of rights is being bought and sold. Even immediate transactions require a clear definition of the buyer's exclusive ownership of a good and the ability to transfer that ownership to the buyer. Property rights provide the common understanding between buyer and seller and thus make exchange possible.[2] Economic analysis demonstrates that market exchange allocates resources to their highest-value use. Property rights that are well-defined are necessary for the economy to achieve an efficient allocation of resources.

Exclusivity and Voluntary Exchange

Property rights help to ensure that market exchange is voluntary. Even if property rights to goods were complete and exclusive, transferability is required for prices to emerge and to enable the market to allocate goods to the highest-value user. Property rights protect individuals from confiscation of property by individuals, companies, or the government. The Supreme Court emphasized in *Dolan* v. *City of Tigard*, as it had in earlier takings cases, that the "right to exclude others is 'one of the most essential sticks in the bundle of rights that are commonly characterized as property.'"[3] The force of that observation, of

---

2. *E.g.*, RICHARD A. POSNER, ECONOMIC ANALYSIS OF LAW 33 (Little, Brown & Co., 4th ed. 1992).

3. 512 U.S. 374, 393 (1994) (quoting Kaiser Aetna *v*. United States, 444 U.S. 164, 176 (1979)).

course, is in no way limited to real property. Any productive activity requires an investment of labor, capital, and other resources, as well as some delay, before one can reap the fruits of those investments.

Incentives for Investment

Property rights are essential for production because they protect individuals and companies that invest resources in productive activities. That is so because property rights guarantee that the investor owns the fruits of his efforts and expenditures. Noting that "[a]ll this has been well known for hundreds of years," Judge Richard A. Posner observes that "without property rights there is no incentive to incur these costs because there is no reasonable assured reward for incurring them."[4] Thus, property rights are the foundation of dynamic allocative efficiency as well as static allocative efficiency.

Without protection of property there would be a reduction in incentives to invest, because there would be an increased risk that others would appropriate the returns to the investment. The classic example is the farmer planting crops in anticipation of reaping the harvest. Those who confiscate property or the productive returns from investment of resources are freeriding on the efforts of others. Free riders create economic inefficiencies because they do not take account of the full costs associated with their behavior.

Similarly, the conservation of natural resources represents an investment in natural resources by leaving mineral resources in the ground for future use or by letting renewable resources such as fish and forests appreciate in value through growth.[5] If an individual does not have ownership of the resource, he is deprived of the incentive to refrain from current consumption. The resource will, therefore, be depleted at a faster rate than is economically efficient. That result is equivalent to underinvestment in the resource. In the absence of complete and exclusive property rights, the well-known "tragedy of the commons" emerges: Free-riding individuals compete to deplete a scarce resource, rather than make efficient use of the resource and invest in its further development.[6]

---

4. POSNER, *supra* note 2, at 32 (citing 2 WILLIAM BLACKSTONE, COMMENTARIES ON THE LAWS OF ENGLAND 4, 7 (1766)).

5. *See, e.g.*, ESSAYS IN THE ECONOMICS OF RENEWABLE RESOURCES (Leonard J. Mirman & Daniel F. Spulber eds., Elsevier-North Holland Publishing Co. 1982).

6. Garrett Hardin, *The Tragedy of the Commons*, 162 SCIENCE 1243 (1968).

The incentive for investment has direct implications for capital markets. Investors in corporations purchase shares to obtain the residual claims on the company's returns—that is, the after-tax profits of the company net of payments to debtholders. Without property protection of returns to equity, investors similarly would have a reduced incentive to invest in stock, which would significantly complicate the raising of funds through financial markets.

THE JUDICIAL RATIONALE
FOR THE TAKINGS CLAUSE

If the institution of property is so salubrious, then it would follow that the uncompensated confiscation of property by the government would be harmful indeed. One would therefore expect the Supreme Court to reiterate the preceding arguments concerning the economic functions of property when answering, in the course of reaching their decisions, the question, Why does the Takings Clause exist? Several lines of reasoning have impressed the Court.

*Prevention of Wasteful
Public Consumption of Resources*

The Court emphasized in *First English Evangelical Lutheran Church* v. *County of Los Angeles* that the Takings Clause "makes clear that it is designed not to limit the governmental interference with property rights per se, but rather to secure *compensation* in the event of otherwise proper interference amounting to a taking."[7] To an economist, the obvious purpose of that rule is to ensure that the government uses property efficiently by being required to pay its opportunity cost.

The Court has evidenced some discomfort with the notion that the government should be constrained to internalize all the costs that its regulatory decisions impose on others. The Court stated in *Andrus* v. *Allard*:

> Government regulation—by definition—involves the adjustment of rights for the public good. Often this adjustment curtails some potential for the use or economic exploitation of private property. To require compensation in all such circumstances would effectively compel the government to regulate by purchase.[8]

---

7. 482 U.S. 304, 315 (1987) (emphasis in original).

8. 444 U.S. at 65; *accord*, Penn Cent. Transp. Co. v. New York City, 438 U.S. 104, 124 (1978); Pennsylvania Coal Co. v. Mahon, 260 U.S. 393, 413 (1922).

That is an embarrassing admission for the Court to make. It would seem that the government, like everyone else, would like to get something for nothing. A government that had to pay its own way would be more circumspect about announcing policies that impose costs on private parties, even though those policies are believed to benefit the public as a whole.

The Transaction Costs of Compensating Private Parties for Changes in Government Policies

There is a more charitable reading that one can give to the Court's statements of aversion to requiring the payment of just compensation in every case of government regulation. In one of the most famous passages in any takings case, Justice Oliver Wendell Holmes observed in *Pennsylvania Coal Co.* v. *Mahon*: "Government hardly could go on if to some extent values incident to property could not be diminished without paying for every such change in the general law."[9] To be sure, regulation affects the value of every business subject to its jurisdiction, and an attempt to compensate for every diminution, however slight, in "values incident to property" would require enormous transaction costs. Consequently, it is efficient that not all uncompensated regulatory changes are deemed to give rise to takings. But that concern about economizing on the costs of compensating diffuse, de minimis diminutions in property values does not describe the situation facing regulated utilities in network industries now undergoing the transformation to competition. The diminution in property values in those industries is large and concentrated among few companies.

Prevention of Free Riding

The limits on government takings do not merely help to ensure economic efficiency in the allocation of resources and development of property through investment. They also prevent the government itself from free-riding on the efforts of individuals. A taking is to be regarded as an exceptional occurrence where public use of the property would increase wealth by being more productive than an alternative use and where there is a severe market failure that prevents the consensual transfer of the property.[10]

---

9. *Id.*

10. This can take the form of holdouts such as the case when the last property owner of a group of properties necessary to effectuate the public use asks for compensation in

Prevention of Disproportionate Burden from
Changes in Government Policies

The Court emphasized in *Armstrong* v. *United States* that the Takings Clause serves "to bar Government from forcing some people alone to bear public burdens which, in all fairness and justice, should be borne by the public as a whole."[11] An economic interpretation of that standard is that it is equivalent to what William J. Baumol has called the *Pareto improvement criterion*, according to which a policy action improves social welfare and therefore may be undertaken if some individuals are made better off and no individuals are made worse off.[12] That criterion rests on consent and unanimity and thus is consistent with voluntary exchange.

Furthermore, if the government failed to compensate for its confiscations of property, the power of eminent domain (as well as the police power, which is at issue in the regulatory takings cases) could become a tool for nothing more than income redistribution, rather than a means to create public goods. The uncompensated confiscation of property (or the uncompensated diminution of property value through exercise of

excess of the alternative use or market value of his single piece of property. *Id.*

11. 364 U.S. 40, 49 (1960). The enunciation of that principle has become boilerplate in the Court's subsequent takings cases. *See, e.g., Penn Central*, 438 U.S. at 123; Webb's Fabulous Pharmacies, Inc. *v.* Beckwith, 449 U.S. 155, 163 (1980); Agins *v.* Tiburon, 447 U.S. 255, 260 (1980); *First English*, 482 U.S. at 318–19; Pennell *v.* City of San Jose, 485 U.S. 1, 9 (1988); *Dolan*, 512 U.S. at 384. In 1994 Judge Jay Plager of the Federal Circuit expressed the principle as follows:

> The question at issue here is, when the Government fulfills its obligation to preserve and protect the public interest, may the cost of obtaining that public benefit fall solely upon the affected property owner, or is it to be shared by the community at large. In the final analysis the answer to that question is one of fundamental public policy. It calls for balancing the legitimate claims of the society to constrain individual actions that threaten the larger community, on the one side, and, on the other, the rights of the individual and our commitment to private property as a bulwark for the protection of those rights. It requires us to decide which collective rights are to be obtained at collective cost, in order better to preserve collectively the rights of the individual.

Loveladies Harbor, Inc. *v.* United States, 28 F.3d 1171, 1175 (Fed. Cir. 1994) (footnote omitted). For an early articulation of the principle, see Monongahela Navigation Co. *v.* United States, 148 U.S. 312, 325 (1893).

12. WILLIAM J. BAUMOL, SUPERFAIRNESS: APPLICATIONS AND THEORY 7–9, 30–37 (MIT Press 1986).

the police power) could become a means to fund government policies in a less transparent, less accountable, off-budget manner.

REGULATORY TAKINGS AND THE DESTRUCTION OF THE INVESTMENT-BACKED EXPECTATIONS OF THE INCUMBENT REGULATED FIRM

Regulatory takings occupy an uneasy place in economic theory and in American constitutional law. The least-protected class of government confiscation of property, regulatory takings have produced an analytical model in the Supreme Court that is only occasionally hospitable to the plight of landowners subjected to land use or environmental restrictions. Nonetheless, the straightforward application of that same model to the state's repudiation of the regulatory contract produces, even at that lowest level of judicial solicitude, powerful protection for the property of the regulated firm.

Weaknesses in the Kaldor-Hicks Compensation Criterion Implicit in the Law of Regulatory Takings

In the typical regulatory takings case the state, relying on the Supreme Court's 1887 decision in *Mugler* v. *Kansas* and its lineage,[13] asserts that it is exercising its police powers in a legitimate fashion such that no compensation need be paid for the resulting diminution in the value of private property.[14] That reasoning implicitly embraces a notion of social welfare that lawyers, economists, and philosophers have subsequently called "Kaldor-Hicks compensation" or "potential Pareto superiority."[15] Strict Pareto efficiency would require the winners from a policy change to use some of their gains to compensate the losers. The requirement that winners pay actual compensation to losers would ensure that the state would undertake only Pareto-efficient policies—that is, only policies that would improve the welfare of at least one person without reducing the welfare of any other person. Faced with the prospect that actual compensation would entail prohibitively high transaction costs and thus limit the discretionary powers of the state to regulate, Nicholas Kaldor proposed in 1939 the criterion of potential Pareto superiority,

13. 123 U.S. 623 (1887).

14. *See, e.g.*, Lucas v. South Carolina Coastal Council, 505 U.S. 1003, 1022 (1992).

15. *See* POSNER, *supra* note 2, at 13–14; WILLIAM A. FISCHEL, REGULATORY TAKINGS: LAW, ECONOMICS, AND POLITICS 68 (Harvard University Press 1995); JULES L. COLEMAN, MARKETS, MORALS, AND THE LAW 81–86 (Cambridge University Press 1988).

under which a policy that would be Pareto superior with the payment of compensation is defended as welfare-enhancing even if winners fail to compensate losers.[16]

Kaldor-Hicks compensation was in perfect synchronicity with the metamorphosis of American constitutional law during the New Deal, a transformation that curtailed protections of contract and property and gave the central government virtually unlimited regulatory powers over economic activity.[17] But the construct created several difficulties for the Takings Clause. First, losses associated with policy changes are true opportunity costs. When they are not compensated, policy change (which is to say, regulation) is overconsumed relative to the level of regulation that would be demanded under a constitutional standard that required actual compensation for Pareto-efficient policy moves.

Second, the Kaldor-Hicks standard is naïve about the public choice aspects of regulation. A principal benefit of requiring the payment of compensation to the losers under regulatory change is to remove their political opposition to Pareto-superior government policies. If property owners know that their losses from regulation will go uncompensated, potential losers will consume their resources in resisting Pareto-improving policies and force potential winners to consume their resources in defending such policies. Consequently, the magnitude of the net benefits to society from such policies will fall.[18]

Third, it is not always the case that the transaction costs of identifying and compensating losers are so prohibitively high that no attempt

---

16. Nicholas Kaldor, *Welfare Propositions of Economics and Interpersonal Comparisons of Utility*, 49 ECON. J. 549 (1939); *see also* John R. Hicks, *Foundations of Welfare Economics*, 49 ECON. J. 696 (1939). A related contemporaneous article is Tibor Scitovsky, *A Note on Welfare Propositions in Economics*, 9 REV. ECON. STUD. 77 (1941). *See also* E. J. MISHAN, INTRODUCTION TO NORMATIVE ECONOMICS 303–14 (Oxford University Press 1981).

17. Although that metamorphosis is most closely associated with the year 1937 (*see* West Coast Hotel Co. *v.* Parrish, 300 U.S. 379 (1937)); NLRB *v.* Jones & Laughlin Steel Corp., 301 U.S. 1 (1937)), the process can be thought to have spanned nearly a decade. By 1937, the Court had already repudiated the Contract Clause in Home Building & Loan Ass'n *v.* Blaisdell, 290 U.S. 398 (1934). The crown jewel of the Court's new jurisprudence, footnote 4 of United States *v.* Carolene Prods., 304 U.S. 144 (1938), came a year later. And Wickard *v.* Filburn, 317 U.S. 111 (1942), eliminated any practical constraint on the scope of the federal commerce power, a development that stood unchecked for more than a half century, until United States *v.* Lopez, 115 S. Ct. 1624 (1995).

18. The result will be reminiscent of the well-recognized dissipation of monopoly rents by firms competing to achieve a monopoly. *See* Richard A. Posner, *The Social Costs of Monopoly and Regulation*, 83 J. POL. ECON. 807 (1975).

should be made to pay compensation. The transaction costs of paying compensation depend in part on how diffusely the loss is spread across the population of property owners. The losses from some regulatory restrictions on the use of property are highly concentrated. If given adequate notice by the state of its pending regulatory change, potential losers who will have concentrated losses can be relied upon to identify themselves.[19] Thus, in the case of concentrated losses—the only kind of takings case that ever gets litigated as a practical matter—the Kaldor-Hicks orientation of the current regulatory takings jurisprudence is likely to violate the principle that the Court announced in *Armstrong* and has reaffirmed many times since—that a small segment of the population should not disproportionately bear public burdens.[20]

Fourth, and most important as a matter of economic theory and constitutional principle, the Kaldor-Hicks criterion fails to put either the winners or the losers to an actual test of their willingness to pay and their willingness to accept, respectively. Do the winners' benefits really exceed the amount that they would be willing to pay? At the same time, would the notional compensation of the Kaldor-Hicks criterion really have been acceptable to the losers? Neither party to that hypothetical bargain actually reveals his preferences in the manner that routinely occurs under voluntary exchange. Furthermore, the government presumably is the entity making the determination of whether that hypothetical bargain would take place. So, if the government's interest is to expand its size by issuing more regulations, it will have an incentive to find that the hypothetical transaction would occur. That is not to say that the Kaldor-Hicks criterion will be used solely to expand the scope of government. That same criterion, based on evaluating net benefits without regard to redistribution of income from winners to losers, underlies the use of cost-benefit analysis to evaluate regulation and other public policies, often in the name of reducing the extent of

---

19. A counterargument in favor of no payment of compensation is that the certainty that losers will receive compensation for regulatory changes will induce moral hazard on the part of property owners. *See* Lawrence E. Blume, Daniel L. Rubinfeld & Perry Shapiro, *The Taking of Land: When Should Compensation Be Paid?*, 99 Q.J. ECON. 71 (1984). The empirical substantiality of such moral hazard is open to question, however, particularly in relation to the moral hazard likely to arise from more explicit forms of government insurance. Which, for example, is more likely to induce risk taking on the part of property owners along the South Carolina coast—the availability of federal disaster relief for hurricane damage or the requirement that the state pay compensation for environmental regulations that it imposes?

20. 364 U.S. at 49.

government regulation. Again, a proper use of cost-benefit analysis should include the actual payment of compensation if takings occur.

Existing Legal Criteria Concerning
Regulatory Takings

The law of regulatory takings has descended from Justice Holmes's "general rule" announced in *Pennsylvania Coal* in 1922, a rule most notable for its utter lack of guidance: "while property may be regulated to a certain extent, if regulation goes too far it will be recognized as a taking."[21] For half a century the Court gave little guidance as to what "too far" meant. In 1978 Justice William J. Brennan, Jr., writing for the Court in *Penn Central Transportation Co.* v. *New York City*, finally attempted to provide such guidance: A regulation constitutes a taking if it denies the property owner "economically viable use" of that property, which is to be determined by examining the following three factors: (1) the "character of the governmental action," (2) the "economic impact of the regulation on the claimant," and (3) the "extent to which the regulation has interfered with distinct investment-backed expectations."[22] The Court has reiterated that three-part test in subsequent decisions.[23]

Scholars have criticized even *Penn Central*'s three-part test for being so vague as to allow inconsistent outcomes and for lacking any indication of the relative weight to be accorded each of those three factors.[24] Although we do not share those scholars' criticisms of the importance of "investment-backed expectations" as one of the relevant factors for the Court to consider, our principal purpose here is not to articulate the "optimal" legal test for regulatory takings. Rather our purpose is to show that the Court's existing legal standard for regulatory takings is even more likely to indicate a need for compensation in the case of breach of the regulatory contract than in the case of burdensome land-use restrictions, which spawned the rule.

---

21. 260 U.S. at 415. For an incisive analysis of the decision, see Robert Brauneis, *"The Foundation of Our 'Regulatory Takings' Jurisprudence": The Myth and Meaning of Justice Holmes's Opinion in* Pennsylvania Coal Co. *v.* Mahon, 106 YALE L.J. 613 (1996).

22. *Penn Central*, 438 U.S. 104, 124 (1978).

23. *E.g.*, Kaiser Aetna v. United States, 444 U.S. 164, 175 (1979); PruneYard Shopping Center v. Robins, 447 U.S. 74, 83 (1980).

24. FISCHEL, *supra* note 15, at 51; Andrea L. Peterson, *The Takings Clause: In Search of Underlying Principles*, 77 CAL. L. REV. 1299, 78 CAL. L. REV. 53 (1989).

The Character of Governmental Action. In a thoughtful opinion for the Federal Circuit in *Loveladies Harbor, Inc.* v. *United States*, Judge Jay Plager described this first of the three *Penn Central* criteria as requiring a court to scrutinize "the purpose and importance of the public interest reflected in the regulatory imposition" and "to balance the liberty interest of the private property owner against the Government's need to protect the public interest through imposition of the restraint."[25] That analysis sounds identical to the means-end scrutiny of economic regulation that courts employ under the Due Process Clauses of the Fifth and Fourteenth Amendments. Implicitly, that means-end analysis takes place at the level of minimum-rationality review. As Judge Plager noted, the Court has considered whether "the avowed need of the Government" to protect some "interest of the public" is indeed "a legitimate interest"[26] and whether "the method of attaining the sought-after goal was reasonably designed to attain it."[27]

Presumably, if the regulation were deficient in either respect (a tall order under minimum rationality), then the regulation would not be a valid exercise of the police power, and compensation would be due the property owner. At the same time, of course, the regulation in question would be invalid on due process grounds. If, as is more likely, the regulation survived review under that minimum rationality standard, the takings analysis would proceed to consideration of *Penn Central*'s other two criteria.

The Economic Impact of the Regulation on the Claimant. This second criterion can be seen as a requirement to minimize the transaction costs of takings claims, along the lines of Justice Holmes's remark in *Pennsylvania Coal* that government "hardly could go on" if made to compensate every diminution in value arising from its regulation.[28] Below a certain cutoff, it would seem, an uncompensated diminution in property value arising from a change in regulation should not consume the resources of the state (as defendant) and the courts. That reasoning is analogous to the requirement that a party plead a minimum amount in controversy to establish jurisdiction.

25. 28 F.3d 1171, 1176 (Fed. Cir. 1994).

26. *Id.* (citing Ruckelshaus v. Monsanto Co., 467 U.S. 986, 1014 (1984)).

27. *Id.* (citing Nollan v. California Coastal Comm'n, 483 U.S. 825, 837 (1987)).

28. 260 U.S. at 413. In *Loveladies*, 28 F.3d at 1176–77, Judge Plager imputed just such a meaning to Justice Holmes's remark.

Interestingly, Judge Plager reasoned in *Loveladies* that *Penn Central*'s overriding requirement—that the payment of compensation for a regulatory taking was conditioned on the property owner's showing that the government had denied him "economically viable use" of his property—was just another way of expressing the idea embodied in *Penn Central*'s second criterion concerning the economic impact of the regulation on the claimant.[29] In Judge Plager's words, both articulations expressed the same "threshold requirement that the plaintiff show a serious financial loss from the regulatory imposition."[30]

Interference with Distinct Investment-Backed Expectations. The remaining criterion in the *Penn Central* test—interference with distinct investment-backed expectations—does all the heavy lifting in a regulatory takings case. If the government has used its police power in a reasonable manner for a legitimate purpose, and if the regulation has diminished the value of private property by a nontrivial amount, then the remaining question is whether the property owner himself has absorbed that diminution or whether he already contracted to accept the diminution if and when it occurred. Again, Judge Plager's formulation in *Loveladies* is particularly lucid.

The requirement that the property owner establish his distinct investment-backed expectations is "a way of limiting takings recoveries to owners who could demonstrate that they bought their property in reliance on a state of affairs that did not include the challenged regulatory regime."[31] Judge Plager elaborated: "In legal terms, the owner who bought with knowledge of the restraint could be said to have no reliance interest, or to have assumed the risk of any economic loss. In economic terms, it could be said that the market had already discounted for the restraint, so that a purchaser could not show a loss in his investment attributable to it."[32]

To that analysis of risk bearing, one can add a related point: The requirement is a means to impose a system of falsifiability on what could otherwise become an inherently subjective inquiry. Without the requirement that the property owner objectively prove, through evidence of investment, that he detrimentally relied on the challenged

29. *Id.* at 1177 (citing Agins v. Tiburon, 447 U.S. 255, 260 (1980); *Nollan*, 483 U.S. at 834).
30. *Id.*
31. *Id.*
32. *Id.*

regulatory regime, how could a court really know whether the regulation at issue had diminished *that person's* wealth at all? Specious claims of lost property value would otherwise inundate the state. That further explanation comports with the Court's observation in *Ruckelshaus* v. *Monsanto Co.* that "[a] 'reasonable investment backed expectation' must be more than 'a unilateral expectation or an abstract need,'"[33] and its statement in *Usery* v. *Turner Elkhorn Mining Co.* that "legislation readjusting rights and burdens is not unlawful solely because it upsets otherwise settled expectations."[34] A private party may have expectations that are, objectively speaking, unreasonable. The Court, not surprisingly, has delivered more guidance on what are *not* reasonable investment-backed expectations than on what are.[35]

Consider the case of changes in American foreign policy with respect to Libya that impaired an American citizen's right to continue receiving the benefits of a contract, signed in 1985, to perform work in Libya for ten years.[36] Such changes in policy did not effect a regulatory taking. The Federal Circuit found in *Chang* v. *United States* that the American citizen had been put on notice—by constitutional provisions, statutes, and court decisions concerning Congress's power to regulate foreign commerce—that U.S. foreign policy could change unexpectedly at any time without giving rise to a right of compensation for contracts thereby impaired.[37] Moreover, it would have been objectively unreasonable to expect that the employment contract would be secure from impairment in light of "the overwhelming public knowledge of strained and deteriorating relations between the two countries existing at the time when the plaintiffs entered their contracts."[38] Whether one has investment-backed expectations thus depends on "the foreseeability of the risk of disruption" of the legal relationships upon which the contract critically depends.[39] The private party must have had a "reasonable expectation" at the time the contract was entered that it "would

---

33. 467 U.S. 986, 1005–06 (1984) (quoting Webb's Fabulous Pharmacies *v.* Beckwith, 449 U.S. 155, 161 (1980)), *quoted in Loveladies*, 28 F.3d at 1177.

34. 428 U.S. 1, 16 (1976).

35. Concrete Pipe & Prods. of Cal., Inc. *v.* Construction Laborers Pension Trust for S. Cal., 508 U.S. 602, 645 (1993); Connolly *v.* Pension Benefit Guaranty Corp., 475 U.S. 211, 226–27 (1986); *see also* Golden Pac. Bancorp *v.* United States, 15 F.3d 1066 (Fed. Cir. 1994).

36. Chang *v.* United States, 859 F.2d 893 (Fed. Cir. 1988).

37. *Id.* at 897.

38. *Id.*

39. *Id.*

proceed without possible hindrance" arising from changes in government policy.[40]

The Investment-Backed Expectations
of a Public Utility

If analyzed as a regulatory taking, the problem of stranded costs is far more compelling than the typical case of land-use restrictions. The regulatory contract is a detailed contract that imposes obligations on the utility, its customers, and the regulatory authority. Moreover, the regulatory contract is subject to executive, legislative, and judicial oversight. The formality and continuity of the contract and its oversight reinforce the conclusion that it is reasonable for a public utility to expect that the regulator will discharge its duties under the contract and that the contract is an agreement that may be enforced against the regulator in court.

Furthermore, the overriding purpose of the regulatory contract is to induce the public utility to make specialized investments. By accepting its franchise, the regulated utility undertakes an obligation to serve—that is, to provide service to any and all customers in its service territory. The utility further agrees to abide by a host of regulations that determine its prices, product offerings, investments, and accounting procedures. Most important, the utility must make long-term investments in highly specialized, immovable facilities. The regulatory contract exists to create the institutional structure of incentives and credible assurances for the public utility to undertake the substantial capital costs required to perform its service obligations. Without those credible assurances, a public utility would not have been willing to incur capital costs to build the facilities needed to satisfy regulatory obligations to serve—including notably the provision of universal service at a uniform price, regardless of incremental cost.

PHYSICAL INVASION
OF NETWORK FACILITIES

In contrast to regulatory takings, government policies that effect physical invasions of property elicit the greatest judicial protection of private property. A physical invasion of property compelled by the state gives rise to an absolute right of compensation.

40. *Id.*

The Loretto *Decision*

The leading decision on takings arising from physical invasion of property is the Supreme Court's 1982 decision in *Loretto* v. *Teleprompter Manhattan CATV Corp.*, which defended that rule even in the case of "a minor but permanent physical occupation of an owner's property authorized by government."[41] The Court announced that "when the 'character of the governmental action,' is a permanent physical occupation of property, our cases uniformly have found a taking to the extent of the occupation, without regard to whether the action achieves an important public benefit or has only minimal economic impact on the owner."[42]

At issue in *Loretto* was a New York statute that required a landlord to permit a cable television (CATV) company to install its CATV facilities upon her property, subject to payment of no greater than "reasonable" compensation set by a state commission. Exclusively franchised to build the CATV system within certain parts of Manhattan, Teleprompter wired Ms. Loretto's five-story apartment building, for which the commission deemed her to be entitled to a one-time payment of one dollar. The motivation for the statute is clear: Before enactment of the statute, Teleprompter routinely paid a property owner 5 percent of the gross revenues received from having access to his property.[43] The statute gave Teleprompter a way to pay a lower price for such access.

Teleprompter's physical invasion of Ms. Loretto's building was minor and consisted of a cable "slightly less than one-half inch in diameter and of approximately 30 feet in length along . . . the roof top," two directional taps on the front and rear of the roof that were four-inch cubes, "two large silver boxes along the roof cables," and the screws, nails, and bolts used to attach those various pieces of infrastructure to the building.[44] Plainly, what motivated Ms. Loretto was not the obtrusiveness of Teleprompter's physical occupation of her property, but rather her opportunity cost (in terms of forgoing a 5 percent share of CATV subscription revenues generated by her tenants) upon being compelled to grant access to her property essentially for free.

41. 458 U.S. 419, 421 (1982).
42. *Id.* at 434–35 (quoting *Penn Central*, 438 U.S. at 124) (citation omitted).
43. *Id.* at 423.
44. *Id.* at 422. Actually, two buildings were involved, but we have simplified the facts here.

In other words, although *Loretto* was in practical terms a simple case of access pricing, the Court chose to make the fact of physical invasion dispositive.[45] Referring to one of *Penn Central*'s three criteria, Justice Thurgood Marshall wrote for the majority that "when the physical intrusion reaches the extreme form of a permanent physical occupation, . . . 'the character of the government action' not only is an important factor in resolving whether the action works a taking but also is determinative."[46] A physical intrusion by government has "unusually serious character" and, if permanent, is "extreme" and fundamentally different from a temporary physical intrusion.[47] "When faced with a constitutional challenge to a permanent physical occupation of real property, this Court has invariably found a taking."[48] Professor Frank Michelman of Harvard Law School, the Court concluded, "accurately summarized" the law on physical invasions of property in his classic article: "The modern significance of physical occupation is that courts . . . *never* deny compensation for a physical takeover. The one incontestable case for compensation (short of formal expropriation) seems to occur when the government deliberately brings it about that its agents, or the public at large, 'regularly' use, or 'permanently' occupy, space or a thing which theretofore was understood to be under private ownership."[49] Unlike the balancing analysis in a regulatory takings case, "a permanent physical occupation is a government action of such a unique character that it is a taking without regard to other factors that a court might ordinarily examine."[50]

---

45. *Id*. at 426 ("a permanent physical occupation authorized by government is a taking without regard to the public interests that it may serve").

46. *Id*.

47. *Id*.

48. *Id*. at 427–28 (distinguishing Pumpelly v. Green Bay Co., 80 U.S. (13 Wall.) 166 (1872) (permanent flooding of private property), from Northern Transp. Co. v. Chicago, 99 U.S. 635 (1879) (temporary flooding of private property)). The Court emphasized that point by relying on additional decisions in which it predicated its finding of a taking on the permanent flooding of private property. *Id*. at 428 (citing United States v. Lynah, 188 U.S. 445, 468–70 (1903); Bedford v. United States, 192 U.S. 217, 225 (1904); United States v. Cress, 243 U.S. 316, 327–28 (1917); Sanguinetti v. United States, 264 U.S. 146, 149 (1924); United States v. Kansas City Life Ins. Co., 339 U.S. 799, 809–10 (1950)).

49. *Id*. at 427 n.5 (quoting Frank Michelman, *Property, Utility, and Fairness: Comments on the Ethical Foundations of "Just Compensation" Law*, 80 HARV. L. REV. 1165, 1184 (1967) (emphasis in original)).

50. *Id*. at 432. The Court likened its rule on permanent physical invasion to a per se rule in antitrust law. *Id*. at 436.

The Court in *Loretto* reached the right result. But it is questionable whether that result flows from either the physical occupation of the property or the permanence of that occupation, rather than from the statute's interference with Ms. Loretto's ability to reap the pecuniary benefits incident to ownership of her property. The Court, for example, said that "constitutional protection for the rights of private property cannot be made to depend on the size of the area permanently occupied."[51] On one level that statement can be taken to be a rhetorical flourish or an absolutist adherence to principle. But on another level, it can be taken to suggest that the concept of permanent physical occupation is a proxy for some other jurisprudential concern, and that the significance of that proxy magnifies as the objective burden of such physical occupation becomes more and more insignificant in terms of its relevant measure of area, volume, or mass. The Court hinted as much in *Loretto* by making light of the factual disagreement between the majority and the dissenters over the volume of the cable boxes attached to Ms. Loretto's building. "The displaced volume . . . [is] not critical: whether the installation is a taking does not depend on whether the volume of space it occupies is bigger than a breadbox."[52] Surely, Ms. Loretto cared less about the permanent clutter that Teleprompter placed on her rooftop than about the 5 percent royalty on gross revenues that she was foreclosed from receiving from the company because New York's statute truncated the charge that she could levy for cable access to her building. The Court did address such issues later in its opinion, but that discussion is evidently dictum in light of the emphatic enunciation of the per se rule that preceded it.

Justice Marshall reasoned that a government policy permitting the permanent physical occupation of private property without compensation would be harmful to society as a matter of first principles and that such considerations animated the precedents upon which the Court relied in *Loretto*. "Property rights in a physical thing," he reasoned, are "the rights 'to possess, use and dispose of it,'" and the government's permanent physical occupation of private property "destroys each of these rights."[53] In support of that proposition, Justice Marshall made three points:

---

51. *Id.* at 436 n.12.
52. *Id.* at 438.
53. *Id.* at 435 (quoting United States *v.* General Motors Corp., 323 U.S. 373, 378 (1945)).

> First, the owner has no right to possess the occupied space himself, and also has no power to exclude the occupier from possession and use of the space. The power to exclude has traditionally been considered one of the most treasured strands in an owner's bundle of property rights.[54]

As we argued earlier, a powerful economic rationale supports Justice Marshall, for the power to exclude is a prerequisite to voluntary exchange, allocative efficiency, and investment. Justice Marshall, however, had considerably more difficulty articulating the importance of protecting the *expectation interest* incident to property ownership:

> Second, the permanent physical occupation of property forever denies the owner any power to control the use of the property; he not only cannot exclude others, but can make no nonpossessory use of the property. Although deprivation of the right to use and obtain a profit from property is not, in every case, independently sufficient to establish a taking, it is clearly relevant.[55]

The nonpossessory use that the owner would presumably make of his property would be to alienate to others the net revenue stream that the property would generate. Yet the Court evidently did not want to follow its reasoning to its logical conclusion and acknowledge that the destruction of the reasonable expectation of that net revenue stream—not the physical invasion of property per se—is the proximate cause of the property owner's diminution in property value and thus the basis for the government's payment of compensation. Such reasoning would have flowed naturally from the 1893 decision in *Monongahela Navigation Co.* v. *United States*, in which the Court held, in the case of the federal government's confiscation of private locks and dams that had made the Monongahela River navigable, that "just compensation requires payment for the franchise to take tolls, as well as for the value of the tangible property."[56]

And indeed Justice Marshall's third point was redolent of the implication that just compensation required protecting the property owner from the full opportunity cost of the physical invasion: "Finally, even though the owner may retain the bare legal right to dispose of the occupied space by transfer or sale, the permanent occupation of that

---

54. *Id.* at 435–36 (citing *Kaiser Aetna*, 444 U.S. at 179–80; RESTATEMENT OF PROPERTY § 7 (1936)).

55. *Id.* at 436 (citing Andrus v. Allard, 444 U.S. at 66) (citation omitted).

56. 148 U.S. 312, 343 (1893).

space by a stranger will ordinarily empty the right of any value, since the purchaser will also be unable to make any use of the property."[57] Physical occupation of the property denies its owner the ability to alienate not only a given right in the bundle (the stream of net revenues from the property), but also the entire bundle of rights.

The closest that the Court came to saying that the Takings Clause protects the owner's expectation interest in his property was Justice Marshall's observation that "an owner suffers a special kind of injury when a stranger directly invades and occupies the owner's property" and that consequently "property law has long protected an owner's expectation that he will be relatively undisturbed at least in the possession of his property,"[58] and that for such an invasion "the property owner entertains a historically rooted expectation of compensation."[59] But, of course, in *Loretto*, more than protecting her expectation to be undisturbed in her possession of her property, the Court was protecting Ms. Loretto's expectation that she would be undisturbed in the *use* of her property (through her ability to negotiate with Teleprompter a better access charge for her building than the one dollar that the statute allowed).

Five years later, the Court considered a similar case. The Pole Attachments Act authorized the FCC to regulate the rates, terms, and conditions of the attachment of cable television wires to utility poles if the state did not engage in such regulation, but the statute did not mandate access.[60] An electric utility challenged the statute as a permanent physical invasion of private property, but the Court ruled in *FCC v. Florida Power Corp.* that *Loretto* did not apply.[61] Justice Marshall, again writing for the majority, reasoned that the statute merely regulated prices in consensual transactions. Unlike the New York statute in *Loretto*, which contained the "element of required acquiescence . . . at the heart of the concept of occupation," the federal law did not compel the property owner to submit to an involuntary transaction.[62]

---

57. *Id.*

58. *Id.* "To require, as well, that the owner permit another to exercise complete dominion literally adds insult to injury." *Id.* (citing Michelman, *supra* note 49, at 1228 & n.110).

59. *Id.* at 441.

60. Pub. L. No. 95-234, § 6, 92 Stat. 35 (1978) (codified at 47 U.S.C. § 224).

61. 480 U.S. 245 (1987).

62. *Id.* at 252. In 1992 the Court reinforced that rationale: Property owners who "voluntarily open their property to occupation by others . . . cannot assert a per se right to compensation based on their inability to exclude particular individuals." Yee *v.*

Florida Power thus does not make *Loretto* any less applicable to mandatory network unbundling, for the introduction of such a regulatory obligation is by definition not voluntary. To the contrary, *Florida Power* has itself become a curio because the Telecommunications Act of 1996 made it *mandatory* for utilities to provide access to their poles, ducts, conduits, and rights of way; furthermore, the statute specified the formula for computing compensation for such mandatory access.[63] Thus, a new wave of pole attachment cases may arise for which *Florida Power* will no longer be dispositive.

Mandatory Interconnection or Unbundling

Because of the technological and economic complexity of interconnection and unbundling in network industries, it is easy to overlook the obvious: Mandatory interconnection and unbundling constitute a government-ordered, physical invasion of the property of the incumbent regulated firm. Electric utilities and local telephone exchange carriers have rights of way, poles, conduits, transmissions lines, switches, central offices, and the like. Indeed, to build that physical infrastructure, an electric utility or a telephone company originally had to acquire the consent of the land owner or, if it was exercising the right of eminent domain, pay just compensation for its taking.[64] Mandatory interconnection or unbundling envisions rivals of the regulated firm having physical access to its property. The Oregon Supreme Court has recognized that fact and, relying upon *Loretto*, held unanimously in 1995 that the state PUC's order that enhanced service providers be allowed to collocate their equipment on the premises of incumbent local exchange carriers constituted a physical invasion that violated the Takings Clause.[65] The court emphasized that "the facts that an industry

Escondido, 503 U.S. 519, 531 (1992).

63. Pub. L. No. 104-104, § 703, 110 Stat. 56, 150 (1996) (codified at 47 U.S.C. § 224(e)).

64. *See Loretto*, 458 U.S. at 429, 437 (citing Western Union Tel. Co. *v.* Pennsylvania R.R., 195 U.S. 540 (1904); Lovett *v.* West Va. Central Gas Co., 65 W. Va. 739, 65 S.E. 196 (1909); Southwestern Bell Tel. Co. *v.* Webb, 393 S.W.2d 117, 121 (Mo. App. 1965); Portsmouth Harbor Land & Hotel Co. *v.* United States, 260 U.S. 327 (1922)). The initial placement of poles for telegraph transmission a century ago generated litigation over whether the telegraph company had to pay a city for the space that its poles would permanently occupy along public streets. St. Louis *v.* Western Union Tel. Co., 148 U.S. 92 (1893).

65. GTE Northwest, Inc. *v.* Public Util. Comm'n of Ore., 321 Ore. 458, 468–77, 900 P.2d 495, 501–06 (1995), *cert. denied*, 116 S. Ct. 1541 (1996).

is heavily regulated, and that a property owner acquired the property knowing that it is heavily regulated, do not diminish a physical invasion to something less than a taking."[66]

Furthermore, a physical invasion of the incumbent firm's property may occur even when the invasion is not visible. The first questions of interconnection pricing in modern regulatory experience arose in connection with the sale of "trackage rights" in the railroad industry. By order of the Interstate Commerce Commission, railroad *A* would be allowed to purchase the right to move its trains over tracks owned by railroad *B*, thus extending the geographic reach of railroad *A*'s rail network beyond its own facilities.[67] One can scarcely imagine a more vivid example of physical invasion than freight trains owned by one railway barreling down another railway's stretch of track.

In electrical or telecommunications networks, the locomotives are electrons or photons. Indeed, the metaphor "information superhighway" derives its saliency from its ability to convey that, no matter how silent or invisible it may be, the physical movement of bits across telephone wires is as tangible as trucks transporting goods across the interstate highway system. In *Loretto* the Court said that the web of cable television infrastructure that constituted a physical invasion of property in that case "could be described as a cable 'highway' circumnavigating the city block."[68] The wheeling of electricity over the transmission grid presents a slightly different case of physical movement through a network. Power flows through multiple paths of least resistance, as determined by Ohm's law, an intrinsic property of all conductors that defines current as a ratio of voltage to resistance. The Court has long recognized the legal implications of the physical properties of current flow for questions for federal jurisdiction,[69] for transmissions of electricity follow unanticipated routes to their final destinations that may cross state boundaries and thereby trigger federal regulation.[70] Nonetheless,

---

66. 321 Ore. at 474, 900 P.2d at 504.

67. *See* WILLIAM J. BAUMOL & J. GREGORY SIDAK, TOWARD COMPETITION IN LOCAL TELEPHONY 95–96 (MIT Press & AEI Press 1994) (citing St. Louis S.W. Ry.—Trackage Rights over Missouri Pac. R.R.—Kansas City to St. Louis, 1 I.C.C.2d 776 (1984), 4 I.C.C.2d 668 (1987), 5 I.C.C.2d 525 (1989), 8 I.C.C.2d 80 (1991)).

68. 458 U.S. at 422.

69. FPC v. Florida Power & Light Co., 404 U.S. 453, 466–69 (1972); *see also* Consolidated Edison Co. v. Public Serv. Comm'n, 63 N.Y.2d 424, 440 (1984).

70. *See, e.g.,* PETER S. FOX-PENNER, ELECTRIC POWER TRANSMISSION AND WHEELING: A TECHNICAL PRIMER 5, 53 (Edison Electric Institute 1990). The phenomenon of parallel flow paths is also said to reflect Kirchhoff's laws. On the pricing of trans-

the condition remains fundamentally the same as the locomotive operating pursuant to trackage rights: A rival's use of the incumbent's network involves occupying the physical capacity of that infrastructure to deliver a service that competes with the incumbent's.

Moreover, it does not matter that the party making the physical invasion of the telephony or electricity network is a private company rather than the state itself. As the Court said in *Loretto*, "A permanent physical occupation authorized by state law is a taking without regard to whether the State, or instead a party authorized by the State, is the occupant."[71]

The Physics of
Network Invasion

Physical Occupation of Electrical Transmission and Distribution Networks. The wheeling of electricity over transmission lines and distribution grids presents an example of physical movement through a network. The intrinsic physical properties of electricity make electric power different from other network supply systems, such as those for water or gas.[72] Efficient electric power transmission requires guidance of transverse electromagnetic (TEM) waves.[73] High-voltage transmission lines serve as the guiding system for that power delivery. Those transmission lines generally consist of parallel conducting wires separated by uniform distances.[74] TEM waves, characterized by electric fields and magnetic fields that are perpendicular to each other and transverse to the direction of propagation, carry electromagnetic power to distant points along transmission lines.[75] Because power travels at nearly the velocity of light, about 3×10^8 meters per second, visual observation of energy flow is difficult. Yet, despite our inability to "see" tangible evidence of energy flow, we can measure the physical presence of power along transmission lines. One can determine the

mission in the presence of parallel flows, see William W. Hogan, *Contract Networks for Electric Power Transmission*, 4 J. REG. ECON. 211 (1992).

71. 458 U.S. at 432 n.9.

72. *See* Hogan, *supra* note 70, at 215.

73. *See* DAVID K. CHENG, FIELD AND WAVE ELECTROMAGNETICS 306–16 (Addison-Wesley Publishing Co. 1983); SIMON RAMO, JOHN R. WHINNERY & THEODORE VAN DUZER, FIELDS AND WAVES IN COMMUNICATION ELECTRONICS 371–415 (John Wiley & Sons, Inc. 1965).

74. CHENG, *supra* note 73, at 371.

75. *Id.* at 370; RAMO, WHINNERY & VAN DUZER, *supra* note 73, at 374.

power being transferred, in an alternating current system, at any instant of time by taking the product of the transmission line's root mean square (rms) voltage and rms current and the cosine of their phase difference.[76]

Given that transmission lines serve as a guiding system for power transfer, is it possible to control completely the route that electricity will travel? Under current technology the answer is no, because transmissions of power follow unanticipated routes to their final destinations. Upon reaching a network of transmission lines with varying impedances, more power will be distributed through wires with smaller impedances. Also, because there exists no economically viable means of storing large quantities of energy, electric power must be produced, transmitted, and instantaneously distributed to meet customer demand, which varies with the time of day and the season of the year.

Because of those unique physical properties of electricity, mandatory retail wheeling, while aimed at fostering competition in the generation of power, would permanently deprive the incumbent local utility of part of its transmission capacity.[77] Furthermore, the incumbent utility would be forced to make available its distribution path for use by a competitor that may become obligated to provide an uninterruptable power supply to the incumbent's former customer. Consequently, the competitor would have the option of using the incumbent utility's capacity at any time the customer requested service.

The incumbent utility would not be the only party adversely affected by the retail power exchange. Another side effect of retail wheeling would be the permanent occupation of some capacity of all the networks involved in the wheeling process. For illustration, consider a customer located in Baltimore that was formerly served exclusively by utility *A*. The customer now desires to purchase power from utility *B*, located in North Carolina. Suppose that there are no direct connections

---

76. *See, e.g.*, Isaak D. Mayergoyz & Wes Lawson, Basic Electric Circuit Theory: A One Semester Text 86–90 (Academic Press 1996).

77. In late 1996 the Vermont Public Service Board rejected the argument that mandatory retail wheeling would constitute a permanent physical invasion of property that would be compensable under *Loretto*. Restructuring of the Electric Utility Industry in Vermont, Dkt. No. 5854, 174 P.U.R. 4th 409 (Vt. Pub. Serv. Bd. Dec. 30, 1996). The board purported to rely on precedent, but the two electricity cases that the board cited, Kansas City Power & Light Co. v. State Corp. Comm'n, 238 Kan. 842, 715 P.2d 19 (1986), *appeal dismissed*, 479 U.S. 801 (1986), and Energy Ass'n of N.Y. State v. Public Serv. Comm'n of N.Y., 169 Misc. 2d 924 (Sup. Ct., Albany County 1996), did not seriously discuss the physics of invasion.

between utilities *A* and *B*. Thus, to reach utility *A*'s distribution grid, power generated by utility *B* must travel cross-country through utilities *C*, *D*, and *E*, which provide interconnection. With the interconnections, it is popularly believed that a direct "contract path" has been established from *B* to *A* via *C*, *D*, and *E*. As explained by Ohm's law and Kirchhoff's laws, however, wheeled power between systems does not flow exclusively over the direct interconnections.[78] Instead, loop flows result that cause power to traverse over many different utilities before reaching the desired buyer. Transmission lines may be connected to other transmission lines with different characteristic impedance or to various customer load resistances.[79] Because of Kirchhoff's laws, not all the power transmitted along a line necessarily goes through the interconnection; some fraction of power may be reflected back.[80] That physical behavior of electric power dispels the notion of a contract path because actual power transmission may and frequently does diverge from a predestined route.[81]

In the example above, assume utilities *F* and *G* are not involved in the wheeling process but are connected to utility *D*. Some amount of power will "mistakenly" travel through *F* and *G* as a result of loop flows. That unintended flow of power affects utilities far removed from the desired route.[82] Utilities that experience uninvited power transfer have less transmission capacity available to serve their own needs.[83]

---

78. Ohm's law holds that "the voltage V_{12} across a resistance R, in which a current I flows from point 1 to point 2 is RI; that is, $V_{12} = RI$." CHENG, *supra* note 73, at 175. Kirchhoff's voltage law

> states that *around a closed path in an electric circuit the algebraic sum of the [electromotive forces] (voltage rises) is equal to the algebraic sum of the voltage drops across the resistances*. It applies to *any closed path* in a network. The direction of tracing the path can be arbitrarily assigned, and the currents in the different resistances need not be the same. Kirchhoff's voltage law is the basis for loop analysis in circuit theory.

Id. at 180 (emphasis in original). Kirchhoff's current law "states that *the algebraic sum of all the currents flowing out of a junction in an electric circuit is zero.* Kirchhoff's current law is the basis for node analysis in circuit theory." *Id.* at 181 (emphasis in original).

79. RAMO, WHINNERY & VAN DUZER, *supra* note 73, at 23–41.

80. *Id.* at 28.

81. Hogan, *supra* note 70, at 216.

82. *See* EDISON ELECTRIC INSTITUTE, ENGINEERING AND RELIABILITY EFFECTS OF INCREASED WHEELING AND TRANSMISSION ACCESS: FACTORS FOR CONSIDERATION 19–22, 24 (Edison Electric Institute 1988) [hereinafter ENGINEERING AND RELIABILITY].

83. M. Granger Morgan & Sarosh Talukdar, *Nurturing R&D*, IEEE SPECTRUM, July 1996, at 32.

Furthermore, power flow along unintended lines could trigger over-loads and power outages throughout all networks directly and indirectly involved in the wheeling process.[84] The magnitude of harm is so great that it must be taken quite seriously even if overloads and outages occur only infrequently.

Under retail wheeling, power would flow through a complex net-work of supply generators, transmission lines, and distribution grids all intricately tied together by hundreds of interconnections. In the exam-ple above, the wheeling utility becomes a composite of *A*, *C*, *D*, *E*, and others. The power flow along all transmission lines is character-ized by a 60 Hz frequency; thus, power wheeled from competitor to customer is physically indistinguishable from the incumbent utility's power. Owing to the homogeneous nature of transmitted power, utili-ties cannot determine the origin of the loop flows and prevent future problems without new technology. In the absence of that technology, utilities could not preserve a high degree of reliability and guard against disruptions in the provision of electric power without maintain-ing a constant reserve of capacity on the their transmission lines for their competitors.

Physical Occupation of Telecommunications Networks. Traditional telecommunications networks consist of three primary components: transmitter, channel, and receiver. The transmitter inputs information and converts it into electromagnetic signals appropriate for transmis-sion.[85] The channel, serving as the bridge between the transmitter and receiver, provides a transmission path for the signal.[86] That signal is a time-dependent value attached to an electromagnetic pulse that carries information.[87] During transmission, the electromagnetic signal may experience distortion and the addition of noise. Upon detection, the receiver extracts the weakened and distorted signal from the channel and amplifies it.[88] Ideally, the regenerated signal remains nearly identi-cal to the original version.

---

84. ENGINEERING AND RELIABILITY, *supra* note 82, at 24; *see also* Benjamin A. Holden, *Did Competition Spark Power Failures?*, WALL ST. J., Aug. 19, 1996, at B1.

85. CLIFFORD R. POLLOCK, THE FUNDAMENTALS OF OPTOELECTRONICS 4–7 (Rich-ard D. Irwin Inc. 1995).

86. *Id.* at 5.

87. JOSEPH A. PECAR, ROGER J. O'CONNOR & DAVID A. GARBIN, MCGRAW-HILL TELECOMMUNICATIONS FACTBOOK 17 (McGraw-Hill Inc. 1993).

88. POLLOCK, *supra* note 85, at 5.

In local voice telephony, the station terminal equipment, in the form of telephone sets, represents the transmitter and receiver.[89] The channel for local communication consists of customer loops, cable pairs that connect the station terminal equipment to a central office, and transmission paths established within a switching system.[90] The switching systems serve to connect a specific terminal of several thousand terminals to the transmitting channel.[91]

The initial stage of voice communication begins at the transmitter station terminal. The microphone in the telephone receiver, the transducer, absorbs sound waves and converts the differences in acoustic pressure into a continuously varying analog electromagnetic signal.[92] The analog signal is partitioned into a train of electrical impulses.[93] Each individual electric energy impulse, commonly called a bit, is characterized by a specific frequency and a specific amplitude corresponding to the unique pitch and unique loudness, respectively, of each sound.[94] The transformation of speech into electricity changes the character of sound from a continuous wave to a discrete number of individual bits. An analog-to-digital (A/D) converter built into the system accomplishes that transformation.[95]

After discretization, electrical impulses are transmitted along the communication channel medium.[96] Bandwidth—that is, the range of allowed frequencies between the lower and upper limiting frequencies that varies with the transmission medium—determines the quantity of information the channel can transmit.[97] Ideally, the bandwidth is as large as possible to allow for greater information transmission capacity, which is defined as the number of bits per second that the channel can

89. 1 Bell Communications Research, Telecommunications Transmission Engineering: Principles 8 (Bellcore 1990).

90. *Id.*

91. *Id.* at 11.

92. Pecar, O'Connor & Garbin, *supra* note 87, at 17.

93. For a graphical interpretation, see Alan V. Oppenheim, Alan S. Willsky & Ian T. Young, Signals and Systems 515–16 (Prentice-Hall Inc. 1983).

94. Pecar, O'Connor & Garbin, *supra* note 87, at 17.

95. For a rigorous description of A/D converters, see Jacob Millman & Arvin Garbel, Microelectronics 719–24 (McGraw-Hill Inc., 2d ed. 1987).

96. *Id.* at 6. The medium for transmitting information is generally copper wire cable or fiber-optic cable. The physical properties of copper wire cable are similar to those of the transmission lines used for power delivery. For a discussion of the physics of fiber-optic cable, see Pollock, *supra* note 85.

97. William L. Schweber, Electronic Communication Systems: A Complete Course 14–15 (Prentice-Hall Inc. 1991).

support.[98] In most telephone networks, bandwidth is set around 3,000 Hz (3 Khz) because the span of 300 Hz to 3 Khz is all that is required to carry voice information.[99]

Upon reaching the desired destination, the train of electric impulses is reconstructed into sound. The Shannon-Nyquist sampling theorem provides the scientific guidelines for recreating continuous sound from instantaneous discrete impulses.[100] The original analog signal can be reconstructed according to the sampling theorem, provided that the sample frequency is at least twice the bandwidth, by generating a periodic impulse train in which the successive impulses have amplitudes that are successive sample values.[101] The sampling frequency must be high enough that the individually sampled pulses do not overlap; if overlap occurs, the original sound cannot be replicated.[102] The sampled signal is processed through a low-pass filter, a mechanism for removing low-frequency noise and distortion, defined by a constant amplification factor and a cutoff frequency that is greater than the bandwidth and less than the difference between the sampling frequency and the bandwidth.[103] The filtered signal is converted back to an analog sound wave by using a digital-to-analog (D/A) converter.[104] The output from the D/A converter should provide a continuous sound wave that is faithful to the unique characteristics of the original transmitted speech.

Unlike electric power transmission, electric impulse trains carrying information must follow predestined routes along the transmission channel of a local exchange carrier's circuit-switched system.[105] Whereas electric power is indistinguishable within a delivery network, each bit

---

98. PECAR, O'CONNOR & GARBIN, *supra* note 87, at 22–24.

99. *Id.* at 14; *see also* DANIEL MINOLI, TELECOMMUNICATIONS TECHNOLOGY HANDBOOK 11 (Artech House 1991).

100. OPPENHEIM, WILLSKY & YOUNG, *supra* note 93, at 514–21.

101. *Id.* at 519.

102. Mathematically, the sampling theorem requires that $f_{\text{samp}} \geq 2f_{\text{sig}}$, where f_{samp} is the sampling frequency and f_{sig} is the signal frequency. The physical phenomenon of overlapping impulses is termed *aliasing*. For a mathematical description, see *id.* at 527–31.

103. The frequencies that pass through the low-pass filter are between $f_{\text{bw}} \leq f_{\text{co}} \leq (f_{\text{samp}} - f_{\text{bw}})$, where f_{bw} represents the bandwidth frequency, f_{co} represents the cutoff frequency, and f_{samp} represents the sampling frequency. *Id.*

104. For a rigorous description of D/A converters, see MILLMAN & GARBEL, *supra* note 95, at 715–19.

105. Different congestion problems arise in packet-switched networks and between such networks and circuit-switched networks. *See* J. Gregory Sidak & Daniel F. Spulber, *Cyberjam: The Law and Economics of Internet Congestion of the Telephone Network*, 20 HARV. J.L. & PUB. POL'Y (forthcoming 1997).

of information representing sound has a unique signature defined by its amplitude and frequency. Because each bit carries unique information, there cannot be more than one train of impulses transmitted along the channel of a circuit-switched network at one time. Consequently, in a market where competitive local telephony takes place over a single network, if a customer chooses to be serviced by a competitor, then the incumbent utility must surrender all use of its transmission channels that connect to that customer. The use of the transmission path is mutually exclusive.

JUST COMPENSATION AND THE REGULATION OF PUBLIC UTILITY RATES

Sandwiched between the strict protection of private property in cases of physical invasions and the minimal protection in cases of regulatory takings are the cases involving the setting of rates for regulated public utilities. Just as property rights are an essential element of private exchange, so also are they required for individuals to transact with the government. Constitutional protections of property rights and due process are the foundation for the administrative process of regulation. Given that the terms of trade between individuals (or companies) are a private matter, how is price regulation to be reconciled with the protection of individual property rights?

Private property protection is the basis for utility regulation. The regulatory contract is subject to the full property protections of the Takings Clause.[106] As explained earlier, investor-owned utilities have a public mandate or obligation to provide service to all in a community who desire such service. In fulfillment of that duty, and in reasonable anticipation of future requests for increased service, the utility purchases and employs specialized assets. Without adequate compensation, the utility will not seek to make investments for expansion or replacement of plant and property and will not be able to raise the necessary capital. Rate regulation controls the returns to investment by the utility's owners; such regulation affects the property's value and therefore must not be confiscatory.[107] The rate of return allowed on property used for

---

106. Chang v. United States, 859 F.2d 893, 894 (Fed. Cir. 1988) ("There is no question that 'valid contracts are property, whether the obligor be a private individual, . . . or the United States.'") (quoting Lynch v. United States, 292 U.S. 571, 579 (1934)).

107. Covington & Lexington Turnpike Road Co. v. Sandford, 164 U.S. 578, 597 (1896) ("a rate that is too low can 'destroy the value of [the] property.'").

public purposes must be sufficient to compensate investors.[108] Sufficiency is measured relative to rates that enable the regulated firm "to operate successfully, to maintain its financial integrity, to attract capital, and to compensate its investors for the risk assumed."[109] Furthermore, the establishment of formal regulatory proceedings with hearings on the record by administrative regulatory agencies reflects the constitutional guaranty that the utility receive due process in ratemaking.

The Duquesne *Test of Fair Return on
Prudently Incurred Investment*

A taking occurs if regulatory authorities interfere with the utility's opportunity to earn a fair return on prudently incurred investment made to carry out regulatory obligations. Because the state regulates the return that the utility can earn, courts have long considered rate regulation of a utility's property to be subject to the Takings Clause. Uncompensatory rate regulation thus requires compensation of the utility's investors for their forgone expected returns. The major takings cases involving regulated utilities, such as *Federal Power Commission* v. *Hope Natural Gas Co.*[110] and *Duquesne Light Co.* v. *Barasch*,[111] do not clearly answer the question of whether the regulator's refusal to allow the public utility the opportunity to recover stranded costs is a taking, for those decisions did not address the consequences of deregulation and wholesale abrogation of the regulatory contract in the name of establishing a competitive marketplace.

In *Duquesne*, the Duquesne Light Company began making investments in new nuclear power plants.[112] Those investments were reasonable (prudent) in light of the current costs of different production tech-

---

108. Duquesne Light Co. *v.* Barasch, 488 U.S. 299, 308 (1989); Smyth *v.* Ames, 169 U.S. 466, 546 (1898). *See generally* Richard J. Pierce, Jr., *Public Utility Regulatory Takings: Should the Judiciary Attempt to Police the Political Institutions?*, 77 GEO. L.J. 2031 (1989).

109. FPC *v.* Hope Natural Gas Co. 320 U.S. 591, 605 (1944); Southwestern Bell Tel. Co. *v.* Public Serv. Comm'n, 262 U.S. 276, 291 (1923) (Brandeis, J., concurring) ("The compensation which the Constitution guarantees an opportunity to earn is the reasonable cost of conducting the business. Cost includes not only operating expenses, but also capital charges. Capital charges cover the allowance, by way of interest, for the use of capital, whatever the nature of the security issued therefor; the allowance for risk incurred; and enough more to attract capital.").

110. 320 U.S. 591 (1944).

111. 488 U.S. 299 (1989).

112. Several other utilities were involved in *Duquesne*. For simplicity, we refer only to Duquesne.

nologies and expected future demand at the time they were made. Changes in the relative costs and risks of nuclear power (for example, the Three Mile Island nuclear mishap) resulted in a further (prudent) decision to abandon the nuclear power plants. Duquesne had spent roughly $35 million in planning and preparation by that time.[113] Duquesne sought to add those sunk-costs to its rate base and to recover them through amortization and the allowed rate of return. Unfortunately for Duquesne, however, after the expenditure but before the inclusion of the nuclear costs in the rate base, Pennsylvania enacted legislation that foreclosed the Pennsylvania Public Utility Commission from granting Duquesne recovery of those costs through higher utility rates.[114]

The Supreme Court examined whether the state legislation caused a taking of the property of Duquesne's shareholders without just compensation. Writing for the Court, Chief Justice William H. Rehnquist noted that Duquesne had "a state statutory duty to serve the public" and that its "assets [were] employed in the public interest," but that the company was "owned and operated by private investors."[115] Those characteristics set the regulated firm apart from others: "This partly public, partly private status of utility property creates its own set of questions under the Takings Clause of the Fifth Amendment."[116]

Whether the allowed rates of a public utility violate the Takings Clause depends on whether they are "confiscatory"[117]—a determination that the Court in 1898 admitted in *Smyth* v. *Ames* to be "always . . . an embarrassing question."[118] The answer to that question, however, does not depend on the use of any single methodology. The *Duquesne* Court reaffirmed the holding in *Hope* that it is the overall effect of rate regulation, not the details or methods, that matter.[119] The question then was whether the rate of return that Duquesne achieved was constitu-

113. 488 U.S. at 302.

114. *Id.* at 303–04.

115. *Id.* at 307.

116. *Id.*

117. *Id.* at 307–08 (citing Covington & Lexington Turnpike Road Co. *v.* Sandford, 164 U.S. 578, 597 (1896); FPC *v.* Natural Gas Pipeline Co., 315 U.S. 575, 585 (1942); FPC v. Texaco Inc., 417 U.S. 380, 391–92 (1974)).

118. 169 U.S. 466, 546 (1898), *quoted in id.* at 308.

119. "[I]t is not theory but the impact of the rate order which counts. If the total effect of the rate order cannot be said to be unreasonable, judicial inquiry . . . is at an end. The fact that the method employed to reach that result may contain infirmities is not then important." *Hope*, 320 U.S. at 602, *quoted in Duquesne*, 488 U.S. at 310. The *Duquesne* Court liked *Hope*'s rhetoric of "theory" and "impact" so much that it quoted the language twice. *Id.* at 314.

tionally sufficient. The Court considered the unrecovered sunk costs as part of the investment on which to measure the overall rate of return.

Distinguishing Stranded Costs from the Unrecovered Prudently Incurred Investment in Duquesne *That Did Not Constitute a Taking*

Five facts convinced the Court that no taking of Duquesne's property had occurred. Those facts look very different in the case of breach of the regulatory contract. First, Duquesne did not claim "that the total effect of the rate order arrived at . . . [was] unjust or unreasonable," and, to the contrary, the Court found that "the overall effect [was] well within the bounds of *Hope*, even with total exclusion" of the prudently incurred costs for the nuclear plants.[120] In contrast, the total exclusion of stranded costs could bankrupt certain regulated firms.

Second, Duquesne's "$35 million investment in the canceled plants comprise[d] roughly 1.9% of its total base."[121] Although the Court here did not cite Justice Holmes's remark in *Pennsylvania Coal* about the transaction costs of compensating trivial takings of private property,[122] that consideration may have been present. It is, however, an odd proposition: If the parties affected by a confiscation are not diffuse, then the government's payment of compensation for a taking should be *less* of a burden (and thus more readily made) as the amount of compensation falls. Moreover, $35 million of property loss is a substantial amount compared with what could conceivably have been at stake in, say, the portentous case of the cable television paraphernalia littering Ms. Loretto's rooftop. And, again, the amount of stranded costs at stake in the electricity and local telephony markets is greater than the $35 million in *Duquesne* by orders of magnitude.

Third, the denial of cost recovery caused by the opportunistic behavior of the Pennsylvania legislature did not threaten Duquesne's financial survival:

> No argument has been made that these slightly reduced rates jeopardize the financial integrity of [Duquesne], either by leaving [it] insufficient

---

120. *Id.* at 311–12. "The Constitution protects the utility from the net effect of the rate order on its property. Inconsistencies in one aspect of the methodology have no constitutional effect on the utility's property if they are compensated by countervailing factors in some other aspect." *Id.* at 314.

121. *Id.* at 312.

122. 260 U.S. at 413.

operating capital or by impeding [its] ability to raise future capital. Nor has it been demonstrated that these rates are inadequate to compensate current equity holders for the risk associated with their investments under a modified prudent investment scheme.[123]

Again, breach of the regulatory contract unquestionably does jeopardize the financial integrity of some regulated firms.

A fourth and related fact upon which the Court relied was that the opportunism exercised by the Pennsylvania legislature was not the most extreme version available to it, given the extent to which a public utility's income depended on the consistency of the rate methodology that its regulator employed:

> The risks a utility faces are in large part defined by the rate methodology because utilities are virtually always public monopolies dealing in an essential service, and so relatively immune to the usual market risks. Consequently, a State's decision to arbitrarily switch back and forth between methodologies in a way which required investors to bear the risk of bad investments at some times while denying them the benefit of good investments at others would raise serious constitutional questions. But the instant case does not present this question.[124]

Justice Antonin Scalia, joined by Justices Sandra Day O'Connor and Byron R. White, concurred but warned, more forcefully than did Chief Justice Rehnquist's opinion for the majority, that the holding in *Duquesne* would not answer the question of whether just compensation would be due in future takings cases where the nature and magnitude of the utility's prudent investment differed substantially from Duquesne's:

> [W]hile "prudent investment" (by which I mean capital reasonably expended to meet the utility's legal obligation to assure adequate service) need not be taken into account as such in ratemaking formulas, it may need to be taken into account in assessing the constitutionality of the particular consequences produced by those formulas. We cannot determine whether the payments a utility has been allowed to collect constitute a fair return on investment, and thus whether the government's action is confiscatory, unless we agree upon what the relevant "investment" is. *For that purpose, all prudently incurred investment may well have to be counted.* As the Court's opinion de-

---

123. 488 U.S. at 312.
124. *Id.* at 315.

scribes, that question is not presented in the present suit, which challenges techniques rather than consequences.[125]

Breach of the regulatory contract *does* present the serious constitutional question that *Duquesne* did not, for it threatens to exploit the utility's irreversible investment to a far greater extent than does the opportunistic disallowance of costs through prudency reviews or other retrospective mechanisms.[126]

Fifth, the Court understood that "utilities are virtually always public monopolies . . . relatively immune to the usual market risks."[127] The new policies mandating interconnection and unbundling, however, will overturn that understanding, for the goal of such policies is to deny current providers of electricity and local telephony their immunity to the "usual market risks" of competition.

In short, although *Duquesne* forced utility investors to bear the losses from unrecovered but prudently incurred sunk costs, the Court's reasoning indicates that the problem of stranded costs arising from breach of the regulatory contract would present a case distinguishable from *Duquesne* in all five respects.

An important implication of *Duquesne* is that utility investors must be compensated in one way or another for prudently incurred sunk costs. One possible method is to include the costs in the investment rate base. A second possible method is to increase the future allowed rate of return sufficiently above the cost of capital that the effect is as if the cost of capital had been allowed on all investments, including sunk-cost losses. A third approach is to increase the allowed rate of return at the time of investment to anticipate the possibility that stranding of investment may occur. What is *not* permitted is switching between rate methodologies in a way that could sometimes require investors to bear the risk of bad investments and at other times deny them the benefit of good investments.[128] The Court indicated that the ratepayers should pay for the sunk costs: The PUC should either ex-

---

125. *Id.* at 317 (Scalia, J., concurring) (emphasis added).

126. Some legal commentators, writing before the current wave of mandatory unbundling in the electric power and telecommunications industries, recommended that the Supreme Court reduce the public utility's protections under the Takings Clause. *See* John N. Drobak, *From Turnpike to Nuclear Power: The Constitutional Limits on Utility Rate Regulation*, 65 B.U.L. REV. 65 (1985); Richard Goldsmith, *Utility Rates and "Takings,"* 10 ENERGY L.J. 241 (1989).

127. 488 U.S. at 315.

128. *Id.*.

plicitly include the investments in the rate base (or allow an ongoing rate of return sufficiently high that the economic effect is equivalent to including costs in the rate base) or should increase the allowed rate of return on an ex ante basis to compensate for the expected cost of stranding.[129] Otherwise, ratepayers must pay the costs of sunk costs when they occur, since investors were not compensated before.

Property protections influence the incentives that utilities and ratepayers have to achieve the economically efficient result. If ratepayers bear prudently incurred sunk costs, they will lobby for abandonment of investments only when the economic value of alternative uses for the asset exceeds the value of the asset's continued use by the utility. That is precisely the efficient result. In contrast, investor-borne prudently incurred sunk costs result in inefficiency because the regulatory commission will be tempted to free ride by confiscating the property of the regulated utility.[130] That danger is particularly acute in the "endgame" that occurs in the transition from regulation to a competitive market.

Uncompensatory Pricing of Interconnection and Unbundled Access

Duquesne fails to address another form of taking that can arise under mandatory unbundling. Apart from being denied the opportunity to recover stranded costs, the incumbent regulated firm may be obliged to sell interconnection to its network or unbundled access to its basic service elements at prices that are uncompensatory. Invariably, the entrant seeks interconnection at (or below) long-run incremental cost (LRIC), with no contribution to the common costs of the incumbent's network. As we demonstrate in our discussion of efficient component

---

129. Some discussion of those issues appears in A. LAWRENCE KOLBE, WILLIAM B. TYE & STEWART C. MYERS, REGULATORY RISK: ECONOMIC PRINCIPLES AND APPLICATIONS TO NATURAL GAS PIPELINES AND OTHER INDUSTRIES (Kluwer Academic Publishers 1993); A. Lawrence Kolbe & William B. Tye, *The* Duquesne *Opinion: How Much "Hope" Is There for Investors in Regulated Firms?*, 8 YALE J. ON REG. 113, 123–27 (1991) [hereinafter *The* Duquesne *Opinion*]; Stephen F. Williams, *Fixing the Rate of Return After* Duquesne, 8 YALE J. ON REG. 159 (1991); *see also* ROGER A. MORIN, REGULATORY FINANCE: UTILITIES' COST OF CAPITAL 38–40 (Public Utilities Reports, Inc. 1994).

130. On the contrasting incentives to achieve the economically efficient result under differing rules for the recovery of stranded costs, see Michael J. Doane & Michael A. Williams, *Competitive Entry into Regulated Monopoly Service and the Resulting Problem of Stranded Costs*, 3 HUME PAPERS ON PUB. POL'Y, no. 3, at 32 (1995).

pricing in chapter 8 and 9, that price induces inefficient entry and threatens to bankrupt the regulated incumbent.

An illustrative example of the failure to recognize the takings implication of interconnection pricing arose in 1995 in a proceeding before the California Public Utilities Commission (CPUC) concerning the method of compensating incumbent local exchange carriers for terminating calls originated by subscribers to new competitive local carriers (CLCs).[131] In 1995 the CPUC adopted rules to authorize prospective CLCs to request certificates of public convenience and necessity to provide local exchange service. Those rules were part of a larger plan to open all of California's telecommunications markets to competition by January 1, 1997. Under the rules, the CLCs were allowed to commence facilities-based local exchange competition on January 1, 1996, and bundled resale-based competition on March 1, 1996.

Before the start of either form of competition, the CPUC adopted for one year, beginning January 1, 1996, "interim" rules concerning the compensation to be paid by carrier A for having carrier B terminate A's calls on B's local exchange network. Rather than order carriers to price terminating access on the basis of some measure of cost (however defined), the CPUC adopted the "bill-and-keep" system advocated by the CLCs, which the commission described as follows:

> "Bill-and-keep" is a method by which each LEC and CLC terminates local traffic for all other LECs and CLCs with which it interconnects, bearing its own capital and operating costs for these functions. Under this approach, individual LECs or CLCs theoretically bear a proportional share of the overall costs associated with reciprocal traffic exchange.[132]

In other words, suppose that 99 percent of calls are placed to subscribers on the network of the incumbent local exchange carrier B, and only 1 percent of calls are placed to subscribers on the network of competitive local carrier A. All other things being equal, a subscriber on A's system would therefore need to terminate calls on B's network 99 per-

---

131. Competition for Local Exchange Service, Decision 95-09-121, R.95-04-043, I.95-04-044, 165 P.U.R.4th 127 (Cal. Pub. Utils. Comm'n 1995).

132. *Id.* at 128. The FCC has also endorsed the use of bill-and-keep as a model of interconnection pricing. Interconnection Between Local Exchange Carriers and Commercial Mobile Radio Service Providers; Equal Access and Interconnection Obligations Pertaining to Commercial Mobile Radio Service Providers, Notice of Proposed Rulemaking, CC Dkt. Nos. 95-185, 95-54, 11 F.C.C. Rcd. 5020 (1996).

cent of the time. Under bill-and-keep, *B* would bear the cost of terminating all calls on its system, including the cost of terminating 99 percent of all calls originating from *A*'s subscribers. Conversely, *A* would bear the cost of terminating the calls from *B*'s subscribers; but by assumption those calls constitute only 1 percent of the total volume of calls placed. Thus, *B* would bear the cost of terminating 99 percent of all traffic and avoid the cost of terminating only 1 percent. Conversely, *A* would avoid the cost of terminating 99 percent of the calls that originated on its network. As *A*'s share of the market grew, its percentage of termination costs avoided would correspondingly fall.

Bill-and-keep is an alternative to explicit mutual compensation by *A* to *B* and *B* to *A*. The method could conceivably economize on transaction costs by obviating the computation and remittance of access charges in settings where the amount owed for flows from *A* to *B* would cancel out the amount owed for flows from *B* to *A*. For that reason, bill-and-keep may be an efficient regime of interconnection pricing in some two-way networks, as in the case of the clearance of checks or transactional paper (credit card receivables) between large numbers of banks. But in local telephony bill-and-keep will produce a lopsided system of implicit compensation, and hence a substantial subsidy to entrants, until the market shares of *A* and *B* become comparable. No doubt it was for that reason that the CPUC's Division of Ratepayer Advocates, which supported bill-and-keep, argued that, in making its interim compensation rule, the CPUC "may well have assumed that the amount of traffic exchanged would be equal in absolute numbers and thus the exchange would be revenue neutral."[133]

Two local exchange carriers, relying on the California Supreme Court's 1913 decision in *Pacific Telephone & Telegraph Co.* v. *Eshleman*,[134] challenged the CPUC's bill-and-keep rule as a taking on the ground that it constituted a forced sharing of their facilities with a competitor without compensation. In *Eshleman* (discussed more fully below) the California court ruled that the state could not subject the property of a public utility to use by its rival without compensation.[135] Yet, in response to the LECs' argument, in 1995 the CPUC ruled that the takings claims were "wholly lacking in merit."[136] One can hardly be surprised when a regulatory commission rejects an argument that it

133. 165 P.U.R.4th at 129.
134. 166 Cal. 640, 137 P. 1119 (1913).
135. 166 Cal. at 665, 137 P. at 1128.
136. 165 P.U.R.4th at 134.

has violated the Constitution. But even with that caveat in mind, the CPUC's treatment of the LECs' takings arguments was notably superficial and dismissive, particularly given the commission's abbreviated discussion of the U.S. Supreme Court's case law on takings.

In three successive paragraphs, the CPUC invoked the physical invasion, regulatory taking, and *Duquesne* lines of cases.[137] Even though the CPUC began its discussion of the law by noting that under *Duquesne* "the U.S. Supreme Court recognized that utility-related taking issues should be analyzed by focusing on whether rates properly compensate utilities for the property they have dedicated to public use," and even though the LECs emphasized the physical invasion of their networks that the interconnection rule entailed (and even though the CPUC *itself* cited *Loretto* as one of "the more important cases"), the commission inexplicably chose to analyze the LECs' taking claim under the standard least favorable to a regulated utility—namely, the three-part test enunciated in *Penn Central* and subsequently used by the Court in regulatory takings cases.[138] Indeed, the CPUC refused to follow *Eshleman* on the grounds that it was no longer in fashion:

> In the early part of this century, the California Supreme Court did hold that when we order a utility to allow its property to be used in a way that exceeds the limits of its "dedicated use," then our order is in effect a taking, even if it appears to be a mere regulation. (The "dedicated use" of a utility property, put simply, is the public purpose for which the utility has agreed to use or "dedicate" its property.) . . . Unfortunately, the *Eshleman* case, which in 1913 was one of the first cases decided under the Public Utilities Act, does not provide clear guidance for contemporary takings questions. While the [California Supreme] Court's wide-ranging discussion of our nature and authority in that case is an important initial construction of the Public Utilities Act, its approach to the taking issue relies on now-outdated principles of jurisprudence and was criticized even by contemporary commentators and jurists.[139]

Given the Court's 1982 decision in *Loretto*, given the five distinguishing factors discussed above that properly inform the limits of the

---

137. *Id.* at 132–33.
138. *Id.*
139. *Id.* at 133 (citing Pacific Tel. & Tel. *v.* Wright-Dickerson Hotel Co. (D. Or. 1914) (no citation given; cased evidently unreported); Annotation, *Right and Duty of Telephone Co. to Make Physical Connection*, 11 A.L.R. 1204, 1213 (1921)) (citation to *Eshleman* omitted).

Court's 1989 *Duquesne* decision concerning uncompensatory rate setting, and given the Court's invigoration of regulatory takings law by 1992 in *Lucas*, there was nothing "outdated" about the takings challenge to the CPUC's bill-and-keep rule. Nor should criticisms that commentators and lower courts lodged against *Eshleman* seventy years earlier trump the logic that motivates the Supreme Court's modern takings jurisprudence.

Instead of analyzing the bill-and-keep rule under the precedent of either the California Supreme Court or the U.S. Supreme Court, the CPUC invoked precedent of its own making in which it had stated:

> The jurisprudence of the takings clause presents scholars with nice doctrinal nuances and fine opportunities for subtle disputation. But we need not join that debate here . . . . Having accepted for so long the benefits of monopoly, [the LEC] may not now reclaim this property as its sole private fief. We may regulate that property pursuant to our authority and in so regulating may diminish its value.[140]

Despite the inherent asymmetry of implicit flows of compensation under bill-and-keep, the CPUC said that "[t]his cost allocation does not result in a diminution of the overall return to the LECs['] shareholders that is so low as to be confiscatory."[141] With that conclusion, the CPUC evidently believed that it had satisfied the requirements of *Duquesne* and *Hope*, for it next purported to apply "established doctrine relating to 'takings' outside the utility arena."[142]

That "established doctrine" consisted not of *Loretto*, but of *Penn Central*'s three-part test. The CPUC first examined the character of its regulation and found that its "regulation of how call termination is handled during the initiation of local exchange competition is a proper exercise of our authority over the LECs who hold their property not as a 'private fief' but in the public trust."[143] For reasons that the CPUC declined to explain, it asserted that "[t]he character of our regulation of call termination is not analogous to *Eshleman*."[144] With respect to the LECs' investment-backed expectations, the CPUC concluded that the LECs would "avoid paying to terminate their customers' traffic on a

---

140. 165 P.U.R.4th at 133 (quoting D.95-05-020, mimeo., at 20, 21).
141. *Id.* at 134.
142. *Id.*
143. *Id.*
144. *Id.*

CLC's network during the year that the requirement is in place" and that, even though the CPUC did "not yet know if 'bill-and-keep' will in fact fully compensate a carrier, it can at least be said that the carriers will receive some benefit."[145] Finally, the CPUC considered the magnitude of the economic harm that bill-and-keep would impose on the LECs:

> [I]t must be kept in mind that without some mechanism in place to deal with mutual call termination, local exchange competition cannot even begin. Moreover, during this first year of local exchange competition, we do not expect viable local competitors to be fully operative before the middle of 1996. Therefore, there is little risk of economic harm to [the LECs] from our interim approach. Even if one assumed that "bill-and-keep" would result in some cost to [the LECs], this cost will most likely be small, and it is a small price for these carriers to pay for the benefit they will gain as a result of the newly competitive environment for local telecommunications. In this new environment, [the LECs] may have much *greater* flexibility to enter new markets and *more control* over the rates which they can charge for their services.[146]

There is more than modest irony in that pronouncement, for the CPUC was in essence saying that the LECs were incapable of recognizing regulatory policies that would serve their self-interest. In the new competitive market that the CPUC described, the LECs could charge no more than competitive prices—namely, the same prices that existing regulation presumably would replicate. But by requiring uncompensatory interconnection pricing regulation on top of the existing regulatory contract, the CPUC was necessarily requiring the LECs to receive something *less* than a competitive return—either in the current regulated environment or in the future competitive environment—at least until the implicit subsidy that bill-and-keep creates for entrants had equalized the volume of calls terminating on the LECs' network and the entrants' networks. Stated differently, a given LEC would receive compensable interconnection prices under bill-and-keep only when it had so subsidized competitive entrants that its share of local exchange terminations had fallen to 50 percent.

The CPUC's decision is most startling for its unexplained refusal to analyze compensation for mandatory interconnection under the one

---

145. *Id.*
146. *Id.* (citation omitted) (emphasis in original).

line of Supreme Court cases most relevant to the facts—namely, *Loretto* and the other decisions concerning physical invasion. As explained earlier, the mandatory interconnection of CLCs to the networks of regulated local exchange carriers entails a physical invasion of the pathways of electrons and photons, just as the trackage rights problem entails the physical invasion of one railroad network by the locomotive owned by the interconnecting railroad. The California Supreme Court had the vision to grasp that point in 1913 in *Eshleman*. Eighty-two years later the state's utility regulators did not—or perhaps the CPUC merely realized that to consider *Eshleman* applicable would necessitate the finding that the bill-and-keep rule was an unconstitutional taking.

In *Eshleman* Justice Henshaw wrote for the California Supreme Court that the "'taking' of property within the meaning of the constitution is not restricted to a mere change of physical possession, but includes a permanent or temporary deprivation of the owner of its use."[147] He then quoted three treatises for the proposition that the mandatory order of trackage rights required the payment of just compensation to the incumbent railroad.[148] Those passages established that:

147. 166 Cal. at 664, 137 P. at 1127.
148. 166 Cal. at 664-65, 137 P. at 1127-28. In part, Justice Henshaw quoted an eminent domain treatise as follows:

[O]ne company cannot be authorized to take the joint use of another's tracks, except by an exercise of the eminent domain power. All the cases practically concede this by holding that compensation must be made. That it is competent for the legislature to authorize a railroad company to take the right to use the tracks of another railroad jointly, upon making compensation as required by the constitution, is a proposition almost unanimously supported by the authorities.

166 Cal. at 664, 137 P. at 1127 (quoting 2 JOHN LEWIS, A TREATISE ON THE LAW OF EMINENT DOMAIN IN THE UNITED STATES § 423 (Callaghan & Co., 3d ed. 1909)). He quoted a treatise on regulated industries as follows:

The principles discussed do not go so far as to give one common carrier the right to demand the use of the facilities of rival common carriers in order to compete against them. Thus it seems plain that one railroad cannot be required to make physical connection with its rival so that it may take its business away from it.

166 Cal. at 664, 137 P. at 1127-28 (quoting 1 BRUCE WYMAN, THE SPECIAL LAW GOVERNING PUBLIC SERVICE CORPORATIONS § 698 (Baker, Voohis & Co. 1911)). Finally, in relevant part, Justice Henshaw quoted a treatise on municipal franchises for the proposi-

This principle, it is to be noted, is not that the legislature, acting directly or through its authorized mandatories, may not subject property
devoted by its owners to a public use to another public use, or to the
same public use by its rivals, but that the doing of this is an act refer-
able to the power of eminent domain and not to the police power, and
that compensation must be made accordingly. Herein lies the vital distinction between the legitimate exercise of the police power and the
exercise of the power of eminent domain. In the former, uncompensated obedience to the order is imperative. In the latter, the order may not
be enforced without compensation first made. And, finally, it may not
be amiss to point out that the devotion to a public use by a person or
corporation of property held by them in ownership does not destroy
their ownership and does not vest title to the property in the public so
as to justify, under the exercise of police power, the taking away of the
management and control of the property from its owners without compensation, upon the ground that public convenience would better be
served thereby, or that the owners themselves have proven false or
derelict in the performance of their public duty. Any law or order seeking to do this passes beyond the ultimate limits of the police power,
however vague and undefined those limits may be.[149]

In *Eshleman* the incumbent local exchange carrier, Pacific Telephone,
also operated long-distance trunk lines. The Railroad Commission of
California, then the regulator of telephone companies, ordered Pacific
to provide interconnection to a competing LEC in each of two counties
and reasoned that Pacific would receive compensation in the form of
toll revenues for long-distance calls originating on the networks of the
competing LECs.

Notwithstanding the CPUC's reading of the case, *Eshleman* was
therefore directly relevant to the CPUC's reasoning in 1995 concerning
bill-and-keep. The commission concluded that the incumbent LECs will
eventually benefit under the flexibility of the new competitive environment even though the CPUC had no idea whether the bill-and-keep

---

tion that "the legislature cannot without compensation to the first company authorize the
second company to take or use the track of the first although with compensation this
might be done under the power of eminent domain if in its judgment the public good
required it." 166 Cal. at 664–65, 137 P. at 1128 (quoting JOHN FORREST DILLON, COM-
MENTARIES ON THE LAW OF MUNICIPAL CORPORATIONS § 727 (Little, Brown & Co., 4th
ed. 1890); JOHN FORREST DILLON, COMMENTARIES ON THE LAW OF MUNICIPAL CORPO-
RATIONS § 1280 (Little, Brown & Co., 5th ed. 1911)).

   149. 166 Cal. at 665, 137 P. at 1128.

arrangement would sufficiently compensate those LECs for providing mandatory interconnection for competitors in the present. Justice Henshaw rejected a similar argument in *Eshleman* when he wrote that "it cannot be contended . . . that an apportionment of rates or tolls for a service to be rendered in the future is a compensation for the present taking of property, and as little can it be said that the allocation of such rates and tolls to be earned in the future can ever measure up to the constitutional requirement that property shall not be taken without compensation first made and paid to the owner."[150]

The concurring opinion by Justice Sloss in *Eshleman* elaborates on the regulated firm's need for cost recovery, the potential for competitors to free ride on its investment, and the contractual purpose for which it dedicated its property for public use:

> By installing its long distance plant for the use of subscribers to its local systems, [Pacific] has developed an element of great value in the conduct of its local business at various points. It has thereby built up for itself an advantage, and a perfectly legitimate one, over competitors who, with a much smaller investment and at far smaller risk, have created only a local system. It has never offered to share this advantage with rival companies. To be compelled to so share it is to subject its property to a new use—and thus, in part, to take it. If the public interest requires the connection, appropriate provision for estimating and paying the damage occasioned thereby must be made.[151]

Whereas the CPUC's discussion of the modern version of such issues dismissed the possibility of a taking as "wholly lacking in merit," Justice Sloss's opinion instead recognized the complexity of determining an access price for mandatory interconnection that would satisfy the Takings Clause:

> A mere division of the tolls, even though the entire toll may be allotted to [Pacific], is not the compensation required as a condition to the taking of property for public use. In the first place, it is uncertain, both as to amount and time. In the next place, the division of tolls will only pay the company for the service actually rendered by it from time to time. It will not afford any compensation for the damage occasioned by the taking, i.e., by the subjecting of its property to the demands of a

---

150. 166 Cal. at 686–87, 137 P. at 1137 (citing Attorney-General *v.* Old Colony R.R., 160 Mass. 62, 35 N. E. 252 (1893)).
151. 166 Cal. at 701, 137 P. at 1143 (Sloss, J., concurring).

public service to which that property was not dedicated. What the measure of such damage is I do not attempt here to define, but it is plain that it includes elements not covered by a mere apportionment of tolls.[152]

One can read that passage to suggest that Justice Sloss intuitively recognized that the interconnection price must compensate the incumbent fully for its opportunity cost of providing network access to its competitor, and not simply for its long-run incremental cost. We return to that question in chapter 8.

UNCONSTITUTIONAL CONDITIONS ON THE
LIFTING OF INCUMBENT BURDENS

In *Dolan* v. *City of Tigard*, the Supreme Court saw a genuine problem of unconstitutional conditions in the much simpler context of land-use regulations: "Under the well-settled doctrine of 'unconstitutional conditions,' the government may not require a person to give up a constitutional right—here the right to receive just compensation when property is taken for a public use—in exchange for a discretionary benefit conferred by the government where the property sought has little or no relationship to the benefit."[153] Similarly, recognizing the potential for unconstitutional conditions in situations involving mandatory access, the Court in *Loretto* said that "a landlord's ability to rent his property may not be conditioned on his forfeiting the right to compensation for a physical occupation."[154] The same reasoning applies to local exchange carriers and electric utilities selling interconnection or unbundled access to competitive entrants into their markets. The government, for example, could not "require a landlord to devote a substantial portion of his building to vending and washing machines, with all profits to be retained by the owners of these services and with no compensation for the deprivation of space."[155] Consistent with its solicitude for property rights when they are physically invaded, the Court has been equally absolutist on the question of unconstitutional condi-

---

152. 166 Cal. at 701, 137 P. at 1143 (citation omitted).
153. 114 S. Ct. 2309, 2317 (1994) (citing Perry *v.* Sindermann, 408 U.S. 593 (1972); Pickering *v.* Board of Ed. of Township High School Dist., 391 U.S. 563, 568 (1968)).
154. 458 U.S. at 438 n.17.
155. *Id.*

tions: "The right of a property owner to exclude a stranger's physical occupation of his land cannot be so easily manipulated."[156]

Those statements put a new face on the relationship between mandatory access and the lifting of incumbent burdens. For example, under the Telecommunications Act of 1996 an RBOC confronts a quid pro quo for removal of the prohibition on its provision of interLATA services: To be granted permission to enter the interLATA market, the RBOC must sell its unbundled service elements at prices that are acceptable to the most formidable of its would-be competitors—namely, interexchange carriers that seek to enter the local access market on a resale basis. Those established interexchange carriers demand the sale of unbundled elements at or below long-run incremental cost, which is not a compensatory price.[157] Thus, for the RBOC the process of securing relief from its incumbent burdens becomes an exercise in unconstitutional conditions.

THE INAPPLICABILITY OF
MARKET STREET RAILWAY

Opponents of stranded cost recovery frequently cite the Supreme Court's 1945 decision in *Market Street Railway Co.* v. *Railroad Commission of California*[158] for the proposition that no taking of property occurs when the government breaches the regulatory contract. That reliance is misplaced for several reasons.

Market Street Railway involved a privately owned railway operating a street car and bus line in and around San Francisco. Increased competition from other forms of transportation, such as buses and automobiles—as well as direct, probably taxpayer-subsidized competition from a municipally owned railway—had eroded the railway's passenger base and financial condition. In 1937 the railway began petitioning the state railway commission for a fare increase from five to seven cents. The commission approved the seven-cent fare in 1939. Initially, the increased fare produced no increase in revenues; passenger traffic continued to decline, no doubt at least partly in response to the higher fare. Meanwhile, the city railway continued to charge only five cents. Al-

---

156. *Id.*

157. PAUL W. MACAVOY, THE FAILURE OF ANTITRUST AND REGULATION TO ESTABLISH COMPETITION IN LONG-DISTANCE TELEPHONE SERVICES 200–10 (MIT Press & AEI Press 1996).

158. 324 U.S. 548 (1945).

though demand subsequently increased as a result of conditions caused by World War II, the commission became concerned about the continued deterioration of service. It instituted an inquiry into both the reasonableness of the rates and the adequacy of service. The commission concluded the inquiry by ordering an experimental decrease in the fare from seven to six cents, partly because it hoped to increase revenues by stimulating demand. The company obtained a delay in implementing the new fare pending judicial review and eventually it sold its properties to the city's municipally owned railway.

The U.S. Supreme Court affirmed the California Supreme Court and ruled that the commission's order that the railway company reduce its base cash fare from seven to six cents did not deprive the Market Street Railway of its property without due process of law under the Fourteenth Amendment of the U.S. Constitution. Although the company advanced numerous procedural and substantive arguments, its central objection was the commission's decision, when calculating the new six-cent fare, to use a rate base of $7,950,000, the amount at which the company had offered to sell its properties to the city. The lower fare, the company argued, compelled the company to operate at a loss. By relying on the sales amount, the company contended that the commission improperly disregarded "reproduction cost, historical cost, prudent investment, or capitalization bases, on any of which under conventional accounting the six-cent fare would produce no return on its property and would force a substantial operating deficit upon the Company."[159]

Three factors distinguish *Market Street Railway* from the present cases of electric utilities and local exchange carriers attempting to recover their stranded costs. First, the company's costs became stranded because of changing economic and technological forces, not because of decisions by the regulatory body or other changes in law and regulation. The Court repeatedly emphasized that the streetcar industry was growing obsolete for reasons beyond the control of either the company or regulators: "It has long been recognized that this form of transportation could be preserved only by the most complete cooperation between management and public and the most enlightened efforts to make the service attractive to patrons."[160] Indeed, a close reading of the case suggests that natural disaster made the Market Street Railway an especially unlucky firm in an already necrotizing industry. The railway

159. *Id*. at 553–54.
160. *Id*. at 565.

"suffered greatly from the earthquake and fire of 1906, but carried out a considerable program of reconstruction between 1906 and 1910."[161] Thus, in an industry already losing customers as the result of exogenous changes in technology and market demand, the devastation of 1906 suddenly required this particular street railway to make substantial *new* investment in nonsalvageable assets. Such investment was directly contrary to the trend of falling (and, by 1916, consistently *negative*) net capital expenditures in that industry.[162] By 1919 the Court noted, the secretary of commerce and the secretary of labor had advised President Woodrow Wilson that the urban street railway industry as a whole was "virtually bankrupt."[163] Because the railway owed its deterioration to industry-wide conditions and market forces rather than any acts or omissions by regulators, there could be no constitutional violation:

> The due process clause has been applied to prevent governmental destruction of existing economic values. It has not and cannot be applied to insure values or to restore values that have been lost by the operation of economic forces.[164]

Unlike the streetcar industry of the early twentieth century, today's electric power industry does not face steadily diminishing demand for electricity and the looming obsolescence of its transmission and distribution infrastructure. The same is true of local exchange telecommunications and the continued demand to use the infrastructure of the incumbent LEC.[165] Not surprisingly, in 1957 the U.S. Court of Appeals

---

161. *Id.* at 555.

162. MELVILLE J. ULMER, CAPITAL IN TRANSPORTATION, COMMUNICATIONS, AND PUBLIC UTILITIES: ITS FORMATION AND FINANCING 402–06 & tab. F-1 (National Bureau of Economic Research & Princeton University Press 1960). Ulmer attributed the decline of the street railway industry as a whole to competition and the industry's inability "to produce services over a range of grades sufficient to counterbalance the tendency toward a declining income elasticity of demand." *Id.* at 89.

163. 324 U.S. at 565 n.8.

164. *Id.* at 567.

165. An earlier Supreme Court decision, Public Serv. Comm'n of Montana v. Great N. Utils. Co., 289 U.S. 130 (1933), is sometimes cited as consistent with *Market Street Railway*. The similarity is merely rhetorical and consists of the statements that "[t]he loss of, or failure to obtain, patronage, due to competition, does not justify the imposition of charges that are exorbitant and unjust to the public," and that takings jurisprudence "does not protect public utilities against such business hazards." *Id.* at 135. The case, however, concerned a municipality's refusal to authorize a utility holding a nonexclusive franchise to *lower* its rates sufficiently to stem the loss of sales to a competing entrant. In apparent disregard for the existence of the antitrust laws, the Court said that the incumbent utility

for the D.C. Circuit ruled that the holding in *Market Street Railway* "has no application, as the opinion shows, to a dynamic industry which is in the midst of phenomenal growth."[166] The court emphasized that predictions of a regulated industry's demise from exogenous forces of technology or competition must have a reasonable time horizon: The holding in *Market Street Railway* "would not have applied to the ordinary metropolitan street railway company at the turn of the century, when the industry was flourishing and traction stocks had gilt edges, on the mere possibility of a drastically depressing economic change such as occurred with the advent of the automobile."[167]

Second, the expected obsolescence of the streetcar infrastructure drastically undermined the Market Street Railway's ability to argue that a higher rate of return was essential to attract future capital investment. As the Court explained, prior decisions involving economically viable utility companies are largely inapplicable to industries shortly to be relegated to the dustbin of history:

> It is idle to discuss holdings of cases or to distinguish quotations in decisions of this or other courts which have dealt with utilities whose economic situation would yield a permanent profit, denied or limited only by public regulation. While the Company does not assert that it would be economically practicable to obtain a return on its investment, it strongly contends that the order is confiscatory by the tests of *Federal Power Commission* v. *Hope Natural Gas Co.*, 320 U.S. 591, 603, 605, from which it claims to be entitled to a return "sufficient to assure confidence in the financial integrity of the enterprise, so as to maintain its credit and to attract capital" and to "enable the company to operate successfully, to maintain its financial integrity, to attract capital, and to compensate its investors for the risks assumed." Those considerations . . . concerned a company which had advantage of an economic position which promised to yield what was held to be an excessive return

"insists that it has a constitutional right by unrestrained cutting of rates to destroy the competitor." *Id.* The facts reported in the Court's opinion, however, confirm that any such predatory scheme, if it indeed was attempted, failed miserably. Moreover, as we note in chapter 3, the durability of the infrastructure built by a facilities-based entrant into a network industry makes predation all the more implausible. Suffice it to say, *Great Northern Utilities* does not illuminate the issue of deregulatory takings, other than to show the Court's inability to recognize in 1933 that minimum price regulation was thwarting the incumbent firm's efforts to mitigate stranded costs by reducing price below its competitor's.

166. Cincinnati Gas & Elec. Co. *v.* FPC, 246 F.2d 688, 692 (D.C. Cir. 1957).

167. *Id.*

on its investment and on its securities. They obviously are inapplicable to a company whose financial integrity already is hopelessly undermined, which could not attract capital on any possible rate, and where investors recognize as lost a part of what they have put in.[168]

Electric utilities and incumbent local exchange carriers, in contrast, are likely after mandatory unbundling to need to raise capital on a routine and recurring basis.

There is a third crucial distinction between Market Street Railway's predicament and the regulatory situation currently facing electric utilities and incumbent local exchange carriers. The regulatory body in *Market Street Railway* apparently was making a good-faith attempt to improve the company's competitive position to the extent feasible in the face of overwhelming competition from other providers. There was no expectation or requirement, however, that the private railway company would be forced to share its bottleneck infrastructure with the municipal railway or other private transportation companies without adequate compensation for forgone revenues or recovery of its sunk costs. In contrast, retail wheeling and unbundling of the local exchange envision an otherwise solvent incumbent firm's being mandated to provide competitors access to its reticulation infrastructure. Had the commission in *Market Street Railway* imposed similar requirements on the company—for example, by forcing it to make its tracks available to the city's cars or its own idle cars available to the city for use on the city's lines—and had the industry otherwise been healthy, the Court would presumably have reached a different result.

Finally, *Market Street Railway* may be distinguishable as a case of opportunistic behavior by the city in operating the municipal railway. The private company competed on some routes against the municipally owned railway, which wanted to expand by acquiring the company's routes. Further, the company charged a higher price than the city line yet was still losing money, which suggests that the city might have been subsidizing the railway's incremental cost of operation through tax receipts—which no private company, of course, could do. The Court paid little attention to the city's competitive privileges. Perhaps it ignored the issue in the recognition that municipalization of the private railway was the only way to preserve the streetcar industry.

In 1997 the Public Utility Commission of Texas read *Market Street Railway* to imply that the Takings Clause does not "guarantee a utility

---

168. 324 U.S. at 566.

a return in the face of a more successful competitor."[169] In 1996 a state trial court in New York, relying on *Market Street Railway*, characterized the question posed by the recovery of stranded costs in the electric power industry as one of "whether utilities, as a matter of law, are entitled to rates that are designed to recover all competitive losses, irrespective of the impact that such rates would have on consumers or a State's economy."[170] Both propositions are red herrings that reveal the depth of the contemporary misunderstanding of *Market Street Railway* that exists among regulators and jurists.[171] *Market Street Railway* did not concern investments by a regulated firm that had become unrecoverable (less "useful" in the jargon of utility regulation) because of a change in *regulatory* policy. To the contrary, the regulatory action taking place in that case was a rate decision that reflected the regulator's conclusion that exogenous changes in the market demand for street railway service had reduced the viability of a regulated enter-

---

169. *E.g.*, Application of Central Power and Light Co. for Authority to Change Rates, Proposal for Decision, Order, Dkt. No. 14965, at 81 ¶ 64 (Pub. Util. Comm'n Tex. Mar. 31, 1997).

170. Energy Ass'n of N.Y. State *v.* Public Serv. Comm'n of N.Y., 169 Misc. 2d 924, 942 (Sup. Ct., Albany County 1996). The opinion begins with a metaphor drawn from Greek mythology:

> In mythological times fire was the exclusive property of the gods. When Prometheus, a Titan, broke the monopoly of the gods and brought the gift of fire to mankind, so incensed were the gods that they caused Prometheus to be chained to a great rock where during the day an eagle devoured his liver. During the night his liver regenerated and the process continued until Prometheus was freed by Hercules.
>
> We turn now to the real world. Fire no longer belongs to the gods, but to the People. The overriding issue of this case is the mode to be followed by the People for generation, transmission and distribution of fire, transmogrified in the context of this case into electric energy—monopolistic or competitive, or some gradation in between. There is no question that the People . . . have the ultimate right to choose . . . what that mode shall look like.

Id. at 927. The court later states: "Prometheus' act of courage and beneficence in breaking the monopoly of the gods by giving electrical energy to mankind—and its terrible consequences to him—may not be demeaned by a mere transfer of that monopoly to the lords of industry, for the benefit only of some and not of all. It was a gift to *mankind*, not a gift to a favored few." *Id.* at 937 (emphasis in original).

171. For similar misinterpretations of *Market Street Railway*, see Restructuring of the Electric Utility Industry in Vermont, Dkt. No. 5854 (Vt. Pub. Serv. Bd. Dec. 30, 1996); Restructuring New Hampshire's Electric Utility Industry, DR 96-150 Order No. 22,514, 175 P.U.R.4th 193 (New Hamp. Pub. Utils. Comm'n 1997).

prise providing such service. If a more successful competitor has arrived, as the Texas commission posits, then the relevant question that *Market Street Railway* poses is, How did the competitor get there in the first place and achieve its success over the incumbent utility? Did the regulator endogenously change the regulatory regime to permit entry that frustrated the incumbent utility's reasonable opportunity for cost recovery, which was the means by which the municipality (and later the state commission) originally induced the utility to make its nonsalvageable investment? If so, then *Market Street Railway* in no way undermines the conclusion that the Takings Clause requires the payment of just compensation. Alternatively, did the utility's revenues collapse in the face of exogenous changes in either technology or market demand—changes that incidentally accrued to the competitor's benefit? If so, then *Market Street Railway* supports the conclusion that the Takings Clause does not require the state to compensate the incumbent utility for its lost opportunity to recover its costs. What if the answer to both questions is yes? In such a case of joint causation—where endogenous regulatory change occurred simultaneously with exogenous changes in technology and market demand—careful factual analysis will be necessary to attribute to each causal factor the correct portion of the incumbent's costs that that particular factor has rendered unrecoverable. The portion attributable to endogenous regulatory change will, of course, deserve just compensation under the Takings Clause.

NORTHERN PACIFIC RAILWAY AND THE REGULATOR'S REDEFINITION OF THE INTENDED USE OF DEDICATED PROPERTY

The Supreme Court's 1915 decision in *Northern Pacific Railway Co. v. North Dakota* has great relevance to the mandatory unbundling of network access now occurring or expected to occur imminently in local telephony and in the electric power industry, for the decision emphasizes that once a regulated utility has dedicated private property to a public purpose, the government cannot appropriate that property for a different purpose.[172] The case involved a challenge by two railroad companies to a North Dakota statute setting maximum rates on the intrastate carriage of coal. The railroads claimed that the rates forced them to carry coal at a loss or at an uncompensatory rate (taking into

---

172. 236 U.S. 585 (1915).

account a competitive return to capital) and therefore constituted a taking of private property. Although the North Dakota Supreme Court agreed that the rates forced the companies to carry coal at a uncompensatory rate, it nonetheless deemed those rates not to be confiscatory because the companies overall continued to earn a reasonable return on their intrastate business.

The Supreme Court reversed. It held that the statute was an attempt to take a carrier's property without due process of law in violation of the Fourteenth Amendment. Although the state enjoys broad power to regulate private property devoted to a public use, Justice Charles Evans Hughes, writing for the eight-member majority, stressed that, "the State does not enjoy the freedom of an owner."[173] That the state may reasonably regulate to ensure that a carrier fairly discharges the obligations of its charter does not mean that state may redefine the public use to which the carrier's property is dedicated, even if the carrier's total business continues to earn a sufficient return:

> The fact that the property is devoted to a public use on certain terms does not justify the requirement that it shall be devoted to other public purposes, or to the same use on other terms, or the imposition of restrictions that are not reasonably concerned with the proper conduct of the business according to the undertaking which the carrier has expressly or impliedly assumed. . . . The public interest cannot be invoked as a justification for demands which pass the limits of reasonable protection and seek to impose upon the carrier and its property burdens that are not incident to its engagement. In such a case, it would be no answer to say that the carrier obtains from its entire intrastate business a return as to the sufficiency of which in the aggregate it is not entitled to complain.[174]

As an example, Justice Hughes stated that if the firm "has held itself out as a carrier of passengers only, it cannot be compelled to carry freight."[175] That simple example from 1915 has a counterpart in the debates of the late 1990s over mandatory unbundling of access to telephony and electric power networks: If the regulated firm has held itself out as an integrated network providing service directly to customers, can it be compelled to rededicate that network to providing service to other (unregulated) firms that compete with the regulated firm for sales

---

173. *Id.* at 595. The lone dissenter, Justice Pitney, wrote no opinion.
174. *Id.* at 595–96.
175. *Id.*

to retail customers? *Northern Pacific Railway* says no. Given the relevance of that answer, it is remarkable that the public debate over the Telecommunications Act of 1996 appears never to have considered the question.

Northern Pacific Railway also established that the proposed redefinition is not made any more constitutionally permissible by the fact that the state intends that redefinition to serve an important public policy goal that materially benefits the state's residents. The Court considered it beside the point that North Dakota believed that the rates would "aid in the development of a local industry," an industry whose "infancy" and potential "to confer a benefit upon the people of the State" were matters of sincere concern to the state.[176] North Dakota's goal of "making the community less dependent upon fuel supplies imported into the State"[177] could not justify its resorting to an appropriation of private property as the means to achieve that objective:

> [W]hile local interests serve as a motive for enforcing reasonable rates, it would be a very different matter to say that the State may compel the carrier to maintain a rate upon a particular commodity that is less than reasonable, or—as might equally well be asserted—to carry gratuitously, in order to build up a local enterprise. That would be to go outside the carrier's undertaking, and outside the field of reasonable supervision of the conduct of its business, *and would be equivalent to an appropriation of the property to public uses upon terms to which the carrier had in no way agreed.*[178]

That passage illuminates the contemporary debate over the regulatory contract because its logic rests on the consensual nature of regulation: The firm dedicates its private property to a public purpose only as the result of voluntary exchange. Justice Hughes emphasized throughout the opinion that, although the legislature's discretion to set both general and particular rates is extremely wide and such rates enjoy a presumption of reasonableness, it is another matter entirely when the state acts to alter fundamentally the obligations imposed on the carrier by its acceptance of the original regulatory contract: "The constitutional guaranty protects the carrier from arbitrary action and from the appro-

176. *Id.* at 598.
177. *Id.*
178. *Id.* (emphasis added).

priation of its property to public purposes outside the under-taking assumed . . . ."[179]

The Court's emphasis on the original understanding of the intended use of regulated property in *Northern Pacific Railway* sheds light on why, and the degree to which, the regulated firm would have willingly opted for asset specificity rather than asset generality in making its investments. If the regulated firm had expected that it could be required to use its dedicated property for a purpose other than that for which such property was originally dedicated, then the firm would have borne the risk that, in the newly designated purpose, the property might fail to earn a sufficient return originally understood by the utility and the municipality to be necessary to allow the firm to recover that capital and a competitive return on such capital over its useful life. Faced with such risk, the firm presumably would have opted instead for a different kind of capital having a lesser degree of asset specificity or a shorter useful life, or both. While investment in that alternative kind of capital would have reduced the risk to the regulated firm of having its regulated property redirected to an originally unintended use, that investment might not have been the most efficient capital in terms of minimizing the cost to society of producing the service in question. If so, then the regulator's rededication of the use of the dedicated property would impose a social cost.

There is an additional implication, relating to entry regulation, of the requirement that the regulator not rededicate the use to which regulated property is to be put. Some states have long forbidden municipalities to grant exclusive franchises for the provision of services such as local telephony and electricity.[180] Given that the absence of franchise exclusivity raised the risk that a utility would not receive a reasonable opportunity to recover its irreversible and nonsalvageable investment in network infrastructure, and given that the utility's rates were regulated not to exceed just and reasonable levels, why would the utility's investors nonetheless have been willing to risk their capital in that manner? Perhaps such investors received a risk premium relative to the return on capital for utilities in jurisdictions that did not forbid franchise exclusivity. But it seems at least as likely that such a premium was unnecessary because the risk was not appreciable. In other words, investors even in jurisdictions that forbade franchise exclusivity may have taken sufficient comfort in knowing that their transaction-specific

179. *Id.* at 604.
180. E.g., TEX. CONST. art. I, § 26.

investments were dedicated to a *specific purpose*—the provision of retail services *directly to customers* in the municipality that granted the franchise. Since the Supreme Court's decision in the *Express Package Cases* in 1885, it had been clear under the common law of common carriage that a public utility could not be required to sell interconnection to another carrier.[181] And early cases such as *Pacific Telephone & Telegraph Co.* v. *Eshleman*, decided by the California Supreme Court in 1913, emphasized that a regulator could not mandate unbundled network access to accommodate a competitor, and that a state legislature could do so *only if* it paid just compensation to the incumbent utility.[182] Thus, when investors built the first local telephone and electricity networks under nonexclusive franchises, it would not have occurred to them, or to the municipality franchising them, that the municipality (or its successor, the state public utilities commission) might subsequently rededicate such regulated property to the purpose of providing a rival firm the infrastructure with which to lure away the incumbent utility's retail customers. Indeed, the early years of local telephony witnessed a race among competing facilities-based LECs with overlapping networks to maximize subscribership within a service area.[183]

The one form of potential competition that the utility and the municipality did originally envision was of a completely different sort. If competition were to occur, it would take the form of another utility's receiving another nonexclusive franchise to build its own transaction-specific infrastructure. Yet, such facilities-based entry was not expected to occur because local exchange carriers and electric utilities were thought to be natural monopolies; indeed, such entry was considered futile and wasteful. That is the reason that entry regulation taking the form of the prior grant of certificates of necessity and convenience placed so much emphasis on avoiding duplicative facilities. In other words, neither the municipality nor the original franchised utility ever expected that competitive entry would take the form of mandated access to the incumbent's network.

Furthermore, if the incumbent's network was to be occupied—in any degree—by some party other than the utility that owned it, that

181. 117 U.S. 1 (1885); *see* MICHAEL K. KELLOGG, JOHN THORNE & PETER W. HUBER, FEDERAL TELECOMMUNICATIONS LAW 13–14 (Little, Brown & Co. 1992).

182. 166 Cal. 640, 664–65, 137 P. 1119, 1127–28 (1913).

183. MILTON L. MUELLER, JR., UNIVERSAL SERVICE: COMPETITION, INTERCONNECTION, AND MONOPOLY IN THE MAKING OF THE AMERICAN TELEPHONE SYSTEM 59–60 (MIT Press & AEI Press 1997).

party was understood to be the municipality itself. Some franchise agreements gave the municipality the option to buy out the utility's network at the end of the franchise term for a price voluntarily negotiated by the parties or, in the case of deadlock, for a price set by arbitration.[184] "Recapture" was the name given that form of public buyout of the utility. As Irston R. Barnes wrote in 1942:

> The long-term franchise may contain a recapture clause, combined with a provision for the amortization of the utility's investment out of its earnings. Such a clause requires the management to use surplus earnings for the amortization of the investment, presumably through the retirement of outstanding securities. At the end of the franchise period, the municipality has the right to assume title to the utility property on payment of the unamortized investment, or the municipality may even have the right to provide for a transfer of the property to another corporation, or the right to recapture may be operative at stated intervals after a designated period.[185]

Of course, at any time *during* the franchise term the municipality independently had the option simply to exercise eminent domain over the utility's network, which would trigger an analogous valuation process for determining just compensation for the forced buyout.

Northern Pacific Railway has relevance to current policies on network unbundling such as the FCC's 1996 interconnection order.[186] To price mandatory access to the incumbent LEC's network elements, the FCC introduced the concept of total *element* long-run incremental cost (TELRIC), which is to be distinguished from total *service* long-run

---

184. *E.g.*, An Ordinance Granting to Central Power and Light Company, Its Successors and Assigns, an Electric Light, Heat and Power Franchise, Corpus Christi, Texas § 4 (July 2, 1935) ("Upon the termination of this grant, the grant as well as the property, if any, of the Grantee in the streets, avenues and other public places, in the then city limits of the City of Corpus Christi, shall thereupon, upon a fair valuation thereof being paid to the Grantee, be and become the property of the City of Corpus Christi, and the Grantee shall never be entitled to any payment or valuation because of any value derived from the franchise or the fact that it is or may be a going concern duly installed and operated, provided, however, it shall be optional with the City of Corpus Christi whether or not it acquires title to said properties in said manner. . . .").

185. IRSTON R. BARNES, THE ECONOMICS OF PUBLIC UTILITY REGULATION 220 (F. S. Crofts & Co. 1942).

186. Implementation of the Local Competition Provisions in the Telecommunications Act of 1996, Interconnection Between Local Exchange Carriers and Commercial Mobile Radio Service Providers, First Report and Order, CC Dkt. Nos. 96-98, 95-185, 11 F.C.C. Rcd. 15,499 (1996).

incremental cost (TSLRIC). TELRIC embodies more than a new kind of costing exercise. It reflects a fundamental redefinition of the output of the regulated local exchange carrier. In the past, the output of a LEC consisted of services. After the FCC's 1996 interconnection order, discussed in chapters 9 and 12, the incumbent LEC's output has been redefined to consist of elements, which are intermediate inputs. The difference is significant in at least two respects.

First, the incumbent LEC built its network in the manner that it did so that it could discharge an obligation to serve—that is, to provide services to consumers. The incumbent LEC, however, now faces both an ongoing obligation to provide services to consumers and a new obligation to supply elements to competitors. The latter was never contemplated when the incumbent LEC dedicated the private property of its investors to a public purpose.

Second, there will likely be significant transaction costs of using the incumbent LEC's network to provide elements rather than services as its intended output. Those new costs are a cost of achieving the benefits that Congress and the FCC envisioned from the mandatory unbundling of local telephony. But it is neither efficient nor constitutional to make the shareholders of incumbent LECs absorb those costs. Rather, such costs must be fully recovered in the rates that an incumbent LEC may charge for unbundled elements. If demand conditions preclude setting prices at a sufficiently high level to recover those costs, then an end-user charge must be employed to recover the residual amount of cost beyond what can be recouped through the market-allowed price.

The Misinterpretation of Judge Starr's Concurrence in *Jersey Central*

Opponents of stranded cost recovery also sometimes cite Judge Kenneth Starr's 1987 concurring opinion in *Jersey Central Power & Light* v. *FERC*[187] as support for their view that there is no constitutional basis for recovery of stranded costs. That reliance is misplaced. It overstates the significance of the concurring opinion and mischaracterizes its meaning.

In *Jersey Central*, the electric utility contested FERC's decision to reduce the company's rates. Jersey Central sought to recover through higher rates a portion of the unamortized costs associated with its sus-

---

187. 810 F.2d 1168 (D.C. Cir. 1987).

pended construction of a nuclear power plant. Although all parties agreed that the investment was prudent when made, political and economic conditions had changed so drastically that Jersey Central after several years decided to abandon the project. The company proposed an arrangement by which investors and consumers would share the losses. FERC summarily rejected the proposal and issued an order that excluded the unamortized portion of the investment in the cancelled plant.

As a result, the company alleged that its financial position was precarious and that it was severely handicapped in raising new capital to meet its statutory obligations. Nonetheless, FERC repeatedly refused to hold an evidentiary hearing on the reasonableness of the rates imposed or to provide the court with a clear and consistent explanation of its position. To the extent that the agency provided an explanation, it appeared to argue that the precedential effect of its prior decisions required application of the "used and useful" test without need of a hearing to consider other factors, such as the impact of its decision on the company's financial status, its investors, and its ability to attract capital.

It bears emphasis that the question of whether FERC's order constituted an unconstitutional taking was *not* before the D.C. Circuit. Rather, the questions the court decided were, first, whether FERC was obligated under *Federal Power Commission* v. *Hope Natural Gas Co.*[188] to provide Jersey Central with a hearing to determine whether its rates were "just and reasonable" and, second, what the proper scope of judicial review of such a determination was. The majority opinion by Judge Robert H. Bork—joined by Judges Laurence H. Silberman, James L. Buckley, and Ruth Bader Ginsburg (now Justice Ginsburg)—analyzed the requirements of *Hope*. The court held that, when a rate is claimed to be beyond "just and reasonable" boundaries, FERC must carefully consider the total impact of the rate—not only on consumers, but on investors as well—and that the agency's findings must be based on substantial evidence in the record.[189] A court reviewing that decision must ensure that the end result of the commission's order "constitutes a reasonable balancing, based on factual findings, of the investor interest in maintaining financial integrity and access to capital markets and the consumer interest in being charged non-exploitative rates."[190]

The court repeatedly stressed that, under *Hope*, the issue is not whether the particular method used to determine the rate is in itself "reasonable," but whether the end result is reasonable in light of all

188. 320 U.S. 591 (1944).
189. 810 F.2d at 1177–78.
190. *Id.* at 1178.

pertinent factors, including the company's financial status. The court further noted that the "used and useful" test has "ceased to have any constitutional significance" and is now "simply one of several permissible tools of ratemaking, one that need not be, and is not, employed in every instance."[191] Additionally, "the commission [is] not obligated to exclude from the rate base all property not presently 'used and useful,' but was free to include prudent but cancelled investments."[192]

In his separate opinion, Judge Starr concurred with both the result and the reasoning of the majority's opinion. He did not depart from or criticize the opinion in any manner, however slight. As in the majority opinion, moreover, Judge Starr chided FERC for appearing to shirk its statutory obligations under *Hope* by summary application of the "used and useful" test. The Commission, he observed, "in order to engage in reasoned decisionmaking, has a duty to consider the entire financial circumstances confronting the utility, . . . not to rely blindly on precedents which do not involve similarly situated utilities facing the most dire financial consequences."[193]

The remainder of Judge Starr's concurring opinion is devoted to an interesting but gratuitous discussion of when a taking of investor property occurs in a rate regulation case—a question that Judge Starr explicitly stated was *not* before the court,[194] but which he felt on remand FERC would have to consider as part of its *Hope* analysis. Judge Starr's view of a proper takings standard in a rate regulation case is indistinguishable from the "just and reasonable" statutory standard set forth in *Hope* and in the majority opinion in *Jersey Central*. A taking occurs, said Judge Starr, "only when a regulated rate is confiscatory, which is a short-hand way of saying that an unreasonable balance has been struck in the regulation process so as unreasonably to favor ratepayer interests at the substantial expense of investor interests."[195]

Judge Starr simply expressed his personal opinion that in a rate case he prefers that constitutional analysis be based on a balancing of interests rather than on mechanical application of any one rule. Moreover, whatever the merits of Judge Starr's approach with respect to losses truly imposed by changes in market conditions, his views provide less

---

191. *Id.* at 1175.
192. *Id.* at 1177 (citing Washington Gas Light Co. *v.* Baker, 188 F.2d 11, 19 (D.C. Cir. 1950)).
193. *Id.* at 1188–89 (Starr, J., concurring).
194. *Id.* at 1189.
195. *Id.*

guidance in determining the proper balance to be struck where the losses have been imposed by the regulator as a result of abrogation of the regulatory contract. Indeed, Judge Starr asserted earlier in his concurrence that, in the case of Jersey Central's canceled nuclear plant, "a taking of investment funds in the . . . project would have occurred if government *so regulated as to prevent the property, in whole or in part, from being employed in the manner desired by the owner.*"[196] Although those conditions did not occur in *Jersey Central*, they obviously are present when regulators order an electric utility to provide access to its facilities to competitors. It could not be clearer that retail wheeling prevents the property "in whole or in part, from being used in the manner desired by the owner." The same is true of mandatory unbundling of the local exchange.

Furthermore, opponents of stranded cost recovery evidently fail to recognize the entire basis for Judge Starr's reasoning that takings analysis in rate cases requires a balancing of interests rather than an application of the prudent investment, used and useful, or other cost recovery rule. The foundation for that conclusion, Judge Starr stated explicitly, is the existence of a regulatory contract:

> The utility business represents a compact of sorts; a monopoly on service in a particular geographical area (coupled with state-conferred rights of eminent domain or condemnation) is granted to the utility in exchange for a regime of intensive regulation, including price regulation, quite alien to the free market. Each party to the compact gets something in the bargain. As a general rule, utility investors are provided a level of stability in earnings and value less likely to be attained in the unregulated or moderately regulated sector; in turn, ratepayers are afforded universal, non-discriminatory service and protection from monopolistic profits through political control over an economic enterprise.[197]

In other words, the foundation for Judge Starr's analysis is the existence of the very regulatory contract that opponents of stranded cost recovery assert does not exist or has no legal effect to ensure that the utility has a reasonable opportunity to recover the full costs of its nonsalvageable investments.

Because the regulatory contract provides the utility the benefits of entry regulation to facilitate recovery of the cost of nonsalvageable

196. *Id.* at 1190 (emphasis added).
197. *Id.* at 1189 (citation omitted).

investments, Judge Starr was understandably concerned that ratepayers not be forced unjustly to bear a disproportionate share of losses that, in an unregulated market, would have been borne entirely by investors and that did not result from any act or omission of regulators. As Judge Starr himself recognized, the analysis necessarily changes in cases where the losses are imposed not by any external market force, but by the regulator's own act or omission. Such an instance would occur when the regulator repudiates the regulatory contract by withdrawing entry regulation without providing for an alternative mechanism to recover the cost of the utility's nonsalvageable investments and to defray the cost of any incumbent burdens that the regulator chooses to leave in place.

CONCLUSION

This chapter has reviewed the economic and legal rationales for protecting property from government confiscation. We have seen how each of the three lines of takings cases would shed light on a deregulatory taking in the telecommunications or electric power industry. A case involving a deregulatory taking would be a case of first impression. Nonetheless, under established takings jurisprudence, a breach of the regulatory contract, including the mandatory unbundling of the utility's infrastructure, would constitute a taking of property if not accompanied by offsetting mechanisms to recover stranded costs and to end continuing incumbent burdens. The government's unilateral repudiation of the regulatory contract would require the payment of just compensation. How one should determine such compensation is the question to which we now turn.

7

Just Compensation for
Deregulatory Takings

AT WHAT MAGNITUDE is the compensation paid for a taking of private property "just"? Compensation for involuntary exchange is just when it is equivalent to the compensation that could be derived from voluntary exchange. Another way of stating the proposition is that the property owner is treated justly when he is made to be indifferent between voluntarily selling his asset in the market and submitting to the state's power of eminent domain to condemn his asset for public use.[1]

A defense raised against claims for compensation for deregulatory takings is that the government has already provided implicit compensation—what might be termed deregulatory "givings"—in return for the takings associated with the changing regulatory regime. Such givings may take several forms, including price deregulation, changes in regulatory obligations, relaxation of incumbent burdens, or lifting of regulatory quarantines. Givings are essentially compensation "in kind." The value of such in-kind transfers and the conditions placed on them determine whether a giving constitutes just compensation for the taking in question. The takings situation differs from the usual rule in contract law, under which a court ordinarily will not review the sufficiency of the

---

1. *See* RICHARD A. EPSTEIN, TAKINGS: PRIVATE PROPERTY AND THE POWER OF EMINENT DOMAIN 182 (Harvard University Press 1985) ("In principle, the ideal solution is to leave the individual owner in a position of indifference between the taking by the government and retention of the property.").

consideration in the contract.[2] In the contractual setting, the sufficiency of the consideration flows directly from the fact that a contract rests on voluntary exchange. At the time of the contract's formation, each party held expectations that the contract would make him better off; otherwise, no consensual transaction would have occurred. In contrast, a taking of property by the government exemplifies involuntary exchange. The coercive nature of the transaction makes it necessary ex post to judge the sufficiency of the giving by which the government claims to have implicitly compensated its taking of private property.

JUST COMPENSATION AND
VOLUNTARY EXCHANGE

The economic reasoning that just compensation should replicate the outcome of voluntary exchange corresponds to the general principle in both American constitutional law[3] and English common law for determining fair compensation for a taking.[4] Australian law, for example, explicitly recognizes that compensation should be based on what the owner of the property could have received for it in voluntary exchange: "As the object is to find the money equivalent for the loss or, in other words, the pecuniary value to the owner contained in the asset, it cannot be less than the money value into which he might have converted his property had the law not deprived him of it."[5] Similarly, in a takings

---

2. RESTATEMENT (SECOND) OF CONTRACTS § 79 (1981).

3. *E.g.*, Olson *v.* United States, 292 U.S. 246, 255 (1934). The Court has also repeatedly stated: "The owner is to be put in the same position monetarily as he would have occupied if his property had not been taken." United States *v.* Reynolds, 397 U.S. 14, 16 (1970); *accord,* United States *v.* New River Collieries Co., 262 U.S. 341, 343 (1922); Seaboard Air Lines Ry. Co. *v.* United States, 261 U.S. 299, 304 (1922). That formulation of compensation should not be confused with reliance damages: If the property owner were restored to the *status quo ante*, he could voluntarily transfer his property to a willing buyer at its expectation value. Thus, the Court's formulation implicitly requires that restoration of the property owner to the *status quo ante* will compensate him for all the opportunity costs of losing his property to government confiscation.

4. English jurists have emphasized that the purpose of compensation is to "give[] to the owner compelled to sell . . . the right to be put, so far as money can do it, in the same position as if his land had not been taken from him." Horn *v.* Sunderland Corp., 1 All E.R. 480, 491 (C.A. 1941) (Scott, J.); *accord,* Maidstone Borough Council *v.* Secretary of State for the Env't, 3 P.L.R. 66 (C.A. 1995); *see also* Nelungaloo Pty. Ltd. *v.* Commonwealth, 75 C.L.R. 495, 571 (Austl. High Ct. 1948) ("[T]he purpose of compensation . . . is to place in the hands of the owner expropriated the full money equivalent of the thing of which he has been deprived.").

5. *Nelungaloo,* 75 C.L.R. at 571 (Dixon, J., dissenting).

case decided in 1897, the Illinois Supreme Court defined market value to be "what the owner, if desirous of selling, would sell the property for; and what reasonable persons, desirous of purchasing, would have paid for it."[6] The Illinois legislature subsequently codified that definition.[7]

What, then, is the price that the property owner would demand before he would voluntarily part with his asset? Another way of phrasing the question is to ask what the full cost would be to the property owner of parting with the asset. The critical insight to answering that question comes once again from Armen A. Alchian's definition that "the cost of an event is the highest-valued opportunity *necessarily* forsaken."[8] The property owner, therefore, would demand the asset's opportunity cost—which, in the absence of regulatory distortions, will usually equal the asset's market value. As a leading textbook on corporate finance explains:

> Sometimes opportunity costs may be very difficult to estimate; however, where the resource can be freely traded, its opportunity cost is simply equal to the market price. Why? It cannot be otherwise. If the value of a parcel of land to the firm is less than its market price, the firm will sell it. On the other hand, the opportunity cost of using land in a particular project cannot exceed the cost of buying an equivalent parcel to replace it.[9]

Again, English common law contains a corresponding expression of that economic reasoning. The property taken is to be valued not merely by reference to the use to which it is being put at the time, but the owner is also entitled to compensation for the potentialities or possibilities of development—that is, the property's opportunity cost.[10] American courts have similarly ruled that the property owner is entitled to compensation

6. Ligare *v.* Chicago, Madison & N. R.R., 166 Ill. 249, 261–62, 46 N.E. 803, 808 (1897); *accord,* Edgcomb Steel Co. *v.* State, 100 N.H. 480, 487 (1957). In his dissent in *Munn* v. *Illinois*, Justice Stephen J. Field made a similar observation about rate regulation: "The amount [of compensation] fixed will operate as a partial destruction of the value of the property, if it fall below the amount which the owner would obtain by contract . . . ." Munn *v.* Illinois, 94 U.S. (4 Otto) 113, 143 (1876) (Field, J., dissenting).

7. 735 Ill. Comp. Stat. 5/7-121 (West 1992) (formerly Ill. Rev. Stat. ch. 110, ¶ 7-121).

8. Armen A. Alchian, *Cost, in* 3 International Encyclopedia of the Social Sciences 404 (David L. Sills ed., Macmillan Co. & Free Press 1968). As we note in chapter 4, Professor Alchian has requested in private correspondence that we add emphasis to the word "necessarily."

9. Richard A. Brealey & Stewart C. Myers, Principles of Corporate Finance 98 (McGraw-Hill, Inc., 4th ed. 1991) (footnote omitted).

10. Robinson Bros. (Brewers) Ltd. *v.* Houghton & Chester—Le-Street Assessment Comm., 2 All E.R. 298 (C.A. 1937), *aff'd,* 2 All E.R. 79 (H.L. 1938).

"for the most profitable purpose, or advantageous use, to which [his property] could be put on the day it was taken."[11]

INVESTMENT-BACKED EXPECTATIONS, OPPORTUNITY COSTS, AND DEREGULATORY TAKINGS

If it has been established that the manner by which the state accomplishes the deregulation of electricity markets or local telecommunications markets constitutes a government taking of the property of the utility's investors, how shall the amount of "just compensation" be determined? The market value of the property is a sufficient measure of just compensation if it happens to take into account the opportunity cost of the taking. Justice Thurgood Marshall observed that "[a]lthough the market-value standard is a useful and generally sufficient tool for ascertaining the compensation required to make the owner whole, the Court has acknowledged that such an award does not necessarily compensate for all values an owner may derive from his property."[12] The notion that the owner should be made whole means that the expected returns to the owner from the property should form the basis of compensation.

In the absence of network congestion, a deregulatory taking does not deprive the shareholders of the utility of the physical assets, including the plant and equipment and transmission system of the utility. Nor does a deregulatory taking deprive shareholders of their ownership share in the regulated firm. Rather, regulators deprive shareholders of the expected returns associated with entry controls and pricing regulations that existed before the deregulation. Thus, it is not necessary to determine the purchase costs of the regulatory assets, nor their resale value, nor their replacement costs. The utility placed the assets in service in expectation of the earnings that would be received. The expected returns of the firm constitute *investment-backed expectations*.

Therefore, just compensation for a deregulatory taking should equal the change in the expected returns to the owners of the property. In the basic example of single-period returns, with compensation paid in the current period, just compensation is the difference between the expected net returns deriving from the property under regulation and the expected net returns under competition:

$$just\ compensation = \Delta.$$

---

11. *E.g.*, Emmons *v.* Power Utils. Co., 83 N.H. 181, 184, 141 A. 65, 67 (1927).
12. United States *v.* 564.4 Acres of Land, 441 U.S. 506, 511 (1979).

Recall from chapter 5 that

$$\Delta \equiv (R_1^e - C_1^e) - (R_2^e - C_2^e),$$

where R_1^e and C_1^e denote expected revenues and costs under regulation, and R_2^e and C_2^e denote expected revenues and costs under competition. If the property is expected to generate returns over multiple periods, those returns should be discounted at the appropriate rate, so that compensation equals the difference between the present discounted value of net earnings expected under regulation and those expected under competition. For investors to be made whole, they should be compensated for the change in the firm's present discounted value of net earnings:

just compensation $= \Delta^*$.

Recall from chapter 5 that

$$\Delta^* \equiv PDV_1 - PDV_2,$$

where PDV_1 denotes the firm's present discounted value of expected net revenues under regulation and PDV_2 denotes the firm's present discounted value of expected net revenues under competition. Therefore, for the one period or the multiperiod case, just compensation for a deregulatory taking exactly equals damages for breach of contract.

Another way to determine the change in investment-backed expectations is to consider the change in the value of the firm to the shareholders as a consequence of deregulation. The value of the firm is the sum of each year's discounted cash flows net of investment requirements.[13] Thus, in the absence of additional investment in the firm, the value of the firm is the present discounted value of expected earnings:

$$V = \sum_{i=0}^{T} \frac{(R_t^e - C_t^e)}{(1+i)^t}$$

The value of the firm differs under regulation from what it is under competition. Let V_1 and V_2 respectively denote the value of the firm calculated for net revenues under regulation and the value of the firm calculated by using expected net revenues under competition. Then, it

---

13. *See, e.g.*, J. Fred Weston, Kwang S. Chung & Susan E. Hoag, Mergers, Restructuring and Corporate Control 138–44 (Prentice Hall 1990).

should be apparent that the change in the value of the firm is the difference between the two present discounted values of cash flows:

$$V_1 - V_2 = \Delta^*.$$

Thus, just compensation for a deregulatory taking from investors is equal to the change in the value of the firm.

DEREGULATORY GIVINGS AND
THE QUID PRO QUO DEFENSE

A defense against the payment of compensation for deregulatory takings is the argument that the regulator (or the legislature) has already provided, or is concurrently providing, other benefits to the regulated firm, benefits whose economic value should be recognized as an offset to any deregulatory takings that might have occurred. Although plausible in principle, that argument will be unpersuasive in practice in many cases in which it is invoked. Our formula for just compensation already incorporates the quid pro quo because that formula accounts for the difference between the present discounted value of net earnings expected under regulation and those expected under competition. Consequently, any increments in net revenues due to increased revenues or lowered costs are automatically taken into account. It bears emphasis that just compensation applies only to the expected net revenues from *regulated* assets; the same restriction should apply to the calculation of offsetting givings.

A number of considerations must go into the proper accounting for deregulatory givings. If regulators confer a benefit on the regulated firm, that benefit must be sufficient to offset the deregulatory taking. That is, the giving's economic value must be fully compensatory. Merely counting up takings and givings in a qualitative sense is not a useful exercise. Instead, it is necessary to place a valuation on those regulated assets affected by the takings and givings, even if economic projections of expected net revenues are necessary. The giving generally should not be retroactive, nor should it double count a quid pro quo that was already struck between the regulator and the firm. For example, the past award of a regulatory franchise or a past rate increase cannot count again today as a giving because the regulator presumably granted each such benefit to the regulated utility not as largess, but in consideration of the public service obligations that the firm agreed to (and subsequently did) perform. Similarly, the firm's ability to recover, through depreciation, the investments in its rate base is a preexisting, bargained-for exchange that has already lessened the firm's unrecovered regulated costs. By the same logic as the preexisting-duty rule in contract law,[14] the government cannot assert that past benefits that it conferred on a regulated firm as part of the regulatory contract may count again as implicit compensation for the government's subsequent taking of the firm's private property.

The preceding caveats should not be taken as disagreement with the basic proposition that deregulation may confer benefits on the incumbent firm that offset potential losses from deregulation. The extent of such offsets, however, depends to a great extent on the nature of the regulatory decisions. That issue relates closely to the duty to mitigate, which we already examined in chapter 4 in the case of the regulatory contract. Thus, if the regulator removes price controls, so that the incumbent firm has pricing flexibility to compete with new entrants, the regulator will enable the firm to mitigate its losses from deregulation and thus reduce its need for compensation for takings. Similarly, the lifting of regulatory obligations borne by the incumbent firm will reduce its costs after deregulation. If the regulator allows the regulated firm to remove cross-subsidies from its rate structure, or if the regulator relaxes incumbent burdens, then the regulator will indeed offset or mitigate the extent to which the taking of the firm's private property is uncompensated. In principle, if deregulatory givings are large enough in their value, the regulator will be able to eliminate the need for any explicit payment of compensation to the regulated firm. To reiterate, however, that analysis will likely require an empirical valuation of the givings that the government claims as offsets to the incumbent firm's taking.

The lifting of regulatory quarantines can provide another example of mitigation of takings under certain conditions. It is critical, however, that the quarantine not be newly imposed as part of the deregulation process. Otherwise, for the regulator to use the lifting of the quarantine as compensation for the taking would create a strong incentive for regulators to impose new and inefficient restrictions simply to lift them later as a form of implicit compensation for *other* regulatory changes that will adversely affect the regulated firm. Such conduct would be little more than regulatory extortion.[15] One could argue, for example, that by ending the Modification of Final Judgment, Congress also opened the long-distance telecommunications markets to entry by the regional Bell operating companies (RBOCs). Whether the RBOCs received a legal

---

14. RESTATEMENT (SECOND) OF CONTRACTS § 73 (1981).

15. *See* FRED S. MCCHESNEY, MONEY FOR NOTHING: POLITICIANS, RENT EXTRACTION, AND POLITICAL EXTORTION (Harvard University Press 1997); Fred S. McChesney, *Rent Extraction and Rent Creation in the Economic Theory of Regulation*, 16 J. LEGAL STUD. 101 (1987).

entitlement that they did not already possess is debatable, however. Indeed, as Paul W. MacAvoy has argued, the Telecommunications Act of 1996 made the RBOCs *worse* off in terms of the regulatory process for supervising their entry into interLATA services.[16] As chapter 3 explains, the Telecommunications Act of 1996 imposed on the RBOCs even more rigorous barriers to entry into interLATA services, in the form of the competitive checklist, than existed under the waiver process applicable to the MFJ's line-of-business restrictions.[17] The FCC further heightened those barriers to entry in its interpretation of the interconnection and access pricing requirements of the 1996 legislation.[18] It is therefore questionable whether the government's lifting of those *new* statutory and regulatory restrictions could be a quid pro quo for the deregulatory takings that the FCC's orders on local exchange competition and on the pricing of interstate access are likely to impose on RBOC shareholders.

In short, the regulator cannot have it both ways. If its lifting of newly created restrictions would have a positive economic value to the incumbent firm, then their imposition must have caused an equal economic cost on the firm. Thus, by imposing and lifting a regulatory restriction in rapid succession, the regulator would achieve a net economic effect on the incumbent firm that should be negligible. Indeed, the transaction costs and financial uncertainty that such actions would entail would more likely impose net costs on the incumbent firm. As a matter of takings jurisprudence, the regulator's claim to having canceled the cost of new restrictions by conferring the benefit of lifting them would be no less specious if the regulator's statutory powers were to permit it to impose such new restrictions.

---

16. PAUL W. MACAVOY, THE FAILURE OF ANTITRUST AND REGULATION TO ESTABLISH COMPETITION IN LONG-DISTANCE TELEPHONE SERVICES 175–212 (MIT Press & AEI Press 1996).

17. 47 U.S.C. § 271.

18. *E.g.*, Access Charge Reform; Price Cap Performance Review for Local Exchange Carriers; Transport Rate Structure and Pricing; Usage of the Public Switched Network by Information Service and Internet Access Providers, Notice of Proposed Rulemaking, Third Report and Order, and Notice of Inquiry, CC Dkt. Nos. 96-262, 94-1, 91-213, 96-263, 11 F.C.C. Rcd. 21,354 (1996); Implementation of the Local Competition Provisions in the Telecommunications Act of 1996 and Interconnection Between Local Exchange Carriers and Commercial Mobile Radio Service Providers, First Report and Order, CC Dkt. Nos. 96-98, 95-185, 11 F.C.C. Rcd. 15,499 (1996); Implementation of the Non-Accounting Safeguards of Sections 271 and 272 of the Communications Act of 1934, as Amended, First Report and Order and Further Notice of Proposed Rulemaking, CC Dkt. No. 96-149, 11 F.C.C. Rcd. 21,905 (1996).

The need to value givings properly and to restrain new regulations that force companies to accept takings would improve the economic efficiency of the deregulation process. The payment of just compensation for takings and the proper economic valuation of givings are necessary to give regulators incentives for efficient behavior, or at least to restrict their inefficient confiscatory actions. Just compensation similarly restrains the government's exercise of its power of eminent domain. Just compensation for deregulatory takings and the proper economic valuation of givings limit the state's power to coerce, constraining what Judge Richard A. Posner has termed "taxation by regulation."[19]

CONCLUSION

Just compensation is predicated on consent, for it is intended to replicate voluntary exchange. In voluntary exchange the price of a good compensates the seller for his opportunity cost. It therefore follows that just compensation must compensate the property owner for the opportunity cost to him of parting with his property. The opportunity cost to the utility of being compelled to sell unbundled network access to competitors is that the firm no longer receives the expected returns that, under regulation, were an actuarially fair means of giving the firm a reasonable opportunity to achieve a return of, and a competitive return on, the specialized investments that the utility made to discharge its obligation to serve. That lost expectation, in turn, corresponds to the diminution in the value of the utility after the introduction of competition. It is equivalent to the difference between the discounted net revenues of the utility before and after the government has compelled the sale of unbundled network access.

In principle, the government can commit givings that offset its takings. The economic valuation of deregulatory takings and givings will not restrict the process of deregulation. Rather, it will motivate regulators to lift incumbent burdens and remaining regulatory obligations, which will hasten the move to a competitive market. The regulator will be less tempted to take actions that confiscate the property of the incumbent firm's shareholders. Instead, the regulator will have an incentive to eschew mere income redistribution in favor of policies that provide consumers with the true benefits of competition.

19. Richard A. Posner, *Taxation by Regulation*, 2 BELL J. ECON. 22 (1971).

8

The Efficient Component-Pricing Rule

DEREGULATION of telecommunications and electric power raises an important question: How should access to the transmission and distribution network of the incumbent utility be priced? If access is priced excessively high, efficient entry may be discouraged and duplicative facilities will be created to bypass the existing network. If access is priced inordinately low, excessive entry and congestion may result, and the incumbent utility might fail to cover its costs. The key issue is how to balance cost recovery for the incumbent with incentives for entrants. The efficient component-pricing rule (ECPR) promises a solution to the access-pricing problem.

The question of how a regulated firm should price its sale of services to competitors arises whenever an incumbent utility is the only supplier of an input used both by itself and by an entrant to provide some final product. If the utility charges its rival more for the input than it implicitly charges itself, it will have handicapped that rival's ability to compete. The reverse will be true if regulation forces the utility to charge the entrant less for the input than the utility charges itself. This chapter examines ECPR pricing for the case in which the incumbent utility serves as the sole supplier of network facilities. In chapter 9 we turn to ECPR pricing when facilities-based competition exists.

The modern analysis of access pricing arose with the purchase of trackage rights by one railroad from another. Soon, the problem manifested itself in telecommunications regulation, as in the case of pricing of access to the local exchange when the local exchange carrier supplies that service to interexchange carriers with which the LEC competes in toll services within a local access and transport area (LATA).

Access has two significant and pertinent attributes. First, access is an intermediate good—an input used in the supply of a final product, such as intraLATA toll service and other final services. Second, the LEC produces that input, which both the LEC and its rivals use in the market for the final product. Analogous pricing problems have arisen with respect to network interconnection by competitive access providers, which compete against the LEC in providing the local transport required for a long-distance call, and with respect to the LEC's sale of unbundled service elements in response to regulatory initiatives to open local exchange telephony to competition.

This chapter derives the access price within the context of specific models of competition. The analysis allows an explicit specification of the access charge that we can use to evaluate efficiency claims for the ECPR. We consider an incumbent subject to break-even price regulation that offers a service that it produces itself and delivers over its own transmission network. Deregulation then takes a specific form. Regulators remove entry barriers and set an access charge for the incumbent's network. Entrants supply a final service (such as local toll calling or delivered bulk power) in competition with the incumbent and transmit the service over the incumbent's network. We derive the access charge by using the efficient component-pricing rule. In each case, more efficient competitors displace sales of the incumbent's final service. Under the ECPR, entry is profitable if and only if there is a production cost efficiency. Thus, the rule ensures proper pricing and efficiency in network access, whether it is a rail system, an electric power grid, or a telecommunications loop.[1] The incumbent's *opportunity cost* is the lost contribution to margin from final sales.

The incumbent has stranded costs resulting from deregulation if the firm's earnings net of operating costs are lower under competition than under regulation. As we emphasize in chapters 3 and 4, the regulatory contract and constitutional protections for private property oblige regulators to provide the regulated firm a reasonable opportunity to recover the shortfall in net earnings. The regulator is assumed to set the access charge to effect the recovery of stranded costs. The access charge thus

---

1. For other demonstrations of the ECPR's efficiency under simpler assumptions of market structure, see WILLIAM J. BAUMOL & J. GREGORY SIDAK, TOWARD COMPETITION IN LOCAL TELEPHONY 105–07 (MIT Press & AEI Press 1994); William J. Baumol & J. Gregory Sidak, *The Pricing of Inputs Sold to Competitors*, 11 YALE J. ON REG. 171, 187–89 (1994); William J. Baumol & J. Gregory Sidak, *Pricing of Services Provided to Competitors by the Regulated Firm*, 3 HUME PAPERS ON PUB. POL'Y, No. 3, at 15 (1995).

equals the incremental cost of access plus stranded costs divided by the total output at the competitive equilibrium. Because the market output and the revenue shortfall depend on the competitive outcome, it follows that the value of the access price is an equilibrium result. We must therefore examine the efficiency of the access charge in the context of the resulting market equilibrium.

To illustrate the effects of entry costs and product differences, we analyze in this chapter the access charge in three competitive settings. The first setting is the contestable markets model of William J. Baumol, John C. Panzar, and Robert D. Willig,[2] which assumes that there are no entry costs and that products are homogeneous. The second model is Cournot-Nash competition with entry, which maintains the assumption of homogeneous products but introduces entry costs. The third model, based on the Chamberlinian competition model of Jeffrey M. Perloff and Steven C. Salop,[3] allows both product differentiation and entry costs.

In each of those settings, several common points emerge. First, the ECPR provides incentives for efficient entry. If more efficient competitors can produce the regulated output at a lower cost, the access charge allows entry to take place. Second, the access charge is consistent with price reduction and output expansion relative to the regulated price and output. By expanding output, entry lowers the incumbent's per-unit opportunity cost and thus lowers the access charge.

Third, we compare the equilibrium access charge with the well-known benchmark case in which the access charge equals the regulated firm's mark-up. In each case, the equilibrium access charge is lower than the benchmark. In the contestable markets case, the reduction of the access charge reflects output expansion due to the cost-efficiency of entrants and lower opportunity cost per unit. That result confirms the observation of Jean-Jacques Laffont and Jean Tirole that under certain conditions the initial price is irrelevant.[4] If there is free entry, entrants do not have market power, and products are perfect substitutes, then the incumbent should supply access only if entrants are more efficient, or the incumbent should supply no access if it is more efficient than

2. WILLIAM J. BAUMOL, JOHN C. PANZAR & ROBERT D. WILLIG, CONTESTABLE MARKETS AND THE THEORY OF INDUSTRY STRUCTURE (Harcourt, Brace, Jovanovich, rev. ed. 1988).

3. Jeffrey M. Perloff & Steven C. Salop, *Equilibrium with Product Differentiation*, 52 REV. ECON. STUD. 107 (1985).

4. Jean-Jacques Laffont & Jean Tirole, *Access Pricing and Competition*, 38 EUR. ECON. REV. 1673 (1994).

entrants. In the Cournot-Nash case, the difference between the benchmark case and the equilibrium ECPR is due to an adjustment for entry costs. In the differentiated products case, the difference in the charges is due to offsetting earnings of the incumbent, which result from lower setup costs.

ECONOMIC ANALYSIS OF THE
EFFICIENT COMPONENT-PRICING RULE

The solution to the recurrent access pricing problem described above is the efficient component-pricing rule, due to Robert D. Willig[5] and William J. Baumol[6] and elaborated on by Baumol and J. Gregory Sidak.[7] A critical requirement for economic efficiency is that the price of any product be no lower than that product's marginal cost. Otherwise, with increasing marginal cost, an excessive amount of output is produced because the returns for the last unit of output are less than the cost of producing the last unit of output. For a fixed level of output, the price of an additional service should cover its average incremental cost.

Economic analysis emphasizes that the pertinent marginal cost as well as the average incremental cost must include all opportunity costs that the supplier incurs in providing the product. Here, opportunity cost refers to all potential earnings that the supplying firm forgoes, either by providing inputs of its own rather than purchasing them or by offering services to competitors that force it to relinquish business to those rivals and thus to forgo the profits on that lost business. In a competitive market, a firm would not accept a price unless it included compensation for such opportunity costs. The efficient component-pricing rule states simply that the price of an input should equal its average incremental cost, including all pertinent incremental opportunity costs:

5. Robert D. Willig, *The Theory of Network Access Pricing, in* ISSUES IN PUBLIC UTILITY REGULATION (H. M. Trebing ed., Michigan State University Public Utuility Papers 1979).

6. William J. Baumol, *Some Subtle Issues in Railroad Regulation*, 10 INT'L J. TRANSP. ECON. 341 (1983).

7. William J. Baumol & J. Gregory Sidak, *The Pricing of Inputs Sold to Competitors, supra* note 1; WILLIAM J. BAUMOL & J. GREGORY SIDAK, TOWARD COMPETITION IN LOCAL TELEPHONY, *supra* note 1.

efficient component price =

the input's direct per unit incremental cost

+   *the opportunity cost to the input supplier of the sale of a unit of input.*

The literature on the economics of price regulation indicates that the pricing principle just described can guide the choice of efficient access charges. The ECPR principle—also known as the *imputation requirement*, the *principle of competitive equality*, or the *parity principle*—is merely a variant of elementary principles for efficient pricing.

Two examples illustrate the basic framework. In the electric power industry, access represents the transmission and distribution lines of the incumbent utility, which supplies access through wholesale or retail wheeling. The final output production is the generation of electric power that is carried out by the integrated utility and independent generators that rely on the utility for transmission and distribution services.

In the telecommunications industry there are many types of network components. One important type of access is the resale of "vertical components," many of which are switching services such as call waiting and call forwarding. In addition, the utility provides access to its transmission facilities and local loops. The final output production could simply be marketing of the vertical components. Alternatively, the final output can be another transmission service, such as long-distance telecommunications, which is bundled with local access.

As applied to network access pricing, the efficient component-pricing rule specifies the access price as the sum of two costs:

access price = incremental cost of providing access

+ *opportunity cost of providing access.*

Charging at least incremental cost for access raises few objections. Moreover, the incremental cost of providing access should be measurable, contingent on defining the access service and correctly measuring network costs. Indeed, most regulated utilities and regulatory commissions have already established procedures for measuring incremental costs. Opportunity costs are more difficult to measure and consequently are the subject of some controversy, as we discuss in chapters 9 and 10.

Since the mid-1990s, the ECPR has generated considerable attention in the academic literature. In chapter 10 we survey the academic proponents and opponents of efficient component pricing, as well as the courts and regulatory agencies that have accepted or rejected the ECPR. The analysis presented here emphasizes pricing access to recover cost and the efficiency of incentives for entry. In that regard, our approach differs from that of Mark Armstrong, Chris Doyle, and John Vickers[8] and of Jean-Jacques Laffont and Jean Tirole,[9] who examine Ramsey-Boiteux pricing as a means of carrying out a second-best allocation of network fixed costs between the incumbent's final output price, the access charge, and the competitor's final output price. The Ramsey-Boiteux prices depend on elasticities of demand. Laffont and Tirole select optimal access charges that depart from the marginal cost of access owing to the cost of public funds needed to cover fixed costs.[10] Armstrong, Doyle, and Vickers impose the standard break-even constraint and show that the second-best optimal access price involves a markup over the marginal cost of access only if the break-even constraint binds. They conclude that if the incumbent's technology has increasing returns to scale, the access charge is set in excess of marginal cost, assuming uniform pricing and ruling out lump-sum transfers.

In their 1996 article, Laffont and Tirole raise three "quibbles" regarding the ECPR.[11] They suggest first that the contestable markets paradigm is of limited value in evaluating the ECPR because it neglects the possibility of entrants' having superior technology, or other factors that create benefits from competition.[12] Second, they state that the ECPR is "only a partial rule as it does not specify how to determine the telephone operator's prices on the competitive segments."[13] Finally, they question whether it makes sense to propose a general access-pricing rule without consideration of the market environment—for example, without considering product differentiation and cost differences.[14]

---

8. Mark Armstrong, Chris Doyle & John Vickers, *The Access Pricing Problem: A Synthesis*, 44 J. INDUS. ECON. 131 (1996); *see also* John Vickers, *Regulation, Competition, and the Structure of Prices*, 13 OXFORD REV. ECON. POL'Y, no. 1, at 15 (1997).

9. Jean-Jacques Laffont & Jean Tirole, *Creating Competition Through Interconnection: Theory and Practice*, 10 J. REG. ECON. 227 (1996) [hereinafter *Creating Competition Through Interconnection*].

10. Laffont & Tirole, *Access Pricing and Competition, supra* note 4.

11. Laffont & Tirole, *Creating Competition Through Interconnection, supra* note 9, at 230.

12. *Id.*

13. *Id.*

14. *Id.*

Our analysis addresses each of those issues. Our model explicitly incorporates technological differences by allowing incumbent and entrant costs to differ. Next, our analysis shows that the ECPR should not be viewed as a "partial" rule because the ECPR allows firms to set prices in the competitive segment at the market equilibrium. Finally, we agree with the need to adjust the access charge to account for the effects of product differentiation and cost differences on the market outcome. Our framework demonstrates how to make those adjustments in the ECPR.

THE BASIC FRAMEWORK

An incumbent utility provides services that it delivers by means of a transmission network. In the case of electricity, the service can be electric power generation. Network transportation is electricity transmission and distribution. In the case of telecommunications, the service can be switching or information services. Network transportation is the transmission of messages over the system lines. In the case of electricity, telecommunications, or natural gas transmission, the service could also be retail marketing and sales of the transportation function.

Let Q represent the output of the service. Assume that each unit of service requires exactly one unit of transmission, so that transmission is an input to the production of the service. The incumbent's unit cost of producing the service is c, and the incumbent's unit cost of producing transmission is b. The incumbent incurs a nonrecoverable capital cost of establishing the network equal to k. Let $Q = D(P)$ be the market demand for the service, where P is its price. The incumbent is subject to rate regulation that sets break-even rates. Then, P_0, the regulated price of services, solves equation (1):

(1) $$(P_0 - c - b) \, D \, (P_0) - k = 0.$$

Let $Q_0 = D(P_0)$ be the output sold by the regulated firm. Assume that the demand function intersects the average investment cost curve from above. Let $P(Q) = D^{-1}(Q)$ be the inverse demand. Then, we require that $P'(Q) + k/Q^2 < 0$.

After the removal of regulatory barriers to entry, entrants are assumed to supply the final service by relying on access to the incumbent's network for transmission of the service to final customers. Entrants purchasing transmission from the incumbent are said to buy *access*. Let X represent the quantity of the service provided by entrants as well as their purchase of access from the incumbent. Entrants supply the final service at cost g, which differs from the incumbent's cost since entrants are not subject to regulatory contraints and have access to technology different from that of the regulated incumbent.

After deregulation, the competitive price is P, with the regulated firm's supplying output Q_1 and entrants' supplying X. With homogeneous products, entry takes place only if the price P offered by competitors does not exceed the regulated price, P_0. Entry is assumed to crowd out the incumbent's sales. Thus, if entry occurs, deregulation lowers the net earnings of the regulated firm by an amount equal to Δ,

$$\Delta = (P_0 - c - b)Q_0 - (P - c - b)Q_1.$$

That amount represents the opportunity cost of deregulation for the incumbent firm.

Let A represent the per-unit price of access to the transmission network. With voluntary exchange, the incumbent firm would only agree to sell access if the price of access covered the incremental cost of providing access plus the opportunity cost of providing access, $A \geq b + \Delta/X$. The *lowest* access price that recovers the incremental cost plus the opportunity cost of the regulated firm is therefore

(2) $$A = b + \Delta/X.$$

The access charge expression in equation (2) is the *efficient component-pricing rule* if it provides incentives for efficient entry. The extent to which efficient entry takes place depends on the type of competition that obtains after deregulation, not just on the type of access pricing that regulators employ. The purpose of the analysis that follows is to explore the performance of the ECPR under various postentry forms of competition.

A BENCHMARK CASE

If entry displaces all the incumbent's sales of the final service, the incumbent's opportunity cost of providing access is the forgone net revenue from sales, $(P_0 - c - b)Q_0$. In the case of the regulated firm we have just described, that happens to equal exactly the incumbent's capital cost:

$$\Delta = k.$$

In that special case, the regulated access charge that recovers the incumbent's operating cost of producing access plus the opportunity cost of access is defined by the following equation:

(3) $A = b + k/X = b + (P_0 - c - b)\, Q_0/X.$

With full displacement, the incumbent supplies access to competitive entrants, with all the final service supplied by entrants. For several reasons, that outcome is not so drastic as it might first appear.

Deregulation may require the incumbent to supply access to entrants on the same terms as it does to itself. For example, the Telecommunications Act of 1996 requires in section 251(e) that a regional Bell operating company:

> (2) shall not provide any facilities, services, or information concerning its provision of exchange access to [its] affiliate . . . unless such facilities, services, or information are made available to other providers of interLATA services in that market on the same terms and conditions;
> (3) shall charge the affiliate . . . or impute to itself (if using the access for its provision of its own services), an amount for access to its telephone exchange service and exchange access that is no less than the amount charged to any unaffiliated interexchange carriers for such service; and
> (4) may provide any interLATA or intraLATA facilities or services to its interLATA affiliate if such services or facilities are made available to all carriers at the same rates and on the same terms and conditions, and so long as the costs are appropriately allocated.[15]

Therefore, for the purposes of our analysis, it is reasonable to assume that the final sales of the incumbent are fully displaced, with the incumbent's deregulated affiliate acting as one of the competitive entrants. We must modify the analysis accordingly if the final sales of the incumbent are only partially displaced and the costs of providing access are not constant, as they are in the present model.

In some cases, the type of displacement observed in the present framework has occurred after deregulation. A notable example is in the market for interstate natural gas, where the major interstate pipelines became transporters of natural gas almost exclusively after the spot and contracts markets for gas largely displaced their merchant services.[16]

15. 47 U.S.C. § 251(e).
16. Michael J. Doane & Daniel F. Spulber, *Open Access and the Evolution of the*

The interstate pipelines have continued to provide some merchant services through marketing affiliates. The case of full displacement is also consistent with the case of partial deregulation, with the incumbent being displaced only from the deregulated or "noncore" portion of the market while it continues to serve regulated or "core" customers.

In the case of full displacement, it is useful to consider a *benchmark case* due to Baumol and Sidak.[17] That case is based on two competitive situations. In the first, suppose that the incumbent faces one or more price-taking entrants acting as a competitive fringe. Alternatively, in the second situation suppose that the incumbent faces a price-setting entrant that prices just below the regulated price level and captures all the incumbent's sales. In either case, the market price does not change after entry, so that the entrant's sales (and purchase of access) exactly equal the incumbent's output before entry, $X = Q_0 = D(P_0)$. In that case, the access charge reduces to

$$(4) \qquad\qquad A_0 = P_0 - c.$$

The entrant's profit is therefore

$$\Pi = (P_o - g - A)X = (c - g)X.$$

Therefore, the competitor finds it profitable to enter the market if and only if the costs of providing the service are less than those of the incumbent, $g < c$. Thus, for the type of competition described in which the market price remains constant, we may conclude that $A_0 = P_0 - c$ is an ECPR. In what follows, we examine the performance of pricing rules that allow recovery of the incumbent's opportunity cost in other competitive settings. We examine various models in which equilibrium entry fully displaces the incumbent from the final service market, thus reducing the incumbent to being a supplier of access.

THE CONTESTABLE-MARKET CASE

Suppose that the market for the service is *contestable* after deregulation: Entrants have identical production costs, and entry does not require any costs to be sunk. In that case, entry will cause prices to fall

---

17. Baumol & Sidak, *The Pricing of Inputs Sold to Competitors*, *supra* note 1; BAUMOL & SIDAK, TOWARD COMPETITION IN LOCAL TELEPHONY, *supra* note 1.

below the regulated price. All the incumbent's sales of services are displaced because the equilibrium price is below the incumbent's break-even price.

The final output price is reduced to the unit cost for an entrant:

$$(5) \qquad\qquad P = A + g.$$

If P is less than the initial regulated price P_0, the incumbent makes no sales. If P falls below P_0, the amount of access sold, $X = D(P)$, exceeds the incumbent's initial output, owing to downward-sloping demand.

If we let $A = b + k/X$ as in equation (2), the market price solves

$$(6) \qquad\qquad P^* = g + b + k/D(P^*).$$

We obtain the equilibrium value of the access price by substituting for the postentry output:

$$(7) \qquad\qquad A^* = b + k/D(P^*).$$

Entry occurs if and only if the entrant's operating costs are lower than those of the incumbent. To establish that result, note that $P^* < P_0$ if and only if

$$g + b + k/D(P^*) < c + b + k/D(P_0).$$

That inequality holds if and only if the entrant's unit cost is less than the incumbent's unit cost,

$$g < c.$$

We illustrate that result in figure 1. Therefore, the access-pricing rule satisfies the efficient entry condition.

The efficient access price is a weighted average of the cost of access and the regulated margin:

$$(8) \qquad\qquad A^* = b \, (1 - Q_0/X) + (P_0 - c) \, Q_0/X^*.$$

Alternatively, from equations (6) and (7), the ECPR equals the margin of the entrant:

$$(9) \qquad\qquad A^* = P^* - g.$$

Notice that the *entrant's* cost is subtracted from the equilibrium price. Compare the efficient access price A^* with the benchmark case. The equilibrium price is lower, but the entrant's costs are lower as well. The net effect is to decrease the efficient access price by $A_0 - A^* = k(1/Q_0 - 1/X^*)$.

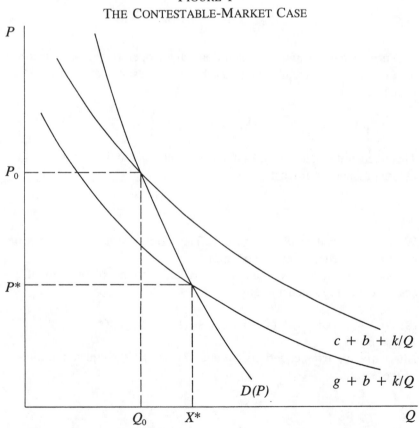

FIGURE 1
THE CONTESTABLE-MARKET CASE

The equilibrium price is increasing in b, g, and k.[18] Thus, the access price is increasing in b, g, and k as well. To verify the effect of the entrant's cost on the equilibrium access price, note that

$$\partial P^*/\partial g = D(P^*) / [(P^* - g - b)D'(P^*) + D(P^*)] > 1$$

so that

$$\partial A^*/\partial g = \partial P^*/\partial g - 1 > 0.$$

The more efficient are potential entrants (that is, the lower g), the lower will be the equilibrium price, and the greater will be output and the corresponding demand for access. That relationship allows the incumbent to recover its costs with a lower unit price of access.

The contestable-market setting shows that access pricing using the ECPR *does* allow prices to fall below the regulated price. The decline in the market price is due to the lower cost of more efficient entrants and to the additional scale economies achieved through higher sales. In the next section, we reexamine the performance of the ECPR without the contestability assumptions.

CAPACITY COMPETITION

The previous section demonstrated the efficiency of the ECPR in a contestable-market setting. This section examines the ECPR's efficiency when entrants must make capacity commitments and entry is costly. We model that situation as a Cournot-Nash equilibrium with entry costs f. Entering firms must make capacity commitments at cost g per unit. The access-pricing rule is efficient if it permits cost-saving entry. Entry reduces costs if the cost savings on the regulated firm's output outweigh total entry costs:

(10) $(c - g) Q_0 \geq nf,$

---

18. Note that

$$\frac{\partial P^*}{\partial g} = \frac{D(P^*)}{[(P^* - g - b)D'(P^*) + D(P^*)]} = \frac{1}{kD'(P^*)/[D(P^*)]^2 + 1} > 0$$

since $kD'(P^*)/[D(P^*)]^2 > -1$ by our earlier assumption.

where n is the equilibrium number of entrants. As in the contestable market case, entry can change the industry's output and price. The condition does *not* state that entry occurs for any pair of entry costs f and market structure n. Rather, the market structure must be an equilibrium that is consistent with entry costs and the access-pricing rule. Thus, given an efficient access-pricing rule, entry occurs if and only if the equilibrium number of firms can produce the incumbent's output at lower cost.

We can interpret the Cournot-Nash equilibrium as the result of capacity competition. David M. Kreps and José A. Scheinkman show that with a particular rationing rule, the Nash equilibrium of a two-stage capacity investment duopoly, with price competition in the second stage, yields the Cournot-Nash outcome.[19] They apply the efficient rationing rule, which specifies that a firm's residual demand equals market demand net of the other firm's capacity. In contrast, Carl Davidson and Raymond Denekere show that the Cournot-Nash outcome fails to occur with different rationing rules.[20]

If the Cournot-Nash equilibrium price exceeds the regulated price, then the market price is the regulated price P_0. If entry occurs, entrants displace the incumbent firm's sales. If entry does not occur, the incumbent supplies the regulated output, Q_0. If the Cournot-Nash equilibrium price is less than or equal to the regulated price, entry occurs and entrants displace the incumbent's sales. The Cournot-Nash equilibrium of the capacity game between entrants has the standard representation. An entering firm maximizes profit by choosing output q given the equilibrium output of the other firms $Q_{\pm}^*$. The firm maximizes profit over q:

$$\Pi(q, Q_{\pm}^*) = (P(q + Q_{\pm}^*) - g - A)q - f.$$

The equilibrium Cournot-Nash output per firm, q^*, solves the following condition:

(11) $$P'(nq^*)q^* + P(nq^*) - g - A = 0.$$

19. David M. Kreps & José A. Scheinkman, *Quantity Precommitment and Bertrand Competition Yield Cournot Outcomes*, 14 BELL J. ECON. 326 (1983).

20. Carl Davidson & Raymond Denekere, *Long-Run Competition in Capacity, Short-Run Competition in Price, and the Cournot Model*, 17 RAND J. ECON. 404 (1986).

Let $X^*(n) = nq^*(n)$ represent industry output and let $P^*(n) = P(nq^*(n))$ be the equilibrium price. Assume that the following condition holds:

(12) $$P''(X)X/n + P'(X) + k/X^2 < 0.$$

That condition is sufficient for the second-order condition of the firm's maximization problem to hold.

If the market price is P_0, the access price is $A = b + k/Q_0$. If the market price is less than P_0, the access price is $A^* = b + k/X^*$, where $X^* = D(P^*)$ is total output. To determine the effect of market structure on the Cournot-Nash equilibrium, it is necessary to take into account the endogenous access price. For ease of presentation, we treat the number of firms as a continuous variable. From equation (11), substituting for $A = b + k/X^*$ and differentiating with respect to n, we obtain:

(13) $\partial X^*/\partial n = [P'(X^*)X^*/n]/$

$$\{[P''(X^*)X^* + P'(X^*)] + n[P'(X^*) + k/(X^*)^2]\}.$$

The numerator is less than zero because demand is downward sloping; the denominator is less than zero by our stability assumption in equation (12). Therefore, total output is increasing in the number of firms, $\partial X^*/\partial n > 0$. Notice that as the number of firms increases, the higher output will lower the access price.

Given the first-order condition in equation (11), we can rewrite the operating return of the firm in equilibrium as

(14) $\pi(n) = (P(X^*(n)) - g - b - k/X^*(n))X^*(n)/n$

$$= - P'(X^*(n)) [X^*(n)/n]^2.$$

Differentiating with respect to the number of firms and using the expression for $\partial X^*/\partial n$ from equation (13), we get

(15) $\pi'(n) = (X^*/n^2)(\partial X^*/\partial n)$

$$\times [P''(X^*)X^* + 2n(P'(X^*) + k/(X^*)^2)].$$

Therefore, $\pi'(n) < 0$ by our earlier assumptions. Thus, for every level of entry cost f, there is a unique market structure $n^* = n^*(f)$ that solves

(16) $\pi(n^*) = f,$

where $n^*(f)$ is strictly decreasing in f. The market structure n^* depends on the access charge $A = b + k/X^*$, which itself is endogenous. Define $q^* = q^*(n)$, $X^* = X^*(n)$, and $P^* = P(X^*(n))$.

Since $X^*(n)$ is increasing in the number of firms, and the equilibrium market structure $n^*(f)$ in turn is decreasing in entry costs, it follows that total output with entry is decreasing in entry cost: $\partial X^*/\partial f < 0$. Let f_0 be the level of entry costs at which total output equals the regulated output:

(17) $X^*(f_0) = Q_0.$

From equations (11) and (16), noting that $A = P_0 - c$, the critical entry cost and corresponding market structure satisfy

(18) $P'(Q_0)Q_0/n_0 + c - g = 0$

(19) $(c - g)Q_0/n_0 = f_0.$

Solving for f_0 and n_0 as functions of the regulated output, we get

(20) $f_0 = (c - g)^2/(-P'(Q_0))$

(21) $n_0 = -P'(Q_0)Q_0/(c - g).$

There are two possibilities. Suppose first that entry costs are greater than or equal to the critical level, $f \geq f_0$. Then, $X^*(f) \leq Q_0$ and $P^*(f) \geq P_0$, so that, were entry to occur, the market price would remain at P_0 and the access charge would equal $A = P_0 - c$. The zero-profit condition for potential entrants is then

(22) $(P_0 - g - A)Q_0/n - f = (c - g)\, Q_0/n - f = 0.$

Therefore, entry occurs if and only if the cost savings on the regulated output cover the cost of entry.

Next suppose that entry costs are less than the critical level, $f < f_0$. Then, $X^*(f) > Q_0$ and $P^*(f) < P_0$. The access charge equals $A^* = b + k/X^*(f)$. The market price equals $P^* = g + b + k/X^* + n^*f/X^*$ from equation (16). Thus, $P^* < P_0$ if and only if

(23) $g + b + k/X^* + n^*f/X^* < c + b + k/Q_0.$

We illustrate the price difference in figure 2. The gap between the two average cost curves widens as output increases. It then follows from $P^* < P_0$ that the regulated firm's average cost must lie above the curve defined by $P = g + b + k/Q + n^*f/Q$ and evaluated at Q_0:

(24) $g + b + k/Q_0 + n^*f/Q_0 < c + b + k/Q_0.$

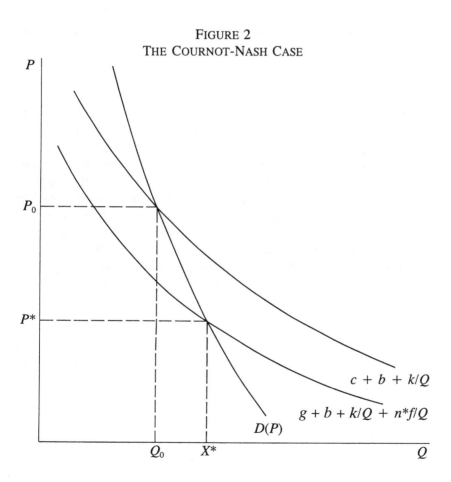

FIGURE 2
THE COURNOT-NASH CASE

Conversely, let $n^*(f)$, $X^*(f)$ be a Cournot-Nash equilibrium, where $(c - g)Q_0 \geq n^*f$. Then, by figure 2, $P^* < P_0$ and $X^* > Q_0$. Thus, the access charge satisfies the cost-efficiency condition in equation (10). Therefore, entry occurs under Cournot-Nash competition if and only if the cost savings on production cover the cost of entry.

The equilibrium ECPR, $A^* = b + k/X^*$, is lower than the benchmark case:

$$A_0 - A^* = k(1/Q_0 - 1/X^*).$$

We can represent the ECPR in two other ways. From the Cournot-Nash entry condition, equation (16), the ECPR equals

(25) $$A^* = P^* (1 - (1/n^*\eta)) - g,$$

where $\eta = - D'(P^*)P^*/X^*$ is the elasticity of market demand. Alternatively, using the entry condition (equation (16)), subtract per-unit entry cost from the entrant's markup:

(26) $$A^* = P^* - g - f/(X^*/n).$$

The ECPR is less than the markup over marginal cost to account for entrants' operating profits, or equivalently, to account for entry costs. That implies that the ECPR is lower than in the benchmark case, $A_0 - A^* = k(1/Q_0 - 1/X^*) > 0$. Therefore, given capacity competition and entry costs, the ECPR should reflect the cost of entry per unit of output.

We can compare the Cournot-Nash ECPR with the contestable-market ECPR by using figures 2 and 1, respectively. The equilibrium output in the contestable-market case is greater because there are no entry costs. Therefore, because $A = b + k/X$, it follows that the ECPR is lower in the contestable-market case compared with the Cournot-Nash case. So, the Cournot-Nash ECPR lies between the benchmark and contestable-market access charges.

PRODUCT DIFFERENTIATION

In this section, we consider a market equilibrium with product differentiation. We apply the Perloff-Salop model,[21] which combines elements

---

21. Perloff & Salop, *supra* note 3.

of Harold Hotelling's spatial competition model[22] and Edward H. Chamberlin's differentiated products approach.[23] The interesting feature of the Perloff-Salop model is that many brands compete for representative consumers. With a finite number of consumers, firms compete for market shares. We show that the access-pricing rule is efficient. That is, prices fall below the regulated level if and only if there are cost savings at the monopoly output. Cost savings occur when operating cost savings at the regulated firm's output level exceed total entry costs.

Before deregulation, all consumers purchase the incumbent's brand. There are L consumers, so that with universal service, $Q_0 = L$. The regulated price is thus $P_0 = b + c + k/L$. After deregulation, the incumbent's brand competes with those of new entrants. Assume that the incumbent pays the same access charge as entrants do for using the network. Moreover, the incumbent supplies the final product through an independent subsidiary that has the same operating cost as entrants, g, presumably because the incumbent avoids costly regulatory constraints and can employ the same technology as entrants. The incumbent incurs a setup cost, h, in establishing its subsidiary, which is less than or equal to that of entrants, because the incumbent already has some facilities in place. The net earnings of the subsidiary are used to offset the incumbent's stranded investment. Thus, the incumbent's net stranded investment is

$$(27) \qquad \Delta = k - \Pi_1,$$

where $\Pi_1 = (P - g - A)Q_1$ is the incumbent's profit from competitive activities. Total output remains at L with competition. Therefore, the access charge is

$$(28) \qquad A = b + k/L - \Pi_1/L = P_0 - c - \Pi_1/L.$$

To examine the postentry equilibrium, we apply the Perloff-Salop model. There are an unlimited number of possible brands, $i = 1, 2, \ldots, n$. There are L consumers, each of whom has a preference vector that assigns relative values to each of the brands, $\theta = (\theta_1, \theta_2, \ldots)$. Given n brands from which to choose, the consumer purchases the brand that maximizes his surplus:

22. Harold Hotelling, *Stability in Competition*, 39 ECON. J. 41 (1929).
23. EDWARD H. CHAMBERLIN, THE THEORY OF MONOPOLISTIC COMPETITION (Harvard University Press 1933).

(29) $s_i = \theta_i - p_i, \quad i = 1, \ldots, n,$

where p_i is the price of brand i and s_i is the surplus from purchasing brand i. As in the Perloff-Salop model, consumers purchase the best buy, regardless of whether surplus may be negative. Each of the elements of a consumer's preference vector, θ_i, are independent draws from the uniform distribution on the unit interval. The preference vectors of each consumer are statistically independent from each other. The demand for firm i's brand is thus

(30) $Q_i\,(p_1, p_2, \ldots, p_n) = \Pr\,(s_i \geq \max_{j \neq i} s_j)\, L.$

Firms choose prices to maximize profits in a Bertrand-Nash equilibrium. Profits are defined by

(31) $\Pi_i\,(p_1, p_2, \ldots, p_n) = (p_i - g - A)Q_i\,(p_1, p_2, \ldots, p_n) - f.$

Perloff and Salop restrict attention to single-price equilibria and show that if such an equilibrium exists, it is unique. Thus, in equilibrium $p_i = P$, $i = 1, \ldots, n$, and output per brand is equal to Q_i,

(32) $Q_i = L \int_0^1 \theta^{n-1} d\theta = L/n.$

The slope of each brand's demand curve is

(33) $\dfrac{\partial Q_i}{\partial p_i} = -(n-1)L \int_0^1 \theta^{n-2} d\theta = -L.$

The equilibrium price solves $p_i(1 - 1/\eta_i) = g + A$ so that

(34) $P^* = g + A + 1/n.$

The competitive single-price equilibrium with entry is determined by equation (34) and the zero-profit condition:

(35) $P^* = g + A + n^*f/L.$

The incumbent firm earns a positive profit if it has lower setup costs than entrants:

(36) $\Pi_1 = (P^* - g - A)L/n^* - h = f - h.$

The access charge is lower than the benchmark by the amount of the incumbent's profit per unit of total output,

(37) $A^* = b + k/L - (f - h)/L,$

or $A^* = P_0 - c - (f - h)/L$. We obtain the equilibrium price by substituting for A in equation (35),

(38) $P^* = g + b + (k + h + (n^* - 1)f)/L.$

The competitive equilibrium price falls below the regulated price if and only if entry is efficient:

(39) $(c - g)L \geq h + (n^* - 1)f.$

Thus, the ECPR retains its efficiency properties in the differentiated products model.

Because products are differentiated, however, consumers also benefit from increased variety. Thus, the value of entry is greater than the cost savings from more efficient entrants. The welfare benefits of entry equal the change in consumer surplus owing to competition, $S^* - S_0$, because profits are zero in equilibrium. The incumbent earns zero profit because the setup cost difference is deducted from net earnings from the access charge. Entrants earn zero profit owing to competition.

Consumer surplus is calculated as follows. Before deregulation, the expected value of the regulated firm's brand to any consumer equals ½ because values of brands are uniformly distributed. So, expected total surplus under regulation is $S_0 = L(½ - P_0)$. With competition, each consumer purchases the brand that yields the greatest surplus. At the single-price equilibrium, the expected value of the best buy for any consumer is the expected value of the maximum-order statistic, which equals $n/(n+1)$ for a sample of size n from the uniform distribution. Thus, expected total surplus under competition is $S^* = (n^*/(n^* +1) - P^*)$. The greater the number of competing brands, the higher the advantage of competition over a single brand available with universal service.

The change in welfare is thus

(40) $S^* - S_0 = L(n^*/(n^* + 1) - \frac{1}{2} + P_0 - P^*)$

$$= L(n^*/(n^* + 1) - \frac{1}{2} + (c - g)) - h - (n^* - 1)f.$$

Consumer surplus can increase even if prices rise as long as the price increase does not exceed the gains from variety:

(41) $$P^* - P_0 \le (n^* - 1)/2(n^* + 1).$$

From equations (34) and (35), the equilibrium market structure is $n^* = (L/f)^{\frac{1}{2}}$. So, in that simple framework, the access charge does not prevent efficient entry. Entry raises consumer surplus by increasing variety even with *less* efficient entrants as long as the cost difference is not excessive. Suppose that $h = f$ for ease of discussion. Then, welfare increases as long as

(42) $$g - c \le n^*/(n^* + 1) - 1/2 - 1/n^*.$$

The right-hand side of (42) is negative if there are three firms or fewer; it is positive if there are four or more firms. So, a cost advantage over the incumbent is necessary with fewer than four firms. If four or more firms can enter, the competitive equilibrium improves consumer surplus, even with entrants that are less efficient than the incumbent. Thus, less cost-efficient entry can occur with differentiated products as long as entry costs are not excessively high. The upper bound on fixed cost such that $n^* = (L/f)1/2 \ge 4$ is $f \le L/16$. In the basic framework, the ECPR does not alter the incentives for efficient entry.

A price cap equal to the regulated price would rule out variety-enhancing entry by less efficient competitors. With both a price cap and the ECPR, entry occurs if and only if there are cost efficiencies. That result suggests that price caps on final output restrict entry and product variety. The ECPR, in contrast, allows competitive entry to determine the appropriate level of product differentiation.

CONCLUSION

Network access charges are a means of recovering the network provider's incremental cost and opportunity costs of service. The opportunity costs of service are due to the loss in net revenue from the displacement of the incumbent's sales, offset by the earnings that the incumbent can achieve from employing its previously regulated assets in the new competitive environment.

Our analysis shows that several common criticisms of the efficient component-pricing rule are misplaced. First, the access price derived from the ECPR permits price to fall and output to expand for the final product relative to the price and output that had obtained under regulation. Second, that result holds under a variety of market structures. In contestable markets, under Cournot-Nash competition, and in markets characterized by product differentiation, the ECPR rewards entry by more efficient rivals and produces lower prices for the final product. The equilibrium access price implied by the ECPR for each of those market structures is lower than the access price that would obtain in the stylized benchmark case in which the incumbent is permitted to receive the regulated markup over the incremental cost of the final service. The greater the output expansion under competition, the lower should be the price that the ECPR implies. The extent of the output expansion depends on the elasticity of demand, the cost efficiency of entrants, and the level of costs that are to be recovered through access charges.

Access charges are compatible with the substantial deregulation that is occuring or has already occurred in telecommunications and electric power. Accordingly, the ECPR can form the basis for setting price caps on access. Such a price cap would allow the incumbent to lower access charges to compete with access alternatives and to expand sales of access. Access price caps can be adjusted by using productivity formulas to account for technological progress in providing access. They can also be adjusted as demand for access expands. They do not, however, need to be adjusted to reflect competitive alternatives for network transmission, because the incumbent already has an incentive to lower its access charges to meet the competition.

Full deregulation of access pricing is feasible if customers have actual or potential transmission alternatives. Controls on access charges can be imposed as a transition device for achieving cost recovery, and phased out as recovery is achieved and competition expands further. If the incumbent utility already has recovered stranded costs, if other provisions for cost recovery have been made, or if competitive returns allow recovery of costs, then there is no longer a need to use access charges for that purpose. In that case, the incumbent utility will set access prices relative to those of competing access providers. The next chapter addresses ECPR pricing in the presence of facilities-based competition. Voluntary exchange is, after all, superior to regulation as a means for determining opportunity costs.

9

The Market-Determined Efficient Component-Pricing Rule

THE TELECOMMUNICATIONS ACT OF 1996 promised to replace nearly a century of monopoly regulation of the local telephone exchange with a regime that Congress said would "promote competition and reduce regulation in order to secure lower prices and higher quality services for American telecommunications consumers and encourage the rapid deployment of new telecommunication technologies."[1] Sections 251 and 252 of the act are the core provisions by which Congress sought to open local telephone markets to competition.[2] Those two sections address the pricing of unbundled access to the network of the incumbent local exchange carrier (LEC). Roughly speaking, there are three ways for a firm to enter local telephony. First, it can build its own network and seek "interconnection" with the network of the incumbent LEC so that the entrant's customers can complete calls to the incumbent's customers. The relevant policy question is how much the incumbent LEC should charge to terminate a call originating on the entrant's network, and vice versa. The second method of entry is through "resale," which means that the entrant buys from the incumbent LEC, at a wholesale price, the basic service provided to the customer. The entrant then retails that service

---

1. Telecommunications Act of 1996, Pub. L. No. 104-104, 110 Stat. 56, 56.

2. 47 U.S.C. §§ 251, 252. In addition, Congress abolished any remaining legal barriers to entry: "No State or local statute or regulation, or other State or local legal requirement, may prohibit or have the effect of prohibiting the ability of any entity to provide any interstate or intrastate telecommunications service." *Id.* § 253(a).

under its own brand name and perhaps combines the service with other offerings. In the case of resale, the pertinent question is the size of the wholesale discount that the entrant should receive from the retail price for the basic service that the incumbent LEC sells to its customers. The third method of entry is through the leasing of unbundled network elements—the building blocks of the local network including loops and switches. The entrant then can build its own network on an à la carte basis by buying some inputs from the incumbent LEC and procuring other inputs from rivals already in the market (such as local transport services provided by competitive access providers) or directly from equipment vendors (such as manufacturers of switches).

If the entrant and the incumbent LEC cannot negotiate mutually acceptable prices, terms, and conditions of interconnection, resale, or unbundling, then the Telecommunications Act directs the state public utilities commission (PUC) to resolve the dispute through compulsory arbitration.[3] It appeared as of late 1996 that entrants and incumbent LECs had been unable to reach any voluntary agreements on the pricing of resale and unbundled network elements. As a consequence, literally hundreds of arbitration proceedings began in the fall of 1996. In most cases, each arbitration was a one-on-one proceeding between a single entrant and the incumbent LEC. Presumably each arbitration will produce an appeal by the loser that will eventually go to the state supreme court. It is also possible that the losers will launch collateral attacks on the state arbitration decisions in federal court. Under either scenario there will likely be conflicts that arise in the interpretation of the Telecommunications Act of 1996. Those conflicts could be between the states, between the federal courts of appeal, or between the state courts and the federal courts. The prospect that the Supreme Court will review the substantive pricing provisions of the Telecommunications Act is therefore highly likely. The appeal would present questions of statutory interpretation under the Telecommunications Act, but it also could pose takings questions presented by incumbent LECs and antitrust questions presented by entrants.

Sections 251 and 252 of the Communications Act, added by the 1996 legislation, provide a skeleton for the pricing of interconnection, resale, and unbundling. Litigation immediately erupted over whether, as a matter of jurisdiction, the proper body for adding the flesh to those provisions is the Federal Communications Commission (FCC) or a state public utilities commission. In what the local exchange carriers and some PUCs re-

---

3. 47 U.S.C. § 252(b). The state commission must rule on the arbitration within nine months of the time that the incumbent LEC was notified of the entrant's request for arbitration. *Id.* § 252(b)(4)(C).

garded as a power grab, the FCC issued its *First Report and Order* in August 1996, a 683-page directive that established pricing rules that the agency expected the states to follow.[4] The grounds for the multiple appeals filed were, generally speaking, that the FCC had exceeded its jurisdiction and that the substantive pricing standards that it adopted were so low as to effect an uncompensated taking of the property of incumbent LECs in violation of the Fifth Amendment.[5] Although in late 1996 the U.S. Court of Appeals for the Eighth Circuit stayed the pricing provisions of the *First Report and Order* pending the court's decision on the merits of the appeal,[6] the Telecommunications Act meanwhile obliged state PUCs to establish prices for resale and unbundled network elements.

In this chapter we focus on the pricing of government-mandated access to unbundled network elements. That topic raises important questions of regulatory economics. But the complexity of those questions should not obscure one simple fact: An incumbent LEC will become insolvent if it cannot recover its total costs. If the government requires the incumbent LEC to sell its inputs to competitors, then the LEC should be reimbursed for all its costs and be allowed the reasonable rate of return expressly authorized by Congress. The prices for unbundled network elements that entrants have proposed in actual arbitration proceedings, however, would deny the incumbent LEC recovery of and a reasonable return on its costs. As a consequence, the incumbent LEC's shareholders would be forced to subsidize competitors as they enter local exchange telephony. The same problems would arise with the pricing rules and default proxy rates that the FCC established in its *First Report and Order*, which the Eighth Circuit stayed. Nonetheless, some states thereafter adopted prices virtually identical to the FCC's proxy prices while purporting to reach that result by some means other than deferring to FCC rules that the federal appellate court had stayed.[7] If imposed on the incumbent LEC, such prices for mandatory network access would raise significant takings questions. In addition, the incumbent LEC's

---

4. Implementation of the Local Competition Provisions in the Telecommunications Act of 1996 and Interconnection Between Local Exchange Carriers and Commercial Mobile Radio Service Providers, First Report and Order, CC Dkt. Nos. 96-98, 95-185, 11 F.C.C. Rcd. 15,499 (1996) [hereinafter *First Report and Order*].

5. U.S. CONST. amend. V ("Nor shall private property be taken for public use, without just compensation.").

6. Iowa Util. Bd. *v.* FCC, 109 F.3d 418 (8th Cir. 1996). As chapter 16 explains, the Eighth Circuit subsequently vacated the FCC's pricing rules.

7. *E.g.*, Application of AT&T Communications of Pa., Inc.; Petition for Arbitration of Interconnection Agreement with GTE North, Inc., Recommended Decision, Dkt. No. A-310125F0002, at 16–17 (Pa. Pub. Utils. Comm'n Oct. 10, 1996).

inability to recover its costs would have serious ramifications for consumers. Just as rent control can harm incentives for investment in maintaining the quality of the housing stock, so also prices for unbundled network elements that impaired the incumbent LEC's financial integrity would discourage investment in the local telecommunications network. That investment, however, is critical not only to replacing the existing infrastructure as it wears out, but also to maintaining and expanding the infrastructure necessary for new competitors to enter the market for local telephony by any means other than building their own network facilities.

This chapter provides a pricing rule for the states to apply when administering sections 251 and 252 that is appropriate on both legal and economic grounds. The rule does not depend on the ultimate resolution by the federal courts of the jurisdictional question concerning the *First Report and Order*. Moreover, our rule anticipates and avoids the takings question, which would otherwise fuel additional litigation once the jurisdictional question has been resolved. Our rule is thus consistent with the principle that a court should construe a statute so as to avoid a "'question of constitutional law in advance of the necessity of deciding it.'"[8] We argue that prices for unbundled network elements should be set according to a standard that we call the market-determined efficient component-pricing rule (M-ECPR). Our rule is a refinement of the efficient component-pricing rule (ECPR) developed by William J. Baumol and Robert D. Willig.[9] As we explain, the M-ECPR satisfies the

---

8. Ashwander *v.* Tennessee Valley Auth., 297 U.S. 288, 341 (1936) (Brandeis, J. concurring) (quoting Liverpool, N.Y. & Philadelphia S.S. Co. *v.* Commissioners of Emigration, 113 U.S. 22, 39 (1885)). That principle applies to takings. *See, e.g.*, United States *v.* Security Indus. Bank, 459 U.S. 70, 78–80 (1982).

9. WILLIAM J. BAUMOL & J. GREGORY SIDAK, TRANSMISSION PRICING AND STRANDED COSTS IN THE ELECTRIC POWER INDUSTRY 115–38 (AEI Press 1995); WILLIAM J. BAUMOL & J. GREGORY SIDAK, TOWARD COMPETITION IN LOCAL TELEPHONY 93–116 (MIT Press & AEI Press 1994); William J. Baumol & J. Gregory Sidak, *The Pricing of Inputs Sold to Competitors*, 11 YALE J. ON REG. 171 (1994); William J. Baumol & Robert D. Willig, Brief of Evidence: Economic Principles for Evaluation of the Issues Raised by Clear Communications, Ltd. on Interconnection with Telecom Corporation of New Zealand, Ltd. (undated) [hereinafter *Baumol-Willig New Zealand Brief*], *submitted in* Clear Communications, Ltd. *v.* Telecom Corp. of New Zealand, Ltd., slip op. (H.C. Dec. 22, 1992), *rev'd*, slip op. (C.A. Dec. 28, 1993), *rev'd*, [1995] 1 N.Z.L.R. 385 (Oct. 19, 1994, Judgment of the Lords of the Judicial Committee of the Privy Council); William J. Baumol, *Some Subtle Issues in Railroad Regulation*, 10 INT'L J. TRANSP. ECON. 341 (1983); *see also* William J. Baumol, Janusz A. Ordover & Robert D. Willig, *Parity Pricing and Its Critics: Necessary Conditions for Efficiency in Provision of Bottleneck Services to Competitors*, 14 YALE J. ON REG. 145 (1997).

FCC's recommendation that prices for unbundled network elements be based on forward-looking costs. The M-ECPR used alone, however, will not allow the incumbent LEC to recover its full forward-looking costs because states typically have mandated cross-subsidies that are embedded in the incumbent LEC's rate structure. For a state PUC to avoid leaving the incumbent LEC uncompensated for a portion of its costs, the commission must also establish a competitively neutral, nonbypassable end-user charge. When the M-ECPR is combined with a system of competitively neutral end-user charges, the rule satisfies Congress's requirement, discussed below, that prices be based on costs and allow for a reasonable profit.

We emphasize at the outset that the M-ECPR differs from the FCC's erroneous description of the ECPR in its *First Report and Order*. To avoid confusion, we call the FCC's mischaracterization of efficient component pricing the FCC-ECPR.[10] Unlike the simplistic FCC-ECPR, the M-ECPR takes full account of competitive entry when setting prices for unbundled network elements. In that respect, the M-ECPR benefits consumers and avoids all the shortcomings that the FCC attributed to the FCC-ECPR in the *First Report and Order*. In contrast, setting prices equal to total service long-run incremental cost (TELRIC), as many entrants have proposed, is inappropriate for pricing unbundled elements, as we show in chapter 12. Such pricing subsidizes entrants and removes the incumbent LEC's opportunity to earn revenues that cover its costs, because TELRIC excludes the LEC's shared costs and common costs.[11]

The first part of this chapter shows that the M-ECPR provides a unified framework for pricing unbundled network elements. We then argue that the *First Report and Order* prevents an incumbent LEC from covering its total costs because the FCC's pricing rules would deny any recovery, through access prices, of the incumbent LEC's historical costs and would ensure that full recovery of its forward-looking costs would be impossible to achieve. The default prices that the FCC established as an "interim" measure would only exacerbate that shortfall in cost recovery.

10. *First Report and Order*, 11 F.C.C. Rcd. at 15,859–60 ¶¶ 708–11; *see also* Implementation of the Local Competition Provisions in the Telecommunications Act of 1996, Notice of Proposed Rulemaking, CC Dkt. No. 96-98, 11 F.C.C. Rcd. 14,171, 14,222 ¶ 147 (1996) [hereinafter *Interconnection NPRM*].

11. The FCC's definition of common costs includes what are sometimes called *shared costs*. *Id*. Shared costs are incurred in the provision of two or more services (but not the collection of all the firm's services) but are not incremental to any individual service. As we show in chapter 12, TELRIC pricing fails to recover any of the firm's shared costs.

PRICING UNBUNDLED NETWORK ELEMENTS

The Telecommunications Act of 1996 added section 252(d)(1) to the Communications Act. That provision states that the price of an unbundled network element "(A) shall be (i) based on the cost (determined without reference to a rate-based proceeding) of providing the . . . network element . . . , and (ii) nondiscriminatory, and (B) may include a reasonable profit."[12] In its *First Report and Order* the FCC related section 252(d)(1) to the agency's notion of total element long-run incremental cost and reasoned "that, under a TELRIC methodology, incumbent LECs' prices for . . . unbundled network elements shall recover the forward-looking costs directly attributable to the specified element, as well as a reasonable allocation of forward-looking common costs."[13]

The M-ECPR satisfies the FCC's recommendation that prices for unbundled network elements be based on forward-looking costs. When combined with a system of competitively neutral end-user charges, the M-ECPR also satisfies the requirement of Congress that prices be based on costs and allow for a reasonable profit.

Cost and Profit Concepts

It is necessary to define key cost and profit concepts before one can understand the debate over the pricing of elements and appreciate how the adoption of the M-ECPR would satisfy sections 251 and 252.

Costs. The *First Report and Order* refers to various cost concepts. The *total service long-run incremental cost* (TSLRIC) of a service sold to end users equals the difference in the firm's total costs with and without the provision of that service. In the *First Report and Order* the FCC coined the term *total element long-run incremental cost* (TELRIC) to describe costs that are incremental (or attributable) to individual network elements.[14] A firm's *joint* costs are those costs incurred when two or more services are produced in fixed proportion.[15] A firm's *common* costs

12. 47 U.S.C. § 252(d)(1).

13. *First Report and Order,* 11 F.C.C. Rcd. at 15,847 ¶ 682.

14. *Id.* at 15,845–46 ¶ 678. We use TELRIC to refer to the long-run incremental cost of an unbundled network element and TSLRIC to refer to the long-run incremental cost of a retail service.

15. As the FCC notes, joint costs have the property that "when one product is produced, a second product is generated by the same production process at no additional cost." *Id.* at 15,845 ¶ 676. Feed for sheep, for example, is a joint cost of mutton and wool.

are costs incurred in the provision of some or all the firm's services that are not incremental to any individual service. Hence, common costs can be avoided only by shutting done the entire firm or by not producing a particular group of services under study. Consistent with the FCC's approach, we use the term *common costs* to refer collectively to all costs that are not incremental costs.[16] In addition, a regulated firm may have *residual costs* caused, for example, by assets that remain on its books even though they have no economic value.

To illustrate the concepts of incremental costs and common costs, consider a street vendor who operates a stand that sells both hot dogs and hamburgers. The incremental cost of a hot dog includes the cost to the vendor of the hot dog, the bun, and condiments. Similarly, the incremental cost of the hamburger includes the ground beef, the bun, and condiments. The common costs include the cost of the grill used to cook the hot dogs and hamburgers, as well as the stand. In the provision of local telephone service, common costs include general and administrative costs (for example, accounting and finance, external relations, and human resources) and support costs, such as general purpose computers. Incremental (or attributable) costs include the costs of central office switching and cable and wire facilities.

Both incremental costs and common costs necessarily include the return on invested capital. For example, the TSLRIC of a service must include a return on capital sufficient to keep those resources in their current employment. If the return on capital invested to provide a service is below the *competitive or fair rate of return,* the capital market will operate to move those investments to other projects that yield (at least) a competitive return. A competitive or fair rate of return is that return that could be earned on an investment of comparable risk.

Profit. Section 252(d)(1) and the *First Report and Order* also refer to "profit."[17] A firm earns a "reasonable profit" when its *economic profits* equal zero. Economic profits are zero when total revenues equal total costs, inclusive of a competitive return on capital. The incumbent LEC's return on capital equals the sum of the return on capital for its incremental costs and common costs. The allowance in section 252(d)(1) for a "reasonable profit" is accomplished when the incumbent LEC's prices for its regulated services are established so that, on average, the LEC earns zero economic profits on the entire array of regulated services that

---

16. *Id.*

17. 47 U.S.C. § 252(d)(1); *First Report and Order*, 11 F.C.C. Rcd. at 15,854 ¶ 699.

it supplies. That is, the firm's rates should be established so that, on average, it earns zero economic profits on its regulated services as a whole. Of course, random market factors may cause the LEC's profits to exceed or fall below that value in any particular period.

At the risk of redundancy four points bear emphasis because they have generated controversy in arbitration proceedings to establish prices for unbundled network elements. First, *firms* earn profits; individual products or services do not. It is therefore an incorrect reading of section 252(d)(1) to say that no individual unbundled network element may earn more than a "reasonable profit." Such a reading of that statute would make economic sense only if each network element were supplied by a firm producing only that element as its output and nothing else. The entire exercise of unbundling addressed in sections 251 and 252 presupposes, to the contrary, that the incumbent LEC is a multiproduct firm. Furthermore, the continuation of regulatory policies that impose public service obligations on the incumbent LEC, and the continuation of any subsidies in the retail rate structure, imply that the incumbent LEC will earn a *negative* contribution to its overall profitability from some services (such as basic local service and service to high-cost customers for whom the incumbent LEC is obliged to serve as the carrier of last resort). Given that regulators continue to embed subsidies into the rate structure, it will necessarily be the case that the incumbent LEC will have to earn returns to certain other services that, if viewed in isolation, would appear to yield positive economic profit. For that reason, the proper reading of section 252(d)(1) corresponds to the economic reality of the situation: Regulators must allow the incumbent LEC the opportunity to earn a "reasonable profit"—a zero economic profit—across the full aggregation of regulated services that the LEC is required to offer.

Second, the only profit that is relevant for purpose of section 252(d)(1) is the profit on the incumbent LEC's *regulated* services. Typically an incumbent LEC is owned by a holding company that has unregulated subsidiaries that make investments in overseas telecommunications ventures or investments in domestic activities that are not regulated. The profit that the incumbent LEC's parent earns from those unregulated subsidiaries is not relevant to the definition of *reasonable profit* under section 252(d)(1) because that profit does not flow from investments made under the regulatory contract in a particular state to discharge the LEC's assumption of public service obligations there. By analogy, the Supreme Court long ago announced as a matter of takings jurisprudence in *Brooks-Scanlon Co.* v. *Railroad Commission of Louisiana* that it is impermissible to judge whether rate regulation is confiscatory by including the returns to unregulated operations of the company in question.[18]

Third, whether the incumbent LEC earns a profit must be determined with respect to its regulated subsidiary *in the particular jurisdiction under consideration.* A state PUC cannot average profit figures across multiple states to determine whether the prices that it sets for unbundled elements in its own state allow the incumbent LEC there the opportunity to earn a reasonable profit. The California Public Utilities Commission, for example, cannot deny an incumbent LEC in California the opportunity to earn a reasonable profit when it sells unbundled elements to entrants in California on the rationale that the Public Utilities Commission of Ohio has allowed the LEC's sister company in Ohio to earn a return there that the California regulators deem to include economic profit. If regulators could do so, they would be tempted to engage in a form of opportunistic behavior: They could "export" to other states the burden of ensuring that the parent company of the various sister LECs achieved revenue adequacy for its local exchange operations as a whole. But, of course, once one state acted in that opportunistic manner, others would follow, and it would be impossible for remaining states to cover the parent company's resulting deficit from its local exchange operations.

A fourth and related point concerns the argument advanced by entrants into local telephony that uncompensatory prices for unbundled network elements (and for resale, for that matter) are legally permissible because the Telecommunications Act of 1996 liberated incumbent LECs to enter other markets—particularly the interLATA long-distance market—as a quid pro quo. That argument is not plausible if one assumes, as the interexchange carriers maintain, that the in-region interLATA market is competitive. That proposition, however, is the subject of bitter controversy as a result of the empirical research by Paul W. MacAvoy suggesting that long-distance markets exhibit tacit collusion among the three major carriers.[19] If interLATA markets are competitive, then simple arithmetic disposes of the quid pro quo argument. By definition, an incumbent LEC that is forced to accept losses in local

---

18. 251 U.S. 396, 399 (1920) (Holmes, J.) ("The plaintiff may be making money from its sawmill and lumber business but it no more can be compelled to spend that than it can be compelled to spend any other money to maintain a railroad for the benefit of others who do not care to pay for it."). *See also* Norfolk & W. Ry. *v.* Conley, 236 U.S. 605, 609 (1915) (Hughes, J.).

19. PAUL W. MACAVOY, THE FAILURE OF ANTITRUST AND REGULATION TO ESTABLISH COMPETITION IN LONG-DISTANCE TELEPHONE SERVICES (MIT Press & AEI Press 1996).

exchange services because of unbundling at uncompensatory prices will earn a return that is below the competitive return on capital. The only way for the incumbent LEC to earn a competitive return overall once it may provide in-region interLATA services is for the LEC to earn supracompetitive returns from those new long-distance services. But if those services are by hypothesis currently earning only a competitive return for the firms providing them, then the incumbent LEC would be averaging a competitive return on capital in the interLATA market and a less-than-competitive return on capital in the local exchange market. The result of that averaging is necessarily an overall return to the LEC that is below the competitive return on capital. In short, the quid pro quo argument is plausible only if those advancing it make what is essentially an admission against interest—namely, that interexchange carriers currently are able to earn supracompetitive returns.[20]

The FCC's Rules for Pricing Unbundled Network Elements

Having defined the relevant cost and profit concepts, we now examine how the FCC sought in its *First Report and Order* to set the price for an unbundled network element at the element's TELRIC plus a reasonable share of the incumbent LEC's forward-looking common costs. In chapter 12 we identify problems that arise as a consequence of the FCC's definition of forward-looking costs.

Calculating Total Element Long-Run Incremental Costs. The first step is to calculate the incumbent LEC's TELRIC for each of its seven unbundled network elements identified in the *First Report and Order*.[21] The FCC defines TELRIC as "the forward-looking cost over the long run of the total quantity of the facilities and functions that are directly attributable to, or reasonably identifiable as incremental to, such element, calculated taking as given the incumbent LEC's provision of other

20. Alternatively, one could argue that the incumbent LEC could earn supracompetitive returns because it would have substantially lower costs of marketing long-distance services to customers than the interexchange carriers have. That assumption is not plausible, however, given that the incumbent LECs would be novices at marketing interLATA services and would face at least four established competitors.

21. The seven network elements are local loops; local switching; dedicated transmission links; shared transmission facilities between tandem switches and end offices; tandem switching; signaling and call-related database services; and collocation. 47 C.F.R. § 51.509 (stayed), in *First Report and Order*, 11 F.C.C. Rcd. at 16,220 app. B.

elements."[22] The *First Report and Order* requires that TELRICs be calculated by assuming the use of the most efficient technology deployed in the incumbent LEC's existing wire centers.[23] In addition, estimations of the incumbent LEC's TELRICs are (1) to assume that in the long run, all costs are avoidable; (2) to exclude common costs; and (3) to use the cost-causation principle, which states that costs caused by the provision of a given network element should be attributable to that element.[24]

Calculating Forward-Looking Common Costs. Second, after calculating all of the incumbent LEC's TELRICs, it is necessary to estimate the LEC's forward-looking common costs, which the *First Report and Order* defines as "economic costs efficiently incurred in providing a group of elements or services (which may include all elements or services provided by the incumbent LEC) that cannot be attributed directly to individual elements or services."[25] A firm's forward-looking common costs are defined as its forward-looking total costs minus its forward-looking attributable costs (equivalently, the sum of the network element TELRICs).

How does one then estimate the incumbent LEC's forward-looking total costs? The economic principles of regulated firms imply that a good approximation of the incumbent LEC's forward-looking total costs are its current revenues. Regulation allows firms the opportunity to earn a fair return on their invested capital.[26] That principle has two important implications: (1) in long-run market equilibrium, regulated firms do not earn positive economic profits; and (2) in long-run market equilibrium, regulated firms are not forced to earn negative economic profits. Thus, regulation provides a firm with sufficient cash flows to replace depreciated capital and to cover its current operating costs, but regulators

22. 47 C.F.R. § 51.505(b) (stayed), in *First Report and Order*, 11 F.C.C. Rcd. at 16,218 app. B.

23. *First Report and Order*, 11 F.C.C. Rcd. at 15,848–49 ¶ 685 ("We . . . conclude that the forward-looking pricing methodology for interconnection and unbundled network elements should be based on costs that assume that wire centers will be placed at the incumbent LEC's current wire center locations, but that the reconstructed local network will employ the most efficient technology for reasonably foreseeable capacity requirements.").

24. *Id.* at 15,850–51 ¶¶ 690–92.

25. 47 C.F.R. § 51.505(c) (stayed), in *First Report and Order*, 11 F.C.C. Rcd. at 16,218, app. B.

26. *See, e.g.,* Hayne E. Leland, *Regulation of Natural Monopolies and the Fair Rate of Return,* 5 BELL J. ECON. 3 (1974); Bruce C. Greenwald, *Rate Base Selection and the Structure of Regulation,* 15 RAND J. ECON. 85 (1984).

constrain the cash flows to prevent the firm from earning positive economic profits.

The cash flows of a regulated firm must allow it to recover its capital costs on a going-forward basis—not just on a historic basis. In other words, the regulated firm's cash flows must be large enough for the firm to replace its capital over time. Thus, a regulated firm's rates of return and depreciation are adjusted so that its cash flows approximately equal those that would result from the use of replacement costs rather than book costs for its invested capital. Of course, replacement costs may vary from book costs because of inflation, changes in relative input prices (for example, rising labor rates or falling capital costs), and changes in technology. Adjusting for those factors, a regulated firm's cash flows should approximate the same cash flows that would result from an explicit, forward-looking calculation of capital costs and operating costs.[27]

Determining the Reasonable Share of Forward-Looking Common Costs to Allocate to Individual Network Elements. Finally, once one has estimated the incumbent LEC's individual TELRICs and its forward-looking common costs, the remaining step in pricing network elements under the FCC's approach is to make "a reasonable allocation of forward-looking common costs" across the various elements.[28] The *First Report and Order* defines a "reasonable allocation" as follows:

> The sum of a reasonable allocation of forward-looking common costs and the total element long-run incremental cost of an element shall not exceed the stand-alone cost associated with the element. In this context, stand-alone costs are the total forward-looking costs, including corporate costs, that would be incurred to produce a given element if that element

27. We therefore do not agree with Janusz A. Ordover when he asserts: "The M-ECPR methodology for estimating forward-looking common costs enables the ILEC [incumbent LEC] to recover its full embedded costs, and not just the forward-looking costs, because it treats revenues, which reflect historic costs, as a proxy for forward-looking economic costs." Prefiled Rebuttal Testimony of Janusz A. Ordover, Petition of AT&T Communications of Wisconsin, Inc. for Arbitration per § 252(b) of the Telecommunications Act of 1996 to Establish an Interconnection Agreement with GTE North, Inc., Nos. 265-MA-102, 2180-MA-100, 41 (Pub. Serv. Comm'n of Wisc., filed Oct. 21, 1996) (prepared for AT&T Communications of Wisconsin, Inc.) [hereinafter *Ordover Rebuttal Testimony*].

28. 47 C.F.R. § 51.505(a) (stayed), in *First Report and Order*, 11 F.C.C. Rcd. at 16,218 app. B.

were provided by an efficient firm that produced nothing but the given element.[29]

In general, there are two approaches to allocating common costs. One can use an arbitrary accounting formula, which produces fully distributed cost pricing. Or one can allocate common costs to individual goods on the basis of actual market forces. The FCC endorses the former, while we endorse the latter.

The Economic Rationale for the M-ECPR

The M-ECPR prices a network element by summing the its direct economic costs and opportunity costs to the incumbent LEC. The opportunity costs of providing an unbundled network element equal the revenues that can be generated by the use of that element, given the presence of all market alternatives, minus the direct economic costs, including the cost of making the element available on an unbundled basis. The opportunity cost of a product or input equals its value in its *best alternative use*, which will change over time. Opportunity costs are therefore by definition forward-looking.

How do companies determine the economic costs of their inputs in practice? Some inputs are purchased on the market. For those inputs the determination of opportunity costs is straightforward because they equal the purchase cost of each input. The market price of the product or service provides the best guide to the economic value of that service because the price results from fundamental supply and demand forces. Consumers' willingness to pay and suppliers' costs are reflected in the price that clears the market.[30]

But not all inputs that a company uses are easily purchased in the marketplace. For inputs not purchased it is necessary to "impute" their cost—that is, to attribute to each such input the value in its best

---

29. 47 C.F.R. § 51.505(c)(2)(A) (stayed), in *First Report and Order*, 11 F.C.C. Rcd. at 16,218 app. B.

30. In a competitive market, the prices for products and services generally reflect their economic cost. If prices do not generate sufficient revenues to cover costs, firms do not have an incentive to provide those products and services. If prices generate revenues that are above costs, price competition between providers and entry of new providers will drive down prices. In a competitive market, price always includes compensation for such economic costs—for example, for the interest forgone by the firm when it supplies funds from retained earnings instead of borrowing them from a bank.

alternative use. When an input is unique to the company or is produced by the company itself, the economically correct price is the best alternative use of that input. Thus, if an owner-manager of a small business puts in time operating the business, the opportunity cost of his time to the business is the best return that he could obtain elsewhere.

The M-ECPR calculates prices for network elements that reflect market opportunities. The M-ECPR is a public interest approach to the problem of how a regulated firm should price unbundled network elements that it sells to a competitor. If a company produces an input and sells that input to another company, what would the economic cost of that input be? In that case, the economic cost would equal the direct cost of making that input plus the earnings forgone elsewhere by making the sale.[31] In other words, the economic cost of the input to be sold by the incumbent LEC to another company is the LEC's direct cost of making the input *plus* the opportunity forgone by the LEC from making the sale. That economic reasoning underlies the M-ECPR formula:

"access" price =   *the incumbent's incremental cost of "access" per unit plus the incumbent's opportunity cost of providing the unbundled input.*

That definition is consistent with the explication of the ECPR by Baumol, Willig, Sidak, and others.[32] In the context of unbundled network elements, the incremental cost of "access" is simply the TELRIC referenced in the FCC's *First Report and Order,* appropriately calculated. Recall that TELRIC represents the forward-looking cost (both capital and operating costs) that is attributable to a particular network element, such as a loop. The M-ECPR, however, imposes a constraint on the magnitude of opportunity costs that the creators of the ECPR overlooked.

---

31. We therefore do not agree with Frederick R. Warren-Boulton when he argues that "M-ECPR pricing is not based on cost" and consequently "is incompatible with the Telecommunications Act of 1996." Rebuttal Testimony of Frederick R. Warren-Boulton, In the Matter of AT&T Communications of the Southwest, Inc.'s Petition for Arbitration Pursuant to Section 252(b) of the Telecommunications Act of 1996 to Establish an Interconnection Agreement with GTE Midwest Inc., Case No. TO-97-63, 10 (Mo. Pub. Serv. Comm'n, filed Oct. 21, 1996) (prepared for AT&T Communications of the Southwest, Inc.) [hereinafter *Warren-Boulton Rebuttal Testimony*].

32. BAUMOL & SIDAK, TOWARD COMPETITION IN LOCAL TELEPHONY, *supra* note 9, at 94–95; Baumol & Sidak, *The Pricing of Inputs Sold to Competitors, supra* note 9, at 178–79; *Baumol-Willig New Zealand Brief, supra* note 9; Baumol, *Some Subtle Issues in Railroad Regulation, supra* note 9, at 353–54.

In the absence of market alternatives that offer end users prices below the incumbent LEC's retail rates, the opportunity cost to the LEC of providing the network element equals forgone revenues (based on the incumbent LEC's tariffed retail rate) less incremental costs.

When market alternatives are present, however, the prices of those alternatives determine the opportunity costs of unbundled network services.[33] The earlier literature on the ECPR did not recognize that constraint on the magnitude of opportunity costs, perhaps because Baumol and Willig developed the ECPR in the context of trackage rights in railroading and interconnection in local telephony—both instances where competition for the bottleneck input was by definition completely foreclosed.[34] We made this opportunity-cost refinement to the ECPR in a submission that we filed before the FCC in May 1996 in its interconnection proceeding.[35] But, as we explain below, the FCC failed to comprehend that such a constraint on opportunity cost exists under efficient component pricing. Instead, the FCC criticized the ECPR for *not* constraining opportunity cost; having incorrectly described the attributes of the rule in that manner, the agency then proceeded to reject the rule. That case of false labeling required us to give the name M-ECPR to our version of efficient component pricing so that it would be clear that opportunity cost, and hence price, are at all times market-determined on a forward-looking basis.

The M-ECPR shows that the economically correct measure of the incumbent LEC's opportunity cost of selling a network element (such as

---

33. Our references to "market alternatives" include both actual and potential alternatives.

34. Baumol and Sidak did acknowledge the quite different limitation on opportunity costs that they termed "virtual regulation":

> [T]he mere threat that the government may begin to regulate the price of the vertically integrated monopolist's final product may suffice to excise some or all of its monopoly rents from the opportunity-cost portion of the efficient component price. Stated differently, the incumbent's expected opportunity cost of providing interconnection to a competitor would exclude the monopoly rent over the final product.

William J. Baumol & J. Gregory Sidak, *The Pricing of Inputs Sold to Competitors: Rejoinder and Epilogue*, 12 YALE J. ON REG. 177, 185 (1995).

35. Michael J. Doane, J. Gregory Sidak & Daniel F. Spulber, An Empirical Analysis of Pricing Under Sections 251 and 252 of the Telecommunications Act of 1996, *appended to* Comments of GTE Service Corporation *in* Implementation of the Local Competition Provisions in the Telecommunications Act of 1996, Federal Communications Commission, CC Dkt. No. 96-98 (filed May 16, 1996).

a loop) is the difference between the market price of the service (inclusive of purchase, installation, and operating costs) and the LEC's incremental costs. With facilities-based competition for loops, the price of the service should be the sum of the LEC's incremental costs and the opportunity cost, which exactly equals the market price.[36] Properly calculated, M-ECPR pricing takes into account market limits on the contribution of revenues to forward-looking common costs. In that respect, the M-ECPR uses market benchmarks to determine the amount of forward-looking common costs that can be "reasonably" allocated to any given element.

Opportunity Cost, Stand-Alone Cost, Competition, and Price

In economics there is also no dispute as to the definition of opportunity costs.[37] The consensus position has been stated by David L. Kaserman and John W. Mayo as follows:

> The economic concept of costs includes the value of all inputs required for production, including the implicit value of those inputs owned by the producer . . . . Thus, economic costs include both implicit and explicit costs . . . . Implicit costs are defined as the opportunity cost of owned resources, where the term *opportunity cost*, in turn, is defined as the value of a resource in its best alternative use. Explicit costs are the out-of-pocket expenditures on inputs purchased by the firm (which, in the short run, include both fixed and variable inputs).[38]

---

36. One can also use the M-ECPR to determine wholesale prices for the resale services offered by incumbent LECs:

wholesale price = retail price − avoided cost of resale.

That method follows precisely section 252(d)(3), which states that "a State Commission shall determine wholesale rates on the basis of retail rates charged to subscribers for the telecommunications service requested, excluding the portion thereof attributable to any marketing, billing, collection, and other costs that will be avoided by the local exchange carrier." 47 U.S.C. § 252(d)(3). Because the method begins with the retail price and subtracts the avoided costs, it is referred to as the "top down" method. *See also* Baumol, Ordover & Willig, *supra* note 9, at 149–50.

37. Again, the classic definition is Armen A. Alchian, *Cost*, *in* 3 INTERNATIONAL ENCYCLOPEDIA OF THE SOCIAL SCIENCES 404, 404 (David L. Sills ed., Macmillan Co. & Free Press 1968).

38. DAVID L. KASERMAN & JOHN W. MAYO, GOVERNMENT AND BUSINESS: THE ECONOMICS OF ANTITRUST AND REGULATION 32 (Dryden Press 1995) (emphasis in original). In light of that universally accepted definition, we cannot accept the criticism of

That standard economic definition of opportunity costs is *not* the definition that the FCC used in its *First Report and Order*. The FCC's definition stated, "Opportunity costs include the revenues that the incumbent LEC would have received for the sale of telecommunications services, in the absence of competition from telecommunications carrier [sic] that purchase elements."[39] The FCC's definition of *opportunity costs* thus explicitly and incorrectly assumes away the existence of competition, whereas the standard economic definition of the term takes as given all competitive options.[40]

Frederick R. Warren-Boulton that by our advocacy of the M-ECPR we "seek[] to avoid the express injunction in the Telecommunications Act that prices be based on costs by introducing the concept of 'opportunity costs.'" *Warren-Boulton Rebuttal Testimony, supra* note 31, at 22.

39. 47 C.F.R. § 51.505(d)(3) (stayed), in *First Report and Order*, 11 F.C.C. Rcd. at 16,219 app. B.

40. In a unanimous 1997 opinion by Judge Douglas H. Ginsburg in a rate case involving landing fees at airports, the U.S. Court of Appeals for the D.C. Circuit chided a regulator, the secretary of transportation, for interpreting "cost" in a way that ignored opportunity cost. City of Los Angeles Dep't of Airports *v.* United States Dep't of Transp., 103 F.3d 1027 (D.C. Cir. 1997). The court noted that when the Supreme Court, in FPC *v.* Natural Gas Pipeline, 315 U.S. 575 (1941), overruled Smyth *v.* Ames, 169 U.S. 466 (1898), it "did not rule fair market value out of cost-of-service rate making; it held only that 'the Constitution does not bind rate-making bodies to the service of any single formula or combination of formulas.'" *Id.* at 1032 (quoting *Natural Gas Pipeline*, 315 U.S. at 586). That subtlety has direct relevance to the use of opportunity cost to approximate the fair market value of the regulated firm's assets:

> Nor has the Court ever held that historic cost represents the only true measure of cost and the Secretary points to no law, regulation, or agency decision to that effect. On the contrary, agencies that regulate utility rates have recognized "opportunity cost" as a factor to be considered when setting rates designed to cover the actual costs incurred to provide a particular service. Economists, too, have argued that opportunity costs should be considered in ratemaking.

Id. (citing Pennsylvania Elec. Co., 60 F.E.R.C. ¶¶ 61,034, 61,120 & n.1 (1992), *aff'd sub nom.* Pennsylvania Elec. Co. *v.* FERC, 11 F.3d 207 (D.C. Cir. 1993); WILLIAM J. BAUMOL & J. GREGORY SIDAK, TRANSMISSION PRICING AND STRANDED COSTS IN THE ELECTRIC POWER INDUSTRY 139 *et seq.* (AEI Press 1995). The court rejected "the view that an opportunity cost is not an 'actual cost,' in law or in economics, because it does not appear as a cash expenditure in the account books of the [regulated firm]." *Id.* The court remanded the case to the secretary of transportation to "confront[] the question of how properly to measure cost under a compensatory fee regime." *Id.* In particular, the court directed the secretary to give "express consideration" to "the testimonial evidence of Professor Kenneth Arrow, a Nobel laureate in economics, to the effect that the methodology [the City of Los Angeles] adopted for [Los Angeles International Airport] would cause the landing fees paid by the airlines to reflect the true cost of the airfield land; namely, 'the

Of course, when one calculates opportunity costs, the revenues that can flow from the use of a network element depend on whether there are market alternatives to the incumbent LEC's retail services and those elements. The magnitude of the incumbent's opportunity costs depends on whether such market alternatives are present or absent. There are therefore two cases to consider when calculating opportunity costs for a given network element. If market alternatives are absent, the incumbent LEC's opportunity costs equal the revenues currently generated in retail rates for services provided by the LEC through the use of that element minus the direct economic costs of the element. In that case the incumbent recovers the same flow of contributions embodied in the existing rate structure. On the other hand, if market alternatives are present, the incumbent LEC's opportunity costs equal the revenues that the LEC can obtain in the market through the use of that element minus its direct economic costs. In that case the presence of facilities-based entry, and the possibility that entrants may purchase services under existing retail rates that are substitutes for the incumbent carrier's unbundled element, reduce the likelihood that the incumbent LEC will recover its total costs. Those forces will necessarily reduce the flow of contributions embodied in the incumbent LEC's existing rate structure.

The *First Report and Order* discussed efficient component pricing only in the circumstance in which no price competition exists. The FCC stated, "The opportunity cost, which is computed as revenues less all incremental costs, represents both profit and contribution to common costs of the incumbent, *given the existing retail prices of the services being sold.*"[41] The agency's proposed rule explicitly assumed the "absence of competition from telecommunications carrier[s] that purchase elements."[42] On the basis of that incorrect definition of opportunity costs, the FCC found:

> We conclude that [the FCC-ECPR] is an improper method for setting prices of interconnection and unbundled network elements because the existing retail prices that would be used to compute incremental

---

value [the City] could have obtained in the best alternative use.'" *Id*. at 1033–34 (quoting Declaration of Kenneth J. Arrow (Mar. 13, 1995)). "This would, the City maintained, ensure that the actual costs of the airfield are borne by those receiving the benefits of the airfield and would create the proper incentive for the City to allocate land to airport use." *Id*. at 1034.

41. *First Report and Order*, 11 F.C.C. Rcd. at 15,859 ¶ 708 (emphasis added).

42. 47 C.F.R. § 51.505(d)(3) (stayed), in *First Report and Order*, 11 F.C.C. Rcd. at 16,219 app. B.

opportunity costs under [the FCC-ECPR] are not cost-based. Moreover, the [FCC-ECPR] does not provide any mechanism for moving prices towards competitive levels; it simply takes prices as given.[43]

The FCC's conclusions follow directly from its incorrect definition of opportunity costs. By ignoring the presence of market substitutes, the FCC found that the ECPR (as the agency misunderstood it) provides no "mechanism for moving prices towards competitive levels." But by no means is that the case. The FCC reached the wrong answer by ignoring fundamental market forces.

In contrast, because it reflects all available market alternatives, the M-ECPR forces rates down when opportunity costs fall in the presence of substitute services. Far from taking "prices as given," the M-ECPR recognizes that an incumbent LEC's ability to sell retail services at existing retail prices depends entirely on whether entrants offer lower prices. If such lower prices are forthcoming in the marketplace, the incumbent LEC's opportunity costs fall, which causes the corresponding rates for unbundled elements to fall as well. In short, the FCC erected a strawman version of the ECPR in its *First Report and Order* and then knocked it down.

Contrary to the FCC's assessment, the M-ECPR method is consistent with the agency's discussion of how forward-looking common costs should be recovered. After discussing various "reasonable" methods for allocating forward-looking common costs, the *First Report and Order* concluded: "In no instance should prices exceed the stand-alone cost for a specific element, and in most cases they should be below stand-alone costs."[44] That outcome is precisely what the M-ECPR method accomplishes when it examines market alternatives. If, for example, an entrant's stand-alone cost of supplying network elements were less than the incumbent LEC's existing wholesale rate, then that condition would reduce the incumbent LEC's existing opportunity costs of supplying the network element to the level of the entrant's stand-alone cost.

Examples of the Market Constraint on Opportunity Costs Inherent in the M-ECPR

Several examples illustrate why the M-ECPR satisfies all the requirements that Congress and the FCC established for pricing network

---

43. *First Report and Order*, 11 F.C.C. Rcd. at 15,859 ¶ 708.
44. *Id.* at 15,854 ¶ 698.

elements. Consider an incumbent LEC that employs a bottleneck input (such as a loop, which we generically call "access") to provide a retail service. The retail service has a regulated price of $10.00 per unit. The incumbent LEC incurs two costs in providing the service: "access," which has an incremental cost of $3.00 per unit, and "transport," which has an incremental cost of $2.00 per unit. Thus, the regulated price provides contribution to the recovery of the LEC's common costs equal to $5.00 per unit (that is, $10.00 − $3.00 − $2.00). In the absence of market alternatives, the M-ECPR price for an unbundled loop is simply $8.00 (that is, $3.00 + $5.00), where $3.00 is the incremental cost and $5.00 is the opportunity cost.

Now suppose that at a cost of $7.00 an entrant can self-supply loops to provide access service. In that case, the incumbent LEC's opportunity cost of selling the services of a loop to a competitor is $7.00 minus $3.00, or $4.00. In this example, the M-ECPR loop price (incremental cost plus opportunity cost) is simply $3.00 + ($7.00 − $3.00) = $7.00. In other words, whenever there are market alternatives, the lowest-priced alternative will determine the M-ECPR price. Suppose, instead, that the entrant buys a loop for $8.00 but then reduces the retail price to $9.00. That reduction in the retail price reduces the opportunity cost of the loop to $4.00, and the M-ECPR price correspondingly falls to $7.00.

The Efficiency of the M-ECPR

A desirable feature of the M-ECPR is that it displaces the incumbent if and only if the entrant is more efficient (has a lower cost) than the incumbent. The efficiency property of the M-ECPR can be easily demonstrated. Assume in the above example that a unit of access not sold to the competitor could generate contribution of $5.00 for the incumbent LEC. Thus, the relevant opportunity cost is $5.00, and the M-ECPR price is $8.00. If the incumbent LEC charges $8.00 per unit of access, then two results will obtain: The incumbent LEC will cover its direct cost of providing access, and entry will occur only if the rival has a lower "transport" cost. To see how M-ECPR promotes efficient entry, assume first that the entrant has the same transport cost as the incumbent LEC (that is, $2.00 per unit). Combining that cost with the M-ECPR access price of $8.00, the entrant can maintain a retail price of $10.00, which is just the initial regulated rate. Therefore, if the entrant has the *same* transport cost as the incumbent LEC, the M-ECPR price allows it to earn zero economic profit.

Suppose now that the entrant has a *lower* transport cost than the incumbent LEC—say, $1.00 per unit, as compared with $2.00 for the incumbent LEC. In that case the entrant can purchase access at the M-ECPR price and set a retail price of only $9.00 per unit. Thus, the more efficient firm can profitably enter and take customers away from the incumbent LEC. Finally, if the entrant's transport cost were *greater* than that of the incumbent LEC—say, $3.00 per unit—it could not profitably enter, which would be the efficient outcome from society's standpoint.

The Opportunity Cost from Forgone Sales of Complementary Services That Alternative Local Exchange Carriers Can Provide by Obtaining Unbundled Elements

Unbundling allows entrants—known as alternative local exchange carriers, or alternative LECs—to enter the local exchange market and provide basic, vertical, and local toll services in a variety of ways.[45] Consider an alternative LEC's options with respect to loop and port/switch facilities. The alternative LEC could construct its own loop facilities and lease port/switch services from the incumbent LEC so as to provide switched services. Alternatively, the alternative LEC could lease the incumbent LEC's loop facilities and obtain its own port/switch facilities to provide those services. An alternative LEC could also obtain loop and port/switch facilities from the incumbent LEC by purchasing at wholesale the incumbent LEC's basic retail services. Of course, an alternative LEC also could construct its own network of loops and port/switch facilities and thereby completely bypass the incumbent LEC's facilities.

When an alternative LEC leases unbundled loops and self-provides port/switch facilities, it can offer basic local service, vertical features, and local toll service (as well as switched access and interLATA toll service) without purchasing any of the incumbent LEC's retail services at wholesale. With unbundling, therefore, alternative LECs can capture the contributions that flow from the incumbent LEC's provision of vertical services as well as local toll, and that opportunity tends to increase the incumbent LEC's forgone revenues from unbundling its network elements.

---

45. Examples of common vertical services are call waiting and call forwarding.

The Determination of a Reasonable
Allocation of Forward-Looking Common
Costs According to the First Report and Order

Following the recommendation in the *First Report and Order* that prices not exceed stand-alone costs, our understanding is that alternative local exchange carriers with demands for port/switching services generally, and local switches and tandem switches in particular, have available market alternatives at competitive prices. Assuming that port/switching services, signaling, and transport can be purchased at competitive prices from third-party vendors of telecommunications equipment, it follows that alternative LECs would have a strong incentive to self-provide those network elements if the incumbent LEC's prices for unbundled elements exceeded the combined cost of purchasing, installing, and operating self-supplied facilities.

Because of that competitive market constraint, an incumbent LEC can allocate relatively little, if any, of its forward-looking common costs to the prices of network elements other than the loop. In contrast, the loop is not so immediately substitutable. Consequently, the incumbent LEC could allocate relatively more of its forward-looking common costs to the price of unbundled loops.

Application of the M-ECPR to
Calculate Unbundled Loop Prices

Consider now a numerical example of the use of the M-ECPR to calculate the price of an unbundled loop used by an incumbent LEC to supply basic service to a business customer. Because the actual data concerning an incumbent LEC's TELRICs and forward-looking common costs may be proprietary, we present suggestive figures that are consistent with data we have observed in actual arbitrations but that do not correspond to any specific LEC in any particular state.

As explained above, the M-ECPR price of a network element depends on the presence or absence of market alternatives. If one assumes away all market alternatives, then he obtains FCC-ECPR prices. But if one considers market alternatives, then he obtains M-ECPR prices. In the next two subsections, we calculate the rates for unbundled loops provided to business customers. First, we assume away all market alternatives to the incumbent LEC's services; then we explicitly consider those alternatives to calculate the M-ECPR rates.

Calculation of FCC-ECPR Prices for Unbundled Loops on the Assumption That No Market Alternatives Exist. Assuming the absence of market alternatives, consider the services provided to an average business customer. Such a customer consumes various services of the incumbent LEC, each having a TSLRIC and each producing a contribution to the LEC's overall revenue adequacy. In addition to consuming the basic retail service (that is, local exchange service), the customer typically consumes local toll service, vertical services, and switched access services. Typically, the incumbent LEC prices local toll, vertical, and switched access services to generate high contribution margins. In addition, the business customer pays the carrier common line charge (which is a federally mandated stream of revenue to the LEC to rebalance local and long-distance rates), which by definition consists entirely of contribution to the LEC.[46] Assume that the total monthly revenues from the services that an average business customer consumes are $60 per line and that the sum of the TSLRICs for providing those services is $25 per line. Thus, the average business customer generates a total contribution of $35 per line per month. As explained earlier, that $35 of contribution is not profit in either the economic or accounting sense of the word. Rather, the $35 reflects compensation for the incumbent LEC's common costs (including the costs of performing its public service obligation and paying the subsidies embedded in the rate structure[47]) and a competitive return to investors. As a practical matter, if the incumbent LEC loses the business customer as a subscriber of basic monthly access service, the LEC will lose the opportunity to sell all the complementary services that such a customer typically consumes.

Assume that the incumbent LEC has correctly estimated the TELRIC of an unbundled loop to be $20 (which would include the incremental marketing cost of providing unbundled loops). The FCC-ECPR, which assumes that no market alternatives exist, would price the unbundled loop by adding the TELRIC of the loop ($20) to the incumbent LEC's opportunity cost ($35 of forgone contribution) of providing the unbundled loop to an alternative LEC, for a total price of $55 per line.[48]

---

46. MICHAEL K. KELLOGG, JOHN THORNE & PETER W. HUBER, FEDERAL TELECOMMUNICATIONS LAW 469–71 (Little, Brown & Co. 1992).

47. Baumol and Sidak have noted that "when a regulated firm has special-service obligations imposed upon it," "[t]hese obligations are appropriately treated as sources of common fixed costs for the firm; the costs must be covered legitimately by the firm's prices . . . ." BAUMOL & SIDAK, TOWARD COMPETITION IN LOCAL TELEPHONY, *supra* note 9, at 108–09.

48. We assume that the alternative LEC bypasses the incumbent LEC's port/switching

Calculation of M-ECPR Prices for Unbundled Loops on the Assumption That Market Alternatives Exist. Now suppose that the entrant's stand-alone cost of supplying its own loop facilities were less than the unbundled loop price for average business customers that was calculated on the assumption that no market alternatives existed for the incumbent LEC's access service. Should regulators give the incumbent LEC the flexibility to lower the price of its unbundled loop facilities? Yes, because otherwise the unbundled loop price would violate the pricing constraint that both the market imposes and the *First Report and Order* recommends—that the price of any unbundled element not exceed its stand-alone cost. Given the presence of market alternatives, the incumbent LEC's M-ECPR price equals its TELRIC for loop service plus the opportunity cost *as constrained by market forces*. A simple example will illustrate the operation of that pricing constraint.

Assume that a facilities-based competitor can self-supply loop facilities to business customers for $38 per line per month. The incumbent LEC's forgone revenues would equal $38 minus its TELRIC of loop service (including marketing costs), which in our example equal $20. Thus, the resulting M-ECPR loop price equals $20 plus $18 (that is, $38 − $20), or simply the entrant's stand-alone cost of $38.

An alternative LEC has other available substitutes for the leasing of unbundled loop facilities besides constructing its own loops. An alternative LEC can acquire basic business service at wholesale rates, which includes the services of both a loop and port/switching services; alternatively, the alternative LEC can purchase two-wire private-line service from the incumbent LEC at that service's tariffed rate. If either alternative has a lower price than the unbundled loop price calculated on the assumption that no such market alternatives existed, then the alternative LEC will choose to purchase the lower-priced alternative. If private-line service is a good substitute for the incumbent LEC's unbundled loops, then the presence of the private-line rate constrains the incumbent LEC's ability to charge a price for an unbundled loop that maintains the level of contribution that the incumbent LEC previously earned from serving the typical business customer. For example, if the

---

facilities so that it obtains no contribution from the provision of those unbundled network elements. If, to the contrary, unbundled prices for port/switching services included some contribution (in other words, if market alternatives were less binding), then that contribution would be subtracted from total forward-looking common costs before determining the unbundled price of the loop. That subtraction would ensure that the contribution provided by unbundled loops and port/switches did not exceed the contribution embodied in the prices of the incumbent LEC's retail services.

incumbent LEC's two-wire private-line rate is $27, then $27 also becomes the highest price that the incumbent LEC can receive for an unbundled loop. The stand-alone cost of the best alternative technology for an unbundled loop, $27, becomes the M-ECPR price.[49]

In sum, given the presence of a two-wire private line service at $27, the FCC-ECPR unbundled loop price is $56, whereas the M-ECPR unbundled loop price is $27. That example illustrates the potentially large differences between FCC-ECPR prices and M-ECPR prices. Those price differences result from the fact the FCC-ECPR explicitly assumes away all competitive market alternatives, while the M-ECPR explicitly takes those alternatives into account. Clearly, the FCC was incorrect in its *First Report and Order* when it rejected efficient component pricing for unbundled elements because the M-ECPR supposedly would use "existing retail prices," which were not cost-based, "to compute incremental opportunity costs" and because the rule supposedly "simply takes prices as given" and "does not provide any mechanism for moving prices towards competitive levels."[50]

The foregoing analysis does not change because differences may exist from an engineering standpoint concerning the provisioning and testing of a two-wire private line versus the (four-wire) unbundled loop. Cellophane, cling wrap, aluminum foil, glass jars, and Tupperware all differ from an engineering perspective in terms of how they are designed,

---

49. Paul W. MacAvoy, in testimony before the Illinois Commerce Commission, has presented the important insight that unadjusted ECPR pricing, which he calls competitive parity pricing (CPP), will fail to deter inefficient bypass:

> In some instances wholesale rates for specific services should be below the CPP level. One special case is when the reseller has the option to self-provide facilities-based wholesale service on a stand-alone basis. If the CPP wholesale price for service exceeds the stand-alone costs of that potential facilities-based carrier, then the CPP rate for that service could generate inefficient bypass.

Prepared Direct Testimony of Paul W. MacAvoy, *attached to* Comments of Ameritech Illinois, Inc. AT&T Communications of Illinois, Inc., Petition for a Total Local Exchange Service Wholesale Tariff from Illinois Bell Telephone Co. d/b/a Ameritech Illinois & Central Telephone Co. Pursuant to Section 13-505.5 of the Illinois Public Utilities Act, Dkt. No. 95-0458, at 10 (Ill. Comm. Comm'n Sept. 1995). MacAvoy notes that "modifications from CPP rates should be undertaken only when necessitated by the possibility of uneconomic bypass by a potential reseller entrant." *Id.* But his correct suggestion that the incumbent has an incentive to reduce prices to compete with potential entrants does not recognize the additional point made here—that the correctly calculated ECPR adjusts price downward because entry changes the incumbent's opportunity cost.

50. *First Report and Order*, 11 F.C.C. Rcd. at 15,859 ¶ 709.

manufactured, tested, packaged, and marketed. But those differences are not relevant to the question of whether, at a particular price, consumers view those five products as substitutes for one another.[51] Typically, in antitrust cases the extent of demand substitutability (commonly called the relevant product market) is evaluated in terms of the goods to which consumers would turn if there were a 5 percent increase in the price of the product sold by the firm under examination.[52] As we have just shown by using stylized figures based on actual arbitration proceedings, the percentage price difference between the FCC-ECPR price and the M-ECPR price for an unbundled loop is likely to be far greater than 5 percent in most states, and therefore the extent of substitution in demand from the unbundled loop to the two-wire private line is likely to be high.

Entrants seeking an even lower unbundled loop price than the M-ECPR price have argued that the two-wire private-line rate is an artificial alternative to the unbundled loop because it is a substitute that the incumbent LEC itself provides to its competitors. Therefore, the argument goes, the incumbent LEC can control the price of the substitute for its bottleneck input, the unbundled loop. That argument is specious on several grounds. First, the incumbent LEC remains subject to price regulation and may not raise the tariff of the two-wire private-line at will. Indeed, in many states the incumbent LEC is subject to rate freezes or price caps that foreclose the possibility of rate increases entirely. And even in those states where no formal rate freeze or price cap is in effect, one must ask, How long ago did regulators permit a general rate increase and how soon are they likely to do so again in the future? Second, before unbundling began, regulators had already approved the two-wire private-line tariff as a "just and reasonable" rate for that service. In economic terms, the two-wire private-line tariff had been set so that it did not exceed stand-alone cost. (In cases where the regulator has set the two-wire private-line tariff below the TSLRIC for that service, it is appropriate for the price to be raised to TSLRIC to ensure that the service is not receiving a subsidy from any other service.) Third, assuming counterfactually that the incumbent LEC did have some ability to raise the two-wire private-line price, how high could the LEC go? Clearly, the incumbent LEC would be constrained to charge no more than the stand-alone cost of the best alternative access technology that the LEC itself did not supply.

51. *See, e.g.*, William E. Landes & Richard A. Posner, *Market Power in Antitrust Cases,* 94 HARV. L. REV. 937 (1981).

52. ANTITRUST DIV., U.S. DEP'T OF JUSTICE, MERGER GUIDELINES § 2.11 (1984), *reprinted in* 4 TRADE REG. REP. (CCH) ¶ 13,103.

To illustrate the constraint on the LEC's pricing, observe that in our example the price would be the $38 stand-alone cost to the alternative LEC of constructing its own loop, although there may subsequently be other access substitutes available at lower cost from third parties, such as competitive access providers. Even if the incumbent LEC could raise the price of its unbundled loop to the alternative LEC's $38 stand-alone cost of constructing a loop, it bears emphasis that *that* price would still be $17 lower than the $55 price that the incumbent LEC would have to charge for its unbundled loop to preserve the contribution that the forgone business customer would have made to the LEC's ability to earn just enough revenue to break even.

The Presence of Market Alternatives Prevents an Incumbent LEC from Recovering Its Forward-Looking Common Costs

When customers can self-supply loops or purchase substitute services from the incumbent LEC at a rate less than the unbundled loop price calculated on the assumption that no market alternatives exist, the M-ECPR prices for loops and other (more substitutable) network elements will not enable the incumbent LEC to recover its forward-looking common costs. M-ECPR prices do enable an incumbent LEC to cover the direct economic cost of providing the unbundled services—the direct incremental cost of providing the service (TELRIC) plus opportunity cost. But M-ECPR prices are not "make whole" prices for the incumbent LEC because they do not enable it to earn revenues equal to its total forward-looking costs. A fortiori the presence of market alternatives prevents an incumbent LEC from recovering its historical costs.

The numerical example above indicates that the incumbent LEC would incur a deficit of $28 (that is, $55 – $27) for each typical business customer that the LEC lost when selling an unbundled loop at the $27 price mandated by the presence of market alternatives.[53] Competitors, of course, generally do not enter markets by first targeting "typical" customers. Rather, entrants characteristically target the highest-margin business customers first. Consequently, in the initial months following competitive entry, the incumbent LEC's average deficit arising from the loss of a business customer due to the sale of unbundled loops would substantially exceed $28 per line. We therefore believe that Janusz A. Ordover is in error when he asserts that a "pricing rule . . . which

---

53. If the incumbent LEC's two-wire private line rate were below its TSLRIC, the deficit would be larger.

combines TELRIC-based pricing with competitively neutral markups subject to stand-alone cost ceiling[s] maintains the ILEC's [incumbent LEC's] opportunity to achieve revenues adequate for the recovery of *all* efficient, forward-looking direct and common costs."[54]

In short, the *First Report and Order* specifies that prices for network elements "shall recover the forward-looking costs directly attributable to the specified element, as well as a reasonable allocation of forward-looking common costs."[55] But market alternatives will likely prevent an incumbent LEC from fully recovering its forward-looking common costs. We must therefore turn to the question of how the FCC's recommendation can be met so that an incumbent LEC can recover its forward-looking common costs and thus maintain its financial viability.

The Role of Competitively Neutral End-User Charges in Recovering the Incumbent LEC's Forward-Looking Common Costs

How should prices for network elements be established to ensure that the incumbent LEC's rates recover its forward-looking common costs? As a general statement, the M-ECPR does not alter in any material way the traditional problems faced by a regulated carrier operating with a rate structure that contains cross-subsidies mandated by regulation. For the firm's rate structure to be preserved and to allow recovery of its total costs, accompanying end-user charges are required. As the example above clearly demonstrates, although the M-ECPR enables the incumbent LEC to recover its incremental costs and opportunity costs of the sale of network elements, it does not enable the incumbent LEC to complete the necessary process of cost recovery, as would regulated rates in the absence of entry. Thus, the M-ECPR does not ensure that the incumbent LEC will be able to recover its historical costs. Generally, facilities-based entry and M-ECPR pricing of network elements result in stranded costs, which are defined as the present value of the incumbent firm's net revenues under regulation minus the present value of the incumbent firm's net revenues under competition. Stranded costs arise because competition that becomes possible as a result of regulatory change immediately reduces the M-ECPR price that the incumbent firm can charge.

The fall in the M-ECPR price provides useful guidance on how to set end-user charges to recover the incumbent LEC's stranded costs. The end-user charge should equal the difference between net revenues ob-

---

54. *Ordover Rebuttal Testimony, supra* note 27, at 22 (emphasis in original).
55. *First Report and Order*, 11 F.C.C. Rcd. at 15,847 ¶ 682.

tained by using the FCC-ECPR (that is, the price based on the regulated rate structure) and the net revenues obtained from the lower, market-constrained M-ECPR price that takes into account the substitutes for the incumbent LEC's elements that are available to the alternative LEC.

What costs does the end-user charge recover? The end-user charge recovers portions of six types of cost burdens that the incumbent LEC cannot recover through competitive, unbundled prices but nonetheless has incurred to discharge its obligation to serve: (1) shared costs of network operation, incurred among two or more (but not all) of the incumbent LEC's services, but not wholly attributable to any single service; (2) common costs of network operation, incurred among all the incumbent LEC's services; (3) losses incurred in providing services to customers at regulated prices that are below the incremental cost of providing such service; (4) costs incurred as a result of incumbent burdens that the incumbent LEC continues to bear after the advent of competition but that entrants are not required to bear, such as universal service obligations; (5) costs incurred by the incumbent LEC to accomplish government-mandated unbundling of network elements or resale of network services; and (6) losses incurred when the incumbent LEC's avoided costs are incorrectly overstated and are used to establish the discount that competitors receive when purchasing wholesale services from the incumbent LEC. If such end-user charges were not put in place, the incumbent LEC would earn *negative* economic profit and therefore would be denied the opportunity to earn the "reasonable profit" envisioned by section 252(d)(3) of the Telecommunications Act of 1996.

Recombination of Unbundled Network Elements, Regulatory Arbitrage, and Statutory Consistency

Entrants into local telephony have argued that they should have the ability to recombine the incumbent LEC's network elements to create a service that would be identical to the service that the LEC offers to entrants at a (discounted) wholesale price.[56] Entrants point to section 251(c)(3), which imposes on the incumbent LEC the following duty concerning resale:

---

56. *See, e.g.,* Petition for Approval of Transfer of Local Exchange Telecommunications Certificate No. 33 from Central Telephone Company of Florida to United Telephone Company of Florida, for Approval of Merger of Certificate No. 33 into United Telephone's Certificate No. 22, and for Change in Name on Certificate No. 22 to Sprint-Florida, Incorporated, Dkt. No. 961362-TL, Order No. PSC-96-1578-FOF-TL, 1996 Fla. PUC LEXIS 2216, at *57 (Fla. Pub. Serv. Comm'n Dec. 31, 1996).

> The duty to provide, to any requesting telecommunications carrier for the provision of a telecommunications service, nondiscriminatory access to network elements on an unbundled basis at any technically feasible point on rates, terms, and conditions that are just, reasonable, and nondiscriminatory in accordance with the terms and conditions of the agreement and the requirements of this section and section 252. An incumbent local exchange carrier shall provide such unbundled network elements in a manner that allows requesting carriers to combine such elements in order to provide such telecommunications service.[57]

Entrants emphasize the second sentence. The incumbent LEC argues in response that Congress intended the entrant to choose the resale alternative if the entrant intended to offer a retail service to customers that consisted entirely of the elements of the incumbent LEC. Recombination, the LEC argues, would defeat that purpose; therefore, consistent with the first sentence of section 251(c)(3), which permits the LEC to impose just and reasonable conditions on the sale of elements, it is lawful for the LEC to refuse to sell elements that will be recombined to simulate resale.

The earlier economic analysis of opportunity cost and recovery of forward-looking common costs elucidates that question of statutory construction. It is telling that recombination is even an issue. The fact that the entrant seeks to establish its right to recombine network elements indicates that the entrant expects that the prices for those elements necessary to provide basic service—the loop and port—will recover a lesser amount of common costs than will the wholesale price of basic service. In other words, the entrant's demand to recombine elements signals the entrant's belief (1) that the incumbent LEC's forward-looking common costs are *not* de minimis, and (2) that summing up the prices of UNEs will allow the entrant to pay a smaller amount toward the recovery of the incumbent LEC's shared costs and common costs than would the entrant's purchase of wholesale service for resale. Viewed in those terms, recombination of network elements is a form of arbitrage induced by distortions in the regulated pricing of those elements and wholesale services.

There is no reason to suppose that Congress wanted to create the opportunity for entrants to engage in such arbitrage. Indeed, the contrary presumption should hold. Sections 252(c)(1) and 252(c)(3) should be read so that regulatory arbitrage is not possible. The prices of those two entry options should yield the same contribution to the recovery of the

---

57. 47 U.S.C. § 251(c)(3).

incumbent LEC's common costs. If they do, then the entrant will face price signals that properly induce the firm to select one entry path over the other solely on the basis of the entrant's own efficiency in the provision of nonbottleneck inputs relative to the incumbent LEC's efficiency. If the prices for wholesale services and for network elements were correctly calculated according to the M-ECPR to reflect in each case the direct cost and the opportunity cost to the incumbent LEC of making the sale to the entrant, and if an end-user charge were imposed to recover the shortfall toward the recovery of common costs that the incumbent LEC could not avoid in its pricing of UNEs, then the incumbent LEC and the entrant would both be indifferent between entry by one method rather than the other. In short, the M-ECPR and end-user charge are necessary policies to permit reconciling the pricing provision for resale in section 252(c)(3) with the pricing provision for network elements in section 252(c)(1). If the two sections were reconciled in that manner, the incumbent LEC would be indifferent whether the entrant purchased a wholesale service or all of the elements necessary to assemble that service. Any other pricing rule is likely to encourage regulatory arbitrage, which is a result that Congress could not have intended.

Summary

We have presented the M-ECPR and shown that it satisfies the FCC's recommendation that prices for unbundled network elements be based on forward-looking costs. When combined with a system of competitively neutral end-user charges, the M-ECPR also satisfies the requirement in section 252(d)(3) that prices be based on costs and allow for a reasonable profit. The M-ECPR is *not* the same as the FCC's misunderstanding of efficient component pricing, which we term the FCC-ECPR. The M-ECPR produces substantially lower prices than the FCC-ECPR because market forces limit the M-ECPR on a continuous, forward-looking basis to the stand-alone cost of the best substitute technology by which an alternative LEC can achieve access to the incumbent LEC's network.[58]

---

58. It is puzzling that Janusz A. Ordover, who endorses efficient component pricing but has nonetheless opposed our M-ECPR in testimony on behalf of AT&T, advocates a pricing rule for UNEs "which combines TELRIC-based pricing with competitively neutral markups subject to stand-alone cost ceiling[s]." *Ordover Rebuttal Testimony, supra* note 27, at 22. That description fits the M-ECPR that Ordover purports to reject.

THE FCC'S *FIRST REPORT AND ORDER* AND RECOVERY
OF THE INCUMBENT LEC'S TOTAL COSTS

The FCC's *First Report and Order* would establish a blueprint for bankrupting incumbent LECs. The order would have that effect because it (1) denied recovery of historic costs incurred by the incumbent LEC to discharge its obligation to serve; (2) forbade the incumbent LEC to recover shared costs and common costs on network elements (particularly loops) that have a low enough price elasticity of demand to bear higher levels of cost recovery without exceeding an entrant's stand-alone cost for that particular element; and (3) forbade the incumbent LEC to pursue cost recovery by charging up to stand-alone cost for unbundled network elements other than loops. Consequently, the FCC has foreclosed the possibility that the incumbent LEC will be able to achieve even the recovery of forward-looking costs that the agency's order purports to endorse. We consider now each of the three preceding factors by which the FCC would deny the incumbent LEC full recovery of all the economic costs that it incurred to discharge its obligation to serve the public.

Prohibition on the Recovery of Historic Costs

The *First Report and Order* precludes the recovery of the incumbent LEC's historic costs through the prices charged for mandatory access to unbundled network elements. The FCC stated that "the sum of the direct costs and the forward-looking common costs of all elements will likely differ from the incumbent LEC's historical, fully distributed costs."[59] Economists testifying on behalf of alternative LECs similarly have rejected using the price of mandatory network access to recover any portion of historic, embedded costs.[60] In the face of that opposition to the incumbent LECs' cost recovery, it bears emphasis that the M-ECPR does *not* guaranty full recovery of historic costs because the market-allowed M-ECPR price of a network element is at all times capped by the entrant's stand-alone cost of supplying that element by the least-cost technology then available. Consequently, as we explained earlier, even a system of M-ECPR prices for network access will have to be accompa-

---

59. *First Report and Order*, 11 F.C.C. Rcd. at 15,854 ¶ 698.

60. *E.g.*, DAVID L. KASERMAN, JOHN W. MAYO, MICHAEL A. CREW, NICHOLAS ECONOMIDES, R. GLENN HUBBARD, PAUL R. KLEINDORFER & CARLOS MARTINS-FILHO, LOCAL COMPETITION ISSUES AND THE TELECOMMUNICATIONS ACT OF 1996, at 12–14 (July 15, 1996) (prepared for AT&T Corp.).

nied by an end-user charge to make the incumbent LEC whole for its stranded costs and thus avoid a taking.

Prohibitions on Pricing of the
Few Network Elements That Can
Contribute to Recovery of Unattributable Costs

The FCC offered two cost-allocation methods that would allow an incumbent LEC to seek to recover forward-looking common costs. The effect of both proposals, however, would be to deny the incumbent LEC any practical ability to recover its unattributable costs.

The first method was a fixed markup: "One reasonable allocation method would be to allocate common costs using a fixed allocator, such as a percentage markup over the directly attributable forward-looking costs."[61] That approach is seductive because of its apparent simplicity. In one of the first state arbitration proceedings under the Telecommunications Act, for example, an administrative law judge of the California Public Utilities Commission ordered that GTE offer unbundled network elements to AT&T at TELRIC plus 16 percent.[62] The practical effect of a fixed percentage markup, however, is to subsidize entrants at the expense of the incumbent LEC. If the fixed percentage produced a price exceeding the entrant's stand-alone cost for the element, then the entrant would self-supply that particular network element rather than buy it from the incumbent LEC. (In addition, as we later explain, the FCC would forbid such a price, assuming unrealistically that the incumbent LEC were so ignorant of basic economics as to attempt to charge a price so high.) If the entrant self-supplied the element, then the incumbent LEC would earn no contribution whatsoever to recovery of its unattributable forward-looking costs. That prospect is real. There are multiple providers of signaling services. There are also competitive commercial providers of switching services—including competitive access providers and the interexchange carriers, which can adapt their long-distance switching facilities to perform local exchange switching. For example, AT&T reportedly intends to use its own switches or those leased from

61. *First Report and Order*, 11 F.C.C. Rcd. at 15,853 ¶ 696.

62. Petition of AT&T Communications of California, Inc. for Arbitration Pursuant to Section 252 of the Federal Telecommunications Act of 1996 to Establish an Interconnection Agreement with GTE California, Inc., Arbitrator's Report, Application 96-08-041, at 13 (Cal. Pub. Utils. Comm'n Oct. 31, 1996). The decision uses TSLRIC terminology rather than TELRIC.

competitive access providers and, as of October 1996, had signed contracts with six providers for such services in over eighty cities.[63]

On the other hand, if the fixed percentage produced a price less than what the incumbent LEC otherwise would charge for the element (bearing in mind that the incumbent LEC in no event could price the element above its stand-alone cost), then the entrant would buy the element from the incumbent LEC rather than self-supply it. In that case, the incumbent LEC would have been forced to forgo a significant share of the overall contribution earned for its recovery of forward-looking common costs. The shortfall in contribution would equal the difference between (1) the element's stand-alone cost and (2) the sum of the element's TELRIC and its fixed-percentage markup over TELRIC. That shortfall to the incumbent LEC is a coerced transfer to, and subsidy for, the entrant.

The FCC's second method for allocating common costs among unbundled network elements was an example of what economists have dubbed "reverse Ramsey pricing" because of its tendency to minimize rather than maximize consumer welfare.[64] The FCC stated:

> We conclude that a second reasonable allocation method would allocate only a relatively small share of common costs to certain critical network elements, such as the local loop and collocation, that are most difficult for entrants to replicate promptly (i.e., bottleneck facilities). Allocation of common costs on this basis ensures that the prices of network elements that are least likely to be subject to competition are not artificially inflated by a large allocation of common costs.[65]

Citing Ramsey pricing specifically, the FCC ruled that "an allocation methodology that relies exclusively on allocating common costs in inverse proportion to the sensitivity of demand for various network elements and services may not be used."[66] Despite the well-recognized welfare-maximizing characteristics of Ramsey pricing principles, the FCC believed that an analogous method of allocating forward-looking

---

63. Catherine Arnst, *AT&T: Will the Bad News Ever End?*, BUS. WK., Oct. 7, 1996, at 122, 128.

64. *See generally* DAVID E. M. SAPPINGTON & DENNIS L. WEISMAN, DESIGNING INCENTIVE REGULATION FOR THE TELECOMMUNICATIONS INDUSTRY 16 (MIT Press & AEI Press 1996).

65. *First Report and Order*, 11 F.C.C. Rcd. at 15,853 ¶ 696.

66. *Id.* (citing Frank P. Ramsey, *A Contribution to the Theory of Taxation*, 37 ECON. J. 47 (1927)).

shared or common costs across network elements would violate the 1996 legislation:

> We conclude that such an allocation could unreasonably limit the extent of entry into local exchange markets by allocating more costs to, and thus raising the prices of, the most critical bottleneck inputs, the demand for which tends to be relatively inelastic. Such an allocation of these costs would undermine the pro-competitive objectives of the 1996 Act.[67]

By imposing that "reverse-Ramsey" constraint on the incumbent LEC's pricing of network elements, the FCC condemned the LEC to insolvency. It is a sham for the FCC to have told incumbent LECs that they can recover their forward-looking common costs only by raising the prices of their most price-sensitive network elements above TELRIC. Such a constraint ensures that the incumbent LEC will be denied the ability to recover any appreciable amount of its unattributable forward-looking costs. That constraint is tantamount to the FCC's ordering every incumbent LEC to write a check to each prospective rival to help pay for its cost of entry into the local market.

Prohibition on Pricing Any
Element at Stand-Alone Cost

Lest any doubt remained concerning the futility of its rules for pricing network elements, the FCC removed that doubt by imposing one final, fatal constraint: "In no instance should prices exceed the stand-alone cost for a specific element, *and in most cases they should be below stand-alone costs.*"[68] The first half of that sentence is superfluous. The laws of economics already prohibit a firm from charging a price exceeding stand-alone cost. The second half of the sentence, however, introduces a serious, new regulatory constraint that ensures that the incumbent LEC would never be able to recover the full amount of its forward-looking common costs.

After forbidding the incumbent LEC to use its pricing of unbundled loops to recover forward-looking shared costs and common costs, the FCC would take away as well the LEC's ability to raise the price of its remaining unbundled elements to *their* stand-alone costs. Given the

---

67. *Id.*
68. *Id.* at 15,854 ¶ 698 (emphasis added).

alternative LEC's ability to combine at will its own self-provision of elements with its purchase of unbundled LEC elements, the FCC would ensure that the incumbent LEC would be prevented from earning the requisite contributions from its sale of unbundled elements to recover the total forward-looking costs of its network.

Paradoxically, the FCC's pricing rules for unbundled network elements would discourage the facilities-based competition in local telephony that the 1996 legislation envisioned. It would, after all, be foolish for any entrant to build its own network from scratch if the incumbent LEC was bound by regulation to sell unbundled network elements below their stand-alone costs, and if, in particular, the LEC was obliged to sell unbundled loops to alternative LECs at a price that was allowed to exceed TELRIC by only a farthing.

CONCLUSION

This chapter has explained the market-determined efficient component-pricing rule and shown how it differs from the original ECPR and from the FCC's incorrect characterization of efficient component pricing. We have examined the pricing provisions for unbundled network elements in the Telecommunications Act of 1996. The FCC's historic *First Report and Order* issued in 1996 recommended an interpretation of those statutory provisions that would produce inefficient and uncompensatory prices. In contrast, the M-ECPR would be efficient and, if accompanied by a competitively neutral and nonbypassable end-user charge, would be compensatory as well. For those reasons the M-ECPR is consistent with the pricing provisions of sections 251 and 252 of the Tele-communications Act.

10

Answering the Critics
of Efficient Component Pricing

SINCE THE EARLY 1990s the efficient component-pricing rule (ECPR) has generated controversy in discussions of regulatory theory and policy. Much of that controversy has resulted from criticism lodged against the ECPR to the effect that the rule is not general in its applicability or not efficient in some respect. The criticism reached a crescendo in 1996, when in the *First Report and Order* the FCC mischaracterized the ECPR and then forbade the states to use the rule that the agency mislabeled as the ECPR. As we note chapter 9, we call *our* rule the M-ECPR to avoid further mislabeling. This chapter addresses the criticisms of M-ECPR pricing raised by economists who have testified on behalf of entrants advocating lower prices for resale and unbundled network elements.[1] We

---

1. *See, e.g.*, DAVID L. KASERMAN, JOHN W. MAYO, MICHAEL A. CREW, NICHOLAS ECONOMIDES, R. GLENN HUBBARD, PAUL R. KLEINDORFER & CARLOS MARTINS-FILHO, LOCAL COMPETITION ISSUES AND THE TELECOMMUNICATIONS ACT OF 1996 (July 15, 1996) (prepared for AT&T Corp.) [hereinafter KASERMAN REPORT]; Rebuttal Testimony of Frederick R. Warren-Boulton, In the Matter of AT&T Communications of the Southwest, Inc.'s Petition for Arbitration Pursuant to Section 252(b) of the Telecommunications Act of 1996 to Establish an Interconnection Agreement with GTE Midwest Inc., Case No. TO-97-63 (Mo. Pub. Serv. Comm'n, filed Oct. 21, 1996) (prepared for AT&T Communications of the Southwest, Inc.) [hereinafter *Warren-Boulton Rebuttal Testimony*]; Prefiled Rebuttal Testimony of Janusz A. Ordover, Petition of AT&T Communications of Wisconsin, Inc. for Arbitration per § 252(b) of the Telecommunications Act of 1996 to Establish an Interconnection Agreement with GTE North, Inc., Nos. 265-MA-102, 2180-MA-100 (Pub. Serv. Comm'n of Wisc., filed Oct. 21, 1996) (prepared for AT&T

show that those critics of M-ECPR pricing do not appreciate that the rule is efficient and compensatory. We then respond to a controversy at the cutting edge of the state and federal efforts to implement the pricing provisions of the Telecommunications Act of 1996: the claim that the principal authors of the efficient component-pricing rule, William J. Baumol and Robert D. Willig, rejected the M-ECPR in favor of TELRIC (total element long-run incremental cost) pricing for unbundled network elements.

THE FCC'S DENUNCIATION OF EFFICIENT
COMPONENT PRICING IN ITS 1996
INTERCONNECTION RULEMAKING

By mid-1996, no proceeding had brought the alleged failings of the ECPR under greater scrutiny than the FCC's proceeding, commenced in April 1996 pursuant to the new Telecommunications Act, on the pricing by incumbent local exchange carriers of interconnection, resale, and unbundled network elements.[2] In its notice of proposed rulemaking, the FCC reached two adverse tentative conclusions concerning the ECPR. First, the FCC asserted that "use of the ECPR or equivalent methodologies to set prices for interconnection and unbundled network elements would be inconsistent with the section 252(d)(1) requirement that prices be based on 'cost.'"[3] Second, the FCC proposed "that states be precluded from using this methodology to set prices for interconnection and access to unbundled elements."[4] In addition, the FCC solicited comment on whether a state's use of the ECPR "would constitute a barrier to entry as under section 253 of the 1996 Act."[5] Those two adverse conclusions, along with the agency's question signaling its predisposition to reach a third adverse conclusion, were predicated on the FCC's misunderstanding of the economic effects of the ECPR and the agency's evident ignorance of the state of academic research on the ECPR.

Communications of Wisconsin, Inc.) [hereinafter *Ordover Rebuttal Testimony*]. A portion of the Kaserman Report was subsequently published as David L. Kaserman & John W. Mayo, *An Efficient Avoided Cost Pricing Rule for Resale of Local Exchange Services*, 11 J. REG. ECON. 91 (1997).

    2. Implementation of the Local Competition Provisions in the Telecommunications Act of 1996, Notice of Proposed Rulemaking, CC Dkt. No. 96-98, 11 F.C.C. Rcd. 14,171 (1996) [hereinafter *Interconnection NPRM*].

    3. *Id*. at 14,222 ¶ 148.

    4. *Id*.

    5. *Id*.

Contrary to the impression that an uninformed reader might have received from the FCC's exiguous discussion of the ECPR, the rule has generated a growing body of academic support. We respond below to the critics of the ECPR as well as to several other familiar canards concerning the rule. Before doing so, however, we review the growing number of academic economists and governmental bodies that endorse the rule.

ACADEMIC PROPONENTS OF EFFICIENT COMPONENT PRICING

Other than referencing several writings by Baumol and Sidak, the FCC did not state or imply in its interconnection proceeding that any other scholar in law or economics had endorsed the ECPR.[6] To the contrary, a substantial body of academic literature has endorsed the ECPR and refined the rule. In addition to the writings and testimony of Baumol, that literature includes books, articles, and working papers by such American academic economists as Michael A. Crew,[7] Jerry A. Hausman,[8] Alfred E. Kahn,[9] Paul R. Kleindorfer,[10] Paul W. MacAvoy,[11]

---

6. *Id.* at 14,222 ¶ 147 & n.207 (citing WILLIAM J. BAUMOL & J. GREGORY SIDAK, TOWARD COMPETITION IN LOCAL TELEPHONY (MIT Press & AEI Press 1994); William J. Baumol & J. Gregory Sidak, *The Pricing of Inputs Sold to Competitors*, 11 YALE J. ON REG. 171 (1994); William J. Baumol, *Some Subtle Issues in Railroad Regulation*, 10 INT'L J. TRANSP. ECON. 341 (1983)).

7. MICHAEL A. CREW & PAUL R. KLEINDORFER, THE ECONOMICS OF POSTAL SERVICE 33 (Kluwer Academic Publishers 1992) ("[T]he basic logic of efficient component pricing appears to be a robust starting point for policies to encourage competition and dynamic efficiency while preserving the natural monopoly efficiencies of the local delivery network."); Michael A. Crew & Paul R. Kleindorfer, *Pricing in Postal Service Under Competitive Entry*, *in* COMMERCIALIZATION OF POSTAL AND DELIVERY SERVICES: NATIONAL AND INTERNATIONAL PERSPECTIVES 117, 122–27 (Michael A. Crew & Paul R. Kleindorfer eds., Kluwer Academic Publishers 1995).

8. Jerry A. Hausman & Timothy J. Tardiff, *Efficient Local Exchange Competition*, 40 ANTITRUST BULL. 529, 539, 544, 552–53 (1995). Hausman and Tardiff propose a pricing rule that is consistent with our M-ECPR, although they distinguish their rule in practice from the benchmark case of the ECPR presented by Baumol and Sidak.

9. Alfred E. Kahn & William Taylor, *The Pricing of Inputs Sold to Competitors: A Comment*, 11 YALE J. ON REG. 225 (1994).

10. CREW & KLEINDORFER, *supra* note 7, at 33; Crew & Kleindorfer, *supra* note 7, at 122–27. Curiously, Crew and Kleindorfer are coauthors of a report prepared for AT&T for submission in state arbitration proceedings that urges regulators to reject the use of efficient component pricing for unbundled network elements. KASERMAN REPORT, *supra* note 1, at 14–17.

11. PAUL W. MACAVOY, THE FAILURE OF ANTITRUST AND REGULATION TO ESTABLISH COMPETITION IN LONG-DISTANCE TELEPHONE SERVICES 209 (MIT Press & AEI Press 1996).

Janusz A. Ordover,[12] John C. Panzar,[13] and Robert D. Willig.[14]

Efficient component pricing has captured the attention of European economists as well. The respected French economists, Jean-Jacques Laffont and Jean Tirole, also endorse the ECPR subject to several caveats that they themselves characterize as academic "quibbles,"[15] notwithstanding the FCC's implication in the interconnection proceeding and in its earlier proceeding on commercial mobile radio service (CMRS) interconnection that Laffont and Tirole opposed the ECPR.[16] As chapter 8 explains, Laffont and Tirole examine Ramsey-Boiteux pricing

12. William J. Baumol, Janusz A. Ordover & Robert D. Willig, *Parity Pricing and Its Critics: Necessary Conditions for Efficiency in Provision of Bottleneck Services to Competitors*, 14 YALE J. ON REG. 145 (1997) [hereinafter *Parity Pricing and Its Critics*]; Janusz A. Ordover & Robert D. Willig, Notes on the Efficient Component Pricing Rule, Paper presented at The Transition Towards Competition in Network Industries, First Annual Conference, PURC-IDEI-CIRANO, Montreal (Oct. 13-14, 1995).

13. John C. Panzar, *The Economics of Mail Delivery, in* GOVERNING THE POSTAL SERVICE 1, 6–10 (J. Gregory Sidak ed., AEI Press 1994); John C. Panzar, *Competition, Efficiency, and the Vertical Structure of Postal Services, in* REGULATION AND THE NATURE OF POSTAL DELIVERY SERVICES 91, 96–98 (Michael A. Crew & Paul R. Kleindorfer eds., Kluwer Academic Publishers 1992).

14. Baumol, Ordover & Willig, *supra* note 12; Ordover & Willig, *supra* note 12.

15. Jean-Jacques Laffont & Jean Tirole, *Access Pricing and Competition*, 38 EUR. ECON. REV. 1673 (1994); Jean-Jacques Laffont & Jean Tirole, Creating Competition Through Interconnection: Theory and Practice 3 (1994) (mimeo, MIT) [subsequently published in 10 J. REG. ECON. 227 (1996)]. Oliver E. Williamson expresses reservations about the ECPR on grounds of its practicality and on grounds of the assumptions that Laffont and Tirole assert are necessary for the rule to be optimal. Oliver E. Williamson, *Deregulatory Takings and Breach of the Regulatory Contract: Some Precautions*, 71 N.Y.U. L. REV. 1007, 1018 (1996) (citing Laffont & Tirole, *Access Pricing and Competition, supra*) [hereinafter *Some Precautions*].

16. *Interconnection NPRM,* 11 F.C.C. Rcd. at 14,222 ¶ 147 & n.209 (citing Laffont & Tirole, *Access Pricing and Competition, supra* note 15). Similarly, in its notice of proposed rulemaking on CMRS interconnection, the FCC erroneously cited Laffont and Tirole as support for the Commission's following assessment of the ECPR:

> Critics . . . have shown that these properties [of economic efficiency produced by the ECPR] only hold in special circumstances. On the other hand, some express concern that the ECPR may inhibit beneficial entry.

Radio Service Providers; Equal Access and Interconnection Obligations Pertaining to Commercial Mobile Radio Service Providers, Notice of Proposed Rulemaking, Dkts. CC No. 95-185, 94-54, 11 F.C.C. Rcd. 5020, 5046 ¶ 53 (1996) (citing Laffont & Tirole, *Access Pricing and Competition, supra* note 15; Laffont & Tirole, *Creating Competition Through Interconnection: Theory and Practice, supra* note 15, at 3) [hereinafter *CMRS NPRM*].

as a means of carrying out a second-best allocation of network fixed costs among the incumbent's final output price, the access charge, and the competitor's final output price. Ramsey-Boiteux prices depend on elasticities of demand. Laffont and Tirole select optimal access charges that depart from the marginal cost of access owing to the cost of public funds needed to cover fixed cost.

In the United Kingdom, Mark Armstrong, Chris Doyle, and John Vickers have similarly examined the theoretical conditions under which the ECPR is obtained within a Ramsey-pricing framework.[17] As we note in chapter 8, they impose the standard break-even constraint and show that the second-best optimal access price involves a markup over the marginal cost of access only if the break-even constraint binds. Assuming uniform pricing and ruling out lump-sum transfers, they conclude that, if the incumbent's technology has increasing returns to scale, the access charge is set in excess of marginal cost.

GOVERNMENT PROPONENTS OF THE ECPR

The ECPR has already advanced from theory to practice in the United States and abroad. The FCC, however, ignored that regulators—including the FCC itself—had already embraced the efficient component-pricing rule, though sometimes giving a different name to the pricing method employed. The Interstate Commerce Commission had applied the rule in several railroad rate cases involving trackage rights.[18] In 1989 the California Public Utilities Commission (CPUC) embraced the rule under a different name—"imputation"—in its reform of regulation of local exchange carriers.[19] In 1994 the CPUC reaffirmed its endorsement of the ECPR.[20] In 1992 New Zealand's High Court adopted, and in 1993 its Court of Appeal rejected, the rule (but not its logic) in antitrust litigation between Clear Communications, Ltd., and the former government telephone monopoly, Telecom Corporation of New Zealand,

17. Mark Armstrong, Chris Doyle & John Vickers, *The Access Pricing Problem: A Synthesis*, 44 J. INDUS. ECON. 131 (1996) .

18. *See* St. Louis S.W. Ry.—Trackage Rights over Missouri Pac. R.R.—Kansas City to St. Louis, 1 I.C.C.2d 776 (1984), 4 I.C.C.2d 668 (1987), 5 I.C.C.2d 525 (1989), 8 I.C.C.2d 80 (1991).

19. Alternative Regulatory Framework for Local Exchange Carriers, Invest. No. 87-11-033, 33 C.P.U.C.2d 43, 107 P.U.R.4th 1 (1989).

20. Alternative Regulatory Framework for Local Exchange Carriers, Invest. No. 87-11-033, Decision 94-09-065 at 204–24 (Sept. 15, 1994). For a discussion of the California imputation ruling, see Hausman & Tardiff, *supra* note 8, at 543–47, 545 n.25, 554–55.

Ltd.[21] In October 1994, however, the Judicial Committee of the Privy Council of the House of Lords reversed in relevant part the decision of the Court of Appeal and, citing academic articles on the ECPR by Baumol and Kahn, held that the rule is compatible with New Zealand antitrust principles governing the pricing of a bottleneck input sold by a vertically integrated firm to its competitors.[22] In March 1996 the National Regulatory Research Institute—the research arm of the National Association of Regulatory Utility Commissioners—endorsed the use of the ECPR for the pricing of unbundled access to transmission facilities in the electric power industry.[23]

Remarkably, despite its own criticisms of its depiction of the ECPR, the FCC in effect adopted the rule in March 1996 for the pricing of mandatory leased access of cable television channels: "We generally agree with Time Warner that the value of leased access channels 'is the opportunity cost imposed on the operator from the lost chance to program these channels.'"[24] The FCC defined opportunity cost in that situation as follows:

> The portion of the maximum rate for leased access channels included in a tier of programming which we propose be paid by the leased access programmer . . . would be based on the reasonable costs (including reasonable profits) that leased access imposes on the operator. These

---

21. Clear Communications, Ltd. *v.* Telecom Corp. of New Zealand, Ltd., slip op. (H.C. Dec. 22, 1992), *rev'd*, slip op. (C.A. Dec. 28, 1993). For discussions of the case, see James Farmer, *Transition from Protected Monopoly to Competition: The New Zealand Experiment*, 1 COMPETITION & CONSUMER L.J. 1 (1993); Baumol & Sidak, *The Pricing of Inputs Sold to Competitors, supra* note 6, at 189–94; Kahn & Taylor, *supra* note 9, at 229 n.10. The rule was rejected because the Court of Appeal held that under New Zealand law no agency has the power to prevent inclusion of monopoly profit in the opportunity-cost component of the input price, a conclusion subsequently rejected by the Judicial Committee of the Privy Council.

22. Telecom Corp. of New Zealand Ltd. *v.* Clear Communications Ltd., [1995] 1 N.Z.L.R. 385, 404–05 (Judgment of the Lords of the Judicial Committee of the Privy Council, Oct. 19, 1994) (citing Baumol & Sidak, *The Pricing of Inputs Sold to Competitors, supra* note 6; Kahn & Taylor, *supra* note 9).

23. ROBERT J. GRANIERE, ALMOST SECOND-BEST PRICING FOR REGULATED MARKETS AFFECTED BY COMPETITION (National Regulatory Research Institute Paper No. NRRI 96-10, Mar. 1996).

24. Implementation of Sections of the Cable Television Consumer Protection and Competition Act of 1992: Rate Regulation Leased Commercial Access, Order on Recons. of the First Report and Order and Further Notice of Proposed Rulemaking, MM Dkt. No. 92-266, CS Dkt. No. 96-60, 11 F.C.C. Rcd. 16,933, 16,958–59 ¶ 61 (1996) (quoting Time Warner comments) [hereinafter *Leased Access Order on Reconsideration*].

costs are specific to the channels designated for leased access. Some of these costs are associated with removing or "bumping" non-leased access programming to accommodate leased access programming; others are the direct costs associated with the specific leased access programmer or its programming. To simplify this discussion, we will refer to all of these costs as opportunity costs.[25]

The FCC further concluded that "any profit which is generated from subscriber revenue could be viewed as an opportunity cost imposed on the operator who forgoes these profits when this channel is used to carry leased access programming."[26] The FCC did not explain why it proposed in its interconnection docket to prohibit the states' use of the same pricing rule for mandatory access that the agency embraced only three weeks earlier and that numerous other regulatory bodies had endorsed as conducive to economic welfare.

In May 1996 the FCC again embraced the ECPR, this time explicitly in a rulemaking concerning open video systems (OVS).[27] The Telecommunications Act of 1996 added section 653 to the Communications Act, which "establishes a new framework for entry into the video programming delivery marketplace—the 'open video system.'"[28] The OVS regulatory regime is intended to create

an option, particularly to a local exchange carrier, for the distribution of video programming other than as a "cable system" governed by all of the provisions of Title VI [of the Communications Act]. If a telephone company agrees to permit carriage of unaffiliated video programming providers on just, reasonable and non-discriminatory rates and terms, it can be certified as an operator of an "open video system" and subjected to streamlined regulation under Title VI.[29]

The OVS proceeding thus considered how a LEC seeking to enter the video marketplace pursuant to Title VI regulation would have to price its carriage of unaffiliated video programming.

25. *Id.* at 16,961 ¶ 69. "[T]he operator would be allowed to recover only those types of opportunity costs which can reasonably be attributed to carriage of the leased access programming and which are reasonably quantifiable." *Id.*
26. *Id.* at 16,964 ¶ 78.
27. Implementation of Section 302 of the Telecommunications Act of 1996; Open Video Systems, Second Report and Order, CS Dkt. No. 96-46, 11 F.C.C. Rcd. 18,223 (1996) [hereinafter *OVS Second Report and Order*].
28. *Id.* at 18,226 ¶ 1.
29. *Id.* at 18,226–27 ¶ 1 (footnotes omitted).

The FCC concluded that "the most effective way to evaluate whether a rate is just and reasonable is to compare it to an imputed carriage rate associated with the open video system operator or its affiliate."[30] The agency called that method the "imputed rate approach" and characterized it as "an application of the Efficient Component Pricing Rule to open video systems."[31] The FCC considered the ECPR to be the appropriate rule for pricing "just, reasonable, and nondiscriminatory" access to an *entrant's* facilities:

> This approach is particularly applicable to circumstances where a new market entrant, the open video system operator, will face competition from an established incumbent, the cable operator. A competitive environment facilitates this approach as market forces limit the ability of the open video system operator to increase its imputed carriage rate. The open video system operator must obtain programming and seek subscribers in a competitive environment, thereby providing a sound basis of comparison to determine whether the unaffiliated rate is just and reasonable. The prices that determine the revenues and costs that make up the imputed carriage rate are effectively set in a competitive market.[32]

But the FCC immediately distinguished that application of the ECPR to a LEC's entering a market from the case of the incumbent LEC's sale of mandatory network access to competing providers of telephony services:

> Use of this approach is appropriate in circumstances where the pricing is applicable to a new market entrant (the open video system operator) that will face competition from an existing incumbent provider (the incumbent cable operator), as opposed to circumstances where the pricing is used to establish a rate for an essential input service that is charged to a competing new entrant by an incumbent provider. With respect to new market entrants, an efficient component pricing model will produce rates that encourage market entry.[33]

---

30. *Id.* at 18,290 ¶ 125.

31. *Id.* ¶ 126 (citing Baumol & Sidak, *The Pricing of Inputs Sold to Competitors, supra* note 6; Kahn & Taylor, *supra* note 9).

32. *Id.*

33. *Id.* at 18,291 ¶ 127. "An open video system operator's price to its subscribers will be determined by several separate costs components. One general category are those costs related to the creative development and production of programming. A second category are costs associated with packaging various programs for the open video system operator's offering. A third category relate[s] to the infrastructure or engineering costs identified with building and maintaining the open video system. Contained in each is a profit allowance attributed to the economic value of each component. When an open video system operator

The FCC's implication is that using the ECPR to price mandatory access to an incumbent LEC's network would discourage entry. As the following section explains, that implied criticism is incorrect. The M-ECPR does not deter entry. Although it benefits consumer welfare for the FCC to embrace the ECPR in at least some contexts, there is no economic justification for the agency to confine the rule's application to the facilities of LECs when they are entrants into other markets. If the FCC were to recognize, as we argue here, that ECPR prices are market-determined and market-constrained on a forward-looking basis, then the commission would be forced to acknowledge that all the criticisms that we examine below do not apply to the M-ECPR.

MISDIRECTED CRITICISMS OF THE ECPR FROM WHICH THE M-ECPR IS IMMUNE A FORTIORI

Despite the distinguished group of economists who have endorsed the ECPR in its original form or in our refined M-ECPR form, and despite the FCC's own use of the ECPR in establishing rules for OVS and for the pricing of leased access to cable channels, the commission argued in its interconnection proceeding that the costs of the ECPR are numerous and that they outweigh the rule's benefits. We consider now the standard criticisms of the ECPR, some of which the FCC did not raise, but all of which can be immediately answered. None of those criticisms accurately describes the properties of the M-ECPR.

The M-ECPR Does Not Preserve Monopoly Rent

The FCC argued that the ECPR will protect monopoly profits if the incumbent LEC is earning them and that the rule does not ensure lower prices and higher outputs in a competitive market:

> Under the ECPR, competitive entry will not place at greater risk the incumbent's recovery of its overhead costs or any profits that it otherwise would forego due to the entry of the competitor. In other words, the incumbent's profitability would not be diminished by providing intercon-

---

provides only carriage through its infrastructure, however, the programming and packaging flows from the independent program provider, who bears the cost. The open video system operator avoids programming and packaging costs, including profits. These avoided costs should not be reflected in the price charged an independent program provider for carriage. The imputed rate also seeks to recognize the loss of subscribers to the open video system operator's programming package resulting from carrying competing programming." *Id.*

nection or unbundled elements or both . . . . The ECPR presupposes that the incumbent is the sole provider of a bottleneck service, and seeks to define efficient incentives for incremental entry based on that assumption. Under the ECPR, competitive entry does not drive prices toward competitive levels, because it permits the incumbent carrier to recover its full opportunity costs, including any monopoly profits.[34]

For four reasons, the FCC's claim that efficient component pricing preserves monopoly rents is erroneous or misdirected. The FCC-ECPR is bad economics, but it is not the ECPR that Baumol, Willig, Sidak, and others advocated. Nonetheless, the *First Report and Order* poisoned the lexicon of efficient component pricing and has obliged us to distinguish our refinement of the ECPR by coining the name M-ECPR to emphasize that its prices are market-determined.

The ECPR with Falling Prices. The first flaw in the FCC's claim that the ECPR preserves monopoly rents is that it fails to account for recent academic research demonstrating otherwise. Contrary to the FCC's claim, the M-ECPR supports both efficient entry *and* falling prices for the end product, as we show in chapter 8.[35]

First, the access price derived from the M-ECPR permits price to fall and output to expand for the final product relative to the price and output that had obtained under regulation. Second, that result holds under a variety of market structures: In contestable markets, under Cournot-Nash competition, and in markets characterized by product differentiation, the M-ECPR rewards entry by more efficient rivals and produces lower prices for the final product. Finally, the equilibrium access price implied by the M-ECPR for each of those market structures is lower than the access price that would obtain in the stylized benchmark case in which the incumbent LEC is permitted (contrary to actual experience in regulated markets) to receive the entire monopoly rent in the ECPR's opportunity-cost component.

34. *Interconnection NPRM*, 11 F.C.C. Rcd. at 14,222 ¶ 147. Similarly, the commission said in its notice of proposed rulemaking on CMRS interconnection: "[B]ecause the ECPR would permit an incumbent carrier to recover its opportunity costs, including any monopoly profits in the sale of the final service, the use of this rule may prevent competitive entry from driving prices towards competitive levels." *CMRS NPRM*, 11 F.C.C. Rcd. at 5046 ¶ 53.

35. *See also* DANIEL F. SPULBER & J. GREGORY SIDAK, NETWORK ACCESS PRICING AND DEREGULATION (J. L. Kellogg Graduate School of Management Working Paper, Northwestern University, Sept. 1996).

The Unrealistic Counterfactual of Unregulated Monopoly Free of Mandated Cross-Subsidies. The second flaw in the FCC's claim that the ECPR preserves monopoly rent is that the agency criticized the rule on the basis of imagined circumstances that do not exist in the real world. To assume that a regulated monopolist routinely and consistently earns monopoly rents is counterfactual: The raison d'être of public utility regulation is to prevent a firm thought to be a natural monopoly from setting the profit-maximizing price of an unconstrained monopolist. Contrary to the FCC's implicit assumption, state regulation in place before the enactment of the 1996 federal legislation should be presumed to have limited rather than to have facilitated the extraction of monopoly rents. Nonetheless, expert witnesses testifying on behalf of entrants in state arbitration proceedings following the *First Report and Order* asserted, without empirical support, that the incumbent LEC "has substantial market power in many areas."[36] If state regulation failed to prevent incumbent LECs from earning monopoly rents, then state regulators should now correct their past failures directly. Indeed, the Telecommunications Act of 1996 commands them to do so if they have not done so already.[37] But even if it a state did permit an incumbent LEC to earn monopoly rents, the need to reform that state's regulation would not justify the FCC's rejecting the ECPR in favor of some other pricing method that will fail to yield efficient and compensatory pricing of mandatory network access.

Moreover, if monopoly rents do persist in the pricing of some final product sold by the regulated incumbent LEC, it is likely that regulators have authorized or mandated the extraction of those rents as part of an overall rate structure that is rife with cross-subsidies from one customer group to another. In other words, the prices for specific services that the regulated incumbent LEC has sold may contain rents extracted from one set of customers that it must dissipate to subsidize other services that the regulator orders the LEC to sell below cost. In that case, the recovery of the contributions to margin on the services supposedly generating the monopoly rents represents nothing more than a preservation of state-mandated cross-subsidies; the FCC should not interpret those positive contributions to margin in isolation as a preservation of monopoly rents that, on balance, flow from the combined classes of all customers to the

---

36. *Warren-Boulton Rebuttal Testimony, supra* note 1, at 7; *see also* KASERMAN REPORT, *supra* note 1, at 6 (describing incumbent LEC services "that remain subject to supply under conditions of significant monopoly power").
37. 47 U.S.C. § 253(a) (abolishing state and local legal barriers to entry).

incumbent LEC's shareholders. In any event, it is surely preferable for the regulator to eliminate the system of cross-subsidies altogether by rebalancing the rate structure, rather than to reject the M-ECPR and instead price network access selectively on the basis of incremental cost while continuing to require the incumbent LEC to price various other services below cost. Such a selective approach would violate sound economic analysis and deny the incumbent LEC the opportunity to recover its costs, which eventually would destroy the LEC's financial solvency and induce disinvestment in the network.

The unsubstantiated assertion that the incumbent LEC enjoys unconstrained market power flies in the face of established thinking in antitrust law. Legal and economic scholars have long recognized that naïve reliance on market shares in antitrust cases can produce diagnoses of monopoly power where none exists. Market power refers to the ability of a firm to raise price above the competitive level without losing so many sales as to make the price increase unprofitable. In terms of maximizing consumer welfare, public policy should ask whether a market produces the textbook result of perfect competition in the sense that price (in an industry without economies of scale or scope) is driven down to marginal cost. Market shares are merely an indirect indicator of whether price is likely to exceed marginal cost. In the stylized, perfectly competitive market, where price equals marginal cost, there are so many firms that no one firm has more than a small share of total sales made in the market.

The danger with market-share analysis, however, is that courts, regulators, and legislators will continue to rely upon it when it produces misleading inferences of market power or when more direct evidence of the margin between price and cost is readily available. The misdiagnosis of market power is especially troublesome in regulated industries like local telephony, which are subject to universal service obligations.

Economists have traditionally measured the market power of some firm i through the Lerner index L_i, named for economist Abba Lerner.[38] The Lerner index is an estimate of the proportion by which firm i's price P_i deviates from its marginal cost C_i' at the firm's profit-maximizing output level:

$$L_i = (P_i - C_i')/P_i.$$

38. Abba Lerner, *The Concept of Monopoly and the Measurement of Monopoly Power*, 1 REV. ECON. STUD. 157 (1934).

In a seminal article published in 1981, William E. Landes and Judge Richard A. Posner derived an equivalent form of the Lerner index that is highly useful in antitrust analysis.[39] It enables one to infer the market power of any firm i by simultaneously considering the entire market's price elasticity of demand ϵ^d_m, firm i's market share S_i, and the price elasticity of supply of the j other firms on the competitive fringe of the market ϵ^s_j:

$$L_i = S_i/(\epsilon^d_m + \epsilon^s_j(1 - S_i)).$$

Through their restatement of the Lerner index, Landes and Posner provided a valuable insight. As long as a court considers all three variables—ϵ^d_m, S_i, and ϵ^s_j—it should arrive at a similar estimate of a firm's market power, regardless of how it defines the relevant market.[40] If one variable (often S_i, the share of the supposedly "relevant" market) is overstated or understated, then the other two variables will assume larger or smaller values that precisely offset the distorted estimate.

Landes and Posner noted that high market shares in a price-regulated industry are either meaningless from a competitive perspective or indicative of prices that are set at or below marginal cost—that is, at or below the price that would obtain in a competitive equilibrium:

> To the extent that regulation is effective, its effect is to sever market power from market share and thus render our analysis inapplicable. This is obviously so when the effect of regulation is to limit a monopolist's price to the competitive price level. A subtler effect should also be noted, however. Regulation may increase a firm's market share in circumstances where only the appearance and not the reality of monopoly power is created thereby. For example, in many regulated industries firms are compelled to charge uniform prices in different product or geographical markets despite the different costs of serving the markets. As a result, price may be above marginal cost in some markets and below marginal cost in others. In the latter group of markets, the regulated firm is apt to have a 100% market share. The reason is not that it has market power but that the market is so unattractive to sellers that the only firm that will serve it is one that is either forbidden by regulatory fiat to leave the market or that is induced to remain in it by the opportunity to recoup its

39. William E. Landes & Richard A. Posner, *Market Power in Antitrust Cases*, 94 HARV. L. REV. 937, 944–45 (1981).

40. The price elasticity of demand, though a negative number, is often expressed as its absolute value, as it is here.

losses in its other markets, where the policy of uniform pricing yields revenues in excess of costs. In these circumstances, a 100% market share is a symptom of a lack, rather than the possession, of market power.[41]

That assessment is directly relevant to the unsubstantiated assertion by numerous economists that the incumbent LEC possesses market power. If an incumbent LEC has a marginal cost of $20 for its providing basic residential service but is ordered by regulators to charge only $15, then the LEC's Lerner index for that service is -0.33. The incumbent LEC has a *negative* markup but virtually 100 percent of the market. Landes and Posner note that in such a case "the causality between market share and price is reversed. Instead of a large market share's leading to a high price, a low price leads to a large market share; and it would be improper to infer market power simply from observing the large market share."[42] The Ninth Circuit comprehended that relationship in *Metro Mobile CTS, Inc.* v. *NewVector Communications, Inc.*, when it said: "Reliance on statistical market share in cases involving regulated industries is at best a tricky enterprise and is downright folly where . . . the predominant market share is the result of regulation. In such cases, the court should focus directly on the regulated firm's ability to control prices or exclude competition."[43]

The ECPR with Facilities-Based Competition for Access. The third flaw in the FCC's claim that the ECPR preserves monopoly rents is that it misapprehends how the rule functions when there is facilities-based competition for the provision of network access. If facilities-based competition is infeasible, then the basis for the opportunity-cost calculation in the M-ECPR is the incumbent LEC's regulated margins. But if access competition is feasible, then the M-ECPR methodology requires pricing at the stand-alone cost of the best alternative technology for providing network access, even if that lower price of access fails to preserve the incumbent LEC's regulated margin. That is why the M-ECPR produces a market-determined price. Thus, contrary to the FCC's claim concerning the ECPR, the M-ECPR cannot and does not protect the incumbent LEC's regulated margins from the downward

41. Landes & Posner, *supra* note 39, at 975–76.

42. *Id.* at 976.

43. 892 F.2d 62, 63 (9th Cir. 1989); *accord*, Consolidated Gas Co. of Fla. *v.* City Gas Co., 880 F.2d 297, 300 (11th Cir.), *vacated and reh'g granted*, 889 F.2d 264 (11th Cir. 1989), *on reh'g*, 912 F.2d 1262 (11th Cir. 1990), *rev'd per curiam on other grounds*, 499 U.S. 915 (1991).

pressure of access competition. Market forces simply will not permit the incumbent LEC to charge a higher price than the stand-alone cost of the best alternative technology for providing network access, even if the incumbent LEC may lawfully attempt in vain to do so.

The existence of access competition also establishes that the incumbent LEC's facilities are not "essential," as that term is used in antitrust law.[44] Entry barriers to facilities-based competition are not insurmountable, as evidenced by the substantial investment in transmission and switching facilities that has already occurred in the local exchange.[45] In addition, technological change has lowered the entrant's need to make irreversible, transaction-specific investment.[46] Wireless technologies lower the specificity of entry costs in comparison with traditional wired technologies. Consequently, there is less reason with each passing day to presume that the wireline facilities of the incumbent LEC, if unregulated by the states, still could generate the monopoly rents that evidently motivated the FCC's opposition to the states' use of the ECPR.

Misdirected Criticism of Policy Instruments. The fourth fallacy in the FCC's claim that the ECPR perpetuates monopoly rents is that the agency attempts to redress a perceived failure of public utility regulation by manipulating the wrong policy instrument. Even if state regulators were to permit an incumbent LEC to earn monopoly rents (net of all government-mandated cross-subsidies), that fact would not undermine the economic efficiency *of the M-ECPR.* The rule's purpose is to reward efficient entry into the market for the end product by ensuring that the incumbent LEC sells network access to itself and to its rivals on the same, nondiscriminatory terms. The M-ECPR accomplishes that task regardless of the market structure and regardless of the presence or absence of economic rents.

The Judicial Committee of the Privy Council of the House of Lords recognized the efficacy of the ECPR when, in *Telecom Corporation of New Zealand, Ltd.* v. *Clear Communications, Ltd.*, that court of last resort considered whether the ECPR would violate section 36 of New Zealand's Commerce Act by allowing Telecom to recover monopoly

44. United States *v.* Terminal R.R. Ass'n, 224 U.S. 383 (1912); MCI Comm. Corp. *v.* American Tel. & Tel. Co., 708 F.2d 1081 (7th Cir.), *cert. denied*, 464 U.S. 891 (1983).

45. Daniel F. Spulber, *Deregulating Telecommunications*, 12 YALE J. ON REG. 25, 45–50 (1995).

46. *Id.* at 56–58.

rents in the opportunity-cost component of the access price that it proposed to charge to the entering local carrier, Clear, for interconnection to Telecom's access network.[47] The committee emphasized that courts applying section 36 "are not acting as regulators" and that "section 36 is only one of the remedies provided by the Commerce Act for the purpose of combatting over-pricing due to monopolistic behavior."[48] Other sections of the Commerce Act, Lord Browne-Wilkinson observed, are available to perform that role:

> Part IV [of the Commerce Act] deals separately with control of prices. Under section 53 the Governor-General, on the recommendation of the Minister, may declare that the prices for goods or services of any description supplied to or for the use of different persons are controlled. Under section 53(2)(a) a Minister cannot make such a recommendation unless he is satisfied the goods or services are supplied in a market "in which competition is limited or is likely to be lessened". Under section 70 the Commission may authorise a price to be charged for controlled services. Therefore section 36 is only part of an overall statutory machinery for dealing with trade practices which operate to the detriment of consumers. Another part of such machinery (Part IV) is specifically directed to the regulation of prices in markets which are not fully competitive.[49]

The Privy Council ruled that "the risk of monopoly rents has no bearing upon the question whether the application of the [ECPR] prevents competition in the contested area."[50] "If *both* Telecom and Clear are charging their customers the same amount in the area in which they are not competitors," Lord Browne-Wilkinson reasoned, "this does not have any effect on their relative competitiveness in the area in which they compete. . . ."[51]

The Mistaken Critique of the ECPR by Economides and White. Beyond positing counterfactual assumptions, the related theoretical case against the M-ECPR makes unrealistic assumptions and errors of reasoning. Nicholas Economides and Lawrence J. White allege that, if the ECPR

---

47. [1995] 1 N.Z.L.R. 385 (Judgment of the Lords of the Judicial Committee of the Privy Council, Oct. 19, 1994); *see also* William J. Baumol & J. Gregory Sidak, *The Pricing of Inputs Sold to Competitors: Rejoinder and Epilogue*, 12 YALE J. ON REG. 177 (1995) (discussing New Zealand interconnection litigation).

48. [1995] 1 N.Z.L.R. at 404.

49. *Id.*

50. *Id.* at 407.

51. *Id.* (emphasis in original).

price is above marginal cost, there is an efficiency distortion.[52] Economides and White reason as follows. Because the M-ECPR price entails a markup above marginal cost (in their model, marginal cost and incremental cost coincide), any lowering of price toward marginal cost must improve welfare. Even entry by a less efficient competitor—a competitor with marginal costs *greater than* those of the incumbent LEC—will lower prices. Therefore, they assert, such inefficient entry improves welfare by lowering prices. Because the M-ECPR deters that type of inefficient entry, they conclude that the M-ECPR must not be efficient.

Each step of that reasoning is flawed. Are all markups above marginal costs inefficient? Surely not, since markups are a common feature of competitive markets, where firms cover fixed costs, or shared costs and common costs, through markups. The Walt Disney Company does not sell videos of *The Lion King* at the marginal cost of a blank video cassette. Ford, General Motors, Chrysler, Nissan, Toyota, and Honda operate in competitive markets, yet each of those multiproduct firms must sell its cars, trucks, and minivans above their respective marginal costs so that the firm can recover shared or common costs incurred across two or more product lines. The objection of Economides and White to the M-ECPR seems to be that it involves a markup over marginal cost. But that objection would apply equally to *all* markups—such as average cost pricing or Ramsey pricing, where fixed costs, or shared costs and common costs, are recovered through markups.

---

52. Nicholas Economides & Lawrence J. White, *Access and Interconnection Pricing: How Efficient Is the "Efficient Component Pricing Rule"?*, 40 ANTITRUST BULL. 557 (1995). Economides has subsequently directed that criticism toward the M-ECPR as well in testimony to the Hawaii Public Utilities Commission. In the Matter of AT&T Communications Co. of Hawaii, Inc., Petition filed Aug. 19, 1996 for arbitration with GTE Hawaiian Telephone Co., Inc., Dkt. No. 96-0329, tr. at 520–34 (Hawaii Pub. Util. Comm'n Oct. 17, 1996). For critiques of Economides and White, see Baumol, Ordover & Willig, *supra* note 12, at 155–56; Alexander C. Larson, *The Efficiency of the Efficient Component-Pricing Rule: A Comment*, 42 ANTITRUST BULL. (forthcoming 1997); William J. Baumol & J. Gregory Sidak, *Pricing of Services Provided to Competitors by the Regulated Firm*, 3 HUME PAPERS ON PUB. POL'Y, No. 3, at 15, 30 (1995). As Larson shows, the model presented by Economides and White suffers from several problematic features: "The three major weaknesses of the analytic framework Economides and White employ are: (1) the assumption of monopoly pricing in the downstream market; (2) the assumption of Bertrand-like limit pricing in the downstream market once entrants purchase the required upstream productive inputs; and (3) the market price elasticities of demand that Economides and White assume for the downstream market." Larson, *supra*, manuscript at 4. Economides and White respond in Nicholas Economides & Lawrence J. White, *The Inefficiency of the ECPR Yet Again: A Reply to Larson*, 42 ANTITRUST BULL. (forthcoming 1997).

That criticism is misguided because it is directed at constant per-unit pricing *in general*, not at M-ECPR pricing in particular. M-ECPR pricing allows any type of pricing to recover incremental cost plus opportunity cost. Firms can charge customers a two-part tariff consisting of a usage charge and a connection charge. The usage charge can be a marginal cost price. The connection charge is a per-customer charge that recovers the difference between the M-ECPR amount and the amount recovered through marginal cost pricing. Then, as is well known, competition between firms offering two-part tariffs ensures an efficient outcome. Two-part tariff competition for the market eliminates excess profit and cross-subsidies and allows efficient entry.[53]

The assertion by Economides and White that inefficient entry improves welfare does not withstand scrutiny. Inefficient entry does nothing more than raise total production costs for the industry. That outcome cannot be desirable. Baumol, Ordover, and Willig sound the following warning, with which we entirely agree:

> It is . . . dangerous to use the bottleneck-service price as a means to stimulate downstream competition because the result must amount to a cross-subsidy to entrants that leads to an excessive allocation of resources into that market . . . . When bottleneck prices are forced to artificially low levels to enable rivals to obtain a foothold, all of the problems entailed in infant-firm subsidies arise. For example, these subsidies undercut the incentives for entrants to reduce their costs.[54]

Nonetheless, the objection of Economides and White to the M-ECPR is that such inefficient entry is deterred. That result cannot be a problem with M-ECPR. Rather, it is a *virtue* of pricing that reflects economic cost. That argument by Economides and White therefore epitomizes the observation by Baumol, Ordover, and Willig (with which we wholeheartedly concur) that any "disagreement between" the academic proponents and opponents of efficient component pricing, "stems largely from their adoption of goals that go beyond attainment of economic efficiency in supply," which Baumol, Ordover, and Willig define to consist "solely of the requirement that access prices do not preclude an efficient firm that is either the owner of the bottleneck or one of its rivals in the final-product market from participating in the supply of the end-user product that utilizes the monopolized input."[55]

---

53. This analysis is performed in DANIEL F. SPULBER, REGULATION AND MARKETS 209–20, 260–61 (MIT Press 1989).
54. Baumol, Ordover & Willig, *Parity Pricing and Its Critics, supra* note 12, at 162.
55. *Id.* at 146 & n.2.

Because Economides and White object to any pricing above marginal cost, they would prefer that all regulated facilities be priced at marginal cost. If the incumbent LEC is not to incur losses, marginal cost pricing requires either instituting a system of two-part tariffs or establishing an alternative means for cost recovery.

Economides and White assume that the incumbent LEC possesses an essential facility that resembles manna from heaven. In their framework, the entrant cannot duplicate the facility at *any* price, yet the incumbent LEC seems to have acquired the facility without incurring any cost. The facility is infinitely costly for the entrant and free for the incumbent LEC. That assumption is certainly unrealistic. In actuality, transmission facilities are costly to establish for incumbent LECs and can be constructed by an entrant at some cost that may be greater than, equal to, or less than that of the incumbent LEC. If the incumbent LEC incurred a cost in constructing the facility, then the alleged "profit" is little more than net revenue. The net revenue of the incumbent LEC could be greater than, equal to, or less than the cost that the incumbent LEC incurred in creating the facilities. Thus, although the incumbent LEC's retail price involves a markup above marginal cost, the incumbent LEC's net revenue does not represent economic profit, but merely a recovery of investment. If the incumbent LEC's net revenue is less than the cost of creating the facilities, including the cost of capital, then the incumbent LEC could be incurring a *loss*, even with a positive markup over marginal cost. By ignoring the costs of establishing facilities in their assertion that the incumbent LEC is making profit (really a short-run operating profit), Economides and White effectively assert that positive operating margins are not efficient, and thus they ignore the recovery of, and return on, capital provided by net revenues.

In sum, although the opportunity cost of selling facilities can include monopoly rents, if such rents are already present, that fact does not indicate a problem with M-ECPR. Rather, it is a feature of the existing market. Yet, such a situation is *not* consistent with effective regulation. If the criticism of M-ECPR is based on the assumption that regulation is ineffective, then the solution is to fix the regulatory problem, not to redistribute income across firms. As Baumol, Ordover, and Willig observe: "If it is the intention of Economides and White to criticize ECPR for its lack of promise as a cure for bottleneck monopoly, they can fault it with equal justice as a poor remedy for inflation or warts."[56]

---

56. *Id.* at 156. The same argument appears in William B. Tye & Carlos Lapuerta, *The Economics of Pricing Network Interconnection: Theory and Application to the Market for Telecommunications in New Zealand*, 13 YALE J. ON REG. 421 (1996), to which Baumol,

Moreover, the opportunity-cost component of the M-ECPR is at all times limited by the cost of the best alternative for network access net of the incumbent LEC's incremental cost. By assuming that competitive alternatives are prohibitively costly, Economides and White stack the deck. As long as there is the potential for entry of facilities-based competitors, the cost of competitive alternatives limits the rents on the incumbent LEC's facilities.

Summary of Monopoly Rent Criticisms. The criticisms of the M-ECPR start from the counterfactual assumption that the incumbent LEC is earning monopoly rents. Presumably, if that were true, it would manifest a failure of regulation that should be corrected directly rather than through access pricing. It is certainly possible that specific services contain markups that are used to provide subsidies for other services that the regulated LEC provides below cost. Then, the recovery of those contributions to margin may represent a preservation of some cross-subsidies that are left in place by rate regulation. It would be misleading, however, to interpret the situation created by the existing regulated rate structure as a preservation of monopoly rents. It is preferable to eliminate the system of cross-subsidies by rebalancing the rate structure, rather than selectively pricing some access services based on costs while simultaneously pricing other services *below* cost. Such a selective approach not only is inconsistent but represents a fundamental breach of the regulatory contract by not allowing the regulated firm the reasonable opportunity to recover its costs.

If facilities-based competition is not feasible, the basis for the opportunity-cost calculation in the M-ECPR is the incumbent LEC's regulated margins. If the LEC is subject to price caps and earnings-sharing rules, then those features further constrain its earnings. Thus, regulation limits the economic rents of the LEC. When there is facilities-based competition, the M-ECPR methodology requires pricing at the best alternative price, even if that price lies below regulated margins. Thus, M-ECPR pricing cannot be said to protect those margins from competition. To the contrary, the M-ECPR method requires repeatedly adjusting the access price to equal the market price of the best alternative.

Ordover, and Willig, *Parity Pricing and Its Critics, supra* note 12, at 159, respond: "To condemn a procedure that performs other useful tasks—the tasks it was designed to carry out—for failing to deal with the monopoly problem as well is patently a *non sequitur.*" *See also* William B. Tye, *The Pricing of Inputs Sold to Competitors: A Response*, 11 YALE J. ON REG. 203 (1994).

The monopoly-rents criticisms of the M-ECPR in deregulated telecommunications markets rely on counterfactual assumptions. Regulation that existed before the opening of the market has served to limit monopoly rents; and if it has not, then any alleged regulatory failures should be corrected directly. Selective departures from an economically efficient pricing method will not yield either efficient or compensatory pricing of network access.

The M-ECPR Does Not
Limit Competitive Entry

Opponents of M-ECPR pricing assert that "ECPR-based prices are designed to keep competitors out of the market."[57] That claim is incorrect. To the contrary, as the Privy Council's analysis in *Telecom* v. *Clear* makes clear, the ECPR does not limit competitive entry in the case of interconnection of local networks to effect terminating access. That result holds a fortiori for the M-ECPR. Likewise, when entry occurs instead by means of resale or unbundled access to network elements, access prices that recover the incumbent LEC's TELRIC and its opportunity costs are no barrier to the entry of competitors that are at least as efficient as the incumbent LEC in the provision of retail services. In all three cases prices that are computed according to the M-ECPR are both efficient and compensatory. By setting access prices that allow the incumbent LEC to recover its costs, retail rates will fall to reflect (1) the efficiencies of resellers and of aggregators of unbundled elements, (2) the increased demand at the lower prices, and (3) the lowering of the cost recovery per unit.[58]

Consider now how competition in the provision of network access affects the M-ECPR and the incentives that it creates for efficient entry. With facilities-based competition, it is evident that the M-ECPR does not impede entry. Setting the M-ECPR at the stand-alone cost of the best alternative technology allows the entry of other companies that are at least as efficient as the entrant that serves as the benchmark. The facilities-based entrant that serves as the benchmark, however, can be less efficient than the incumbent LEC because the ECPR price does not undercut that entrant's incremental cost.

57. *Warren-Boulton Rebuttal Testimony, supra* note 1, at 24.

58. For a technical economic analysis demonstrating these assertions, see chapter 8 and SPULBER & SIDAK, *supra* note 35.

It is sometimes asserted that the ECPR excludes entrants that have the *potential* in the long run of becoming more efficient providers of some end service than the incumbent LEC. Perhaps the same argument would be directed at the M-ECPR. Proponents of that view are implicitly advocating an entry subsidy. The fallacy in that position, however, is that no one, including the regulator, can distinguish ex ante between those entrants that have such potential and those that do not. Furthermore, the incumbent LEC's forced subsidization of entrants is an undertaking that fundamentally differs in character from mandating that the LEC interconnect the networks of competing carriers, that it offer its retail services to competitors at wholesale, and that it offer its network elements to competitors on an unbundled basis. By effecting that subsidy, the regulator would force the incumbent LEC to fund a kind of public good: the entry of a multitude of inefficient firms into the local exchange market in the hope that one would eventually discover a lower-cost production technology than the incumbent LEC's for delivering an end service to consumers.

That end may be laudable in the minds of some persons—but the means should not be, for two reasons. First, the M-ECPR already rewards such innovation and does so in a neutral manner that does not condition the benefits that the innovating firm may reap from its achievement of cost-reducing breakthroughs on whether the innovator is the incumbent LEC or a new entrant. Second, if the government considers the quest for lower-cost technologies to be an endeavor likely to benefit the citizenry as a whole, it should expressly pay for the production of that public good, just as it might choose to subsidize other R&D activities believed to have potential public benefit. For the regulator, however, to require the incumbent LEC to subsidize its rivals' quest for superior production technologies is not only to impose a perverse regulatory policy, but also to confiscate the property of the incumbent LEC's shareholders and transfer it to shareholders of that class of favored entrants.

The M-ECPR Does Not Impede Dynamic Efficiency

The FCC asserted in the notice of proposed rulemaking for its 1996 interconnection proceeding, "In general, the ECPR framework precludes the opportunity to obtain the advantages of a dynamically competitive marketplace."[59] That adverse result supposedly obtains because, according to the

---

59. *Interconnection NPRM*, 11 F.C.C. Rcd. at 14,222 ¶ 147.

FCC, the incumbent LEC makes the same profits whether it provides the entire service or sells network access to entrants. In the FCC's view, that condition of indifference gives the incumbent LEC no incentive to reduce costs by introducing new technology or to provide better services. That reasoning, however, finds no support in either theory or experience.

Like the argument that the ECPR preserves monopoly rent, the argument that the rule (or the M-ECPR) impedes dynamic efficiency depends on a counterfactual assumption: Regulators are either indifferent to the incumbent LEC's total factor productivity or ineffectual in creating incentives for productivity growth. Such an assumption ignores the prevalence of price caps, rate freezes, and other incentive regulation schemes that reward greater efficiency.[60] Nothing prevents regulators from building incentive mechanisms of that sort into their regulation of the pricing of mandatory network access under the M-ECPR.

Furthermore, the FCC's claim of lost dynamic efficiency under the ECPR is controverted by the actual experience in New Zealand, the first nation to embrace the rule in local telephony. By any measure, Telecom New Zealand's investment and productivity gains have been substantial, and the country's telecommunications network is one of the most advanced in the world. From the beginning of deregulation in 1987 through the end of 1994, Telecom New Zealand invested over NZ$4.1 billion in network modernization and service enhancement.[61] By the end of 1994, more than 97 percent of access lines were connected to digital switches; in 1995 it was projected that in three years Telecom New Zealand's telephone network would be entirely digitally switched.[62] In addition to that investment in infrastructure, there has been an "introduction of a growing range of new services such as call diversion, audio conference and call waiting."[63]

To be sure, it would be an overstatement to attribute all New Zealand's gains in efficiency to its judiciary's support of the ECPR. Telecom New Zealand subsequently agreed to a confidential interconnection contract that was rumored not to rely explicitly on the ECPR. The levels of investment observed in New Zealand may nonetheless reflect the salutary effect of the parties' bargaining in the shadow of the

60. *See generally* DAVID E. M. SAPPINGTON & DENNIS L. WEISMAN, DESIGNING INCENTIVE REGULATION FOR THE TELECOMMUNICATIONS INDUSTRY (MIT Press & AEI Press 1996).

61. NEW ZEALAND MINISTRY OF COMMERCE, TELECOMMUNICATIONS REFORM IN NEW ZEALAND: 1987–1994, TELECOMMUNICATIONS LEAFLET NO. 5, at 4 (Jan. 19, 1995).

62. *Id.*

63. *Id.*

ECPR rather than in the shadow of TELRIC pricing or the FCC's even lower default prices. At a minimum the empirical evidence shifts the burden of proof back onto the FCC and other opponents of the M-ECPR to substantiate their sweeping assertion that the states' use of the M-ECPR would entail a sacrifice in dynamic efficiency.

The M-ECPR Does Not Require Difficult Measurement of Future Earnings Forgone

The FCC argued that the difficulty of accurately measuring the incumbent LEC's loss of revenue would make the ECPR difficult to employ: "[A]s an administrative matter, it would be difficult for a regulatory agency to determine a carrier's actual opportunity cost."[64] That criticism is doubly unpersuasive. First, it fails to explain why the estimation of forgone net revenue would be any harder than the typical test-year calculations that are routinely conducted in rate proceedings, or the estimates of productivity growth that are made to compute the "X factor" in price-cap regulation.

Second, the FCC's complaint is inconsistent with its own detailed discussion of how to compute opportunity cost when determining the mandatory price of leased access to cable channels.[65] In its March 29, 1996, order, the FCC devoted eleven paragraphs consisting of more than 2,000 words to a discussion of how to compute "net opportunity costs" for purposes of pricing leased access. In contrast, the FCC devoted only one sentence to the analogous issue concerning mandatory access to the local exchange network and gave no indication of why, only three weeks after its pronouncements on leased access, state and federal regulators should find the definition and measurement of opportunity costs to be an insuperable challenge.

Moreover, *any* method for computing prices for network access will entail some nontrivial amount of administrative costs. The relevant objective, which the FCC seemed not to recognize, is not to minimize the regulator's administrative costs, but rather to maximize the gains in economic welfare from the access-pricing rule chosen, net of such administrative costs.[66] Regulators may understandably aspire to the quiet

---

64. *Interconnection NPRM*, 11 F.C.C. Rcd. at 14,222 ¶ 147. Oliver E. Williamson similarly asserts that there "are severe measurement problems posed" by efficient component pricing. Williamson, *supra* note 15, at 1019.

65. *Leased Access Order on Reconsideration*, 11 F.C.C. Rcd. at 16,964–68 ¶¶ 79–89.

66. That principle is simply a variant on the argument, familiar in antitrust policy, that

life that they enjoyed with the monopolists that they oversaw for decades. But if a particular access-pricing rule stifles efficient entry or bankrupts efficient incumbents, it is hardly an endorsement for that rule that it requires few of the regulator's resources to administer.

The M-ECPR Does Not Recreate Cost-of-Service Regulation

The M-ECPR is a method of pricing access that a regulator can use to unbundle an incumbent LEC's network. The rule is intended to produce efficient access and entry decisions and to compensate the incumbent LEC for the incremental cost and the opportunity cost of being compelled to allow a competitor to use the LEC's network. If, because of access competition, even the M-ECPR cannot produce an access price for the incumbent LEC's network that is compensatory in terms of recovering total costs, then the regulator must take an additional step to ensure that the LEC can achieve full recovery of the cost of providing mandatory network access to its competitors. The regulator can do so by imposing an end-user charge equivalent to the amount of the shortfall remaining after computation of the access price implied by the M-ECPR.

From that brief recapitulation, it should be clear that the M-ECPR does not recreate cost-of-service regulation. To the extent that regulated retail rates remain in force, the M-ECPR provides a means to translate those rates into access charges for unbundled network elements. The continuation of regulated retail rates is a regulatory decision that is independent of the regulator's application of the M-ECPR to calculate the price of unbundled network elements.

a liability rule should minimize the combined costs of false positives (type I errors), false negatives (type II errors), and the costs of administration. *See* Paul L. Joskow & Alvin K. Klevorick, *A Framework for Analyzing Predatory Pricing Policy*, 89 YALE L.J. 213, 223 (1979); *see also* Frank H. Easterbrook, *Predatory Strategies and Counterstrategies*, 48 U. CHI. L. REV. 263, 318–19 (1981); Richard L. Schmalensee, *On the Use of Economic Models in Antitrust: The* ReaLemon *Case*, 127 U. PA. L. REV. 994, 1018–19 n.98 (1979). For extensions to telecommunications regulation, see BAUMOL & SIDAK, TOWARD COMPETITION IN LOCAL TELEPHONY, *supra* note 6, at 131–32; MACAVOY, *supra* note 11, at 177–79; Kenneth J. Arrow, Dennis W. Carlton & Hal S. Sider, *The Competitive Effects of Line-of-Business Restrictions in Telecommunications*, 16 MANAGERIAL & DECISION ECON. 301, 305 (1995) ("The goal of public policy in telecommunications should not be simply to minimize potential regulatory problems but instead to maximize net benefits to society."); J. Gregory Sidak, *Telecommunications in Jericho*, 81 CAL. L. REV. 1209, 1216–17 (1993).

To be sure, the calculation of prices for network elements does depend on the incremental cost and the opportunity cost borne by the regulated incumbent LEC. In the absence of regulation, the incumbent LEC would determine its own access charges in a similar manner. The regulation of prices for those elements necessarily creates the need for the incumbent LEC to present cost information to the regulator as part of the process of administering the M-ECPR—or, for that matter, any other rule for access pricing. The relaxation of cost-of-service regulation, on the other hand, would allow the incumbent LEC to set its access charges without presenting cost information to its regulator.

With facilities-based entry, the M-ECPR bases rates on the cost of the best alternative technology for the provision of network access. That computation requires an estimation of the *competitor's* incremental cost. Such an exercise differs substantially from regulation based on the costs of the firm being regulated—namely, the incumbent LEC. Consequently, when firms compete to provide network access, the regulator's application of the M-ECPR fundamentally departs from traditional cost-of-service regulation.

The M-ECPR Is Not Fully Distributed Cost Pricing

Janusz A. Ordover warns, "To the extent that there are non-trivial common or shared costs among network elements, strict limits on their recovery are appropriate in order to avert *arbitrary* additives significantly above TELRIC and the inefficiencies of pricing based on fully distributed costs."[67] That statement is a non sequitur. The need to price above TELRIC is not equivalent to a need to resort to fully distributed cost (FDC) pricing. And, in any event, Ordover's concern is not an indictment of the M-ECPR, because the rule is not a form of FDC pricing. To be sure, the M-ECPR is based on costs because it prices any network component at the sum of its incremental cost and its opportunity cost. That exercise, however, need not entail the use of an arbitrary FDC allocation of joint and common costs. If the regulator preserves a structure of regulated rates, then any underlying cost allocation will be reflected in the calculation of prices for unbundled elements. Any problems with the outcome in that case result not from the M-ECPR, but from the regulator's failure to rebalance regulated rates.

---

67. *Ordover Rebuttal Testimony, supra* note 1, at 21 (emphasis in original).

With resale competition and flexible prices the M-ECPR adjusts downward to reflect falling retail prices. That adjustment does not imply any reliance upon an FDC methodology. Similarly, if there is facilities-based competition, no FDC methodology motivates the result under the M-ECPR that the incumbent LEC should price access at the incremental cost of the best alternative technology for providing network access.

The M-ECPR Is Not Ramsey Pricing

The M-ECPR is not Ramsey pricing.[68] Ramsey pricing is a method of allocating nonattributable costs to the individual products of a multiproduct regulated firm. If the firm experiences economies of scale or scope, marginal cost pricing yields insufficient revenues to cover the firm's total cost. Prices must therefore exceed marginal cost for the firm to recover its common costs and thus continue to supply the goods in question. Ramsey pricing denotes those second-best prices that are Pareto optimal, subject to the requirement that they yield revenues sufficient to cover the total costs incurred by the supplier of the products in question. The damage to welfare from deviating from marginal cost pricing is minimized if the firm's revenue shortfall is covered through smaller relative increases in the prices of the goods whose demands are elastic and through larger relative increases in the prices of goods whose demands are inelastic.[69] Ramsey prices are usually obtained by maximizing the sum of consumer surplus and producer surplus *subject to the constraint that the revenues generated by the firm must cover its costs.*

Like Ramsey pricing, the M-ECPR allocates common costs to unbundled network elements in inverse relation to each element's price elasticity of demand. But the similarity between Ramsey pricing and the M-ECPR ends there. Unlike Ramsey pricing, prices for unbundled

68. *Cf.* INGO VOGELSANG & BRIDGER M. MITCHELL, TELECOMMUNICATIONS COMPETITION: THE LAST TEN MILES 61 (MIT Press & AEI Press 1997) ("The efficient component-pricing rule is identical to the Ramsey rule if retail service prices are Ramsey-efficient, if the interconnector competes with the LEC on a price basis, and if the retail services supplied by both firms are identical and produced in fixed proportion to the interconnection service.").

69. *See* Frank P. Ramsey, *A Contribution to the Theory of Taxation*, 37 ECON. J. 47 (1927). For a review of the subsequent literature, see William J. Baumol, *Ramsey Pricing*, in 4 THE NEW PALGRAVE: A DICTIONARY OF ECONOMICS 49–51 (John Eatwell, Murray Milgate & Peter Newman eds., Macmillan Co. 1987); William J. Baumol & David F. Bradford, *Optimal Departures from Marginal Cost Pricing,* 60 AM. ECON. REV. 265 (1970).

network elements that are calculated according to the M-ECPR cannot ensure that the firm will cover its costs. In that respect we agree with Baumol, Ordover, and Willig that a "Ramsey price can be expected to violate ECPR"—as long as one does not equate their reference to the ECPR with the FCC-ECPR.[70] As shown earlier, the price that an incumbent LEC can charge for an unbundled network element is capped by the stand-alone cost of the next-best alternative technology. In the presence of facilities-based substitutes for the incumbent LEC's supposedly bottleneck elements, the M-ECPR will produce prices that fail to cover the LEC's total costs. The M-ECPR cannot make the incumbent LEC whole. Rather, it produces the *loss-minimizing* set of prices for the incumbent LEC's unbundled network elements. In that respect we would *not* agree with Baumol, Ordover, and Willig that "Ramsey-adjusted ECPR prices can be expected to be even higher" than ordinary ECPR prices—*if* Baumol, Ordover, and Willig were to include M-ECPR prices in their definition of "Ramsey-adjusted ECPR prices."[71]

The M-ECPR Does Not
Violate the Diamond-Mirrlees
Principle for Pricing Intermediate Goods

Some have argued that the price for an unbundled element should not exceed its TELRIC on the ground that a higher price would distort input choices in production.[72] That argument is an adaptation of an article by Peter A. Diamond and John A. Mirrlees concerning optimal principles of taxation.[73] As Baumol and Sidak have argued,[74] however, the Diamond-Mirrlees argument does not apply to the pricing of unbundled network access. Four considerations support that conclusion.

First, by virtue of its enactment of the Telecommunications Act of 1996, Congress redefined the incumbent LEC's output. Before 1996 the incumbent LEC provided telecommunications services to customers. Network elements were the inputs for the production of those services.

70. Baumol, Ordover & Willig, *Parity Pricing and Its Critics, supra* note 12, at 153 n.11.

71. *Id.* (emphasis suppressed).

72. KASERMAN REPORT, *supra* note 1, at 13–14 & n.14; *see also* Hausman & Tardiff, *supra* note 8, at 549; *Ordover Rebuttal Testimony, supra* note 1, at 22.

73. Peter A. Diamond & John A. Mirrlees, *Optimal Taxation and Public Production, II: Tax Rules,* 61 AM. ECON. REV. 261 (1971).

74. BAUMOL & SIDAK, TOWARD COMPETITION IN LOCAL TELEPHONY, *supra* note 6, at 106 n.4.

Since the enactment of the new legislation, however, the incumbent LEC has been obligated to sell elements directly to competitors, which in turn will assemble their own retail services for sale to customers. Under that new regime the incumbent LEC's network elements have become its outputs. Because the Diamond-Mirrlees principle applies to inputs rather than outputs, the principle does not apply after the 1996 telecommunications legislation to the LEC's pricing of unbundled network elements.

Second, Diamond and Mirrlees presented an argument why Ramsey pricing should not be used to price inputs. But, as explained earlier, the M-ECPR differs from Ramsey pricing. The purpose of Ramsey pricing is to set prices for multiple goods produced by a given firm in a manner that maximizes consumer welfare subject to the constraint that the firm break even. Ramsey pricing, in other words, is predicated on the requirement that the firm's total revenues equal its total costs. The M-ECPR, however, cannot guarantee that the incumbent LEC will break even when it sells unbundled elements to its competitors. Thus, the Diamond-Mirrlees principle is a criticism lodged at a method of pricing that is not the method embodied in the M-ECPR.

Third, even if the Diamond-Mirrlees principle were applicable to the case of unbundling in local telephony, it is nonetheless true, as Baumol and Sidak have noted,[75] that there is no markup over the marginal cost of an unbundled element for purposes of the Diamond-Mirrlees analysis when one correctly includes in the definition of marginal cost the marginal *social opportunity cost* of the sale of an input to a competitor. That marginal social opportunity cost reflects the effect of the sale of the input on the LEC's continued ability to fund through its regulated rate structure the recovery of its common costs of operating the network and of providing services that regulators require (such as subsidized services to certain customers, universal service, and carrier-of-last-resort functions). Setting prices for inputs according to the M-ECPR does not entail any markup over marginal cost when that cost is correctly defined to reflect the marginal opportunity cost *to society* that arises when the incumbent LEC is compelled by law to sell an input to a competitor.

Fourth, as Baumol and Sidak have also noted,[76] the Diamond-Mirrlees analysis ignores the case of scale economies—which likely describes the cost characteristics of many of the incumbent LEC's inputs. Instead, Diamond and Mirrlees assume that marginal cost exceeds average cost.[77]

75. *Id.*

76. *Id.*

77. Diamond & Mirrlees, *supra* note 73, at 278.

Thus, they do not consider the critical implications for cost recovery of a regulatory policy that requires the firm to price at marginal cost even if the firm's marginal cost is less than its average cost.

The M-ECPR Does Not Rest on a Divergence of Social Opportunity Cost from Private Opportunity Cost

Some critics of the M-ECPR argue that its opportunity-cost component overstates the opportunity cost to society of providing unbundled network elements. Those critics assert that the social opportunity cost of providing the network element is its TELRIC, whereas the M-ECPR gives the incumbent LEC its private opportunity cost, which assertedly contains monopoly rent. David L. Kaserman has observed:

> The ECPR, in all its versions, including the one proposed here, is an attempt to perpetuate the recovery of monopoly rents of an incumbent monopolist despite competition in complementary markets. The ECPR renames the "monopoly rents" of the incumbent as its "opportunity costs," and demands their recovery. There is no efficiency basis at all for such a demand. Although *social* opportunity costs are the appropriate measure of costs for an unbundled network element (and these are precisely what TSLRIC [total service long-run incremental cost] represents), *private* opportunity costs have, in general, no relationship to social opportunity costs. In fact, ECPR-based prices are bound to be higher than efficient prices based on social opportunity costs (TSLRIC-prices) because the ECPR rule—contrary to any notion of efficiency—adds the private opportunity costs of the incumbent monopolist to social opportunity costs.[78]

Similarly, Frederick R. Warren-Boulton has written that, while "the private opportunity costs to [the incumbent LEC] of competition would include any reduction in profits which it earns as the dominant firm or costs it might incur in enhancing its efficiency," "these are not social opportunity costs."[79] Though similar to the earlier argument that the

78. Rebuttal Testimony of David L. Kaserman, In the Matter of the Interconnection Contract Negotiation Between AT&T Communications of the Midwest, Inc., and GTE Midwest Inc. Pursuant to 47 U.S.C. Section 252, Dkt. No. ARB-96-3, at 8 (Iowa Util. Bd. filed Oct. 7, 1996) (emphasis in original) (filed on behalf of AT&T Communications of the Midwest, Inc.). Kaserman uses TELRIC and TSLRIC synonymously when discussing the pricing of elements. Identical language, updated to reflect the FCC's coining of the term *TELRIC*, appears in *Warren-Boulton Rebuttal Testimony, supra* note 1, at 24.

79. *Id.; accord,* Henry Ergas & Eric Ralph, Pricing Network Interconnection: Is the

M-ECPR protects monopoly rent, that argument is one that turns on an interpretation of opportunity costs that is at odds with the accepted meaning of that concept among economic and legal scholars. As Judge Richard A. Posner has observed, "Cost to the economist is 'opportunity cost'—the benefit forgone by employing a resource in a way that denies its use to someone else."[80] Similarly, Joseph E. Stiglitz, the former chairman of the Council of Economic Advisers, writes in his textbook that "when rational firms and individuals make decisions—whether to undertake one investment project rather than another, whether to buy one product rather than another—they take into account *all* of the costs, the full opportunity costs, not just the direct expenditures."[81] Finally, it is a matter of textbook economics that "opportunity cost is the same from the private and social points of view in the absence of external economies and diseconomies."[82] With those textbook definitions of *opportunity cost* in mind, the fallacy in Kaserman's and Warren-Boulton's argument is self-evident.

The opportunity cost of taking an action should be determined from the point of view of the decision maker. In the absence of externalities such as environmental pollution, economic costs are the costs to individual consumers and firms bearing those opportunity costs. The notion that there is a distinction between social opportunity cost and private opportunity costs whenever market power is present opens the door to public regulation of any industry that departs in some way from the ideal of perfect competition. The market price of a good remains the best indicator of opportunity cost, whether or not the company selling the good has market power.

Economic analysis defines the value of a product or service as its market price. If value were based on any other yardstick than market price, economic value would be cast adrift without the foundation of market exchange, which reflects what consumers are willing to pay to obtain the good and what producers are willing to accept in return for

Baumol-Willig Rule the Answer? (Feb. 24, 1994) (mimeo, Australian Trade Practices Comm'n).

80. RICHARD A. POSNER, ECONOMIC ANALYSIS OF LAW 6 (Little, Brown & Co., 4th ed. 1992).

81. JOSEPH E. STIGLITZ, ECONOMICS 44 (W.W. Norton & Co. 1993) (emphasis in original). That definition coincides with the definition in Kaserman's own text. *See* DAVID L. KASERMAN & JOHN W. MAYO, GOVERNMENT AND BUSINESS: THE ECONOMICS OF ANTITRUST AND REGULATION 32 (Dryden Press 1995).

82. JAMES M. HENDERSON & RICHARD E. QUANDT, MICROECONOMIC THEORY: A MATHEMATICAL APPROACH 302 (McGraw-Hill, Inc., 3d ed. 1980).

supplying the good. The profitability of an economic activity does not alter the fundamental identity between economic value and market price. Market prices cannot be said to reflect value only when there is zero economic profit. Moreover, even if it were desirable to exclude monopoly profit from valuation, how could it be determined whether or not a firm were earning monopoly profit? The returns earned by a firm include not only the returns to invested capital, but also the returns to innovation, entrepreneurship, arbitrage, brand equity, goodwill, creativity, managerial effort, and other intangible factors. The economic value of those inputs is best determined with reference to market prices.

Not only is it impractical to exclude monopoly profit from valuation, it is meaningless to do so. A firm evaluates a forgone opportunity in the same manner whether the firm is a monopolist or whether it faces many competitors. As Judge Posner has observed:

> Another weakness in the theory that monopoly leads to slack and waste is its inconsistency with the fundamental economic principle that an opportunity forgone is a cost analytically different from a loss incurred; indeed forgone opportunity *is* the economic definition of cost. For a monopolist to fail to obtain another $100 in profit by failing to exploit some new process costs him $100, and this is the same amount that is lost by a competitive firm in failing to exploit an opportunity for a $100 cost reduction or product improvement.[83]

Therefore, a distinction between opportunity costs for a monopolist versus a competitive firm has no economic content.

Markups over marginal cost due to market power may be distortionary relative to the perfect competition ideal under some circumstances.[84] Monopoly potentially imposes a social cost in terms of the welfare triangle lost from pricing above marginal cost. That loss is attenuated or eliminated through price discrimination and nonlinear pricing such that the revenue from the marginal unit is closer to marginal

---

83. RICHARD A. POSNER, ANTITRUST LAW: AN ECONOMIC PERSPECTIVE 16 (University of Chicago Press 1976).

84. Judge Posner makes the case for antitrust law by noting that monopoly profit as a whole can be a source of social cost if firms engage in "rent-seeking" activities to obtain a monopoly. POSNER, ECONOMIC ANALYSIS OF LAW, *supra* note 80, at 257. The solution to that problem is to enforce antitrust laws or to avoid government creation of barriers to entry, not to engage in rent-control activities. Indeed, rent seeking is not unique to potential monopolists. Because rent control by government also creates income transfers from firms to consumers or other firms, rent control is at least as likely to engender rent-seeking activities on the part of beneficiaries.

cost. Moreover, monopoly profits provide economic incentives for competition over time, creating incentives for innovation, investment, and market entry.

The notion that some regulatory "social opportunity cost" could provide a better indicator of market value than market prices not only is economically incorrect, it leads to interventionist policy recommendations. Such a notion would provide a justification for regulating prices of companies in any industry in which firms are judged to exhibit market power. "Rents earned on services sold at supracompetitive prices are not a social opportunity cost," argues Warren-Boulton.[85] Such an incorrect interpretation of opportunity cost would lead to absurd, confiscatory results. Kaserman's and Warren-Boulton's rule would require Microsoft to sell Windows 95 at its incremental cost of production or the Walt Disney Company to sell videos of *The Lion King* at the incremental cost of copying the motion picture to cassettes. Presumably Kaserman and Warren-Boulton would even advocate TELRIC as the price for competitor access to lines of code contained in Microsoft's Windows 95 operating system. The disincentive to investment and to R&D under policies based on such a misinterpretation of opportunity cost would be profound. Thus, the incorrect distinction between social and private opportunity cost creates a justification for arbitrarily extending rent control to practically any industry. That is clearly inconsistent with a free-market economy.

As we note in chapter 9, for inputs that are purchased, the market price of the input provides the best indicator of the opportunity cost of using an input in production, while for inputs that are made by the firm that uses them, it is necessary to impute the value by determining the best opportunity forgone due to the use of that input in production. The opportunity cost of selling inputs to competitors depends on the opportunities forgone when the competitor rather than the firm itself uses the input. The M-ECPR approach recognizes the need to constrain the price of inputs sold to competitors by the market price of such inputs. A firm providing a product or service, whether voluntarily or under regulatory compulsion, cannot expect to make any sales unless that input is priced at or below the market price for comparable goods. Opportunity costs of selling inputs should be defined according to the choices of individual firms based on relative prices in both input and output markets. Efficient network access pricing requires voluntary transactions rather than compulsory pricing and forced sales.

---

85. *Warren-Boulton Rebuttal Testimony, supra* note 1, at 28–29.

Full Recovery of Forward-Looking
Costs through a Combination of the M-ECPR and
an End-User Charge Is Not Tantamount to "Indemnification"

Some respected regulatory economists have misunderstood the inability of efficiently determined prices for unbundled network elements to achieve full recovery of the incumbent LEC's forward-looking costs. For example, Warren-Boulton has asserted that "[t]he FCC's TELRIC-based pricing proposal would permit the ILEC [incumbent LEC] to recover all of its forward-looking, efficient costs, including any joint and common costs, and it would be poor economic policy to indemnify any competitor against losses associated with competition."[86] That assessment is incorrect on multiple grounds.

First, Warren-Boulton is incorrect to suggest that the incumbent LEC is simply "any competitor," for its unique characteristic in the marketplace is that it continues to bear incumbent burdens (and indeed acquired new ones under the Telecommunications Act of 1996), despite the lifting of entry regulation that formerly provided regulators the mechanism by which they could credibly commit to giving the incumbent LEC a reasonable opportunity to recover its total costs. Second, given the inability of even the M-ECPR to ensure full cost recovery, it follows a fortiori that TELRIC pricing (which Warren-Boulton favors over the M-ECPR) would not suffice to recover all the incumbent LEC's forward-looking costs.

Third, at a more substantial level, Warren-Boulton's criticism seems more plausibly redirected at the competitively neutral end-user charge. But even then, can the end-user charge fairly be said to "indemnify" the incumbent LEC in the face of competitive entry so that its incentives for efficiency evaporate? One would think that the risk is not substantial, for Warren-Boulton has nonetheless endorsed in principle the concept of an end-user charge to achieve cost recovery for the incumbent LEC.[87] Likewise, the end-user charge has received the endorsement of William J. Baumol, Janusz A. Ordover, and Robert D. Willig, who advocate TELRIC pricing of network elements notwithstanding their endorsement in other forums of efficient component pricing in other markets.[88] The

---

86. *Id.* at 4. "Offering a guarantee to *any* firm that it will be able to recover 'all its costs,'" Warren-Boulton continues, "is incompatible with competition and market discipline." *Id.* at 5 (emphasis in original). Warren-Boulton was formerly chief economist of the Antitrust Division of the U.S. Department of Justice.

87. *Id.* at 23, 31.

88. *Ordover Rebuttal Testimony, supra* note 1, at 6; Affidavit of William J. Baumol,

end-user charge therefore appears to be uncontroversial among the regula-tory economists who have considered it, even those who oppose the M-ECPR.[89]

Furthermore, the extent to which an end-user charge might blunt the incumbent LEC's incentive to achieve greater efficiency would depend on the specific design of that charge. If the regulator credibly committed itself not to adjust the end-user charge for an extended period of time, then the familiar efficiency incentives of regulatory lag would manifest themselves.[90] Alternatively, regulators could explicitly structure the end-user charge as a price cap, in which case the possible variations in design and the resulting incentives would be considerable.[91]

Warren-Boulton bases his argument against full cost recovery for the incumbent LEC on its supposed inefficiency: "To the extent [the incumbent LEC] is currently inefficient or its costs reflect investments in facilities which are not required to service telephone demand, these costs should not be recovered via the prices for . . . unbundled network elements."[92] David L. Kaserman, John W. Mayo, and others make the same argument when urging that the wholesale discount for resale of LEC services be increased by netting out monopoly rents and inefficiencies.[93] That argument invites three responses. First, to date, the economists who allege that incumbent inefficiency have not provided factual, let alone empirical, support for their allegation. Second, it is easy to assert that a regulated firm like a local exchange carrier *must* be inherently inefficient, since regulation is inferior to competition and cannot replicate its disciplines; nonetheless, it bears emphasis that the investments of the incumbent LEC that the M-ECPR's detractors would characterize as inefficient (and thus costs that would become stranded in the face of competition) are investments that regulators approved beforehand as "prudent." The argument is thus one of massive, persistent regulatory failure—for which opponents of the M-ECPR implicitly argue that the incumbent LEC should be held financially responsible.[94] Third, if they

Janusz A. Ordover, and Robert D. Willig on behalf of AT&T Corporation 21–22 (May 17, 1996) [hereinafter *Baumol-Ordover-Willig Affidavit*], submitted in *Interconnection NPRM*, *supra* note 2.

89. Warren-Boulton's criticism of the end-user charge is limited to the uncertainty concerning the "nature . . . and application" of the charge and to the possibility of double recovery of costs. *Warren-Boulton Rebuttal Testimony, supra* note 1, at 33–34.

90. *See, e.g.*, BAUMOL & SIDAK, TOWARD COMPETITION IN LOCAL TELEPHONY, *supra* note 6, at 88–89.

91. *See* SAPPINGTON & WEISMAN, *supra* note 60.

92. *Warren-Boulton Rebuttal Testimony, supra* note 1, at 5–6.

93. KASERMAN REPORT, *supra* note 1, at 17–19.

94. As we have previously noted, that argument distills to the assertion that the

existed, inefficiencies in the incumbent LEC's cost structure could take the form of incremental costs as well as common costs. Pricing at TELRIC would not eliminate inefficiency that occurred incrementally with respect to the provision of a network element.

The Nonexistence of Natural Monopoly
Does Not Imply That the Incumbent LEC's
Forward-Looking Common Costs Are Insignificant

Some economists who oppose the M-ECPR assert that the argument that an incumbent LEC has substantial forward-looking common costs to recover is really an argument that the firm is a natural monopoly. Those economists then attempt to rebut the existence of common costs by arguing that empirical evidence compiled by Richard T. Shin and John S. Ying indicates that local exchange telephony is not a natural monopoly.[95] If an incumbent LEC is not a natural monopolist, the reasoning goes, then it cannot have substantial common costs.[96] And, if the

---

democratic institutions that produced public utility regulation and that have been politically responsible for overseeing the performance of regulators have failed miserably. J. Gregory Sidak & Daniel F. Spulber, *Deregulatory Takings and Breach of the Regulatory Contract*, 71 N.Y.U. L. REV. 851, 991–93 (1996). We address that issue in chapter 13.

95. *See* KASERMAN REPORT, *supra* note 1, at 12 & n.11 (citing Richard T. Shin & John S. Ying, *Unnatural Monopolies in Local Telephone*, 23 RAND J. ECON. 171 (1992)). The Shin-Ying study used data from 1976 to 1983 and found that LEC costs were not subadditive before the AT&T divestiture. In subsequent empirical research, Ying similarly concluded that over the periods 1976–1983 and 1984–1991, LECs were not natural monopolies. Affidavit of John S. Ying, Motion of Bell Atlantic Corp., BellSouth Corp., NYNEX Corp., and Southwestern Bell Corp. to Vacate the Decree, United States *v.* Western Elec. Co., No. 82-0192 (D.D.C. filed July 6, 1994). Previous studies of natural monopoly conducted on the Bell System reached conflicting results. *Compare* Laurits R. Christensen, Diane C. Cummings & Philip E. Schoech, *Econometric Estimation of Scale Economies in Telecommunications*, in ECONOMIC ANALYSIS OF TELECOMMUNICATIONS (Léon Courville, Alain de Fontenay & Rodney Dobell eds., North-Holland 1983) (AT&T had scale economies) *with* David S. Evans & James J. Heckman, *A Test for Subadditivity of the Cost Function with an Application to the Bell System*, 74 AM. ECON. REV. 615 (1984) (AT&T's costs were not subadditive).

96. David L. Kaserman has testified that "Shin and Ying . . . found that [local telephony is] not a natural monopoly, and if it's not a natural monopoly then the economies of scale and scope cannot be very large." Testimony of David L. Kaserman, In the Matter of AT&T Communications of the Midwest, Inc.'s Petition for Arbitration with Contel of Minnesota, Inc., Pursuant to Section 252(b) of the Federal Telecommunications Act of 1996, OAH Dkt. No. 9-2500-10733-2, MPUC Dkt. Nos. P-442, 407, M-96-939, at vol. 4B, Tr. 111 (Minn. Office of Admin. Hearings/Minn. Pub. Util. Comm'n, Oct. 22, 1996).

incumbent LEC has only insignificant common costs, then TELRIC pricing is efficient and compensatory, and the M-ECPR is unnecessary.

That argument is incorrect because it conflates economies of scope and natural monopoly. Plainly, it is possible for a firm to experience economies of scope without being a natural monopoly. Multiproduct firms—such as Ford, RJR Nabisco, and Hewlett Packard—are prevalent despite the obvious available alternative of organizing the same economic activities in a multitude of single-product firms. The persistence of multi-product organization of production strongly suggests that even firms in competitive markets experience economies of scope. But those economies need not be so large as to lead ineluctably to natural monopoly.

Summary of Misdirected Criticisms

The FCC's abbreviated discussion of efficient component pricing in the notice of proposed rulemaking in its 1996 interconnection proceeding did not do the concept justice. The ECPR is neither flawed nor impractical, as the FCC implied. Nor has the rule withered under the glare of academic scrutiny. To the contrary, it has blossomed. A rapidly growing body of economic analysis confirms the robust efficiency characteristics of the ECPR. That analysis makes clear that our refined M-ECPR not only is socially beneficial, but also is practical enough for the FCC and the state public utilities commissions to employ without undue administrative burden.

Contrary to the impression that competitive entrants sometimes create in regulatory proceedings, substantial intellectual support exists for efficient component pricing among academics and governmental bodies. In addition, the alleged shortcomings of the ECPR (or of the M-ECPR) that are commonly raised in the academic literature and in regulatory proceedings in fact do not withstand close scrutiny. In short, despite the fusillade of criticisms lodged against the ECPR, the intellectual health of the rule in our refined M-ECPR version remains robust.

DID THE CREATORS OF THE
ECPR REJECT THE M-ECPR?

In an affidavit filed on behalf of AT&T Corporation in the FCC's 1996 interconnection proceeding, William J. Baumol, Janusz A. Ordover, and Robert D. Willig endorsed the use of the ECPR for pricing mandatory network access but concluded that the proper price for the incumbent LEC to charge for mandatory network access under the Telecommunications Act of 1996 is total service long-run incremental cost.[97] The Baumol-Ordover-Willig affidavit prompted other economists retained by AT&T to assert in subsequent arbitration proceedings, "Even the creators of ECPR, Drs. Baumol and Willig, note in a recent submission to the FCC that it is inappropriate to apply the ECPR to telecommunications to derive prices of unbundled elements."[98]

That assertion misapprehends both the ECPR and the caveats that Baumol, Ordover, and Willig expressed concerning the rule. Moreover, the actual evidence on the existence of shared costs or common costs in the incumbent LEC's network revealed the factual error in the assumption that motivated the qualification raised by Baumol, Ordover, and Willig. Once the significance of that factual error is comprehended, there dissolves any apparent disagreement that might have existed between our assessment that the M-ECPR is appropriate for pricing the components of the local exchange network and the seemingly contrary assessment by Baumol, Ordover, and Willig. Indeed, Baumol, Ordover, and Willig have subsequently written that "among uniform, non-negotiated, and non-discriminatory pricing mechanisms, *only* pricing of access to the bottleneck-input service satisfying ECPR can ensure avoidance of . . . inefficiency. In this sense, ECPR is indeed a necessary efficiency requirement."[99] Once those points of empirical misunderstanding are clarified, any apparent disagreement between our position and that of Baumol, Ordover, and Willig is revealed to be a false conflict, and it becomes clear that economic welfare would suffer if regulators rejected the M-ECPR in favor of a rule that priced mandatory access to the incumbent utility's network at TSLRIC or TELRIC.

Baumol, Ordover, and Willig Endorsed the ECPR for Pricing Mandatory Network Access

In recognition of the seminal contribution that Baumol and Willig have made to the theory of network pricing, scholars and jurists routinely call the ECPR the "Baumol-Willig rule." Predictably, Baumol, Ordover, and Willig said in their 1996 affidavit that they "continue to believe that

97. *Baumol-Ordover-Willig Affidavit, supra* note 88.

98. KASERMAN REPORT, *supra* note 1, at 15 (citations omitted).

99. Baumol, Ordover & Willig, *Parity Pricing and Its Critics, supra* note 12, at 148 (emphasis in original).

principles of ECPR are valid and serve a useful regulatory role."[100] The FCC's unsophisticated caricature of the ECPR, however, naturally caused Baumol, Ordover, and Willig to applaud the agency's tentative rejection of the ECPR "in a form *supposedly* advocated by us" and to state politely that the FCC's rejection of the ECPR "[was] proper, although for reasons that differ somewhat from those articulated in the Notice."[101] In other words, Baumol, Ordover, and Willig evidently concluded that the FCC's stated criticisms of the pricing rule *that the agency incorrectly described as being the ECPR* were misplaced.

Given that the FCC's stated reasons for rejecting its understanding of the ECPR (what we call the FCC-ECPR) did not motivate Baumol, Ordover, and Willig to conclude that application of the rule (as they originally and correctly defined it) would not serve the public interest in the pricing of unbundled network elements, then by what rationale did they decline to apply to local telephony in the United States the same rule for pricing inputs that they advocated in railroading, in electric power, and in local telephony in New Zealand? The answer lay in the critical assumptions that Baumol, Ordover, and Willig made in their 1996 affidavit concerning the size and makeup of the opportunity-cost component of the ECPR in the specific context of local telephony.

Data filed in actual state PUC proceedings revealed that the critical cost assumption made by Baumol, Ordover, and Willig was empirically unsupported.[102] Cost and price data from local exchange companies, typified by GTE Florida Inc., for example, confirm (1) that there are significant shared costs and common costs among network elements, such that pricing the incumbent LEC's wholesale and unbundled services at or near long-run incremental costs would fail to meet the statutory requirement that rates be just and reasonable and, in the case of unbundled elements, would exclude the reasonable profit allowed by statute; and (2) that there would be stranded costs *even if* the prices of wholesale and unbundled services were set according to the M-ECPR.[103]

100. *Baumol-Ordover-Willig Affidavit, supra* note 88, at 8 ¶ 20.

101. *Id.* (emphasis added).

102. For example, joint (or shared) costs are 12 percent, and common costs are 15 percent, of the total costs of Ameritech Illinois. Only 55 percent of the Ameritech Illinois's total costs are incremental to specific services as defined by the Illinois Commerce Commission. Comments of Ameritech Corporation at 63, submitted in *Interconnection NPRM, supra* note 2.

103. Michael J. Doane, J. Gregory Sidak & Daniel F. Spulber, An Empirical Analysis of Pricing Under Sections 251 and 252 of the Telecommunications Act of 1996, *appended*

Had Baumol, Ordover, and Willig been aware of such empirical evidence of the existence of economies of scope when assessing the suitability of the ECPR to the pricing of unbundled network elements in local telephony, their analysis would have led them to the same conclusion contained here: Pricing mandatory access to the incumbent LEC's network at TSLRIC would be insufficient on economic grounds to produce efficient incentives for entry and would be insufficient on economic (and constitutional) grounds to produce just compensation for government-ordered use of the LEC's property by its competitors.

Does Stand-Alone Cost Equal Incremental Cost, and Are Shared Costs and Common Costs Trivial?

A supplier would not voluntarily invest in a transaction unless he expected the returns from the transaction to cover all its economic costs, including a competitive return on invested capital. As noted earlier, the supplier's cost of investing in the transaction would include the highest net benefit of all opportunities forgone—that is, its *opportunity cost*. The ECPR and M-ECPR extend that logic to the mandatory sale of network access by specifying: "optimal input price = the input's direct per unit incremental cost + the opportunity cost to the input supplier of the sale of a unit of input."[104]

If the firm has economies of scale or scope, then its sale of network inputs to a competitor at incremental cost would not give the firm a sufficient contribution to cover its total costs. The sale of the input at incremental cost would entail an opportunity cost in the amount of the contribution to revenue adequacy that the regulated firm would forgo by selling the network element to a competitor rather than using that input itself to produce a final product whose price incorporated the requisite contribution margin. Stated differently, in the absence of government compulsion and of facilities-based competition, no firm would sell an input to its competitor for less than the price that Baumol and Willig specified in their original exposition of the ECPR. The ECPR and

---

to Comments of GTE Service Corporation *in* Implementation of the Local Competition Provisions in the Telecommunications Act of 1996, Federal Communications Commission, CC Dkt. No. 96-98 (filed May 16, 1996).

104. BAUMOL & SIDAK, TOWARD COMPETITION IN LOCAL TELEPHONY, *supra* note 6, at 94.

M-ECPR, in other words, replicate the price that would result from voluntary exchange.

At the same time, as chapter 11 shows, the M-ECPR (1) establishes the proper incentives for efficient entry into the regulated market and (2) ensures, when there are no competitive alternatives to the facilities necessary for access, that the price of government-mandated network access will not be so low as to be confiscatory under the Fifth Amendment. Consequently, regulators must scrutinize any pricing proposal for mandatory network access that would deviate from the M-ECPR to ensure that the proposal would not violate sound economic principles *and* constitutional protections against the uncompensated taking of private property.

The 1996 affidavit by Baumol, Ordover, and Willig, however, failed to provide either assurance. It assumed that an incumbent LEC would bear no opportunity cost by being required to sell unbundled network elements at TSLRIC. But that critical assumption had no empirical basis; indeed, subsequent arbitration proceedings before state PUCs produced considerable empirical evidence substantiating the existence of shared costs and common costs in the provision of network elements necessary for local telephony. Stated differently, in their 1996 affidavit Baumol, Ordover, and Willig asserted that, if the ECPR were adjusted in the case of local telephony to reflect what they supposed was an absence of opportunity costs of any significant magnitude, the rule would yield the following formula:

efficient price of aggregate network element = TSLRIC of aggregate network element + 0.

Indeed, that formula had to be the correct interpretation of the Baumol-Ordover-Willig position, because the term *opportunity costs* did not appear in their affidavit despite its frequent use in their previous writings and testimony concerning the ECPR. Baumol, Ordover, and Willig were able to conclude that the efficient price of unbundled network elements was TSLRIC and to reach that conclusion in a manner consistent with their previous work on efficient component pricing, *only* because they assumed—incorrectly, as it turned out—that the incumbent LEC had "minimal or nonexistent" joint and common costs.[105]

Suppose, counterfactually, that the critical assumption of zero shared costs or common costs were true. In that case, several remarkable condi-

---

105. *Baumol-Ordover-Willig Affidavit, supra* note 88, at 13 ¶ 35.

tions would obtain: (1) the local exchange would have no economies of scope; (2) the local exchange market could be served just as efficiently by single-product firms, consistent with the classical definition of a perfectly competitive market; and (3) such technological conditions would obviate the access-pricing regime of the Telecommunications Act of 1996, as the services of the incumbent LECs' networks would be easily supplanted by competitive small-scale, single-product firms. If such a state of affairs existed, it would have been unnecessary for Baumol previously to have written:

> [E]ven if every one of a firm's services is sold at a price equal to its average-incremental cost, the firm's total revenues may not cover its total costs. Consequently, it is normal and not anticompetitive for a firm to price some or all of its products to provide not only the required profit component of incremental cost, but also some contribution toward recovery of common fixed costs that do not enter the incremental costs of the individual products. . . . Any service whose price exceeds its per-unit incremental cost provides such a contribution in addition to the profit required on the incremental investment contained in the incremental cost.[106]

The opportunity-cost component of the ECPR and the M-ECPR seeks to generate for the firm the contribution to margin essential to recover the firm's unattributable costs and thus to ensure its continued solvency. As we explain in chapter 9, however, the M-ECPR cannot ensure full cost recovery for the incumbent LEC.

Common Costs and Shared Costs between Aggregative Categories and between Individual Network Elements

Baumol, Ordover, and Willig asserted that, with regard to *aggregative* categories of network elements (loop, switching, transport, signaling), "[e]conomies of scope, or cost subadditivities, among these categories are likely to be minimal or nonexistent."[107] Actual empirical evidence submitted in subsequent state arbitration proceedings contradicted that assertion, however. But even if it were empirically supported, that assertion by Baumol, Ordover, and Willig would not preclude the existence of shared costs or common costs *within* any one of the

---

106. BAUMOL & SIDAK, TOWARD COMPETITION IN LOCAL TELEPHONY, *supra* note 6, at 102.

107. *Baumol-Ordover-Willig Affidavit, supra* note 88, at 13 ¶ 35.

aggregative categories of network elements. In other words, even if the statement by Baumol, Ordover, and Willig had been correct on its face as an empirical matter, it still could simultaneously be true that appreciable economies of scope exist among individual network elements within an aggregative category, such that setting prices at TSLRIC for unbundled services would surely fail to recover the totality of shared costs and common costs within that aggregative category. The incumbent LEC, after all, is not being asked by its rival to price *all* loops taken together or *all* switching taken together as a bundle, but rather to offer significantly finer disaggregations of its services. It is therefore significant that Baumol, Ordover, and Willig recognized: "The competitive price for any such subcomponent must lie between the subcomponent's unit long run incremental cost and SAC [stand-alone cost]."[108] In other words, by their own analysis Baumol, Ordover, and Willig acknowledged that pricing unbundled network access at TSLRIC cannot recover shared costs and common costs.

Baumol, Ordover, and Willig further argued that the prices for unbundled network services should be priced above their incremental costs to recover shared costs and common costs, which within their framework equals "the difference between the TSLRIC of an aggregate of outputs, and the sum of the TSLRICs of each subset of those outputs."[109] According to Baumol, Ordover, and Willig, those costs "should be assigned to individual network elements on an efficient and competitively neutral basis."[110] Likewise, our earlier discussion of the M-ECPR showed that those costs should be recovered through prices on unbundled network services that exceed the TSLRICs for those services. Those costs should be recovered whether they are small or significantly large—in which case, as Baumol, Ordover, and Willig observe, "the method of revenue recovery should be consistent with allocative and competitive efficiency."[111] That outcome could only be achieved by pricing above the incremental costs of the unbundled network services, according to the formula that Baumol and Willig had previously advocated elsewhere:

efficient price of unbundled network element = TSLRIC of unbundled network element + opportunity cost.

---

108. *Id.* at 5 n.1.
109. *Id.* at 14 ¶ 37.
110. *Id.*
111. *Id.*

Our analysis concurs with the conclusion by Baumol, Ordover, and Willig that such recovery of costs should be bounded above by stand-alone cost, which would properly include any shared costs and common costs, and that the access price "should be no higher than the imputed price charged by the ILEC to itself in the context of a competitive offering."[112]

In light of the analysis contained in the affidavit by Baumol, Ordover, and Willig, how did AT&T propose in the FCC's interconnection proceeding to assign those shared costs and common costs to the unbundled network services? AT&T advocated a form of FDC pricing known as the attributable cost method.[113] Such a pricing rule, however, could not be extrapolated from anything that Baumol, Ordover, and Willig had advocated in their affidavit, for the distinguishing feature of FDC pricing is that the allocation of common costs is done without reference to any economically meaningful criterion. Indeed, Baumol and Willig had previously shown that various FDC methods were arbitrary and could produce widely different results.[114]

Can Incumbent LECs
Earn Monopoly Profits?

Baumol, Ordover, and Willig expressed concern in their 1996 affidavit that existing rate structures for incumbent LECs included monopoly profits, which they believed could be passed on to entrants in access prices determined according to the ECPR.[115] That assertion, however,

---

112. *Id.* at 14 n.7.

113. "[T]he Commission should establish a presumption that such costs will be assigned on an equiproportional basis relative to causally attributable costs . . . ." AT&T Corporation Comments at 63, submitted in *Interconnection NPRM, supra* note 2.

114. In a frequently cited article criticizing FDC pricing, Baumol and Willig wrote:

> The "reasonableness" of the basis of allocation selected makes absolutely no difference except to the success of the advocates of the figures in deluding others (and perhaps themselves) about the defensibility of the numbers. There just can be no excuse for continued use of such an essentially random, or, rather, fully manipulable calculation process as a basis for vital economic decisions by regulators.

William J. Baumol, Michael F. Koehn & Robert D. Willig, *How Arbitrary Is "Arbitrary"?—or, Toward the Deserved Demise of Full Cost Allocation*, 21 PUB. UTIL. FORTNIGHTLY, Sept. 3, 1987, at 16; *accord,* WILLIAM J. BAUMOL & J. GREGORY SIDAK, TRANSMISSION PRICING AND STRANDED COSTS IN THE ELECTRIC POWER INDUSTRY 55–64 (AEI Press 1995).

115. *Baumol-Ordover-Willig Affidavit, supra* note 88, at 8 ¶ 23.

like their earlier assertion that shared costs and common costs in local telephony were insignificant, did not rest on any empirical evidence. Further, it was inconsistent with the history of price regulation of incumbent LECs, which has controlled their earnings either through traditional cost-of-service regulation or through incentive regulation. Finally, Baumol, Ordover, and Willig have subsequently made clear that the existence of monopoly rent does not justify the rejection by regulators of efficient component pricing: "It is our position . . . that distortion of access prices *is the wrong instrument* for elimination of monopoly power or monopoly profit."[116] We agree.

Moreover, any returns that the LECs might have obtained from achieving cost efficiencies under incentive regulation were an intended consequence of such regulation; for the regulator to eliminate those returns retroactively would amount to a breach of the most essential element in the bargain that the LEC and the regulator struck when replacing rate-of-return regulation with incentive regulation. In any case, sharing rules and other regulatory constraints have limited those returns.

Finally, the assertion that regulators had been allowing incumbent LECs to earn monopoly profits was inconsistent with the incumbent LECs' existing and continuing obligations to serve. The opportunity-cost component of the ECPR will necessarily be positive, Baumol previously noted, "when a regulated firm has special-service obligations imposed upon it,"[117] as has been the case with any incumbent LEC. Elaborating on that point, Baumol wrote:

> Examples include the arrangement under which the input supplier is also forced to serve as the "carrier of last resort," or when, as in the case of Telecom Corporation of New Zealand, the carrier is required to supply services to residential customers at rates that it claims to be insufficient to cover the pertinent incremental costs. *These obligations are appropriately treated as sources of common fixed costs for the firm; the costs must be covered legitimately by the firm's prices* and be taken into account in calculating its stand-alone-cost ceilings [for final-product prices].[118]

116. Baumol, Ordover & Willig, *Parity Pricing and Its Critics, supra* note 12, at 147 n.3 (emphasis in original).

117. BAUMOL & SIDAK, TOWARD COMPETITION IN LOCAL TELEPHONY, *supra* note 6, at 108.

118. *Id.* at 108–09 (emphasis added) (citing Clear Communications, Ltd. *v.* Telecom Corp. of New Zealand, Ltd., slip op. (H.C. Dec. 22, 1992)).

In their 1992 testimony concerning the interconnection of Clear Communications to the local network of Telecom New Zealand, Baumol and Willig even more clearly endorsed the proposition that the opportunity-cost component of the ECPR must permit the incumbent LEC to recover the cost of government-mandated subsidies to residential customers:

> In the case at hand, a crucial issue is, if Telecom New Zealand provides interconnection to its local loops for the local loops that belong to Clear Communications, whether the price that Telecom New Zealand charges for this service should include any contribution toward coverage of the cost of the cross-subsidy to residential customers that is imposed by the government upon Telecom New Zealand. The question to be answered, then, is whether the price charged for interconnection should or should not include such a contribution. Once again, the competitive market standard provides an unambiguous answer: such a contribution is not merely permissible, it is *mandatory*.[119]

Far from reducing the size of such public service obligations borne by incumbent LECs, the Telecommunications Act of 1996 increased their obligations by creating new unbundling requirements and more expansive universal service obligations.

Stranded Cost Recovery through Competitively Neutral End-User Charges

In their 1996 affidavit, Baumol, Ordover, and Willig advocated keeping cross-subsidies to a minimum: "A deliberate wedge between prices and TSLRIC is most likely to result from a decision to subsidize universal service or other regulatory goals."[120] That is so because pricing below incremental costs for some services requires obtaining subsidies elsewhere, encourages excess demand for those services, and harms the

---

119. William J. Baumol & Robert D. Willig, Brief of Evidence: Economic Principles for Evaluation of the Issues Raised by Clear Communications Ltd. on Interconnection with Telecom Corporation of New Zealand Ltd. 21–22 ¶ 40 (emphasis in original) (undated) [hereinafter *Baumol-Willig New Zealand Brief*], *submitted in* Clear Communications, Ltd. *v.* Telecom Corp. of New Zealand, Ltd., slip op. (H.C. Dec. 22, 1992), *rev'd*, slip op. (C.A. Dec. 28, 1993), *rev'd*, [1995] 1 N.Z.L.R. 385 (Judgment of the Lords of the Judicial Committee of the Privy Council, Oct. 19, 1994). Ordover has taken a contradictory position in an unbundling arbitration under the Telecommunications Act: "In my view, until the end-user rates are aligned with the underlying costs, M-ECPR and ECPR are not appropriate methodologies for setting rates for unbundled network elements." *Ordover Rebuttal Testimony, supra* note 1, at 47.

120. *Baumol-Ordover-Willig Affidavit, supra* note 88, at 21 ¶ 60.

financial solvency of the incumbent, thus placing it at a disadvantage relative to entrants. Furthermore, obtaining those subsidies by adding overcharges to other services inefficiently reduces demand for those facilities and places the incumbent at a competitive disadvantage to entrants that can price flexibly, which leads to inefficient bypass of existing network facilities. That analysis by Baumol, Ordover, and Willig concurs with our conclusion in chapters 2 and 15 and in our previous writings[121] that regulators should rebalance the rates of the incumbent LECs to eliminate cross-subsidization.

Baumol, Ordover, and Willig also advocated competitive neutrality of funding and distribution mechanisms. That goal requires that regulatory obligations, price regulations, and unbundling requirements neither penalize nor reward incumbents or entrants. Baumol, Ordover, and Willig cautioned that deviations between prices and economic costs should not be allowed to distort competition between the incumbent LEC and its potential rivals: "To be competitively neutral, a regulatory wedge between prices and TSLRIC must never favor entrants over incumbents, or *vice versa*."[122] They elaborated:

> The reason is obvious: any such departures from competitive neutrality tend to channel business to inefficient suppliers. This inefficient allocation of business will raise costs, repress innovation and investments and—as usual when competition is subverted—needlessly burden consumers.[123]

But as Baumol had previously emphasized elsewhere, economic logic implies that that principle be applied not only to specific subsidies (for example, universal service), but to *all* pertinent costs, including the cost of regulatory obligations—past, present, and future. The entry of competitors not burdened by such expenses raises the prospect that such costs borne by the incumbent firm will be stranded:

> Stranded costs can be defined as those costs that the utilities are currently permitted to recover through their rates but whose recovery may be impeded or prevented by the advent of competition in the industry. Those costs represent expenditures incurred by a utility in the past in meeting its obligation to serve all customers within the area in which it held an exclusive franchise, granted to it under the traditional regulatory regime.[124]

---

121. Sidak & Spulber, *supra* note 94, at 872–74.

122. *Baumol-Ordover-Willig Affidavit, supra* note 88, at 21 ¶ 61.

123. *Id.*

124. BAUMOL & SIDAK, TRANSMISSION PRICING AND STRANDED COSTS IN THE ELECTRIC POWER INDUSTRY, *supra* note 114, at 98.

Baumol argued that such stranded costs should be recovered:

> The cost of recoupment of stranded costs can be considered part of the common costs to which the price of inputs supplied by the utility to other firms can appropriately contribute or even cover completely. A cost imposed by regulatory arrangements is as real a cost for the enterprise as any other, and an input price that helps to cover that cost is merely contributing to adequacy of revenues for the firm.[125]

If regulators "omit or limit recovery of portions of opportunity costs," Baumol concluded, their "pricing policies will undermine economic efficiency."[126]

As stated earlier, the ECPR and the M-ECPR imply that an incumbent LEC's price for an unbundled network element should equal its long-run incremental costs plus its opportunity cost. But competition constrains the latter: The presence of facilities-based entry, and the possibility that entrants may purchase services under existing retail rates that are substitutes for the unbundled network elements of the incumbent LEC, reduce the likelihood that the incumbent LEC will recover its total costs. That is so because the incumbent LEC's price will be constrained by the stand-alone cost of the best alternative for network access. It therefore bears repeating that M-ECPR pricing is not fully compensatory. Thus, as Baumol, Ordover, and Willig advocated, state regulators should consider rate rebalancing *before* imposing a system of prices for wholesale services and unbundled network elements. If, however, the state regulator chooses not to rebalance rates, then, to preserve the existing contribution in the incumbent LEC's existing rate structure, a system of end-user charges must accompany the pricing of wholesale services and unbundled network elements. As Baumol argued in 1995, "The efficient component-pricing rule, and the competitive market model of which it is a constituent part, equip [regulators] to resolve [network] pricing and stranded cost disputes in the public interest."[127]

Baumol, Ordover, and Willig emphasized in their 1996 affidavit that cost must be examined on a forward-looking basis. That position necessarily applies to the future cost of regulatory obligations newly imposed on incumbent LECs by the Telecommunications Act of 1996. The act places obligations on incumbent LECs, all of which will impose costs on a forward-looking basis that potential entrants will not bear. One such

125. *Id*. at 147.
126. *Id*.
127. *Id*. at 158.

costly obligation is the duty to provide interconnection to any requesting telecommunications carrier at "any technically feasible point within the carrier's network."[128] Equivalent access requirements apply to unbundled network elements. The costs of those newly established obligations will be stranded unless they are either (1) recovered through competitively neutral charges, as Baumol, Ordover, and Willig advocated in their affidavit[129] and as we advocate here, or (2) included in the TSLRIC for a service.

In sum, our analysis is consistent with the recommendation of Baumol, Ordover, and Willig that the wedge between prices and costs be recovered in a competitively neutral manner. The relevant cost need not equal the incumbent's TSLRIC, however, but rather may equal the stand-alone cost of the best alternative for network access. In their 1996 affidavit, Baumol, Ordover, and Willig accepted unquestioningly that the incumbent LEC's TSLRIC exactly equaled the stand-alone costs of potential entrants. In contrast, as our previous analysis implies, we regard that question as an empirical matter to be determined in competitive markets. Contributions to universal service funds, to shared costs and common costs (which will be present if the incumbent LEC's TSLRICs are less than the entrant's stand-alone costs), and to other regulatory obligations that cannot be recovered in competitive markets are appropriately collected through competitively neutral charges that do not distort consumption and investment decisions. That was precisely the recommendation of Baumol, Ordover, and Willig in their 1996 affidavit when one follows their proposal for universal service funding to its logical economic conclusion.

CONCLUSION

We have answered the critics of efficient component pricing, both in academia and government. Moreover, we have shown that those critics, particularly the FCC, have failed to give appropriate consideration to the numerous writings of the scholars who endorse such pricing and the governmental bodies that have employed it.

Did the creators of the ECPR reject the application of that rule or of the M-ECPR to the pricing of unbundled network elements in local telephony? Contrary to the assertions of some economists, the answer is

128. 47 U.S.C. § 251(c)(2)(B).
129. *Baumol-Ordover-Willig Affidavit, supra* note 88, at 21–22; *see also Ordover Rebuttal Testimony, supra* note 1, at 22–23.

no. The analysis of Baumol, Ordover, and Willig in their 1996 affidavit can be entirely reconciled with our M-ECPR analysis here. On the two most important regulatory questions concerning competition in local telephony, Baumol, Ordover, and Willig were in agreement with our analysis presented here. First, efficient component pricing is the proper method to price mandatory network access; mandatory access to the incumbent LEC's network should be no exception. Second, even when the ECPR is correctly administered to take the form of our M-ECPR, its automatic adjustment of the incumbent LEC's opportunity costs on a forward-looking basis will require regulators to impose competitively neutral charges to recover the incumbent LEC's stranded costs. The price of unbundled access must permit a market-allowed contribution to shared costs and common costs, over and above TSLRIC.

11

The Equivalence Principle

AN EQUIVALENCE EXISTS between (1) damages for breach of the regulatory contract; (2) just compensation for a regulatory taking; (3) the change in investor valuation of the utility after deregulation; and (4) pricing policies that promote efficient entry and interconnection in network industries opened to competition by using the incumbent's facilities. Those identities constitute the *equivalence principle*.

In this chapter we set out the equivalence principle within the context of the basic deregulation model. The equivalence translates readily to a multiperiod setting where the firm's opportunity cost is the difference between the present discounted value of regulatory returns and the present discounted value of competitive returns, where each stream of returns is discounted at the rate appropriate for the riskiness of the stream of returns.

The common thread is the interplay between economic expectations and opportunity costs. Economic agents make choices by comparing the expected net benefits of available alternatives. All economic choices are "forward looking," with the preferred choice yielding the greatest expected benefits. The opportunity cost of the preferred choice is the value of the best alternative. By definition, the expected benefits of the preferred choice exceed its opportunity cost. Although we focus on transitional remedies for unexpected deregulation, the equivalence principle applies equally to remedies for breach of private contract and property protections for competitive firms.

The equivalence principle establishes that the compensation of regulated firms when making the transition to a competitive market can be calculated by using either a contract damages approach or a property compensation approach. Moreover, the financial valuation approach that the firm uses provides another forward-looking measure for determining the expected effects of deregulation. Finally, the access charge that the regulated firm would voluntarily accept to offer its competitors access to its network will yield the same expected returns that it would have received under regulation. That access charge presumes the absence of facilities-based competition. As chapter 9 demonstrates, facilities-based competition requires additional end-user charges to protect expectation interests during the transition to competition.

EXPECTATION DAMAGES

Regulators and utilities in the electricity and telecommunications industries entered into a regulatory contract with regulatory commissions. The contract included entry controls, rate regulation, and service obligations. Entry controls were intended to protect the earnings of the regulated utility and to allow it to achieve cost savings derived from natural monopoly and to carry out the regulator's social objectives, including cross-subsidization, rate averaging, universal service, carrier-of-last-resort obligations, and special programs such as energy conservation in the electric power industry. Rate regulation limited the earnings for utilities with a protected franchise to ensure customers of "reasonable" rates while giving investors an opportunity to earn a "fair" or competitive rate of return on their investment. In addition, rate regulation involved the specification of a rate structure that allocated costs across services and customer classes. Finally, the utility undertook an obligation to serve, meeting regulatory requirements for service quality, capacity investment, universal service, and related common carrier obligations.

Deregulation that does not allow the utility to recover its investment costs leads to the problem of stranded costs for the utility and constitutes a breach of the regulatory contract. By analogy to private contracts, an expectation damage remedy for breach of the regulatory contract serves to mitigate opportunism by regulatory commissions while protecting the expectation interests of the parties. Parties breach if and only if it is economically efficient to do so, which happens when the benefits from breach exceed expectation damages. As chapter 5 shows, the damage remedy that restores the expectations of the regulated firm equals the shortfall of net earnings due to deregulation, $\Delta = (R_1^e - C_1^e) - (R_2^e - C_2^e)$:

$$expectation\ damages = \Delta.$$

Damages for breach of the regulatory contract equal Δ^* in the multiperiod case, which is the difference between expected discounted net earnings under regulation and those under deregulation.

The key point is that private contracts and the regulatory contract are intended to protect the expectation interests of the parties to the contract. Contracts do not protect the costs incurred by the parties but rather the expected value of the transaction-specific investment. Otherwise, the parties would reduce their investments or make different types of investments that had a greater market value and a correspondingly lower value for the specific transaction. Protection of the expectation interests allows the parties to a contract to make those investments that enhance the gains from trade within the contract. The regulatory contract is not simply the procurement of service by the regulatory authority. Rather, the regulated firm makes transaction-specific investments to satisfy obligations to serve and specific performance requirements created by the regulatory process. Otherwise, the regulated firm and its investors would not have made the same types of investments to provide utility services. For example, the regulated firm might have built facilities that provided services to different geographic areas than those under regulation, favoring those areas with higher margin customers, rather than facilities required to provide universal service. The regulated firm might have chosen facilities to provide service with a lower level of reliability or lower capacity, rather than to maintain excess capacity for full service during periods of peak demand. Alternatively, the regulated firm might not have been vertically integrated; it might have purchased some services instead of investing in production, transmission, and distribution facilities.

The expectation interests of parties to a contract are those that induced the parties to enter into the contract. The opportunity cost to utility investors is the competitive rate of return on capital investment. Investors compare risks and returns of alternative investment opportunities. The regulated firm's investors expected net revenues under regulation to be sufficient so that they would recover the cost of investment and earn a competitive return on their invested capital.

In *Duquesne Light Co.* v. *Barasch*, the Supreme Court stated that determinations of the rates of return for regulated utilities "should be commensurate with returns on investments in other enterprises having corresponding risks" and should not "jeopardize the financial integrity of the companies . . . by impeding their ability to raise future capital."[1] If the regulator were to require the utility to sell unbundled access to its basic service elements at a price that did not include the utility's full opportunity cost, the utility's shareholders would suffer a corresponding forfeiture in their share price. That forfeiture in turn would cause future investors to demand a risk premium from the utility—which is to say that the company would face a higher cost of capital that reflected the risk that the regulator might unexpectedly take future actions, contrary to the regulatory contract, that would arbitrarily expropriate shareholder wealth.

JUST COMPENSATION

Just compensation for a deregulatory taking equals the value that the owner of the property would voluntarily accept in the market, which reflects not simply the market value of the assets but the opportunity cost to the owner. Thus, as chapter 7 shows, the compensation for the investors of the regulated firm equals the difference between the net earnings under regulation and net earnings under competition:

$$just\ compensation\ =\ \Delta.$$

Just compensation for a deregulatory taking equals Δ^* when paid in advance in the multiperiod case.

Thus, the amount of compensation for a deregulatory taking restores the "investment-backed expectations" of the regulated firm. The returns to the assets under competition correspond to mitigation in the case of contract damages. Of course, as in the calculation of contract damages, that logic requires that employing the assets to provide services under competition is the best alternative use of those assets once deregulation has occurred. If there are better alternatives, including scrapping the assets or resorting to some type of divestiture, those alternatives would determine the proper calculation of just compensation.

It should not be surprising that the contract and property approaches yield the same outcome. The property owner decides which alternative use of the property yields the greatest expected net benefits. Investors in the regulated industry compare the expected net benefits of their investments with market alternatives. The investment-backed expectations were the net expected earnings of the regulated firm. Investment

---

1. 488 U.S. 299, 312, 314 (1989).

was attracted to the industry because investors expected to recover their investment plus a competitive return.

INVESTOR VALUATION

Because the value of the firm is the present discounted value of returns, the change in the market value of the utility upon deregulation is exactly equal to the opportunity cost of deregulation. Therefore, as chapter 7 shows, the change in the market value of the firm provides another approach to estimating contract damages or just compensation:

$$change\ in\ the\ firm's\ market\ value\ =\ \Delta^*.$$

The change in the firm's market value is reflected in writeoffs of the regulated firm's capital upon deregulation. If competitive markets generate greater uncertainty, thus raising the cost of capital, that consideration will be reflected in the amount of capital that the regulated firm writes off.

Those calculations ultimately will require the use of accounting data. That analysis entails using information based on the activities of the firm were it to continue as a regulated enterprise in combination with information on a firm that has a mixture of regulated and competitive activities or even a firm that exclusively carries on competitive activities if deregulation is complete. The forward-looking approach that compares present discounted values of cash flows is the economically correct comparison. Translating that comparison into accounting data will inevitably require a number of compromises, particularly because a forward-looking calculation is called for and accounting measures emphasize past performance. Moreover, some accounting conventions can differ for the regulated firm and the competitive firm. Nonetheless, it is useful to examine a few basic issues in measurement of damages.

Let K denote the value of the rate base, which could represent the book value of capital, and let D represent the depreciation determined by a given accounting schedule. Under rate-of-return regulation, the regulator specifies the maximum allowed rate of return. The regulated firm's allowed rate of return generally will be greater than or equal to the firm's expected rate of return. The regulator approves rates that are designed to yield the allowed rate of return. In other words, the rates are set so that they equal the utility's revenue requirement: $R = C + D + rK$. The firm's accounting rate of return for a given period thus equals the accounting profit (equal to the net revenues earned in a period) minus depreciation divided by the book value of capital employed at the beginning of the period. Thus, r denotes the regulated firm's return on investment:

$$r = (R - C - D)/K.$$

Under competition, suppose that the utility were to retain the same initial capital stock and depreciation schedule. Suppose, however, that competition lowers market revenues net of operating costs, thus lowering the rate of return. Define r_2 as the rate of return of the firm under competition:

$$r_2 = (R_2 - C_2 - D)/K.$$

Define r_1 as the rate of return of the firm under regulation:

$$r_1 = (R_1 - C_1 - D)/K.$$

Then, we can represent the decline in the firm's net revenues as a fall in the rate of return multiplied by the firm's capital investment:

$$\Delta = (r_1 - r_2)K.$$

Therefore, we can represent stranded investment as a decline in the regulated firm's rate of return.

The allowed rate of return under regulation is intended to represent the cost of capital. Suppose for the moment that the firm's cost of capital does not change after the transition from competition to regulation. Suppose also for simplicity that depreciation is otherwise equal under regulation and competition. By lowering the firm's net revenue, the introduction of competition may require the firm (pursuant to accounting conventions) to write off its capital investment to maintain the same rate of return to capital. Let K_2 denote the firm's capital after it takes the required writeoffs:

$$K_2 = (R_2 - C_2 - D)/r.$$

Let K_1 denote the initial capital investment, which corresponds to the regulated rate base. Then, we can represent the decline in the firm's net revenues as a fall in the firm's capital:

$$\Delta = r(K_1 - K_2).$$

That formulation makes clear the use of the term *stranded investment*.

Generally speaking, the change in the firm's net revenues should be represented as a combination of changes in both the rate of return and the firm's investment. The increased risk under competition is generally associated with a greater cost of capital. Let r_1 represent the rate of return of the firm under regulation. Under rate-of-return regulation, revenues net of operating cost equal the rate of return multiplied by the rate base plus depreciation, $(R_1 - C_1) = r_1 K_1 + D_1$. Next, let r_2 represent the cost of capital under competition. As a consequence of the higher cost of capital, the firm will have to take an even greater write-off of capital under standard accounting rules. So, given the competitive cost of capital r_2, the capital stock under competition must satisfy the condition $K_2 = (R_2 - C_2 - D_2)/r_2$. We can represent the change in the firm's net revenues as:

$$\Delta = r_1(K_1 - K_2) - (r_2 - r_1)K_2 + (D_1 - D_2).$$

Therefore, the firm's expected loss under competition equals the regulated rate of return times the amount of capital written off, minus the increase in cost of capital multiplied by the depreciated rate base, plus changes in the amount of depreciation. That formula shows that the regulated rate of return multiplied by the write-off of capital investment overstates stranded investment. That is so because part of the write-off is due to higher rates of return in the competitive markets. For that reason, it is necessary to subtract the change in the rate of return times the new book value of capital.

Calculation of damages or compensation will encounter the usual difficulties in extending to multiple periods the comparison of economic and accounting losses attributable to competition. Those difficulties are due to problems that arise in determining present discounted values by using accounting profitability data.[2] There are also problems in determining the losses to the owner of assets from his being deprived of assets or of some uses of assets. A standard objection raised to "value to the owner" rules is that in contrast to historical costs, the forward-looking determination of earnings is necessarily subjective because it

---

2. *See, e.g.*, JEREMY EDWARDS, JOHN KAY & COLIN MAYER, THE ECONOMIC ANALYSIS OF ACCOUNTING PROFITABILITY (Clarendon Press 1987).

depends on estimating cash flows and discount rates.[3] Such problems are present in any legal damage calculation, however. Although the deregulation of an industry presents additional complications, the conceptual problems are similar to those encountered in standard damage calculations. Moreover, the estimation of revenues and costs relative to a "test year" has long been a feature of the regulatory process.[4]

THE EFFICIENT COMPONENT-PRICING RULE

Access pricing that promotes only *efficient* entry, interconnection, and bypass in the market at issue also serves to compensate the utility for its opportunity cost, when entrants rely on the incumbent's network. As a rule for computing an interconnection price, the efficient component pricing rule (ECPR) serves the same function as contract damages or just compensation. Therefore, under the efficient component-pricing rule, interconnection prices are not confiscatory under the Takings Clause. If the regulator imposes an access-pricing rule that fails to compensate the utility for the opportunity costs of the resources used to provide unbundled access, then the regulator will have given the utility less compensation for that involuntary exchange than the amount to which it would be entitled under established takings jurisprudence. In the presence of competitive alternatives to the incumbent's network, however, efficient access pricing generally is not equivalent to the contract and takings results because the access price is capped by the stand-alone costs of competing facilities. We examine the case of facilities-based entry in greater detail in our discussion of the market-determined efficient component-pricing rule (M-ECPR) in chapter 9.

The ECPR determines the price of access as the sum of the incumbent's direct incremental cost of providing access plus the incumbent's opportunity cost of supplying access to its competitors. The firm's opportunity cost of supplying network access to its competitors in the absence of competitive alternatives is the change in the incumbent's net revenues due to retail competition. Thus, the incumbent firm's opportunity cost equals Δ. The incumbent firm's unit access costs equal b, and sales of access equal X. By the definition of the ECPR, the access charge then equals

---

3. *Id.* at ch. 3; *see also* EDWARD E. ZAJAC, THE POLITICAL ECONOMY OF FAIRNESS 204 (MIT Press 1995).

4. *See, e.g.,* 1 ALFRED E. KAHN, THE ECONOMICS OF REGULATION: PRINCIPLES AND INSTITUTIONS 26 (John Wiley & Sons, Inc. 1970) (MIT Press, rev. ed. 1988).

$$A = b + \Delta/X.$$

Thus, the net earnings from the sale of access recover the firm's opportunity cost:

$$(A - b)X = \Delta.$$

If the regulator orders the utility to provide unbundled access to its basic service elements at a price less than that implied by the efficient component-pricing rule, the regulator will effect an uncompensated taking of the utility's property.

The efficient component-pricing rule recovers the utility's opportunity cost of entry in each period. By applying the ECPR over time, the utility recovers the net present value of expected revenues. In each period, the utility's expected net earnings from selling its final output plus the net earnings from selling access equal the net earnings it expected to have obtained under regulation:

$$(R_2^e - C_2^e) + \Delta = R_1^e - C_1^e.$$

Thus, the present value of the utility's total net earnings equals the present value of the earnings that it expected under regulation, PDV_1. Applying the ECPR in each period to recover opportunity costs thus is equivalent to a one-time payment of Δ^* in the initial period. The relevant opportunity cost subject to full compensation will not be a static one, but rather a dynamic one that takes into consideration, in the case of a local exchange carrier, the profits that the utility will forgo from lost sales of interactive narrowband, interactive broadband, and enhanced services supported by the advanced information network. In short, if the regulator orders the utility to provide unbundled access to its basic service elements at a price less than that implied by the efficient component-pricing rule, the regulator will effect an uncompensated taking of the utility's property.

CONCLUSION

The damages for breach of the regulatory contract, just compensation for a taking, the change in the value of the firm due to competition, and net revenues from efficient access pricing are equivalent because they all equal the firm's opportunity cost. The opportunity cost of supplying access to the firm's facilities equals the net revenues forgone owing to competition. Compensating the firm for its lost opportunity does not mean preventing or delaying the benefits of competition. On the contrary, compensating the firm for the change in expected net revenues is efficient because regulators proceed to breach the regulatory contract only if there are efficiency gains from doing so—that is, if a competitive industry is expected to be more efficient than a regulated utility industry subject to entry controls. Equivalently, if the regulator must pay just compensation, the regulator will not grant competitors access to the utility's facilities unless such access brings those same efficiency gains. Finally, by allowing the incumbent to price access to its facilities in a manner that leaves it indifferent between selling retail services and selling access to its competitors, market entry will occur only if it is efficient.

Compensating the incumbent for opportunity costs recognizes the economic costs of access. If regulators were not obliged to compensate the incumbent firm for its opportunity costs, they would be tempted to act opportunistically by opening utility markets to competition after the utility had made irreversible investments in facilities investment. Similarly, without efficient access pricing, granting competitors access to an incumbent's facilities would constitute a government taking and lead to free riding by competitors.

12

TSLRIC Pricing and the
Fallacy of Forward-Looking Costs

PROSPECTIVE ENTRANTS into local exchange telephony advocate
that the prices for unbundled network elements be set equal to the total
element long-run incremental cost (TELRIC) or that the prices for
services be set at their total service long-run incremental cost (TSLRIC)
per unit. To be sure, TSLRIC or TELRIC pricing is simple to understand. It would be a mistake, however, to equate simplicity with
accuracy. Although employing a simple pricing mechanism may result
in some savings in administration, those possible cost savings are trivial
compared with the short-term and long-term market distortions that
would be certain to result from taking the easy way out. TSLRIC or
TELRIC pricing is overly simplistic because it is simply the wrong
pricing policy.

The problem with TSLRIC or TELRIC pricing generally is that it
does not equal economic costs. Thus, such pricing creates economic
inefficiencies. The problems with TSLRIC or TELRIC pricing outlined
below stem from that basic defect. Those defects are evidently not obvious, for a number of distinguished economists have overlooked them.[1]

---

1. In 1996, for example, five former chief economists of the Antitrust Division of the
Department of Justice wrote to the chairman of the Federal Communications Commission
"to declare [their] support for both the principles behind TELRIC and the feasibility of
implementing the TELRIC approach." Letter from Bruce Owen, Lawrence J. White,
Frederick R. Warren-Boulton, Bobby Willig, and Janusz A. Ordover to Reed E. Hundt,
Chairman, Federal Communications Commission, at 1, Dec. 2, 1996. For a response to
that letter that comports with the analysis presented in this chapter, see Letter of Alfred E.

To avoid redundancy, and because the economic analysis is the same in either case, we subsume our critique of TELRIC pricing within that of TSLRIC pricing. There is an important difference between TSLRIC and TELRIC that should be noted, however. The FCC introduced the term *TELRIC pricing* in August 1996 in its *First Report and Order* to emphasize the costs of providing unbundled network elements.[2] The duty to provide unbundled elements to the competitors of the local exchange carriers represents a significant extension of regulation from the traditional focus on services, which are the *outputs* of a telecommunications firm, to elements, which are the productive *inputs* of the firm. Thus, the vertically integrated LEC becomes separated into a firm that provides both outputs and inputs. Regulation of the pricing and provision of inputs represents a significant increase in the regulatory control of the LEC. Ultimately, the services sold to competitors are also inputs because they are the wholesale version of services provided to the LEC's retail customers. But unbundling the components of the network that are used to provide retail services represents an additional level of regulatory intrusiveness. In any case, the basic problems with the pricing approach are present whether it is applied to inputs or to outputs.

PROBLEMS WITH TSLRIC PRICING OF MANDATORY NETWORK ACCESS

Our critique of TSLRIC pricing of mandatory network access presupposes that incremental costs are calculated correctly. Incorrect calculation of incremental costs exacerbates the problems with TSLRIC pricing that we identify. The FCC introduced the notion of "forward-looking costs" as a means of estimating incremental costs. While all economic costs are forward-looking, the regulatory application of that concept departs from economic notions of costs. Intended to value facilities at their replacement costs, rather than historic costs, the regulatory application of

Kahn to Reed E. Hundt, Chairman, Federal Communications Commission, Jan. 14, 1997.

2. Implementation of the Local Competition Provisions in the Telecommunications Act of 1996 and Interconnection Between Local Exchange Carriers and Commercial Mobile Radio Service Providers, First Report and Order, CC Dkt. Nos. 96-98, 95-185, 11 F.C.C. Rcd. 15,499 (1996) [hereinafter *First Report and Order*]. A LEXIS search of all publicly available FCC documents reveals that the first usage of "TELRIC" or "total element long-run incremental cost" appeared in an August 1, 1996, press release announcing the agency's decision in the *First Report and Order*. Commission Adopts Rules to Implement Local Competition Provisions of Telecommunications Act of 1996 (CC Docket No. 96-98), 1996 FCC LEXIS 4029, Aug. 1, 1996.

forward-looking costs goes further by considering costs that are irrelevant to economic decisions and ignoring costs that are relevant. Thus, with inaccurate estimates of incremental costs, the application of TSLRIC pricing to compulsory network access is likely to introduce additional economic inefficiencies.

TSLRIC or TELRIC pricing refers to pricing at the *average attributable cost* of each service or element. Thus, such pricing is highly preferable to alternatives that would force prices below average attributable cost, such as pricing that would average costs across services, or alternatives that would simply force pricing below average attributable cost. Attributable cost is perhaps a desirable price floor since it guarantees that a service at least covers those costs that can be properly assigned to that service. As we observe shortly, however, average attributable cost by itself does not provide sufficient information or guidance for the pricing of inputs or outputs.

TSLRIC Pricing Does Not Reflect the Incumbent LEC's Total Direct Costs

The incremental cost of production is of value to the firm when it makes decisions comparing incremental revenue with incremental cost. Because a multiproduct firm has shared costs and common costs, however, TSLRIC pricing does not provide a complete picture of the firm's direct costs.

Certainly, there are circumstances in which TSLRIC pricing equals the firm's economic costs of production. If the firm provides only one service, then the incremental cost and stand-alone cost of the service are equal, and incremental pricing provides an accurate estimate of the firm's costs of production. Incremental cost pricing may also be appropriate for a regulated firm, such as a natural gas pipeline, that provides transportation services and then undertakes an expansion project to provide a new service. In that case, incremental cost pricing is preferable to averaging the cost of the expansion service with that of the existing service, which can lower the price of the new service below incremental cost because of the low book value of the existing facility.[3] The expansion project should be priced at least at its incremental cost. If the firm provides multiple services, but the services have no shared costs or common costs—that is, there are no economies of scope—then

---

3. Daniel F. Spulber, *Pricing and the Incentive to Invest in Pipelines After* Great Lakes, 15 ENERGY L.J. 377 (1994).

incremental cost pricing provides an accurate estimate of the costs of production. Those circumstances do not describe the technology and cost of local exchange telecommunications, however.

If a firm sold all its services at their TSLRICs, then it would not cover its total costs. The difference between a firm's total costs and the sum of its incremental costs equals the firm's shared costs and common costs. Thus, under TSLRIC pricing the firm would incur losses exactly equal to that remainder—that is, the firm's shared costs and common costs.

The firm's shared costs and common costs are precisely its economies of scope, which means that they are the firm's efficiency gains from jointly producing multiple services. To price without regard to those costs is to penalize a firm for its efficiencies.

Because TSLRIC pricing fails to recover any of the incumbent LEC's shared costs or common costs, it interferes with the incumbent LEC's opportunity to earn a fair rate of return on its investment or even to recover its investment. That outcome violates section 252(d)(1), added to the Communications Act in 1996, which calls for the firm to recover its costs with pricing that may include a reasonable profit.[4] TSLRIC pricing *guarantees* losses and thus is inherently confiscatory. A policy that required TSLRIC pricing would therefore violate section 252(d)(1) and constitute a taking.

Some would suggest that the firm subject to TSLRIC pricing could make up its losses elsewhere, perhaps from retail sales or from the "next fertile field" that the incumbent LEC might enter in the newly deregulated environment. Although appealing on the surface, such a suggestion requires that earnings from other services be sufficient to cover shared costs and common costs. Such an unfounded belief can easily fail to correspond to market conditions. Competition may but need not lower margins on those services that competitors identify in their unbundling requests and is just as likely to do so on the remaining services. Indeed, with TSLRIC pricing, competitors are most likely to purchase those services that would have a markup in a competitive market, so as to free ride on the incumbent LEC. Competitive firms are able to stay in business when they recover common costs and shared costs through revenues above incremental costs. The market-allowed contribution of "other services" cannot be predicted a priori. What *is* certain is that a

---

4. 47 U.S.C. § 252(d)(1).

firm that does not cover its common costs and shared costs will not remain in business for very long.

TSLRIC Pricing Does Not Reflect the Incumbent LEC's Economic Costs

TSLRIC pricing is not efficient because it does not reflect the LEC's economic costs, which include the direct incremental cost *plus* the opportunity costs of the facilities to which the incumbent LEC provides access. The TSLRIC pricing method is neither efficient nor compensatory because the incumbent LEC will not be allowed the opportunity to recover its economic costs.

The definition of attributable cost is partly at issue. The attributable economic cost of providing a service should not be limited to its direct costs, or equivalently its accounting cost. To calculate economic cost, it is necessary to impute the opportunity cost of inputs that the firm manufactures or develops, rather than purchases. Moreover, as Ronald H. Coase emphasized in his classic article, the purchase price of inputs may not reflect their full cost because of the transaction costs associated with obtaining those inputs, including search and bargaining costs.[5] Those transaction costs may not be explicitly accounted for because they involve the use of scarce resources within the firm, such as managerial effort. Those inputs have opportunity costs that must be included in the economic costs of providing the service. In addition, the purchase cost of inputs may not reflect the opportunity costs of inputs once the inputs have been obtained, because securing additional inputs may involve delays. Such delays in obtaining inputs may, in turn, retard production and result in missed sales and forgone earnings.

Pricing the firm's outputs sold to customers differs from pricing the firm's inputs sold to competitors. The economic costs can be expected to differ. The incremental economic costs of inputs sold to competitors must equal the direct economic costs plus the opportunity costs to the firm of those inputs. That necessarily includes forgone sales to customers. To exclude the firm's opportunity costs in one's definition of costs, as do advocates of TSLRIC pricing, is simply an expedient by which regulators give competitors a free ride. It is not an assertion about economic efficiency.

---

5. Ronald H. Coase, *The Nature of the Firm,* 4 ECONOMICA 386 (1937).

TSLRIC Pricing Should Not Be
Confused with Competitive Pricing

Some economists and regulators justify TSLRIC pricing by analogizing it to marginal cost pricing.[6] David L. Kaserman, for example, asserts with respect to local telephony that "with common costs present . . . the long-run competitive equilibrium . . . yields prices equal to marginal cost and a full recovery" of the incumbent LEC's total costs.[7] That justification for TSLRIC pricing rests on a misunderstanding of one the most basic principles of economics. It is true, of course, that when price exceeds the marginal cost of production, there may be additional benefits to consumers from expanding output to the point where marginal cost equals price. That condition does not imply, however, that utility regulators should set prices for any and all services at their marginal cost (the cost of producing the last unit). Moreover, it does not imply that prices should be set at average incremental cost (the incremental cost of producing the service divided by the number of units of the service provided), which is what TSLRIC pricing represents. There are several fundamental problems with jumping to that conclusion.

With marginal cost pricing, costs are not covered in the presence of economies of scale (or, in the case of a multiproduct firm, when there are economies of scale and scope). Economists are familiar with the problem of pricing a bridge that costs $100 to build. The marginal cost

---

6. *E.g.*, DAVID L. KASERMAN, JOHN W. MAYO, MICHAEL A. CREW, NICHOLAS ECONOMIDES, R. GLENN HUBBARD, PAUL R. KLEINDORFER & CARLOS MARTINS-FILHO, LOCAL COMPETITION ISSUES AND THE TELECOMMUNICATIONS ACT OF 1996, at 6 & n.4 (July 15, 1996) (prepared for AT&T Corp.) [hereinafter KASERMAN REPORT].

7. Testimony of David L. Kaserman, AT&T Communications P–140, sub. 51, vol. 2, tr. 19 (N.C. Util. Comm'n Oct. 24, 1996) [hereinafter *Kaserman North Carolina Testimony*]. Kaserman's support for that proposition is Glenn M. MacDonald & Alan Slivinski, *The Simple Analytics of Competitive Equilibrium with Multiproduct Firms*, 77 AM. ECON. REV. 941 (1987), but MacDonald and Slivinski develop a model of a two-product firm in which they assume that "the marginal cost of producing either [product] *rises*, and does so nonnegligibly." *Id.* at 945 (emphasis added). Thus, they assume a condition in which the marginal cost curve will intersect a product's average total cost curve at its minimum, such that marginal cost pricing can enable the firm to earn zero economic profit and thus break even. *Id.* at 944. Similarly, Kaserman asserts: "If the TSLRIC . . . [prices are] increasing, then even in the presence of common cost, even in the presence of large common cost, TSLRIC prices can be fully compensatory." *Kaserman North Carolina Testimony, supra*, vol. 2, tr. 31 (citing MacDonald & Slivinski, *supra*). The fallacy in Kaserman's reasoning, and in his reliance on the article by MacDonald and Slivinski, is that an incumbent LEC is uniformly believed to operate over an output range in which marginal cost is *below* average total cost.

of providing the services of the bridge are zero. What should the price of crossing the bridge be?[8] Efficiency considerations alone might suggest pricing at zero. Yet, the bridge then would not be economically viable. One solution would be to finance the bridge by using general taxation. That policy, however, would transfer income to users of the bridge from those taxpayers who are not users of the bridge. Whether one views such a solution as efficient depends on how he evaluates income transfers in determining the effect on social welfare. Those income transfers have consequences for economic efficiency. Accordingly, it is often desirable for users of the bridge to pay for the cost of the bridge.

To illustrate further how TSLRIC pricing fails to be a useful solution when there are significant shared costs and common costs, suppose that the bridge accommodates both passenger cars and pedestrians. Again, the incremental costs of allowing each type of service equal zero. The shared costs and common costs are $100. Advocates of TSLRIC pricing would suggest pricing the bridge at zero for both passenger cars and pedestrians. As before, the bridge would not remain economically viable.

The analogy between competitive markets and regulated pricing as a guide to efficient pricing is somewhat strained. Even in the ideal case of "perfect competition" covered in basic economics textbooks, one cannot say that competitive firms price at marginal cost. Rather, the "perfectly competitive firm" takes the market price as a given and offers its output for sale at the market price. The firm, in that theoretical ideal case, sets its *output* level such that the firm's marginal cost equals the market price.[9] That is how in equilibrium the marginal cost of the firm equals the market-clearing price. That situation is different from the problem of a regulator's seeking to determine the regulated firm's marginal cost, which will vary depending on the types of services and the volume of services that the firm offers. For regulators to determine what price equals the firm's marginal cost, *at the level of services demanded at that price*, is a fundamentally different and more complex problem. To make that determination, regulators not only would have to predict marginal costs at each level of output over a relevant range, but also would have

8. Jules Dupuit, *On the Measurement of the Utility of Public Works* (1844), in READINGS IN WELFARE ECONOMICS 255 (Kenneth J. Arrow & Tibor Scitovsky eds., Irwin 1969); Harold Hotelling, *The General Welfare in Relation to Problems of Taxation and of Railway and Utility Rates*, 6 ECONOMETRICA 242 (1938).

9. *E.g.*, PAUL A. SAMUELSON & WILLIAM D. NORDHAUS, ECONOMICS 130 (McGraw-Hill, Inc., 15th ed. 1995).

to make projections of the quantity demanded of those services at the relevant prices to determine the equilibrium prices.

Finally, when textbooks speak of the marginal cost or incremental cost of the firm, they are referring to the firm's marginal *economic* cost. As any textbook will indicate, economic costs of the firm's inputs refer to the direct cost of purchasing the inputs or the imputed *opportunity cost* of inputs that are not purchased. The firm's costs refer to the costs of the inputs used by the firm, with the cost function of the firm defining the minimum cost of producing output, given the firm's technology and cost of inputs.

TSLRIC Pricing Promotes
Free Riding by Competitors

TSLRIC pricing fails to address the problem of selling inputs to competitors. To illustrate those issues clearly, recall the fast-food stand that offers both hot dogs and hamburgers, each of which is cooked on the same grill. The unit incremental cost of cooked hot dogs to the firm is $1, and the unit incremental cost of cooked hamburgers is $2. The total cost of the grill is $100. The fast-food stand charges its customers $1.50 and $2.60 for hot dogs and hamburgers, respectively, allowing the firm to cover its shared costs and common costs.

Proponents of TSLRIC pricing would have that fast-food stand sell cooked hot dogs and hamburgers to rival fast-food sellers at $1 and $2, respectively, ignoring the shared costs and common costs of the grill, which is the capital of the fast-food stand. The rivals could then offer the cooked hot dogs and hamburgers to the firm's customers at prices that are equal to or lower than the prices of the fast-food stand. Without question, that free riding would increase competition for the fast-food stand that owns the grill, so much so that the firm would be driven out of business. But such a pricing solution does not conform with any pricing behavior actually observed in a competitive market, and it cannot be justified on grounds of economic efficiency.

TSLRIC Pricing
Subsidizes Entrants

Some proponents of TSLRIC pricing may argue that prices set at TSLRIC do not involve cross-subsidies, so that TSLRIC pricing would rebalance rates. That claim is false. The incremental cost test for cross-subsidization requires that each service, *and each combination of services*, must cover its incremental cost.[10] That outcome easily fails to occur with TSLRIC pricing as soon as the firm produces more than two services and any group of services has shared costs. That result is illustrated by the following example with three services:

incremental cost of service *A*	=	$1
incremental cost of service *B*	=	$1
incremental cost of service *C*	=	$1
shared cost of services *A* and *B*	=	$5

total cost of all services	=	$8

The example shows that the incremental cost of services *A* and *B* taken together is $1 + $1 + $5 = $7. TSLRIC pricing would set the price of each service at $1. Services *A* and *B* taken together would have revenues of $2, which would fail to cover their $7 incremental cost. Thus, TSLRIC pricing creates cross-subsidies.

In a general sense, TSLRIC pricing creates cross-subsidies when multiple services are available that have shared costs or common costs. Those costs do not magically disappear. Failure to cover those costs makes those services available collectively at less than their total costs.

What are the consequences of cross-subsidization? Entrants will make efficient decisions about the mix of resale and facilities-based competition only if their access to existing networks is provided at prices that accurately reflect economic costs. Subsidizing services by pricing them at TSLRIC sends the wrong price signals and leads to incorrect decisions. Prices below economic costs lead to excessive use of under-priced facilities and distort the decisions of resellers. Thus, underpriced facilities not only encourage but also finance the entry and expansion of resellers.

Moreover, pricing network services below economic cost is likely to discourage the building of competing facilities. Thus, TSLRIC pricing thwarts rather than stimulates facilities-based competition. Why should an entrant seek a competitively priced alternative when it can free ride on the incumbent LEC's facilities at prices that are below cost? TSLRIC pricing turns out to be a misnomer: It should more appropriately be

10. *See, e.g.*, WILLIAM J. BAUMOL & J. GREGORY SIDAK, TOWARD COMPETITION IN LOCAL TELEPHONY 69–72 (MIT Press & AEI Press 1994).

termed "individual-service LRIC," for it ignores the incremental costs of *combinations* of services.

Indeed, unbundling "at any technically feasible point," as envisioned by the Telecommunications Act of 1996, compounds the problem.[11] Finer and finer partitioning of services wrings out the shared costs from TSLRIC prices and thus increases the subsidies inherent in such pricing. In the limit, the finer partitioning of services creates TSLRIC prices that will not cover the incremental costs of *any* pair or group of services that have shared costs.

*TSLRIC Pricing Creates Incentives
for Excessive Unbundling*

TSLRIC pricing creates incentives for excessive unbundling because it ignores the fact that unbundling shifts costs from attributable costs to shared costs and common costs. A firm cannot apply any pricing methodology independent of the characteristics of the products and services for which prices are being chosen. On the demand side, the characteristics of the products and services will affect the willingness of consumers to pay for those products and services. On the supply side, if the firm sets prices subject to regulatory controls based on its costs of service, then the definitions of the products and services will significantly affect the costs that are attributable to those products and services.

The pricing methodology that regulators adopt for resale and unbundled network elements should be flexible enough to adapt to the regulations governing the extent of unbundling. Efficient and compensatory pricing must allow the firm to recover its economic costs, including both its attributable costs and its unattributable costs. The firm's unattributable costs are its shared costs and common costs.

The measurement of costs depends on the definition of the firm's services. For a multiproduct firm, changes in the definition of classes of services and individual services will affect measures of incremental cost. Generally speaking, the more services that are defined by subdividing sets of services, the lower the attributable costs of individual services, and the higher the shared costs and common costs of those services. Without any increase or decrease in total costs, it is simply more difficult to identify the attributable costs of a particular service as one moves toward higher levels of disaggregation in the classification of services.

Suppose, for example, that a company produces services that are

---

11. 47 U.S.C. § 251(c)(3).

grouped into two categories, *A* and *B*, and each category of services is sold as a bundle. The average incremental cost of category *A* is $10. The same is true of the average incremental cost of category *B*. Moreover, the firm has common costs of $20. Suppose that there are two services within category *A*, each of which has an incremental cost of $4, and that the two services have shared costs of $2, for a total of $10. By unbundling services in category *A*, the shared costs and common costs of the firm rise by $2 to $22. In state arbitration proceedings under section 252 of the Communication Act, for example, entrants have requested incumbent LECs to engage in "subloop unbundling," so that pieces of the loop (such as the network interface device, or NID, on the side of one's home) can be obtained independently of a "NID-less" loop and other subelements.[12] One would expect subloop unbundling to raise the incumbent LEC's proportion of unattributable costs.

Unbundling therefore has the effect of decreasing the proportion of costs that are attributable and of correspondingly increasing the proportion of total costs that are classified as shared or common. To the extent that the degree of unbundling follows regulatory dictates, the resulting service definitions may bear little relation to technological and managerial measurements of costs. Consequently, it becomes increasingly difficult to identify the firm's underlying cost components. Reliance on regulatory accounting measures, based on regulatory service classifications and unbundling requirements, is likely to cause inefficient decisions concerning the pricing of network components. That inefficient outcome is particularly likely to occur if, as one would expect, the packages of retail services that the LEC offered before the imposition of mandatory unbundling were intended to facilitate optimal management decisions about pricing and service offerings.

That effect of unbundling on cost calculations counsels regulators to take careful account of the interplay between unbundling requirements and pricing. Competing carriers have an incentive to request pricing at incremental cost to the incumbent LEC as a means of obtaining network services in a manner that avoids paying for the LEC's shared costs and

---

12. For examples of arbitration decisions ordering subloop unbundling, see Petition of MCI Telecommunications Corp., Pursuant to Section 252(b) of the Telecommunications Act of 1996, for Arbitration to Establish an Intercarrier Agreement Between MCI and New York Telephone Co., Case 96-C-0787, Op. No. 96-33, 1996 N.Y. PUC LEXIS 702, at *43, *70 (N.Y. Pub. Serv. Comm'n Dec. 23, 1996); Petition of MCI Metro Access Transmission Services, Inc. for Arbitration of Its Interconnection Request to Bell Atlantic-Pa., Inc., Dkt. No. A-310236F0002, 1996 Pa. PUC LEXIS 161, at *76 (Pa. Pub. Util. Comm'n Nov. 7, 1996).

common costs. Further, by requesting a finer and finer partition of the incumbent LEC's services into unbundled components, competitors shift costs away from measures of incremental cost and toward measures of shared costs and common costs. In the limit, groups of services may individually have negligible incremental costs, even though as a group, their shared costs and common costs are significant.

TSLRIC pricing thus creates a perverse incentive. Unbundling requests from competitors using LEC services may be strategic actions, rather than legitimate requests for access to network services. Competitors not only avoid paying a portion of shared costs and common costs, but also have an incentive to request ever finer partitions of services, and interconnection at every technologically feasible point, so as to shift costs farther away from incremental costs and into shared and common costs. That strategic opportunity allows competitors to free ride on the incumbent LEC.

M-ECPR pricing avoids those perverse incentives because competitors must pay for the costs of the services that they purchase—both the incremental costs and a portion of the shared costs and common costs. By allocating shared costs and common costs in a competitively neutral manner, M-ECPR pricing eliminates the incentive for competitors to make strategic requests for excessive unbundling. Instead, a competitor will purchase resale and unbundled network elements on the basis of its market prospects rather than as an attempt to game the regulatory system.

TSLRIC Pricing Fails to Include Increases in Shared Costs and Common Costs That Result from Unbundling

Unbundling has costs. The provision of resale services and unbundled network components entails two types of costs: transaction costs and production costs. Unbundling should not be an end in itself, because the bundling of products and services reduces customer transaction costs and enhances convenience. Access to a few types of local network elements is sufficient to achieve the objectives of deregulation. Competitive markets are capable of resolving the tradeoff between the need to customize offerings and the advantages of bundling. The costs of mandated unbundling must be reflected in estimates of the incumbent LEC's incremental costs, shared costs, and common costs and thus included in the prices for resale and unbundled network elements.

Excessive government-mandated unbundling of services provided by the LECs may lead to higher prices and customer inconvenience. Competition in the local exchange obviates much of such mandated unbundling. Bundling in a competitive market is self-regulating because customer demand will determine which bundles of services a firm must offer to remain competitive. Regulatory commissions can therefore achieve their open-access goals with limited unbundling; they need only selectively target several points of entry to the local exchange network that are shown not to be competitive and then price that network access at compensatory levels. The Canadian Radio-television and Telecommunications Commission adopted such a policy in May 1997, when (in contrast to the U.S. approach in the Telecommunications Act of 1996) the agency ordered that incumbent LECs "should generally not be required to make available facilities for which there are alternative sources of supply or which [competitive local exchange carriers] can reasonably supply on their own."[13] Mandatory unbundling in Canada will extend only to the incumbent LEC's "essential" facilities.[14]

Unbundling entails more transaction costs than do goods and services that are sold together, because the firm must break down ordering, purchasing, billing, and pricing information for individual components. Most products and services offered by competitive companies are bundles of attributes or features. Customers benefit from the convenience of purchasing a range of products and services from the same supplier that offers lower transaction costs through "one-stop shopping" for bundled products and services. Companies compete by offering packages of goods and services that enhance customer convenience.

For those reasons, many goods and services are sold as packages. Imagine buying an automobile or even a computer part by part. The final product not only is a physical package of components, but also is sold as a single product requiring only one set of transactions. Even when automobiles are customized with options, customers receive discounts when they choose standardized options packages. The greater the extent of standardization of bundles of features offered to either the customers or the competitors of the incumbent LEC, the lower will be the transaction costs associated with offering those features. Conversely, the more that regulatory commissions require that each retail service or network component be sold separately, or in individually customized service packages, the greater will be the associated transaction costs.

Excessive unbundling not only is inefficient and unnecessary, but entails production costs as well. To unbundle retail services and network components, the incumbent LEC often needs to install complex switching

---

13. Local Competition, Telecom Decision CRTC 97-8, at ¶ 74 (Canadian Radio-television & Telecommunications Comm'n May 1, 1997).
14. *Id.*

equipment and to provide additional interconnection facilities for competitors. As with transaction costs, the more such resale and access facilities can be standardized, the lower will be the associated costs. If unbundling and regulated pricing requirements shift the costs to the incumbent LEC, then competitors will have an additional strategic incentive to demand unique, customized wholesale and access services from the LEC.

The transaction costs and production costs due to unbundling represent *wholesaling* costs for the incumbent LEC. The incremental wholesaling costs that are attributable to individual services or elements must be included in the LEC's prices. In addition, any increase in shared costs or common costs that results from unbundling also should be reflected in the prices for resale and unbundled network elements. A competitive firm would not provide a service if it did not generate sufficient revenues to cover its costs. Regulators should account for wholesaling costs in their pricing rules. If competitors do not bear the full economic costs of the services that they purchase, they will not make efficient purchasing and investment decisions.

TSLRIC pricing will capture wholesaling costs if and only if all those costs are attributable. But it will not capture those transaction costs and production costs due to wholesaling that increase shared costs or common costs. Thus, TSLRIC pricing will fail to reflect the full economic costs of unbundling.

The inefficiencies associated with the transaction costs and production costs of specialized services under mandatory unbundling are a problem when costs are shifted to the incumbent LEC's other customers or when the LEC is expected to shoulder those costs as a means of easing the transition to competition. Unbundling becomes an incumbent burden that potentially hinders the incumbent LEC's ability to compete and subsidizes new entrants, thereby distorting their decisions about how much to invest in competing facilities. Just as overpriced network services can induce inefficient bypass decisions, so also can subsidized wholesale services induce underinvestment in facilities and overuse of network components relative to less costly alternatives.

TSLRIC Pricing Creates Incentives for the Incumbent LEC to Reduce Common Costs or Shared Costs

Because TSLRIC pricing fails to compensate the incumbent LEC for its shared costs and common costs, adoption of such pricing would create an incentive for the LEC to reconfigure its network and change the structure of the company to increase the proportion of costs that would be attributable to those services priced at TSLRIC and to lower costs that would be classified as shared costs or common costs. That shift in the incumbent LEC's cost structure would not represent efficiency gains: By lowering shared costs or common costs, the company would potentially increase *total* costs because it would lose some of the benefits of economies of scope. Moreover, the reductions in uncompensated shared costs or common costs that are necessary to enable the firm to break even could result in a lowering of the quality of service or the elimination of some services that are uncompensated. Thus, TSLRIC pricing creates a situation that is ripe for the law of unintended consequences.

TSLRIC Pricing Lacks Dynamic Pricing Flexibility and Creates Incumbent Burdens

TSLRIC pricing lacks dynamic flexibility, for there is no room for price adjustment. Pricing at the lowest possible level is not sustainable in the long run because no company can continue to operate indefinitely without covering its shared costs and common costs.

Proponents of TSLRIC pricing argue that because prices in competitive markets tend toward incremental costs, regulators should immediately reduce price to its lowest level. That argument is flawed because it presupposes that a competitive market eliminates all margins over marginal cost. To the contrary, competitive markets determine the size of relative margins on products depending on many factors, including the extent of shared costs and common costs, demand elasticities, product differentiation, transaction costs, and marketing and sales efforts. Moreover, the argument presupposes that regulators can discern competitive price levels more accurately than the market can—a proposition forcefully rebutted by Friedrich A. Hayek and many after him.[15]

A system of price caps protects consumers from price increases while allowing competitive price decreases. TSLRIC, however, is inconsistent with price caps. It does not allow prices to be adjusted in response to competition. Regulators should not adopt TSLRIC pricing to pursue a mistaken representation of how markets operate. Instead, regulators should let competition determine the margins on unbundled services.

15. Friedrich A. Hayek, *The Use of Knowledge in Society*, 35 AM. ECON. REV. 519 (1945). For a summation of Hayek's theories on the superiority of markets over state control of production, see FRIEDRICH A. HAYEK, THE FATAL CONCEIT: THE ERRORS OF SOCIALISM (W.W. Bartley III ed., Routledge 1988).

TSLRIC pricing, by automatically eliminating *all* margins, leaves the incumbent LEC no room for competitive price adjustment and thus creates a competitive disadvantage relative to new entrants.

The Telecommunications Act of 1996 offers an unprecedented opportunity for further growth of competition in local exchange telecommunications. As a precondition, however, the act requires additional regulation of prices for resale and unbundled network elements. To achieve the intended benefits of competition, it is essential that regulatory commissions grant incumbent LECs sufficient flexibility to adjust their prices for resale and for unbundled network elements to reflect customer demand and market conditions. Regulatory rules for pricing resale and unbundled network elements should allow the incumbent LECs to recover their economic costs, including the additional costs of following unbundling rules. If prices for resale and unbundled network elements are to be regulated, then price controls should not discriminate against the incumbent LECs by placing them at a competitive disadvantage in the marketplace.

Regulatory commissions should allow the incumbent LECs the same flexibility in pricing and defining unbundled services that is available to the competitive local exchange carriers. Regulators should not mandate excessive unbundling of the "components" of demonstrably competitive services, for competitive markets suffice to determine the efficient extent of unbundling.

Whether the incumbent LEC is providing services to retail customers or to other telecommunications companies, negotiation and competition should be relied upon as much as possible to price services and to resolve whether particular services should be offered in combination with others or à la carte. TSLRIC pricing is an extreme negotiating position taken by competitive local exchange carriers seeking access to network services and elements at prices below economic costs.

A regulatory commission should not establish pricing and unbundling restrictions that bias decisions about the type of technology that a carrier may employ to offer local telephone service. The absence of such restrictions should apply equally to the incumbent LEC and alternative local exchange carriers. Customer choice and competitive interaction between the incumbent LEC, the alternative local exchange carriers, and the many other providers of transmission capacity should determine the pricing of unbundled network elements. TSLRIC pricing can bias technology choice by eliminating the rewards from economies of scope, thereby encouraging separation of network services into components associated with incremental costs.

TSLRIC Pricing Is Discriminatory

TSLRIC pricing is discriminatory because it creates subsidies for entering competitive local exchange carriers at the expense of the incumbent LECs. As we have demonstrated, TSLRIC pricing does not cover the incumbent LEC's direct economic costs, because it ignores shared costs and common costs. Moreover, TSLRIC pricing creates cross-subsidies because it yields revenues that fail to cover the incremental costs of any two or more services that have shared costs. TSLRIC pricing further fails to cover the incumbent LEC's economic costs because it ignores the LEC's opportunity costs when it is compelled to sell inputs to competitors.

No competitive firm would agree to price below costs. No competitive firm could offer services that subsidize one another or that contain subsidies for competitors and thus encourage free riding on the firm's facilities. By forcing the incumbent LEC to accept prices to which a competitive firm would never agree, TSLRIC pricing places the LEC at a competitive disadvantage. Facilities-based competitors certainly will not be subject to such pricing regulations. The discriminatory impact on the incumbent LEC of TSLRIC pricing is undeniable.

Regulated Network Pricing and the Fallacy of Forward-Looking Costs

We have just seen that TSLRIC or TELRIC pricing of mandatory network access suffers from a number of specific problems. Those problems are compounded if regulators base measures of incremental cost on irrelevant costs. As a general rule, one should not base economic decisions on costs and benefits that are irrelevant to those decisions; correspondingly, one should take into account all the costs and benefits that each decision entails. Thus, when comparing two alternatives, one should compare the benefits and costs associated with each decision, not the benefits or costs incurred in the past, present, or future that are not directly caused by the decisions.

First, consider costs that already have been incurred and are not recoverable. After costs are sunk, economic decisions should be based on *quasi rent*—that is, revenues net of avoidable cost. The *fallacy of sunk costs* refers to decision making that takes into account irreversible expenditures.[16] That is a fallacy because those expenditures do not affect

---

16. *E.g.*, Joseph E. Stiglitz, Economics 44–45 (W.W. Norton & Co. 1993).

the benefits and costs associated with later decisions; thus, such expenditures should not enter into one's decision-making process.

But cost fallacies need not center only on past costs. What we term the *fallacy of forward-looking costs* bases pricing and other economic decisions on future costs that are not related to those decisions, and it ignores costs that *are* related to those decisions. In its network pricing rules, the FCC's notion of "forward-looking costs" is intended to emphasize that the fallacy of sunk costs should be avoided—that is, only the avoidable or future costs of decisions should be taken into account. The FCC, however, gets so carried away with projected costs that it recommends making decisions based on future costs that also are not affected by current decisions. Moreover, the fallacy of forward-looking costs ignores other costs that are affected by current decisions. The fallacy of forward-looking costs thus has two aspects. First, the decision maker takes into account costs that are irrelevant to the decision. Second, the decision maker ignores costs that are relevant to the decision, especially opportunity costs.

What are forward-looking costs? In its *First Report and Order* on interconnection, the FCC defines forward-looking costs as "the costs that a carrier would incur in the future."[17] That definition is fine as far as it goes. The FCC then proposes three alternative measures for the cost of interconnection and unbundled network elements for local exchange carriers: (1) "the most efficient network architecture, sizing, technology, and operating decisions that are operationally feasible and currently available to the industry,"[18] (2) "existing network design and technology that are currently in operation,"[19] and (3) "the most efficient technology deployed in the incumbent LEC's current wire center locations."[20] The FCC selected a measure that is a hybrid of options (1) and (3) consisting of "costs that assume that wire centers will be placed at the incumbent LEC's current wire center locations, but that the reconstructed local network will employ the most efficient technology for reasonably foreseeable capacity requirements."[21] That measure of costs rests on economic fallacies.

17. *First Report and Order*, 11 F.C.C. Rcd. at 15,848 ¶ 683.
18. *Id.*
19. *Id.* at 15,848 ¶ 684.
20. *Id.* ¶ 685.
21. *Id.* at 15,849 ¶ 685.

Putting the Cart before the Horse

A decision entails costs. The FCC, however, puts the cart before the horse *by embedding a decision within its definition of costs*. The decision is whether or not to expand capacity, contingent on two preconditions: that the LEC's current wire center locations are given and that the LEC has fully flexible capacity. Not coincidentally, those two assumptions correspond to a model employed by AT&T and other interexchange carriers known as the Hatfield model, which assumes a "scorched-node" network, as if there were no existing loops or switches in place.[22] Such assumptions are only meaningful if that is indeed the relevant decision, such as might be the case in rebuilding a local exchange network that had been seriously damaged by war or natural disaster. Otherwise, the FCC's cost definition will be off the mark. One could perhaps defend the need to make some choices as a means of operationalizing the cost measurement. The question, however, is whether the FCC's particular set of assumptions corresponds to the decisions to which the cost measure would be applied.

Such a hybrid cost measure is necessarily off the mark. First, it cannot represent the costs of an entrant, which can choose where to locate its wire centers, as in option (1). Thus, the cost measure is not relevant to the entry and operating decisions of a competitive entrant. Second, the cost measure cannot represent the costs of the incumbent, because the incumbent already has loops and switches in place, as in option (2). Thus, the cost measure is not relevant to the expansion and operating decisions of an incumbent LEC.

Jumping the Gun

The forward-looking cost rhetoric is aimed at estimating the replacement cost of network assets, a laudable objective. In its pricing recommendations and cost estimation methods, however, the FCC paints an incorrect portrait of how competitive pricing works. Technology and competitive entry occur with lags in competitive markets. Setting prices on the basis of competitors' costs is a good competitive strategy, but only when market alternatives are available. To use a "most efficient technology" standard, as the FCC recommends, is to jump the gun, because that standard is at variance with competitive markets.

---

22. HATFIELD ASSOCIATES, DOCUMENTATION OF THE HATFIELD MODEL, VERSION 2.2, RELEASE 1 (Hatfield Associates May 16, 1996).

To take a simple example, consider the evolution of semiconductors. The speed and computing power of each generation of computer chip has increased as chip manufacturers have developed new products such as Intel's 286, 386, 486, Pentium, and P6 chips. The price of a computer chip is highest when it is first introduced. The chip's price then begins a decline that depends in part on the rate of development of the next generation of chip; after the new chip is introduced, the price of the previous generation depends in part on the availability of the new chip. Thus, the pricing of chips is affected by the lags in developing new technology and lags in introducing products that embody the new technology. Existing products are not immediately devalued by new and improved substitutes. Rather, the adjustment process often is gradual.

If prices did not adjust gradually, there would be no incentive to engage in research and development or to invest in costly manufacturing to introduce any generation of products bearing new technology. Industry would be waiting for the next development before making a commitment. Thus, no progress would occur. Instead, because of lags, companies earn a return to the current technology in the interim period before the new technology becomes available; after the new technology is introduced, the development cycle continues. To imagine that prices fall immediately as a new technology is spotted over the horizon would be to eliminate any incentives for R&D and investment in production.

Consider pricing when technological change occurs that changes the cost of production. The firm expects its operating cost to be c_0. Technological change occurs, and the operating cost of entrants is lower than that of the incumbent, say c_1. Suppose that incumbents and entrants have the same entry costs k (although the same argument applies if entry costs change as well). The incumbent expects to charge a price p. Should it change its price after the technological change occurs and the entrant's alternative makes its appearance? If the entrant does not have any capacity constraints, then c_1 will be the new market price. If the entrant does face capacity constraints, then c_1 will not be the new market price, which instead will fall with a lag. The lag is due to the adjustment costs of entry, which should be counted as part of the cost of the competitive alternative. Therefore, the price should not fall so as to reflect the entrant's economic costs as well as to provide incentives for entrants to incur the adjustment cost of entry. The incumbent's expectations would have taken that market lag into account. Thus, the best technology available is not a proper yardstick for the incumbent until the market alternative is no longer capacity-constrained. Put differently, the current market price reflects the projected cost of the alternative plus the adjustment cost associated with installing and adapting to the new production method.

The FCC jumped the gun by recommending that access to the local exchange network reflect the most efficient technology before the market makes that technology available. The consequences of jumping the gun are to eliminate incentives for incumbents to expand and upgrade their networks and for entrants to establish facilities. The prices of existing network facilities should adjust at market-determined rates that reflect the availability of facilities that embody the most efficient technology available. Jumping the gun could slow the introduction of the most efficient technology that the FCC uses as its benchmark.

Moreover, how will the FCC know what is really the most efficient technology? Experience in telecommunications shows that there is rapid technological change in computers, optical transmission, wireless transmission, and network design. It is not realistic to presume that a government agency is better equipped than market participants to sort out those technological changes to determine which technology is the best available or most efficient. The process of price adjustment to technological change cannot be predetermined by government fiat; it can only be revealed through market competition. Not only are there incentive problems that could forestall the very innovation that the FCC is attempting to predict, but the information required to make the prediction is beyond the capabilities of administrative decision making.

Ignoring Investment-Backed Expectations

Consider a basic example. Suppose that to carry out production a firm must invest k dollars. Suppose that the investment k is irreversible, so that k represents sunk costs. The firm has operating costs c and expects to earn revenues R. The firm's economic rent is defined as revenues net of operating cost and investment cost, $R - c - k$. Economic rent provides the incentive for entry. The firm's economic quasi rent is defined as net revenue, $R - c$. The quasi rent provides incentives to stay in the industry after entry costs have been sunk. Having sunk k, the firm decides whether or not to produce on the basis of its comparison of R and c only. It would manifest the fallacy of sunk costs for the firm to base the production decision on the magnitude of k. Thus, after k is sunk, only quasi rents—not economic rents—affect the firm's decision whether or not to produce the good.

That condition does not mean that pricing should not take into account sunk costs k. The fallacy of forward-looking costs ignores the expectations of the investor when the decision to invest k is made. Thus, the fallacy of forward-looking costs would be to base the investment decision on quasi rents alone, ignoring the magnitude of k. *Before* the firm has sunk k, it is economic rents that count, not quasi rents.

Buyers and sellers enter into contracts on the basis of economic rents. The purpose of contract law is to allow efficient contracts to form. Otherwise, without the protection of contract law, buyers and sellers would be tempted to behave opportunistically, taking advantage of the reliance or irreversible investment of the other party. To illustrate that point, suppose that R is determined by a buyer and seller negotiating a contract before k is sunk. After the parties enter into the contract, one of the parties sinks cost k. The other party then has an incentive to behave opportunistically by offering a payment that is only slightly above c, thus capturing the investor's quasi rent. That situation cannot be justified by giving c the new label "forward-looking economic costs." Contract law protects the expectation, $R - c$, which equals the investor's quasi rent. If the seller anticipated that the buyer could reduce the payment to c after the contract was formed, then the seller would have no incentive to make a transaction-specific investment in the first place.

To complicate matters, suppose that a new technology appears such that the replacement cost of capacity is lower than k, say k_1. Suppose that operating costs continue to equal c. The forward-looking costs of production are then equal to $c + k_1$. Again, that condition would not mean that the contract price should be reduced to forward-looking costs. The purpose of the contract is to protect the expectation interests of the buyer and seller. Thus, the price should remain at R. Forward-looking economic costs are not simply the firm's avoidable costs after it has made investments. If that were the case, there would be no transaction-specific investments.

It is now possible to see the efficiency of the expectation damage measure in contract law and its relation to the pricing of the regulated services of incumbent LECs, including interstate access. Suppose that the buyer contracts to pay R to the seller and another seller later appears with a better offer, R_1. In other words, R_1 is less than R. Contract law ensures efficient breach by allowing breach only if the buyer pays the original seller's expectation of $R - c$. That payment leads to efficient breach decisions because the buyer will breach the contract only if the offer from the new seller is lower than the operating cost of the original seller.[23] The offer of the entrant must be lower than the avoidable cost

---

23. That result obtains because the buyer will choose to breach if and only if $R > R -$

of the incumbent for breach to be efficient. Contract law does not require paying the incumbent the offer of the entrant. To do so would simply be a transfer of income from the seller to the buyer and would not lead to efficient breach decisions. If the seller anticipated that the buyer could breach or pay the going rate whenever a lower price appeared, then the seller would have no incentive to make a transaction-specific investment.

In the regulated context, the expected revenue of the incumbent LEC happens to be based on embedded costs because, under cost-of-service regulation, the LEC's capital costs are necessarily used to calculate revenue requirements. That calculation does not mean that embedded costs are part of the firm's economic cost. Nevertheless, because the regulated firm's expected revenues reflect those costs, the expected revenues should be used to compensate the firm. The fact that the regulated firm's capital has a lower (or higher) replacement value in comparison with embedded cost is not relevant to the compensation decision. The embedded cost is a part of cost recovery because it underlies the incumbent firm's investment-backed expectation.

The Janus Artifice

Accompanying the fallacy of forward-looking costs is an inconsistency between the many cost definitions that regulators use and their analysis of competition. The Romans built temples to Janus, the most ancient king who reigned in Italy, who was often represented with two faces because he was believed to know the past and the future.[24] Like Janus, regulators alternate between past and future perspectives on markets as doing so serves their purpose. The result, which we call the Janus artifice, is an inconsistent economic analysis of competition and pricing. When evaluating the prospects for competition, regulators often look to the past, emphasizing the sunk costs of the incumbent LECs and past market share. For pricing purposes, however, regulators look to the future, promoting their notion of forward-looking costs. Regulators can only compound the fallacies inherent in the forward-looking cost approach when they engage in shifts in perspective that are meant to facilitate desired policy outcomes. At a minimum, regulators should apply the forward-looking cost approach's yardstick in a consistent manner.[25]

$c + R_1$. That condition is equivalent to $c > R_1$.

24. LEMPRIÈRE'S CLASSICAL DICTIONARY OF PROPER NAMES MENTIONED IN ANCIENT AUTHORS WRIT LARGE 304 (1788) (F. A. Wright ed., Routledge & Kegan Paul, 3d ed. 1984).

25. Children know the Janus artifice as the Pushmi-Pullyu phenomenon, named for "the

CONCLUSION

The supposed efficiency of TSLRIC pricing and TELRIC pricing for mandatory network access is a mirage. Such pricing suffers from a host of specific shortcomings. It would not cover the firm's total direct costs, nor would it compensate the firm for its economic costs inclusive of opportunity costs. Competitive pricing does not emulate TSLRIC or TELRIC pricing. To the contrary, such pricing would invite free riding and would subsidize entrants, both conditions that competitive markets do not willingly tolerate. The imposition of TSLRIC or TELRIC pricing would create the perverse incentive for the incumbent LEC to reduce its common costs and shared costs. That action would be the direct response to the tendency of such pricing to shift attributable costs to shared costs and common costs, and to increase the incumbent LEC's shared costs and common costs as a result of unbundling. In addition to those failings, TSLRIC or TELRIC pricing does not permit the incumbent LEC to have dynamic pricing flexibility. Such pricing discriminates in favor of entrants and against the incumbent LEC. In short, the call to apply TSLRIC or TELRIC pricing to resale and unbundled network elements is a mantra that misapprehends the most basic principles of price theory.

TSLRIC or TELRIC pricing creates inefficiencies because it confuses average attributable cost with economic cost. Setting prices for mandatory network access on the basis of irrelevant costs manifests what we have dubbed "the fallacy of forward-looking costs." The forward-looking approach, as put forward by the FCC, departs further from economic costs in several ways. It specifies costs for a type of network expansion that is unlikely to occur. The forward-looking regulatory approach eagerly anticipates the effects of technological change before the market would make those innovations available. The forward-looking approach also ignores investment-backed expectations. Therefore, despite the appealing label, regulated pricing based on the FCC's forward-looking costs approach fails to reflect economic costs and necessarily departs from market pricing.

rarest animal of all," "now extinct," that "had no tail, but a head at each end." HUGH LOFTING, THE STORY OF DR. DOOLITTLE 73 (Bantam Doubleday Dell Publishing Group 1988) (1920). The pushmi-pullyu was very difficult to catch "because, no matter which way you came toward him, he was always facing you." *Id.*

13

Deregulatory Takings and Efficient Capital Markets

THE EXISTENCE of efficient capital markets raises several important questions concerning stranded costs and deregulatory takings. After briefly reviewing the implications of capital market efficiency, we examine whether the regulated firm has already been compensated for stranded costs, when claims of deregulatory takings are ripe for adjudication, whether it truly serves the private interests of competitive entrants to oppose stranded cost recovery by the incumbent regulated firm, and whether a principled argument against stranded cost recovery can be predicated on the political objective of minimizing the size of the regulatory state. Finally, we discuss the securitization of stranded costs.

A Brief Review of the Theory of Efficient Capital Markets

A capital market is said to be "efficient" if the strategy of "buy and hold" cannot be outdone by buying and selling securities on the basis of various sorts of information.[1] The earliest efficient-market studies—all

---

1. *See* Eugene F. Fama, *Efficient Capital Markets: A Review of Theory and Empirical Work*, 25 J. FIN. 383 (1970); Ronald J. Gilson & Reinier H. Kraakman, *The Mechanisms of Market Efficiency*, 70 VA. L. REV. 549, 554–65 (1984). That usage of *efficiency* differs from the word's usage in price theory, where efficiency implies that all resources are allocated to their highest-valued use. The following review of the literature draws upon J. Gregory Sidak & Susan E. Woodward, *Takeover Premiums, Appraisal Rights and the Price Elasticity of a Firm's Publicly Traded Stock*, 25 GA. L. REV. 783 (1991).

empirical analyses of the serial properties of asset prices—examined whether past price and volume information could be used to predict future prices. The first important paper asked whether security prices exhibit zero serial correlation or, alternatively, a random walk.[2] The research, conducted mostly by statisticians, continued in that same vein until the 1950s. The explanation for the observed results was so simple that it defies identification with any one theorist: There is no serial correlation in returns on securities (nor any predictable patterns in prices) because, "If we knew that the price would rise, it would have already risen." If price patterns existed, investors would buy (or sell short) securities to exploit those patterns and continue buying (or selling) until the patterns were no longer present—and consequently until the information, having been fully exploited, was no longer useful.

That early research addressing the question of whether one could beat the market by using price and volume information came to be called the "weak form" of the efficient capital market hypothesis (ECMH). Next came the "semistrong form," which hypothesized that not only were price and volume information useless in devising superior investment strategies, but all publicly available information was useless as well. The story was the same: If we knew that the price would rise (due to some piece of information), it would have already risen. At the same time, researchers began developing a "strong form" hypothesis that addressed the question of whether prices reflect all information, public or not.[3]

Once research shifted to those event-oriented versions of the ECMH, analysts could examine the appropriateness of the assumption of instantaneous reaction of markets to news. The earliest studies of stock splits, earnings announcements, and other price-influencing events showed that many announcements do generate an immediate flurry of trading, often accompanied by an unusually high return variance for a day or two.[4] But neither during nor after that flurry is it possible to predict the future movement of the price contingent on the event. The correct interpretation of evidence on the weak and semistrong versions of the ECMH is not that all securities prices are "right" at all times, but that prices are unbiased

2. LOUIS BACHELIER, THEORY OF SPECULATION (1900), *reprinted in* THE RANDOM CHARACTER OF STOCK MARKET PRICES 17 (Paul Cootner ed., MIT Press 1964).

3. Fama, *supra* note 1, and Gilson & Kraakman, *supra* note 1, survey the literature presenting and supporting the weak, semistrong, and strong forms of the ECMH.

4. *See generally* R. Ball & P. Brown, *An Empirical Evaluation of Accounting Income Numbers*, 6 J. ACCT. RES. 159 (1968); Eugene F. Fama, Lawrence Fisher, Michael C. Jensen & Richard Roll, *The Adjustment of Stock Prices to New Information*, 10 INT'L ECON. REV. 1 (1969).

predictors of future values. Securities on average are priced correctly as present values of the cash flows currently expected to be received on them. Sometimes they may be excessively high or overly low, but mere mortals cannot tell when; the prices are sufficiently accurate in reflecting currently available public information, thus allowing no systematic strategy for predicting which way prices will subsequently move.

Although research supports the hypothesis that securities markets are efficient in the weak and semistrong form, analysis has refuted the strong-form hypothesis. Information that is not publicly available can be used to earn abnormally high returns.[5] The many semistrong-form studies of various sorts of announcements imply forcefully that someone possessing information before its public announcement could earn abnormal returns by buying or shorting before the announcement is made. For example, studies of price movements before tender offers show that prices and volumes both rise, suggesting strongly that information is leaking out and being acted upon. Prices do not necessarily reflect everything insiders know; indeed, securities prices may not reflect any inside information at all or may only partially reflect that information.

That research on the ECMH subsequently led to the formation of efficient portfolio theory and the capital asset pricing model (CAPM). Harry Markowitz's pioneering insight was to exploit the covariances among security returns to identify those portfolios having the maximum expected return for a given risk (variance of return) or the minimum variance for a given expected return.[6] Markowitz called those portfolios "efficient,"[7] but that portfolio theory was not a theory of prices or returns. It was simply an algorithm for computing an optimal portfolio, given estimates of the means, variances, and covariances of returns on individual securities. The CAPM, the natural extension of Markowitz's portfolio theory, posed the following questions: What if everybody follows Markowitz's method for computing an optimal portfolio?[8] What

5. *E.g.*, H. N. Seyhun, *Insider's Profits, Costs of Trading, and Market Efficiency*, 16 J. FIN. ECON. 189, 196–99, 210–11 (1986).

6. Harry Markowitz, *Portfolio Selection*, 7 J. FIN. 77, 79–82 (1952).

7. *Id.* at 82.

8. John Lintner, *The Valuation of Risk Assets and the Selection of Risky Investments in Stock Portfolios and Capital Budgets*, 47 REV. ECON. & STATISTICS 13, 13–15 (1965); William F. Sharpe, *Capital Asset Prices: A Theory of Market Equilibrium Under Conditions of Risk*, 19 J. FIN. 425, 426–27 (1964). A third seminal paper, by Jack Treynor, was not published. *See* RICHARD A. BREALEY & STEWART C. MYERS, PRINCIPLES OF CORPORATE FINANCE 129 n.17 (McGraw-Hill, Inc., 4th ed. 1991). To make the CAPM tractable, it was assumed that everyone in the market has homogeneous

will be the nature of the resulting equilibrium? The CAPM yielded a startling insight: Average return will indeed be related to risk if market participants are risk averse; but only nondiversifiable risk matters. A security that is risky in isolation, but uncorrelated with the market, has nothing but diversifiable risk, and it will earn a return on average no higher than the return on riskless investments. The value of the CAPM lies not in the veracity of the assumptions used to derive it, but rather in its success in helping to explain and understand the pricing of securities. Can investors who are not insiders improve on the strategy of buying and holding a fully diversified portfolio? The voluminous efficient markets literature made possible by the CAPM strongly suggests that they cannot.

HAS THE UTILITY ALREADY BEEN COMPENSATED FOR BEARING THE RISK OF STRANDED COSTS?

Some argue that its allowed cost of capital has already compensated the incumbent regulated firm for the risk that the regulator will breach the regulatory contract before the incumbent has had the opportunity to recover the cost of nonsalvageable assets acquired in detrimental reliance on the continued operation of that regulatory contract. The most articulate proponent of that view, Irwin M. Stelzer, writes:

> Every utility executive has always known, and many have loudly proclaimed, that regulators are fickle, responding to changing fashions, the political winds, and, often at the urging of industry, to changing economic circumstances. Surely, it is not implausible to assume that intelligent investors factored the risk of rule changes into the return they have demanded for exposing their capital to the tender mercies of Huey Long's successors in the regulatory profession (the Kingfish's first elective office was as a utility regulator).[9]

Consequently, Stelzer argues, "it is not at all clear just how far the 'you can't change the rules in mid-investment' argument carries the case that shareholders should not be the ones to bear the costs of the effect of competition on the value of their investments."[10] He continues:

---

beliefs about the means, variances, and covariances of returns.

9. Irwin M. Stelzer, *What Happens When the Rules Are Changed and the Plug Is Pulled on Electric Utilities?*, AM. ENTERPRISE, Nov.–Dec. 1994 at 76, 81 [hereinafter *When the Plug Is Pulled*]; *see also* Irwin M. Stelzer, *A New Era for Public Utilities*, PUB. INTEREST, Fall 1994, at 81.

10. Stelzer, *When the Plug Is Pulled, supra* note 9, at 81.

Is it not equally plausible to argue that investors knew that regulatory rules change, that they made their investments forewarned of that possibility, and that they have in the past been compensated for the risks for such changes? . . . [U]tility shares have often sold at prices that suggest that shareholders anticipated and received earnings well above those that strict regulation might produce. So in the swings and roundabouts of regulation—lean years, fat years—it is arguable that investors have received rewards that have amply compensated them for the risk that rules would be changed.[11]

Elsewhere, Stelzer has argued in effect that the regulatory contract was breached before the restructuring of the 1990s, when "the wave of *ex post* prudence hearings served notice that recoupment of investment was far from certain."[12] Thereafter, he argues, the utility's new investment (other than expenditures mandated by regulators) should be "borne by the shareholders who, it can be argued, by that time had fair warning that all was not well with the regulatory compact."[13]

Stelzer is the intellectual successor to James C. Bonbright, who disputed in his 1961 treatise that "the principles of American rate regulation were so unchanging and so determinate in their measurement of a fair return that all public utility investors could be deemed to have been put on constructive notice of the restrictive character of the regulation prior to their commitment of capital."[14] Bonbright considered rate regulation of public utilities to be neither constant nor determinate: "In the first place, there have occurred important retroactive shifts in the 'rules of the game'—shifts such as that from a 'fair-value' rate base to an 'actual-cost' rate base, or from retirement-expense accounting to accrued-depreciation accounting. And in the second place, the rules themselves, at any given time and in any single jurisdiction, are too

---

11. *Id.* More generalized versions of that argument against compensation on grounds of rational expectations and moral hazard appear in Susan Rose-Ackerman, *Against Ad Hocery: A Comment on Michelman*, 88 COLUM. L. REV. 1697 (1988); Louis Kaplow, *An Economic Analysis of Legal Transitions*, 99 HARV. L. REV. 509 (1986); Lawrence E. Blume & Daniel L. Rubinfeld, *Compensation for Takings: An Economic Analysis*, 72 CAL. L. REV. 569 (1984). For a critical assessment of that theoretical literature, see WILLIAM A. FISCHEL, REGULATORY TAKINGS: LAW, ECONOMICS, AND POLITICS 184–88 (Harvard University Press 1995).

12. Irwin M. Stelzer, *Restructuring the Electric Utility Industry: Further Tentative Thoughts*, ELEC. J., Oct. 1994, at 36, 38.

13. *Id.*

14. JAMES C. BONBRIGHT, PRINCIPLES OF PUBLIC UTILITY RATES 156 (Columbia University Press 1961).

indefinite to predetermine the reasonable expectancies of the purchasers of utility securities except within fairly wide limits."[15]

Though Bonbright thought that American rate regulation was fickle and indeterminate, his prescription was certainly not the abrupt repudiation of the regulatory contract. To the contrary, Bonbright exhorted regulators to rededicate themselves to holding *better* rate cases. "The best prospect of minimizing these frustrating issues" of fairness to investors and consumers, he wrote, "lies in the gradual development of more definite rules, which may become more and more firmly established as their application stands the test of experience."[16] Thus, within a span of three pages Bonbright chided investors for expecting regulators to commit credibly to any particular policy and put his own faith in the "gradual" perfectibility of regulatory rules that "experience" would validate. If Bonbright recognized the contradiction, he gave no explanation. Why, for example, would the same regulatory commissions that had supposedly produced, from roughly 1907 to 1961, the inconstant and indeterminate hodgepodge upon which Bonbright believed no investor should reasonably rely, change their spots and from 1961 onward converge upon regulatory perfection? Bonbright himself must have doubted the plausibility of his own prescription, for he wrote: "Investors in utility securities, notably in common stocks, must therefore take their chances as to the effect of future rate cases, or even of future amendments to regulatory law, on the earning power of the companies in which they invest."[17] Bonbright's view of the future circa 1961 is informative for what it did *not* include. Despite Bonbright's skepticism about what the capital markets conveyed to investors about the risks of rate regulation, one cannot read his 1961 treatise to imply that investors were on notice that regulators might breach the regulatory contract. The thought that regulators would simply abrogate the regulatory contract would have violated Bonbright's expectations of the "gradual" refinement of regulation, of "future rate cases," and of "amendments to regulatory law" as opposed to its outright elimination.

Inferences from Stock Prices

What can stock price fluctuations tell us about deregulatory takings? Establishing causation between regulatory actions and changes in the market value of the firm involves using a sophisticated empirical

15. *Id.*
16. *Id.* at 158.
17. *Id.* at 157.

procedure that financial economists call an "event study." That procedure requires, first, netting out price movements attributable to movements in the stock market as a whole and other industry-specific events
on the relevant trading days and, second, demonstrating that the residual
movement in the share value of the affected companies corresponds to
key regulatory announcements.[18]

It is important to separate the effects of deregulatory announcements
on the returns to regulated capital investment from the effects on the
utility's other lines of business. Many regulated utilities engage in
diverse competitive activities not subject to regulation. Deregulation may
benefit those activities while it penalizes regulated service. Thus, the net
effect of a deregulatory announcement on the market value of the firm
may be ambiguous. For example, a local exchange company may
experience reduced earnings in local exchange services as a result of deregulation. At the same time, deregulation may allow the firm to expand
its already unregulated businesses, such as video or information services.

Some might argue that no deregulatory taking can occur in the absence
of substantial stock price movements, since competitive gains offset losses
on regulated services. That reasoning is incorrect. What must be
determined is the change in the utility's expected earnings from its
regulated assets. The utility's returns to unregulated investment are no
more relevant to that determination than are the returns to the investments
of an unrelated firm operating in some other industry. Moreover, it is
essential to separate the effects of multiple regulatory announcements and
to evaluate the steady release of information through regulatory hearings,
court decisions, filings made by the regulated firm and its adversaries in
litigation, and so forth. Event study methodology builds on efficient
capital market theory to measure the change in firm value in response to
unanticipated events. To measure the magnitude of a regulatory taking
through stock prices, one must be able to link the market's move to
competition to readily identifiable but unanticipated regulatory events
whose abnormal effects on firm value can be measured.

Regulatory Risk Premium

Some might argue that investors need not be compensated if they have
already received a regulatory risk premium. The notion that compensation has already occurred raises three questions. First, was deregula-

---

18. *See* John J. Binder, *Measuring the Effects of Regulation with Stock Price Data*,
16 RAND J. ECON. 167 (1985); G. William Schwert, *Using Financial Data to Measure
Effects of Regulation*, 24 J.L. & ECON. 121 (1981).

tion foreseen when the utility made its irreversible investment in specialized assets? Second, did the wave of prudency disallowances foreshadow deregulation? Third, if deregulation was foreseen, did investors receive from the regulator compensatory rewards through adjustments in the rate of return to compensate for regulatory risk?

The Foreseeability of Deregulation. Whether deregulation was foreseen when the utility made its investment may be difficult to determine. To establish that deregulation was foreseen requires explicit recognition of deregulation in rate hearings and other regulatory proceedings. Often, the record is clear that the public utilities commission has no intention to depart substantially from traditional regulation. Evidence of the commission's continuing fidelity to the regulatory contract would include its continuing enforcement of entry controls, rate regulation, and the utility's obligation to serve. In other cases, the commission has deregulated part of the market under its jurisdiction, such as intraLATA toll in telecommunications. But such a development hardly signals the regulator's imminent abrogation of the regulatory contract, for the commission and the regulated firm may both expect regulation to continue for a large segment of the market, such as the local exchange.

Moreover, as we explain in our discussion of contract modification in chapter 5, the introduction of different forms of regulation, such as price caps or incentive regulation, does not provide conclusive evidence of removal of entry controls, for the commission typically retains all the elements of the regulatory contract while altering only the rate-setting process. For the regulated firm to form a useful prediction that the public utilities commission will breach the regulatory contract and cause stranded costs to arise, regulators and the utility would need to be able to foresee the full extent of deregulation—that is, the elimination of entry barriers into all segments of the utility's franchise markets, including markets for its so-called core customers.

The Improbability That Prudency Disallowances Signaled Deregulation. Contrary to Stelzer's assertion, the wave of prudency disallowances did not foreshadow deregulation. A. Lawrence Kolbe and William B. Tye examined compensation for the regulatory risk associated with cost disallowances.[19] They found an increase in regulatory risk and a worsen-

---

19. *See* A. Lawrence Kolbe & William B. Tye, *It Ain't in There: The Cost of Capital Does Not Compensate for Stranded-Cost Risk*, PUB. UTIL. FORTNIGHTLY, May 15, 1995, at 26.

ing of the regulatory climate for investors, who consequently demanded a higher rate of return to compensate for that heightened risk. Prudency hearings are well within the regulatory contract, but they do not in themselves signal an end to the bargain. Entry controls, rate restrictions, and obligations to serve continue. Indeed, prudency disallowances generally are interpreted as *stricter* regulation—a tightening of controls on the regulated utility, not the loosening of controls that supposedly presages the move to a competitive market. The elimination of entry controls, the corresponding relaxation of pricing restrictions, and the sharing across suppliers of any remaining obligations to serve represent a sea change in the regulatory regime that the regulated firm could not have foreseen by examining past regulatory activities for clues.

Moreover, it is inaccurate to characterize the move to competition as an expansive form of cost disallowance. The opening of the industry to competition certainly will cause write-offs of regulatory assets and capital facilities better adapted to regulation than to competition. After the utility has made investments to comply with prior regulatory obligations, it would be circular reasoning for the regulator then to disallow those costs as imprudently incurred on the ground that they are not suited—"used and useful," in regulatory jargon—to the new environment. Whether particular investments were prudent is a question already resolved in prior adversarial hearings. Whether deregulation effects a taking by breaching the regulatory contract is a different question entirely.

If the utility could not foresee deregulation when it made its long-lived investments, then the utility is entitled to receive its investment-backed expectations. Alternatively, suppose that the utility did foresee deregulation, but only *after* the utility had made its investments. In that case, the regulator can and should compensate the utility for the greater regulatory risk that it now bears. The regulator can modify the regulatory contract in a number of ways to achieve that purpose, including adjusting the firm's rate of return or allowing the firm accelerated depreciation of its regulated assets.

Compensatory Rewards for Foreseeable Regulatory Risk. Even if it had been foreseeable that the public utilities commission would breach the regulatory contract, that fact would not excuse the regulator from its preexisting obligation to allow the utility the opportunity to earn a competitive rate of return and to recover all the capital costs of its regulatory assets. To excuse the regulator in that situation would be analogous in a private contract to allowing the promisor to breach on the ground that the promisee should have known when the contract was formed that the promisor would behave opportunistically. That reasoning is, to put it mildly, circular. It would imply in essence that, at the time the parties entered into their contract, the promisee (the utility) waived its standard contract remedy of expectation damages in the event of breach by the promisor (the public utilities commission) in return for a risk premium's being added to the price under the contract.

How great would that risk premium have to be? The regulator would have to make the utility indifferent ex ante between (1) the regulator's performance of the contract and (2) the situation in which the regulator might breach the contract with some likelihood and the utility has waived its right to damages for its lost expectation. Therefore, the regulator's consideration paid to the utility for waiving its right to expectation damages would have to exceed, by the discounted present value of the utility's expectation damage measure, the price at which the contract otherwise would fully compensate the utility. The price otherwise necessary to compensate the utility would be that which gave it a competitive rate of return on its invested capital and returned that capital by the end of the useful lives of the assets that the utility placed in service with the use of that capital. In other words, the utility would have accepted a risk premium ex ante in lieu of its right to receive expectation damages for breach ex post if and only if the regulator in effect prepaid the discounted present value of that damage remedy. If the regulator had done so, however, it would in effect be conceding the existence of the very regulatory contract that opponents of stranded cost recovery assert does not exist. That is so because the price premium that would result from voluntary bargaining between the regulator and the utility would be the present value of the precise amount that is in dispute in the current debate over stranded costs.

Efficient Risk Bearing for Exogenous and Endogenous Shocks

Regulators set the allowed rate of return to reflect the utility's cost of capital. The rates that the firm is allowed to charge are set such that the firm's expected revenues equal its estimated revenue requirement. The allowed rate of return is generally an average of the costs of debt and equity weighted by the relative proportions of debt and equity, usually measured at book value. That procedure is followed not only under rate-of-return regulation, but also under price-cap regulation because regulatory commissions often set the initial price caps on the basis of the firm's cost of capital. For example, the FCC sets price caps for interstate access rates and cable television services by using cost-of-capital estimates. The cost of debt usually is taken to equal total interest payments per unit of the book value of debt. The estimated cost of equity is derived in a variety of ways, including the discounted-cash-flow method and the earnings-price-ratio method. Estimates of the cost of equity are generally based on regulatory assessment of investor expectations regarding the future performance of the firm and thus depend on future regulatory policies.[20] Alternative approaches based on comparable earnings require the regulator to identify firms with comparable risks. The regulator's pricing policy affects the firm's expected earnings; in turn, earnings affect the firm's cost of capital. The circularity of that process suggests that the regulated firm, the capital market, and regulators take into account the interrelated determination of the cost of capital and regulated prices.

The utility's cost of capital depends on the expected returns of the utility and the riskiness of the stream of returns. Utility earnings are risky owing to two types of risk: *exogenous* shocks, which depend on market uncertainty and other factors beyond the firm's control, and *endogenous* shocks, which are subject to some control, particularly those due to regulatory policies. Exogenous shocks are external effects such as fluctuations in market demand, variations in the costs of labor, equipment, and technology, and environmental factors such as the effects of weather on electric power usage, or the effects of adverse weather conditions on the operation of the utility's facilities. Endogenous shocks are determined by the effect of the regulator's actions on the riskiness of the utility's stream of earnings over time. If regulators pursue predictable policies and if investors do not anticipate fluctuations in earnings caused by disallowances of capital expenditures through prudency reviews, endogenous risk is minimized.

Creating uncertainty due to unexpected shifts in regulatory policies raises the cost of capital to the utility. Those costs must be reflected in future rates because, if the utility expects to attract any further investment, it must compensate investors for the opportunity cost of capital on comparable investments. Therefore, it is inefficient for regulators to create unnecessary uncertainty for the utility's investors. There are few if any benefits from that risk, and the costs can be high. A relatively small likelihood of capital disallowance can entail a correspondingly high

---

20. For additional discussion of this point, see Daniel F. Spulber & Yossef Spiegel, *The Capital Structure of a Regulated Firm*, 25 RAND J. ECON. 424 (1994); Stewart C. Myers, *The Application of Finance Theory to Public Utility Rate Cases*, 3 BELL J. ECON. 58 (1972); Richard H. Pettway, *On the Use of β in Regulatory Proceedings: An Empirical Examination*, 9 BELL J. ECON. 239 (1978).

increase in the allowed rate of return that is required to compensate investors, as Kolbe and Tye have shown.[21] That does not mean that regulators should be denied flexibility of action. Echoing Justice Oliver Wendell Holmes's remark about transaction costs in *Pennsylvania Coal Co. v. Mahon,*[22] Judge Stephen F. Williams has observed: "A judicial requirement of compensation for every adverse change, no matter how slight, would freeze the system."[23] He cautions, however, that "[i]f there were evidence that jurisdictions engaging in de facto but not de jure wealth confiscation pay in full for their self-indulgence, states would presumably take heed."[24]

Presumably, the increase in the allowed rate of return that would have been required to compensate utility investors for the possibility of breach of the regulatory contract would be substantial. There is little evidence that such large-scale increases occurred or were even contemplated by state regulatory commissions. But the point is not simply the magnitude of such increases in the allowed rate of return. The question is whether such increases in the allowed rate of return, passed on to utility customers through rate increases, would be an efficient way to approach prospective deregulation. Regulators would be creating unnecessary risk, which would then require compensating investors for the risks of loss if markets were to be opened to competition. That is not an efficient way to manage the transition to competition. It is less costly for regulators to make deregulatory policies clear and then to compensate investors for diminished expectations, without engaging in a "randomized" strategy. The availability of a less costly alternative makes it unlikely that, as Stelzer suggests, regulators deliberately increased the allowed rate of return to compensate investors for the "risk" of future deregulation.

THE JUSTICIABILITY
OF DIMINISHED EXPECTATIONS

A recurring problem in takings litigation is whether regulation that threatens to impair the value of property has in fact done so. In *Pennell*

---

21. A. Lawrence Kolbe & William B. Tye, *The* Duquesne *Opinion: How Much* "Hope" *Is There for Investors in Regulated Firms?*, 8 YALE J. ON REG. 113 (1991).

22. 260 U.S. 393, 413 (1922) ("Government hardly could go on if to some extent values incident to property could not be diminished without paying for every such change in the general law.").

23. Stephen F. Williams, *Fixing the Rate of Return After* Duquesne, 8 YALE J. ON REG. 159, 162 (1991).

24. *Id.* at 163.

v. *City of San Jose*, for example, the Supreme Court in 1988 considered a rent control ordinance that contained a "tenant hardship" provision, which the city could use to order a lesser annual rent increase than that which otherwise would be permissible.[25] At the time that landlords challenged the hardship provision as a taking, the city had not relied on the provision in any case to order a lower rent for a tenant. Consequently, the Court concluded, no possible taking of property had yet occurred, and the lawsuit was not ripe for adjudication.[26]

The significance of the ripeness rule in *Pennell* to deregulatory takings becomes clearer when one considers that regulatory announcements that may implicate takings can reduce the value of publicly traded companies by billions of dollars in a single day. For example, the April 1994 announcement by the California Public Utilities Commission that it would begin proceedings leading to the introduction of retail wheeling of electricity caused Pacific Gas & Electric, SCEcorp., and San Diego Gas & Electric to lose $4.4 billion in equity value, or roughly 20 percent, virtually overnight.[27] Note that, in contrast to our discussion of cost disallowance decisions by the PUCs, the CPUC's announcement on retail wheeling was a formal notice to all utilities subject to that regulator's jurisdiction (and, hence, their investors) that the regulator might unilaterally seek to rewrite material terms of the regulatory contract.

The Court's reasoning in *Pennell* ignores that an efficient market values an asset today on the basis of the expectation of the discounted net profit that the asset will generate in the future. Therefore, for purposes of reducing the value of property today, it is does not matter whether or not a provision in a statute that might some day give rise to a taking has in fact been relied upon to effect such a taking. The market anticipates the cost associated with the taking (should it occur), assigns the best estimate today of the probability that such a taking will actually occur in the future, discounts the (lower) net profit to its present value, and lowers the current market value of the asset accordingly. The result is that the owner of the property experiences *today* a diminution in the value of property subject to the statute. It follows, consequently, that as a legal matter it is fallacious to reason, as the Court in *Pennell* did, that the property owner has not yet suffered a harm giving rise to a justiciable controversy within the meaning of Article III of the Constitution.

25. 485 U.S. 1 (1988).

26. *See generally* Gregory M. Stein, *Regulatory Takings and Ripeness in the Federal Courts*, 48 VAND. L. REV. 1 (1995).

27. Benjamin A. Holden, *California's Struggle Shows How Hard It Is to Deregulate Utilities*, WALL ST. J., Nov. 28, 1995, at A1.

Indeed, the alternative approach—to wait until the statute is actually applied and has diminished property values—is deceptive. In the interim, other circumstances may have changed as well and thus may confound the process of isolating the diminution in market value attributable solely to the statute. Assessing the diminution in property value at the time that the statute is enacted reduces that problem of eliminating "noise" in the price fluctuations of the asset subject to the regulation. In addition, contemporaneous assessment has the advantage of being an evaluation made ex ante: both the property owner and the state remain shrouded in the Rawlsian veil of ignorance concerning the eventual effect on individual property owners in individual cases. By securing contemporaneous assessment, the property owner runs the risk that the market has underestimated the loss that he will actually suffer under the regulation; conversely, the state runs the risk that the market has exaggerated that loss.

But there is no reason to believe that the market is consistently biased in either the property owner's or the state's favor. The market price today reflects the consensus of best estimates and conjectures *held today* of the asset's future stream of net profits. Like any estimation process, the market price will yield deviations of the actual outcome from the predicted outcome. But errors of overestimation will cancel out errors of underestimation, so that the market price today is, on average and in aggregate, an unbiased predictor at that moment of the future stream of net profits to be earned by the asset.

As we already noted, the market price of the firm's shares depends on endogenous factors, such as regulatory policy and judicial decisions. The net revenue impact of regulatory decisions therefore requires independent estimation on the basis of projections of consumer demand, incumbent sales, the incumbent's costs, and other market factors. Such economic projections, although inexact, constitute a standard feature of the regulatory process.

Is Competitor Opposition to Recovery of Stranded Costs Farsighted or Myopic?

Typically, competitive entrants oppose a policy of stranded cost recovery. Those companies believe that stranded cost recovery would not be in their interests, evidently on the assumption that they would have a price advantage over the incumbent with high stranded costs. That assessment, however, is arguably myopic for two reasons.

First, suppose that the regulator denies an incumbent firm having low long-run incremental costs but high stranded costs the opportunity to recover those stranded costs. In the most dire scenario, the incumbent goes bankrupt, and its shareholders are wiped out. But the firm's physical assets do not evaporate. Instead, those assets emerge from either liquidation or reorganization without the burden of recovering the stranded costs any longer. The assets still have the same long-run incremental cost.

Stated differently, while the regulator's decision whether or not to allow recovery of stranded costs will affect future decisions to invest in long-lived assets, it will not affect the efficiency of existing assets for providing local telephony or generating electricity. In that respect, the entrant reaps no competitive advantage by having the incumbent regulated firm denied recovery of its stranded costs. Under the market-determined efficient component-pricing rule and a competitively neutral end-user charge, the recovery of stranded costs would not impede the ability of the access charge to reward the entrant whenever it is more efficient than the utility in assembling the retail product sold to consumers.[28]

Second, the entrant opposed to stranded cost recovery may ignore that the consequences of the regulator's not allowing the incumbent to recover stranded costs would be to raise the cost of capital for *all* firms in the market, including entrants that do not have stranded costs. The reason why that is so is that, while stranded costs are sunk costs that cannot be undone, recovery of such costs *is* a policy decision that regulators have the power to make going forward into the future. Consequently, asset values and economic decisions will be affected by the regulator's prospective decision to honor the regulatory contract in the sense of permitting the incumbent the opportunity to recover its stranded costs. If the regulator does not allow such recovery, then the capital markets will recognize that transaction-specific investments being made today and in the future will be subject to a similar risk of regulatory expropriation, regardless of the current representations of the regulators.

That risk will not fall exclusively on the incumbent regulated firm saddled with stranded costs from the past. Rather, such risk will fall on *all* firms subject to that regulator's jurisdiction. In that respect, entrants that argue against stranded cost recovery are, paradoxically, arguing for a regulatory policy that would raise their own cost of capital.

Perhaps, however, such firms intend to enter the market by using production technologies that entail a lesser degree of asset specificity

---

28. *See* WILLIAM J. BAUMOL & J. GREGORY SIDAK, TRANSMISSION PRICING AND STRANDED COSTS IN THE ELECTRIC POWER INDUSTRY 144–47 (AEI Press 1995).

than that reflected in the incumbent's production technology. Examples would include entry into the local loop through wireless technology or through the purchase of resale capacity from the incumbent LEC. An entrant with low asset specificity may believe that it can avoid the higher capital cost necessitated by regulatory opportunism, since its lower proportion of specialized investment implies a lower proportion of total firm value subject to expropriation. Further, such entrants may expect *never* to be subject to regulation by the same regulator. Rather, they may expect to be able to exploit asymmetry in the regulatory burden and in the degree of asset specificity required for entry. Even if the entrant can succeed in that strategy, it will at a minimum bear the cost of persuading the capital markets that the risk of regulatory opportunism should not be imputed to its cost of debt and equity. In that sense, the entrant still bears some implicit cost as a result of regulatory opportunism. The empirical magnitude of that cost is unclear.

THE ANARCHIC ARGUMENT
AGAINST COMPENSATION

One argument against stranded cost recovery is notable for its sophistication and cynicism. A prominent libertarian economist has argued to us that, even if one can show that a regulatory contract exists between the state and the regulated firm, takings jurisprudence should not require the state to compensate the firm for its stranded costs.[29] As faithfully and objectively as we can, we summarize the person's argument as follows:

> The so-called regulatory contract has harmed the consumers it was intended to benefit. The sooner the state replaces regulation with competition, the better for consumer welfare. The state, however, will be forced to postpone or forgo achieving all the benefits of competition in the regulated network industries if it must compensate public utilities for investments in facilities rendered obsolete by competition. It makes no difference that regulators mandated those investments or approved them as prudent, for those regulatory mandates and prudency reviews merely exemplify the extent to which the old regulatory regime deviated from efficient resource allocation. The only possible reason to compensate incumbent public utilities for their stranded costs is to buy their cooperation so that they do not block policies to open electric power and local telephony markets to competition. Moreover, if the state did not

---

29. To our knowledge, this person has not publicly expressed his views in print. For that reason, we do not identify him.

allow recovery of stranded costs, private parties would doubt that the state would abide by any future regulatory contract into which it might seek to enter. That would be a good result. Those private parties would be less inclined to engage in rent-seeking activities because they could not be sure that the state would stand behind its representation to use its regulatory powers to protect monopoly rents from competition. Relative to the status quo, private parties entering into any new relationship with the regulator would face a higher cost of capital for investments made in reliance on the regulator's assurances that it would protect a market from competitive entry. That result would be desirable because it would reduce reliance on the state and discourage rent seeking.

The foregoing argument is literally anarchic in that it seeks to impair the government's ability to substitute its regulatory policies for the voluntary association of private individuals and institutions. However much one may value individual liberty and prefer the private rather than public ordering of economic activity, the argument is misguided for five reasons.

First, it is a utopian argument in which the ends justify the means. In this case, the ends are the creation of competitive markets for electricity and local telephony, which will increase consumer welfare relative to the current regulatory regime. No one can quibble with those ends, but the means to achieving them are breach of contract, destruction of investment, and expropriation of wealth. The argument does not seek to comply with neutral principles of law, nor does it respect the historical evidence that the current regime arose from explicit voluntary exchange. The argument relies on economic analysis only in the narrow sense that such analysis can be used to predict the disincentives to bargaining with the state that repudiation of the regulatory contract would produce.[30] In those respects, the argument is not fundamentally different from more ignominious utopian arguments, situated elsewhere on the political spectrum, that sacrificed the sanctity of property and the rule of law for a vision of the greater good of society.

Second, because the argument is predicated on the state's making a Pareto-superior policy move without bothering to compensate losers from the gains enjoyed by winners, it embodies all the problems of the Kaldor-Hicks standard of potential Pareto superiority that we criticized in chapter 6 in our analysis of the law of regulatory takings. It is ironic that the call

---

30. The argument is similar, for example, to the argument that the best way to restrain the growth of the federal government is for it to repudiate some amount of its debt: A government that acted opportunistically with respect to its creditors would thereafter face a higher cost of borrowing, which would limit its ability to finance expenditures with debt.

for repudiating the regulatory contract and ignoring its takings implications should come from market liberals who have staunchly defended the rights of property owners to compensation for regulatory takings.

Third, for all of its intricacy, the argument naïvely assumes that the need for regulation can be extinguished entirely. To put the matter in economic terms, the argument assumes that the regulatory game is over, that there will be no more repeated play between the regulator and the regulated firm. The experience of deregulation, however, suggests that the just the opposite will happen: Regulation tends to persist in some residual form, even in markets that supposedly have undergone the transition to competition.

Fourth, if some form of residual regulation remains, private parties will need to be able to trust the regulator's representations. If they cannot, private parties will eschew investments in the specialized assets so often found in network industries. Instead, incentives will exist to channel private investment into production technologies that have low degrees of asset specificity, a result that may not lead to the lowest cost of production. An anarchic desire to destroy the power of the regulatory state to make credible commitments may therefore have serious unintended consequences for consumer welfare.

Fifth, the argument ultimately is a complaint about the failure of democratic institutions. The regulators who entered into the regulatory contract with public utilities were appointed by democratically elected governors or were directly elected by the voters themselves. The state legislatures exercised regular oversight of the public utilities commissions, if not also periodic oversight through the process of confirming commissioners for the PUCs. State supreme courts, occupied by justices similarly appointed by democratically elected governors, reviewed the major policies of the state PUCs. Perhaps one may justly criticize public utility regulation as a defective product of those various democratic processes. But if democratic processes have produced a defective product that harms consumers, it is hardly fair or efficient that the costs of that political failure be placed on the firms that bargained at arm's length with the state and thereafter made irreversible investments in detrimental reliance on the state's representations.

RESTORING CREDIBLE COMMITMENTS THROUGH THE SECURITIZATION OF STRANDED COSTS

Chapter 9 shows that the recovery of stranded costs requires a competitively neutral and nonbypassable end-user charge, even if the regulator permits the incumbent utility to employ M-ECPR pricing. One would expect the specific design of the end-user charge to differ from one jurisdiction to the next, just as the specific design of incentive regulation already does. But one development from the restructuring of the electricity industry in Pennsylvania—the issuance of *transition bonds*—may emerge as a dominant feature in the overall design of such cost recovery programs. Perhaps because of the novelty of the Pennsylvania approach, state public utilities commissions and the FCC seem not to have considered the relevance of transition bonds to resolving the disputes over cost recovery that have arisen under the pricing provisions of the Telecommunications Act of 1996.

Under the transition bond approach, the electric utility establishes in a regulatory proceeding the extent of its recoverable stranded costs, given the pricing regime that regulators have imposed for mandatory unbundled access to the firm's network. Under Pennsylvania's Electricity Generation and Customer Choice and Competition Act of 1996,[31] that amount of recoverable costs becomes *intangible transition property*.[32] The regulator then authorizes the utility to securitize those stranded costs and issues, on a expedited basis, via a qualified rate order permitting the utility to service the resulting bonds through a new *intangible transition charge* that the utility will impose on end users in a competitively neutral and nonbypassable manner.[33] The regulator designs the intangible transition charge to expire as the transition bonds mature. Intangible transition property represents "the irrevocable right of the electric utility or an assignee to receive through intangible transition charges amounts sufficient to recover all its qualified transition expenses."[34]

31. 1996 PA. LAWS 138 (codified at 66 PA. CONS. STAT. § 2801 *et seq.*).

32. 66 PA. CONS. STAT. § 2812(c).

33. *Id.* The Pennsylvania legislation defines intangible transition charges as "[t]he amounts authorized to be imposed on all customer bills and collected, through a non-bypassable mechanism by the electric utility or its successor or by any other entity which provides electric service to a person that was a customer of an electric utility located within the certificated territory of the electric utility on the effective date of this chapter or that, after this effective date of this chapter, became a customer of electric services within such territory, and is still located within such territory, to recover qualified transition expenses pursuant to a qualified rate order." *Id.* § 2812(g). The statutory definition includes the following proviso concerning cross-subsidies: "The amounts shall be allocated to customer classes in a manner that does not shift inter-class or intra-class costs and maintains consistency with the allocation methodology for utility production plant accepted by the commission in the electric utility's most recent base rate proceeding." *Id.*

34. *Id.*

What do the creation of intangible transition property and the issuance of the transition bonds accomplish that the regulator could not accomplish simply by authorizing the utility to impose a (correctly calculated) end-user charge and to use the proceeds to recoup its stranded costs over time? The answer relates to the ability of government to make credible commitments, which chapter 4 shows was critical to eliciting the private investment in nonsalvageable infrastructure that was the raison d'être of the regulatory contract a century ago. The proceeds from the bond issuance would enable the incumbent utility to recoup its stranded costs immediately. The utility would use the bonds to shift the risk of stranded cost recovery from current shareholders to a new class of consenting bondholders, whose recourse relative to other creditors would presumably be limited to the stream of revenues that the intangible transition charge would produce. The incumbent utility could no longer oppose immediate competitive entry on grounds of cost recovery. But how could the new holders of transition bonds be confident that the regulator would not destroy the value of those bonds by reneging on the intangible-transition-charge rate order—all in the name of lowering the consumer's total bill for electricity? What would prevent the regulator from simply substituting his repudiation of the intangible transition charge for his repudiation of the underlying regulatory contract?

Under the Pennsylvania plan, the commonwealth does not guaranty the transition bonds. Nonetheless, the capital markets would provide, through the price that it set for those marketable securities, a continuous estimate of the likelihood that the state would renege on its promise embodied in the rate order authorizing the securitization and the intangible transition charge. Moreover, services such as Moody's and Standard & Poor's would continuously rate the risk that the state would interfere with the sole revenue stream servicing the transition bonds. Through bond prices and bond ratings, the capital markets would quantify the expectation of regulatory opportunism on a state-by-state basis, much in the way that the premiums for political risk insurance vary from one country to the next. The issuance of transition bonds would create a security for which the principal risk would be relatively free from "noise" and causal ambiguity. Risk would not arise from competitors or from exogenous changes in technology or market demand, but rather from regulatory opportunism. Transition bonds, in short, would enable the capital markets to regulate the regulators.

Given the capital markets' intense level of scrutiny, regulatory opportunism by the state commission or the Commonwealth of Pennsylvania would incur an immediate, conspicuous cost to reputation that would be continuously measurable through the price of the transition bonds. Not surprisingly, therefore, the Pennsylvania legislation contains the following promise that the commonwealth will refrain from regulatory opportunism:

> The Commonwealth pledges to and agrees with the holders of any transition bonds issued under this section and with any assignee or financing party who may enter into contracts with an electric utility under this section that the Commonwealth will not limit, or alter or in any way impair or reduce the value of intangible transition property or intangible transition charges approved by a qualified rate order until the transition bonds and interest on the transition bonds are fully paid and discharged or the contracts are fully performed on the part of the electric utility. Subject to other requirements of law, nothing in this paragraph shall preclude limitation or alteration if adequate compensation is made by law for the full protection of the intangible transition charges collected pursuant to a qualified rate order and of the holder of this transition bond and any assignee or financing party entering into contract with the electric utility.[35]

The interpretation and enforceability of *that* regulatory promise would surely admit less gainsaying by lawyers than the regulatory contract's earlier promise to the utility that the regulator would permit the firm a reasonable opportunity to recover it costs and earn a competitive return on such costs. In short, Pennsylvania's novation of the regulatory contract, backed by the discipline of the capital markets, would increase the likelihood of preserving the original investment-backed expectations of utility shareholders.

CONCLUSION

The existence of efficient capital markets adds a layer of complexity to the question of compensation for a deregulatory taking or breach of the regulatory contract. In this chapter we have argued that it is improbable that stock price adjustments have already implicitly compensated the

---

35. *Id.* § 2812(c)(2). In addition, the legislation gives the state commission greater power to commit itself credibly to the recovery of stranded costs: "Notwithstanding any other provision of law, the Commission has the power to specify that all or a portion of a qualified rate order shall be irrevocable. To the extent so specified, neither the order nor the intangible transition charges authorized to be imposed and collected under the order shall be subject to reduction, postponement, impairment or termination by any subsequent action of the Commission. Nothing in this paragraph is intended to supersede the right of any party to judicial review of the qualified rate order." *Id.* § 2812(b)(4).

shareholders of regulated firms for the risk that changes in regulatory policy would prevent the firm's recovery of its full economic costs of providing service. The signals that regulators gave capital markets before the Telecommunications Act of 1996 and before the current effort to restructure the electric power industry did not include a clear message that the government would repudiate its preexisting obligations under the regulatory contract so as to thwart the incumbent firm's ability to recover the costs of its investments to provide service. Once such a message becomes clear, however, a court need not wait until the competitive transformation of the industry is complete to estimate the loss to shareholders of the regulated firm and to order that the government pay them just compensation for the confiscation of their private property. In an efficient capital market, there is no merit after that moment to the argument that the takings claim of a publicly traded utility is not yet ripe for adjudication. Finally, there is some hope that the issuance of transition bonds that securitize stranded costs will harness the considerable monitoring power of the capital markets to reduce the problem of regulatory opportunism.

14

Limiting Principles for
Stranded Cost Recovery

THE PRECEDING CHAPTERS define deregulatory takings and demonstrate the equivalence that exists between damages for breach of the regulatory contract, just compensation for a taking of property, changes in investor expectations, and (under certain conditions concerning the stand-alone cost of substitute technologies) the efficient pricing of network access. Such an analysis would not be complete without specifying the limits on stranded cost recovery. What conditions are *sufficient* for a regulatory action to constitute a deregulatory taking? What conditions are *necessary* for a deregulatory taking? The answers to those questions will give regulators, legislators, and judges guidance as to whether eliminating taxicab medallions, agricultural production quotas, or occupational licensure, to take three common examples, would engender compensable stranded costs. The answers also will clarify whether stranded costs are more likely to arise in one regulated network industry (such as electricity) than in another (such as local exchange telephony). We emphasize at the outset that the questions addressed in this chapter are subtle on both legal and economic grounds, and they will likely acquire greater complexity as the restructuring of network industries continues to unfold. As with any question of first impression, the delineation of limiting principles for stranded cost recovery will be an iterative process that will likely take a number of years to achieve convergence. Our analysis in this chapter is therefore not the final word, but only the beginning of what we are confident will be an extended undertaking.

NECESSARY AND SUFFICIENT CONDITIONS
FOR THE RECOVERY OF STRANDED COSTS

Four conditions appear to be both necessary and sufficient to establish a deregulatory taking: (1) the existence of a regulatory contract; (2) evidence of investment-backed expectations; (3) the elimination of regulatory entry barriers; and (4) a decline in the regulated firm's expected revenues. Our discussion in the preceding chapters establishes that those conditions are sufficient for recovery of stranded investment. We now show that those conditions are also necessary to support a claim, under contract principles or takings jurisprudence, for recovery of stranded investment. The absence of any one condition implies that a firm's claim that it has suffered a deregulatory taking should fail.

The Existence of a Regulatory Contract

The existence of a regulatory contract is a necessary condition for the recovery of stranded investment. There must have been a clear understanding of the terms and conditions of regulation with respect to entry controls, rate regulation, and service obligations. If any of those three essential components is absent, a regulatory contract has not been formed, and a deregulatory taking could not have occurred.

Consider the first element of the regulatory contract. If a market has no regulatory entry controls, then increased competition in the market cannot be attributed to changes in regulatory policy concerning entry. Steel producers and agribusinesses, for example, may benefit from barriers to entry taking the form of import controls. But those firms have not entered into any regulatory contract with the state to assume public service obligations and to submit to rate regulation in exchange for the imposition of those entry barriers. Consequently, those firms could not make claims of deregulatory takings on the government if it were to remove those barriers and allow increased freedom of trade.

Regulation of maximum rates is the second essential aspect of the regulatory contract. It is closely associated with the regulator's responsibility to allow the utility's investors a reasonable opportunity to earn a competitive rate of return. If rate regulation is absent, then no deregulatory taking can arise because it is unlikely that private parties entered into any regulatory contract with the government.

The obligation to serve is the third component necessary to the formation of the regulatory contract. It follows that no deregulatory taking can occur if service obligations are absent. Such obligations must exist because stranded investment is the utility's cost of facilities and other expenditures made to perform its obligation to serve. The obligation to serve (through common carrier, universal service, or carrier-of-last-resort rules) generally does not exist in isolation from entry and rate controls.

Some statutory entitlements to welfare benefits and the like do constitute property for purposes of due process.[1] But, if it is withdrawn by the government, such a benefit concerning economic activity should not support a claim of deregulatory taking unless the statute was part of a voluntary exchange between the state and the regulated firm. The potential for ambiguity and dispute under any lesser standard is suggested by Justice Potter Stewart's remark in *Board of Regents* v. *Roth* that, to have a property interest in a statutory entitlement, a person's claim to it must rest not on a mere "unilateral expectation" but on "a legitimate claim of entitlement to it" that reflects the goal of property law "to protect those claims upon which people rely in their daily lives, reliance that must not be arbitrarily undermined."[2]

Relative to Justice Stewart's inquiry, our requirement that a regulatory contract exist is more demanding and less ambiguous. Our criterion avoids inquiry into the reasonableness or legitimacy of unilateral expectations; instead, it focuses on the existence of demonstrable evidence of a voluntary exchange between the state and a private firm to produce services that benefit consumers, on whose behalf the state has negotiated as agent. The formality of the regulatory process—with notice, written comments, and hearings on the record—provides the mechanism for verifying the mutuality of voluntary exchange and a meeting of the minds. The past decisions and method of operation of the regulatory agency, and the legal framework within which the regulatory agency operates, are essential aspects of the regulatory contract that must be identified before a deregulatory taking can be established.[3]

1. Goldberg v. Kelly, 397 U.S. 254, 262 (1970) (welfare payments); Wheeler v. Montgomery, 397 U.S. 280 (1970) (old-age benefits); Fusari v. Steinberg, 419 U.S. 379 (1975) (unemployment benefits); Goss v. Lopez, 419 U.S. 565, 574 (1975) (public education); Mathews v. Eldridge, 424 U.S. 319, 332 (1976) (social security disability benefits); Bishop v. Wood, 426 U.S. 341, 344 (1976) (tenured public employment).

2. 408 U.S. 564, 577 (1972).

3. By emphasizing the existence of a regulatory contract, we do not mean to imply that stranded costs could not be recovered under an equitable theory of promissory estoppel in the absence of a showing that the regulator and the utility had formed a contract. We would expect that many utilities would be able to prove to a court that they had enforceable regulatory contracts. Moreover, we would expect as a practical matter that the evidentiary

Investment-Backed Expectations

Investment-backed expectations are the second of the four necessary preconditions for a deregulatory taking. If a firm simply produces a regulated service and can recover all its economic costs as they are incurred, then the firm cannot suffer a deregulatory taking if the state removes entry controls. The foundation for compensation for stranded costs is the regulated firm's substantial *irreversible* investment in facilities to discharge its regulatory obligation to serve. In the language of contract law, the grounds for compensating stranded costs are detrimental reliance, as manifested in the firm's irreversible investment to perform the contract. Without such objectively verifiable reliance on the part of the regulated firm, there can be no deregulatory taking.

Here we have the basis for distinguishing open-access regulation in network industries from, say, the abolition of entry controls for taxicabs in New York City. One might plausibly argue that taxi companies entered into a regulatory contract with the city: They received entry regulation in return for submitting to rate regulation and the public service obligation to carry any passenger to any neighborhood in New York, no matter how rough it might be. Even so, taxicabs currently bearing medallions in New York are not *irreversible* investments. To the contrary, they are inherently mobile assets that can be redeployed for the same use in another city or for a different use in New York. Moreover, a fleet of taxicabs is divisible; it does not have the "lumpiness" of an integrated network for the provision of electricity or local telephony. To only a slightly lesser extent the same points regarding reversibility of investment are true of the garage and radio communications investments of the taxicab company. (Indeed, some entrepreneurs have become rich redeploying the specialized mobile radio frequencies used for the dispatching of taxicabs to higher-valued forms of digital mobile communications.[4]) In short, one can reach either of two conclusions that have essentially the same economic and legal significance: (1) taxicab regulation in New York City is not a regulatory contract because it does

---

showing necessary for a utility to prove the existence of a regulatory contract would not be substantially more demanding than the showing necessary to establish the utility's right to compensation under the doctrine of promissory estoppel.

4. *See, e.g.*, Richard Ringer, *Nextel Is Set for Wireless U.S. Network*, N.Y. TIMES, Aug. 6, 1994, at 33; Leslie Helm, *Fleet Thinking Helps Tiny Nextel Make Big Waves; Telecommunications: The Maker of Low-Tech Radio Dispatch Equipment Aims to Create a National System to Rival Cellular's*, L.A. TIMES, Dec. 5, 1993, at D1.

not induce investment that is irreversible and transaction-specific or (2) such regulation does establish a regulatory contract, but one that can give rise to only negligible stranded costs because the firm's capital can be so thoroughly and immediately redeployed in alternative uses. The degree of asset specificity is low; hence the firm's opportunity to mitigate stranded costs is great. If one prefers the second interpretation, it is important not to succumb to the incorrect argument that, so too, the transmission and distribution network of an electric utility or the loops and switches of a local exchange carrier are thoroughly and immediately redeployed when used on an unbundled or wholesale basis by a competitor. The grant of substantially more taxi medallions by New York City, like the award by the Federal Communications Commission of substantially more spectrum licenses, dissipates the rents that existing holders of medallions or licenses can earn. But such expansion of supply by government fiat is not the same as mandatory unbundling. The award of more medallions does not compel Yellow Cab to make its taxicabs available to Checker Cab at wholesale rates. The elimination of government restrictions on capacity is not the same as the government's order that existing capacity be made available to the incumbent's competitors for use as an input in the supply of an end product.

Thus, a related aspect of investment-backed expectations is that the regulated capital of the incumbent firm not be rededicated to a public purpose other than the one to which shareholders originally intended. If the regulator or legislature has redefined the public purpose to which the incumbent firm's private property shall be dedicated, then the Supreme Court's decision in *Northern Pacific Railway Co.* v. *North Dakota* requires that compensation be paid to the firm for any diminution in its ability to recover the costs of, and return on, its invested capital.[5] Put differently, the government cannot erase the investment-backed expectations of a regulated firm's shareholders by redefining the public purpose to which they dedicated their capital.

Although investment-backed expectations provide the standard for objectively verifying the need for stranded cost recovery, that criterion does not imply that the calculation of compensation should be based on an appraisal of the assets in the deregulated environment. As chapter 5 shows, the correct basis for compensation for breach of the regulatory contract is the change in the firm's expected net earnings from its *regulated* assets.

5. 236 U.S. 585 (1915).

Elimination of Regulatory
Barriers to Entry

By definition, deregulation that eliminates regulatory entry barriers is a third necessary condition for a deregulatory taking. The regulatory authority must have taken some action that removes regulatory control of entry into the utility's franchise territory in such a way that eliminates revenue protections for the firm. The utility then faces increased competition as a result of either the removal of regulatory entry constraints or the regulator's issuance of certificates of public convenience and necessity to other firms so that they can enter the market.

In contrast, removing other types of regulatory restrictions on utilities, such as relaxation of constraints on pricing flexibility or elimination of service obligations, does *not* suggest the need for cost recovery. Such actions do not diminish the earnings of the incumbent utility. To the contrary, they are likely to enhance the utility's earnings. Thus, although such constraints are part of the regulatory contract, they are not the *benefits* of the bargain from the perspective of the regulated firm. Rather, they are burdens that the regulated firm would gladly avoid. Consequently, no compensation is required when the regulator removes them.

Furthermore, most types of deregulation cannot form any part of the basis of a taking under the theory that we have developed in the preceding chapters. For example, the removal or relaxation of environmental regulations, or changes in rules concerning product or workplace health and safety, are exercises of the police power that would not seem to provide grounds for a deregulatory taking action, even if a company had relied on those rules' remaining in place when it invested in equipment to comply with the rules.

Decline in Expected Revenues

The fourth and final necessary condition for a company to recover stranded costs is that its expected revenues must decline when deregulation opens the market to competition: The change in expected revenues net of mitigation, which we have denoted as Δ^* in the previous chapters, must be positive. If instead the company, using formerly regulated assets, experiences gains under competition that offset losses in regulated services, then there is no basis for recovery. That result would include any deregulatory "givings" of the sort that chapter 7 discusses.

One must carefully scrutinize the offsetting gains to the firm that purportedly flow from deregulation, however. The company's earnings from investments that were never treated as part of the regulatory rate base should not be considered to have mitigated its stranded costs. Regulatory authorities may be tempted to identify the company's profits from its unregulated activities as a potential source of stranded cost recovery. The reason advanced for such an action is that the formerly regulated company benefits from new competitive opportunities in the market due to deregulation. Such reasoning is flawed, however, because the company's benefits from the newly deregulated market are by no means a "gift" conferred on it by the regulatory commission, even if the company is allowed to enter the market by removal of a regulatory quarantine. Instead, a company's earnings in deregulated markets are simply a return of, and on, the capital invested in those markets. Such investments are not included in the rate base; in regulatory parlance, they are "below the line." The company assumes all the risk of loss on such investments in competitive markets and consequently is entitled to the full returns earned from those investments. For the regulator to appropriate the returns to such investment to pay for the recovery of stranded costs or to subsidize continuing regulatory obligations would itself constitute a taking. The capital invested in unregulated markets is private property that the firm has never dedicated to *any* public purpose. To count the return of, and on, such capital toward the recovery of stranded costs would be tantamount to the regulator's conscripting private property for dedication to a public purpose to which the owners of the property never consented.

As a general proposition, deregulation that primarily involves the lifting of price controls, such as housing rent control or natural gas field prices, does not create a deregulatory taking. After such deregulation, companies can adjust prices in response to market competition, and prices more closely reflect supply and demand conditions. Even if the ultimate result of competition is falling prices, as occurred in natural gas, the reductions in revenues should not be interpreted as a taking.

REGULATORY CONTRACTS, STATUTORY GRATUITIES, AND STATE-MANAGED CARTELS

The regulatory contract is a bargained-for exchange between the state and individual firms that is intended to benefit consumers. That relationship between the private firm and the state differs fundamentally from the relationship that frequently exists when, as in the notorious case of the California raisin cartel given state-action immunity from the federal antitrust laws in *Parker* v. *Brown*,[6] the state or federal government confers a statutory gratuity on a firm or permits (or even encourages) the government's use of its regulatory prerogatives to cartelize an industry and shield private firms from the antitrust liability that would otherwise arise from such horizontal coordination on decisions concerning pricing and output.[7] Far from benefiting consumers, a state-managed cartel of that sort harms them. In 1991 the Supreme Court was asked to lift antitrust immunity to state-managed restraints of trade in cases in which the state action creating those restraints resulted from a conspiracy against consumers or competitors into which public officials and private actors had entered. Justice Antonin Scalia, writing for the Court, refused to extend the antitrust laws to reach such conduct:

> Few governmental actions are immune from the charge that they are "not in the public interest" or in some sense "corrupt." The California marketing scheme at issue in *Parker* itself, for example, can readily be viewed as the result of a "conspiracy" to put the "private" interest of the State's raisin growers above the "public" interest of the State's consumers. The fact is that virtually all regulation benefits some segments of the society and harms others; and that it is not universally considered contrary to the public good if the net economic loss to the losers exceeds the net economic gain to the winners.[8]

If the state faces no obligation under federal antitrust law to compensate losers when it restrains trade and reduces consumer welfare for the purpose of transferring wealth to a favored constituency, then surely the state need not compensate winners when it subsequently reverses course and terminates their previously granted statutory gratuity or state-managed cartel. To be sure, the private firms that benefited from the prior state of affairs will have lost an economic expectation. That expectation may have even led to some measure of irreversible investment. The

---

6. 317 U.S. 341 (1943).

7. *E.g.*, Bates *v.* State Bar of Ariz., 433 U.S. 350 (1977); California Retail Liquor Dealers Ass'n *v.* Midcal Aluminum, Inc., 445 U.S. 97 (1980); Hoover *v.* Ronwin, 466 U.S. 558 (1984); Southern Motor Carriers Rate Conf. *v.* United States, 471 U.S. 48 (1985); 324 Liquor Corp. *v.* Duffy, 479 U.S. 335 (1987); City of Columbia *v.* Omni Outdoor Advertising, Inc., 499 U.S. 365 (1991); FTC *v.* Ticor Title Ins. Co., 504 U.S. 621 (1992). Similarly, the antitrust laws do not constrain the sincere attempts of private actors to petition government to crush their competitors. Eastern R.R. Presidents Conf. *v.* Noerr Motor Freight, Inc., 365 U.S. 127 (1961); United Mine Workers *v.* Pennington, 381 U.S. 657 (1965).

8. City of Columbia *v.* Omni Outdoor Advertising, Inc., 499 U.S. 365, 377 (1991).

grapevines that bore the cartelized raisins in *Parker* v. *Brown* obviously could not be moved and would have had value in a competitive market only to the extent that the market price of grapes or raisins exceeded the incremental cost of production. It bears emphasis, however, that the expectation held by members of a state-managed cartel is entirely different from the expectation of a regulated utility, which is rooted in the law of contract and property and predicated on the recovery of the cost of transaction-specific investment made to discharge a public purpose. Thus, the state's decision to terminate or interfere with the expectation of a formerly state-sanctioned cartel, even an *investment-backed* expectation, would not support a claim for breach of a regulatory contract or for a deregulatory taking. That distinction helps to clarify the meaning of the four limiting principles for stranded cost recovery, and it will help to reconcile our theory of stranded cost recovery with the actual outcomes in other industries that have experienced deregulation.

"No person," wrote Justice Mahlon Pitney in 1917 in *New York Central Railroad* v. *White*, "has a vested interest in any rule of law entitling him to insist that it shall remain unchanged for his benefit."[9] In regulatory proceedings concerning the unbundling of network industries, that proposition is cited more frequently than it is understood. No serious student of the issue would assert that the regulatory contract entitles the regulated utility to insist that the law shall remain unchanged for the firm's benefit. Rather, that contract—to paraphrase Justice Oliver Wendell Holmes's famous aphorism about contracts generally and damages for breach of contract—merely entitles the regulated utility to the payment of damages if the state chooses to breach the contract.[10] As Judge Richard A. Posner has recognized, there is the fundamental symmetry between the logic underlying Justice Holmes's observation and the proposition that the government avoids a taking by paying just compensation for its changes in regulation:

> The essence . . . of a breach of contract is that it triggers a duty to pay damages for the reasonably foreseeable consequences of the breach. If the duty is unimpaired, the obligation of the contract cannot be said to have been impaired. In Holmes's vivid formulation, the obligation created by a contract is an obligation to perform or pay damages for nonperformance, and if the second alternative remains, then, since it is an alter-

---

9. 243 U.S. 188, 198 (1917).

10. Oliver Wendell Holmes, *The Path of the Law*, 10 HARV. L. REV. 457, 462 (1897) ("The duty to keep a contract at common law means a prediction that you must pay damages if you do not keep it—and nothing else.").

native, the obligation created by the contract is not impaired. The analogy to the principle that government does not violate the takings clause if it stands ready to pay compensation for its takings should be evident.[11]

Judge Posner's insight applies directly to deregulatory takings and breach of the regulatory contract. It is up to the state to decide whether to exercise its police power in a manner that abrogates the regulatory contract, subject to the resulting obligation to compensate the utility for its lost expectation of cost recovery. The existence of a regulatory contract thus clarifies the distinction between the Takings Clause and the state's police power to impose or remove entry regulation.

Our conclusion that breach of the regulatory contract obligates the state to compensate the regulated firm is entirely congruent with the well-established principle in constitutional law that the termination of statutory gratuities, such as welfare and pension rights, is not compensable under the Takings Clause.[12] Such relationships between the state and private parties do not seem to rise to the level of a contract, even though those relationships doubtless induce some degree of detrimental reliance by private parties and thus might sustain a claim for recovery predicated on promissory estoppel. There is no obvious consideration flowing from the recipient of such benefits to the state, as there is in the case of a public utility, which accepts an obligation to serve all customers in its area at regulated rates. In short, a deregulatory policy that eliminated entry barriers that had gratuitously benefited a particular business or industry would not produce a deregulatory taking.

The presence of maximum rate regulation clarifies another basis for distinguishing regulatory changes that would necessitate the payment of compensation from those that would not. Although the imposition of price controls can be problematic because they remove the opportunity to earn returns for businesses, the *elimination* of such controls, by itself, cannot indicate a deregulatory taking. To the contrary, the lifting of price regulation unambiguously benefits the regulated firm—unless, of course, such regulation facilitated collusion and generated supracompetitive re-

11. Horwitz-Matthews, Inc. *v.* City of Chicago, 78 F.3d 1248, 1251 (7th Cir. 1996) (citing Ruckelshaus *v.* Monsanto Co., 467 U.S. 986, 1016 (1984); Coniston Corp. *v.* Village of Hoffman Estates, 844 F.2d 461, 463 (7th Cir. 1988); citation to Holmes, *supra* note 10, omitted).

12. United States *v.* Teller, 107 U.S. 64, 68 (1882); Lynch *v.* United States, 292 U.S. 571, 576–77 (1934); Railroad Retirement Bd. *v.* Fritz, 449 U.S. 166, 174 (1980); Bowen *v.* Gilliard, 483 U.S. 587, 604, 607 (1987); Hoffman *v.* City of Warwick, 909 F.2d 608, 616–17 (1st Cir. 1990).

turns for the very firms that ostensibly were being regulated in the public interest.[13] In an oligopolistic market (as opposed to a purely monopolistic one), tariffing requirements (which require advance posting and approval of price changes before they may take effect), price floors, and regulatory standardization of product quality and other nonprice attributes can all facilitate explicit or tacit collusion among regulated firms. Indeed, the justification for such regulation in a market populated by multiple firms is inherently suspicious on economic grounds. In such circumstances, the regulatory body functions as the cartel manager. Classic examples of such regulatory perversion include the Civil Aeronautics Board's past regulation of airlines' routes and fares and the Interstate Commerce Commission's past regulation of interstate trucking.

To identify the limits on stranded cost recovery, it is critical to comprehend the difference between the regulatory contract that we describe in the preceding chapters and the phenomenon of cartelization by regulation. In a comment on our earlier article on deregulatory takings and the regulatory contract, Judge Stephen F. Williams posed the following questions concerning the potential recovery of stranded costs by a third party who purchases a taxi franchise, which then is subject to the elimination of entry regulation:

> [Sidak and Spulber] set forth the existence of a franchise as a limit to their proposal, but also seem ready to embrace franchises generally, *i.e.*, to see franchises as manifesting the sort of regulatory bargain that calls for their solution. What of taxi franchises, held now not by the original rent-seekers but by people who have bought their franchises at market rates, *i.e.*, rates that capitalized the value of the artificially created scarcity? Those purchases were transfer payments induced by regulation. Must the state provide compensation for losses in franchise value that will flow from any increase in the number of taxi franchises? Perhaps compensation should be excluded here because the medallion owners' payments have been made outside the system, somewhat like the payments by which particular investors in a utility become stockholders, as opposed to the investments of the utility itself (just as, today, a firm purchasing a regulated utility does not get a stepped-up "rate base" merely by paying more than book value for the firm's assets). Or perhaps compensation should be denied on the ground that such purchasers were obviously buying the capitalized value of prior rent-seeking, and thus, the

13. *See* Paul W. MacAvoy, The Failure of Antitrust and Regulation to Establish Competition in Long-Distance Telephone Services (MIT Press & AEI Press 1996).

argument would run, an asset that is not only self-evidently hazardous but one of questionable social utility.[14]

We agree with Judge Williams's intuition that the losses that a third-party buyer of a taxi franchise experiences upon deregulation should not be considered compensable stranded costs. We do not quarrel with Judge Williams's grounds for distinguishing the taxi medallion case from the case of the mandatory unbundling of the electricity and local telephony industries. But we believe that our second criterion—that investment-backed expectations be based on the deployment of irreversible capital—is sufficient to distinguish the case, provided that we clarify the criterion in one respect: The irreversible investment cannot consist solely of a franchise right to receive supracompetitive returns. That qualification helps to distinguish the taxicab example from the regulatory contract in electric power and local telephony, which was formed in the late 1800s and early 1900s in response to the need of municipalities to induce private investors to make asset-specific investments in network infrastructure. The regulation of taxicabs, in contrast, was directed at industries with far lower levels of asset specificity. As we noted earlier, taxicabs are inherently mobile assets that can be immediately redeployed for other uses and in other geographic markets. (The same is true, of course, of airplanes, trucks, ferries, ships, and railroad rolling stock.[15]) The problem of inducing investment and of credibly committing the regulator not to act opportunistically once the firm had made nonsalvageable investments does not exist to the same degree in the taxicab industry—or in airlines, trucking, and other regulated or formerly regulated industries—relative to the situation in the electric power and local telephony industries. That fundamental economic difference corresponds to a basic historical difference. The use of regulation to cartelize competitive industries largely occurred during the New Deal,[16]

---

14. Stephen F. Williams, *Deregulatory Takings and Breach of the Regulatory Contract: A Comment*, 71 N.Y.U. L. REV. 1000, 1004–05 (1996).

15. In 1930, for example, the Supreme Court of California affirmed the regulator's grant to an entrant of a certificate of public convenience and necessity to provide ferry service across San Diego Bay, notwithstanding the incumbent's recent purchase of an expensive, new ferryboat. San Diego & Coronado Ferry Co. *v.* Railroad Comm'n of Cal., 210 Cal. 504, 292 P. 640 (1930). That result is consistent with our limiting principles because a ferryboat is inherently mobile. A firm that no longer needs a ferry in San Diego can readily shift the asset to San Francisco, Seattle, or Vancouver.

16. *See, e.g.*, RICHARD A. POSNER, ECONOMIC ANALYSIS OF LAW 628 (Little, Brown & Co., 4th ed. 1992).

well after investors had already supplied the affected industries with the requisite capital to commence production of their services.

It is true that a subsequent buyer of a taxi medallion cannot mitigate the loss in value of that franchise if the regulator permits firms to expand aggregate supply in the market. But the asset that the buyer acquires is a specialized, irreversible investment *only* in the sense that it embodies the naked demand that the law not change to the detriment of the franchise holder. As Justice Pitney observed, no one has a vested right of that sort. A simple rule of thumb is that the government owes no compensation for changes in regulatory policy that expand output and lower price while preserving the ability of the incumbent firm to recoup the costs of irreversible investments in infrastructure and other essential or government-mandated inputs.

THE DEREGULATORY EXPERIENCE
IN OTHER NETWORK INDUSTRIES

We have set forth four conditions that appear to be both necessary and sufficient for a deregulatory taking: the existence of a regulatory contract, evidence of investment-backed expectations, the elimination of regulatory entry barriers, and a decline in expected revenues. The analysis in the preceding chapters indicates that those conditions apply to the deregulation of local exchange telecommunications and electric power. To determine the general applicability of our limiting principles, we consider briefly the deregulation of several other network industries where those four conditions either do not apply or apply only to a limited extent: private municipal railways, airlines, and railroads. We also examine the AT&T divestiture. Finally, we analyze the policies of the Federal Energy Regulatory Commission (FERC) concerning open-access transportation of natural gas and mandatory wholesale wheeling of electricity. We consider whether our conditions allow a determination of whether or not a deregulatory taking occurred; we further consider how policymakers and the companies involved addressed the regulatory transition.

Private Municipal Railways

The demise of privately owned municipal railways during the first half of the twentieth century presented the question of stranded cost recovery, although the judicial discussion of the issue did not use such terminology. As we note in chapter 6, the Supreme Court's 1945 decision in *Market Street Railway Co.* v. *Railroad Commission of California* affirmed a state rate decision that the Court recognized would not permit the owner of the municipal railway to recover the cost of its investment.[17] That outcome is consistent with the limiting principles that we propose here. As chapter 6 explains, Market Street Railway's sunk costs became unrecoverable because of changing economic and technological forces that were making privately owned municipal railways obsolete and infeasible. The elimination of regulatory entry barriers into the municipal railway industry was not the cause of the regulated firm's inability to recover its costs. Nor was cost recovery rendered impossible by a new regulatory mandate to unbundle the incumbent firm's network for use by its competitors.

Opponents of stranded cost recovery in network industries such as local telephony and electric power often quote the Court's observation in *Market Street Railway* that although "[t]he due process clause has been applied to prevent governmental destruction of existing economic values," that constitutional provision "has not and cannot be applied to insure values or to restore values that have been lost by the operation of economic forces."[18] That statement, however, is entirely compatible with our own limiting principles for stranded cost recovery. If "governmental destruction of existing economic values" results from breach of the regulatory contract, then it is emphatically *not* the case that economic values "have been lost by the operation of economic forces." The government's promise to allow a regulated firm the reasonable opportunity to achieve sufficient earnings to recover its invested capital and to earn a competitive return on it is a promise that presumes that sufficient market demand will continue to exist for the service produced by the firm, at least over the useful life of the physical capital employed to provide that service. Exogenous factors may cause demand for the regulated service to collapse before the firm has achieved full capital recovery; but, absent explicit evidence to the contrary, we would assume that that particular risk is not one that the government assumed under the regulatory contract. Therefore, the fact that the regulated firm may not invoke the Constitution to compel the government to ensure full recovery of costs that exogenous market forces have made unrecoverable in no way negates the conclusion that, when the government has breached the regulatory contract, the regulated firm may indeed invoke the Constitution to compel full recovery of the costs that are consequently stranded.

17. 324 U.S. 548 (1945).
18. *Id.* at 567.

Surely in the electric power and local telecommunications industries there is no realistic expectation today that demand for use of the incumbent's network will collapse in the manner that demand for use of the Market Street Railway did by World War II. To the contrary, there will be a continuing need to invest in the local exchange network and the transmission and distribution network of the incumbent electric utility to accommodate the expected increase in demand. Electric utilities and LECs will need to return repeatedly to the capital markets to finance the investment needed to provide the network capacity to serve the higher levels of expected demand. It is therefore not the case, as it was for the Market Street Railway in 1945, that the LEC or electric utility today is "a company whose financial integrity already is hopelessly undermined, which could not attract capital on any possible rate, and where investors recognize as lost a part of what they have put in.[19]

In short, the costs that were unrecoverable in *Market Street Railway* were not, strictly speaking, stranded costs because they were not rendered unrecoverable by a change in regulation that breached the existing regulatory contract. A regulator in 1945 could no more ensure the recovery of Market Street Railway's costs in the face of dwindling demand than it could force automobile and bus commuters to revert to travel by horse-drawn buggy.[20]

Airline Deregulation

Airline deregulation does not satisfy the criteria for a deregulatory taking. A brief review of the opening of airline markets helps to clarify the limits of the takings argument.[21] Formal airline regulation did not

---

19. *Id.* at 566.

20. For similar reasoning concerning the collapsing demand for steam service, see Rochester Gas & Elec. Corp. *v.* Public Serv. Comm'n, 108 A.D.2d 35, 37, 488 N.Y.S.2d 303, 304–05 (3d Dept. 1985). For a similar decision concerning a natural gas company that experienced a massive decline in demand for throughput due to "economic conditions in the market . . . [that] could hardly have been less propitious," see Proceeding on the Motion of the Commission as to the Minor Rate Filing of Finger Lake Gas Co., Inc. to Increase Its Annual Gas Revenues by $99,999, or 24.0%, Case 93-G-0885, 1994 N.Y. PUC LEXIS 40, at *7 (N.Y. Pub. Serv. Comm'n 1994).

21. On the economic consequences of airline regulation, see REGULATION OF PASSENGER FARES AND COMPETITION AMONG THE AIRLINES (Paul W. MacAvoy & John W. Snow eds., American Enterprise Institute 1977); GEORGE W. DOUGLAS & JAMES C. MILLER III, ECONOMIC REGULATION OF DOMESTIC AIR TRANSPORT: THEORY AND POLICY (Brookings Institution 1974); STEPHEN G. BREYER, REGULATION AND ITS REFORM 197–221 (Harvard University Press 1982).

begin until the passage of the Civil Aeronautics Act of 1938, which created the Civil Aeronautics Board (CAB).[22] The CAB oversaw entry restrictions, route assignments, and prices. Airline regulation continued for over four decades until the passage of the Airline Deregulation Act of 1978,[23] which opened the passenger airline markets, with the eventual sunset of the CAB in 1984.[24] Deregulation of the airlines brought about the elimination of entry barriers and a decline in the expected revenues of the airlines, thus satisfying two of our four criteria for the recovery of stranded costs. Airline deregulation cannot be characterized as a government taking, however, because of the limited nature of the regulatory contract and the weak evidence of investment-backed expectations.

The CAB exercised entry controls and denied seventy-nine entry applications between 1950 and 1974.[25] The CAB imposed some obligations to serve by controlling the abandonment of routes. Although CAB oversight had some of the earmarks of a regulatory contract, that oversight fundamentally differed from utility regulation. Despite entry and route restrictions, some competition between incumbent airlines continued under regulation. Ratemaking set fares across markets rather than on an individual route basis, and it created a pattern of subsidizing short hauls by above-cost fares on long hauls. In over forty years of CAB control, there were only two brief periods of utility-style ratemaking. In 1956, as the major carriers began a costly program of purchasing jet aircraft, the CAB instituted its *General Passenger Fare Investigation* of 1960.[26] The other ratemaking exercise occurred in 1970

22. 52 Stat. 973. Congress substantially reenacted the 1938 legislation in the Federal Aviation Act of 1958, 72 Stat. 731.

23. Pub. L. No. 95-504, 92 Stat. 1705 (1978).

24. There is a large literature on the economics of airline deregulation. *See* STEVEN A. MORRISON & CLIFFORD WINSTON, THE EVOLUTION OF THE AIRLINE INDUSTRY (Brookings Institution 1995); JOHN R. MEYER & CLINTON V. OSTER, JR., DEREGULATION AND THE FUTURE OF INTERCITY PASSENGER TRAVEL (MIT Press 1987); STEVEN A. MORRISON & CLIFFORD WINSTON, THE ECONOMIC EFFECTS OF AIRLINE DEREGULATION (Brookings Institution 1986); ELIZABETH E. BAILEY, DAVID R. GRAHAM & DANIEL P. KAPLAN, DEREGULATING AIRLINES (MIT Press 1985); JOHN R. MEYER & CLINTON V. OSTER, JR., DEREGULATION AND THE NEW AIRLINE ENTREPRENEURS (MIT Press 1984); AIRLINE DEREGULATION: THE EARLY EXPERIENCE (John R. Meyer & Clinton V. Oster, Jr., eds., Auburn House Publishing Co. 1981); Elizabeth E. Bailey & Jeffrey R. Williams, *Sources of Rent in the Deregulated Airline Industry*, 31 J.L. & ECON. 173 (1988); Michael A. Levine, *Airline Competition in Deregulated Markets: Theory, Firm Strategy and Public Policy*, 4 YALE J. ON REG. 393 (1987).

25. Daniel P. Kaplan, *The Changing Airline Industry, Case 2*, *in* REGULATORY REFORM: WHAT ACTUALLY HAPPENED 72 (Leonard Weiss & Michael W. Klass eds., Little, Brown & Co. 1986).

26. 32 C.A.B. 291 (1960); *see also* RICHARD K. VIETOR, CONTRIVED COMPETITION:

with the five-year *Domestic Passenger Fare Investigation*, which led to a reduction of airline price discounts.[27] The investigation determined an *industry revenue requirement* based on a reasonable rate of return, *industry* rate base, prudency review of investment, and fixed industry load factor.[28] The CAB's brand of managed competition differed substantially from the complex rate-of-return regulation traditionally found in the electric and telephone utilities. Because the CAB suppressed some forms of price competition, while allowing others such as discounts, the CAB's pricing policies were applied across the board instead of being tailored to the capital costs and operating costs of individual airlines, as would be the case with utility regulation.

Airline fare regulation was more a cartel-like coordination mechanism than a contractual approach to procuring services from a firm arguably exhibiting the characteristics of natural monopoly. According to Justice Stephen G. Breyer, writing as a Harvard professor in 1982, "The problem of high fares was essentially a problem of low load factors, which reflected excessive scheduling, which in turn resulted from CAB action that inhibited price competition."[29] Justice Breyer observed that although the statute did not forbid price cutting and price competition, the CAB limited such competition, because it eschewed rate hearings and instead pursued a policy of negotiation and private meetings.[30] The U.S. Court of Appeals for the D.C. Circuit eventually held those informal meetings to be unlawful.[31] That type of cartelistic procedure cannot be justified as a regulatory contract, for it is antithetical to the welfare of consumers.

What were the economic effects of deregulation on the airlines? In any regulated industry, regulated firms make investments based on their expectations about future regulation and deregulation. The extent to which airline investors were deprived of their investment-backed expectations, however, was limited. There is no question that the capital equipment of the airlines was not well adapted for competition.[32] The choice of aircraft was better suited for point-to-point service than the

REGULATION AND DEREGULATION IN AMERICA 38 (Belknap Press & Harvard University Press 1994).

27. Civil Aeronautics Board, *Domestic Passenger Fare Investigation: January 1970 to December 1974* (1976); *see also* BREYER, *supra* note 21, at 211–12.

28. BREYER, *supra* note 21, at 211.

29. *Id.* at 210.

30. *Id.* at 211.

31. Moss *v.* Civil Aeronautics Bd., 430 F.2d 891, 901 (D.C. Cir. 1970).

32. *See* VIETOR, *supra* note 26, at 61.

hub-and-spoke service that was to emerge with deregulation. The airlines had to reconfigure their fleets of aircraft to adapt to new route structures and the effects of competition on load factors. Moreover, additional investment in gates and terminals was required to update or replace existing ground facilities. Despite the fact that the capital investment undertaken by the airlines before deregulation was not well adapted for competition in the ways described above, their investment differed in a significant respect from the investment in other network industries, such as electric power transmission and local telephony. Like the investment in taxicabs in New York City, the investment in aircraft before deregulation was not market-specific. Airplanes have been called "capital with wings," and the airlines were able to redeploy some airplanes to other routes for which they were better suited and to realize some scrap value by resale into other markets. Moreover, the capital investment in aircraft has a shorter economic life than that of investment in utility plants and equipment, given aircraft lives and technological change in air travel.

Most airlines suffered substantially reduced earnings in the aftermath of deregulation. Two major carriers, Braniff and Continental, went bankrupt. Some of those effects were due to high oil prices that coincided with deregulation, although incumbent airlines also felt the effects of high labor costs under contracts entered before deregulation. It is difficult to discern, however, whether the declines in earnings were already expected by the time that deregulation occurred. Certainly, the financial impacts of deregulation were mitigated by removing any regulation that would hinder the incumbents. The CAB eliminated service obligations on the incumbent airlines, allowed them to abandon routes and change the time of individual flights, and lifted price controls so that the airlines could adjust fares to meet the competition.

Railroad Deregulation

Railroad regulation was the first major federal regulation of industry. Regulation of the railroads began in 1887 with the Interstate Commerce Act, which established the Interstate Commerce Commission (ICC).[33] The Railroad Revitalization and Regulatory Reform Act of 1976[34] was an initial attempt at railroad deregulation that left many regulatory con-

---

33. Interstate Commerce Act, 24 Stat. 379 (1887). On railroad regulation, see RAILROAD REVITALIZATION AND REGULATORY REFORM (Paul W. MacAvoy & John W. Snow eds., American Enterprise Institute 1977).
  34. Pub. L. No. 94-210, 90 Stat. 31 (codified at 49 U.S.C. § 10701).

trols in place. Railroads were substantially deregulated by the Staggers Rail Act of 1980[35] and by the sunset of the ICC at the end of 1995 and its replacement by the creation of the Surface Transportation Board within the Transportation Department,[36] which continues oversight of railway rates.

Railroad regulation imposed substantial financial costs on the railroad industry. Railroads faced increasing competition from trucking, air transport, pipelines, and barges. The regulated rate structure of railroads constrained their pricing flexibility and created rates that were not competitive. The setting of across-the-board rates by regulators severely constrained the rate-setting ability of individual railroads. Freight rates involved a complex system of cross-subsidies between shippers, subsidies that could not be sustained in the presence of intermodal competition. Moreover, restrictions on abandonment forced the railroads to maintain unprofitable routes. Other regulations restricted the types of services that railroads could offer and constrained their entry into trucking. Regulation also controlled the ability of railroads to merge with one another. Limits on end-to-end mergers prevented carriers from achieving efficiencies from vertical integration that would have addressed the high transaction costs of forwarding shipments from one carrier to another. Limits on mergers, both parallel and end-to-end, constrained the efficiency gains from consolidation of duplicate facilities. Against that background of incumbent burdens, a number of railroads, including the Penn Central, went bankrupt.[37]

The Staggers Rail Act and ICC decontrol gave the railroads increased ability to adjust freight rates, loosened restrictions on "piggy-back" traffic of containers, and authorized contracting with shippers.[38] By freeing railroads from restrictions on rates, abandonments, and mergers, deregulation has allowed railroads to adapt their prices to market forces by rebalancing rates. Mergers have created more efficient and financially stronger carriers. The Chessie System and Seaboard Coast Line merged to form CSX in 1980; the Burlington Northern merged with the Santa

---

35. Pub. L. No. 96-448, 94 Stat. 1895 (codified in scattered sections of 49 U.S.C.).

36. ICC Termination Act of 1995, Pub. L. No. 104-88, 109 Stat. 803 (codified at 49 U.S.C. § 201).

37. The bankrupt railroads included the Erie Lackawanna, the Boston & Maine, the Central of New Jersey, the Lehigh Valley, and the Reading. *See* Agis Salpukas, *Born in Crisis, Conrail Defies Skeptics with Turnaround*, N.Y. TIMES, Oct. 16, 1996, at D8.

38. *See* Thomas Gale Moore, *Rail and Trucking Deregulation, Case 1, in* REGULATORY REFORM: WHAT ACTUALLY HAPPENED, *supra* note 25, at 14, 23–24.

Fe; and the Union Pacific merged with both the Southern Pacific and the Chicago and North Western Transportation Company.[39]

The federal regulation of railroads—with control of entry, rate regulation, and obligations to serve that included common carrier regulations and restrictions on abandonments—was indeed a form of regulatory contract. But it was a regulatory contract that differed from the individually tailored state regulation of electric and natural gas utilities and of local exchange carriers. The unchanging terms of the regulatory contract for railroads became increasingly onerous and outdated over a century of regulation, in large part owing to exogenous technological change and intermodal competition. Consequently, it became mutually beneficial for regulators, railroads, and shippers to renegotiate or simply terminate the regulatory contract. Certainly, the expenditures for railroad trackage and rolling stock manifested investment-backed expectations. But the same could be said of the trackage and rolling stock of the Market Street Railway in the early 1940s. Investment-backed expectations by themselves do not establish that it is the regulator's action—and not some exogenous force—that has upset those expectations. Continuation of railroad regulation would have meant further financial difficulties for the incumbent railroads and additional increases in their cost of capital.

Put differently, the elimination of regulatory barriers to entry was not a significant issue in railroad deregulation. Railroads already faced competition from other modes of transportation.[40] As evidenced by the series of rail mergers that followed deregulation, the rail industry itself sought to reduce and consolidate capacity. Railroad deregulation did not cause expected revenues to fall. Exogenous forces of intermodal competition did. To the contrary, railroad deregulation conferred pricing flexibility that allowed revenues to increase or mitigated their decline. In short, the deregulation of railroads did not appear to produce stranded costs. It therefore did not constitute a deregulatory taking.

That conclusion does not necessarily answer, however, whether a *new* regulatory policy requiring a railroad to provide shippers access to unbundled elements of its rail network would cause a deregulatory taking today. Alfred E. Kahn, for example, has defended stranded cost recovery for local exchange carriers and electric utilities, but he has rejected the

---

39. *Rebuilding the Nation's Railroads*, J. Com., Jan. 6, 1997, at 18C; Barnaby J. Feder, *How Conrail Became a Hot Ticket; Global Trade, High Tech Lift Railroad "Basket Case,"* N.Y. Times, Nov. 1, 1996, at D1.

40. *See, e.g.*, Eastern R.R. Presidents Conf. *v.* Noerr Motor Freight, Inc., 365 U.S. 127 (1961).

proposition put before the Surface Transportation Board in 1996 that railroads would suffer stranded costs if made to price unbundled access to bottleneck routes at (lower) local tariffed rates.[41] Railroads sought deregulation, Kahn reasoned, and through such policy reform have avoided the continuation of incumbent burdens of the sort borne by the LECs and electric utilities:

> The railroad industry . . . was deregulated more than 16 years ago, at the industry's own request. Railroads have since had the freedom to set discriminatory rates, to enter into transportation contracts free from government regulation and to abandon non-profitable segments and enter new ones, largely as they see fit, all without any overall cap on their earnings. Moreover, railroads were never subject to the sort of thorough regulatory oversight as continues to characterize the electric and telephone utilities.[42]

The absence of mandatory cross-subsidies in current regulated rates is, in Kahn's view, another basis for distinguishing the case of railroads from that of local exchange carriers:

> The continuing obligation to serve includes, at least in the telephone case, an obligation to charge rates to large bodies of customers below economically efficient levels and even below incremental costs, with the clear expectation of the companies being permitted to charge rates for other regulated services correspondingly above those levels. As I understand it, the railroads have been subject to no such obligations. The ceilings on the only railroad rates that continue to be capped—for services to captive shippers—far from being held below incremental costs, are set at the *maximum* level beyond which the shipper would be deprived of the benefits of economies of scale, density or scope.[43]

In response, William J. Baumol and Robert D. Willig have argued that railroads also enjoy a regulatory contract, which would be breached by mandatory unbundling of bottleneck routes:

> Contrary to Dr. Kahn's apparent understanding, railroads, too, have been subject to a regulatory compact that would be unravelled by the proposal advocated by Dr. Kahn. Investment has long been attracted to

---

41. Verified Statement of Alfred E. Kahn (Nov. 27, 1996), in Central Power & Light Co. *v.* Southern Pac. Transp. Co., Dkt. Nos. 41242, 41295, 41626, 1996 STB LEXIS 358 (Surface Transp. Bd. Dec. 27, 1996).

42. *Id.* at 18.

43. *Id.* (emphasis in original).

the railroads under the consistent understanding that only rates for end-to-end movements, and not rates for segments, would be regulated. (We are advised that the Supreme Court so stated in 1925 in *Louisville & Nashville R.R.* v. *Sloss-Sheffield Steel & Iron Co.*, and that the ICC repeatedly reaffirmed this point—for example, in a number of merger cases in the past decade.) On that understanding, investors have committed vast sums to provide efficient *networks*, and not merely segments. That is no less a regulatory compact than those described by Dr. Kahn for the electricity and telephone industries. That compact was, of course, reinforced still further by the Staggers Rail Act of 1980, which directed the ICC to provide railroads the opportunity to attain revenue adequacy; and it was not changed by the ICC Termination Act of 1995.[44]

Which of those two assessments is wrong? Neither, for in a sense the two opinions are talking past one another. Baumol and Willig do not agree with Kahn on the question of whether, before deregulation, railroads faced the same kind of regulatory contract as telephone companies and electric utilities. If Kahn is correct, then it follows even more forcefully that we are correct in concluding that the railroads did not suffer a deregulatory taking as the result of rail deregulation. But even if Baumol and Willig are correct, it is still possible for the reasons we have presented that the railroads suffered no deregulatory taking with rail deregulation.

But the resolution of that dispute concerning the regulatory contract circa 1980 would *not* shed light on whether, well after rail deregulation, a railroad would suffer stranded costs if it were forced to unbundle its network and to price its unbundled bottleneck routes at levels that would prevent the railroad from recovering all its economic costs. Baumol and Willig in effect frame the following significant proposition about deregulatory takings: The fact that a network industry has completed a transition to a more deregulated status does not imply that the regulator may thereafter freely redefine the public purpose to which the firm's private capital has been dedicated. Deregulation, in other words, does not automatically suspend the constitutional protection of regulated property that the Supreme Court articulated in *Northern Pacific Railway*. Baumol and Willig correctly note that the Staggers Rail Act and the ICC

---

44. Response of William J. Baumol and Robert D. Willig to the Verified Statement of Alfred E. Kahn 8 (Dec. 13, 1996), Central Power & Light Co. *v.* Southern Pac. Trans. Co., Dkt. Nos. 41242, 41295, 41626, 1996 STB LEXIS 358 (Surface Transp. Bd. Dec. 27, 1996) (emphasis in original; citation to 269 U.S. 217, 231–34 (1925) omitted) [hereinafter *Baumol-Willig STB Response*].

Termination Act did not erase the investment-backed expectations of shareholders who supplied capital to provide consumers railroad *networks* rather than to provide shippers or other railroads access to unbundled rail *segments*. It should be obvious, moreover, that a subsequent round of railroad "deregulation" that took the form of mandatory unbundling would produce far different issues of stranded costs than did railroad deregulation in 1980, for such unbundling would diminish the revenues attainable from immovable trackage. Asset specificity and regulatory holdup would be a serious concern.

The AT&T Breakup

It is sometimes observed, as apparent support for the proposition that it is unnecessary for the state and federal governments to worry about stranded cost recovery, that the breakup of AT&T precipitated write-offs by that company for which it received no special opportunity for cost recovery. The comparison of the AT&T divestiture with the current form of unbundling taking place in the local telephony and electric power industries is inapt for numerous reasons.

First, the AT&T divestiture was not a regulatory action. It was an antitrust case prosecuted by the U.S. Department of Justice. A federal prosecutor is not a regulator exercising a broad mandate to promulgate myriad policies that advance the public interest. Rather, the Antitrust Division prosecutes violations of civil and criminal law. It was the federal government's contention that AT&T was acting *unlawfully* under existing legal standards. Indeed, Assistant Attorney General William F. Baxter believed that the successful conclusion of the AT&T litigation would *reduce* the need for regulation in the future.[45] The divestiture decree was not an attempt to modify the existing regulatory contract that AT&T had formed with the FCC and the state PUCs. Throughout the critical negotiations leading to the agreement between the government and AT&T to divest the local operating companies from the rest of AT&T's businesses, the Justice Department kept the FCC uninformed of what was occurring.[46] The culmination of those negotiations was a consent decree between the government and AT&T to settle the antitrust

---

45. MacAvoy, *supra* note 13, at 20–24; Gerald W. Brock, Telecommunications Policy for the Information Age: From Monopoly to Competition 164, 166 (Harvard University Press 1994); Peter Temin, The Fall of the Bell System: A Study in Prices and Politics 282 (Cambridge University Press 1987).

46. *Id.*

case. AT&T remained free to spurn settlement and to present its defense at trial, although that alternative may have been unappealing. AT&T freely chose not to do so.

Second, even if one prefers to view the AT&T litigation as a de facto form of regulation, it is nonetheless clear that the divestiture was the outcome of voluntary exchange. It resulted in a consent decree, a judicially enforceable contract between an antitrust defendant and the federal government. Charles L. Brown, chairman of AT&T, *wanted* to divest his local exchange companies in the belief that they were a stagnant business.[47] The attractive opportunities for AT&T, in Brown's estimation, lay in long-distance and in the ability to focus the substantial research and development capabilities of Bell Laboratories and Western Electric on the computer industry.[48] But a 1956 consent decree into which AT&T had entered to settle a previous federal antitrust prosecution forbade the company from entering the computer business.[49] Brown therefore willingly offered to divest AT&T's local operating companies in return for having the 1956 decree vacated.

In time, many errors became apparent in key assumptions that AT&T's managers held at the time of the divestiture concerning the future of the telecommunications industry and AT&T's abilities to enter other product markets. AT&T failed to recognize the future role of wireless as a means of local access. By 1994, however, AT&T paid nearly $12 billion in stock to purchase McCaw Cellular Communications,[50] the nation's largest cellular telephone company. AT&T's management overestimated AT&T's potential in the computer industry. By October 1995, AT&T announced that it would voluntarily undergo another divestiture that would separate equipment manufacturing, long-distance services, and network services into three independent companies.[51] AT&T decided to reorganize, purportedly to transform itself into leaner, more aggressive companies better able to compete in the global telecommunications market.[52] In addition, AT&T announced that it would exit the computer business entirely. The framers of the

47. MacAvoy, *supra* note 13, at 24–27.

48. *Id*. at 25.

49. United States *v*. Western Elec. Co., 1956 Trade Cas. (CCH) ¶ 68,246 (D.N.J. 1956).

50. Andrew Kupfer, *AT&T's $12 Billion Cellular Dream*, Fortune, Dec. 12, 1994, at 106.

51. AT&T Corp., 1996 SEC Form 10-K, at 3 (1997).

52. *Id*.

divestiture had believed, of course, that by freeing AT&T to enter the computer business, the 1984 divestiture decree would enable AT&T to become a potent competitor of IBM. Instead, personal computer producers came to dominate the computer industry, and AT&T, even after its purchase of NCR, proved to be an ineffective competitor in a market characterized by low margins and very rapid product innovation.

Third, AT&T needed no compensation for being ordered to jettison its local operating companies, for they were *recipients* of cross-subsidies flowing from long-distance services. Starting in the mid-1960s, the FCC began using the "separations" process to assign an increasing share of common costs (known as "non-traffic-sensitive" costs) to the interstate portion of AT&T's business, for recovery through the pricing of interstate long-distance service.[53] The result was increasing pressure from state regulators for LECs to price local services at or below their economic costs. It was far better, from Brown's perspective, for AT&T to be a company capable of paying regulatory subsidies than a company that could not be financially viable without the receipt of them. The new AT&T suffered no decline in the expected revenues of the assets assigned to it by the plan of reorganization. Moreover, technological change (particularly the conversion from microwave to fiber-optic cable) was reducing the cost of interexchange services, so even continued FCC rate regulation (before the advent of price caps) led to larger margins.[54]

Fourth, the divestiture did nothing to open the local exchange to competition. Another prerequisite for stranded cost recovery—the elimination of regulatory barriers to entry into the regulated firm's market—was therefore absent. There continued to be one and only one Bell operating company in each service territory. As we examine in chapter 3, the prevailing assumption among AT&T, the Department of Justice, and Judge Harold H. Greene was that local telephony was and would remain a natural monopoly. That assumption became a principal justification for the regulatory quarantine imposed on the RBOCs. The divestiture structurally separated AT&T's long-distance network from its local exchanges but did not require any unbundling of those exchanges.

53. MILTON L. MUELLER, JR., UNIVERSAL SERVICE: COMPETITION, INTERCONNECTION, AND MONOPOLY IN THE MAKING OF THE AMERICAN TELEPHONE SYSTEM 159–60 (MIT Press & AEI Press 1997); ROBERT W. CRANDALL, AFTER THE BREAKUP: U.S. TELECOMMUNICATIONS IN A MORE COMPETITIVE ERA 26 (Brookings Institution 1991); TEMIN, *supra* note 45, at 24–27.

54. MACAVOY, *supra* note 13, at 93–98.

In short, the AT&T divestiture was not a case of a deregulatory taking for which no compensation was forthcoming for stranded costs. The breakup was a bargain to which the regulated firm consented, on terms that appeared to its managers at the time to be in the best interests of the firm's shareholders. The agreement did not lift entry barriers into the local exchange, nor did it reduce the revenues that could be earned from the assets of the new AT&T.

Open-Access Transportation
of Natural Gas

Open-access transportation of natural gas represented a partial deregulation of interstate natural gas pipelines that involved stranded costs, although most of those costs were contractual rather than stranded investment.[55] Thus, it is more appropriate to characterize the firm's expectations as contractual in nature rather than investment-backed. Regulation of interstate natural gas provides evidence for the existence of a regulatory contract. Open-access transportation eliminated regulatory entry barriers only for the merchant functions of interstate pipelines. After the adoption of FERC Order 636, the pipelines were left with the costs of high-priced gas-purchase contracts. FERC recognized those stranded costs and allowed the pipelines to pass them through to consumers.

Major regulatory changes in both pricing and transportation began in 1978 with the passage of the Natural Gas Policy Act (NGPA).[56] The NGPA, partly in response to natural gas shortages in the 1970s, decontrolled the wellhead prices of certain categories of natural gas. The NGPA created pricing categories on the basis of production methods, whether the gas was sold under a prior interstate contract, and other factors. Gas was divided into old, new, and "high-cost" gas, and many subcategories were created.[57] Pipelines sought to increase their contractu-

---

55. The following discussion draws upon Michael J. Doane & Daniel F. Spulber, *Open Access and the Evolution of the U.S. Spot Market for Natural Gas*, 37 J.L. & ECON. 477 (1994).

56. Pub. L. No. 95-261, 92 Stat. 3397 (1978) (codified as amended at 15 U.S.C. §§ 3301–3432). The NGPA was accompanied by a host of other legislative actions concerning energy: the National Energy Conservation Policy Act, Pub. L. No. 95-619, 92 Stat. 3206 (1978); the Public Utility Regulatory Policies Act, Pub. L. No. 95-617, 92 Stat. 3117 (1978); and the Powerplant and Industrial Fuel Use Act, Pub. L. No. 95-620, 92 Stat. 3289 (1978).

57. Old gas referred to gas dedicated to interstate commerce before the NGPA and

al purchase of gas in anticipation of future gas shortages in the early 1980s. Pipelines faced contractual obligations for resale and were able to recover the cost of purchased gas through cost-of-service rate regulation and minimum bill contracts with local distribution companies. The purchasing policies of many pipelines created severe distortions in wellhead prices as a consequence of the partial deregulation brought about by the NGPA.

Since the NGPA maintained strict controls on old gas, and relaxed controls on new gas and deregulated deep gas, pipelines seeking to contract for additional supplies bid up the prices of new and deep gas substantially above market-clearing levels. Since high-cost and low-cost supplies were "rolled in" by average cost price regulation, the pipelines purchased expensive new and deep gas. Furthermore, "most-favored-nation clauses" in many contracts caused prices to soar for other pipelines that had not bid for additional supplies but that had high cost supplies already under contract. To compound the problem further, take-or-pay clauses in those contracts bound pipelines to take deliveries of gas at those higher prices—often significantly above resale market price levels.

Those pipelines with smaller "cushions" of old gas faced higher average gas purchase costs. That led to many contract disputes as pipelines sought to avoid losses from take-or-pay obligations. Those losses were either in the form of payments for gas not taken, above-market payments for gas that was taken, or payments to settle contract disputes. Take-or-pay obligations increased significantly in 1984 when FERC issued Order No. 380, which eliminated the variable cost component of the minimum bill obligations of pipeline customers.[58] By removing the costs associated with maintaining the supplies of gas available for purchase from pipelines' minimum commodity bills, Order No. 380 effectively eliminated the requirement that customers of interstate pipelines purchase any minimum quantity of natural gas from their interstate pipelines. By the end of 1986, $10 billion worth of

---

rollover contracts and was subject to price controls. New gas primarily referred to new wells and was allowed a phased decontrol. High-cost gas included "deep" gas (from wells to a depth greater that 15,000 feet), which was deregulated.

58. Order No. 380, Elimination of Variable Costs from Certain Natural Gas Pipeline Minimum Commodity Bill Provisions, [Regs. Preambles 1982–85] F.E.R.C. Stats. & Regs. (CCH) ¶ 30,571, *order on reh'g*, Order No. 380-A, [Regs. Preambles 1982-85] F.E.R.C. Stats. & Regs. (CCH) ¶ 30,584, *order on reh'g*, 29 F.E.R.C. ¶ 61,076, *order on reh'g*, [Regs. Preambles 1982–85] F.E.R.C. Stats. & Regs. (CCH) ¶ 30,607, *order on reh'g*, 29 F.E.R.C. ¶ 61,332 (1984), *aff'd in part and remanded in part sub nom.* Wisconsin Gas Co. *v.* FERC, 770 F.2d 1144 (D.C. Cir. 1985).

contracts were involved in take-or-pay disputes.[59] Pipelines encountered difficulties in recovering contractual take-or-pay obligations. The contractual problems of producers and pipelines were an important factor in the creation of the spot market in that the gas supplies purchased in the infant spot market in late 1983 and early 1984 included the original, refused takes of the pipelines. An important motivation for later FERC Order Nos. 436 and 500 was to alleviate take-or-pay obligations by allowing pipelines to pass along the costs of buying out contracts.

On the transportation side, the NGPA allowed producers and resellers of gas other than pipelines and local distribution companies to be exempt from the certificate of convenience and necessity requirements of the Natural Gas Act of 1938 (NGA).[60] Furthermore, the NGPA, under section 311, allowed pipelines to transport gas interstate without the certification requirements of the NGA. The NGPA was followed by various orders by FERC. Under Order No. 46 in 1978, FERC could authorize interstate and intrastate pipelines to transport gas for each other.[61] FERC Order No. 27 in 1979 allowed essential agricultural users, schools, and hospitals to develop gas themselves or to buy directly from producers and authorized interstate pipelines to transport such gas.[62] FERC Order No. 30 in 1979 extended transportation programs to end users substituting natural gas for fuel oil during the fuel oil emergency.[63] FERC also allowed interstate pipeline companies to sell gas directly to end users not normally served, a practice referred to as "off-system sales."[64]

---

59. Matthew L. Wald, *Gas Producers See an End to Disputes with Pipelines*, N.Y. TIMES, Nov. 7, 1988, at D1.

60. 52 Stat. 821, ch. 556 (1938) (codified as amended at 15 U.S.C. §§ 717-717w).

61. Order 46, Order Amending Part 284 and Issuing Subparts A, B, C and E on Final Regulations, Dkt. No. RM79-75, 8 F.E.R.C. ¶ 61,238 (1979).

62. Order 27, Certification of Pipeline Transportation for Certain High-Priority Users, 44 FED. REG. 24,825 (1979).

63. Order 30, Transportation Certificates for Natural Gas for the Displacement of Fuel Oil, 45 FED. REG. 70,712 (1980).

64. FERC took two intermediate steps toward open-access transportation in 1983. FERC Order No. 319 introduced the use of blanket certificates for the transport of gas for high-priority users. Order No. 319, Sales and Transportation by Interstate Pipelines and Distributors, [Regs. Preambles 1982–85] F.E.R.C. Stats. & Regs. (CCH) ¶ 30,477, *order on reh'g*, Order No. 319-A, [Regs. Preambles 1982–85] F.E.R.C. Stats. & Regs. (CCH) ¶ 30,512 (1983). The transporter did not need to obtain separate authorization for each transaction. FERC Order No. 234-B allowed the use of blanket certificates for the transport of gas for nonpriority users. Order No. 234-B, Interstate Pipeline Blanket Certificates for Routine Transactions and Sales and Transportation by Interstate Pipelines and Distributors, [Regs. Preambles 1982–85] F.E.R.C. Stats. & Regs. (CCH) ¶ 30,476 (1983). That development created a spot market of direct sales from producers and other intrastate

FERC took the major step toward open-access transportation by issuing Order No. 436 in 1985, which allowed pipelines to become open-access transporters for gas bought directly from producers by all classes of customers.[65] That order institutionalized the separation of the merchant and transportation functions of interstate pipelines. In addition, FERC Order No. 500 (which in 1987 superseded Order No. 436) offered blanket certificates for transportation of gas, provided that the pipeline company agreed to allow all customers access to the service.[66] Order No. 500 allowed pipelines to reduce their rates while permitting customers to convert the contractual delivery requirements for gas that were placed on pipelines (known as "contract demand" volumes) to "firm transportation" volumes, thus allowing pipelines to shift their responsibilities from merchant functions to transportation. As a consequence, within roughly five years, beginning in the mid-1980s, major interstate pipelines went from being primarily buyers and sellers of gas, bundled with transportation services, to being primarily transporters of gas. Pipelines continued to provide merchant services through marketing affiliates, but they faced a host of competitors, including direct transactions between buyers and gas suppliers, brokers, and gas marketers. With the enactment of the Natural Gas Wellhead Decontrol Act of 1989, Congress repealed the remaining price controls on wellhead gas.[67] After the NGPA

suppliers to industrial boiler fuel users. Gas could be sold and transported for up to 120 days without prior approval.

65. Order No. 436, Regulation of Natural Gas Pipelines After Partial Wellhead Decontrol, [Regs. Preambles 1982–85] F.E.R.C. Stats. & Regs. (CCH) ¶ 30,665, *order on reh'g*, Order No. 436-A, [Regs. Preambles 1982–85] F.E.R.C. Stats. & Regs. (CCH) ¶ 30,675 (1985), *order on reh'g*, Order No. 436-B, [Regs. Preambles 1986–90] F.E.R.C. Stats. & Regs. (CCH) ¶ 30,688, *order on reh'g*, Order No. 436-C, 34 F.E.R.C. ¶ 61,404, *order on reh'g*, Order No. 436-D, 34 F.E.R.C. ¶ 61,405, *order on reh'g*, Order No. 436-E, 34 F.E.R.C. ¶ 61,403 (1986), *vacated and remanded sub nom.* Associated Gas Distribs. *v.* FERC, 824 F.2d 981 (D.C. Cir. 1987), *cert. denied*, 485 U.S. 1006 (1988).

66. Order No. 500, Regulation of Natural Gas Pipelines After Partial Wellhead Decontrol, [Regs. Preambles 1986–90] F.E.R.C. Stats. & Regs. (CCH) ¶ 30,761, *order on reh'g*, Order No. 500-A, [Regs. Preambles 1986–90] F.E.R.C. Stats. & Regs. (CCH) ¶ 30,770, *order on reh'g*, Order No. 500-B, [Regs. Preambles 1986–90] F.E.R.C. Stats. & Regs. (CCH) ¶ 30,772, *order on reh'g*, Order No. 500-C, [Regs. Preambles 1986–90] F.E.R.C. Stats. & Regs. (CCH) ¶ 30,786 (1987), *order on reh'g*, Order No. 500-D, [Regs. Preambles 1986–90] F.E.R.C. Stats. & Regs. (CCH) ¶ 30,800, *order on reh'g*, Order No. 500-E, 43 F.E.R.C. ¶ 61,234, *order on reh'g*, Order No. 500-F, [Regs. Preambles 1986–90] F.E.R.C. Stats. & Regs. (CCH) ¶ 30,841 (1988), *order on reh'g*, Order No. 500-G, 46 F.E.R.C. ¶ 61,148, *vacated and remanded sub nom.* American Gas Ass'n *v.* FERC, 888 F.2d 136 (D.C. Cir. 1989).

67. Pub. L. No. 101-60, 103 Stat. 157 (1989).

began the process of decontrolling the wellhead prices of natural gas in 1978, open-access transportation led to the rapid development of a national spot market for gas.[68]

In 1992 FERC issued Order No. 636, which mandated that pipelines separate gas sales from transportation.[69] The order, in effect, completed the policy actions that FERC adopted throughout the 1980s. The traditional merchant function of pipelines included the management of a complex portfolio of purchase and sales contracts, brokerage between suppliers and customers, and financing of gas transactions that were almost exclusively tied to the pipelines' transportation of gas. The NGPA and subsequent FERC orders dramatically altered the structure of the industry and the role of pipelines. The separation of marketing and transportation allowed customers to purchase and resell gas and then contract for transportation. Specialized middleman, consisting of gas brokers and other marketers, arose to service those transactions. Pipelines were reduced largely to common carrier status, transporting gas for other buyers and sellers.

FERC addressed stranded cost recovery in the wake of Order 636, thus avoiding a deregulatory taking.[70] Michael J. Doane and Michael A. Williams have observed that

> the Commission recognized unbundling would create four types of costs: (1) unrecovered gas purchase costs resulting from the adoption of market-based gas pricing in lieu of a purchased gas adjustment mechanism; (2) gas supply realignment ("GSR") costs resulting from the need to revise or terminate existing contracts with gas suppliers; (3) costs incurred in connection with providing bundled sales service that could not be directly assigned to customers of bundled service (which the FERC explicitly labeled "stranded costs"); and (4) costs of new facilities required to implement the Order.[71]

---

68. *See* Doane & Spulber, *supra* note 55.

69. Order No. 636, Pipeline Service Obligations and Revisions to Regulations Governing Self-Implementing Transportation Under Part 284 of the Commission's Regulations, and Regulation of Natural Gas Pipelines After Partial Wellhead Decontrol, [Current] F.E.R.C. Stats. & Regs. (CCH) ¶ 30,939, *order on reh'g*, Order No. 636-A, [Current] F.E.R.C. Stats. & Regs. (CCH) ¶ 30,950, *order on reh'g*, Order No. 636-B, 61 F.E.R.C. ¶ 61,272 (1992), *reh'g denied*, 62 F.E.R.C. ¶ 61,007 (1993).

70. FERC exacerbated the problem by removing the variable cost component of minimum-bill obligations for pipeline customers in Order 380, *supra* note 58.

71. *See* Michael J. Doane & Michael A. Williams, *Competitive Entry into Regulated Monopoly Services and the Resulting Problem of Stranded Cost*, 3 HUME PAPERS ON PUB. POL'Y, no. 3, 32, 36 (1995).

FERC allowed the pipelines to recover those costs through the fixed-charge element of straight fixed-variable transportation rates for natural gas. FERC learned from its earlier experience when, in *American Gas Distributors* v. *FERC*, it was faulted by the U.S. Court of Appeals for the D.C. Circuit for not addressing the pipelines' take-or-pay problems that had occurred in the early 1980s.[72] FERC had some incentive to deal with stranded cost recovery because the rate regulation of pipeline transportation continued after the institution of open-access transportation. Nonetheless, the agency significantly relaxed controls on the entry of interstate pipelines while incumbent pipelines continued to face rate controls and other incumbent burdens.[73] That situation suggested that there could be continued concerns over deregulatory takings in the natural gas pipeline industry. FERC allayed those concerns by expressly providing for full recovery of gas supply realignment costs. As the D.C. Circuit noted in 1996 in *United Distribution Companies* v. *FERC*:

> Instead of refusing to establish a mechanism for pipelines to recover their take-or-pay costs, as it originally had in Order No. 436, FERC authorized pipelines to bill their customers separately for 100% of their GSR costs. This policy was, in fact, a substantial change from even Order No. 500, which permitted pipelines to surcharge their transportation customers for take-or-pay costs only if they agreed to absorb between 25 and 50% of those costs.[74]

As the D.C. Circuit noted, FERC later modified Order 636 by requiring pipelines "to bill 10% of their GSR costs to interruptible transportation customers."[75] The court, however, remanded the decision to FERC for a fuller explanation of its rationale for that method of cost recovery.

Wholesale Wheeling of Electricity

FERC has explicitly endorsed the recovery of stranded costs occasioned by the mandatory wholesale wheeling of electricity. The agency ruled in Order 888 in 1996 that "[i]f a former wholesale requirements customer

72. 824 F.2d 981, 998 (D.C. Cir 1987).

73. *See* Paul W. MacAvoy, Daniel F. Spulber & Bruce E. Stangle, *Is Competitive Entry Free?: Bypass and Partial Deregulation in Natural Gas Markets*, 6 YALE J. ON REG. 209 (1989).

74. 88 F.3d 1105, 1177 (D.C. Cir. 1996).

75. *Id.*

or a former retail customer uses the new open access" mandated by FERC, pursuant to the Energy Policy Act of 1992, "to reach a new supplier" of electricity, then "the utility is entitled to recover legitimate, prudent and verifiable costs that it incurred under the prior regulatory regime to serve that customer."[76] The agency concluded that "utilities that entered into contracts to make wholesale requirements sales under an entirely different regulatory regime should have an opportunity to recover stranded costs that occur as a result of customers leaving the utilities' generation systems through Commission-jurisdictional open access tariffs or . . . orders [under section 211 of the Federal Power Act], in order to reach other power suppliers."[77] FERC characterized the situation as one of *regulatory* change rather than strictly exogenous changes in market demand or technology:

> [W]e do not believe that utilities that made large capital expenditures or long-term contractual commitments to buy power years ago should now be held responsible for failing to foresee the actions this Commission would take to alter the use of their transmission systems in response to the fundamental changes that are taking place in the industry. We will not ignore the effects of recent significant statutory and regulatory changes on the past investment decisions of utilities. While . . . there has always been some risk that a utility would lose a particular customer, in the past that risk was smaller. It was not unreasonable for the utility to plan to continue serving the needs of its wholesale requirements customers and retail customers, and for those customers to expect the utility to plan to meet future customer needs. With the new open access, the risk of losing a customer is radically increased.[78]

FERC explicitly stated that "the electric industry's transition to a more competitive market is driven in large part by statutory and regulatory changes beyond the utilities' control."[79] The commission reiterated its earlier conclusion that electric utilities had been subject to a regulatory regime that "that, on the one hand, imposed an obligation to serve, and,

---

76. Promoting Wholesale Competition Through Open Access Non-Discriminatory Transmission Services by Public Utilities; Recovery of Stranded Costs by Public Utilities and Transmitting Utilities, Final Rule, Order No. 888, Dkt. Nos. RM95-8-000, RM94-7-001, 61 FED. REG. 21,540, 21,630 (1996) (construing Pub. L. No. 102-486, 106 Stat. 2776 (1992) (codified at 15 U.S.C. § 79z-5a, 16 U.S.C. §§ 796, 824)).
    77. *Id.* at 21,629.
    78. *Id.* at 21,629–30.
    79. *Id.* at 21,630 n.583.

on the other hand, permitted recovery of all prudently incurred costs."[80]
Stranded cost recovery also had an implication for the efficient and
equitable treatment of various customer classes, for "if customers leave
their utilities' generation systems without paying a share of these costs,
the costs will become stranded unless they can be recovered from
other customers."[81]

FERC believed that its experience in addressing stranded costs in
natural gas transportation following Order 636 had demonstrated the
need to include stranded cost recovery as part of the agency's initiatives
to order open-access transmission of wholesale power:

> We learned from our experience with natural gas that, as both a legal
> and a policy matter, we cannot ignore these costs. During the 1980s and
> early 1990s, the Commission undertook a series of actions that contribut-
> ed to the impetus for restructuring of the gas pipeline industry. The
> introduction of competitive forces in the natural gas supply market as a
> result of the Natural Gas Policy Act of 1978 and the subsequent
> restructuring of the natural gas industry left many pipelines holding
> uneconomic take-or-pay contracts with gas producers. When the
> Commission initially declined to take direct action to alleviate that
> burden, the U.S. Court of Appeals for the District of Columbia Circuit
> faulted the Commission for failing to do so. The court noted that
> pipelines were "caught in an unusual transition" as a result of regulatory
> changes beyond their control.[82]

FERC concluded that the D.C. Circuit's "reasoning in the gas context
applies to the current move to a competitive bulk power industry."[83] The
agency emphasized that it sought to avoid problems that it had created
in deregulating natural gas transportation by not addressing stranded
costs from the beginning:

> [B]ecause the Commission failed to deal with the take-or-pay situation in
> the gas context, the court invalidated the Commission's first open access
> rule for gas pipelines. Once again, we are faced with an industry
> transition in which there is the possibility that certain utilities will be left
> with large unrecoverable costs or that those costs will be unfairly shifted
> to other (remaining) customers. That is why we must directly and timely

80. *Id.* at 21,628.
81. *Id.*
82. *Id.* at 21,629 (quoting *American Gas Distributors*, 824 F.2d at 1027; other citations
omitted).
83. *Id.*

address the costs of the transition by allowing utilities to seek recovery of legitimate, prudent and verifiable stranded costs.[84]

At the same time, FERC emphasized that its rule for stranded cost recovery would not "insulate a utility from the normal risks of competition, such as self-generation, cogeneration, or industrial plant closure," which FERC emphasized "do not arise from the new availability of non-discriminatory open access transmission."[85] Just as our limiting principles would imply, FERC concluded that "[a]ny such costs would not constitute stranded costs for purposes of" the agency's rule for cost recovery.[86] Thus, FERC's decision in Order 888 was consistent with the limiting principle inherent in the correct interpretation of *Market Street Railway*, which would deny a utility recovery of costs that had become unrecoverable as a result of exogenous changes in technology or market demand.

Recapitulation of Deregulatory Experiences in Other Network Industries

Private municipal railways did not experience deregulatory takings because their inability to recover costs did not result from a change in regulatory policy. Airline deregulation did not satisfy the criteria for a deregulatory taking, in large part because a key characteristic of that industry is a limited degree of asset specificity. Railroad deregulation also did not effect a deregulatory taking, for the lifting of regulatory controls benefited the railroad industry by allowing it pricing and contracting flexibility to compete more effectively with other modes of transportation that had already imposed exogenous downward pressure on profitability. The AT&T divestiture did not effect a deregulatory taking for a number of reasons, including the fact that AT&T was released from incumbent burdens that had been imposed by regulation and an earlier antitrust consent decree. Open-access deregulation in natural gas transportation also did not satisfy the criteria for a deregulatory taking because FERC made explicit provisions for addressing stranded costs associated with supply contracts for gas that were priced above the deregulated market level. Thus, FERC avoided the takings issue through appropriate cost-recovery procedures. FERC chose the same course of action with respect

84. *Id.*
85. *Id.*
86. *Id.*

to stranded costs arising from mandatory wholesale wheeling of electricity.

CABLE TELEVISION FRANCHISES
AND MILITARY BASE CLOSINGS

The end of the Cold War precipitated a kind of stranded-cost problem concerning cable television franchises on military bases. The parallels to abrogation of the regulatory contract are strong. In a 1996 advisory opinion, Chief Judge Loren A. Smith of the Court of Federal Claims in effect ruled that the federal government was liable for the cable operators' stranded costs resulting from the military base closings.[87] Cable operators entered into franchise agreements with the federal government to serve military bases in a manner reminiscent of the grant of early utility franchises by municipalities: "the cable operator builds the infrastructure at its own cost, and is given a franchise to provide cable service for a term of years in which to recoup its costs and make a reasonable return on its investment."[88] The end of the Cold War, however, forced the federal government to close various military bases, an act with a "potentially devastating" effect on cable operators, who "had already made the up-front capital expenditures to build the cable system infrastructure, but often did not have enough time to recoup their costs by selling cable services on the bases."[89] The government took the position that the cable franchise agreements were "not contracts for goods or services" but "merely confer[red] upon the franchisee a non-exclusive right to enter the base to construct, install, maintain, and operate the facilities and equipment necessary to provide cable services."[90] Consequently, the government refused to accept any responsibility for a cable operator's unrecouped capital expenditures when a base was closed.

Chief Judge Smith rejected the government's position as a matter of law and equity. He believed that the "franchise agreements at issue are much more than mere easements: they create reciprocal rights and

---

87. In the Matter of the Department of Defense Cable Television Franchise Agreements, National Defense Authorization Act for Fiscal Year 1996—Section 823, 36 Fed. Cl. 171 (Ct. Fed. Claims 1996). The Court of Federal Claims may issue advisory opinions because it is an Article I court, not an Article III court. For simplicity, we ignore the various questions of government procurement law not critical to the decision's relevance, by analogy, to the regulatory contract.

88. *Id.* at 173–74.

89. *Id.* at 174.

90. *Id.*

responsibilities and include enforceable terms and conditions . . . that have nothing to do with easements or rights-of-way."[91] His rebuke of the government's position was reminiscent of contemporary arguments that the municipal franchises of electric utilities and telephone companies consist of nothing more than a permit to use public rights of way:

> [T]he government's argument that the franchise agreement is nothing more than a non-exclusive right of entry to construct, install, and maintain a cable system simply does not reflect the nature of the franchise agreement standing alone. The franchise agreement does contain such a right of entry, but this is only a portion of its scope. The agreement also memorializes the corresponding rights of the parties, and the obligations of the cable operator in actually operating the system. This goes far beyond a mere right-of-way . . . . [A] military base enters into a franchise agreement for the purpose of purchasing a service—the ability to have access to cable television for its direct use and the use of the base population. In consideration the cable operator is granted a specific term of years—embodied in the contract and enforceable by the cable operator—in which to make a return on its capital investment by selling subscriptions. It is true that the military is not obligated to purchase cable service under the terms of these franchise agreements, but the reality is that both the cable operator and the base know that sales to the base of cable service will be a natural consequence of the franchise agreement, and are expected to occur under the agreement.[92]

Chief Judge Smith noted that "the government's position would be far more plausible if it had merely provided a right-of-way, revocable at the government's option, for a cable operator to build, construct, and install a cable system," but that "a rational cable operator would never enter into such an agreement because it could have no guarantee that its investment would be protected."[93] Just as in the early Supreme Court decisions concerning municipal franchises, Chief Judge Smith's reasoning emphasized the necessity of cost recovery: "The consideration a cable operator receives in the franchise agreement is the term of years, which gives the cable operator the opportunity to recoup its investment and make a return on that investment."[94] And, just like the Supreme Court in the 1902 decision in *Detroit Citizens' Street Railway*,[95] Chief

---

91. *Id.* at 177 (citations omitted).
92. *Id.* at 178–79.
93. *Id.* at 179.
94. *Id.*
95. City of Detroit *v.* Detroit Citizens' Street Ry., 184 U.S. 368, 384–85 (1902) ("It

Judge Smith relied on proof by contradiction to establish that the bargain at issue must have envisioned that the franchisee would receive the reasonable opportunity to recover its costs:

> It is . . . instructive to see if the franchise agreement can be viewed rationally under the government's interpretation. Under the government's theory, cable operators are permitted to build and maintain a cable system at the cable operator's cost, while at the same time the contractor has no idea whether the term of years needed to recover its investment will take place. Moreover, the government at any time can close the base and eliminate the opportunity for the cable operator to recoup its costs. It appears clear to the court that no rational actor would agree to such terms; it would face unquantifiable risks and uncompensable damages. This approach would turn a cable franchise at a military base into a pure gamble.[96]

In short, the form of exchange that the government depicted would have been involuntary—and thus counterfactual in an economy where there is no conscription of private capital.

Chief Judge Smith then considered the foreseeability of the risk of base closure, the issue in the case analogous to the claim in the case of telephone and electric power industries that the regulator's abrogation of the regulatory contract was foreseeable. The government understandably took the position that "the risk of base closure was a legitimate business risk that cable operators assumed when entering into these agreements."[97] Chief Judge Smith disagreed:

> Aside from the fact that it was very unlikely that base closure was ever contemplated by either the government or cable operators as a real possibility when these agreements were executed, this cannot be considered a legitimate business risk. No person would argue that cable operators are guaranteed a profit; they are susceptible to the traditional risks all businesses face. Things such as changing costs, the ability to attract customers, and the estimates and projections on which bids are

would hardly be credible that capitalists about to invest money in what was then a somewhat uncertain venture, while procuring the consent of the city to lay its rails and operate its road through the streets in language which as to the rate of fare amounted to a contract, and gave the company a right to charge a rate then deemed essential for the financial success of the enterprise, would at the same time consent that such rate then agreed upon should be subject to change from time to time by the sole decision of the common council.").

96. 36 Fed. Cl. at 179.
97. *Id.*

made all are business variables that are inherent to any business venture. The closure of the military base, however, is *a unilateral act by a party to the bargain that deprives cable operators not only of any opportunity to make a profit but of any opportunity to recover fixed and sunk costs.* Such action by one party to a bargain that can directly damage the other cannot be considered to fall under the rubric of legitimate business risk.[98]

Chief Judge Smith concluded that "impacted cable operators are entitled as a matter of law to termination for convenience costs for the unamortized and unreturned portion of their capital investments."[99]

Chief Judge Smith also concluded that the cable operators had "a strong equitable claim to compensation regardless of the status of the law."[100] He reiterated that "the cable operator needs the term of years under the franchise agreement to recoup its capital investment and make a return on that investment" and that "the possibility of major base closure was simply not seriously considered by either franchisors or franchisees as defense spending continued to increase prior to the end of the Cold War."[101] His comments about the unpredictability of the end of the Cold War echo the comments about the unpredictability of regulatory change's scrapping the old paradigm and mandating unbundled network access in local telephony and electric power:

> There was simply no consideration that the military would shrink rapidly, necessitating the closure of bases while cable operators were still trying to recoup their investments. Further, the closing of the bases, which effectively denied the cable operators on impacted bases the opportunity to recoup their investments, was, of course, without any fault by the cable operators nor within their control. Closure means the subscriber population literally disappears, leaving the cable operator with a ghost system.[102]

Chief Judge Smith concluded his advisory opinion by recommending that Congress enact legislation to permit cost recovery for the cable operators, and he even suggested a formula for achieving that purpose.

---

98. *Id.* (emphasis added).

99. *Id. Convenience costs* is a term of art in procurement law. *See* Torncello *v.* United States, 681 F.2d 756, 759 (Fed. Cir. 1982).

100. 36 Fed. Cl. at 180.

101. *Id.*

102. *Id.*

The cable operators affected by military base closings do not, of course, strictly satisfy all four of our limiting principles for stranded cost recovery. As Chief Judge Smith's advisory opinion makes clear, those operators have an enforceable contract similar in nature to the regulatory contract. Their cable infrastructures are ample evidence of investment-backed expectations. And they will assuredly suffer a decline in their expected revenues following the base closings. But, unlike a utility undergoing deregulation, those cable operators did not experience the elimination of regulatory entry barriers. Instead, they experienced the complete elimination of demand for their services due to the government's unilateral actions. Nonetheless, the legal analysis of the rights of cable operators affected by military base closings helps to illuminate the regulatory contract, for the decision to abrogate that contract, like the decision to close a particular base, is a "unilateral act by a party to the bargain that deprives" the regulated firm "not only of any opportunity to make a profit but of any opportunity to recover fixed and sunk costs."[103]

RETROACTIVE PRUDENCY REVIEWS AS A CONDITION FOR RECOVERY OF STRANDED COSTS

In Order 888 FERC ruled that stranded costs associated with a departing customer could be recovered only if they were "legitimate, *prudent* and verifiable costs" that the electric utility "incurred under the prior regulatory regime to serve that customer."[104] That condition raises the question of whether prudency of investment should be a limiting principle for stranded cost recovery in addition to the four principles that we have identified in this chapter. Our view, which we express in chapter 5, is that it would be superfluous to require the utility to prove for a second time the prudency of the investments whose costs are stranded by the elimination of entry regulation or mandatory unbundling. The regulator already passed on the prudency of those investments before the utility made them and was allowed to include them in its regulated capital account. Despite our initial resistance to making a retroactive prudency review a precondition or limiting principle for the recovery of stranded costs, Judge Stephen F. Williams has criticized our earlier writings as insufficiently attentive to the need for such a review.[105]

---

103. *Id.* at 179.
104. Order No. 888, 61 FED. REG. at 21,630 (emphasis added).
105. Williams, *supra* note 14.

Judge Williams's "central concern" with our analysis "is the question of why the old utility may not be in a good position to compete with new entrants."[106] He disagrees with our analysis to the extent that he considers it to be limited by "the failure to sift out and deny compensation for sunk but inefficient capital costs."[107] (Oliver E. Williamson, also responding to our earlier article, suggests that regulatory inefficiencies might excuse deregulatory takings.[108]) Apart from that concern, however, Judge Williams agrees that, if the utility's inability to compete after deregulation has resulted from mandatory cross-subsidies in the rate structure or other incumbent burdens, we are

> surely right, at least as a first approximation, in saying that compensation is economically sound. When "deregulation" exposes the regulated firm to what is called cream-skimming, *i.e.*, to market prices in the markets where it has been collecting rents that the regulator has doled out to someone else, the authors' case for compensation is powerful. And a duty to provide compensation will create pressure on the regulators to protect the utility by *rebalancing* the pricing, *i.e.*, by using rebalancing to satisfy the compensation requirement (in whole or in part).[109]

Judge Williams, however, expresses skepticism that the losses from deregulatory unbundling flow only from such distortions mandated by regulation. "It is a commonplace of regulatory literature," he notes, "that the price-regulated natural monopoly is likely to be run inefficiently and with a degree of gold-plating—lavish executive offices, corporate jets, etc."[110] Judge Williams therefore disputes the propriety of compensating the incumbent utility for its inability to recover certain kinds of costs of a competitive environment:

> [T]ake the case of the electric utility that is suddenly required to wheel electricity for other entrants and finds its own power uncompetitively expensive. Part of its plight may well be due to obligations to sell to privileged customers at inadequate prices, but part of it may be due to inefficiencies generally associated with price-regulated natural monopo-

---

106. *Id.* at 1000.

107. *Id.* at 1005.

108. Oliver E. Williamson, *Deregulatory Takings and Breach of the Regulatory Contract: Some Precautions*, 71 N.Y.U. L. REV. 1007, 1013–14 (1996).

109. Williams, *supra* note 14, at 1001 (emphasis in original).

110. *Id.* (citing Bernard S. Black & Richard J. Pierce, Jr., *The Choice Between Markets and Central Planning in Regulating the U.S. Electric Industry*, 93 COLUM. L. REV. 1339, 1345 (1993)).

lies. Can one clearly say that there is a compelling principle of political economy requiring compensation for one hundred percent of the losses attributable to inefficiency?[111]

Complicating the equitable case for recovery of the costs of the utility's inefficient practices, in Judge Williams's view, is the possibility that the utility "captured" the very regulators who subsequently found the firm's inefficient investments to be prudent or, worse, never bothered to enquire into the matter:

> Now it is quite true that the *stockholders* will have gained nothing from the inefficiencies (though gold-plating will have benefited management). So, lapsing from efficiency to equity, I can see some equitable claim. But by the same token, it is not clear that customers necessarily bear any more responsibility for this perversity. One might say that regulation had been embarked upon in their name, so they should bear the costs of transition. But even this equitable argument is undercut if you accept commonly held stories of regulation as a benefit for the regulated firms, deliberately secured by them in the political market. If the equities are uncertain, there surely is ground to resist a compensation rule that projects the ill effects of regulation-induced inefficiencies into the future.
>
> The problem is further complicated by the very source of these inefficiencies. If regulators were thoroughly adept at spotting inefficiencies, they wouldn't have existed in the first place—the regulators would have screened them out as impermissible costs. In fact, one of the arguments for deregulatory unbundling is precisely the tendency of regulation to cause inefficiencies. So there may be considerable difficulty separating the portion of the firm's losses due to embedded inefficiencies and the portion due to pricing imbalance.[112]

Judge Williams further notes that as an empirical matter, "costs are commonly not evaluated by the regulatory agency at all unless an issue has been made of them in a rate case."[113] He therefore disputes the factual premise of our earlier discussion in which we argue that conditioning stranded cost recovery on an ex post prudency review is to

---

111. *Id.* at 1001–02.

112. *Id.* at 1002–03 (emphasis in original). As Judge Williams notes, *id.* at 1003 n.8, one of us has written that the opportunity cost component of the efficient component-pricing rule *"must exclude any monopoly profits or excessive costs attributable to inefficiency."* WILLIAM J. BAUMOL & J. GREGORY SIDAK, TRANSMISSION PRICING AND STRANDED COSTS IN THE ELECTRIC POWER INDUSTRY 117 (AEI Press 1995) (emphasis in original).

113. Williams, *supra* note 14, at 1003.

give the regulator (and consumers) two bites at the investment apple. Two bites would not be objectionable in the abstract, but in practice several costs would arise.

To respond to Judge Williams's criticism, let us first consider cases in which prudency reviews did precede the construction or inclusion in the rate base of substantial investments that have become uneconomic in the competitive market. We continue to believe that it would be inefficient in such cases to require a retroactive prudency review as a condition of stranded cost recovery. Four kinds of unnecessary costs would attend such proceedings. First, at the time that the utility made its investment in nonsalvageable assets, the expectation of a second prudency review years after the utility had made its investment in long-lived assets would shift risk from consumers to the utility and thus raise the utility's cost of capital relative to what it would be in the absence of such a procedure. To the extent that the cost of capital had not compensated the utility's shareholders for that allocation of risk, the retroactive prudency review would effect a wealth transfer after the utility had invested in asset-specific capital. Going forward, of course, investors would explicitly demand such a risk premium.

Second, a retroactive prudency review conducted years after the utility had made its investment in long-lived assets would be a fact-intensive proceeding that would have the high transaction costs and evidentiary complications inherent in any commercial litigation concerning business decisions that had been made decades earlier. *Every* state and federal unbundling proceeding in the electric power and local telephony industries could be expected to generate protracted litigation over the prudency of investments that had long before been the basis for the calculation of rates that regulators had approved as just and reasonable. As a legal matter, the prudency of those investments is and should be *res judicata*.[114] As a broader matter of public policy, all the arguments that justify doctrines of issue preclusion in civil procedure would militate against relitigating the prudency of investments that regulators evaluated years or decades earlier. Note also that the retroactive prudency review is inherently an asymmetric process. No one is suggesting that, at the time it seeks to recover its stranded costs, a utility should be allowed to revisit the question of whether investments previously determined to have been imprudently incurred were in fact erroneously disallowed by the regulator. That asymmetry means that those seeking retroactive prudency reviews would have nothing to lose,

114. *See, e.g.*, Ryan v. New York Tel. Co., 62 N.N.2d 494, 499 (1984).

except their own transaction costs. Consequently, their demand for such reviews would be excessive.

Third, a retroactive prudency review would implicitly focus on an asset-by-asset summation of stranded costs. As chapter 5 argues, however, that approach is inferior on both theoretical and computational grounds to an estimation of the diminution of the utility's net revenues after mitigation.

Fourth, a retroactive prudency review presents a question that goes to the heart of identifying and compensating stranded costs: Prudent *for what purpose?* The answer to that question returns us to *Northern Pacific Railway*. It is not legitimate to ask whether a set of transaction-specific investments that were designed to provide an integrated network to end customers also happens to embody an efficient design for the same utility now to supply unbundled network segments or elements to its competitors. As Baumol and Willig observe in the case of railroads, "investors have committed vast sums to provide efficient *networks*, and not merely segments."[115] It would contravene takings jurisprudence and sound economic policy for regulators or courts to use retroactive prudency reviews as camouflage while they proceeded to redefine without just compensation the public purpose to which the utility had originally dedicated its private property.

Those four considerations imply that, with respect to any investment for which the utility already underwent a prudency review, it would be inappropriate to require another, retroactive prudency review as a condition for permitting the utility to recover its stranded costs. One may continue to object that the regulator that passed on the prudency of the utility's investment was captured by the firm that it purported to regulate or was too inept to regulate it in a manner truly in the public interest. Judge Williams observes that, "if one of the defects of regulation is that we doubt the ability of the regulators to identify inefficiency, the fact of their failure to do so proves little."[116] But, as chapter 13 argues, that lament is really one that concerns the failure of democratic institutions. The legislators and regulators entrusted to design effective regulation failed in their task. Moreover, if the regulator demonstrated its susceptibility to type I errors by incorrectly determining imprudent investment to be prudent, what confidence could we have that, in subsequent determinations attending proceedings for stranded cost recovery, the same regulators would not also commit type II errors by retroactively

---

115. *Baumol-Willig STB Response*, *supra* note 44, at 8 (emphasis in original).
116. Williams, *supra* note 14, at 1003.

reclassifying prudent investment as imprudent and hence ineligible for stranded cost recovery? Alternatively, an appellate court might have the wisdom and insulation from interest-group politics to commit far fewer type I and type II errors than a regulatory commission. But for a court to displace the public utilities commission in that manner and to insinuate itself so deeply and expansively into the technicalities of public utility regulation would, in effect, reinforce the conclusion that the democratic processes that created the regulatory process had failed.

Now consider cases where prudency reviews did *not* precede the construction or inclusion in the rate base of substantial investments that became uneconomic in the competitive market. Here, for the reasons that Judge Williams identified, a regulator would have a stronger rationale for requiring a retroactive prudency review as a condition for stranded cost recovery. Yet even in such cases the rationale for a retroactive prudency review is far from compelling. Judge Williams may be correct that "costs are commonly not evaluated by the regulatory agency at all unless an issue has been made of them in a rate case."[117] But public utility regulation implicitly contains a private enforcement mechanism in the form of intervention by large, well-organized customers. Judge Williams's legitimate observation therefore invites one to ask why the utility's large business and industrial customers failed to act in their own self-interest by intervening in the very rate cases in which the regulator approved, as just and reasonable, prices that provided for cost recovery for the investments that those customers subsequently contend, in stranded cost proceedings, were imprudently incurred. On such facts it would appear that, as evidenced by their own behavior, large customers in such rate cases did not consider the investments at issue to have implications for the regulated price of service that were significant relative to the costs of intervening in the rate proceeding. In that case, it would hardly be appropriate to make the past inaction of such customers a factor that favored revisiting the prudency question today.

Judge Williams questions whether ongoing operating costs due to past regulatory decisions should be counted as part of stranded costs. He offers the example of inefficient natural gas procurement contracts entered into under regulation.[118] In our view, the operating costs due to past regulatory decisions remain the responsibility of regulators, and such was the case with FERC's handling of the transition costs in natural gas. Judge Williams points out that the recovery mechanism will affect the economic outcome. If the regulator allows the regulated firm to

117. *Id.* at 1003.
118. *Id.* at 1003–04.

recover those costs as they are incurred, that policy could dull the incumbent's incentives to mitigate those costs, while reimbursement of those costs upon deregulation would transfer to the utility any costs savings from mitigation. The problem is how to preserve incentives for mitigation by the firm while sharing the gains from mitigation with consumers. That is a thorny problem that raises both economic efficiency and equity issues. The incentive effects of pay-as-you-go compensation are essentially those of standard cost-of-service regulation. If the main concern is equity, then pay-as-you-go is the right approach, with regulators' attempting to mitigate costs by using any leverage over the parties to the contracts to renegotiate. If the main concern is efficiency, then a fixed payment will cause the incumbent to renegotiate, as Judge Williams observes. The two objectives can be reconciled by choosing a fixed payment that takes into account the likelihood and magnitude of future mitigation. The expected value of costs to be recovered then would be deducted from the estimated payment for stranded costs. In that way, consumers would recover the *expected* gains from mitigation, and the incumbent's incentives for mitigation would be preserved.

CONCLUSION

The repudiation of the regulatory contract in local telephony and the electric power industry presents the same fundamental admonition that Justice Oliver Wendell Holmes issued in *Pennsylvania Coal Co. v. Mahon* in 1922: "We are in danger of forgetting that a strong public desire to improve the public condition is not enough to warrant achieving the desire by a shorter cut than the constitutional way of paying for the change."[119] If, as appears to be the case, those network industries cease to exhibit conditions of natural monopoly in their production technologies, then no disagreement can remain on economic grounds that competition is superior to regulated monopoly. Only the proper means to achieve that end are in dispute. Just as Holmes recognized, "the question at bottom is upon whom the loss of the changes should fall."[120] The answer that regulators, legislators, and the Supreme Court ultimately give to that question will affect more than perceptions of the fairness of past regulatory policies. That answer will also affect the economic efficiency of future regulatory policies, as well as perceptions of the trustworthiness of government when it makes future commitments to

119. 260 U.S. 393, 416 (1922).
120. *Id.*

private parties. The proper treatment of stranded costs, in short, concerns the future as much as the past.

To establish a deregulatory taking, it should be necessary and sufficient for a regulated firm to show the existence of a regulatory contract; evidence of investment-backed expectations; the elimination of regulatory entry barriers; and a decline in the regulated firm's expected revenues. Actual experience in a number of regulated industries indicates that regulators have repeatedly recognized the implications of stranded cost recovery and have allowed such recovery in a manner consistent with our four limiting principles. Consistent with the facts and circumstances of particular industries, those regulators have afforded the incumbent utility the opportunity to recover costs stranded by regulatory change rather than exogenous declines in demand for the utility's services.

15

Deregulation and Managed Competition in Network Industries

HOW SHOULD REGULATORS approach the competitive transformation of network industries? The temptation is to "manage" the competitive transition so as to determine the *outcome* of competition. Thus, paradoxically, the process of deregulation often brings about increased regulatory intervention in the marketplace and correspondingly greater administrative costs and market inefficiencies. The result is neither fish nor fowl, neither a regulated market nor a competitive one. The benefits of competition do not materialize. Partial deregulation distorts economic incentives in a manner that is far worse than traditional rate-of-return regulation or newer forms of incentive regulation. The staffs and budgets of the regulatory agency swell as they undertake the impossible task of managing markets. The problem is akin to privatization in planned economies. Government policymakers must be willing to forsake power and influence over the economy, and to trust what they sometimes view as the "chaos" of the marketplace.

Regulators are concerned with achieving competition "fairly," yet markets are well known for their efficiency properties, rather than the equity of the outcomes that they produce.[1] Economists may posture as purists and assert that it is misguided for regulators to pursue any goal other than economic efficiency. However correct that position may be as

---

1. The California Public Utilities Commission, for example, "shall take steps to ensure that competition in telecommunications markets is fair and that the state's universal service policy is observed." CAL. PUB. UTIL. CODE § 709.5.

a matter of theory, it does not take the institutional setting of regulation as it really is. Consequently, although economists may consider the definition of "fair competition" to be an oxymoronic undertaking, it is nonetheless necessary to supply regulators with an operational definition of fairness that does not attempt to specify outcomes. They need a set of objectives that does not perpetuate regulation but rather lets regulation recede as competition progresses. This chapter proposes three general principles for providing such a definition and thus facilitating the regulator's role in the competitive transformation of network industries.

Free-market competition likely will bring significant benefits to consumers by enhancing the productive efficiency of companies in telecommunications, electric power, and other network industries. Competition will increase the variety of products and services that are offered and stimulate technological innovation. Achieving the benefits of market allocation, however, does not mean that regulators should transfer income from regulated utility investors to consumers. Regulators should not confuse such income transfers with efficiency gains. Instead, regulators should establish basic rules for an orderly transition to competition that rely on competitive innovation and cost cutting as the sources of consumer benefits. To achieve fully the benefits of competition while preserving fairness, regulators should observe three fundamental principles:

Economic incentive. To preserve economic incentives requires cost recovery for past, present, and future regulatory obligations. The regulated incumbent would not undertake significant expenditures to perform its regulatory service obligations or continue to incur such expenses without economic incentives. Eliminating cost recovery for regulatory obligations will induce free riding by entrants and regulators, and it will make it difficult for regulators to achieve future agreements with private firms. The consequences of reducing or eliminating those economic incentives would be to raise the incumbent firms' cost of capital, to reduce the quality of their service, to discourage their innovation and investment, and ultimately to deprive markets of the competitive effort and technological expertise of the incumbents.

Equal opportunity. To achieve the benefits of competition fairly requires that regulations fall evenly on both competitive entrants and the formerly regulated incumbent. In practice, that even-handedness means that incumbent burdens must be either dismantled or shared equally across market participants and that any competitive flexibility possessed by entrants must be accorded to incumbents.

Impartiality. Regulatory commissions cannot "pick winners" in terms of technology, products and services, individual companies, or market institutions. Regulators can achieve the benefits of competition only by refraining from market interventions that favor particular competitors, by avoiding attempts to manage competitive outcomes, and by dismantling regulation in demonstrably competitive markets— that is, where there are actual and potential alternatives.

In this chapter we examine the economic incentive principle, set out its underpinnings based on the regulatory contract, and assess the implications for competition, investment, innovation, and quality of service if competitive rules reduce economic incentives for incumbents. We then examine the equal opportunity principle, identify its relationship to competitive entry, and explore its implications for the removal and sharing of incumbent burdens and the removal of regulatory restrictions on incumbent utilities. Finally, we examine the impartiality principle and explain the need for regulators to remove excessive regulation.

A consistent application of those three principles would provide an essential set of guidelines for the restructuring of regulations governing network industries that would yield the benefits of competitive markets. For ease of exposition, we cast much of our discussion in terms of local telephony and local exchange carriers (LECs), although our analysis is intended to, and does, extend equally to investor-owned electric utilities, as well as other investor-owned public utilities that may face partial or total deregulation of their network industry.

THE ECONOMIC INCENTIVE PRINCIPLE

The *economic incentive principle* requires that the regulatory commission give the local exchange carrier the incentive to discharge its regulatory obligations. We consider the consequences for telecommunications markets of competitive rules that would deprive the incumbent LEC of the economic incentives to compete in the market, invest in expanding and upgrading facilities, maintain quality of service, and obtain investment capital. We then examine the implications of that principle for the design of competitive rules governing the local telecommunications market.

Incentives for Voluntary
Exchange and Investment

Economic analysis of how consumers, companies, investors, and other market participants make choices rests on the notion of response to incentives. A consumer purchases goods and services only if he anticipates gains from trade—that is, only if he expects the transaction to yield positive net benefits for him. Companies supply products and services in the hope of earning economic profits—that is, earnings beyond what is necessary to keep all factors of production employed in their current use. It follows that a supplier will not invest in a transaction unless he expects the returns from the transaction to recover all economic costs, including a competitive return to invested capital. Investors supply funds to projects in expectation of earning a competitive return on their investment—that is, a return that equals the return on other investment opportunities of comparable risk. Markets function on the basis of those economic incentives.

Economic incentives imbue contract law. As we discuss in chapter 4, a contract must provide *consideration* to each of the parties. Parties generally will not make promises gratuitously—that is, without a contract that provides them with economic incentives to supply goods or services or other performance specified in the contract.[2] Damage remedies for breach of contract also contain economic incentives. Without such incentives, a party to the contract would be tempted to behave in an opportunistic fashion: He would break the contract (without cost to himself) when it was advantageous for him to do so; and, by unilaterally forcing a renegotiation of the contract terms, he would take advantage of the irreversible commitments made by the other party to the contract. Without such incentives to honor the terms of efficient contracts, parties would decline to enter into contractual commitments, and society would lose the many benefits of contractual exchange.

As chapters 4 and 6 explain in detail, legal protections of private property rest on economic incentives. Without property protections, individuals and businesses would not have an incentive to invest in improvements of their property. Without property protections for the residual returns from investment projects, companies would not have the incentive to undertake those productive activities. Economic incentives therefore affect the production and investment behavior of any firm, whether or not that firm is subject to regulation. Federal and state regulation of pubic utilities takes account of the economic incentive principle. A utility would not have undertaken the extensive investments required to provide regulated service within its franchise region without

2. In chapter 4 we also discuss the relevance of gratuitous promises to the regulation of network industries. We show that the law of gratuitous promises also protects economic incentives of investors in public utilities.

the necessary economic incentives. Removing such incentives would eliminate the impetus for a regulated company to undertake new expenditures to satisfy regulatory obligations.

Regulatory Opportunism and the Cost of Capital

As the telecommunications industry becomes deregulated, the incumbent LEC cannot be asked to provide services in the competitive market at regulated prices that are uncompensatory—that is, at prices that preclude any reasonable opportunity for full cost recovery. The destruction of economic incentives that would result from depriving a utility of the reasonable opportunity to earn a fair return on its investment would reduce the utility's ability—and hence its willingness—to continue providing service. By a "fair return" we mean the return that investors expect to receive in comparison with competitive alternatives of comparable risk. Accordingly, we use the terms *fair return* and *competitive return* interchangeably. If competitive rules deny the utility the reasonable opportunity to earn a fair return on its investments made under the previous regulatory regime (and thus cause stranded costs to materialize), the regulator's attenuation of economic incentives will create additional efficiency problems.

If the regulator's rule for deregulating the industry destroys the economic incentives facing the utility, then the regulator will create a temptation for opportunism and free riding; the regulator will also raise the cost of capital, deprive the market of some effective competitors, reduce the quality of service, and deter innovation. Concerns over reputation effects normally keep regulatory commissions from behaving opportunistically. If the regulatory commission were to behave opportunistically, there would be several related consequences. If a regulated firm were made to anticipate renegotiation of rate agreements after it had made irreversible investments, it would have an incentive to underinvest. Moreover, by raising the risks to investors through such opportunistic behavior, the regulator would necessarily raise the cost of capital to the regulated firm. That risk premium would apply to both debt financing and equity financing of utility investment.[3]

---

3. For a more technical discussion of the effects of imperfect regulatory commitment on the utility's capital structure and its cost of capital, see Yossef Spiegel & Daniel F. Spulber, *The Capital Structure of a Regulated Firm*, 25 RAND J. ECON. 424 (1994).

Denying the utility's investors the reasonable opportunity to earn a fair rate of return on their investments not only lowers the value of the utility's equity but also increases its cost of raising capital because investors must be compensated for the increased risk that they are made to bear. Thus, the inability of a utility to recover stranded investment would increase its capital costs. A regulatory commission must be aware that its reputation and the regulatory climate of its state affect the anticipated risk to potential investors. For the utility to be able to continue to attract capital, its rate of return must be competitive with other investment opportunities. If the regulator disappoints current investor expectations, investors will revise their assessment of the risks involved in continuing to invest in regulated companies in that state. In short, contrary to the simplistic assessment that stranded costs are sunk costs whose recovery does not affect the current and future decisions of economic actors, it is clear that the recovery of the utility's historic costs (also called embedded costs) is an issue whose treatment by the regulator during the transition to competition affects the utility's investment decisions and cost of capital on a forward-looking basis.

To the extent that some services provided by utilities continue to be regulated, the regulator's failure to address the problem of stranded costs harms the long-term interests of ratepayers. If the regulator does not protect the expectation interest of utility investors, then customers in competitive telecommunications markets may receive short-term gains at the long-term expense of other customers in segments of the market that continue to be regulated. That scenario represents an income transfer from one group of customers to another, rather than a benefit of deregulation.

Impairment of Competition

Reducing or eliminating the economic incentives for utilities will deprive local telecommunications markets of effective competitors. If those competitors would be able to bring specialized service capabilities and competencies to the market, then the variety of service offerings could decline appreciably. Customers would lose the opportunity to have the full range of choices of telecommunications carriers.

Eliminating the benefits of competition would raise prices for given levels of services and result in lower net benefits to consumers and reduced access to services. Eliminating the incumbent LECs as effective competitors would foreclose their providing the full benefit of their experience to the marketplace. That forgone participation in the marketplace could reduce the vigor and extent of competition as companies enter the market. Although entrants will compete vigorously for a share of the telecommunications market, the full participation of the incumbent LECs would further stimulate such competition.

Disincentive to Investment

Removing the returns to investment and denying the specific recovery of past investments would cause the incumbent LEC to reduce or eliminate the construction of transmission and switching facilities that are necessary to supply telecommunications services. That disincentive to investment would halt or slow the growth of existing networks and could reduce maintenance expenditures and delay the upgrading of transmission technology. Although competitors could be expected to supply some of the needed transmission technology, the extent of such supply of new facilities will depend critically on the pricing of unbundled network elements and wholesale services; even if competitors do become facilities-based entrants, the market would again be denied the benefits of having the incumbent LECs present as substantial and experienced rivals. Without a fair return on investment, the incumbent LECs would not continue to build facilities to accommodate growth in demand for their services; nor would the incumbent LECs enhance the capabilities of those facilities to respond to changing customer transmission requirements.

Utilities will participate in providing services only where they have an economic incentive to do so—that is, they will supply services only where they can earn a competitive return. If the competitive rules were to deny the incumbent LEC a fair return, those rules would impair the LEC's ability to compete and remove its incentive to participate in some types of service. With reduced market participation by the incumbent LEC, customers would have fewer choices of suppliers for particular services.

The investment in and maintenance of facilities entails economic costs—both operating costs and investment costs—including a fair return to invested capital. Reducing the earnings of the firm such that it could not earn a fair return on its invested capital would be a myopic policy that would prevent the firm from financing its maintenance and quality-enhancing activities.

One might argue that because capital facilities are nonrecoverable or sunk costs, the incumbent LEC would continue to operate as long as it had earnings that equal or exceed its operating costs. Could not the incumbents depreciate or "write off" all nonrecoverable capital costs already incurred without harming the incentives for continued operation?

That perspective assumes that, once in place, capital facilities continue to provide services without a continual need for maintenance, upgrading, and eventual replacement. If deprived of a return to capital facilities after capital has been sunk in irreversible investments, or if faced with reduced returns to such investments already made, any economically rational company will have the incentive to eliminate or reduce future capital investments of a like nature. Instead, the company will invest in more promising telecommunications ventures in Chile or New Zealand or Hungary. Such elimination or reduction of investment would diminish the quality of service for customers relying on the incumbent LEC's obligation to serve.

The incumbent LEC invests not only in facilities and maintenance of service quality, but also in the creation and deployment of innovative services. A firm invests in the risky process of product innovation only if it anticipates positive expected earnings on its new or enhanced services. The incumbent LEC also invests resources in "process" innovation—that is, in efficiency-enhancing or cost-reducing innovation. If it cannot obtain those returns to innovation, the incumbent LEC would have a reduced incentive to devote those resources to product and process innovation.

Summary of the
Economic Incentive Principle

The economic incentive principle implies that, if regulators do not allow incumbent utilities the opportunity to recover their stranded investment or the costs of satisfying additional regulatory requirements, then the service and investment incentives of those utilities will be severely impaired. In designing competitive rules, regulators should take account of the consequences caused by denying incumbent utilities the economic incentives to carry out their obligations to serve, to maintain quality of service, to raise capital for investment, to innovate, and to participate actively in deregulated telecommunications and energy markets. Without such incentives, one cannot expect utilities to continue making investments in regulated services. Moreover, regulators must honor their obligations to allow utilities a competitive rate of return on investments made to carry out regulated service obligations.

It is in the regulator's interest to renegotiate the regulatory contract only in a way that makes customers better off while maintaining economic incentives for the utility providing regulated services to continue investing in those services and preserving economic incentives for the investors who supply the utility with capital. That objective requires the regulator to enlist the support of the incumbent utilities in the transition to competition because they provide substantial transmission facilities and other network facilities for use in the competitive market, and they bring expertise and experience obtained from operating those facilities. If the regulator fails to give due regard to the recovery of stranded investment, he may inadvertently delay or forfeit the full economic gains from competition.

By adhering to the economic incentive principle, the regulator will ensure that he will not precipitate a reduction in the quality of service, that he will maintain incentives for innovation, that his policies will not elevate the incumbent LEC's cost of capital, and that one class of customers will not shift costs to core customers during any transition period. Continuing service requirements imposed on the incumbent LECs, particularly the obligation to provide unbundled network access, should be priced in a fashion that maintains the incumbent LEC's incentives to provide service. To do so requires compensating the incumbent LEC for all of its continuing and future regulatory obligations to serve, including its universal service obligation. As chapter 9 explains, if the price of unbundled network elements cannot provide the incumbent LEC with the level of contribution necessary to recover its forward-looking shared costs and common costs, then the regulator must implement a competitively neutral, nonbypassable end-user charge that is sufficient to offset the operating deficit that the incumbent LEC will incur on a going-forward basis. Similarly, the regulator must adopt a competitively neutral, nonbypassable mechanism that gives the incumbent LEC the reasonable opportunity to recover the substantial capital that it invested *before deregulation* to fulfil its obligation to serve, along with a competitive return on that invested capital.

By preserving economic incentives for the incumbent LEC, the regulator will not have an incentive to behave opportunistically by unilaterally rewriting the regulatory contract. Competitive rules should not deprive the incumbent LEC of the opportunity to earn a fair rate of return on its investments made to satisfy past, continuing, and future regulatory obligations.

THE EQUAL OPPORTUNITY PRINCIPLE

To achieve the economic benefits of competition, regulators must give the incumbent LEC an opportunity to compete that is equal to that given entrants. To do so requires modifying or eliminating regulatory rules that fall unevenly on the incumbent and the entrant, including rules that prevent the incumbent and the entrant from exercising the same flexibility in pricing, service offerings, investment, and choice of technology. The *equal opportunity principle* requires regulations to fall evenly on entrants and incumbents. That principle has two closely related implications. First, regulatory requirements imposed on the incumbent LEC that the regulator wishes to continue when the market is opened to competition should be imposed on all entrants. Second and conversely, the regulator should extend any flexibility and freedom from regulation that entrants possess to the incumbent LEC by removing the pertinent regulations that apply exclusively or disproportionately to the incumbent LEC.

Regulations create costs and constraints for market participants. Regulations that favor incumbents over entrants will create regulatory *barriers to entry* that reduce market competition and potential entry. That situation can create inefficiencies in the protected market, with or without regulatory safeguards, in comparison with the outcome of a competitive market. Government regulation that takes the form of rules applying unevenly to incumbents and entrants can create additional costs for entrants. Government regulation can also restrict market entry outright, so much so that George J. Stigler referred to licenses as "absolute barriers to entry."[4]

In contrast, regulations that favor entrants over the incumbent limit the incumbent's ability to compete, and thus they create *incumbent burdens*, as chapter 2 discusses. Deregulation requires the removal of utility regulations that are not imposed on entrants, including continuing obligations to serve, liabilities undertaken in response to regulatory requirements or in reasonable expectation of a continuation of regulatory policy, and restrictions on the utility's pricing and its product and service offerings. Incumbent burdens provide incentives for inefficient bypass of the incumbent's transmission facilities by taxing the incumbent and by creating corresponding subsidies for entrants.[5] As one of us has previously noted:

> The benefits of entry, including survival of low-cost producers and efficient pricing, may not be achieved if the incumbent must satisfy

---

4. GEORGE J. STIGLER, THE ORGANIZATION OF INDUSTRY 123–25 (Richard D. Irwin, Inc. 1968).

5. *See* Paul W. MacAvoy, Daniel F. Spulber & Bruce E. Stangle, *Is Competitive Entry Free?: Bypass and Partial Deregulation in Natural Gas Markets*, 6 YALE J. ON REG. 209, 228 (1989).

regulations not imposed on entrants. Costly duplication of capital facilities may occur. Loss of economies of scope may create welfare losses for the remaining customers served by the incumbent firm. Thus, deregulation does not merely require competitive opportunities for entrants; it also requires an equal lifting of restrictions placed on established firms.[6]

To satisfy the equal opportunity principle requires designing regulatory rules that create neither undue entry barriers nor incumbent burdens.

Accordingly, regulators should eliminate any incumbent burdens that impose costs that entrants do not bear. Any continuing obligations to serve that incumbents currently shoulder should be shared equally with competitors or eliminated entirely. The regulator should not impose new asymmetric liabilities on the incumbent in response to regulatory requirements or in anticipation of a continuation of regulatory policy; if such new liabilities are absolutely necessary, the regulator should design them to impose equal costs on the incumbent and entrants. Finally, the regulator should remove or redesign regulations to guarantee that the incumbent has the same regulatory flexibility in terms of pricing and service offerings that entrants have. If regulators constrain the incumbent's ability to compete, they will not secure for consumers the full benefits of competition.

The Economic Basis for Achieving the Benefits of Competition and Entry

Regulators can achieve the economic benefits of competition and entry only if all companies have an equal opportunity to compete. Competition means that the most efficient and creative firms prosper. The market cannot be expected to discover the best competitors unless all companies begin on an equal regulatory footing. We consider now the economic benefits of competition—lower prices, cost efficiency, product variety, and innovation—and explain why regulators must follow the equal opportunity principle to achieve those benefits. Eliminating regulations also creates direct benefits, including more efficient investment, lower administrative costs, flexibility in pricing and product offerings, and elimination of cross-subsidies in pricing.

The incumbent LEC is an important competitor with technological experience, management expertise, knowledge about customers in its

---

6. DANIEL F. SPULBER, REGULATION AND MARKETS 624 (MIT Press 1989).

service regions, ready access to financial capital, and transmission facilities. To deprive the market of the incumbent LEC's services and expertise would reduce competition. That outcome would disadvantage consumers and reduce the competitive stimulus to entrants. Regulators should not design competitive rules to eliminate the incumbent LEC from any part of the market, for that would waste valuable expertise, technology, and transmission facilities. Moreover, it is not necessary to limit the incumbent LEC's ability to compete as a means of encouraging new entry. As in any other business, the market returns that can be earned by providing telecommunications services are reward enough to encourage entry. Placing restraints on the incumbent LEC that confer an advantage on entrants does nothing but impede competition.

The Incumbent Should Have the Same Pricing Flexibility as Entrants

When companies compete to provide local telecommunications services, prices are driven down toward costs. Regulators, however, will not achieve the full benefit from competition if they continue price controls on the incumbent. The maintenance of price controls—not only price caps, but also price floors—prevents the incumbent from responding competitively to the price offers of entrants. That minimum-price constraint can prevent the incumbent's participation in important market segments, for the constraint provides an umbrella under which entrants can price without fear of retaliation from the incumbent.[7]

Price constraints on the incumbent also effectively discourage competition. It is well known that in price regulation "a ceiling can become a floor and a floor can become a ceiling." With regulatory price floors set on the incumbent, entrants could price just below the floor, tacitly coordinate their prices, and capture customers from the incumbent while avoiding competition among themselves. Eliminating the incumbent's price floor injects the incumbent into the market as a credible rival and allows the market price to fall freely, as true competition requires.

Price caps will discourage competition as well if regulators maintain them for the incumbent but do not require them for entrants. If a price cap prevented the incumbent from recovering its full economic costs, the cap could induce the incumbent to exit the market segment covered by

---

7. For an analogous assessment of the untoward consequences of the FCC's asymmetric regulation of AT&T in the interexchange market, see PAUL W. MACAVOY, THE FAILURE OF ANTITRUST AND REGULATION TO ESTABLISH COMPETITION IN LONG-DISTANCE TELEPHONE SERVICES (MIT Press & AEI Press 1996).

the cap (if the firm were permitted by law to do so), again depriving the market of an important competitor.

Further, a price constraint imposed on an unbundled service should not allow an entrant to offer the service as part of a bundle that competes effectively with the incumbent's bundled service strictly because of the price constraint. Unbundling should not imply that regulation prevents the incumbent from offering any bundled services; rather, unbundling should merely enable entrants to have access to components of the incumbent's bundled service. If there are competitive markets for those components, then regulators should eliminate the price constraints. In any case, if prices for components continue to be regulated, then they must allow the incumbent to recover its costs. Otherwise, if entrants can buy the components in a way that is uncompensatory for the incumbent, the result will simply be an income transfer from the incumbent's shareholders to the entrants' shareholders and the exit of the utility from market segments, again reducing the vigor of competition.

To increase profits and to achieve competitive advantage, companies continually strive to lower their costs and prices. They do so by acquiring new technology and by deploying their technology in the most efficient manner. Price caps and sharing rules are meant to provide incentives for regulated firms to improve cost efficiency because companies can retain a share of their cost savings from cost-reducing investment.[8] Price caps and sharing rules lose some of their incentive properties, however, if applied in a competitive market. The reason is that, if the incumbent utility must share the gains from investment while competitors may retain all their earnings, then the incumbent will have a relatively smaller incentive to provide the service. The sharing rule will function as a tax on the incumbent utility's earnings, thus reducing the incumbent's return on investment in comparison with that of competitors. Sharing rules should be eliminated so that the incumbent LEC and entrants have equal incentives to reduce costs, invest, expand, and compete for customers.

Limits on Pricing Flexibility Can Create
Inefficiencies in Entry and Investment

Regulators should not constrain the incumbent's price responses to entry to a greater extent than do the antitrust laws already. The incumbent

---

8. *See generally* DAVID E. M. SAPPINGTON & DENNIS L. WEISMAN, DESIGNING INCENTIVE REGULATION FOR THE TELECOMMUNICATIONS INDUSTRY (MIT Press & AEI Press 1996).

utility faces a set of incumbent burdens associated with the regulatory rate structure. Those burdens concern the *horizontal* rate structure (the relative rates charged to the utility's customer classes) and the *vertical* rate structure (the relative prices for network components and retail services). Entrants are free to set prices as market conditions change and to negotiate contractual agreements and discounts with individual customers. In contrast, the utility must file tariffs with the regulator and charge prices that are nondiscriminatory. Regulated rate structures therefore constrain the timing and substance of the price responses available to the incumbent once competition begins.

The utility's rate structure generally is based on cost allocation rules that determine the relative prices charged to various customer groups; or that rate structure contains price caps that continue to reflect past cost allocation rules. Those cost allocation rules often entail cross-subsidies. As chapter 2 explains, a regulated break-even rate structure is said to be free of cross-subsidies only if the revenues from each service, or combination of services, are less than or equal to the stand-alone cost of that service or combination of services. Under cost-of-service regulation, with a break-even rate structure, business customers are subsidizing other services if the revenues from business customers exceed the stand-alone costs of serving those customers. In that case business customers would be better off if they were to receive stand-alone service. Therefore, the presence of cross-subsidies provides opportunity for bypass of the incumbent's network. A stand-alone entrant can undercut the incumbent's rates and serve major customers while still earning economic profit.

The existence of cross-subsidies across customer classes creates incentives for bypass. Customers contract with entrants and bypass the facilities of the incumbent. At least initially, entrants serve those customers who had provided cross-subsidies. That selection bias in the class of customers served by entrants can lead to uneconomic bypass. The incumbent's facilities may be able to serve the market at least cost. But because regulation distorts relative prices across the incumbent utility's customer classes, the prices charged some customer classes do not reflect the incumbent's cost advantage. That artificial disparity between cost and regulated price allows some types of inefficient entry to occur that a competitive market would not tolerate. Total industry capacity may be excessive as a consequence. The industry's total costs of service can rise because the incumbent's facilities are not priced competitively and thus are employed below their most efficient scale of operation.

If rate restrictions remain on the incumbent LEC, then the outcome that results when regulators open the local telecommunications market to competition will not necessarily be efficient. The rate structure will prevent the incumbent LEC from responding to competition. That problem is exacerbated by cost-of-service regulation that is based on recovery of sunk costs or by incentive regulation that continues to reflect embedded-cost components. Valuation of the rate base using historical costs, rather than market value, further increases the distortion. Moreover, if the regulated utility faces a two-tier market divided into core and business customers, with price restrictions remaining in both market segments, its pricing decisions in the business market will be affected.

The Regulator Should Eliminate
Vertical Cross-Subsidies

The incumbent LEC's rate structure also contains vertical cross-subsidies: Some components, functions, or elements of telecommunications services are sold below cost and receive subsidies from other components or elements. For transfer revenues to be free of vertical cross-subsidies, the transfer revenue for a service must not exceed its stand-alone cost and must cover the incremental cost to the vertically integrated firm of producing the service.[9]

Suppose that a firm uses an input X to produce a retail service Q. Let $C(X)$ be the stand-alone cost of producing X. Let $C(Q)$ be the cost of producing Q by using the input X, *but excluding the cost of producing the input* X. Finally, let C be the total cost to a vertically integrated firm of producing both the input X and the final service Q by using the input X. Then, the transfer revenues must not exceed the stand-alone cost of the input, $C(X)$. Moreover, the transfer revenues must be greater than or equal to the incremental cost of the input to the vertically integrated firm, which equals C minus $C(Q)$.

Clearly, the regulated revenues from the final service should equal the total cost of providing the final service. Suppose that the input and the final service are unbundled, so that a purchaser buying the final service pays the sum of two charges. Then, if transfer revenues are subsidy-free, the separate charge for the final service cannot exceed the stand-alone cost of providing the downstream service (excluding the cost of the input). Moreover, the separate charge for the final service must be greater than or equal to the incremental cost of producing the final service for the vertically integrated firm.

9. That concept is defined formally in SPULBER, *supra* note 6, at 120.

Using the same notation as above, the separate revenues for the downstream service are less than or equal to the stand-alone cost. Then, the transfer revenues must not exceed the stand-alone cost of the output, excluding the cost of the input, $C(Q)$. Moreover, the transfer revenues must be greater than or equal to the incremental cost of the output to the vertically integrated firm, which equals C minus $C(X)$.

Unbundling Requirements Should Not Create Incumbent Burdens

Most products and services, from automobiles to piano lessons, are bundles of attributes or features. Customers also benefit from the convenience of purchasing a range of products and services from the same supplier that offers lower transaction costs through "one-stop shopping" and bundling of products and services. Companies compete by offering creative packages of goods and services that enhance customer convenience. Regulations on the incumbent LEC that prevent it from bundling, or that deny it access to services that are an important component of the product bundle, block incumbent entry into the market and can reduce the vigor of competition in such services.

If the incumbent LEC cannot provide interexchange services, for example, other firms will be able to resell bundles of services that include interexchange services without facing competition from the LEC. The interexchange carrier that bundles services will bid away customers by offering the convenience of one-stop shopping, not because the carrier has any inherent competitive advantage in providing local exchange services—or interexchange services for that matter. Rather, the competitive advantage is due to regulations that impose asymmetric unbundling requirements: The incumbent LEC cannot offer such a bundle while the interexchange carrier can. As a consequence, seemingly neutral unbundling requirements determine the outcome of competition. Moreover, the unbundling requirements become onerous when coupled with quarantines on the incumbent LEC that prevent its resale or provision of interexchange services. The result is a diminution in competition for a broad range of services relative to a market in which the incumbent LEC has an equal opportunity to compete.

Besides harming competition, asymmetric unbundling requirements are necessarily arbitrary. Excessive unbundling eliminates the benefits of reduced transaction costs from bundling features that increase consumer convenience. Furthermore, standardized bundles of product features and services lower the marketing and sales costs of the supplier, thus creating cost efficiencies. Forced unbundling is not a means by which regulators can replicate the functioning of competitive markets. To the contrary, because bundling is a standard aspect of competition, forced unbundling can achieve precisely the opposite result—it will eliminate product and service bundles that would have been offered in an unregulated market.

Unbundling of services is inconsistent with cross-subsidies. A regulator who orders unbundling cannot maintain cross-subsidization through geographic rate averaging or other rate-structure distortions such as business-to-residential cross-subsidies. Without limits, unbundling will eliminate the distinction between flat-rate and usage-sensitive pricing. Entrants will invariably purchase below-cost services and network elements and then provide their own bundled or unbundled services in competition with above-cost services. As a consequence, the incumbent will inevitably incur losses that will exacerbate the problem of stranded investment. As we have emphasized, cross-subsidies are an incumbent burden that can induce inefficient entry. Coupled with unbundling, cross-subsidies effectively disable the incumbent's ability to compete. To pursue a consistent deregulation strategy, the regulator must couple any unbundling policy with rate deregulation in the appropriate services that supply or receive cross-subsidies.

Elimination of Restrictions on Service Offerings by the Incumbent LEC

Competitive companies increase their returns by offering customers differentiated products. Customers benefit from greater product variety because they can purchase products that are better tailored to their preferences. Restrictions placed on the types of products and services that the incumbent LEC can offer again deprive the market of a potentially effective competitor. Although other competitors eventually may fill gaps in product and service offerings, consumers will lose the near-term benefits of such vigorous competition from the incumbent LEC.

Competition creates dynamic efficiencies as companies invest in research and development of new production processes that lower costs and deliver enhanced services with higher value to consumers. Regulations that limit the incumbent LEC's ability to compete, however, will reduce or eliminate that firm's incentive to invest in innovation, which in turn will create opportunities for entry and growth of competitors. The market will not achieve its full potential for consumers if regulation discourages the innovative contributions of the incumbent LEC.

A competitive market can exacerbate the unintended consequences of regulation. As chapter 3 explains, the Modification of Final Judgment (MFJ) contained a line-of-business restriction that prevented any regional Bell operating company (RBOC) from providing long-distance service from one local access and transport area (LATA) to another; the Department of Justice attempted to justify that restriction as a means of enhancing competition in the long-distance market.[10] That restriction, however, had the unintended (but, in retrospect, entirely predictable) consequence of reducing competition in the long-distance market; and unless the successor provision in section 271 of the Telecommunications Act of 1996 is construed in a more competitive manner, it will have the effect of also impairing the incumbent LEC's ability to compete in local exchange, much to the detriment of consumers.[11]

Rate regulation that creates cross-subsidies and other constraints on the pricing of the incumbent LEC place it at a disadvantage relative to entrants. To achieve the benefits of competition, regulators must give all competitors equal pricing flexibility. If allowed to persist, cross-subsidies built into the incumbent LEC's rate structure will encourage entrants to target the incumbent's above-cost customers in the markets for intraLATA toll services, switched access, vertical features, and the like. The incumbent LEC would be unable to change its regulated rate structure in response to such targeted entry, and its shareholders would be forced to absorb the economic loss arising from reduced revenues and fewer customers.

Quarantines, such as those contained in the MFJ and continued in the "checklist" provisions of section 271 of the Telecommunications Act of 1996, could prevent the RBOCs from offering competitive service packages. Interexchange carriers entering the local exchange market may bundle the RBOCs' local exchange services (purchased on an unbundled or wholesale basis) with their own long-distance service and thus offer their customers one-stop shopping. In other words, an interexchange carrier could package its own interLATA service with an RBOC's local exchange service that had been sold at wholesale (or recreated through the recombination of unbundled network elements) at less than that service's true economic cost. Given the prohibition against a public utility's unilaterally modifying its rate structure, that asymmetric ability to bundle services would place the RBOC at a severe competitive disadvantage. Regulators should not permit that distorted version of

10. *See* MacAvoy, *supra* note 7, at 175–212.
11. 47 U.S.C. § 271.

competition to obtain. Regulators should prevent an entrant from exploiting the horizontal subsidies that regulation has imposed across the incumbent LEC's services, as well as the vertical cross-subsidies built into the LEC's regulated transfer prices.

The regulatory obligation to serve should not unevenly distribute the burden of the social objectives of regulation between the incumbent LEC and entrants. Entrants generally can establish their own service areas, which allows them to target pockets of high-volume customers within the incumbent LEC's service area while neglecting less profitable customers in rural or high-cost locations. Meanwhile, the incumbent LEC retains the burden of serving those customers whom entrants find unprofitable to serve.

Regulators should carefully specify an entrant's service requirements. If an entrant's application to the regulator to provide local exchange service specifies a class of customers that the entrant intends to serve, and all customers outside that class could be denied the entrant's service regardless of their proximity to the entrant's facilities, such selectivity in the entrant's offering of service would disadvantage the incumbent LEC in favor of entrants. Again, entrants would provide service only to the most profitable customers and would leave the high-cost, low-volume users to be served by the incumbent LEC. The regulator should therefore create symmetric service obligations or provide a common fund to compensate the incumbent LEC for the full costs of satisfying its universal service obligation.

Another burden that the incumbent LEC shoulders is to serve as the carrier of last resort. Mandating that the incumbent LEC alone act as the carrier of last resort forces the firm to hold capacity in reserve to meet demand at peak load. An entrant, however, need not hold capacity in reserve because it does not serve as the carrier of last resort; the entrant can simply purchase capacity for resale from the incumbent LEC at peak demand. The entrant thus benefits from the implicit form of insurance provided to its customers without charge by the incumbent LEC's standby service.

Unless the regulatory framework adjusts to actual and impending competition, it can create incumbent burdens that artificially place the existing utility at a competitive disadvantage. The regulator should eliminate those asymmetric rules and avoid adopting new ones that deny the incumbent an equal opportunity to compete. For example, the lesser degree of pricing flexibility allowed the incumbent LEC enables entrants to adjust their prices in response to changing market conditions much faster than can the incumbent. That difference is a regulation-induced competitive advantage for entrants that comes at the incumbent's expense. In addition, regulators typically do not require entrants to provide cost studies to support their proposed rates, even though the incumbent LEC must provide such studies. Entrants derive an additional competitive advantage over the incumbent by virtue of their unreciprocated access to its cost studies. Furthermore, without proper safeguards applied equally to all local exchange carriers, entrants (which will include established firms such as AT&T and Time Warner) can exploit the regulatory constraints on the incumbent LEC in their design of pricing programs and service offerings. For example, the cost-study requirements borne by the incumbent LEC create delay that entrants can easily exploit in marketing new services. Unencumbered by those rules, entrants could be performing market research on new products while the incumbent LEC was still awaiting the regulator's permission.

The equal opportunity principle is essential to achieving the full benefits of competition. Regulators should dismantle incumbent burdens and remove regulations that impede the competitive flexibility of the incumbent LEC relative to entrants, including pricing flexibility and choice of service offerings. Regulators should allow the incumbent LEC the same flexibility in bundling services that is available to the entrants, for differences in the ability to bundle confer significant competitive advantages. Regulators should not mandate the unbundling of the components of demonstrably competitive services, for competitive markets suffice to determine the efficient extent of unbundling. Unbundling should not be an end in itself, for bundling products and services reduces customer transaction costs and enhances convenience. Numerous combinations and permutations on modes of access to local network services are not necessary to achieve regulatory objectives. Regulators should equitably distribute the obligation to serve among all competitors in the market, including the obligation to be the carrier of last resort. By pursuing those steps toward assuring equal opportunity in the marketplace, regulators will avoid creating or perpetuating incumbent burdens that entrants can evade and thereby achieve an artificial competitive advantage.

Caveats Concerning the Evolving Standard of Universal Service

The Telecommunications Act of 1996 codified and expanded the concept of universal service to be an evolving standard that advances with new technology.[12] If, as a matter of social policy, it is decided that a particular group of consumers should be subsidized in their use of interactive broadband services, it is preferable for government to fund those subsidies explicitly through its power to tax and appropriate funds from the public treasury. Regulators should resist the temptation to fund the subsidies by distorting the prices charged other consumers of interactive broadband services.

Some of the most notable statements by senior policymakers concerning telecommunications policy have referred to "information haves" and "information have-nots."[13] Those remarks imply that any disparity in access to interactive broadband services must be avoided as part of a technologically revised policy of universal service. There are several risks in viewing universal service through that lens. First, it is doubtful that, relative to private firms, government policymakers will have superior knowledge of the interactive broadband services that consumers will ultimately demand. If we do not even know what the "information haves" are likely to demand, the government can hardly know what to prescribe to improve the relative standing of the "information have-nots."

Second, consumer tastes are heterogeneous across the population. Consequently, it does not necessarily reflect a failure of government policy or an inequitable distribution of income that some consumers demand sophisticated communications products while others do not. Forcing all consumers to receive the same package of services is likely to cause providers of interactive broadband services to gravitate to the lowest common denominator. The result will be that interactive broadband services will be less diverse and less responsive to niche markets.

Third, the "information have-nots" may lack other important resources that impede their economic advancement, such as literacy, education, and work experience. If so, then the substantial cost of subsidizing interactive broadband access to their homes may actually divert the public's attention and financial resources from other policies that would materially improve conditions for those persons in a shorter period of time. It may be counterproductive as well as foolhardy to oversell the ability of the information highway to cure social ills.

12. 47 U.S.C. § 254. This discussion draws upon Robert W. Crandall & J. Gregory Sidak, *Competition and Regulatory Policies for Interactive Broadband Networks*, 68 S. CAL. L. REV. 1203, 1217–20 (1995).

13. Edmund L. Andrews, *The Media Business: New Plan for Phone and Cable*, N.Y. TIMES, Dec. 22, 1993, at D1 (reporting speech by Vice President Albert Gore).

Fourth, if universal service becomes the predominant public policy concern regarding the deployment and operation of interactive broadband networks, regulators may inadvertently foreclose the possibility of intermodal competition among rival networks in their attempt to use the information superhighway as a tool to redistribute income. A report by McKinsey & Company speculated how that state of affairs could arise:

> [T]he [Clinton] Administration has . . . stressed the need for universal access as a way to avoid the segregation of society into information "haves" and "have nots." This goal is likely to conflict with facilities-based competition. Market forces may well lead to the early deployment of two full-service networks in affluent areas, but preclude investment in costly-to-serve rural areas or impoverished inner-city neighborhoods. As the potential for conflict becomes more apparent, there may be a shift in regulatory policy toward a more heavily regulated, "one wire" approach, which avoids redundant investments in a second broadband network and gives greater emphasis to the policy objective of universal access.[14]

From the perspective of maximizing consumer welfare, it would be regrettable if the commitment to empowering disadvantaged segments of the population were to have the unintended effect of denying *all* segments of the population the substantial benefits that would flow from having two or more facilities-based providers of interactive broadband services rather than one.

Summary of the
Equal Opportunity Principle

On the basis of the equal opportunity principle, regulators should restructure regulation to ensure that all competitors enter the market on an even regulatory footing. Regulators should dismantle any incumbent burdens that deprive incumbent utilities of an equal opportunity to compete. For example, if regulators insist on market intervention to achieve universal service objectives, they should create a common fund, with equitable contributions made by all competitors to cover the cost of such service. Moreover, it is essential for regulatory commissions to eliminate horizontal and vertical cross-subsidies and to grant incumbent utilities the same pricing and service flexibility offered to competitors.

---

14. John Hagel III & Thomas R. Eisenmann, *Navigating the Multimedia Landscape*, MCKINSEY Q., June 22, 1994, at 39.

THE IMPARTIALITY PRINCIPLE

If regulators follow the economic incentive principle and the equal opportunity principle, they will establish the preconditions for achieving competition. Regulators will then face the challenge of making policies as market forces begin to supplant regulatory oversight, whether in the form of traditional cost-of-service regulation or incentive regulation. Society can realize the benefits of competition and deregulation only if regulators remain above the fray and decline, even in the face of unanticipated developments, the invitation of market participants to direct the outcome of competition. Regulators should take the initiative to "sunset" portions of regulation and exercise their full statutory authority to forbear from regulation. In so doing, regulators will allow competition and customer choice to determine market outcomes rather than administrative bargaining and rulemaking.

Once all market participants receive from regulators an equal opportunity to compete, what should happen after deregulation occurs and competition continues to increase? For markets to function properly, government cannot direct the outcomes without incurring high administrative costs and constraining customer choice and company innovation. The *impartiality principle* is therefore a fundamental component of public policy: Regulators should not "pick winners" in terms of technology, products and services, companies, or market institutions.

Deregulation should not be viewed as a type of industrial policy in which the government attempts to dictate or even gently nudge market outcomes, favoring one technology or mode of transmission over another. Regulators should not create artificial boundaries between modes of transmission, or artificial distinctions between services, customers, or carriers. Moreover, the deregulatory process should not be designed to favor specific services such as voice, data, or video transmission. Needless to say, the existence of the First Amendment testifies to the fact that, subject to very narrow qualifications, regulators *must* be impartial about the content of the information transmitted over the network.

By definition, the outcomes of technological innovation are unanticipated. Moreover, an important benefit of competition is that rival companies create unexpected products and services. That result is particularly salutary because neither regulators nor anyone else can easily predict the choices of individual customers. The regulator should resist the temptation to manage the rate and direction of technological innovation or to favor one mode of transmission or type of service over another. For regulators to do otherwise could force consumers to forgo the benefits of valuable innovation.

The impartiality principle is a policy prescription that recognizes the process of "creative destruction" that Joseph A. Schumpeter described in 1942.[15] He argued that the pursuit of market power is a creative, dynamic force that "incessantly revolutionizes the economic structure *from within*, incessantly destroying the old one, incessantly creating a new one."[16] Schumpeter saw such rivalry as "the essential fact about capitalism."[17] Creative destruction means that a firm's acquisition or possession of market power can be fleeting. In the most famous passage of Schumpeter's classic discussion on creative destruction, he wrote:

> [S]ince we are dealing with an organic process, analysis of what happens in any particular part of it—say, in an individual concern or indus-try—may indeed clarify details of mechanism but is inconclusive beyond that. Every piece of business strategy acquires its true significance only against the background of that process and within the situation created by it. It must be seen in its role in the perennial gale of creative destruction; it cannot be understood irrespective of it or, in fact, on the hypothesis that there is a perennial lull.
>
> But economists who, *ex visu* of a point in time, look for example at the behavior of an oligipolistic industry—an industry which consists of a few big firms—and observe the well-known moves and countermoves within it that seem to aim at nothing but high prices and restrictions of output are making precisely that hypothesis. They accept the data of the momentary situation as if there were no past or future to it and think that they have understood what there is to understand if they interpret the behavior of those firms by means of the principle of maximizing profits with reference to those data. The usual theorist's paper and the usual government commission's report practically never try to see that behavior, on the one hand, as a result of a piece of past history and, on the other hand, as an attempt to deal with a situation that is sure to change presently—as an attempt by those firms to keep on their feet, on ground that is slipping away from under them. In other words, the problem that is usually being visualized is how capitalism administers existing structures, whereas the relevant problem is how it creates and destroys them.[18]

15. JOSEPH A. SCHUMPETER, CAPITALISM, SOCIALISM AND DEMOCRACY 81–86 (Harper & Row 1942).

16. *Id.* at 83 (emphasis in original).

17. *Id.*

18. *Id.* at 83–84.

Unless government imposes artificial barriers to market entry—as it did in 1956, when an antitrust decree forbade AT&T to enter the computer business—actual and potential competitors will repeatedly challenge and inevitably supplant the incumbent. That version of competition, Schumpeter explained, "commands a decisive cost or quality advantage and . . . strikes not at the margins of the profits and outputs of the existing firms but at their foundations and their very lives."[19] Such competition, moreover, "acts not only when in being but also when it is merely an ever-present threat. It disciplines before it attacks."[20] Creative destruction thus implies that basing regulatory or antitrust policy on static analysis of today's market conditions can be seriously misleading.

If they must base regulatory intervention on predictions of dynamic trends in markets, government officials should proceed with the knowledge that their crystal ball may be just as cloudy as the one employed by the drafters of the AT&T divestiture. Government cannot ordain how the technologies of communications shall evolve, nor can government expect to remove the economic distortions that its regulations have created simply by ordering the industry to be restructured. The world's largest providers of telecommunications and information services are now locked in a tournament to offer consumers a new generation of interactive broadband services. It would harm consumers for regulators to exclude *any* firm from that tournament. The impartiality principle envisions that the regulator will impartially permit firms to compete for the market dominance that Schumpeter described, an ephemeral dominance from which they may be unseated by the next wave of product innovation.

The Benefits of Deregulation

We have identified some of the benefits of competition. There are many additional efficiency gains that deregulation can achieve. Those benefits include greater efficiency in entry and investment decisions, lower administrative costs, elimination of pricing distortions, increased innovation, and greater opportunities for customer choice. Under regulation, the incumbent LEC invested in facilities to perform its obligation to serve and to achieve regulatory objectives, including the provision of universal service. The possibility that stranded costs will arise as regulators permit competition in the market for local telephony indicates that such investment may not have been economically effi-

19. *Id* at 84.
20. *Id*. at 85.

cient—that is, it may fail to be the case that the incremental benefits to consumers exceed the incremental costs of the investment. Through their performance of prudency reviews and used and useful tests, regulators attempted to guard against inefficient investment that did not satisfy regulatory criteria. Those safeguards, however, were significantly different from a full test of economic efficiency. The deregulation of telecommunications now forces companies investing in facilities for access, switching, transmission, and other functions to subject their investment decisions to a more rigorous market test to determine whether the investment project is tailored to the task at hand and is justified by the value of the services that customers will receive.

Deregulation yields benefits by reducing or eliminating the administrative costs associated with traditional rate-of-return regulation as well as those associated with incentive regulation. In particular, deregulation obviates rate hearings, which entail costs for the regulator's staff as well as for the utilities, the intervenors for customers, and competitors. To achieve those benefits requires the regulator to reduce its oversight role in competitive segments of the formerly regulated marketplace rather than to create complex rules requiring increased intervention in market activities.

Deregulation enhances economic efficiency by eliminating cross-subsidies. Cross-subsidies cause economic losses by distorting customer decisions because prices fail to convey accurate signals about costs. Services that receive the subsidy are priced inordinately low, which encourages excessive purchases of that service and displaces potentially more efficient alternative products or services. Services that generate the subsidy are priced overly high, which discourages purchases of that service and can lead customers to seek alternatives that would otherwise not be purchased.

Deregulation promotes innovation. With many competitors' entering the market, there will be myriad competing solutions to telecommunications problems. Solutions may involve not only new technologies, but also widely differing mixtures of software, equipment, network connections, and transmission media. Under regulation, universal service requirements and an absence of competition leads to a "one-size-fits-all" approach. Regulated telecommunications providers have concentrated in large part on upgrading system capacity, enhancing reliability, and achieving the objectives mandated by regulatory commissions. In contrast, a competitive market responds to changing customer preferences and tailors capacity, reliability, and service offerings to the disparate needs of individual market segments.

Deregulation can enhance customer choices. Under the monopoly of the former Bell System, customers could purchase only basic types of telephones. The proliferation of customer premises equipment since the Department of Justice broke up AT&T and the FCC deregulated such equipment indicates how the market responds to customer requirements by offering a variety of choices and investing in research and development to widen those choices still further.[21]

For the market to innovate in such a responsive manner, and for customers to have access to a variety of telecommunications choices, regulators must have the courage and forbearance to allow multiple telecommunications solutions to emerge. Regulators should remove regulations that artificially impose distinctions on the basis of products, services, transmission modes, or content. Thus, regulators should allow twisted copper pair, coaxial cable, fiber optics, wireless, satellite, and other media of transmission to compete and combine without restriction or encouragement. Alternative types of content (including voice, data, and video) should not trigger regulatory distinctions. Firms should be neither favored nor handicapped, whether they are incumbent utilities, entrants, or new forms of service providers.

As deregulation proceeds, some urge regulators to take an activist role to manage the transition so as to "promote" or "protect" competition. That view is misguided. *Regulation should recede as competition progresses.* There is no need for regulators to promote competition because the returns that firms expect to earn from serving customers provide sufficient incentives for those firms to compete in providing telecommunications services. Indeed, the attempt to manage competition not only entails administrative costs, but also prevents the market from achieving the benefits of competition that regulators wish to attain for consumers.[22]

---

21. *See* PETER W. HUBER, MICHAEL K. KELLOGG & JOHN THORNE, THE GEODESIC NETWORK II: 1993 REPORT ON COMPETITION IN THE TELEPHONE INDUSTRY 2.12 to 2.13, 6.52 to 6.71 (Geodesic Co. 1992); ROBERT W. CRANDALL, AFTER THE BREAKUP: U.S. TELECOMMUNICATIONS IN A MORE COMPETITIVE ERA 11, 88–97, 149–53 (Brookings Institution 1991).

22. Elsewhere we have written of the need to protect private firms from anticompetitive behavior by the U.S. Postal Service. J. GREGORY SIDAK & DANIEL F. SPULBER, PROTECTING COMPETITION FROM THE POSTAL MONOPOLY (AEI Press 1996). As we make clear in our previous book, the situation of the Postal Service is entirely distinguishable from that of a regulated investor-owned utility. The Postal Service is a public enterprise that cannot be assumed to maximize profit; the regulatory authority to which it is subject lacks the essential powers of a typical state PUC. The Postal Service enjoys not only a statutory monopoly, but also many other privileges and immunities relative to private firms,

Regulation Does Not
Replicate Competition

Regulators need not protect or safeguard competition. Market incentives are sufficient to allow competition to flourish. If regulators act in a partial manner, either by picking winners or by protecting less successful firms from their own inefficiency, then the benefits of competition will diminish. Moreover, antitrust laws serve to protect competition from monopolization and other anticompetitive practices. Regulatory attempts to supplant that role of antitrust law would, if anything, preempt its proper functioning.

Competition is desirable in local exchange telecommunications for the same reasons that it is desirable in any market. Competitive markets are the preferable economic mechanism for achieving allocative, productive, and dynamic efficiency. Allocative efficiency is present when goods and services are allocated to the uses in which they have the highest value. Productive efficiency is present when producers use goods and services in such a manner as to minimize costs, subject to technological constraints. Dynamic efficiency refers to decisions made over time and includes efficiencies in investment and technological innovation.

Excessive regulatory intervention during the competitive transformation of network industries often seems designed to promote competitors, not competition. That distinction should be familiar from antitrust, where the view that antitrust exists to protect "small dealers and worthy men"[23] has been replaced by an understanding that antitrust should set the rules of the game, not determine its outcome.[24] Markets tend to achieve efficient allocations of resources because of competition among firms. Firms compete by offering lower prices, improvements on products and services, customer convenience, product variety, marketing, and sales services. When companies offer similar products to their customers, competition tends to lower prices toward production costs, as firms bid against each other to make sales to customers. Firms face competition from other firms operating in the same market, from firms that offer substitutes for their products, and from potential entrants that will respond to the perceived needs of consumers. All of that competitive ferment happens because consumers seek to maximize their well-being

---

and it exercises the authority to define the scope of its own monopoly. Moreover, there is no indication that the delivery of letter mail will soon undergo a transition to competition.

23. United States *v.* Trans-Missouri Freight Ass'n, 166 U.S. 290, 323 (1897).

24. *E.g.*, Continental T.V., Inc. *v.* GTE Sylvania, Inc., 433 U.S. 36 (1977).

subject to their budgets and because firms seek to maximize their profit. It was in that sense that Adam Smith wrote in *The Wealth of Nations* of an "invisible hand" that guides every individual so that "[b]y pursuing his own interest he frequently promotes that of the society more effectually than when he really intends to promote it."[25]

Competitive markets are preferable to government allocation of goods and services because they produce economic transactions at the least cost and thus allow individual customers and competitors the freedom to make economic choices. Economic analysis and historical experience conclusively demonstrate that even with its imperfections, a competitive market outperforms government regulation or central planning as a mechanism to allocate resources. Competition is the best mechanism for stimulating research and development and for resolving uncertainty about evolving technology. Technological change and uncertainty surely characterize the telecommunications industry. As Friedrich A. Hayek powerfully argued, markets create and process vast quantities of information, which necessarily would overwhelm the conscious efforts of any central economic planner.[26] Experience in regulated markets—from airlines to railroads to natural gas—confirms that pricing and other command-and-control restrictions imposed by regulators are associated with high administrative costs and an economically inefficient allocation of resources.

As chapter 9 explains, the Federal Communications Commission, while singing the praises of competition and market allocation of resources, promptly proposed after the enactment of the Telecommunication Act of 1996 an entirely new genre of price regulation for inputs in local telephony.[27] That price regulation was on a scale unprecedented in the telecommunications industry—or any other U.S. industry, for that matter. The regulation of markets for resale and unbundled network services supplants the determination of pricing and service offerings by firms competing in the market. That new form of government intervention extends regulation beyond the previous system addressing final

---

25. ADAM SMITH, AN INQUIRY INTO THE NATURE AND CAUSES OF THE WEALTH OF NATIONS 423 (Modern Library 1937) (1776).

26. Friedrich A. Hayek, *The Use of Knowledge in Society*, 35 AM. ECON. REV. 519 (1945).

27. Implementation of the Local Competition Provisions in the Telecommunications Act of 1996 and Interconnection Between Local Exchange Carriers and Commercial Mobile Radio Service Providers, First Report and Order, CC Dkt. Nos. 96-98, 95-185, 11 F.C.C. Rcd. 15,499, *stayed pending appeal sub nom.*, Iowa Util. Bd. v. FCC, 109 F.3d 418 (8th Cir. 1996).

telecommunications services to include new controls of the underlying factors of production. Entrants into local telephony, such as the major interexchange carriers and competitive access providers, may now urge regulators to determine how productive inputs shall be priced, provided, and employed in the production of telecommunications services. Telecommunications regulation has thus expanded to encompass control of technology, capital equipment, and other productive inputs. Contrary to the popular conception created by the passage of the Telecommunications Act, the new unbundling obligations of the 1996 legislation represent a significant and qualitative extension of regulation from outputs to productive inputs.

In the wake of the 1996 telecommunications legislation, some economists endorsed the proposition that regulators are necessary to "jumpstart" competition in the new environment of mandatory network access. John W. Mayo, for example, has argued that regulators should implement regulations that achieve competitive outcomes:

> A primary goal of public utility pricing is to achieve an allocation of resources similar to that which would result in competitive markets. Because effectively competitive markets automatically generate efficient prices (the fundamental virtue of the invisible hand), it is essential that regulators understand the basic characteristics of such prices if they are to replicate competitive outcomes in regulated markets.[28]

Thus, in Mayo's view, regulators of telecommunications markets should seek to achieve an outcome similar to that which one would observe in a competitive market. Regulators are to achieve that desired outcome, however, not by letting the forces of competition operate freely, but instead by relying upon some unspecified system of government "replication." That prescription raises two fundamental questions.

First, is a competitive allocation of resources the primary goal of regulators? There are many reasons to doubt the validity of that proposition. Economic analysis establishes that cross-subsidies in the prices offered by a company cannot survive in a competitive market. First, no firm in a competitive market would voluntarily cross-subsidize

---

28. Opening Testimony of John W. Mayo on Behalf of AT&T Communications of Cal., at 24, *in* Rulemaking on the Commission's Own Motion to Govern Open Access to Bottleneck Services and Establish a Framework for Network Architecture Development of Dominant Carrier Networks; Investigation on the Commission's Own Motion into Open Access and Network Architecture Development of Dominant Carrier Networks, Dkt. No. R.93-04-003, I.93-04-002 (filed Cal. Pub. Utils. Comm'n, June 14, 1996).

its own product offerings because it would sooner have an incentive to cease offering services whose incremental revenues did not cover their incremental costs. Moreover, the firm would lose customers of those services providing cross-subsidies to competitive entrants. Regulated markets, however, differ markedly from competitive markets in that the former commonly contain cross-subsidies, as regulators seek to achieve perceived fairness and other social objectives, such as universal service.[29] Regulated prices for local telecommunications services, for example, typically contain cross-subsidies due to geographic averaging, subsidies from business customers to residential customers, and subsidies from vertical services to basic services.

Second, could regulators "replicate" competitive outcomes in regulated markets even if they were inclined to do so? It is doubtful. Competitive markets require continual adjustment of prices and product offerings to respond to changes in customer tastes, incomes, and technological innovation. The informational requirements of such adjustments are not compatible with the costly, complex, and protracted administrative procedures that regulatory rulemaking requires. Regulators cannot be expected to react to, let alone anticipate, changes in customer preferences and supplier technology. To the contrary, excessive regulation can discourage innovation and capital investment and thus lock in obsolete technologies. In short, transaction costs and information processing costs make it unworkable for regulators to attempt to supplant or recreate competitive outcomes. To suggest that regulators can replicate the "invisible hand" of the market fundamentally contradicts Adam Smith's original point (expressed on the same page of *The Wealth of Nations*) that policymakers should not interfere with the functioning of competition:

> The statesman, who should attempt to direct private people in what manner they ought to employ their capitals, would not only load himself with a most unnecessary attention, but assume an authority which could safely be trusted, not only to no single person, but to no council or senate whatever, and which would nowhere be so dangerous as in the hands of a man who had folly and presumption enough to fancy himself fit to exercise it.[30]

Regulation is at best an imperfect proxy for competition, not a *replica* of it.[31] Rather than attempt to replicate the market, regulators surely

---

29. *See, e.g.*, WILLIAM J. BAUMOL & J. GREGORY SIDAK, TOWARD COMPETITION IN LOCAL TELEPHONY 24–25 (MIT Press & AEI Press 1994).

30. SMITH, *supra* note 25, at 423.

31. One of us has previously advocated with William J. Baumol that regulators should

recognize that achieving market outcomes requires removing regulatory restrictions as telecommunications markets become increasingly competitive. Expanding the scope of regulation will only make it less, not more, plausible that regulators will be able to achieve market outcomes.

Congress, the states legislatures, and regulators have opened the local exchange market to competition. If they now establish unbiased rules that allow entrants and the incumbent an equal opportunity to compete, regulators can rely on market incentives to produce competitive outcomes. Firms compete when and where they discern opportunities for profit. They compete by investing in facilities to produce goods and services. They compete by making process innovations so that prices can be lower than competitors'. They compete by undertaking research and development to provide improvements and innovations in existing products and services. They compete by differentiating their product offerings from their rivals'. Competition takes place in markets without the need for government promotion. Rather, competition is the spontaneous and natural outcome of private companies seeking to obtain a competitive return on the investment of their shareholders. There is no more need for the government actively to promote competition than there is need for it to exhort Olympic athletes to remember to compete with each other. Competition occurs because of the economic rewards that firms expect to obtain by satisfying the demands of their customers.

The Infant Industry Argument

Some assert that competition in a newly deregulated market, such as local telephony, differs from competition in other industries because the incumbent LEC has been subject to a regulated monopoly and because competition in the local exchange market is "nascent." The fact that the incumbent LEC held a regulated monopoly in the past is not an indicator that regulators need to promote competition. The fallacy of the conclusion that regulatory nurturing is necessary for competition to blossom is evident from making a counterfactual assumption for the sake of

pattern regulation according to the *competitive-market standard*, which asserts that "the regulator's task is to serve as a proxy for competition—to stand *in loco* [*competitionis*], preventing all actions that competition would have precluded, and requiring all courses of economic behavior that competition would have imposed." BAUMOL & SIDAK, *supra* note 29, at 28. Just as a guardian who stands *in loco parentis* cannot replicate for an orphan the essence of his deceased parents, neither can a regulator replicate the essence of a competitive marketplace. Accordingly, the first principle of the competitive-market standard provides: "Where competitive forces are adequate and effective, the regulator should eschew all forms of intervention." *Id.*

argument. Suppose that the incumbent LEC acted as a classic monopolist and withheld services, increased prices substantially, and reduced the quality of customer service. Those actions would increase the incentives for the entry of new competitors. Past monopoly, far from being a hindrance to competition, is an important stimulus to competition, as entrants seek to bid away customers by outperforming the pricing, product availability, and service quality of the former monopolist. Past monopoly requires no corrective action by regulators in terms of subsidizing, supporting, or otherwise promoting competitors.

Students of economic history will immediately recognize the "nascent competition" argument in a newly deregulated industry as a variation on the "infant industry" argument employed to justify entry barriers in international trade.[32] The infant industry argument is advanced by those who believe that domestic industry should be subsidized and otherwise protected from international competitors until it grows sufficiently. The argument has little merit, and it certainly does not apply to the regulated network industries. In telecommunications the entrants into local exchange telephony include AT&T, MCI, Sprint, Time Warner, and others. They are not infants. To the contrary, those companies are notably large, well established, well funded, and innovative. They are experienced in telecommunications, and their competitive efforts are far from nascent. They do not need subsidies, assistance, or special privileges. Even relative newcomers to telecommunications are perfectly capable of purchasing the requisite equipment and obtaining the required technological and marketing expertise to pursue their objectives.

If, contrary to the weight of economic analysis, regulators choose to subsidize entrants, it bears emphasis that *that* decision in no way answers the question of who should pay the subsidy. In particular, it in no way follows logically that the subsidy must be a wealth transfer from the incumbent LEC to entrants. In the United Kingdom, for example, the regulatory body, the Office of Telecommunications (OFTEL), requires British Telecom (BT) to provide interconnection to its network to cable television systems that have telephony capabilities and compete against BT's provision of voice and data services. Although the interconnection charge includes a component representing the entrant's payment of BT's contribution to universal service obligations, the director general of OFTEL has exercised his discretion to waive payment of that "access deficit contribution" until the entrant has achieved a market share of 10 percent.[33] A subsidy financed in that manner in the United States would raise takings concerns of the sort analyzed in chapters 6 and 7. If there is to be a subsidy, it should instead be politically transparent. The legislature, for example, could explicitly subsidize entrants by paying the incumbent LEC the difference between the price and the economic cost of providing interconnection.

The interconnection charge is not the only place where regulators might attempt to impose a subsidy. If regulators force the incumbent LEC to sell unbundled network elements to competitors at prices below the economic costs of those elements (that is, below the sum of each element's incremental cost and its opportunity cost), then regulators will effect a transfer of income from the incumbent LEC to its competitors. Such pricing is neither efficient nor compensatory. Efficiency requires that the incumbent LEC price any inputs sold to a competitor at the input's economic costs, as we emphasize in earlier chapters.

Even if an infant industry argument were applicable to telecommunications (which it decidedly is not), when do such advantages for the competitors of the incumbent LEC cease? How would their duration be specified in advance? The government's commitment to ending the entrant's infant-industry status at a date certain or upon the attainment of some objective level of market penetration must be credible and binding. That political task would be difficult to accomplish, however. Consequently, the recommendations for regulatory promotion of competition appear to create open-ended commitments for the regulator. Such open-ended commitments are poorly suited to allowing regulation to recede as competition increases.

Price Caps and Competition

Policies designed to promote competition and establish prices for resale and unbundled network services do not in themselves increase competition. Instead, such policies may hinder competition. The genius of competition is that the market discovers prices. Regulating prices constrains competition by interfering with the competitive process of firms as they bid against each other to serve their customers. For regulators accurately to determine the prices that competition would produce presumes that regulators can foresee the underlying determinants

---

33. *See* Crandall & Sidak, *supra* note 12, at 1235–37.

of pricing—including demand, costs, technology, product features, and competitive strategy. Such central planning is not only incapable of setting prices efficiently, but also incompatible with competitive markets.

If regulators are concerned that competition will not be sufficiently vigorous following their removal of entry barriers, then they should rely on price caps and allow competition (if it takes hold) to set prices below the cap. Moreover, the caps should be phased out as rapidly as possible because many factors other than imperfect competition (such as rising input costs, capacity shortages, or product enhancements) can cause market prices to rise. Adjustments to price caps based on productivity and inflation indexes are unlikely to achieve the flexibility required for the regulated firm to keep pace with changing market conditions.

Implications for the Design of Rules Governing Access and Unbundling

As they dismantle entry barriers, regulators should commit to curtailing their future market intervention. They should neither attempt to manage competition nor retain rules that arbitrarily favor one market outcome over another. The competitive market is an allocation mechanism that generates and uses tremendous amounts of information about the preferences and purchasing patterns of individual consumers, as well as the technology and supply patterns of many diverse competitors. Although the regulation of a franchise monopoly utility generates a large amount of technical and economic information, competitive markets that are growing and innovative generate quantities of information that are orders of magnitude greater than what any regulatory commission can assimilate. The regulator must be prepared for the increased complexity of competitive markets by withdrawing entirely its supervision and management of the pricing and other strategic decisions made in any market that is demonstrably competitive. The lifting of regulation, of course, does not mean that the incumbent LEC in a newly competitive market is freed of the antitrust laws.

The markets served by the incumbent LEC are not homogeneous. The cost of serving different market segments varies widely depending on the type of service offered, customer density, and the regulatory obligations associated with the particular service. Similarly, the revenues from various customer groups differ substantially, in large part because of the structure of regulated rates. Because of that heterogeneity of costs and revenues, the incumbent LEC faces selective entry by firms seeking to serve the high-margin customers. Such entry is undeniably competitive in the sense that it drives down the prices of certain services closer to cost; but the selective focus of such entry results directly from government policies manifested in the rates and service obligations that the regulator has demanded of the incumbent LEC—rates and service obligations that a competitive marketplace most assuredly would *not* demand of any firm. Stated differently, regulators have imposed homogeneous pricing and service obligations across heterogeneous segments of customers. Competitive markets do the just the opposite: They allow firms to make heterogeneous supply and pricing responses to heterogeneous customer demand. Regulators should therefore eliminate the rate imbalances and service obligations that induce selective entry and thus preordain the outcome of competition.

The common name given to selective entry of markets served by an incumbent utility is "cream skimming" or "cherry picking." For a typical incumbent LEC, 80 percent of its revenues may come from 20 percent of its customer accounts, which in turn will be concentrated in metropolitan areas. Entrants can minimize their marketing costs by focusing on those high-margin customers. Selective entry also reduces the network costs for entrants, particularly facilities-based entrants.

Selective entry is a normal method of market competition that should not be impeded. For such entry to be efficient, however, regulators should not create or perpetuate rules that impair the ability of any firm, including the incumbent LEC, to respond to that form of competition with its own flexible pricing and service offerings. Moreover, the selectivity of entrants should be based on economic considerations such as customer demand and costs of service. Selectivity should not be based on regulatory loopholes that encourage the entrant to serve only certain customers or geographic locations so as to avoid the burden of public service obligations. Entry decisions should not be strategic responses by firms to incumbent burdens that competitively handicap the incumbent LEC. Eliminating cross-subsidies and other service requirements that fall asymmetrically on the incumbent LEC will allow regulators to use undistorted market considerations to determine the pattern of competitive entry.

Impartiality further requires that regulators refrain from imposing new product and market definitions on the basis of past regulatory considerations. Perpetuating such distinctions would lead to balkanized markets and would deter both intermodal competition and technological innovation. For example, traditional regulation in telecommunications has distinguished between telecommunications services on the basis of the mode of transmission (copper wire, coaxial cable, or wireless), the type of communication (voice, data, or video), and regulatory customer class (residential or business). Markets for the transmission of voice, data, video, and other types of information will combine those types of communication in new and unexpected ways, providing specialized services to satisfy the needs of diverse market segments comprising households and businesses. Regulators should dismantle to the maximum extent possible the artificial distinctions between types of information transmitted so as not to bias the types of products and services that firms will be free to offer to consumers.

California has provided a commendable example of regulatory impartiality by enacting legislation providing that "[t]o the extent possible, competition in intraexchange telecommunications markets shall be coincident with competition in video markets."[34] The statute further provides:

> If any local exchange telephone company obtains the right to offer cable television or video dialtone service within its service territory from a regulatory body or court of competent jurisdiction, any cable television corporation or its affiliates may immediately have the right to enter into the intraexchange market within the service territory of the local exchange carrier by filing for approval of a certificate of public convenience and necessity, if necessary, which shall be expeditiously reviewed by the commission.[35]

Finally, the statute specifies that the California Public Utilities Commission's standards for the interconnection of networks, network unbundling, and service quality applied to the LECs shall apply equally to cable television companies.[36] Thus, California's legislature stated its laudable intent that competition in video, cable television, and video dialtone should be fair in that competitors should be free to enter each other's markets and that regulations and standards should apply symmetrically.

Another area where regulatory impartiality is sorely needed concerns the boundary between local and long-distance telephony. Distinctions between interexchange, intraLATA toll, and intraexchange service, although having some basis in technology and regulatory history, have little economic foundation. Regulators should allow companies to offer the full range of services without regard to the distance traveled or the types of switches used. Indeed, the clear trend in telecommunications is to erase any distinctions among interLATA, intraLATA, or local exchange service.[37] Companies seek to provide connections between customers—what AT&T calls "anywhere, anytime" communications. If

---

34. CAL. PUB. UTIL. CODE § 709.5(b).

35. *Id.* § 709.5(d).

36. *Id.* § 709.5(e).

37. *See, e.g., A Survey of Telecommunications: The Death of Distance*, THE ECONOMIST, Sept. 30–Oct. 6, 1995 (unnumbered) (special insert).

regulators continue to impose detailed restrictions on the service offerings of incumbent LECs that do not recognize that evolution in the market, then regulators will place the LECs at a competitive disadvantage and will have effectively, albeit unintentionally, preordained the success or failure of individual firms in the market.

The same point applies to modes of transmission, including the twisted copper pair, coaxial cable, fiber optics, cellular, PCS, and satellite systems. Technological change in software and switching systems allows the near-seamless integration of networks consisting of diverse transmission elements and the connection of multiple networks with each other. An incumbent LEC must have the same flexibility as other firms to employ and combine modes of transmission in constructing networks for its services. Any artificial distinctions between modes of transmission or means of switching and routing information across networks will place the incumbent LEC at a competitive disadvantage.

Another issue of impartiality arises with respect to facilities-based competition and resale. A resale market for the facilities of any carrier is desirable for achieving efficient use of existing facilities and efficient investment in new facilities. As we emphasize in chapter 9, however, the regulator's rules for unbundling and resale must not place uneconomic requirements on the incumbent LEC. Excessive unbundling does not enhance economic efficiency. Moreover, government-mandated access to network facilities at rates that do not recover the incumbent LEC's economic costs will induce inefficient decisions by entrants concerning whether to build facilities or merely to resell services that use the incumbent's existing facilities. Overpriced services and facilities will encourage entrants to underuse existing facilities and could induce the incumbent to overinvest, whereas underpriced services and facilities will force the incumbent to subsidize entrants and could induce its underinvestment in network facilities.

Access and unbundling requirements should not require the incumbent to offer resale of any newly created products or services. The incumbent LEC should have no lesser property rights in its innovations than the rights that any other company enjoys with respect to its proprietary products and services. It is imperative to protect the incumbent LEC's right to recover the market value of its innovations—whether through the incumbent's voluntary decision to engage in resale of the innovation to competitors or by the incumbent's choice to employ the innovation exclusively. If regulators were to deny the incumbent LEC that discretion over the use of its intellectual property, resale requirements would severely reduce incentives for the LEC to invest in research and development. Such disincentives to invest in R&D would deprive the market of the efforts of experienced and creative companies and thereby could decrease innovation. That concern has particular relevance to telecommunications, where many companies are engaged in substantial innovative efforts.

Impartiality requires that all firms involved in originating, transporting, or terminating calls be compensated on the basis of network usage and services provided. Given the complexity of network interconnection and transactions that will likely emerge in a competitive market, revenue-sharing arrangements should be the outcome of voluntary agreements between carriers, customers, and other market participants. When multiple carriers are involved in the transmission of communications, they should all receive compensation. The regulator should resist allowing traffic flow imbalances to benefit some competitors at the expense of others.

Summary of the Impartiality Principle

Following the impartiality principle means that regulators should not attempt to influence the eventual outcome of competition or to micromanage the evolving telecommunications and electric power markets. Regulators should rapidly phase out their industry oversight and regulatory activities to avoid the possibility of biasing competitive outcomes. To unleash the efficiencies and innovation of competitive markets in telecommunications, for example, regulators should eliminate regulations that draw artificial distinctions between modes of transmission, types of communications, or services that are performed within or across the boundaries of a local access and transport area. It is overwhelmingly an artifact of regulatory convenience rather than economic or technological necessity that regulators continue to draw distinctions between interLATA, intraLATA, and local exchange services. To maintain impartiality and to avoid stifling innovation, regulators should avoid or limit as much as possible forced access and unbundling that will reduce the returns to innovation and competitively disadvantage incumbent carriers.

CONCLUSION

The Telecommunications Act of 1996 got off to a rocky start because federal and state regulators were reluctant to relinquish control of the industry. The result was wrangling between incumbents and entrants before regulatory commissions and in the courts, as well as disagreement between Congress and the Federal Communications Commission over interpretation of the statute. The resulting litigation will delay the benefits that competition will bring. Federal and state deregulation of the electric power industry lies ahead. It would be unfortunate if legislators and regulators were to repeat in that industry the same mistakes being committed in the competitive restructuring of local telecommunications. We therefore propose three principles for legislators and regulators to follow to ensure that their deregulation of those two industries will indeed bring consumers the benefits of competition.

The economic incentive principle rests on the recognition that economic gains from trade drive market transactions and that economic incentives underlie the regulatory contract as well. If the competitive rules were to deprive the incumbent LEC of economic incentives, that outcome would harm the firm's ability to enter competitive markets, to raise capital to finance investment projects, to innovate, to provide a diversity of services offerings, and to perform its regulatory obligations.

Regulators cannot achieve the economic benefits of competition without adhering to the equal opportunity principle. They should scrupulously design rules that create no advantage for the entrant over the incumbent, or vice versa, but instead place all competitors on an even regulatory footing. Regulators should dismantle regulatory constraints as necessary to ensure that any opportunity or independence enjoyed by the entrants extends as well to the incumbent. The incumbent LEC should receive the same flexibility and autonomy as entrants in choosing its prices, negotiating with customers, altering service offerings, and making any other relevant business decision.

Regulators following the impartiality principle will refrain from interfering with innovative competition. Regulators should resist appeals from entrants to aid their cause by continuing to monitor competitive outcomes. Because competition is a process of innovation, it is not possible for regulators to predict accurately the prices, products, services, technology, and network characteristics that will result. Regulations that are dismantled should remain so. They should not be kept in reserve if the outcomes differ from regulators' expectations. Regulators must not create rules that favor particular companies, technologies, service offerings, or other market outcomes. They should "sunset" regulations in competitive segments of the local telecommunications market.

In short, by allowing economic incentives for the incumbent LEC to compete and perform regulatory obligations, by giving all firms in the local telecommunications market an equal opportunity to compete, and by remaining impartial as that competition progresses, regulators will attain the goal of achieving competition fairly.

16

The Tragedy of the Telecommons

PROPERTY RIGHTS are the foundation of a market economy. Only a well-defined system of property rights allows for the exchange of goods and services in the marketplace and provides incentives for investment in all manner of business ventures. Our theme is the economic importance of legal protection of property rights from government takings. We express concern that as deregulation proceeds in telecommunications and electric power, regulatory agencies are attempting to erode those constitutional protections for private property and are pursuing a government taking of unprecedented proportions through a carefully structured sequence of deregulatory programs.

FOUR EPIGRAMS FOR PROTECTING
PRIVATE PROPERTY IN NETWORK INDUSTRIES

The analysis that we present is neither an apologia for regulation nor a defense of monopoly. To the contrary, our overriding concern is the protection of private property as the foundation of a competitive economy. Our analysis of deregulatory takings in the light of the constitutional defense of property rights is meant as a criticism of regulators who seek to use their authority to effect taxes and income transfers "off the books." We strongly favor moving from a regulated regime to a competitive market in the network industries as quickly as possible. That transition, however, requires loosening regulatory controls not only on entry, but also on the incumbent utilities. The need to compensate the incumbent utility for past, present, or future regulatory obligations does not mean that competition should be delayed. Rather, it means that regulators should recognize the full economic costs of the services that are procured through regulatory fiat and the consequences of income transfers obtained through distorted rate structures. If the economic costs of regulation are explicitly recognized, rather than obscured in a manner that facilitates income transfers to the investors of entrant firms and to some fortunate subset of the customers of incumbent utilities, then there will be greater political scrutiny of regulatory decisions, and policymakers will redesign or remove regulations accordingly.

Defending property rights does not entail endorsing monopoly. The rights to returns on investment for any type of firm sustain competition and eliminate monopoly power. Certainly monopoly rents can represent an inefficient transfer from consumers to the monopoly firm that results in a loss of consumer surplus under some pricing policies. It is the earnings of incumbent monopolies, however, that provide incentives for competitors to enter markets, to invest in productive capacity, to innovate, to market products, and to offer lower prices and higher quality to consumers. Moreover, a regulated monopoly is not the same thing as the textbook monopolist. Regulated utilities, while benefiting from entry controls, are subject to price controls and limits on their rate of return, and they must meet regulatory obligations such as universal service and quality standards. It is false and misleading to equate regulated monopoly with the textbook monopolist because the firm's pricing and supply decisions are completely different in the two cases. Whereas the textbook monopolist restricts supply to drive up the price, the regulated monopoly is held to cost-based pricing to drive prices as low as possible to increase supply so as to achieve universal service.

Clearing the books by offering just compensation to utility investors for their expected earnings would hasten the move to competitive markets. Attempts to confiscate the incumbent utility's property will delay the move to competition because such takings will surely be challenged in court and are likely to be found unconstitutional. If the regulator renegotiates the regulatory contract, then the transition to competition can be accelerated, the opposition of incumbents can be eliminated, and the incumbent firm can join the competitive fray on an even footing. Removing incumbent burdens, such as price controls and asymmetric service obligations, allows market incentives to operate so that competition can flourish. Compensation for yesterday's investment does not insulate today's incumbent monopolist from the hazards of tomorrow's competitive marketplace. The decision to permit the incumbent utility the reasonable opportunity to recover the full economic cost of investments undertaken to render service to the public was a decision made long ago, when the system of regulated utilities was instituted. Paying for the incumbent's stranded costs—that is, its expected earnings under regulation net of expected earnings under competition—addresses the problem of unamortized investment. Only a *continuation* of regulation would create de facto protections for incumbents. Going forward, after the resolution of outstanding regulatory obligations, the incumbent then confronts the same vagaries of the marketplace as do entrants.

The cost of compensation for takings need not prevent or delay deregulation. The economic benefits of competition provide a source of funds for compensating investors who relied on the regulatory contract. Cost efficiencies and innovative technologies brought by entrants lower industry costs. There is room for competitively neutral end-user charges to recover stranded costs while still allowing lower prices. As chapter 5 emphasizes, that effect is similar to paying expectation damages for breach of contract. The returns to *efficient* breach cover the damage payment, yielding all the efficiency gains as surplus. The faster that regulators relax incumbent burdens, the greater the mitigation of damages that would otherwise arise from continuing regulatory asymmetry. The mere fact that companies can enter new lines of business, however, is not a sufficient quid pro quo for deregulation, for competitive firms *already* have the right to enter new markets. It is instead the relaxation of government-mandated cross-subsidies and other regulatory restrictions that minimize the cost of compensating incumbents for the regulator's abrogation of the regulatory contract.

Thus, the "greater good" of competition does not necessitate a deregulatory taking, because paying compensation and moving to competition are compatible. Moreover, the inefficiencies of regulation do not provide a basis for refusing to compensate incumbents. The inefficiencies of regulation are manifest, including the transaction costs of regulatory hearings and regulatory accounting. The distortions in incentives created by rate-of-return regulation of capital-intensive firms are generally understood. Moreover, the capital equipment of regulated firms cannot reasonably be expected to be free of technological obsolescence or to be immune from the possible superior performance of new entrants. Those inefficiencies are beside the point, however. Deregulation requires the state to compensate for past contractual obligations made to private investors and to think carefully before creating new ones.

Our analysis can be summarized in four familiar epigrams. First, "a deal is a deal." The government entered into a regulatory contract with utilities in the network industries that consists of entry controls, rate regulation, and obligations to serve. The contract can be renegotiated bilaterally to prepare the ground for competition, but the voluntary exchange inherent in such renegotiation will require compensating utility investors for the loss of their investment-backed expectations.

Second, "there is no such thing as a free lunch." Someone must pay the costs of publicly mandated services. The facilities of the regulated network industries did not fall like manna from heaven, but rather were established by incumbent utilities through the expenditures of their investors. Utilities made past expenditures to perform obligations to serve in expectation of the reasonable opportunity to recover the costs of investment plus a competitive rate of return. Investors must be compensated for those past costs; it follows a fortiori that investors must be offered additional compensation if existing responsibilities are perpetuated or new burdens are imposed. Reed E. Hundt, chairman of the Federal Communications Commission, revealed his lack of understanding of that principle when he declared at the end of 1996 that opening the local exchange should not be called a free lunch: "The rate payers paid for this network . . . . My argument is that it's been a nice lunch for the entire country."[1]

Contrary to that reasoning, the benefits of deregulation are the result of free markets, not the expropriation of investor wealth. A telephone customer has acquired no ownership in the local exchange network by virtue of his having paid regulated rates for service from an investor-owned local exchange carrier, just as he could not expect to have acquired any ownership interest in Texaco by virtue of having purchased gasoline from that company over a period of years. Chairman Hundt's comment fundamentally misapprehends the legal and economic significance, traceable to *Munn* v. *Illinois*[2] and to earlier English common law, of dedicating *private* property to a public purpose. In addition, his remark shows that he does not recognize that investment in a network industry does not happen only once.

Third, "an ounce of prevention is worth a pound of cure." If regulators adopt the correct pricing policies for mandatory access to network facilities and accompany such pricing rules with competitively neutral and nonbypassable end-user charges, then they will avoid the takings issue. That advice is consistent with the prudential rule, common-

---

1. Mark Landler, *The Bells Want F.C.C. to Make Providers Share Internet Costs*, N.Y. TIMES, Dec. 25, 1996, at C1 (quoting Reed E. Hundt, Chairman, Federal Communications Commission).

2. 94 U.S. 113, 125–26 (1877).

ly attributed to Justice Louis Brandeis's 1936 concurrence in *Ashwander* v. *Tennessee Valley Authority*,[3] that courts (and a fortiori regulatory agencies, we would add) should read statutes to avoid having to decide constitutional questions. The deregulation of network industries in the United States should not have come to that. Regulators should have taken care to read statutes, such as the local competition provisions of the Telecommunications Act of 1996, in a way that would have obviated litigation over takings questions that arose as a result of the FCC's actions. In short, this third epigram is necessary advice to dispense because the FCC and many state PUCs have ignored the constitutional precedent concerning regulated industries that makes clear that investors in public utilities are entitled to the reasonable opportunity to recover their investment and a competitive return.

Fourth, regulators should heed the advice, "Look before you leap." Before creating new forms of regulation of network industries, such as cable reregulation in 1992 or the unbundling requirements of the Telecommunications Act of 1996, regulators should compare the costs and benefits. It does little good to protest the high cost of deregulation or the inefficiencies of regulation *after the fact*. Optimization is achieved as the result of decisions made *before* networks are created and costs are sunk. After costs are sunk, protections against regulatory opportunism and deregulatory takings come into play to preserve *future incentives* for private parties to invest in network infrastructure and to enter into efficient agreements with regulatory agencies.

What does it mean to protect private ownership of the telecommunications network? Ownership of an economic asset has two aspects: rights to residual returns and rights of residual control.[4] Residual returns refer to the returns from an asset after all prior claimants have been paid; thus, equityholders in a corporation obtain the returns after debtholders and other creditors have been paid. Residual control refers to the control of the asset for the purposes of the owners, subject to legal and other prior (contractual) restrictions. Protection of private property from government takings means protection of investors' residual returns, as well as protection of their residual control in the absence of just compensation.

---

3. 297 U.S. 288, 347 (1936) (Brandeis, J., concurring) (citing Liverpool, N.Y. & Philadelphia S.S. Co. *v.* Commissioners of Emigration, 113 U.S. 22, 39 (1885)).

4. *See* OLIVER HART, FIRMS, CONTRACTS, AND FINANCIAL STRUCTURE 5–6, 63–66 (Oxford University Press 1995); Eugene F. Fama & Michael C. Jensen, *Agency Problems and Residual Claims*, 26 J.L. & ECON. 327, 328 (1983). The parties entitled to the firm's residual return are called *residual claimants*.

Ownership can be either public or private, or some mixture of the two. The ownership of companies, including those in the network industries, has important implications for economic efficiency. In the remainder of this concluding chapter, we review some of the consequences of the structure of ownership in light of our analysis of deregulatory takings. We begin with changes in public ownership through privatization or nationalization. We then consider the hazards of government policies that would convert the assets of competitive firms or regulated firms to a commons. We emphasize that the protection of property rights is a crucial determinant of efficiency in network industries.

OWNERSHIP AND STRANDED COSTS

Around the world, governments are privatizing public enterprises, particularly those in the network industries. That reversal of the earlier nationalization of industry reflects an understanding that private ownership and control increase cost efficiency and innovation and thus eradicate poor service and the need for costly public subsidies. As with regulated firms, public enterprises usually have facilities that are not well adapted to competitive markets. Consequently, stranded costs will also arise in the public sector when technological or regulatory change permits new forms of competition to take root.

What is the optimal ownership structure of a network industry such as telecommunications? Who should own the telecommunications system: investors, customers, the government? There are at least four possibilities:

Private Ownership and Control. Private rights to residual returns and primarily private control apply to companies in competitive markets subject to lighter forms of regulatory control. Ostensibly, the Telecommunications Act of 1996 foresees that situation as the industry becomes more competitive and as regulatory controls are relaxed or eliminated.

Private Ownership and Public Control. To date, the telecommunications system in the United States has been characterized by a system of private ownership and public control—that is, private property dedicated to public use. That state of affairs means that investors in the utility have rights of management control and rights to residual returns, subject to public regulatory control over rates and service obligations.

Public Ownership and Control. Public ownership of an enterprise unites claims on the residual returns from the enterprise with control in the hands of the government. Many countries (including France, Germany, and Japan) have for decades favored government ownership of the telecommunications system. Public enterprises in the United States include the U.S. Postal Service, Amtrak, and the Tennessee Valley Authority, a supplier of electric power.

The Commons. The telecommunications system could be operated as a publicly owned commons, with free or below-cost access to everyone. That state of affairs would be analogous to the existing interstate highway system.

In the case of the commons, access is rationed through delays or reduction in service quality rather than through prices. The government is responsible for the cost of the system—in effect, there is no positive residual return. At the same time, the unlimited and diffuse private control of the asset creates the possibility of congestion and other negative externalities that one observes on freeways and in public parks. Although a commons is incompatible with private ownership, the open access and unbundling provisions of the Telecommunications Act of 1996, if applied without efficient pricing for network access, could replicate the outcome of a commons.

We have ranked the four alternative ownership structures in declining order of economic efficiency. The combination of public or private rights over returns and control has important implications for the economic performance of an industry. Competitive companies should achieve the most efficient performance because private owners will exercise their control rights to maximize their residual returns. Next, regulated companies should be relatively less efficient, because regulators have some say in managing the company, though without direct reference to the consequences of their actions for residual returns. (The most direct consequences of regulation for residual returns would presumably arise under incentive regulation plans that explicitly encompass earnings sharing.[5]) A regulated company would generally be expected to operate more efficiently than a public enterprise because the latter need not pursue profit maximization; indeed, it can run losses and receive

5. *See* DAVID E. M. SAPPINGTON & DENNIS L. WEISMAN, DESIGNING INCENTIVE REGULATION FOR THE TELECOMMUNICATIONS INDUSTRY 75–79 (MIT Press & AEI Press 1996).

subsidies, as has been the case with the U.S. Postal Service.[6] Moreover, control of a public enterprise may be diffuse owing to political constraints on the firm's managers. Finally, a commons is the least efficient ownership structure: Although the public sector is responsible for incurring costs and receiving any revenues that the asset generates, the diffusion of control among numerous private users will quickly cause crowding and degradation of the asset. In the economic history of the United States, that scenario has repeatedly played out in diverse settings ranging from the harvesting of oysters in the Chesapeake Bay to the extraction of natural gas in Texas.

The record of public ownership of telecommunications systems is decidedly mixed in developed economies and certainly is poor in current or former centrally directed economies and developing nations. Telecommunications services in developing countries, most of which are still provided by state-owned enterprises, have poor economic performance owing to day-to-day government interference, sluggish bureaucratic controls, and limited management flexibility.[7] Another source of inefficiency has been that many developing countries inherited the combination of postal and telecommunications services in a single public enterprise that improperly matches labor-intensive postal systems having relatively slow rates of technological innovation with capital-intensive telecommunications services for which it is necessary to keep pace with rapid technological innovation.[8] A World Bank study observed that in many Asian, African, and Latin American countries, public ownership of telecommunications has led to insufficient funds for capacity investment, particularly through the discouragement of private-sector investment: "Altogether, private investment (voluntary and mandatory) probably did not account for more than 5 percent of total telecommunications investment in the developing world during the 1980s."[9] That situation has changed dramatically in the developing countries that have opted for privatization of telecommunications, which has attracted private

---

6. J. GREGORY SIDAK & DANIEL F. SPULBER, PROTECTING COMPETITION FROM THE POSTAL MONOPOLY 67, 88–89, 105 (AEI Press 1996); Paul W. MacAvoy & George S. McIsaac, *The Current File on the Case for Privatization of the Federal Government Enterprises*, 3 HUME PAPERS ON PUB. POL'Y, no. 3, 121 (1995); *see also* HART, *supra* note 4, at 12.

7. ROBERT J. SAUNDERS, JEREMY J. WARFORD & BJÖRN WELLENIUS, TELECOMMUNICATIONS AND ECONOMIC DEVELOPMENT 65 (World Bank & Johns Hopkins University Press, 2d ed. 1994).

8. *Id.* at 67.

9. *Id.* at 79.

capital for expansion and modernization. Although progress has occurred in Mexico and other countries that have privatized, still roughly 80 percent of developing countries have yet to restructure their telecommunications sector.[10]

The problems of recovering stranded costs in the face of competitive entry assume a different character when the utility is publicly rather than privately owned. Many public enterprises have no shareholders, other than the citizenry as a whole.[11] Under public ownership, the cost of mandating access prices at a level lower than that required by the market-determined efficient component-pricing rule is to make taxpayers as a whole subsidize competitive entry into the market. If the incumbent public enterprise fails to recover its full economic costs, then taxpayers as a whole will bear the burden of stranded costs, which will be reflected in the diminished value of the state's equity interest in the enterprise. Unlike the investor-owned utility, the public enterprise does not have a set of private investors who could be coerced to bear the burden of either the enterprise's unrecovered stranded costs or the cost of subsidizing the growth of a competitive market.

That unique characteristic of public enterprises has an important implication for public policy concerning the transition to competition in network industries. First, if a government is contemplating privatizing a public enterprise—say, Germany's sale of Deutsche Telekom, which commenced in 1996—it is better to complete all policies of stranded cost recovery or subsidy of competitive entry *before* the enterprise is sold to private investors. By so doing, the government will spread the cost of the transition to competition (including any subsidies to entrants) across all consumers, rather than leave that cost to be spread later across a more concentrated and organized set of private shareholders in the privatized utility. That method of spreading transition costs will mitigate the public choice problems that would otherwise arise if the public enterprise were privatized and its exclusive franchise were then phased out. The commercialization of Telstra Corporation, the state-owned telephone company in Australia, roughly fits the preceding description.[12] Australia's commitment to eliminate all remaining entry controls in telecommunications by 1997—which turned out to be sooner than the date by which privatization of Telstra commenced—surely reduced uncertainty

---

10. *Id.* at 303–31.
11. *See, e.g.,* SIDAK & SPULBER, *supra* note 6, at 88–95.
12. *See* TELSTRA CORP. LTD., 1994 ANNUAL REP. (1994).

about the future returns to the network assets of a privatized Telstra and thus enabled the capital markets to value the firm more accurately.

Because the greatest economic efficiency is likely to be achieved through competition between privately owned firms, the protection of private property rights in the transition from regulation to competition assumes added significance. Deregulation accompanied by takings does not represent a move to unfettered competition. Rather, the reduction in the value of the regulated incumbent as a consequence of remaining regulations is a form of nationalization of industry. Thus, deregulation in a manner that creates a taking runs contrary to the global trend of privatization in the sense that it confiscates private property for a supposedly public purpose.

Indeed, if such "nationalization" is attractive to public policymakers in the United States, then they should make their choice explicit. If a state chooses to abrogate its regulatory contract with an investor-owned utility, one alternative (particularly in the face of the utility's possible bankruptcy) is to nationalize the utility and thus pass the stranded costs and entry subsidies on to taxpayers as a whole in their new capacity as implicit shareholders in the public enterprise. Thereafter, the state would resell the public enterprise to investors after all such costs had been recovered and subsidies ended. Essentially, the state, acting like a leveraged buyout firm, would undertake a going-private transaction followed by an initial public offering. That strategy is one possible interpretation that can be given to former Governor Mario Cuomo's proposal that the state of New York buy Long Island Lighting Co. (LILCO).[13]

The possibility of switching back and forth between public and private ownership introduces an intriguing possibility for addressing the problem of stranded costs.[14] When faced with onerous land-use restric-

13. *The Governor's Plan for LILCO*, N.Y. TIMES, Oct. 20, 1994, at A26. The Long Island Power Authority is statutorily empowered to condemn LILCO. *See* Dan Barry, *Takeover of LILCO by Brooklyn Gas Faces Vote Today*, N.Y. TIMES, Dec. 29, 1996, at 1, 29.

14. Oliver Hart has observed as a general proposition that the government's capacity to change the ownership of property raises the specter of opportunism that we examine throughout this book in the specific case of the regulated network industries:

[W]hat ensures that the government respects an agreed-upon allocation of property rights? The government, unlike a private agent, can always change its mind: it can nationalize assets it has privatized or privatize assets it has nationalized.

HART, *supra* note 4, at 12. Of course, the fact that the government has the power to condemn private property opportunistically does not imply (nor do we understand Hart to imply) that government will never use its condemnation power beneficently.

tions, some property owners have sued the regulatory body for inverse condemnation—that is, they have sued to force the state to buy the property at its fair market value before the imposition of the restrictions. By analogy, an investor-owned utility that remained subject to incumbent burdens after the regulator had permitted competitive entry could sue the state on an inverse condemnation theory and demand that the state buy the utility and internalize the costs of the regulator's breach of the regulatory contract. That alternative is a variant on the nationalization option, but it would be a buyout that the utility would compel the state to undertake, rather than vice versa.

In any case, nationalization is not a desirable option—not only because it contradicts the global trend toward privatization, but also because public management is likely to be substantially less efficient than private management. The clearly preferable alternative is for the regulator to adopt policies for network pricing and cost recovery that prevent takings from occurring during the transition to competition.

THE TELECOMMONS

The purpose of the Telecommunications Act of 1996 was to deregulate the telecommunications industry and to open its various markets to competition. Within a matter of months, however, it became clear that the legislation could not properly be called deregulation. Rather, it reified that Orwellian oxymoron, "managed competition." If they adopt inappropriate pricing standards for resold services and unbundled network elements, regulators may precipitate a deterioration of the local telecommunications network that we call *the tragedy of the telecommons*. In that scenario, the financial nonviability of the private firm that owned and operated the network used for local exchange telephony would necessitate direct public intervention. The Telecommunications Act of 1996 could therefore lead to a de facto government takeover of the local exchange. Few anticipated those consequences—not the members of Congress who passed the Telecommunications Act, not the telecommunications companies that lobbied for (and presumably drafted) the legislation, not the FCC regulators who interpreted the legislation, not the telecommunications companies that lobbied *against* the legislation, and not the equity analysts at the investment banks who were expected to translate the turmoil in the industry into the stark metric of share prices.

By the tragedy of the telecommons we are alluding, of course, to the 1968 article by biologist Garrett Hardin in which he argued that there was no technical solution to the problem of overpopulation.[15] The article, however, is more memorable for presenting a succinct, popular discussion of how the absence of property rights can induce the overconsumption and ultimate ruin of a public resource. Hardin's example was a pasture owned by the public in common. Individually, it would be in the interest of each herdsman to increase the size of his herd grazing on the publicly owned commons, notwithstanding the fact that collectively the overgrazing of the commons would reduce and eventually destroy its value for all herdsmen. Hardin, of course, was not first to recognize the problem of externalities that arise from public ownership. Ronald H. Coase, Harold Demsetz, and Armen A. Alchian had all explained how the absence of property rights induces the overconsumption of a resource,[16] and the basic insight can be traced to Alfred Marshall, A. C. Pigou, and other pioneers of economic theory.[17] What Hardin did was to popularize the concept and add a philosophical twist. By describing what happens to the commons as a "tragedy," he did not intend the colloquial meaning of the word, but rather the meaning that philosopher Alfred North Whitehead imparted to the word: "The essence of dramatic tragedy is not unhappiness. It resides in the solemnity of the remorseless working of things."[18]

The slow understanding of the implications of the Telecommunications Act fits Whitehead's definition of tragedy. One senses "the solemnity of the remorseless working of things" when, to their surprise, business executives, legislators, and regulators began to realize in the summer of 1996 that the new legislation had turned the local telecommunications network into a kind of commons. What once was private property (subject to regulation, of course) had become a lesser form of private property: It was now property that had excised from its essential elements the prerogative of the owner to exclude others at will. (Whether Congress has the power to effect that transmogrification without the payment of just compensation is doubtful for the reasons discussed at length in earlier chapters, but it is not the central question that we wish to address here.)

---

15. Garrett Hardin, *The Tragedy of the Commons*, 162 SCIENCE 1243 (1968).

16. Ronald H. Coase, *The Problem of Social Cost*, 3 J.L. & ECON. 1 (1960); Harold Demsetz, *Toward a Theory of Property Rights*, 57 AM. ECON. REV. PAPERS & PROC. 347 (1967); Armen A. Alchian & Harold Demsetz, *The Property Rights Paradigm*, 33 J. ECON. HIST. 16 (1973).

17. ALFRED MARSHALL, PRINCIPLES OF ECONOMICS (Macmillan 1922); A. C. PIGOU, THE ECONOMICS OF WELFARE (Macmillan, 4th ed. 1932).

18. Hardin, *supra* note 15, at 1244 (quoting ALFRED NORTH WHITEHEAD, SCIENCE AND THE MODERN WORLD 17 (Mentor 1948)).

The fundamental change that Congress made to the private ownership of the telecommunications network would be less significant were it not that the terms of the transaction by which another firm may acquire access to the incumbent's network are mandated by regulation of the sort specified in sections 251 and 252 of the Communications Act.

When economists speak of network externalities, they usually refer to positive spillovers that arise from higher levels of network access and usage.[19] Network externalities are benefits to society that accrue as the size of a network grows: An individual consumer's demand to use the telephone network increases with the number of other users on the network whom he can call or from whom he can receive calls.[20] Usually, we think of the network externality in telecommunications as occurring when another access line or another node (exchange) is added to the network. As Bridger M. Mitchell and Ingo Vogelsang observe: "When a new node is added, the externality is reflected in the number of calls made between any existing nodes and the new node (not an increase in

19. *See* Stanley M. Besen & Joseph Farrell, *Choosing How to Compete: Strategies and Tactics in Standardization*, J. ECON. PERSPECTIVES, Spring 1994, at 117; Michael L. Katz & Carl Shapiro, *Systems Competition and Network Effects*, J. ECON. PERSPECTIVES, Spring 1994, at 93; Michael L. Katz & Carl Shapiro, *Product Innovation with Network Externalities*, 40 J. INDUS. ECON. 55 (1992); Joseph Farrell & Carl Shapiro, *Standard Setting in High-Definition Television*, 1992 BROOKINGS PAPERS ON ECON. ACTIVITY: MICROECONOMICS 1; Stanley M. Besen & Garth Saloner, *The Economics of Telecommunications Standards*, *in* CHANGING THE RULES: TECHNOLOGICAL CHANGE, INTERNATIONAL COMPETITION, AND REGULATION IN COMMUNICATIONS 177 (1989); Janusz A. Ordover & Garth Saloner, *Predation, Monopolization, and Antitrust*, *in* 1 HANDBOOK OF INDUSTRIAL ORGANIZATION 537 (Richard L. Schmalensee & Robert D. Willig eds., North-Holland 1989); Michael L. Katz & Carl Shapiro, *Product Compatibility Choice in a Market with Technological Progress*, 38 OXFORD ECON. PAPERS 146 (1986); Michael L. Katz & Carl Shapiro, *Technology Adoption in the Presence of Network Externalities*, 94 J. POL. ECON. 822 (1986); Joseph Farrell & Garth Saloner, *Installed Base and Compatibility: Innovation, Product Preannouncements, and Predation*, 76 AM. ECON. REV. 940 (1986); Joseph Farrell & Garth Saloner, *Standardization, Compatibility, and Innovation*, 16 RAND J. ECON. 70 (1985); Michael L. Katz & Carl Shapiro, *Network Externalities, Competition, and Compatibility*, 75 AM. ECON. REV. 424 (1985).

20. *See* INGO VOGELSANG & BRIDGER M. MITCHELL, TELECOMMUNICATIONS COMPETITION: THE LAST TEN MILES 51–53 (MIT Press & AEI Press 1997); LESTER D. TAYLOR, TELECOMMUNICATIONS DEMAND IN THEORY AND PRACTICE 9 (Kluwer Academic Publishers 1994); BRIDGER M. MITCHELL & INGO VOGELSANG, TELECOMMUNICATIONS PRICING: THEORY AND PRACTICE 11 (Cambridge University Press 1991); JEAN TIROLE, THE THEORY OF INDUSTRIAL ORGANIZATION 405 (MIT Press 1988); Jeffrey Rohlfs, *A Theory of Interdependent Demand for Telecommunications Service*, 5 BELL J. ECON. & MGMT. SCI. 16 (1974).

the calls between existing nodes)."[21] Some telecommunications regulations, such as policies promoting universal service, are justified as a means to capture for consumers as a whole the benefits of network externalities that accrue as the size of the network grows.[22] Such externalities will vary with both the number of consumers having access to the network and the amount by which each consumer uses the network. Network externalities become less important as more and more subscribers are connected to the network. With respect to the narrowband network for voice telephony, once subscription rises to more than 95 percent of all households, the remaining positive externalities that may be achieved on the margin surely become quite small.

Economists have given less attention to the negative externalities from higher levels of network usage. Nonetheless, negative network externalities relating to congestion plainly arise notwithstanding the conventional view that networks have such expansive economies of scale that capacity is seemingly unlimited.[23] That cheerful view overlooks that the design of local telecommunications networks is predicated on probabilistic estimates of congestion in the use of familiar functions (such as dialtone when one picks up the telephone receiver) that consumers may have come to assume are available at all times on an unlimited basis.[24] As S. J. Liebowitz and Stephen Margolis critically observe of network externalities arguments: "Constant or decreasing marginal cost, which is the assumption that has most commonly been made in the network externality literature, converts the problem to one of natural monopoly."[25]

The recent fascination of policymakers with arguments of network externalities has also caused them to overlook that the consumption of network access and network usage, like the consumption of any normal good, will rise as price falls. Only a few regulatory economists—Robert

---

21. MITCHELL & VOGELSANG, TELECOMMUNICATIONS PRICING, *supra* note 20, at 11.

22. *See, e.g.*, MILTON L. MUELLER, JR., UNIVERSAL SERVICE: COMPETITION, INTERCONNECTION, AND MONOPOLY IN THE MAKING OF THE AMERICAN TELEPHONE SYSTEM (MIT Press & AEI Press 1997).

23. For further criticism of the network externalities literature along those lines, see S. J. Liebowitz & Stephen E. Margolis, *Network Externality: An Uncommon Tragedy*, J. ECON. PERSPECTIVES, Spring 1994, at 133.

24. BELL COMMUNICATIONS RESEARCH, BOC NOTES ON THE LEC NETWORK—1994, at 4–24 (Bellcore 1994) (describing blocking probabilities for trunking); 1 BELL COMMUNICATIONS RESEARCH, TELECOMMUNICATIONS TRANSMISSION ENGINEERING: PRINCIPLES 604 (Bellcore 1990) ("[E]xcessively high traffic . . . has its greatest impact on switching system operation. This form of overload causes blocking of calls and a breakdown of service.").

25. Liebowitz & Margolis, *supra* note 23, at 143.

W. Crandall in particular—have recognized the potential for excessively low prices for network access to stimulate inefficiently high levels of use of the incumbent LEC's network by competitors.[26] Pricing network access below cost is likely to lead to congestion externalities by failing to send correct pricing signals to consumers and by removing entry and investment incentives from suppliers. In the local exchange, flat-rate pricing encourages the usage of the local exchange services. Lowering access prices below cost not only would encourage excessive use of the local exchange network but also would discourage investment in competing facilities.

The problem of the telecommons is evident in developing countries, where consumers wait months or years for service owing to shortages of telephone lines and where it is difficult to complete a call because networks are heavily congested, especially during business hours.[27] Moreover, congestion at major centers or on long-distance routes tends to propagate across entire national systems.[28] Robert J. Saunders, Jeremy J. Warford, and Björn Wellenius argue that the solution to the problems observed in developing countries is imposing market prices for scarce lines and charging for local calls to reduce congestion:

> [I]n a situation of unserved demand, setting the price of telecommunications services on the basis of calculated long-run marginal costs is not necessary. Instead, price can serve as a rationing mechanism. Scarce telephone lines can thus be allocated to customers who will derive the highest value from their use by charging prices above cost to the point where the level of unmet demand is almost eliminated and additional funds are generated for the enterprise.[29]

The problems of pricing and congestion in developing countries are a harbinger of the future even for the advanced U.S. telecommunications system if regulated pricing recreates the typical problems that accompany rent control.

The network outage experienced in August 1996 by the Internet access provider America Online[30] may be an imperfect analogy to the

---

26. Statement of Robert W. Crandall on Interconnection Policies for CMRS (Mar. 4, 1996), *submitted in* Interconnection Between Local Exchange Carriers and Commercial Mobile Radio Service Providers; Equal Access and Interconnection Obligations Pertaining to Commercial Mobile Radio Service Providers, Notice of Proposed Rulemaking, CC Dkt. No. 95–185, 11 F.C.C. Rcd. 5020 (1996).

27. SAUNDERS, WARFORD & WELLENIUS, *supra* note 7, at 274.

28. *Id.* at 15.

29. *Id.* at 274.

30. *Big On-Line Crash Frustrates Businesses*, N.Y. TIMES, Aug. 8, 1996, at A1.

congestion externality that may beset the local exchange network in the new era of unbundled access, but it nonetheless provides vivid evidence that congestion externalities can and do occur—even without regulatory intervention that stimulates demand for network access by virtue of having set access prices below the incumbent network operator's full economic cost of providing unbundled functions to competitors. Not long after the passage of the Telecommunications Act of 1996, Pacific Bell reported that roughly 15 percent of local calls were not being successfully completed in the Silicon Valley area of California because Internet usage there, while still a small fraction of total telephone subscribers, had risen to such a high level that it was seriously congesting the capacity of the local exchange.[31]

A 1996 study by Bell Atlantic found that the prices of its lines offered to Internet service providers was well below its cost of service.[32] The reason was that vastly increased usage of the local exchange system due to Internet usage had required Bell Atlantic to add new equipment to central offices, increase the number of trunk lines, deploy more efficient Internet transport technologies (such as switched multimegabit data service), and increase maintenance expenditures. Long-run solutions to the problems of network congestion posed by Internet usage will require the use of more advanced network architecture tailored for data transmission. One problem faced by the LECs is that Internet service providers use the FCC's enhanced service provider exemption to purchase primary-rate integrated service digital network lines, business dial tone lines, and other facilities to receive access to the local telephone network without charge to obtain a dedicated direct connection to the switch—all of which eliminate the incentives of Internet service providers to seek alternative access.[33] According to Bell Atlantic, without changes in pricing policies, such Internet traffic risks overwhelming the local telephone network.

---

31. James Kim, *Net Use Strains Phone Lines*, USA TODAY, Oct. 30, 1996, at 1A; *see also* Michael Fitzpatrick, Internet's Pricing Structure, Not Flood of Users, Is Threat to Its Survival (Pacific Telesis Oct. 23, 1996) (available on the Internet at http://www.pactel.com/cgi-bin/getrel?1321); J. Gregory Sidak & Daniel F. Spulber, *Cyberjam: The Law and Economics of Internet Congestion of the Telephone Network*, 20 HARV. J.L. & PUB. POL'Y (forthcoming 1997).

32. REPORT OF BELL ATLANTIC ON INTERNET TRAFFIC (Bell Atlantic Corp. Mar. 1996) (available on the Internet at http://www.ba.com/ea/fcc/report.htm); *see also Superhighway Traffic Taxes Current LEC Networks*, TELEPHONY, July 29, 1996, at 35.

33. *Id.*

The tragedy of the telecommons also implies underinvestment in the maintenance, replacement, and enhancement of the local telecommunications network. If the incumbent LEC, the putative owner of the local network, no longer can recover the costs of investments that it would make on a forward-looking basis—let alone keep any economic rents accruing to such investments—then entrants seeking access to the local exchange become free riders, and the incumbent LEC's incentive to make further investment in the local exchange network evaporates.

To avoid congestion externalities, access should be priced to allocate consumer demand and to provide incentives for producers to expand transmission capacity. The capacity of a commons can never keep up with demand—even if telecommunications capacity initially appears limitless. New uses develop, and substitution away from more costly alternatives further stimulates demand.

Carried to its logical conclusion, the tragedy of the telecommons implies that the owner of the local exchange network will go broke and the quality of the network will deteriorate. Given the preference of regulators to combine incremental cost pricing for access and unbundled network elements while refusing to impose a new competitively neutral, nonbypassable end-user charge (or increasing an existing charge of that sort, such as the subscriber line charge), the incumbent LEC will consistently fail to earn revenues from its local exchange operations that will cover their total forward-looking costs. Having imposed such regulatory policies concerning unbundling, the state will not be able to expect *any* private investor to take over operation of the local network in the absence of the payment of an explicit subsidy to cover operating losses. The alternative thus becomes public ownership of the network: The logical culmination of unbundling (accompanied by below-cost and flat-rate pricing) and continuing asymmetric regulation of the incumbent LEC would be the need for some public entity to buy the network and assume financial responsibility for its operating deficits. Paradoxically, the great unbundling experiment in the Telecommunications Act of 1996 showed indications before its first anniversary of producing not deregulation, but subsidized competition and public control of private enterprise on an unprecedented scale.

REGULATORY DIVESTITURE

The creation of a telecommons through forced unbundling of the local telecommunications network at uncompensatory prices may impel incumbent local exchange carriers to resort to a radical restructuring of their operations. The generic transaction, which could be undertaken by any incumbent LEC required by regulation to give competitors access to its network at regulated prices, would aim to preserve economic incentives for investment.

In brief, the transaction would spin off ownership of the incumbent LEC's network facilities from its branded retailing activities and value-added services. The new retailing entity would buy network usage on the same terms that the new entrants (such as AT&T, Time Warner, and MFS) could and then resell it as a branded, bundled service to customers. The reseller resulting from the spinoff would be the successor to the brand name of the formerly integrated incumbent LEC (such as "Bell Atlantic" or "BellSouth" or "GTE") and would receive the LEC's existing retail customer accounts. The network operator would assume a new name. Complete separation of the two entities, with wholly separate management, would be necessary to overcome the serious burdens of asymmetric regulation of the incumbent LEC. If undertaken by an incumbent LEC, the spinoff would create a segregation of assets with a corresponding public offering or tax-free distribution of stock in a new and independent company.[34]

The Telecommunications Act of 1996 creates *diseconomies* of scope and vertical integration for any firm satisfying the definition of an "incumbent local exchange carrier."[35] That problem appears not to have been recognized by legislators, regulators, or even investment analysts.[36] The conventional wisdom was that the new legislation on balance benefited the RBOCs by freeing them (eventually) to enter the

---

34. There would be no conflict between that form of spinoff and a merger between a major interexchange carrier and an incumbent LEC, such as the merger between AT&T and SBC that was rumored in May 1997 to be under consideration but abandoned a month later. *See* John J. Keller, *AT&T and SBC Are Holding Talks to Merger in Transaction Valued at More Than $50 Billion*, WALL ST. J., May 27, 1997, at A3; Robert E. Allen, *For Ma Bell, the Bell Tolled Long Ago*, WALL ST. J., June 23, 1997, at A15; Leslie Cauley & John J. Keller, *AT&T-SBC Plan Is Ended by Phone Call*, WALL ST. J., June 30, 1997, at A3. Moreover, such a spinoff would improve the ability of such a merger to gain the approval of antitrust authorities.

35. 47 U.S.C. § 251(h).

36. *See, e.g.,* MERRILL LYNCH & CO., UNITED STATES TELECOM SERVICES—RBOCs & GTE (May 14, 1996) ("In our view, the high incremental margins and low capital intensity of long distance enables RBOCs and GTE to gain enough to offset the pain of losing (what we believe will be) comparable market share in the local telephone market. Indeed, because it is likely that the RBOCs will enjoy more of a buyers' market for long distance than the new entrants in the local market will for local capacity, we are able to reach our counterintuitive conclusions.").

interLATA long-distance market. But that view overlooked that, until permitted to enter the interLATA market, the RBOCs could be forced by regulators to subsidize the entry into the local market of rivals such as AT&T and Time Warner at prices for network interconnection, unbundled elements, and wholesale services that would prevent the RBOCs from covering their total costs. As chapter 6 shows, if that state of affairs persists, bankruptcy becomes a genuine danger for RBOCs, just as it already has been for some electric utilities subject to regulatory policies mandating the transmission of competitively generated power for sale to retail customers.

The value from our suggested divestiture transaction would come from five sources. First, when setting prices for network access, the state public utilities commission would be limited, relative to the status quo, in the amount of harm that it could inflict on the incumbent LEC's shareholders. If the owner of the local exchange network divested itself of all high-margin, unregulated service offerings, then the regulator would have no safety margin when it ordered the firm to sell network access to new entrants at uncompensatory prices. The absence of a pool of positive net revenues that could offset the network owner's losses from the sale of unbundled elements and wholesale services would mean that the PUC would, with a high degree of certainty, render the network operator insolvent if the commission tried to force the incumbent to subsidize competitive entry. A PUC would be reluctant to do that. Moreover, under those same facts, a regime of uncompensatory access prices would be far more likely to produce a winning argument in court for the network operator that its property had been confiscated without just compensation in violation of the Fifth Amendment. To avoid the possibility of losing such a lawsuit, which could produce liability in the billions of dollars, the PUC would be more likely to mandate access to the incumbent's network *only* at prices that did not threaten the incumbent's financial viability. The divestiture would stop the financial hemorrhaging that the incumbent LEC suffers because of the subsidies that regulators have required it to pay to competitors. For that reason, we would expect entrants vigorously to oppose the incumbent LEC's proposal to restructure in that manner.

The second source of value from the divestiture transaction would flow from the fact that the Telecommunications Act of 1996 requires an incumbent LEC to pass along to competitors seeking network access any economies of scale or scope that the LEC has achieved for itself. The legislation added section 259 to the Communications Act, which provides in subsection (a):

> The Commission shall prescribe, within one year after the date of enactment of the Telecommunications Act of 1996, regulations that require incumbent local exchange carriers (as defined in section 251(h)) to make available to any qualifying carrier such public switched network infrastructure, technology, information, and telecommunications facilities and functions as may be requested by such qualifying carrier for the purpose of enabling such qualifying carrier to provide telecommunications services, or to provide access to information services, in the service area in which such qualifying carrier has requested and obtained designation as an eligible telecommunications carrier under section 214(e).[37]

In turn, section 259(b) provides in part that the FCC's regulations promulgated pursuant to section 259(a) shall "ensure that such local exchange carrier makes such infrastructure, technology, information, facilities, or functions available to a qualifying carrier on just and reasonable terms and conditions that permit such qualifying carrier to fully benefit from the economies of scale and scope of such local exchange carrier, as determined in accordance with guidelines prescribed by the Commission in regulations issued pursuant to this section . . . ."[38] Finally, section 259(d) defines a "qualifying carrier" to be "a telecommunications carrier that (1) lacks economies of scale or scope, as determined in accordance with regulations prescribed by the Commission pursuant to this section; and (2) offers telephone exchange service, exchange access, and any other service that is included in universal service, to all consumers without preference throughout the service area for which such carrier has been designated as an eligible telecommunications carrier under section 214(e)."[39] Those statutory provisions fundamentally alter the ownership and control characteristics of the network assets that the incumbent LEC ostensibly holds as private property dedicated to a public purpose: Congress so expanded the scope of the public purpose as to swallow the remaining attributes of private ownership and control.

The FCC has added by regulation a similar gloss to other provisions of the Telecommunications Act of 1996. For example, an incumbent LEC "may not withhold any information necessary to provide number portability on the grounds that such data are combined with other information in its downstream database."[40] An entrant, however, faces

---

37. 47 U.S.C. § 259(a).
38. *Id.* § 259(b)(4).
39. *Id.* § 259(d).
40. Telephone Number Portability, First Report and Order and Further Notice of

no similar obligation with respect to the incumbent LEC. Because such regulatory asymmetry would permit the entrant to free ride on the incumbent LEC's investments in software enhancements to improve service quality and reliability, the FCC in effect has created a disincentive for the LEC to undertake such investments because they cannot give the LEC any competitive advantage.

Similarly, the Telecommunications Act of 1996 added section 272 to the Communications Act, which governs the entry of the RBOCs into interLATA services and provides in part: "A Bell operating company and an affiliate that is subject to the requirements of section 251(c) . . . shall charge the affiliate . . . , or impute to itself (if using the access for its provision of its own services), an amount for access to its telephone exchange service and exchange access that is no less than the amount charged to any unaffiliated interexchange carriers for such service . . . ."[41] Although imputation is a desirable policy with respect to the pricing of a bottleneck facility on an efficient and nondiscriminatory basis, by its very nature imputation eliminates the advantages that a firm might achieve by vertically integrating instead of relying on arms-length contracting.

In short, regulation has consciously eliminated for the incumbent LEC many benefits from scale, scope, and vertical integration. To make matters worse, an incumbent LEC continues to bear incumbent burdens in the form of public-service obligations and carrier-of-last-resort obligations that new entrants can avoid. In short, the operating structure for an incumbent LEC after the Telecommunications Act of 1996 entails greater costs and no benefits relative to competitors. Consequently, any divestiture of assets away from the legally disfavored incumbent LEC structure would increase the value of those assets by reducing the extent of regulation over them and by protecting them to a greater extent from attempts by competitors to use the regulatory system to free ride on the incumbent firm's investments.

The third source of value from our suggested divestiture transaction would come from superior pricing of capital assets. In light of the deteriorating regulatory environment for incumbent LECs following the Telecommunications Act of 1996, investors in those firms have been made to bear financial risk inefficiently. Currently, those investors hold a single security that is in essence a blend of a security in a network operator and a security in a retailer of network services. That blend

Proposed Rulemaking, CC Dkt. No. 95-116, 11 F.C.C. Rcd. 8352, 8404 ¶ 100 (1996).
   41. 47 U.S.C. § 272(e)(3).

obscures the very different risk-return characteristics of the two constituent parts. It affords investors less transparency and choice than they would have if they could instead hold one share of an incumbent network operator and a separately traded share of an unregulated reseller of network services. The spinoff would produce that transparency and choice for investors.

The fourth source of value would flow from the ability to contain the deleterious effects on the incumbent LEC of subsidized pricing of mandatory network access. If, after the proposed spinoff, the regulator forced the incumbent LEC to sell network services below cost, then at least the LEC's newly divested reseller would be able to buy that access at the same subsidized rate as the other major market entrants. That result would stand in stark contrast to the current situation in which the incumbent LEC's retail operations in effect subsidize rivals when the state PUC mandates interconnection, unbundling, and resale at uncompensatory prices.

The fifth source of value relates only to the regional Bell operating companies. If an RBOC could shed itself of ownership of its local exchange network, it would have a powerful basis for arguing that it should be free immediately to offer in-region interLATA service, notwithstanding the onerous "checklist" procedure specified in section 271 of the Communications Act.[42] For an RBOC, rapid entry into the interLATA market would be a major accomplishment, for securing the permission to enter that long-distance market was the principal objective that the RBOCs sought in the 1996 legislation. Following the spinoff transaction, an RBOC would no longer own bottleneck facilities in the local market. As a mere reseller of local exchange services, the post-spinoff RBOC would have no ability to exclude competitors, as regulators have perennially feared. In other words, the RBOC would shed itself of the distinguishing characteristic that provided the rationale both for the imposition of the interLATA restriction in the Modification of Final Judgment and for the subsequent checklist procedure in the 1996 legislation for lifting that restriction. Nonetheless, the RBOC would retain a valuable brand name with which to market lucrative interLATA services within the states in which it formerly provided local exchange services. In short, the RBOC's means of lifting the regulatory quarantine is divestiture.

The spinoff transaction would separate the LEC's network facilities from its retailing activities. Needless to say, the retailing entity would

---

42. *Id.* § 271.

also retain ownership of all other businesses (such as wireless) that were inessential to operation of the local network. Indeed, a first approximation for dividing the incumbent LEC's assets between the network facilities operator and the reseller of network services would come from answering the following question: What assets are *not* necessary for the incumbent LEC to provide resale, interconnection, or unbundled network access to a competing telecommunications carrier?

The proposed spinoff could have a geographic scope as well. A state PUC would be most likely to be dissuaded from acting opportunistically with respect to the setting of access prices for an incumbent LEC if the adverse consequences of doing so would be felt entirely within that state and could not be "exported" to stakeholders in other jurisdictions. That result would most likely obtain if the LEC were a separate publicly traded company providing service only in that state. Under those circumstances the financial consequences of the PUC's setting of uncompensatory access prices would have the most pronounced political ramifications for the commission, for financial losses that the network operator incurred in that state could not be offset by superior returns in another state.

THE EIGHTH CIRCUIT'S 1997
DECISION IN *IOWA UTILITIES BOARD*

In July 1997 the U.S. Court of Appeals for the Eighth Circuit issued its long-awaited decision in *Iowa Utilities Board* v. *FCC*,[43] in which the court vacated, after having stayed nine months earlier,[44] the pricing provisions of the FCC's *First Report and Order*.[45] In an opinion by Judge David R. Hansen, the court held that "the FCC exceeded its jurisdiction in promulgating the pricing rules regarding local telephone service."[46] Accordingly, the court vacated the FCC's pricing rules "on that ground alone" and did not review the rules on their merits.[47]

---

43. 1997 U.S. App. LEXIS 18183 (8th Cir. July 18, 1997).

44. Iowa Utils. Bd. *v.* FCC, 109 F.3d 418 (8th Cir. 1996).

45. Implementation of the Local Competition Provisions in the Telecommunications Act of 1996 and Interconnection Between Local Exchange Carriers and Commercial Mobile Radio Service Providers, First Report and Order, CC Dkt. Nos. 96-98, 95-185, 11 F.C.C. Rcd. 15,499 (1996) [hereinafter *First Report and Order*].

46. 1997 U.S. App. LEXIS 18183 at *7.

47. *Id.* at *34. The rules vacated were 47 C.F.R. §§ 51.501–51.515 (inclusive, except section 51.515(b)), 51.601–51.611 (inclusive), and 51.701–51.717 (inclusive). 1997 U.S. App. LEXIS 18183 at *34 n.21.

Nonetheless, the court upheld certain key provisions of the *First Report and Order* concerning unbundling of network elements, on which the court concluded the FCC did have jurisdiction and was entitled to the reviewing court's deference under the *Chevron* doctrine.[48]

The Eighth Circuit's affirmation of those unbundling provisions may prove to be more important than its invalidation of the FCC's pricing rules. By the end of 1996, most state commissions had issued interim pricing orders for unbundled elements and resale that mirrored the TELRIC methodology and proxy rates of the *First Report and Order* without purporting to be legally bound by the order. The FCC, in other words, succeeded in setting the intellectual agenda for state regulators, even if the agency was destined to lose the turf battle over jurisdiction. At the same time, the Eighth Circuit deferred to the FCC's unbundling rules and embraced the reasoning of the agency and entrants concerning the probable effects of those rules on competition, investment, and innovation.

The court did not consider whether the FCC's unbundling rules effected a taking, because the court ruled the question not yet ripe for adjudication.[49] In a footnote, the court noted but did not evaluate the argument advanced by incumbent LECs "that the TELRIC method underestimates their costs to provide interconnection and unbundled access and results in prices that are too low, effectively requiring them to subsidize their new local service competitors."[50]

We consider now how several of the Eighth Circuit's more significant rulings concerning the FCC's unbundling rules relate to the major themes that we have developed in this book.

The Scope of the Definition of a Network Element

The Eighth Circuit agreed with the FCC's decision to define *network element* broadly.[51] The court ruled that "the Act's definition of network

---

48. Chevron U.S.A. Inc. *v.* Natural Resources Defense Council, Inc., 467 U.S. 837, 842–45 (1984).

49. 1997 U.S. App. LEXIS 18183 at *100.

50. *Id.* at *9 n.8.

51. *Id.* at *62 (citing *First Report and Order*, 11 F.C.C. Rcd. at 15,633–34 ¶ 263, 15,707 ¶ 413). The Telecommunications Act defines a network element as "a facility or equipment used in the provision of a telecommunications service. Such term also includes features, functions, and capabilities that are provided by means of such facility or equipment, including subscriber numbers, databases, signaling systems, and information suffi-

elements is not limited to only the physical components of a network that are directly used to transmit a phone call from point *A* to point *B*."[52] Rather, the definition "includes the technology and information used to facilitate ordering, billing, and maintenance of phone service—the functions of operational support systems."[53] The Eighth Circuit also concluded that the information and databases of such systems "constitute features, functions, and capabilities that are provided through the use of software and hardware that is [sic] used in the commercial offering of telecommunication services to the public."[54] The court similarly concluded that operator services, directory assistance, caller I.D., call forwarding, and call waiting are network elements that are subject to unbundling, even if one were to label those capabilities "services" rather than "elements."[55]

The conclusion that technology or information can constitute a network element subject to mandatory unbundling has broad implications. As chapter 9 explains, dynamic inefficiency would result from mandating access to the incumbent's information at prices set at TELRIC plus a slight contribution to common costs, for the firm's underlying decision to make the investment necessary to create the technology or information would depend on its expectation of earning economic rent on its outlays. As chapter 12 explains, without the prospect of earning economic rent, there would be no incentive for those investments. Because it had invalidated the FCC's pricing rules, the Eighth Circuit evidently presumed that it did not need to devote any special consideration to the peculiar problem of mandating access to information at regulated prices. Yet those regulated prices would threaten to deny the incumbent LEC its expectation of earning the economic rents that were the prerequisite for its making that investment.

"Technically Feasible" Unbundling

The Eighth Circuit affirmed the FCC's interpretation of the statutory requirement that interconnection and unbundled access occur "at any technically feasible point."[56] The agency had ruled that "determination

---

cient for billing and collection or used in the transmission, routing, or other provision of a telecommunications service." 47 U.S.C. § 251(c)(3).

52. 1997 U.S. App. LEXIS 18183 at *64.
53. *Id.* at *65.
54. *Id.*
55. *Id.* at *68–*69.
56. 47 U.S.C. §§ 251(c)(2), (3).

of technical feasibility does not include consideration of economic, accounting, billing, space, or site concerns."[57] As chapter 12 explains, however, finer and finer partitioning of the network into technically feasible unbundled elements increases the likelihood that pricing based on the FCC's TELRIC methodology will fail to compensate the incumbent LEC for shared costs incurred across subsets of the firm's elements.

In concluding that the FCC's definition of *technically feasible* was reasonable and entitled to deference under *Chevron*, the Eighth Circuit did not consider the difficulty that the incumbent LEC might encounter in recovering that cost by noting that the LEC was entitled to compensatory prices for its unbundled elements.[58] If the process of cost recovery were that simple—and if it were clear that "the FCC's definition of 'technically feasible' [would] not unduly burden the incumbent LECs," as the Eighth Circuit concluded[59]—then the local competition provisions of the 1996 legislation would not have become mired in litigation within weeks of the FCC's release of the *First Report and Order*. In essence, the Eighth Circuit took the rather unrealistic view that the FCC's unbundling rules and the pricing of unbundled elements (according to either FCC or state PUC rules) operate independently of one another. That assumption is false. The lower the price of unbundled elements, the greater the amount and scope of network unbundling that entrants will demand. And the greater the extent of unbundling, the harder it will become for the incumbent LEC to recover its total forward-looking costs.

The Quality of Unbundled Access and
Its Relationship to Forward-Looking Costs

The Eighth Circuit vacated the FCC's rule that incumbent LECs provide unbundled access "at levels of quality that are superior to those levels at which the incumbent LECs provide these services to themselves, if

---

57. 47 C.F.R. § 51.5.

58. "Although economic concerns are not to be considered in determining if a point of interconnection or unbundled access is technically feasible, the costs of such interconnection or unbundled access will be taken into account when determining the just and reasonable rates, terms, and conditions for these services. Under the Act, an incumbent LEC will recoup the costs involved in providing interconnection and unbundled access from the competing carriers making these requests." 1997 U.S. App. LEXIS 18183 at *70 (citing 47 U.S.C. §§ 251(c)(2), (3)).

59. *Id.*

requested to do so by competing carriers."[60] Those rules "violated the plain terms" of section 251(c) of the Telecommunications Act, which provides instead that unbundled access be "at least equal in quality" to the access that the incumbent LEC supplies to itself.[61] That ruling is also relevant to the FCC's approach to calculating forward-looking costs. As chapter 12 explains, the *First Report and Order* defines forward-looking costs as "the costs that a carrier would incur in the future,"[62] based on the critical "scorched-node" assumption that "wire centers will be placed at the incumbent LEC's current wire center locations, but that the reconstructed local network will employ the most efficient technology for reasonably foreseeable capacity requirements."[63] After noting as a matter of statutory construction that section 251(c) "mandates only that the quality be equal—not superior," the Eighth Circuit added that "subsection 251(c)(3) implicitly requires unbundled access only to an incumbent LEC's *existing* network—not to a yet unbuilt superior one."[64]

The court did not need to explain the implications of that insight for the FCC's method of calculating forward-looking costs, because the court had already vacated on jurisdictional grounds the pricing rules that were the reason for the FCC's cost calculations in the first place. Nonetheless, if the incumbent LEC need not offer unbundled access to a "yet unbuilt superior" network, it would be surprising if it had to price access to its *existing* network on the basis of the projected costs of that "yet unbuilt superior" network. In short, even without addressing the merits of the FCC's pricing rules, the Eighth Circuit cast doubt on the lawfulness of calculating prices for unbundled elements on the basis of the FCC's scorched-node version of forward-looking costs.

Recombination of Unbundled Elements

The Eighth Circuit affirmed the FCC's ruling that the Telecommunications Act permits a firm to offer telecommunications services that consist entirely of a recombination of the incumbent LEC's unbundled elements.[65] Incumbent LECs had argued that Congress intended resale of

60. *Id.* at *78 (citing 47 C.F.R. §§ 51.305(a)(4), 51.311(c)).
61. *Id.* (citing 47 U.S.C. § 251(c)).
62. *First Report and Order*, 11 F.C.C. Rcd. at 15,848 ¶ 683.
63. *Id.* at 15,849 ¶ 685.
64. 1997 U.S. App. LEXIS 18183 at *79–*80 (emphasis in original).
65. *Id.* at *83–*86 (citing *First Report and Order*, 11 F.C.C. Rcd. at 15,666–71 ¶¶ 328–41). The court held that "under subsection 251(c)(3) a requesting carrier is entitled to gain access to all of the unbundled elements that, when combined by the requesting car-

services to be the exclusive means by which entry would occur if the entrant provided no elements on its own. As chapter 9 notes, the controversy over recombination of elements has practical competitive significance *only* if the regulator forces the incumbent LEC to compute the price of either resale or unbundled elements incorrectly and thus creates an opportunity for entrants to engage in arbitrage.

Although linguistic analysis ostensibly sufficed to produce the Eighth Circuit's holding that the FCC had reasonably interpreted section 251(c)(3), the court nonetheless attempted to bolster its holding with economic reasoning. That economic analysis, however, reflected the fact that, by disposing of the *First Report and Order*'s pricing rules on jurisdictional grounds, the court evidently did not fully comprehend (because it had no need) how those rules would influence entry and investment. The court reasoned:

> Carriers entering the local telecommunications markets by purchasing unbundled network elements face greater risks than those carriers that resell an incumbent LEC's services. A reseller can more easily match its supply with its demand because it can purchase telephone services from incumbent LECs on a unit-by-unit basis. Consequently, a reseller is able to purchase only as many services (or as much thereof) as it needs to satisfy its customer demand. A carrier providing services through unbundled access, however, must make an up-front investment that is large enough to pay for the cost of acquiring access to all of the unbundled elements of an incumbent LEC's network that are necessary to provide local telecommunications services without knowing whether consumer demand will be sufficient to cover such expenditures. Moreover, our decision requiring the requesting carriers to combine the elements themselves increases the costs and risks associated with unbundled access as a method of entering the local telecommunications industry and simultaneously makes resale a distinct and attractive option. With resale, a competing carrier can avoid expending valuable time and resources recombining unbundled network elements.[66]

The Eighth Circuit's economic reasoning is not persuasive for the reasons that chapter 3 examines. First, the entrant will surely target its entry, such that its scale and geographic focus will permit it to buy or lease elements (such as switches) as soon as it becomes more efficient for

---

rier, are sufficient to enable the requesting carrier to provide telecommunications services."
Id. at *87.

66. *Id.* at *87–*89.

the firm to do so. Regulators will typically not force a competitive local exchange carrier to serve all segments of the market. The entrant is free to use a combination of resale and unbundling. It will purchase elements where its expected scale of operation permits (such as in business districts) and procure the incumbent LEC's service on a wholesale basis elsewhere. Thus, the entrant's risk will be lower, even when assembling unbundled elements, than the Eighth Circuit's discussion presumes.

Second, nothing prevents several entrants from reducing risk by sharing a switch and spreading its fixed cost among their respective customers. Similarly, there are facilities-based providers of local transport—such as MFS and Teleport—that can lease capacity to the entrant. Certainly in the case of competitive access providers, the fiber-ring architecture of those firms' networks may make the firms more efficient suppliers of transport than the incumbent LECs.

Third, scale is surely not an issue for the most important unbundled element—the customer loop. The risk to the entrant of leasing an unbundled loop to serve a particular customer is minimal. If the customer were to switch to another carrier, the entrant would simply not renew its lease of that loop from the incumbent LEC.

Unbundling and the Purpose
of the Telecommunication Act of 1996

Near the end of its opinion, the Eighth Circuit offered an extended discussion of the role that mandatory network unbundling plays in the Telecommunications Act of 1996. The court rejected arguments that, under the FCC's unbundling rules, "competing carriers will have no incentive to construct their own facilities" and "neither the competing carriers nor the incumbent LECs will attempt to innovate their technology."[67] The Eighth Circuit believed that those arguments assumed "that the FCC's unbundling rules would operate in conjunction with the Commission's proposed pricing rules."[68] The court reasoned that, because it had "vacated the FCC's pricing rules and determined that the Act requires state commissions to set the rates that competing carriers must pay for access to incumbent LECs' networks,"[69] the court could not "know what the state-determined rates will be."[70] Oddly, the court did

---

67. *Id.* at *91.
68. *Id.* at *91–*92.
69. *Id.* at *92.
70. *Id.*

not mention the pricing methodology that the state PUCs had employed in their many interim rate decisions on resale and unbundling in late 1996 and early 1997. Instead, the Eighth Circuit concluded that the argument that "competing carriers will incur only minimal costs in gaining access to incumbent LECs' networks and have no incentive to build their own is merely speculative at best."[71]

The Eighth Circuit next stated that, "[e]ven if the states establish 'inexpensive' rates," the unbundling rules in the *First Report and Order* would not violate the Telecommunication Act's purpose because, the court concluded, that legislation's "exclusive goal" is not to promote facilities-based competition.[72] To the contrary, the court reasoned, "Congress recognized that the amount of time and capital investment involved in the construction of a complete local stand-beside telecommunications network are substantial barriers to entry, and thus required incumbent LECs to allow competing carriers to use their networks in order to hasten the influence of competitive forces in the local telephone business."[73] The court's reasoning, however, contained several flaws. As chapter 9 shows, it is unlikely that any one entrant would construct "a complete local stand-beside telecommunications network" employing the same technology as the incumbent LEC. For the entrant the relevant entry cost is the stand-alone cost of the network of *its* intended scale and geographic coverage, not the stand-alone cost of replicating the incumbent's network. Moreover, as chapter 3 shows, the barrier to entry argument is incorrect because entrants have already incurred substantial sunk costs to build overlapping networks employing multiple wireline and wireless technologies. Finally, as chapters 9 and 12 show, the combination of the FCC's unbundling rules and TELRIC-based pricing administered by the states will not replicate competitive markets.

The Eighth Circuit also concluded that the unbundling rules would not "hinder the development of facilities-based competition or impede innovation in telecommunications."[74] The court stated:

> Even in light of the unbundling rules, we believe that competing carriers will continue to have incentives to build their own networks. Once a new entrant has established itself and acquired a sufficient customer base to justify investments in its own facilities, a carrier that develops its own

71. *Id.*
72. *Id.* at *93.
73. *Id.* at *93–*94 (citation omitted).
74. *Id.* at *94.

network gains independence from incumbent LECs and has more flexibility to modify its network elements to offer innovative services.[75]

It is unclear, however, what value "independence from incumbent LECs" has for the entrant if the pricing rules for unbundled elements produce prices below the incumbent LEC's respective TELRICs for its network elements and groups of elements. Typically, the recipient of a subsidy does not yearn for independence of the sort that terminates that subsidy. The Eighth Circuit reiterated its belief that "the increased incentive to innovate resulting from the need of a carrier to differentiate its services and products from its competitors' in a competitive market will override any theoretical decreased incentive to innovate resulting from the duty of a carrier to allow its competitors access to its network elements."[76] Over time, the court's hypothesis will be empirically testable. Chapters 9 and 12, however, suggest why one might expect that hypothesis ultimately to be rejected.

The Eighth Circuit's decision highlights how the pricing of network access is inextricably linked to the scope of mandatory unbundling. One cannot say whether or not a particular unbundling obligation is just and reasonable unless one knows how the regulator will permit the incumbent firm to price the mandatory network access associated with that obligation. Because of the jurisdictional basis for its decision on the *First Report and Order*'s pricing rules, the Eighth Circuit avoided the takings issues posed by the confluence of the FCC's unbundling rules and the state PUCs' pricing rules. As a matter of *statutory* interpretation at least, the court treated the local telecommunications network as the commons that the Telecommunications Act had made it—yet without deciding whether, in light of the practical interaction of state and federal regulation, that transformation was an unconstitutional confiscation of private property. Thus, the Eighth Circuit left for a later day—and a different court—the demanding task of resolving the takings and contract issues that result from the competitive transformation of network industries.

CONCLUSION

Network infrastructure has always been the hallmark of civilization. The Romans' systems of aqueducts, sewers, and roads were signs of social progress. Systems of telecommunications, electric power transmission,

75. *Id.*
76. *Id.*

transportation, water services, and other networks have been central to modern economic development. The National Telecommunications and Information Administration observed in 1991 that "telecommunications facilities and services will be as important to the future performance of the U.S. economy as transportation systems have been in the past."[77]

During the twentieth century, U.S. network industries, including telecommunications and electric power, developed under a system of private ownership with public regulation. The dominant mode of regulation has been the regulatory contract: private property dedicated to a public purpose. As the twenty-first century approaches, technological change and market developments allow for network services to be competitively supplied. Achieving the benefits of competition, however, will be feasible only if private property rights are maintained, so that market incentives can be translated into efficient consumption and investment decisions. Unfortunately, the Telecommunications Act of 1996 appears unlikely to produce that salutary outcome in the near term.

Successful deregulation avoids the pitfalls of government takings. Just compensation for stranded investment preserves private property rights. Maintaining economic incentives for private investment averts the inefficiencies associated with public ownership or public subsidies. Finally, market-determined pricing of access to networks achieves economic efficiency and prevents the tragedy of the telecommons.

77. U.S. Department of Commerce, National Telecommunications and Information Administration, Telecommunications in the Age of Information 21 (Government Printing Office 1991).

References

Airline Deregulation: The Early Experience (John R. Meyer and Clinton V. Oster, Jr., eds., Auburn House Publishing Co. 1981).

Alchian, Armen A., "Cost," in *International Encyclopedia of the Social Sciences* (David L. Sills ed., Macmillan & Free Press 1968).

Alchian, Armen A., "Vertical Integration and Regulation in the Telephone Industry," 16 *Managerial and Decision Economics* 323 (1995).

Alchian, Armen A., and Harold Demsetz, "The Property Rights Paradigm," 33 *Journal of Economic History* 16 (1973).

Areeda, Phillip, and Donald F. Turner, "Predatory Pricing and Related Practices under Section 2 of the Sherman Act," 88 *Harvard Law Review* 637 (1975).

Armstrong, Mark, Chris Doyle, and John Vickers, "The Access Pricing Problem: A Synthesis," 44 *Journal of Industrial Economics* 131 (1996).

Arrow, Kenneth J., Dennis W. Carlton, and Hal S. Sider, "The Competitive Effects of Line-of-Business Restrictions in Telecommunications," 16 *Managerial and Decision Economics* 301 (1995).

Bachelier, Louis, *Theory of Speculation* (1900), reprinted in *The Random Character of Stock Market Price* 17 (Paul Cootner ed., MIT Press 1964).

Bailey, Elizabeth E., and Jeffrey R. Williams, "Sources of Rent in the Deregulated Airline Industry," 31 *Journal of Law and Economics* 173 (1988).

Bailey, Elizabeth E., David R. Graham, and Daniel P. Kaplan, *Deregulating Airlines* (MIT Press 1985).

Baird, Douglas G., "The Law and Economics of Contract Damages," University of Chicago Law and Economics Working Paper No. 30 (2d series) (1994).

Ball, R., and P. Brown, "An Empirical Evaluation of Accounting Income Numbers," 6 *Journal of Accounting Resources* 159 (1968).

Barnes, Irston R., *The Economics of Public Utility Regulation* (F. S. Crofts & Co. 1942).

Bauer, John, "Public Utilities: United States and Canada," *in* 12 *Encyclopaedia of the Social Sciences* 677 (Edwin R. A. Seligman & Alvin Johnson eds., Macmillan 1934).

Baumol, William J., "Ramsey Pricing," in 4 *The New Palgrave: A Dictionary of Economics* 49 (John Eatwell, Murray Milgate & Peter Newman eds., Macmillan 1987).

Baumol, William J., "Some Subtle Issues in Railroad Regulation," 10 *International Journal of Transport Economics* 341 (1983).

Baumol, William J., *Superfairness: Applications and Theory* (MIT Press 1986).

Baumol, William J., and David F. Bradford, "Optimal Departures from Marginal Cost Pricing," 60 *American Economic Review* 265 (1970).

Baumol, William J., and Thomas W. Merrill, "Deregulatory Takings, Breach of the Regulatory Contract, and the Telecommunications Act of 1996," 72 *New York University Law Review* (forthcoming 1997).

Baumol, William J., and J. Gregory Sidak, "The Pricing of Inputs Sold to Competitors," 11 *Yale Journal on Regulation* 171 (1994).

Baumol, William J., and J. Gregory Sidak, "The Pricing of Inputs Sold to Competitors: Rejoinder and Epilogue," 12 *Yale Journal on Regulation* 177 (1995).

Baumol, William J., and J. Gregory Sidak, "Pricing of Services Provided to Competitors by the Regulated Firm," 3 *Hume Papers on Public Policy*, no. 3, at 15 (1995).

Baumol, William J., and J. Gregory Sidak, "Stranded Costs," 18 *Harvard Journal of Law and Public Policy* 835 (1995).

Baumol, William J., and J. Gregory Sidak, *Toward Competition in Local Telephony* (MIT Press & AEI Press 1994).

Baumol, William J., and J. Gregory Sidak, *Transmission Pricing and Stranded Costs in the Electric Power Industry* (AEI Press 1995).

Baumol, William J., and Robert D. Willig, "Fixed Costs, Sunk Costs, Entry Barriers and Sustainability of Monopoly," 96 *Quarterly Journal of Economics* 405 (1981).

Baumol, William J., Michael F. Koehn, and Robert D. Willig, "How Arbitrary Is 'Arbitrary'?—or, Toward the Deserved Demise of Full Cost Allocation," 21 *Public Utilities Fortnightly*, Sept. 3, 1987, at 16.

Baumol, William J., Janusz A. Ordover, and Robert D. Willig, "Parity Pricing and Its Critics: Necessary Conditions for Efficiency in Provision of Bottleneck Services to Competitors," 14 *Yale Journal on Regulation* 145 (1997).

Baumol, William J., John C. Panzar, and Robert D. Willig, *Contestable Markets and the Theory of Industry Structure* (Harcourt Brace Jovanovich, rev. ed. 1988).

Bell Communications Research, *Telecommunications Transmission Engineering: Principles* (Bellcore 1990).

Berg, Sanford V., and John Tschirhart, "A Market Test for Natural Monopoly in Local Exchange," 8 *Journal of Regulatory Economics* 103 (1995).

Berg, Sanford V., and John Tschirhart, *Natural Monopoly Regulation: Principles and Practice* (Cambridge University Press 1988).

Besen, Stanley M., and Joseph Farrell, "Choosing How to Compete: Strategies and Tactics in Standardization," 8 *Journal of Economic Perspectives* 117 (1994).

Besen, Stanley M., and Garth Saloner, "The Economics of Telecommunications Standards," in *Changing the Rules: Technological Change, International Competition, and Regulation in Communications* (Robert W. Crandall & Kenneth Flamm eds. Brookings 1989).

Binder, John J., "Measuring the Effects of Regulation with Stock Price Data," 16 *RAND Journal of Economics* 167 (1985).

Birmingham, Robert, "Notes on the Reliance Interest," 60 *Washington Law Review* 217 (1985).

Bishop, William, "The Choice of Remedy for Breach of Contract," 14 *Journal of Legal Studies* 299 (1985).

Blackmon, Glenn, and Richard Zeckhauser, "Fragile Commitments and the Regulatory Process," 9 *Yale Journal on Regulation* 73 (1992).

Blume, Lawrence E., and Daniel L. Rubinfeld, "Compensation for Takings: An Economic Analysis," 72 *California Law Review* 569 (1984).

Blume, Lawrence E., Daniel L. Rubinfeld, and Perry Shapiro, "The Taking of Land: When Should Compensation Be Paid?" 99 *Quarterly Journal of Economics* 71 (1984).

Bonbright, James C., *Principles of Public Utility Rates* (Columbia University Press 1961).

Bork, Robert H., *The Antitrust Paradox: A Policy at War with Itself* (Free Press, rev. ed. 1993) (Basic Books 1978).

Bowman, Ward S., "Tying Arrangements and the Leverage Problem," 67 *Yale Law Journal* 19 (1957).

Braeutigam, Ronald R., "Optimal Policies for Natural Monopolies," in 2 *Handbook of Industrial Organization* 1289 (Richard Schmalensee & Robert D. Willig eds., North-Holland 1989).

Brandon, Paul S., and Richard L. Schmalensee, "The Benefits of Releasing the Bell Companies from the Interexchange Restrictions," 16 *Managerial and Decision Economics* 349 (1995).

Brauneis, Robert, "'The Foundation of Our Regulatory Takings Jurisprudence': The Myth and Meaning of Justice Holmes's Opinion in *Pennsylvania Coal Co.* v. *Mahon*," 106 *Yale Law Journal* 613 (1996).

Brealey, Richard A., and Stewart C. Myers, *Principles of Corporate Finance* (McGraw-Hill, 4th ed. 1991).

Brennan, Timothy J., and James Boyd, "Political Economy and the Efficiency of Compensation for Takings," Resources for the Future Discussion Paper 95-28 (June 1995).

Breyer, Stephen G., "Antitrust, Deregulation, and the Newly Liberated Marketplace," 75 *California Law Review* 1005 (1987).

Breyer, Stephen G., *Regulation and Its Reform* (Harvard University Press 1982).

Brock, Gerald W., *Telecommunications Policy for the Information Age: From Monopoly to Competition* (Harvard University Press 1994).

Brozen, Yale, *Concentration, Mergers, and Public Policy* (Macmillan 1982).

Calhoun, George, *Wireless Access and the Local Telephone Network* (Artech House 1992).

Carlton, Dennis W., and Jeffrey M. Perloff, *Modern Industrial Organization* (Harper Collins College Publishers, 2d ed. 1994).

Cellular Telecommunications Industry Association, *State of the Cellular Industry* (1992).

Chamberlin, Edward H., *The Theory of Monopolistic Competition* (Harvard University Press 1933).

Cheng, David K., *Field and Wave Electromagnetics* (Addison-Wesley Publishing Co. 1983).

Christensen, Laurits R., Diane C. Cummings, and Philip E. Schoech, "Econometric Estimation of Scale Economies in Telecommunications," in *Economic Analysis of Telecommunications* (Léon Courville, Alain de Fontenay & Rodney Dobell eds., North-Holland 1983).

Civil Aeronautics Board, *Domestic Passenger Fare Investigation: January 1970 to December 1974* (1976).

Clemens, Eli Winston, *Economics and Public Utilities* (Appleton-Century-Crofts 1950).

Coase, Ronald H., "The Nature of the Firm," 4 *Economica* 386 (1937).

Coase, Ronald H., "The Problem of Social Cost," 3 *Journal of Law and Economics* 1 (1960).

Coleman, Jules L., *Markets, Morals, and the Law* (Cambridge University Press 1988).

Council of Economic Adivsers, *Economic Report of the President* (Government Printing Office 1996)

Crandall, Robert W., *After the Breakup: U.S. Telecommunications in a More Competitive Era* (Brookings Institution 1991).

Crandall, Robert W., and Harold Furchtgott-Roth, *Cable TV: Regulation or Competition?* (Brookings Institution 1996).

Crandall, Robert W., and J. Gregory Sidak, "Competition and Regulatory Policies for Interactive Broadband Networks," 68 *Southern California Law Review* 1203 (1995).

Crandall, Robert W., and Leonard Waverman, *Talk Is Cheap: The Promise of Regulatory Reform in North American Telecommunications* (Brookings Institution 1996).

Crew, Michael A., and Paul R. Kleindorfer, *The Economics of Postal Service* (Kluwer Academic Publishers 1992).

Crew, Michael A., and Paul R. Kleindorfer, "Pricing in Postal Service Under Competitive Entry," in *Commercialization of Postal and Delivery Services: National and International Perspectives* 117 (Michael A. Crew & Paul R. Kleindorfer eds., Kluwer Academic Publishers 1995).

Crocker, Keith J., and Scott E. Masten, "Regulation and Administered Contracts Revisited: Lessons from Transaction-Cost Economics for Public Utility Regulation," 9 *Journal of Regulatory Economics* 5 (1996).

Currie, David P., *The Constitution in the Supreme Court: The Second Century, 1888–1986* (University of Chicago Press 1990).

Davidson, Carl, and Raymond Denekere, "Long-Run Competition in Capacity, Short-Run Competition in Price and the Cournot Model," 17 *RAND Journal of Economics* 404 (1986).

Dawson, John P., William Burnett Harvey, and Stanley D. Henderson, *Cases and Comment on Contracts* (Foundation Press, 6th ed. 1993).

Demsetz, Harold, "Toward a Theory of Property Rights," 57 *American Economic Review Papers and Proceedings* 347 (1967).

Demsetz, Harold, "Why Regulate Utilities?" 11 *Journal of Law and Economics* 55 (1968).

Diamond, Peter A., and John A. Mirrlees, "Optimal Taxation and Public Production, II: Tax Rules," 61 *American Economic Review* 261 (1971).

Doane, Michael J., and Daniel F. Spulber, "Open Access and the Evaluation of the U.S. Spot Market for Natural Gas," 37 *Journal of Law and Economics* 477 (1994).

Doane, Michael J., and Michael A. Williams, "Competitive Entry into Regulated Monopoly Service and the Resulting Problem of Stranded Costs," 3 *Hume Papers on Public Policy*, no. 3, at 32 (1995).

Dobbs, Dan B., *Remedies: Damages, Equity, Restitution* (West Publishing Co. 1973).

Dorau, Herbert B., *Materials for the Study of Public Utility Economics* (Macmillan 1930).

Douglas, George W., and James C. Miller III, *Economic Regulation of Domestic Air Transport: Theory and Policy* (Brookings Institution 1974).

Drobak, John N., "From Turnpike to Nuclear Power: The Constitutional Limits on Utility Rate Regulation," 65 *Boston University Law Review* 65 (1985).

Dupuit, Jules, "On the Measurement of the Utility of Public Works" (1844) in *Readings in Welfare Economics* 255 (Kenneth J. Arrow & Tibor Scitovsky eds., Irwin 1969).

"The Duty of a Public Utility to Render Adequate Service: Its Scope and Enforcement," 62 *Columbia Law Review* 312 (1962).

Easterbrook, Frank H., "Predatory Strategies and Counterstrategies," 48 *University of Chicago Law Review* 263 (1981).

Easterbrook, Frank H., and Daniel R. Fischel, *The Economic Structure of Corporate Law* (Harvard University Press 1991).

Economides, Nicholas, and Lawrence J. White, "Access and Interconnection Pricing: How Efficient is the Efficient Components Pricing Rule?" 40 *Antitrust Bulletin* 557 (1995).

Economides, Nicholas, and Lawrence J. White, "The Inefficiency of the ECPR Yet Again: A Reply to Larson," 42 *Antitrust Bulletin* (forthcoming 1997).

Edison Electric Institute, *Engineering and Reliability Effects of Increased Wheeling and Transmission Access: Factors for Consideration* (Edison Electric Institute 1988).

Edwards, Jeremy, John Kay, and Colin Mayer, *The Economic Analysis of Accounting Profitability* (Clarendon Press 1987).

Eisenberg, Melvin, "Donative Promises," 47 *University of Chicago Law Review* 1 (1979).

Energy Information Administration, *Electric Trade in the United States* (1994).

Epstein, Richard A., *Takings: Private Property and the Power of Eminent Domain* (Harvard University Press 1985).

Ergas, Henry, and Eric Ralph, "Pricing Network Interconnection: Is the Baumol-Willig Rule the Answer?" Mimeo, Australian Trade Practices Commission (1994).

Essays in the Economics of Renewable Resources (Leonard J. Mirman and Daniel F. Spulber eds., Elsevier-North Holland Publishing Co. 1982).

Evans, David S., and James J. Heckman, "A Test for Subadditivity of the Cost Function with an Application to the Bell System," 74 *American Economic Review* 615 (1984).

Fama, Eugene F., "Efficient Capital Markets: A Review of Theory and Empirical Work," 25 *Journal of Finance* 383 (1970).

Fama, Eugene F., and Michael C. Jensen, "Agency Problems and Residual Claims," 26 *Journal of Law and Economics* 327 (1983).

Fama, Eugene F., Lawrence Fisher, Michael C. Jensen, and Richard Roll, "The Adjustment of Stock Prices to New Information," 10 *International Economic Review* 1 (1969).

Farnsworth, E. Allan, "Legal Remedies for Breach of Contract," 70 *Columbia Law Review* 1145 (1970).

Farrell, Joseph, and Garth Saloner, "Installed Base and Compatibility: Innovation, Product Preannouncements, and Predation," 76 *American Economic Review* 940 (1986).

Farrell, Joseph, and Garth Saloner, "Standardization, Compatibility, and Innovation," 16 *RAND Journal of Economics* 70 (1985).

Farrell, Joseph, and Carl Shapiro, "Standard Setting in High-Definition Television," 1992 *Brookings Papers on Economic Activity: Microeconomics* 1 (1992).

Feinman, Jay M., "Promissory Estoppel and the Judicial Method," 97 *Harvard Law Review* 678 (1984).

Field, Oliver P., "The Withdrawal from Service of Public Utility Companies," 35 *Yale Law Journal* 169 (1925).

Fischel, William A., *Regulatory Takings: Law, Economics, and Politics* (Harvard University Press 1995).

Fisher, Franklin M., Robert J. Larner, Michael Hunter, and Amy Salsbury Serrano, "BOC Manufacture of Telecommunications Equipment: An Assessment of Benefits and Competitive Risks," 16 *Managerial and Decision Economics* 439 (1995).

Fitzpatrick, Michael, "Internet's Pricing Structure, Not Flood of Users, Is Threat to Its Survival," Pacific Telesis (Oct. 23, 1996).

Fox-Penner, Peter S., *Electric Power Transmission and Wheeling: A Technical Primer* (Edison Electric Institute 1990).

Frankfurter, Felix, and Henry M. Hart, Jr., "Rate Regulation," *in* 13 *Encyclopædia of the Social Sciences* 104 (Edwin R. A. Seligman & Alvin Johnson eds., Macmillan Co. 1934).

Fuller, Lon, and William Perdue, "The Reliance Interest in Contract Damages," 46 *Yale Law Journal* 52 (1936).

Gabel, David, "Competition in a Network Industry: The Telephone Industry, 1894–1910," 54 *Journal of Economic History* 543 (1994).

Gilson, Ronald J., and Reinier H. Kraakman, "The Mechanisms of Market Efficiency," 70 *Virginia Law Review* 549 (1984).

Goldberg, Victor P., "Regulation and Administered Contracts," 7 *Bell Journal of Economics* 426 (1976).

Goldberg, Victor P., "Relational Exchange: Economics and Complex Contracts," 23 *American Behavioral Scientist* 337 (1980), reprinted in *Readings in Contract Law* (Victor P. Goldberg ed., Cambridge University Press 1989).

Goldsmith, Richard, "Utility Rates and 'Takings,'" 10 *Energy Law Journal* 241 (1989).

Graniere, Robert J., Almost Second-Best Pricing for Regulated Markets Affected by Competition, National Regulatory Research Institute Paper No. NRRI 96-10 (Mar. 1996).

Greenstein, Shane, Susan McMaster, and Pablo T. Spiller, "The Effect of Incentive Regulation on Infrastructure Modernization: Local Exchange Companies' Deployment of Digital Technology," 4 *Journal of Economics & Management Strategy* 187 (1995).

Greenwald, Bruce C., "Rate Base Selection and the Structure of Regulation," 15 *RAND Journal of Economics* 85 (1984).

Griffith, Janice C., "Local Government Contracts: Escaping from the Government/Proprietary Maze," 75 *Iowa Law Review* 277 (1990).

Hagel, John, III, and Thomas R. Eisenmann, "Navigating the Multimedia Landscape," *McKinsey Quarterly*, June 22, 1994, at 39.

Hall, Ford P., "Discontinuance of Service by Public Utilities," 13 *Minnesota Law Review* 181 (1929).

Hardin, Garrett, "Tragedy of the Commons," 162 *Science* 1243 (1968).

Hart, Henry M., "The Power to Limit the Jurisdiction of Federal Courts: An Exercise in Dialect," 66 *Harvard Law Review* 1362 (1953), reprinted in Paul M. Bator, Paul J. Mishkin, David L. Shapiro, and Herbert Wechsler, *Hart and Wechsler's The Federal Courts and the Federal System* (Foundation Press, 2d ed. 1973).

Hart, Oliver, *Firms, Contracts, and Financial Structure* (Clarendon Press, Oxford 1995).

Hatfield Associates, *Documentation of the Hatfield Model, Version 2.2, Release 1* (Hatfield Associates May 16, 1996).

Hausman, Jerry A., "Competition in Long-distance and Telecommunications Markets: Effects of the MFJ," 16 *Managerial and Decision Economics* 365 (1995).

Hausman, Jerry A., and Timothy J. Tardiff, "Efficient Local Exchange Competition," 40 *Antitrust Bulletin* 529 (1995).

Hayek, Friedrich A., *The Fatal Conceit: The Errors of Socialism* (W. W. Bartley III ed., Routledge 1988).

Hayek, Friedrich A., "The Use of Knowledge in Society," 35 *American Economic Review* 519 (1945).

Henderson, James M., and Richard E. Quandt, *Microeconomic Theory: A Mathematical Approach* (McGraw-Hill, 3d ed. 1980).

Hicks, John R., "Foundations of Welfare Economics," 49 *Economic Journal* 549 (1939).

Hogan, William W., "Contract Networks for Electric Power Transmission," 4 *Journal of Regulatory Economics* 211 (1992).

Holmes, Oliver Wendell, "The Path of the Law," 10 *Harvard Law Review* 457 (1897).

Hopper, Jack, "A Legislative History of the Texas Public Utility Regulatory Act of 1975," 28 *Baylor Law Review* 777 (1976).

Horngren, Charles T., George Foster, and Srikant M. Datar, *Cost Accounting: A Managerial Emphasis* (Prentice Hall, 8th ed. 1994).

Horwitz, Robert Britt, *The Irony of Regulatory Reform: The Deregulation of American Telecommunications* (Oxford University Press 1989).

Hotelling, Harold, "The General Welfare in Relation to the Problems of Taxation and of Railway and Utility Rates," 6 *Econometrica* 242 (1938).

Hotelling, Harold, "Stability in Competition," 39 *Economic Journal* 41 (1929).

Huber, Peter W., Michael K. Kellogg, and John Thorne, *The Geodesic Network II, 1993 Report on Competition in the Telephone Industry* (Geodesic Co. 1992).

Huber, Peter W., Michael K. Kellogg, and John Thorne, *The Telecommunications Act of 1996: Special Report* (Little, Brown & Co. 1996).

Hyman, Leonard S., *America's Electric Utilities: Past, Present, and Future* (Public Utilities Reports, 5th ed. 1994).

Irwin, Douglas A., *Against the Tide: An Intellectual History of Free Trade* (Princeton University Press 1996).

Ivins, William M., and Herbert Delavan Mason, *The Control of Public Utilities* (Baker, Voorhis, and Co. 1908).

Johnson, Leland L., *Toward Competition in Cable Television* (MIT Press & AEI Press 1994).

Jones, William K., *Regulated Industries: Cases and Materials* (Foundation Press 1976).

Joskow, Paul L., "Asset Specificity and the Structure of Vertical Relationships: Empirical Evidence," 4 *Journal of Law, Economics, and Organization* 95 (1988).

Joskow, Paul L., "Contract Duration and Durable Transaction-Specific Investments: The Case of Coal," 77 *American Economic Review* 168 (1987).

Joskow, Paul L., "Vertical Integration and Long Term Contracts: The Case of Coal-Burning Electric Generating Plants," 1 *Journal of Law, Economics, and Organization* 33 (1980).

Joskow, Paul L., and Alvin K. Klevorick, "A Framework for Analyzing Predatory Pricing Policy," 89 *Yale Law Journal* 213 (1979).

Joskow, Paul L., and Richard Schmalensee, "Incentive Regulation for Electric Utilities," 4 *Yale Journal on Regulation* 1 (1986).

Joyce, Joseph A., *A Treatise on Franchises* (Banks Law Publishing Company 1914).

Kahn, Alfred E., *The Economics of Regulation: Principles and Institutions* (John Wiley & Sons 1970) (MIT Press, rev. ed. 1988).

Kahn, Alfred E., *How to Treat the Costs of Shared Voice and Video Networks in a Post-Regulatory Age* (Cato Institute Nov. 27, 1996).

Kahn, Alfred E., and William E. Taylor, "The Pricing of Inputs Sold to Competitors: A Comment," 11 *Yale Journal on Regulation* 225 (1994).

Kaldor, Nicholas, "Welfare Propositions of Economics and Interpersonal Comparisons of Utility," 49 *Economics Journal* 549 (1939).

Kaplan, Daniel P., "The Changing Airline Industry, Case 2," in *Regulatory Reform: What Really Happened* 72 (Leonard Weiss & Michael W. Klass eds., Little, Brown, & Co. 1986).

Kaplow, Louis, "An Economic Analysis of Legal Transitions," 99 *Harvard Law Review* 509 (1986).

Kaserman, David L., and John W. Mayo, "An Efficient Avoided Cost Pricing Rule for Resale of Local Exchange Services," 11 *Journal of Regulatory Economics* 91 (1997).

Kaserman, David L., and John W. Mayo, *Government and Business: The Economics of Antitrust and Regulation* (Dryden Press 1995).

Kaserman, David L., John W. Mayo, Michael A. Crew, Nicholas Economides, R. Glenn Hubbard, Paul R. Kleindorfer, and Carlos Martins-Filho, *Local Competition Issues and the Telecommunications Act of 1996* (July 15, 1996) (prepared for AT&T Corp.).

Katz, Michael L., and Carl Shapiro, "Network Externalities, Competition, and Compatibility," 75 *American Economic Review* 424 (1985).

Katz, Michael L., and Carl Shapiro, "Product Compatibility Choice in a Market with Technological Progress," 38 *Oxford Economic Papers* 146 (1986).

Katz, Michael L., and Carl Shapiro, "Product Innovation with Network Externalities," 40 *Journal of Industrial Economics* 55 (1992).

Katz, Michael L., and Carl Shapiro, "Systems Competition and Network Effects," 8 *Journal of Economic Perspectives* 93 (1994).

Katz, Michael L., and Carl Shapiro, "Technology Adoption in the Presence of Network Externalities," 94 *Journal of Political Economy* 822 (1986).

Kellogg, Michael K., John Thorne, and Peter W. Huber, *Federal Telecommunications Law* (Little, Brown & Co. 1992).

Kolbe, A. Lawrence, and William B. Tye, "The *Duquesne* Opinion: How Much '*Hope*' Is There for Investors in Regulated Firms?" 4 *Yale Journal on Regulation* 113 (1991).

Kolbe, A. Lawrence, and William B. Tye, "It Ain't in There: The Cost of Capital Does Not Compensate for Stranded-Cost Risk," *Public Utilities Fortnightly*, May 15, 1995, at 26.

Kolbe, A. Lawrence, William B. Tye, and Stewart C. Myers, *Regulatory Risk: Economic Principles and Applications to Natural Gas Pipelines and Other Industries* (Kluwer Academic Publishers 1993).

Krattenmaker, Thomas G., and Steven C. Salop, "Anticompetitive Exclusion: Raising Rivals' Cost to Achieve Power over Price," 96 *Yale Law Journal* 209 (1986).

Kreps, David M., *A Course in Microeconomic Theory* (Princeton University Press 1990).

Kreps, David M., and José A. Scheinkman, "Quantity Precommitment and Bertrand Competition Yield Cournot Outcomes," 14 *Bell Journal of Economics* 326 (1983).

Kronman, Anthony T., "Specific Performance," 45 *University of Chicago Law Review* 351 (1978).

Kumm, Harold F., "The Legal Relations of City and State with Reference to Public Utility Regulation," 6 *Minnesota Law Review* 32 (1922).

Laffont, Jean-Jacques and Jean Tirole, "Access Pricing and Competition," 38 *European Economic Review* 1673 (1994).

Laffont, Jean-Jacques, and Jean Tirole, "Creating Competition through Interconnection: Theory and Practice," Mimeo, Massachusetts Institute of Technology (1994).

Laffont, Jean-Jacques, and Jean Tirole, *The Theory of Incentives in Procurement and Regulation* (MIT Press 1993).

Landes, William E., and Richard A. Posner, "Market Power in Antitrust Cases," 94 *Harvard Law Review* 937 (1981).

Larson, Alexander C., "The Efficiency of the Efficient Component-Pricing Rule: A Comment," 42 *Antitrust Bulletin* (forthcoming 1997).

Leland, Hayne E., "Regulation of Natural Monopolies and the Fair Rate of Return," 5 *Bell Journal of Economics and Management Science* 3 (1974).

Lemprière's Classical Dictionary of Proper Names Mentioned in Ancient Authors Writ Large (1788) (F. A. Wright ed., Routledge & Kegan Paul, 3d ed. 1984).

Lerner, Abba, "The Concept of Monopoly and the Measurement of Monopoly Power," 1 *Review of Economic Studies* 157 (1934).

Levine, Michael A., "Airline Competition in Deregulated Markets: Theory, Firm Strategy and Public Policy," 4 *Yale Journal on Regulation* 393 (1987).

Levy, Brian, and Pablo T. Spiller, "The Institutional Foundations of Regulatory Commitment: A Comparative Analysis of Five Country Studies of Telecommunications Regulation," 10 *Journal of Law, Economics, and Organization* 201 (1994).

Liebowitz, S. J., and Stephen E. Margolis, "Network Externality: An Uncommon Tragedy," 8 *Journal of Economic Perspectives* 133 (1994).

Lintner, John, "The Valuation of Risk Assets and the Selection of Risky Investments in Stock Portfolios and Capital Budgets," 47 *Review of Economics and Statistics* 13 (1965).

Lofting, Hugh, *The Story of Dr. Doolittle* (Bantam Doubleday Dell Publishing Group 1988) (1920).

MacAvoy, Paul W., *The Failure of Antitrust and Regulation to Establish Competition in Long-Distance Telephone Services* (MIT Press & AEI Press 1996).

MacAvoy, Paul W., and George S. McIsaac, "The Current File on the Case for Privatization of the Federal Government Enterprises," 3 *Hume Papers on Public Policy*, no. 3, at 121 (1995).

MacAvoy, Paul W., Daniel F. Spulber, and Bruce E. Stangle, "Is Competitive Entry Free? Bypass and Partial Deregulation in Natural Gas Markets," 6 *Yale Journal on Regulation* 209 (1989).

MacDonald, Glenn M., and Alan Slivinski, "The Simple Analytics of Competitive Equilibrium with Multiproduct Firms," 77 *American Economic Review* 941 (1987).

Maloney, Michael T., and Robert E. McCormick with Raymond D. Sauer, *Customer Choice, Customer Value: An Analysis of Retail Competition in America's Electric Industry* (Citizens for a Sound Economy Foundation 1996).

Markowitz, Harry, "Portfolio Selection," 7 *Journal of Finance* 77 (1952).

Marshall, Alfred, *Principles of Economics* (Macmillan 1922).

McChesney, Fred S., *Money for Nothing: Politicians, Rent Extraction, and Political Extortion* (Harvard University Press 1997).

McChesney, Fred S., "Rent Extraction and Rent Creation in the Economic Theory of Regulation," 16 *Journal of Legal Studies* 101 (1987).

McDonald, Forrest, *Insull* (University of Chicago Press 1962).

Merrill Lynch & Co., *United States Telecom Services—RBOCs & GTE* (May 14, 1996).

Meyer, John R., and Clinton V. Oster, Jr., *Deregulation and the Future of Intercity Passenger Travel* (MIT Press 1987).

Meyer, John R., and Clinton V. Oster, Jr., *Deregulation and the New Airline Entrepreneurs* (MIT Press 1984).

Michaels, Robert J., "Stranded Investment Surcharges: Inequitable and Inefficient," *Public Utilities Fortnightly*, May 15, 1995, at 21.

Michelman, Frank, "Property, Utility, and Fairness: Comments on the Ethical Foundations of 'Just Compensation' Law," 80 *Harvard Law Review* 1165 (1967).

Milgrom, Paul, and John Roberts, *Economics, Organization, and Management* (Prentice Hall 1992).

Mill, John Stuart, *Principles of Political Economy* (W. J. Ashley ed., Augustus M. Kelly 1961) (1848).

Miller, Geoffrey P., "Comment on Priest, 'The Origins of Utility Regulation and the *Theories of Regulation* Debate,'" 36 *Journal of Law and Economics* 325 (1993).

Millman, Jacob, and Arvin Garbel, *Microelectronics* (McGraw-Hill, 2d ed. 1987).

Minoli, Daniel, *Telecommunications Technology Handbook* (Artech House 1991).

Mishan, E. J., *Introduction to Normative Economics* (Oxford University Press 1981).

Mitchell, Bridger M., and Ingo Vogelsang, *Telecommunications Pricing: Theory and Practice* (Cambridge University Press 1991).

Moore, Thomas Gale, "Rail and Trucking Deregulation, Case 1," *in Regulatory Reform: What Actually Happened* 14 (Leonard Weiss & Michael W. Klass eds., Little, Brown, & Co. 1986).

Morin, Roger A., *Regulatory Finance: Utilities' Cost of Capital* (Public Utilities Reports 1994).

Morrison, Steven A., and Clifford Winston, *The Economic Effects of Airline Deregulation* (Brookings Institution 1986).

Morrison, Steven A., and Clifford Winston, *The Evolution of the Airline Industry* (Brookings Institution 1995).

Mueller, Milton L., Jr., *Universal Service: Competition, Interconnection, and Monopoly in the Making of the American Telephone System* (MIT Press & AEI Press 1996).

Myers, Stewart C., "The Application of Finance to Public Utility Rate Cases," 3 *Bell Journal of Economics and Management Science* 58 (1972).

National Association of Regulatory Utility Commissioners, *The Status of Competition in Intrastate Telecommunications* (1994).

New Zealand Ministry of Commerce, "Telecommunications Reform in New Zealand: 1987–1994," Telecommunications Leaflet No. 5 (Jan. 19, 1995).

Niskanen, William A., "A Case against Both Stranded Cost Recovery and Mandatory Access," *Regulation*, 1996 no. 1, at 16 (1996).

Noam, Eli M., "Network Tipping: The Rise and Fall of the Public Network Monopoly," in *Telecommunications in Europe* (Oxford University Press 1992).

Oppenheim, Alan V., Alan S. Willsky, and Ian T. Young, *Signals and Systems* (Prentice Hall 1983).

Ordover, Janusz A., and Garth Saloner, "Predation, Monopolization, and Antitrust," in 1 *Handbook of Industrial Organization* 537 (Richard Schmalensee ed., North-Holland 1989).

Ordover, Janusz A., and Robert D. Willig, "Notes on the Efficient Component Pricing Rule," paper presented at The Transition towards Competition in Network Industries, First Annual Conference, PURC-IDEI-Cirano, Montreal, October 13–14, 1995.

Owen, Bruce M., and Steven S. Wildman, *Video Economics* (Harvard University Press 1992).

Panzar, John C., "Competition, Efficiency, and the Vertical Structure of Postal Services," in *Regulation and the Nature of Postal Delivery Services* 91 (Michael A. Crew & Paul R. Kleindorfer eds., Kluwer Academic Publishers 1992).

Panzar, John C., "The Economics of Mail Delivery," in *Governing the Postal Service* 1 (J. Gregory Sidak ed., AEI Press 1994).

Pecar, Robert A., Roger J. O'Connor, and David A. Gurbin, *Telecommunications Factbook* (McGraw-Hill 1993).

Perloff, Jeffrey M., and Steven C. Salop, "Equilibrium with Product Differentiation," 52 *Review of Economic Studies* 107 (1985).

Peterson, Andrea L., "The Takings Clause: In Search of Underlying Principles," 77 *California Law Review* 1299 (1989).

Pettway, Richard H., "On the Use of β in Regulatory Proceedings: An Empirical Examination," 9 *Bell Journal of Economics* 239 (1978).

Phillips, Charles F., Jr., *The Regulation of Public Utilities* (Public Utilities Reports, 3d ed. 1993).

Pierce, Richard J., Jr., *Economic Regulation: Cases and Materials* (Anderson Publishing Co. 1994).

Pierce, Richard J., Jr., "Public Utility Regulatory Takings: Should the Judiciary Attempt to Police the Political Institutions?" 77 *Georgetown Law Journal* 2031 (1989).

Pierce, Richard J., Jr., "The Regulatory Treatment of Mistakes in Retrospect," 132 *University of Pennsylvania Law Review* 497 (1984).

Pigou, A. C., *The Economics of Welfare* (Macmillan, 4th ed. 1932).

Pleitz, Dan, and Robert Randolph Little, "Municipalities and the Public Utility Regulatory Act," 28 *Baylor Law Review* 978 (1976).

Pollack, Clifford R., *The Fundamentals of Optoelectronics* (Richard D. Irwin 1995).

Pond, Oscar L., *A Treatise on the Law of Public Utilities Operating in Cities and Towns* (Bobbs-Merrill Co. 1913).

Posner, Richard A., *Antitrust Law: An Economic Perspective* (University of Chicago Press 1976).

Posner, Richard A., *Economic Analysis of Law* (Little, Brown & Co., 4th ed. 1992).

Posner, Richard A., "Gratuitous Promises in Economics and Law," 6 *Journal of Legal Studies* 411 (1977).

Posner, Richard A., "Natural Monopoly and Its Regulation," 21 *Stanford Law Review* 548 (1969).

Posner, Richard A., "The Social Costs of Monopoly and Regulation," 83 *Journal of Political Economy* 807 (1975).

Posner, Richard A., "Taxation by Regulation," 2 *Bell Journal of Economics* 22 (1971).

Posner, Richard A., and Andrew M. Rosenfield, "Impossibility and Related Doctrines in Contract Law: An Economic Analysis," 6 *Journal of Legal Studies* 83 (1977).

Priest, George L., "The Origins of Utility Regulation and the 'Theories of Regulation' Debate," 36 *Journal of Law and Economics* 289 (1992).

Railroad Revitalization and Regulatory Reform (Paul W. MacAvoy & John W. Snow eds., AEI Press 1977).

Ramo, Simon, John R. Whinnery, and Theodore Van Duzer, *Fields and Waves in Communication Electronics* (John Wiley & Sons 1965).

Ramsey, Frank P., "A Contribution to the Theory of Taxation," 37 *Economic Journal* 47 (1927).

The Random Character of Stock Market Prices (Paul Cootner ed., MIT Press 1964).

Regulation of Passenger Fares and Competition among the Airlines (Paul W. MacAvoy & John W. Snow eds., AEI Press 1977).

Report of Bell Atlantic on Internet Traffic (Bell Atlantic Corp. Mar. 1996).

"Right and Duty of Telephone Co. to Make Physical Connection," 11 *American Law Reports* 1204 (1921).

Rohlfs, Jeffrey H., "A Theory of Interdependent Demand for Telecommunications Service," 5 *Bell Journal of Economics and Management Science* 16 (1974).

Romano, Roberta, *The Genius of American Corporate Law* (AEI Press 1993).

Rose, Kenneth, *An Economic and Legal Perspective on Electric Utility Transition Costs* (National Regulatory Research Institute July 1996).

Rose-Ackerman, Susan, "Ad Hocery: A Comment on Michelman," 88 *Columbia Law Review* 1697 (1988).

Rose-Ackerman, Susan, *Rethinking the Progressive Agenda: The Reform of the American Regulatory State* (Free Press 1992).

Rubin, Paul H., and Hashem Dezhbakhsh, "Costs of Delay and Rent-Seeking under the Modification of Final Judgment," 16 *Managerial and Decision Economics* 385 (1995).

Samuelson, Paul A., and William D. Nordhaus, *Economics* (McGraw-Hill, 15th ed. 1995).

Sappington, David E. M., "Revisiting the Line-of-Business Restrictions," 16 *Managerial and Decision Economics* 291 (1995).

Sappington, David E. M., and Dennis L. Weisman, *Designing Incentive Regulation for the Telecommunications Industry* (MIT Press & AEI Press 1996).

Saunders, Robert J., Jeremy J. Warford, and Björn Wellenius, *Telecommunications and Economic Development* (World Bank & Johns Hopkins University Press, 2d ed. 1994).

Schelling, Thomas C., *The Strategy of Conflict* (Oxford University Press 1960).

Schmalensee, Richard, *The Control of Natural Monopolies* (Lexington Books 1979).

Schmalensee, Richard L., "On the Use of Economic Models in Antitrust: The ReaLemon Case," 127 *University of Pennsylvania Law Review* 994 (1979).

Schumpeter, Joseph R., *Capitalism, Socialism and Democracy* (Harper & Row 1942).

Schwartz, Alan, "The Case for Specific Performance," 89 *Yale Law Journal* 271 (1979).

Schweber, William L., *Electronic Communication Systems: A Complete Course* (Prentice Hall 1991).

Schwert, G. William, "Using Financial Data to Measure Effects of Regulation," 24 *Journal of Law and Economics* 121 (1981).

Scientific Atlanta, *CoAccess: CATV Telephone System: A Dual-Service Telephony/Video System for CATV Networks* (1993).

Scitovsky, Tibor, "A Note on Welfare Propositions in Economics," 9 *Review of Economic Studies* 77 (1941).

Seyhun, H. N., "Insider's Profits, Cost Trading, and Market Efficiency," 16 *Journal of Finance and Economics* 189 (1986).

Sharpe, William F., "Capital Asset Prices: A Theory of Market Equilibrium under Conditions of Risk," 19 *Journal of Finance* 425 (1964).

Shavell, Steven, "The Design of Contract Remedies for Breach," 99 *Quarterly Journal of Economics* 121 (1984).

Sherman, Roger, *The Regulation of Monopoly* (Cambridge University Press 1989).

Sidak, J. Gregory, "Debunking Predatory Innovation," 83 *Columbia Law Review* 1121 (1983).

Sidak, J. Gregory, "The President's Power of the Purse," 1989 *Duke Law Journal* 1162 (1989).

Sidak, J. Gregory, "Telecommunications in Jericho," 81 *California Law Review* 1209 (1993).

Sidak, J. Gregory, and Daniel F. Spulber, "Cyberjam: The Law and Economics of Internet Congestion of the Telephone Network," 20 *Harvard Journal of Law and Public Policy* (forthcoming 1997).

Sidak, J. Gregory and Daniel F. Spulber, "Deregulation and Managed Competition in Network Industries," 15 *Yale Journal on Regulation* (forthcoming 1998).

Sidak, J. Gregory, and Daniel F. Spulber, "Deregulatory Takings and Breach of the Regulatory Contract," 71 *New York University Law Review* 851 (1996).

Sidak, J. Gregory, and Daniel F. Spulber, "Givings, Takings, and the Fallacy of Forward-Looking Costs," 72 *New York University Law Review* (forthcoming 1997).

Sidak, J. Gregory, and Daniel F. Spulber, *Protecting Competition from the Postal Monopoly* (AEI Press 1996).

Sidak, J. Gregory, and Daniel F. Spulber, "The Tragedy of the Telecommons: Government Pricing of Unbundled Network Elements Under the Telecommunications Act of 1996," 97 *Columbia Law Review* 1081 (1997).

Sidak, J. Gregory, and Susan E. Woodward, "Takeover Premiums, Appraisal Rights and the Price Elasticity of a Firm's Publicly Traded Stock," 25 *Georgia Law Review* 783 (1991).

Smith, Adam, *An Inquiry into the Nature and Causes of the Wealth of Nations* (Modern Library 1937) (1776).

Spiller, Pablo T., "Institutions and Regulatory Commitment in Utilities' Privatizations," 2 *Industrial and Corporate Change* 387 (1993).

Spulber, Daniel F., "Deregulating Telecommunications," 12 *Yale Journal on Regulation* 25 (1995).

Spulber, Daniel F., "Pricing and the Incentive to Invest in Pipelines after *Great Lakes*," 15 *Energy Law Journal* 377 (1994).

Spulber, Daniel F., *Regulation and Markets* (MIT Press 1989).

Spulber, Daniel F., and J. Gregory Sidak, "Network Access Pricing and Deregulation," J. L. Kellogg Graduate School of Management Working Paper, Northwestern University (Sept. 1996).

Spulber, Daniel F., and Yossef Spiegel, "The Capital Structure of a Regulated Firm," 25 *RAND Journal of Economics* 424 (1994).

Stein, Gregory M., "Regulatory Takings and Ripeness in the Federal Courts," 48 *Vanderbilt Law Review* 1 (1995).

Steinberg, Jeffrey G., "Promissory Estoppel as a Means of Defeating the Statute of Frauds," 44 *Fordham Law Review* 114 (1975).

Stelzer, Irwin M., "A New Era for Public Utilities," *Public Interest*, no. 117, at 81 (Fall 1994).

Stelzer, Irwin M., "Restructuring the Electric Utility Industry: Further Tentative Thoughts," *Electricity Journal*, vol. 7, no. 8, at 36 (Oct. 1994).

Stelzer, Irwin M., "What Happens When the Rules Are Changed and the Plug Is Pulled on Electric Utilities?" *American Enterprise*, vol. 5, no. 6, at 76 (Nov./Dec. 1994).

Stigler, George J., *The Organization of Industry* (Richard D. Irwin 1968).

Stigler, George J., "*United States* v. *Loew's, Inc.*: A Note on Block Booking," 1963 *Supreme Court Review* 152 (1963).

Stiglitz, Joseph E., *Economics* (W.W. Norton & Co. 1993).

Stoebuck, William B., "A General Theory of Eminent Domain," 47 *Washington Law Review* 553 (1972).

Stoebuck, William B., "The Property Right of Access versus the Power of Eminent Domain," 47 *Texas Law Review* 733 (1969).

Taylor, Lester D., *Telecommunications Demand in Theory and Practice* (Kluwer Academic Publishers 1994).

Temin, Peter, *The Fall of the Bell System: A Study in Prices and Politics* (Cambridge University Press 1987).

Tirole, Jean, *The Theory of Industrial Organization* (MIT Press 1988).

Train, Kenneth E., *Optimal Regulation: The Economic Theory of Natural Monopoly* (MIT Press 1991).

Trebilcock, Michael J., *The Limits of Freedom of Contract* (Harvard University Press 1996).

Tribe, Lawrence H., *American Constitutional Law* (Foundation Press, 2d ed. 1988).

Tye, William B., "The Pricing of Inputs to Competitors: A Response," 11 *Yale Journal on Regulation* 203 (1994).

Tye, William B., and Carlos Lapuerta, "The Economics of Pricing Network Interconnection: Theory and Application to the Market for Telecommunications in New Zealand," 13 *Yale Journal on Regulation* 421 (1996).

Ulen, Thomas S., "The Efficiency of Specific Performance: Toward a Unified Theory of Contract Remedies," 83 *Michigan Law Review* 341 (1983).

Ulmer, Melville J., *Capital in Transportation, Communications, and Public Utilities: Its Formation and Financing* (National Bureau of Economic Research & Princeton University Press 1960).

United States Telephone Association, *Phone Facts* (1995).

U.S. Department of Commerce, National Telecommunications and Information Administration, *Telecommunications in the Age of Information* (Government Printing Office 1991).

Vickers, John, "Regulation, Competition, and the Structure of Prices," 13 *Oxford Review of Economic Policy*, no. 1, at 15 (1997).

Vietor, Richard K., *Contrived Competition: Regulation and Deregulation in America* (Belknap Press & Harvard University Press 1994).

Vogelsang, Ingo, and Bridger M. Mitchell, *Telecommunications Competition: The Last Ten Miles* (MIT Press & AEI Press 1997).

Walras, Leon, *Etudes d'Economie Sociale: Theorie de la Repartition de la Richesse Sociale* (F. Pichon 1896).

Weiman, David F., and Richard C. Levin, "Preying for Monopoly? The Case of Southern Bell Telephone Company, 1894–1912," 102 *Journal of Political Economy* 103 (1994).

Weisman, Dennis L., "Default Capacity Tariffs: Smoothing the Transitional Regulatory Asymmetries in the Telecommunications Market," 5 *Yale Journal on Regulation* 149 (1988).

Weston, J. Fred, Kwang S. Chung, and Susan E. Hoag, *Mergers, Restructuring and Corporate Control* (Prentice Hall 1990).

Wilcox, Delos F., *Municipal Franchises* (Gervaise Press 1910).

Williams, Stephen F., "Deregulatory Takings and Breach of the Regulatory Contract: A Comment," 71 *New York University Law Review* 1000 (1996).

Williams, Stephen F., "Fixing the Rate of Return after *Duquesne*," 8 *Yale Journal on Regulation* 159 (1991).

Williamson, Oliver E., "Deregulatory Takings and Breach of the Regulatory Contract: Some Precautions," 71 *New York University Law Review* 1007 (1996).

Williamson, Oliver E., *The Economic Institutions of Capitalism: Firms, Markets, and Relational Contracting* (Free Press 1985).

Williamson, Oliver E., "Franchise Bidding for Natural Monopolies—In General and with Respect to CATV," 7 *Bell Journal of Economics* 73 (1976).

Williamson, Oliver E., *Markets and Hierarchies: Analysis and Antitrust Implications* (Free Press 1975).

Williamson, Oliver E., *The Mechanisms of Governance* (Oxford University Press 1996).

Williamson, Oliver E., "Transactions-Cost Economics: The Governance of Contractual Relations," 22 *Journal of Law and Economics* 233 (1985).

Willig, Robert D., "The Theory of Network Access Pricing," in *Issues in Public Utility Regulation* (H. M. Trebing ed., Michigan State University Public Utility Papers 1979).

Zajac, Edward E., *The Political Economy of Fairness* (MIT Press 1995).

Zupan, Mark A., "Cable Franchise Renewals: Do Incumbent Firms Behave Opportunistically?" 20 *RAND Journal of Economics* 473 (1989).

Case and Regulatory Proceeding Index

Name Index

Subject Index